U.S.

GARDENING GUIDE

Everything You Need to Know
About How to Make Things Grow

COMPILED BY *Jeffrey Feinman*

SIMON AND SCHUSTER · NEW YORK

Published by Simon and Schuster
A Division of Gulf & Western Corporation
Simon & Schuster Building
Rockefeller Center
1230 Avenue of the Americas
New York, New York 10020

Designed by Libra Graphics, Inc.
Manufactured in the United States of America
1 2 3 4 5 6 7 8 9 10

Library of Congress Cataloging in Publication Data

Main entry under title:

U.S. gardening guide.
"This compilation is an edited version of pamphlets, brochures, and publications of the U.S. Government."
Includes index.
1. Gardening. I. Feinman, Jeffrey.
SB453.U54 635 78-21235

ISBN 0-671-24026-9

Contents

Preface 7
Introduction by Harold Givens 9

I CARING FOR YOUR PLANTS 11
1 Transplanting Ornamental Trees and Shrubs 13
2 Mulches for Your Garden 21
3 Green Thumb Tips for Growing House Plants 23

II GROWING ANNUALS 37
4 Flowering Annuals 39

III GROWING PERENNIALS 51
5 Flowering Perennials 53

IV GROWING BULBS 75
6 Spring-flowering Bulbs 77
7 Summer-flowering Bulbs 85
8 Iris in the Home Garden 92

V GROWING ORNAMENTALS 97
9 Ornamentals in Urban Gardens 99
10 Selecting Shrubs for Shady Areas 110
11 Shrubs, Vines and Trees for Summer Color 115
12 Pruning Ornamental Shrubs and Vines 125

VI GROWING TREES 133
13 Selecting and Growing Shade Trees 135
14 Trees for Use and Beauty 141
15 Dwarf Fruit Trees: Selection and Care 146
16 Flowering Crabapples 150
17 Flowering Dogwood 155
18 Magnolias 160
19 Growing Apricots for Home Use 164

VII GROWING PLANT SPECIALTIES 169
20 Azaleas and Rhododendrons 171
21 Bonsai 175
22 Boxwoods 188
23 Camellias 193
24 Chrysanthemums 199
25 Dahlias 203
26 Ground Covers 207
27 Hollies 214
28 Lilacs 218
29 Pansies 222
30 Peonies 226

VIII GROWING BERRIES 233
31 Blackberries 235
32 Thornless Blackberries for the Home Garden 239
33 Raspberries 243

IX GROWING GRAPES AND WALNUTS 249
34 American Bunch Grapes 251
35 Black Walnuts 256

X GROWING VEGETABLES 259
36 Vegetables in the Home Garden 261
37 Minigardens for Vegetables 298
38 Cauliflower and Broccoli 303
39 Table Beets 306
40 Tomatoes in the Home Garden 309
41 Insects and Diseases of Vegetables 314

Index 343

Preface

"WHY ANOTHER GARDEN BOOK?" That's a fair question. There has been a huge outpouring in recent years of books on plants. They have been written by experienced growers, successful amateurs and self-proclaimed experts. This book, however, is different. This compilation is an edited version of pamphlets, brochures and publications of the U.S. Government. The reality is that no writer, publisher or gardener has the financial and manpower resources of the U.S. Department of Agriculture.

Government publications contain the best possible in-depth research. What your editor has done is wade through the literally thousands of Government publications to provide the most usable information. Reprinted are the facts you need to be a successful indoor and outdoor gardener.

Unfortunately, the Government does little to promote and distribute its fine work. In fact, the Government Printing Office has no central listing of publications on the subject. What is required is painstaking library research to cull out the potentially interesting (e.g., "Growing Shade Trees") from the unmistakably dull (e.g., "Commercial Carrot Production").

This one volume is the "Best of the Best." That is, it has culled and edited, from millions of words, only the data that will help the garden enthusiast succeed.

May your garden grow and flourish!

JEFFREY FEINMAN

January 1979

Introduction

THIS BOOK WAS WRITTEN by specialists to properly guide us in developing and maintaining truly efficient and enjoyable gardens—the kind we are proud of. Gardens have significant recreational value and can become a satisfying emotional outlet for everyone. As we stroll through a beautiful garden, we experience the kind of exhilarating peacefulness that comes from observing the graceful natural forms and harmonious color blendings of living plants. Such aesthetic responses immediately make us feel good.

But this is not enough. To derive the full benefit, we must become a part of the garden. The plants become our friends. We assume responsibility for their well-being. We select their climate, provide them with food and drink, bind their wounds, protect them from enemies; prune them for better form, flower and fruiting potential; and blend their floral colors to our liking.

To carry out these fascinating duties properly, most of us need help. This book is for that very purpose—to guide us along the various avenues of gardening and to cause us to realize that nature has prescribed certain requirements for individual species and conditions—a no-nitrogen fertilizer for rhododendrons after buds form, or the proper depth to plant peonies, for example. The majority of us do not have the technical know-how to fulfill all these requirements, nor do we have the scientific answers at our fingertips. We rely upon ways and formulas from experts in the plant world.

This book is such a dependable guide. It provides logical answers and vital information on a select list of garden subjects common to gardeners everywhere. Through diligent use, it will guide your garden to new heights and satisfactions, and will make your adventure with growing plants richly rewarding.

HAROLD GIVENS

I

CARING FOR YOUR PLANTS

CHAPTER 1

Transplanting Ornamental Trees and Shrubs

WHY DO YOU WANT TO TRANSPLANT? You might need to move a plant because it is too crowded, because it gets too much or too little shade, or simply because it may be more appealing or useful in another place. Whatever the reason, you begin to dig up that tree or shrub you want to move.

If, at this point, you tell yourself that transplanting is nothing more than digging up and planting again, you may be disappointed when your newly transplanted tree or shrub doesn't grow well or when it dies during the first year. There are, however, many things you can do to help ensure successful transplanting.

WHAT TO TRANSPLANT

Successful transplanting can depend entirely on the individual plant you select to move. The kind of tree or shrub, however, isn't always as important as its age, size and condition. For instance, young plants and small plants can be transplanted with less risk than older or larger ones. Also, healthy plants are more likely to survive the shock of transplanting than unhealthy ones.

In some cases, however, you might want to move an unhealthy plant to a more suitable location. Transplanting for this reason may be especially helpful for plants that manage to survive in their present environment but lack vigor. A change of environment more suited to the needs of the plant often can restore its vitality.

Good indicators of a plant's health and vigor are the length of annual twig growth, the condition of buds and flowers, the number of dead branches and the size and color of the leaves. Wilting, stunted growth, malformation and disease spots are signs of poor health.

Hardy Plants

Plants are considered hardy when they can withstand various extremes of environmental conditions, such as very low winter temperatures and extreme summer heat and drought.

Moving a plant from one part of your property to another should not affect its hardiness unless there are extreme changes in wind and sun exposure.

If you wish to move a plant from one part of the country to another, make sure that the plant will be hardy in its new location. If temperature differences are too extreme at the new location, the plant will not survive.

Temperature zones affecting plant hardiness are indicated on the plant hardiness map (page 14). Perhaps the best way to tell whether your plant will survive in a certain area of the country is to consult the nurseries in that area. The trees and shrubs nurserymen raise and sell should be hardy for their areas.

WHEN, WHERE AND HOW TO TRANSPLANT

The best time for transplanting is when plants are still dormant in early spring or after they have become dormant in the fall. How long they are dormant depends upon the climate as well as the kind of plant.

In the spring, deciduous trees and shrubs should be moved before the buds start to grow. In the fall, they should be moved only after their leaves turn color and drop off. Transplant only when the ground is not frozen and is workable.

Spring planting is advisable in areas that have severe winters. Transplant in the spring if you live in an area with strong, drying winter winds, deficient soil moisture or deeply frozen ground during the winter months. This applies to evergreens as well as to deciduous plants.

Evergreens can be transplanted earlier in the fall and later in the spring than deciduous plants. They may be moved from early September to June if the weather is not too severe.

If you transplant in the summer, make sure that the rootball is kept moist while it is out of the ground. Because of high temperatures in summer, plants have a greater tendency to lose too much moisture through evaporation.

You can cut down this water loss by using a transpiration-inhibiting chemical. Antitranspirants can be purchased at nurseries or garden supply stores. When sprayed onto the plant, the chemical coats the leaves and reduces moisture loss.

Another method of reducing water loss is to shade the plant for the first few days after replanting. One way of shading is to cover the plant with burlap.

Select the planting site carefully. Consider not only where a plant would look good, but also where it will grow most successfully. Make sure that your plant can adapt to any changes in sun, shade, wind exposure and soil moisture. In addition, avoid these common mistakes: placing plants too close together in an effort to get quick screening effects, setting young trees under windows, and crowding the walls of buildings.

At the new site, provide enough space above and below the ground to allow for future spreading and growth of the top and roots of the plant. Later crowding may deform it, stunt its growth or eventually even kill it.

Digging

When digging up a deciduous tree or shrub, avoid injuring as many roots as possible. Start digging from the outer edge of the crown and carefully remove the soil while working toward the trunk until the main roots are found.

Transplanting from the Wild

With amateur handling, such plants as dogwoods, oaks and maples will usually die when moved from the woods. The key to successfully moving wild trees and shrubs is root pruning well before you move them.

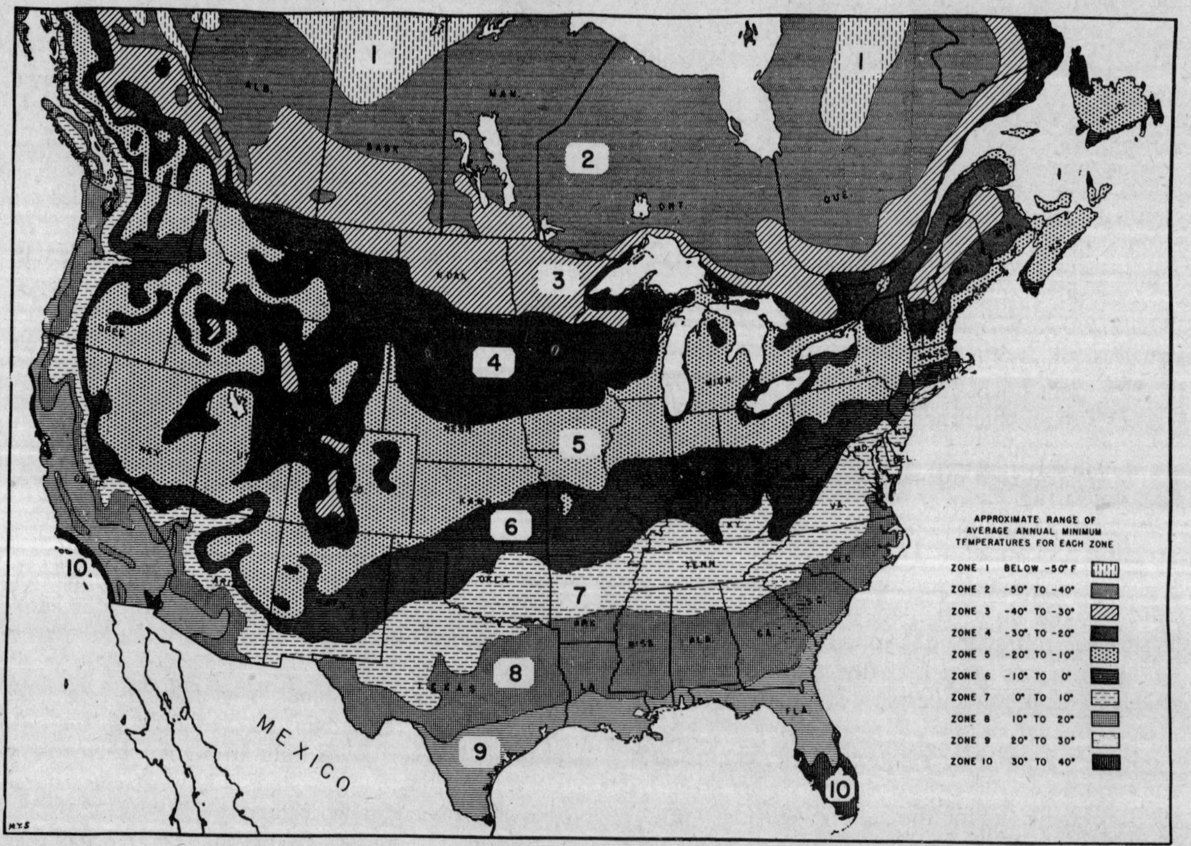

Plant Hardiness Map

To root-prune, cut all roots with a sharp spade at the same distance from the trunk as when you are digging a rootball. Go out from the trunk 1 foot for each inch of diameter of the trunk before you start cutting the roots. Next, make sure that the roots beneath the plant are also cut. Then, lift the plant slightly to make sure all the roots are free. Drop the plant back into position, firm the soil around it, and see that it is watered during dry periods.

If you intend to move your wild plant in the fall, then root-prune the previous spring. Likewise, if you intend to move the plant in the spring, root-prune the previous fall.

Though most plants can be successfully transplanted this way, plants that have very dominant top roots, such as hickory and sassafras, may not survive.

Remember, however, that when you move a plant from a wild to a cultivated environment, such as your lawn, you may be changing its environment to such an extent that the plant may lose its hardiness and die. For example, if you move a plant that is adapted to a lot of shade and shelter in the woods to an open, sunlit spot, the tree may die through overexposure. If it is necessary to move the wild tree to a more exposed place, protect the trunk by wrapping it with a strip of burlap.

Dig the soil from around the roots of deciduous trees—without completely baring them—with a minimum of bruising and cutting. Any extra soil will help to retain the fine "hair" roots which absorb moisture from the soil.

Evergreens, on the other hand, must have a lot of soil around the roots. For this reason they must be dug with a rootball. The size of the rootball will vary with the size of the plant and the type of soil around it. Normally, however, a rootball of 1 foot in radius to each inch of trunk diameter is recommended.

Although evergreens require a rootball and deciduous plants normally do not, some deciduous plants are exceptions to the general rule. Deciduous plants need a rootball when they:

- Have a trunk diameter greater than 3 inches.
- Are considered difficult to transplant, such as dogwoods and magnolias.
- Are transplanted in the summer or when they are in full leaf.

Whether your plant requires a rootball or whether you can move it bare-rooted, always keep the roots moist. If they dry out while the plant is out of the ground, the plant is likely to die.

Heeling-In

If replanting is delayed for a few days, keep the roots and top moist by putting the plant in a protected place, sheltered from exposure to sun and wind. Cover the roots with moist peat, burlap, wet leaves, or waterproof plastic sheets.

If replanting is delayed two or three weeks, "heel-in" the plant. First, choose a shady area away from drying winds. Then, dig a trench to accommodate the roots and slope one side 45 degrees or lower. Place the roots in the trench and rest the trunk or stem against the sloping side. Cover the roots with loose soil and keep them moist. Evergreens should be heeled-in upright and placed close together if there are more than one.

Heel-in your tree or shrub if replanting is delayed.

After heeling-in your plant, you may cover the roots with burlap in order to reduce evaporation of water from the roots.

Preparing the Soil

In most cases soil composition, texture, aeration and drainage can be improved at the new planting site. The purpose of good soil preparation is to promote root growth of the newly transplanted tree or shrub.

Well-prepared soil will provide adequate drainage, moisture retention, aeration and the proper degree of soil acidity.

The texture and composition of the soil affects drainage and aeration. If drainage is poor, water will collect around the roots and cause them to rot. If aeration is poor, oxygen cannot reach the roots through the soil and the plant will suffocate. This is particularly true when transplanting into heavy clay soil.

If soil is not heavy or dense enough, it will not hold soil nutrients and an adequate amount of water around the roots. This is a problem with very sandy soils.

TRANSPLANTING ORNAMENTAL TREES AND SHRUBS

digging up

1

Before you start to dig, go out 1 foot for each inch of trunk diameter.

2

Dig with the back of the spade toward the plant to avoid prying up uncut roots. After the rootball is cut, trim and shape the ball, and undercut the roots.

3

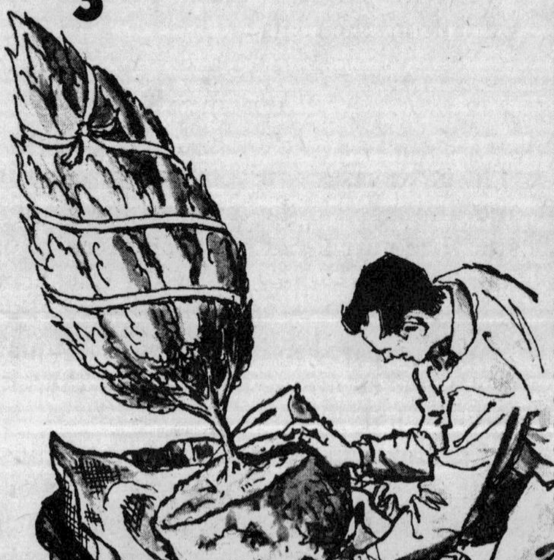

Tip the ball and tuck a roll of burlap under it. Tip the ball in the opposite direction; unroll and pull the burlap under the ball.

4

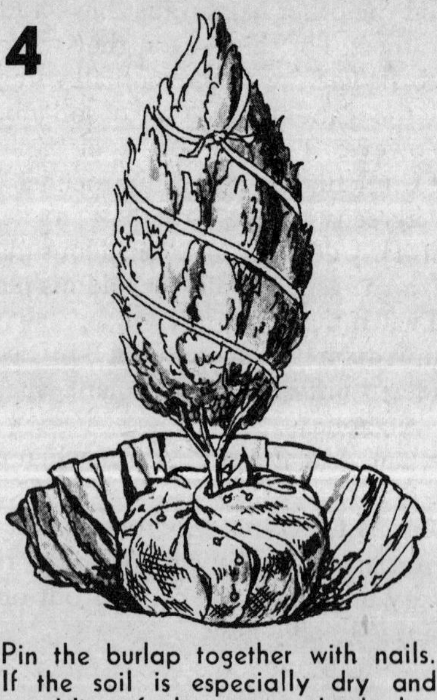

Pin the burlap together with nails. If the soil is especially dry and crumbling, further secure the burlap with a nylon cord or small rope. Do not lift the plant by its trunk or branches. Lift small plants by the rootball and larger ones by prying up with 2 spades.

planting

1

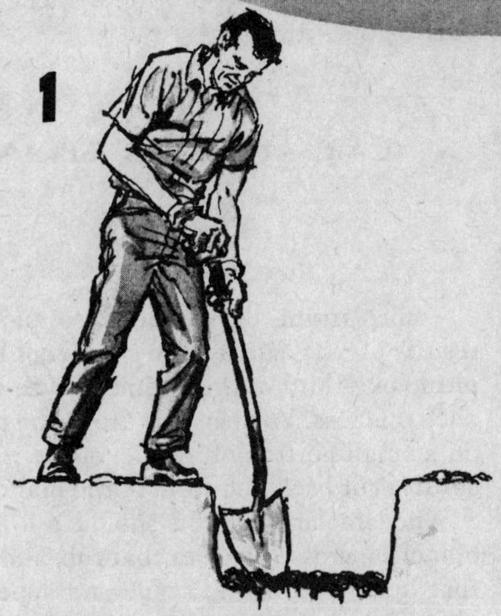

Dig the hole a foot deeper than the height of the roots, and twice as wide as the root span, or the rootball. Loosen several inches of soil at the bottom of the hole to facilitate drainage.

2

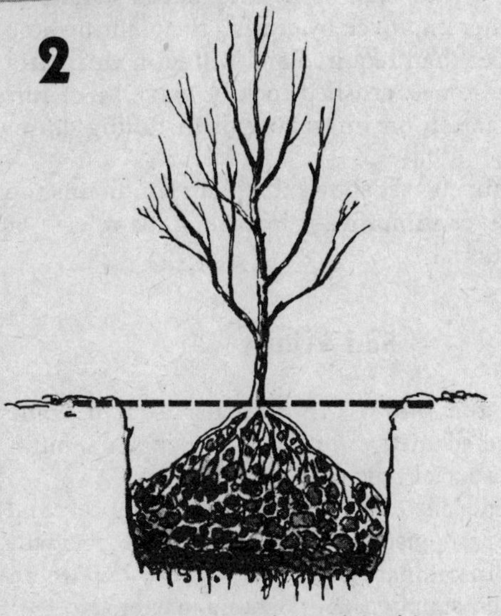

Add soil to the hole and build it up in a mound beneath the plant, so that the plant sits at the same level as before it was moved.

3

Fill three-fourths of the hole with soil, then water.

4

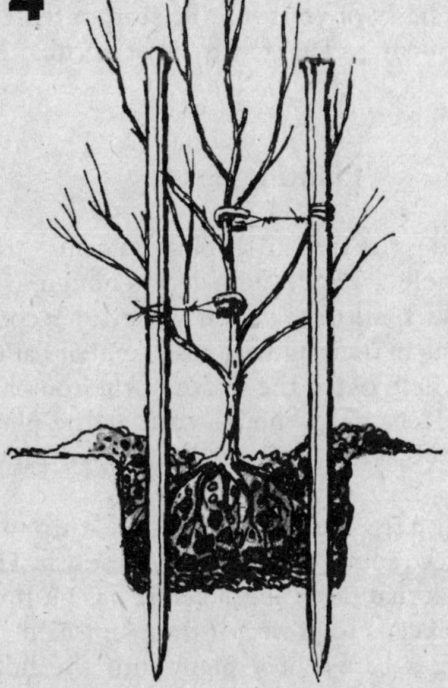

Fill the remaining part of the hole with soil, then for small plants drive in stakes to secure them. For securing large plants, use guy wires.

To test for drainage, dig a hole a foot or more deep and fill it with water. The next day, fill the hole with water again and see how long the water remains. If the water is absorbed in eight to ten hours, soil drainage is adequate for planting.

If water remains in the hole more than ten hours, you can improve drainage by altering the consistency and composition of the soil. To do this, mix the clay soil with sand or organic matter. Drainage can be further improved by digging the planting hole a foot deeper than required and filling in this extra space with stones, crushed rock or gravel. (For further information on improving or installing drainage, see page 138.)

If the drainage test shows that your soil drains too rapidly, you can improve it by adding loam, clay or organic material.

Soil Acidity

Most of the woody ornamentals used in home planting are adapted to ordinary garden soils, but a few need a special type.

Rhododendrons, azaleas, mountain laurel and their relatives constitute a class of plants that will not thrive in ordinary sweet soil. These require an acid soil well supplied with organic matter.

You can make soil more acid by mixing it with decayed leaves from oak woods or old thickets of mountain laurel, decayed leaf mold or peat.

To find out if you have acid soil, consult your county agricultural agent or your local nurseryman about soil testing. If necessary, get directions for changing the acidity of your soil. Be sure to tell the person testing your soil which trees or shrubs you want to grow.

Planting

Before planting the tree or shrub, make sure that the planting hole is wide and deep enough. For bare-rooted plants, allow sufficient room to accommodate the roots in their natural position. For balled plants, dig the hole twice the width of the rootball. The hole should be deep enough so that the plant can be set at the same level it was planted previously.

Before setting a tree into a planting hole, turn it so the side that faced south before still faces south. The side of the trunk that faced south before has built up an extra layer of cells to protect it from sunscald.

After placing a bare-rooted plant into the hole, press the soil firmly around the base of the roots. Work the soil under the trunk or center of the plant to support it. This also keeps the plant from settling too much.

Set a balled plant in the hole and keep the burlap covering intact. Cut the twine from the stem or trunk and draw the covering back from the rootball.

Fill in with soil around the roots or rootball until the hole is about three-quarters full. Then pour in water. The water helps to bring soil particles into direct contact with the roots. The water will also settle the surface soil 1 or 2 inches. Fill in this depression with soil.

CARE AFTER TRANSPLANTING

Pruning

Transplanting deciduous trees and shrubs often results in root damage and some root loss. For trees, prune one-third of the lateral growth to counterbalance this loss. You can also "top" the tree by cutting off a small portion of the top of the main stem. For shrubs, cut back one-third of the branches.

When replanting, you should prune off diseased branches, cross-branches that rub, and any branches that detract from the shape and appearance of the plant. Be careful not to overprune. If overpruned, the plant will be set back since you are removing the foliage that produces its food. Plant growth is then slowed down, depending on how many leaves you prune off.

Not all trees and shrubs must be pruned after transplanting. Evergreens, for example, may not need it because the rootball normally protects the roots from injury. Deciduous plants may not need pruning if they are planted in humid areas of the country. Where it is humid, new roots usually will be formed within a few weeks and will restore adequate water absorption from the soil.

Watering

Be careful to avoid extremes in watering. Too little water will cause the roots to dry up and die, and too much water may rot them away.

Newly transplanted trees and shrubs need regular watering during the spring, summer, and fall of the first year, unless you plant in an area where rainfall is abundant.

In winter, evergreens retain their leaves and continue to lose water through them. For this reason evergreens should be watered during dry winter periods. Deciduous plants do not need watering in the winter since they are dormant and will not lose any moisture.

Do not water plants every day. Allow the soil to dry at the surface before you water again. Test the soil for dryness by crumbling it through your fingers. The amount of water needed is the amount that the soil can absorb. Stop watering when water no longer seeps rapidly into the soil.

Mulching

After planting, mulch the soil beneath the branches with a 3-inch layer of peat moss, leafy mold or forest litter. Use only well-decayed material because the decomposition of such material as fresh manure, green plants or fresh grass clippings releases by-products that can be harmful to the roots.

To reduce damage by mice and decay, keep the mulch about a foot away from the trunk or stem of larger plants. Make sure that the mulch covers the area occupied by the roots. For small or young trees, reduce the depth of the mulch near the trunk or stem.

Fertilizing

If you use plenty of rich soil for back-filling, newly transplanted trees and shrubs are not likely to need fertilizer for the first year. However, if immediate growth seems stunted or leaves are paled, fertilizing is advisable.

Apply fertilizer in fall or early spring in the following way:

For trees: Measure the diameter of the trunk 3 feet above the ground; use 2 pounds of 5–10–5 fertilizer for each inch of diameter. For trunks with a diameter of less than 3 inches, use ½ pound for each inch.

Using a soil auger, crowbar or posthole digger, make holes 15 to 24 inches deep and 18 to 24 inches apart around the drip line of the tree (the area beneath the ends of the longest branches). Also fertilize a few feet beyond the drip line, especially for young trees.

Distribute the fertilizer equally among the holes, using ¼ cup per hole. Then fill the holes with soil. A mixture of equal parts of topsoil, sand, and peatmoss is a good filling.

For shrubs: Scatter fertilizer on the surface over the root area, then scratch it in. Use one or two handfuls of fertilizer, depending on the size of the shrub.

Protecting from Sun and Wind Damage

Young trees or those dug from shady areas may easily be damaged by sudden exposure to the sun. If you replant them in an open area, protect them by

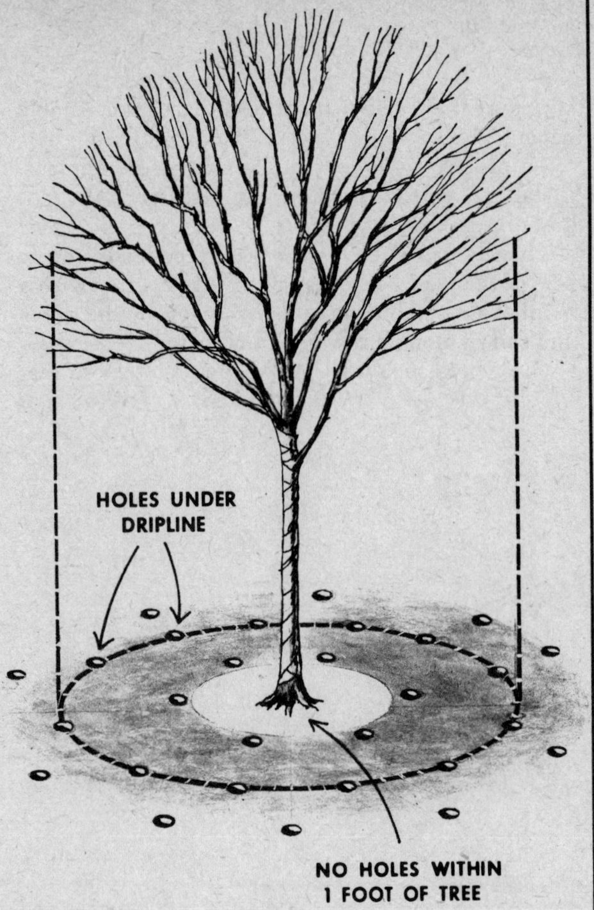

To fertilize, make holes under the drip line first. Use these as a guide for digging evenly spaced holes to a foot from the trunk. Then, dig holes a few feet beyond the drip line so that new root growth will be fertilized.

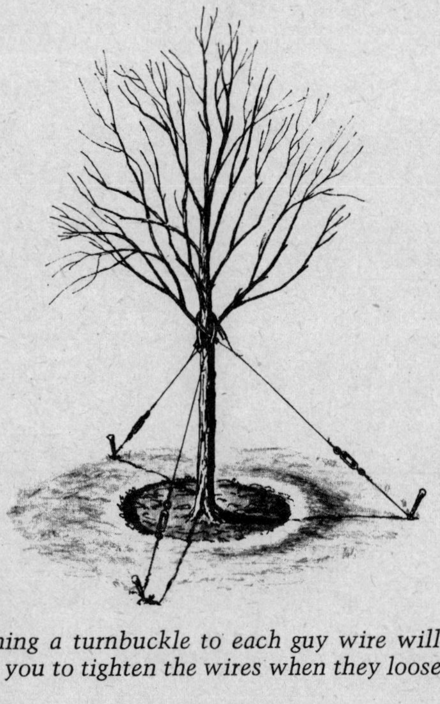

Attaching a turnbuckle to each guy wire will enable you to tighten the wires when they loosen.

wrapping the trunks with strips of burlap or durable paper.

To protect trees and shrubs from wind damage, install guy wires to hold them in place until the root system regenerates.

The number of guy wires needed depends on the size of the plant. You may wish to use wires with a turnbuckle so you can adjust the pull of the wires and can tighten them when they become loose.

Guy wires should be placed high enough so that leverage of the top does not loosen them. A crotch is a good place to anchor the wires.

Use a short length of rubber hose around each wire to protect the bark from injury. Do not wrap the loop so tightly that the growth of the bark is restricted.

Fasten the wires securely to sturdy stakes or other solid anchors. If you use three guy wires, space anchors evenly. Place one anchor against the prevailing winds.

CHAPTER 2

Mulches for Your Garden

USING A MULCH in your flower or vegetable garden may well be your most valuable garden practice. A good mulch can reduce blowing and washing away of soil, suppress weeds, keep the soil moist and cool and add organic matter to it.

Grass clippings, sawdust, straw, and compost make excellent mulches. And they are easy to apply. Simply spread a 3- to 6-inch layer of one of these organic materials on the soil surface around your plants, making certain you do not cover the plants. Keeping the layer deep enough to do the job is important too. This means that you will need to add more mulching material over the old layers to get all the benefits of mulching.

Mulching with grass clippings is a good way to dispose of some of your clippings. But you may need to mix them with other mulch materials to keep them from packing down and preventing water from entering the soil.

Sawdust makes a better mulch if it is well rotted, or if you add 1 to 2 cups of ammonium sulfate or sodium nitrate to each bushel of fresh sawdust before applying the mulch. Weed-free straw is excellent, but loose straw can be a fire hazard and, to some, it may be unsightly.

Compost is probably the best mulch you can use. And you can make it yourself from leftover plant materials from your garden.

Mulches prevent loss of moisture from the soil by evaporation. Moisture moves by capillary action to the surface and evaporates if the soil is not covered by a mulch. Sun and wind hasten this loss of moisture.

You can reduce evaporation and control weeds by stirring the soil an inch or so deep, but plant roots cannot develop in this soil layer. A layer of organic material on the surface gives the same benefits and allows normal plant-root development.

Energy from falling raindrops is dissipated on a mulched soil. The result is less soil erosion and less soil compaction.

Mulches suppress weeds, thus saving you a lot of work. An occasional weed may poke through the mulch but it is easily pulled out.

Mulches keep the soil from getting hot under intense sunlight. Many plants, including vegetables and flowers, need a cool surface soil.

Mulches, especially grass clippings and compost, add organic matter to the soil and furnish food for earthworms, which are valuable in aerating the soil. The organic matter helps to keep the soil crumbly and easy to work. Farmers call this "good tilth." At the end of the growing season the mulch can be worked into the soil to supply organic matter the following year.

If you use a mulch around perennials in the winter, remove it in the spring to let the soil thaw out and warm up.

Many organic materials, such as straw and autumn leaves, are rich in carbohydrates and low in nitrogen. Usually you will find it beneficial to add nitrogen fertilizer to the material before applying it as a mulch. One to 2 cups of fertilizer high in nitrogen (ammonium sulfate) for each bushel of organic

Raindrops splashing on bare soil detach soil particles, which are carried away by surface water.

material is about right. To avoid burning the plants, do not let the fertilizer touch them.

To provide a source for one of the best mulches, every gardener should have a compost bin—preferably two—for making compost from organic materials. You can make the bins yourself by attaching ordinary wire fence or boards to solid posts or open brickwork. Each bin should be 4 to 6 feet high, 3 to 5 feet wide, and any convenient length. And one side of each should be removable for convenience in building up the compost material and for taking it out. In late fall, a temporary piece of wire fence may be used to increase the height about 2 feet. By March, after the material has settled, the piece of fence can be removed.

Two bins permit turning compost by moving it from one bin to the other.

Compost is not only an excellent mulch but it is also a good fertilizer and soil conditioner when it is worked into the soil.

Leaves, grass clippings, stems and stalks from harvested vegetables, corn husks, pea hulls and fine twigs are good materials for composting. You should always compost leaves before using them as a mulch. Raw leaves are flat and map keep water from entering the soil. Avoid using any diseased plants.

The ideal way to make compost is to use two bins. Fill one with alternate layers of organic material 6 to 12 inches thick and garden soil about 1 inch thick. To each layer of organic material, add chemicals at the following rate:

Chemical	*Rate in Cups per Bushel of Organic Material*[1]
Method 1:	
Ammonium sulfate	1
or	
Ammonium nitrate	½
Ground dolomitic limestone[2]	⅔
or	
Wood ashes[2]	1½
Superphosphate	½
Magnesium sulfate (epsom salts)[3]	[4] 1/16
Method 2:	
Mixed fertilizer 5-10-5	3
Ground dolomitic limestone[2]	⅔

[1] Packed tightly with your hands.
[2] For acid compost (for azaleas and rhododendrons), omit lime, limestone, and wood ashes.
[3] Add epsom salts only if dolomitic limestone is unavailable and ordinary limestone is used (at same rate).
[4] Equivalent to 1 tablespoonful.

Be sure to moisten the organic material thoroughly. Repeat this layering process until the bin is full or you run out of organic material. Pack the material tightly around the edges but only lightly in the center so that this area settles more than the edges and the water does not run off.

After three to four months of moderate to warm weather, commonly in June, begin turning the material by moving it from the first bin into the second one. Before turning, it is a good idea to move the material added the previous fall from the edges, which dry out first, to the center.

In areas that have cool frosty winters, compost made from leaves in November and December can be turned the following May or June.

CHAPTER 3

Green Thumb Tips for Growing House Plants

HOW TO BUY A HOUSE PLANT

Rule of Thumb: Be Choosy When You Buy Plants.

Look for plants that are healthy and insect free. It is best to avoid plants showing any of the following telltale signs: spindly growth, yellowing leaves, unnatural blotches, speckles, wilted or artificially waxed leaves. When you check for signs of insects, look on the underside of foliage and in the joints of the leaves, stems and branches. If possible, buy plants during their growth season. Look for signs of leaf buds on foliage plants and flower buds on blooming ones.

LOCATION

Rule of Thumb: Choose the Right Plant for the Growing Conditions You Have to Offer.

Particularly note the light and temperature your plant will receive. When you choose plants for your home or office, know what conditions you have and what plants will do well in that environment.

Light is the factor over which you have the least control. To determine the amount of light you have, use the shadow test. Hold a piece of paper up to the light and note the shadow it makes. A sharp shadow means that you have bright or good light, and a barely visible shadow means dim light.

If directions for your plant note direct or full sun, that means your plant will need sun for at least half of the daylight hours. Indirect or partial sun indicates that the sunlight should be filtered through a curtain. Bright light means no direct sunlight but that the room should be bright and well lighted. Shade-loving plants should be kept in a well-shaded part of your room.

Temperature is a very important factor when dealing with plants. Most plants do not like sudden changes in temperature. Generally speaking, plants do not want a temperature variable of more than a few degrees. Average household temperatures range between 60 and 75 degrees during the winter months.

House plants are usually grouped in three temper-

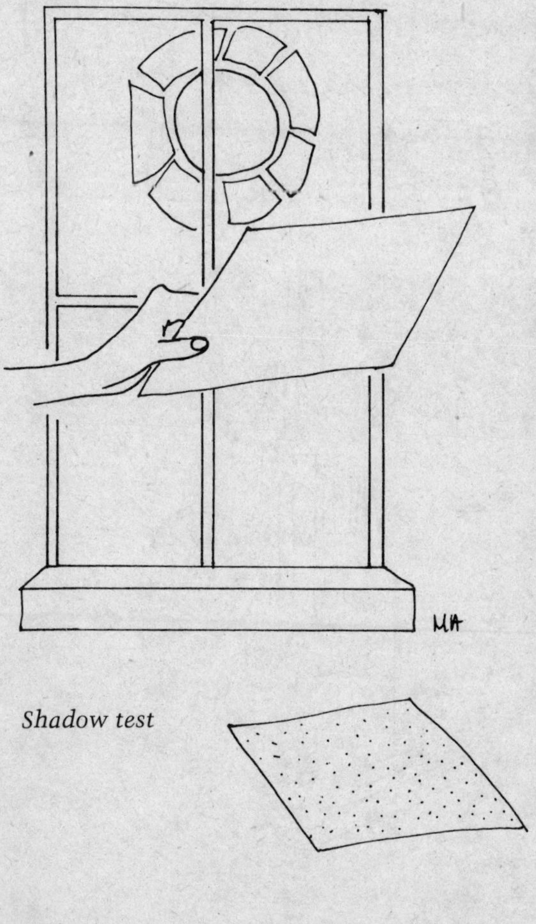

Shadow test

ature categories: cool, moderate, and warm. Cool temperatures range from 50 to 60 degrees and should not go below 45 degrees. Moderate temperatures are from 60 to 70 degrees and should not be below 50 degrees. Warm temperatures range from 70 to 80 degrees and should not go below 60 degrees.

GROOMING AND TOOLS

Rule of Thumb: Establish a Regular Weekly or Monthly Routine for Plant Care. A Groomed Plant Is a Healthy Plant.

Remove all wilted or withering leaves, stems and flowers with a sharp scissors or knife. This is a good time to look at how the plant is growing. If it is getting leggy, pinch out new growth. This will force the plant to branch out and form a more compact shape.

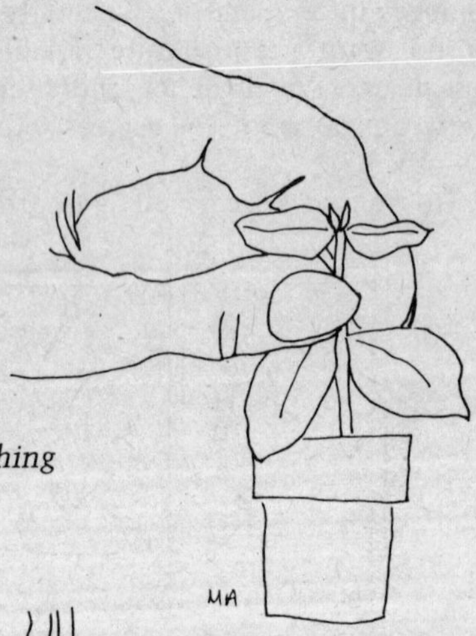

Pinching

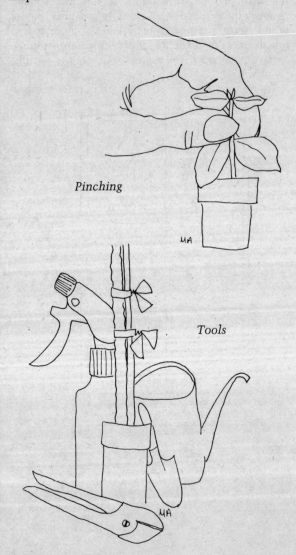

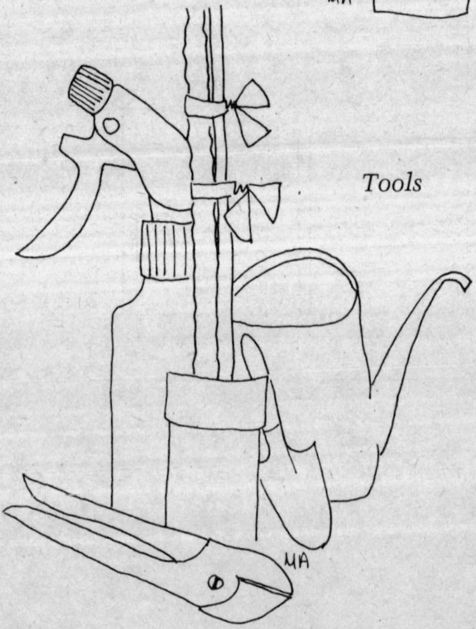

Tools

When staking your plants, do it early in their development. It is easier to keep the stem straight than to straighten a crooked one. Some plants need support for heavy flower heads or dense growth at the top of the stem. Thin bamboo stakes are useful and twistums or the paper-coated wire found in boxes of plastic bags are excellent for staking and tying the plant. Climbing and trailing plants such as philodendron need to have a piece of bark or totem pole for climbing.

Once the plant has been groomed, place the pot in the sink and gently wash the leaves to remove dust and insects. Using a fork for a cultivator, loosen the surface soil in the pot.

Useful tools to have on hand for your indoor gardening are a trowel or large spoon and fork for working the soil. You will need pruning shears, a pair of sharp scissors or a sharp knife to cut off dead leaves and stems and to do the pruning and grooming your plant requires. A watering can with a long thin spout is best for watering. However, you can use a pitcher or even a recycled bottle. A daily misting is beneficial to most plants as they thrive in a humid environment. (Note there are exceptions such as cactus and African violets.) Good, inexpensive plastic-bottle misters can be bought at hardware and garden-supply stores; or convert an old cleaned-out spray bottle into a mister.

POTS, TRAYS AND SAUCERS

Rule of Thumb: Use Pots with Drainage Holes.

The unglazed clay pot exchanges the air in the soil readily. The clay evaporates the moisture through the walls of the pot, and it is less likely to become waterlogged. In summer these pots dry out in the heat and breezy weather and must be watered more frequently.

Plastic pots require less frequent watering because the moisture evaporates from the soil surface only. It is important to provide a plant in this type of pot with well-drained soil and a layer of drainage material in the bottom of the pot. The soil will get waterlogged from too frequent watering and the plant will suffer.

Decorative glazed pots can be used for planting if there are drainage holes in the bottom and the plant has well-drained soil. If you have a favorite pot that does not provide adequate drainage there are several ways to make it a usable planter. It may be advisable to fit a properly drained container for the plant inside your pot. It might be possible to drill a hole in the bottom. If these suggestions will not work, place a thick layer of fine gravel in the bottom of the pot and then set the plant in. Be very careful not to overwater.

To protect your windowsill or table, place pots in trays or saucers. These are available in plastic, rubber, glazed or unglazed clay. The unglazed clay must be waterproofed with a sheet of plastic or painted with waterproof paint.

POTTING

Rule of Thumb: The Diameter of the Pot Generally Should Be One Third the Height of the Plant.

Cover each drainage hole with a pebble or piece of broken pot to allow water to seep out but to keep the soil in place. Add a layer of gravel, crushed brick, or bits of broken clay pots for additional drainage. This is particularly important when you are using plastic pots. Cover the drainage material with a layer of soil. The depth of the layer will be determined by the size of the plant's rootball. The plant should sit in the pot so that when the pot is filled with soil the level is one inch below the rim. Set the plant gently but firmly in the pot and work the soil down into the roots. A sharp rap or two on the work surface will help to settle the soil. Do this a couple of times as you fill the pot with soil. Soak the freshly potted plant in water until soil is thoroughly moistened.

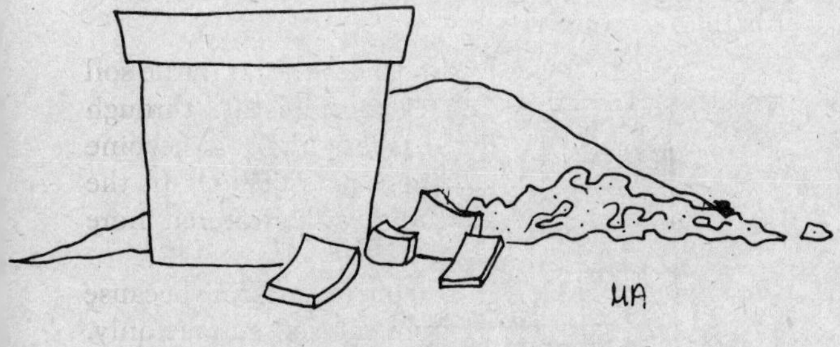

Pot and drainage material

Occasionally plants may outgrow their pots. In general, repotting is done in the spring or the fall. Flowering plants are best repotted after the flowers have faded. As you prepare the plant for repotting, take a careful look at the roots. Check for insects and signs of root damage such as root rot. Remove anything that looks or feels unhealthy. There are some plants that are happy being potbound and some that do not bloom unless they are. Be sure to check a plant book for the likes and dislikes of your specific plant.

SOILS

Rule of Thumb: Be Sure to Select the Correct Soil Mixture for Your Plants.

There are several readily available ingredients that are fairly common to all soil mixtures. However, the proportions used and those to include and leave out differ from plant to plant. These ingredients and their functions are:

Peat moss: This provides rich organic content for the soil. It also helps to prevent the soil from packing into a hard mass around the roots. Peat moss retains moisture and will prevent the soil mixture from drying out.

Potting soil or garden loam: This is the dense, black soil available in variety and plant stores. Used alone, it is too rich, dense and heavy for most plants but provides body and nutrients for many plant varieties.

Coarse sand, perlite or vermiculite: Any of these organic materials will loosen your soil mixture so that air and water are readily available to the roots. Coarse sand is prefered by some people, especially in mixtures for cacti and succulents. Perlite, a white volcanic substance, will not pack or soak up moisture, but it keeps the soil porous. Vermiculite, an expanded mica, does soak up and retain moisture.

Activated charcoal and bone meal: These are extra ingredients and are not mandatory in a soil mixture. They help, however, in keeping the soil fresh and they promote root growth.

If obtained prepackaged in a plant or variety store, the above ingredients have the advantage of being sterilized. This will ensure that there will be no harmful fungii or pests in the planting mixture. If you wish to sterilize your own soil, place it in a shallow baking pan and add one cup of water for each gallon of soil. Bake it in the oven at 180 degrees for 45 minutes. The soil must be cooled for at least 24 hours before using.

WATERING

Rule of Thumb: Do Not Water Too Much. More Plants Die of Overwatering Than from Any Other Cause.

Always water your plants in the morning with room-temperature water. Plants take in moisture and minerals which are most useful in combination with light energy. Know the needs of your plant and its environmental conditions. Factors such as humidity, sunlight, seasonal variations, and type of pot

Plants in an attractive arrangement

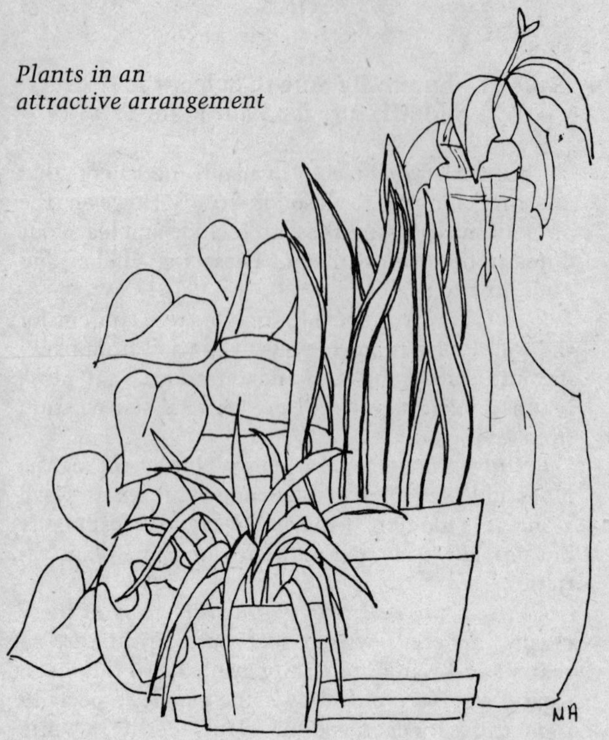

used must influence your decision concerning the amount of the water to give your plant. Here are some basic guidelines. When the plant is growing new leaves or producing flowers it needs more water than during its resting period. A cool environment requires less water than a hot, dry one. Plants with hairy, thorny or waxy leaves need less water than the thin-leaved varieties. Plants are specially adapted to meet specific needs. Inform yourself of the needs and adaptations of your individual plants.

There are several ways of watering your plants. The basic thing to remember about watering is to wet the soil in the pot until the excess drains off. One way of being sure the soil is thoroughly wet is to soak the pot in a bucket of tepid water for half an hour, remove the pot, and drain. If you prefer to water from the top, pour the water slowly onto the soil, fill the pot up to the top with water and allow it to absorb it until excess drains from the hole in the bottom. Otherwise there is the danger that the water will not penetrate the rootball, particularly after repotting. Use a knitting needle or other sharp implement to poke a few holes in the soil ball to channel the water to the roots.

All pots should have a layer of drainage material in the bottom to keep the plant from getting root rot from soggy soil. The plastic pot does not allow the moisture to evaporate through the walls; do not be too generous with water. Too much water clogs the soil and cuts down on the supply of air to the roots.

HUMIDITY

Rule of Thumb: Most Plants Like High Humidity and Will Benefit from a Daily Misting. This Does Not Replace Watering.

Creating a humid environment for your plants can be achieved in several ways. Locate the plants in the area of your house where the humidity is high, such as the bathroom. Placing a collection of plants in a glass baking dish filled with pebbles that are kept partially covered with water is helpful in making a more humid atmosphere around the plants. Cluster your plants together and they will benefit from the moisture each gives off. Misting the foliage daily is beneficial to practically all the house plants except African violets, cacti, and some succulents. Use your mister or recycled spray bottle as described under "Grooming and Tools."

FERTILIZING

Rule of Thumb: Establish a Regular Routine for Feeding Your Plants, and Do Not Fertilize Your Plants When the Soil Is Dry.

A quick intake of the fertilizer solution when the soil is dry causes burned roots and leaf edges.

When plants are actively growing (usually between March and October), they should be fertilized every four to six weeks. Do not fertilize when the plant is not producing new buds and leaves, because it is then resting.

Fertilizing

Flowering plants will need more fertilizer. When the plant has set flower buds, fertilize every two weeks while the plant is in bloom. After the flowers have faded, remove the flower stalks and stop feeding the plant for a month to six weeks. This will give the plant a chance to rest.

There are a variety of plant foods available at plant and garden-supply stores and variety stores. Fish emulsion is a safe organic plant food that most plants respond well to. If you prefer to use a chemical fertilizer, follow the directions exactly. It is better to feed too little than too much. Too rich a diet can surely kill your plant.

PLANTS FOR THE INDOOR GARDEN

African Violet (*Saintpaulia*)

The African violet, a longtime favorite houseplant, does insist on a certain amount of care and attention, but its beautiful blossoms make the effort worthwhile.

Temperature: African violets are most contented and grow best within a temperature range of 65 to 80 degrees. Be careful that your plants are not in an open window in cold weather, or in a draft.

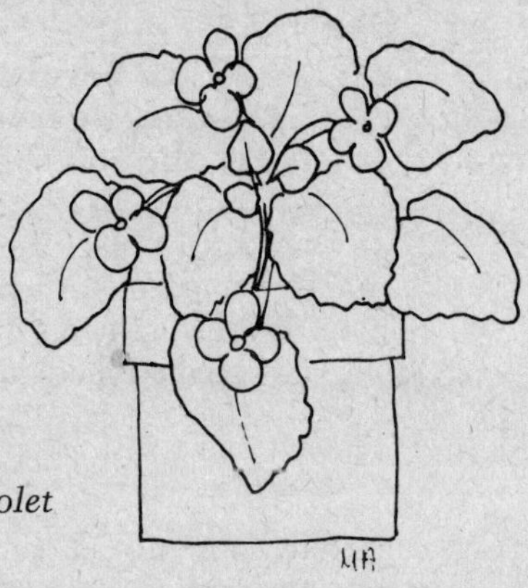

African violet

Light and sun: The African violet enjoys a place in an east or west window. Direct sun is too strong, unless filtered through a curtain. Excess sun will cause spotting and loss of color, and too little light causes elongated stems and no blooms.

Water and humidity: African violets should be watered from the saucer underneath, in the morning, with *lukewarm* water. Water when the soil beings to dry out. Do not keep it soggy. If the air is dry in your home, place the potted plant in a tray of moistened pebbles.

Soil: Rich but light and crumbly (add some coarse sand and leaf mold to achieve this) or use commercial African violet mix.

How to start new plants: If more crowns develop on your plant, separate them from plant with some root attached, and pot. Or cut off a healthy leaf with 1-inch stem attached and set in rooting medium—tiny plantlets will develop from leaf and can be potted. Plants propagated from crowns may flower as soon as a month; plantlets from leaf may take a year or more to flower.

Aralia, False
(*Dizygotheca elegantissima*)

A plant of grace and elegance with narrow, ribbonlike, notched leaves of dark green, usually born on slender, single stems. The false aralia is attractive if two or three plants are planted together in one pot. It grows very quickly, so prune the stem tips from time to time to prevent the foliage from thinning at the bottom.

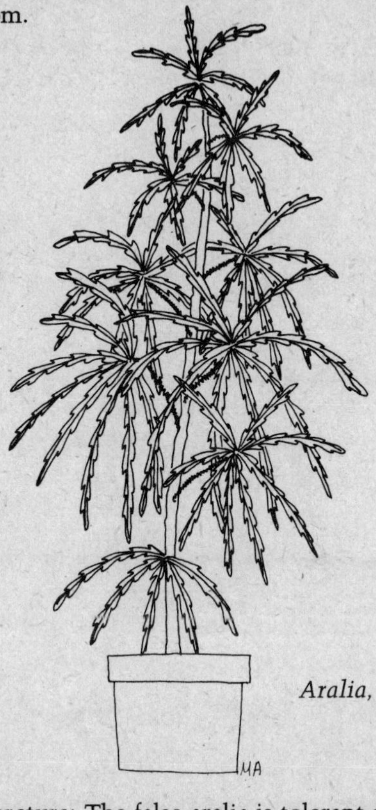

Aralia, false

Temperature: The false aralia is tolerant of warm temperatures if there is plenty of humidity.

Light and sun: The plant likes a semisunny (or semishady) window; an east or west window is ideal.

Water and humidity: Keep the soil damp but not soggy. The false aralia likes a humid atmosphere. Place your plant on a pebble tray and mist the foliage daily.

Soil: The soil should be equal parts loam, sand and peat moss.

Special care: You can rejuvenate leggy plants by drastically cutting the stems back to four to six inches from the pot. Do this in the spring and leave the plant in a sheltered location, being sure to fertilize and water frequently.

Asparagus Fern, Emerald Feather
(*Asparagus sprengeri*)

This delightful, feathery, plant is best displayed in a hanging container. The long branches drape gracefully and are studded with tiny white flowers that ripen into red-orange berries.

Temperature: Asparagus fern is not fussy about temperatures, but prefers a range of 60 degrees to 68 degrees.

Light and sun: The filtered sun of an east or west window is a good location.

Water and humidity: Soak the soil in the pot thoroughly and allow it to become dry to the touch before rewatering.

Soil: A well-drained potting soil or a mixture of equal parts of loam, peat moss and sand or perlite.

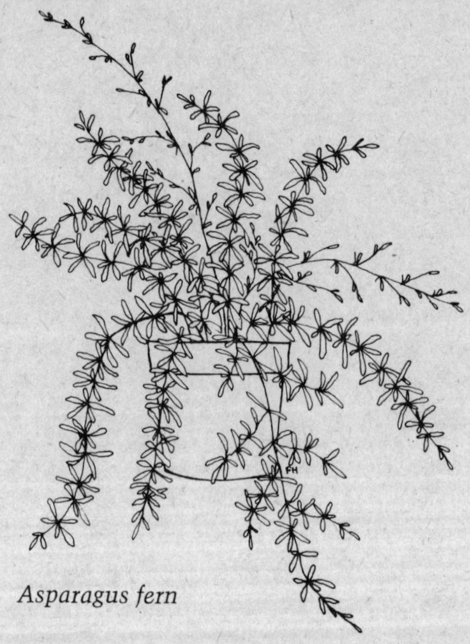

Asparagus fern

How to start new plants: Allow the berries to ripen and when dry sow the seeds they contain. Asparagus fern can usually be grown from seed quite well. The whole berry may also be planted. Or take root cuttings from large plants.

Avocado (*Persea americana*)

The avocado comes easily from seed and is grown for its ornamental foliage. It makes a nice tree for your indoor garden. Allow the plant to reach the desired height and then begin regular pinching to force branching and encourage bushy growth.

Temperature: Temperatures between 60 and 70 degrees suit the avocado well.

Light and sun: Keep your avocado in bright light but protected from direct sun. Avocados are easily sunburned, indoors or out.

Water and humidity: Use tepid water and keep the soil moist. Place the plant on a pebble tray to raise the humidity level around it. This plant likes a fair amount of humidity and benefits from regular misting. Any signs of browning or crispness at the tips and along the edges of the leaves means the plant needs more humidity.

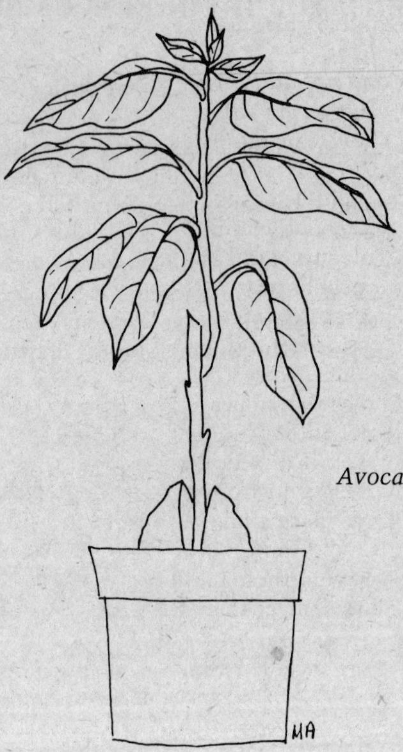

Avocado

Soil: Use a mixture consisting of equal parts of sand, loam and peat moss.

How to start new plants from seed: There are two ways of starting the seed. You can germinate it in a glass of water. Placing the pointed end up, stick three or four toothpicks around the middle of the seed to support it on the rim of the glass. Keep the water fresh. If you prefer to start the seed in soil, place it in a pot, pointed end up, allowing one third of the seed to stick out of the soil. Avocados come easily from seed but patience is important. Sometimes it takes two months for the seed to germinate.

Boston Fern
(*Nephrolepis exaltata 'Bostoniensis'*)

Exaltata is a good adjective for this family of ferns that can fill a corner with rich green foliage. These are excellent for hanging baskets. Initially the ferns may need a lot of attention until the right combination of environmental factors is achieved but the effort is well worth it. The leaflets grow on a midrib that is covered with fine brown hairs, and vary from smooth-edged to feathery and even ruffled. A mature fern can have fronds ranging in length from 2 to 3 feet and 2 to 3 inches across.

Temperature: With lots and lots of humidity, ferns will do well in house temperatures in the 60-to-70-degree range.

Light and sun: Ferns need a location with good bright light, but this means *filtered* sunlight. *Avoid direct sunlight.*

Water and humidity: It is essential that the roots never dry out at any time. Soak the soil regularly. Clay pots and hanging baskets can be soaked in a bucket or the sink for half an hour and then drained. The soil should be checked daily to make sure that it is not drying out. Humidity is the most important ingredient in successful fern growing. Place pots of ferns on a pebble tray. Mist the foliage daily with room-temperature water.

Soil: Ferns need a soil that is loose and easily penetrated by their dense root systems. The soil mixture should be rich in peat moss and organic matter with a liberal amount of sand for drainage. A sprinkling of charcoal mixed in the soil helps to keep it from becoming sour from frequent watering. When potting ferns, place a layer of bits of broken pots or gravel in the bottom of the pot. Ferns do not take kindly to having their roots tampered with, so be careful not to damage them when repotting.

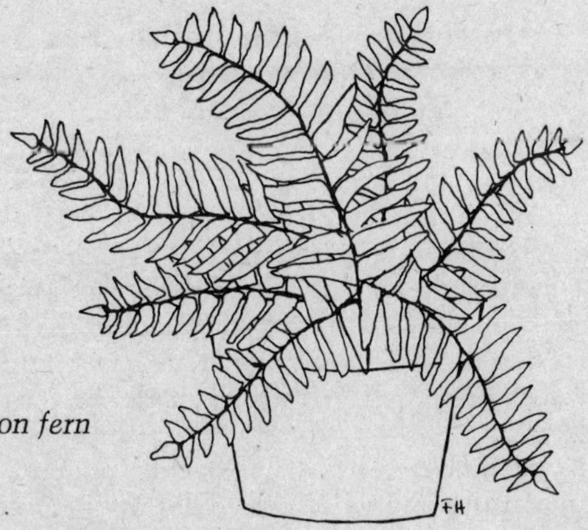

Boston fern

How to start new plants: An easy way is to divide roots when repotting large plants and to pot these divisions separately.

Chinese Evergreen
(*Aglaonema* varieties)

This beautiful foliage plant has waxy dark-green leaves. The leaves grow on a cane-like stem and are oblong, tapering to a thin tip. Some of the varieties are variegated with splashes of creamy white or yellow. Under optimal conditions, it will produce a flower spike surrounded by a white or greenish-white spathe. The flower is similar to a calla lilly. The great thing about this plant is that it will adapt to a variety of environments—which makes it a good plant for a beginner or in a difficult location.

Temperature: A range of 60 to 70 degrees suits this plant well.

Light and sun: A shady spot, under artificial light, or any other location will suit this plant. The Chinese evergreen is an excellent plant for a north window.

Water and humidity: Keep the soil moist but not soggy. To avoid waterlogged soil, allow the surface soil to become dry to the touch before rewatering. The Chinese evergreen can be grown in water. The roots are attractive so a clear glass container shows them off to best advantage. It is important to wash the leaves regularly to keep them dust free.

Soil: The soil should be equal parts of garden loam, peat moss and sand—but any average garden soil will do.

How to start new plants: This plant has a tendency to get leggy. To start a new plant, make a diagonal cut 2 inches below the foliage and root in water. Additional new plants can be started from 2-inch lengths of stem set in moist sand or soil.

Dracaenas

There are several varieties of dracaenas differing in foliage color, variegation and size. Here are three that are commonly available. *Dracaena deremensis 'Warneckei'* is a good choice for a location without much light. The gray-green foliage is striped with white and gray. *Dracaena marginata* has clusters of narrow deep-green leaves edged with red, and gray stems strongly marked with leaf scars. This variety will reach a height of five or six feet. *Dracaena sanderiana* resembles a corn plant in the brightness of the green and the size and shape of the leaves, with the difference that the leaves are striped with white.

Temperature: Moderate household temperatures in the 60-to-70-degree range suit these plants best. It is important to keep plants away from heating vents.

Light and sun: The *marginata* and *sanderiana* should get only filtered sun or bright light. The *'Warneckei'* will fare well in a spot with very little light; it will flourish when more light is available.

Water and humidity: All these plants like soil that is kept evenly moist but not soggy. Soak the soil in the pot thoroughly and rewater only when the soil surface feels dry to the touch. Humidity is a must. Brown crispy leaf tips and margins mean too little moisture in the air. It is a good idea to place the dracaenas in pebble trays and mist the foliage daily.

Soil: Commercial potting soil or ordinary garden soil are adequate, but added drainage material such as sand or perlite is advisable.

How to start new plants: By air-layering or stem cuttings.

Dracaena marginata

Dracaena sanderiana

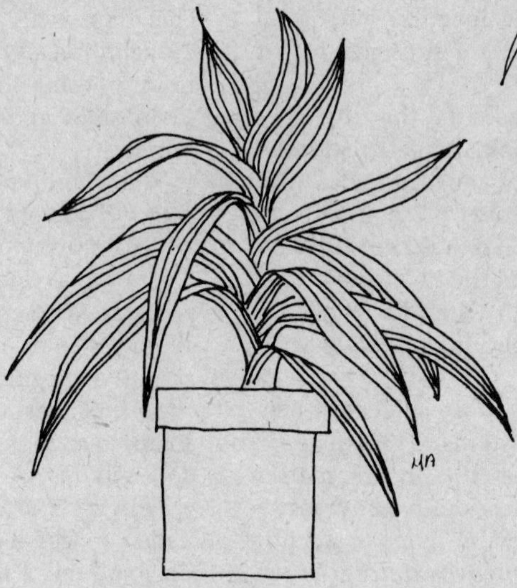

Dracaena deremensis 'Warneckei'

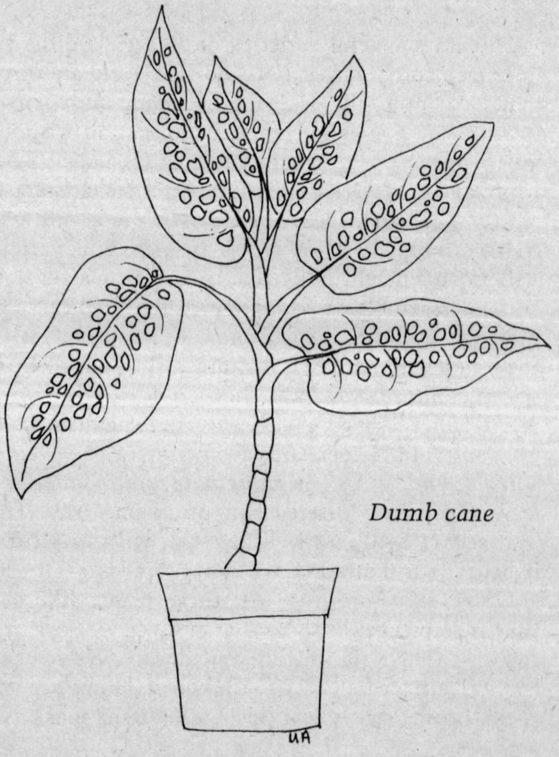

Dumb cane

Dumb Cane, Mother-in-Law Plant, Dieffenbachia
(*Dieffenbachia maculata*)

The cool-looking foliage of this plant is yellow-green mottled with white. The leaves are pointed ovals that become quite large as the plant matures. The names "dumb cane" and "mother-in-law plant" come from the fact that when a piece of the stem is placed on the tongue it causes temporary numbness and loss of speech. *All joking aside, this plant is poisonous.*

Temperature: The dieffenbachia prefers warm temperatures and will tolerate hot dry places if additional humidity is supplied.

Light and sun: This plant does well in an east or west window where it can bask in the sun for a few hours.

Water and humidity: The soil should be allowed to dry out for a few days before rewatering. The plants indicate a need for water when the leaves show signs of dropping. Regular misting keeps the foliage dust free and luxuriant.

Soil: A porous soil of equal parts loam, peat moss, and sand is fine.

How to start new plants: If the plant is too tall and the stem is bare and unsightly, cut the top on a diagnonal and root it in water. The old stem will probably sprout, so do not throw it out.

Gardenia (*Gardenia jasminoides*)

This lovely, fragrant plant is truly a challenge to the indoor or outdoor gardener. But what a reward in the creamy scented flowers and the glossy foliage.

Temperature: The temperature must be kept above 65 degrees to maintain healthy foliage and flower buds. These plants hate drafts. Loss of flower buds is often due to sudden changes in temperature.

Light and sun: The gardenia needs lots of light; but avoid strong sun, which may burn the leaves.

Water and humidity: The soil must be kept constantly moist without becoming soggy. Submerge the pot in a bucket of lukewarm water and allow it to soak for half an hour, or until the soil is moist on the surface. Do not allow the pot to sit in water, as that will cause the roots to rot. Gardenias need very high humidity at all times. Place the pot in a tray of moistened pebbles. Mist the foliage daily with tepid water. Leaf or bud drop indicate that the air is too dry.

Soil: Potting soil should be a mixture of equal parts peat moss, loam and well-decayed manure, with sand or perlite added for drainage.

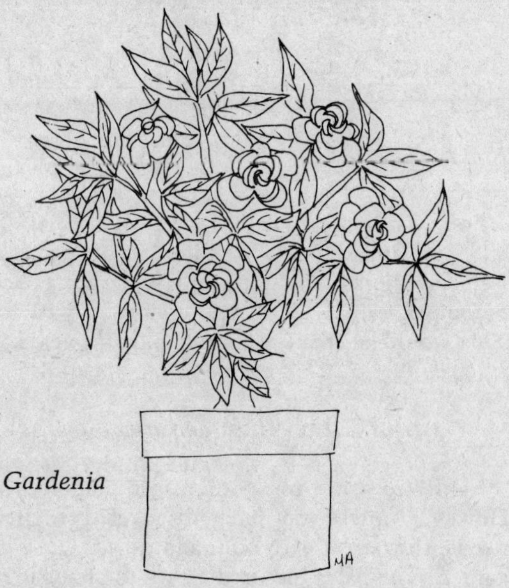

Gardenia

How to start new plants: Root cuttings in vermiculite, sand or water.

Special requirements: The gardenia needs to have lots of pampering to encourage it to flower. It is necessary to provide plenty of light, a uniform temperature and moisture level, and high humidity. Loss of buds and blackening of the leaves and new growth result from a sharp change in temperature or from insufficient light and humidity.

Grape Ivy (*Cissus rhombifolia*)

Grape ivy is a climber or trailer. The olive-colored green leaves look a bit like those of holly but without the stiffness or the sharp tips. The leaves form attractive groups of three and are accompanied by furry tendrils.

Temperature: The plant is fairly tolerant of a wide temperature range. Increase the amount of humidity as the temperature goes up.

Light and sun: Grape ivy will do all right in low light and is often used in low-light areas. But it flourishes in bright light or filtered sunlight.

Water and humidity: Soak pot and soil thoroughly; allow the soil to become dry to the touch before rewatering. Mist frequently and wash the foliage regularly to remove dust and restore the luster of the leaves.

Soil: A potting soil that is rich in organic matter is the best. Be sure to add plenty of drainage material to the soil mixture.

How to start new plants: Six-inch cuttings will root slowly in water; or take root cuttings from large plant when repotting.

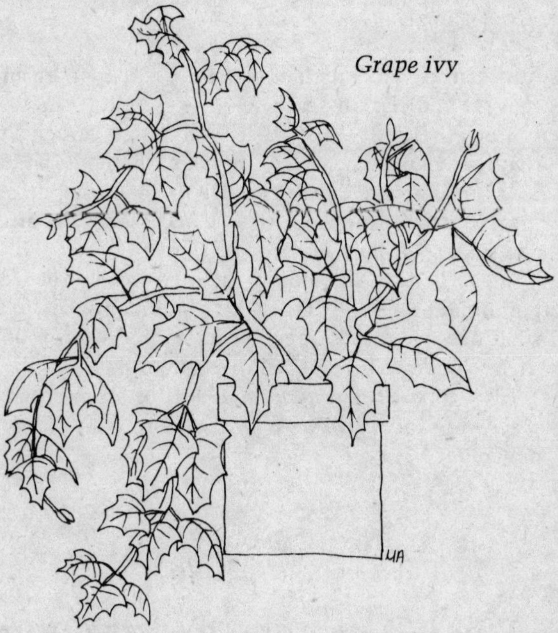

Grape ivy

Jade Plant (*Crassula arborescens*)

This sturdy succulent can grow into a shapely miniature tree. Mature plants (six to eight years) will produce clusters of star-shaped flowers with care and luck.

Temperature: Temperatures ranging from 65 to 75

degrees are fine. Lower and higher temperatures will be tolerated.

Light and sun: In the house, the jade plant does best in full sunlight, with shade at midday if possible. A west or south window is a good location. If you put the plant outside in the summer, place it in a lightly shaded spot.

Water and humidity: The soil should remain dry for several days between waterings. The fleshly leaves soak up the water in the soil and store it for

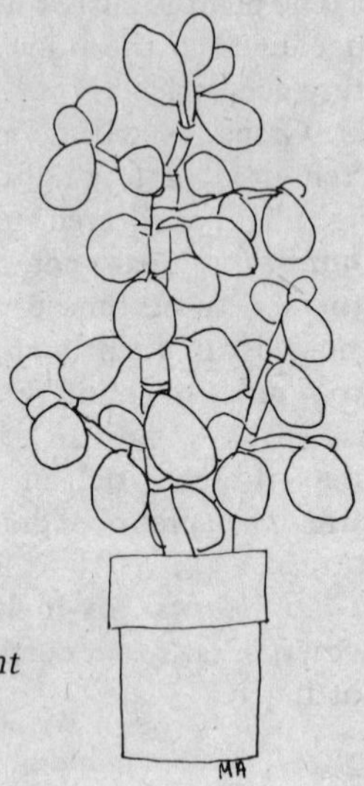

Jade plant

future use. Too much water will cause stem and root rot and certain death.

Soil: The jade plant will do well in rich garden soil that has coarse sand or fine bits of broken pots added to it for drainage. Each year give the pot a top dressing of humus. A new pot will be necessary only after about three or four years.

Special care: The jade plant must be thoroughly potbound to bloom. Once your plant approaches the right age, let the pot become crammed with roots; then it will produce its delicate flowers.

How to start new plants: A leaf or stem cutting placed in sandy, gritty soil will take root and form a new plant.

Norfolk Island Pine
(*Araucaria excelsa*)

The delightful symmetry of this evergreen makes it a desirable house plant. The branches grow in tiers of about six, each tier representing a year's growth. The bright-green needles are soft and pleasant to touch.

Temperature: The ideal temperature is between 50 and 60 degrees. High temperatures are tolerated when sufficient humidity is available.

Light and sun: The filtered sun of an east or west window is best. Yellowing of the needles might mean too much sun.

Water and humidity: Provide the plant with a well-drained soil and pot. Water thoroughly and allow the soil surface to become dry before rewatering. Daily misting is necessary for the warmer temperatures of most houses and offices. A pebble tray will help to add more moisture to the air around the plant.

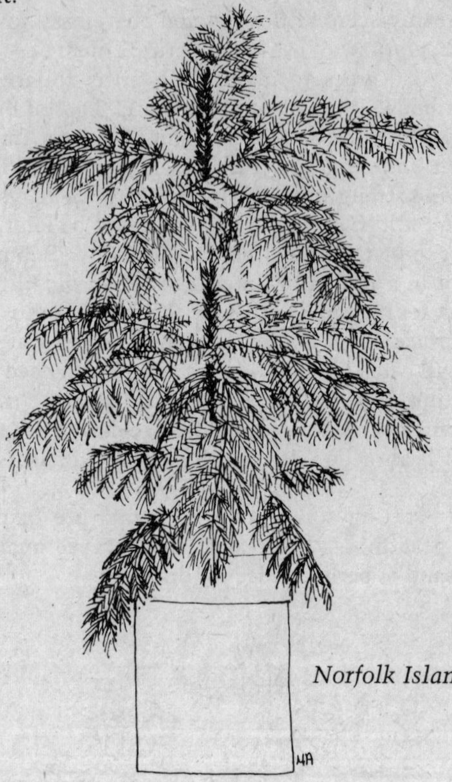

Norfolk Island pine

Soil: Garden loam mixed with equal parts of sand and peat moss makes a suitable potting mixture. Repot Norfolk Island pine only when it has become potbound (when the pot is crammed with roots). This would be about every two or three years.

Parlor Palm (*Chamaedorea elegans*)

Palm trees are not the easiest plants to grow. However, once you have discovered their basic needs, they are a delightful addition to your indoor garden. The palm pictured grows to about four feet tall. It is most attractive when two or three plants are grouped together in a pot. The long feathery fronds grow out of a single stem. Other varieties to try are *C. seifrizii, C. erumpens,* and *C. costarincana.*

Temperature: The best growing temperatures for palms range between 60 and 75 degrees.

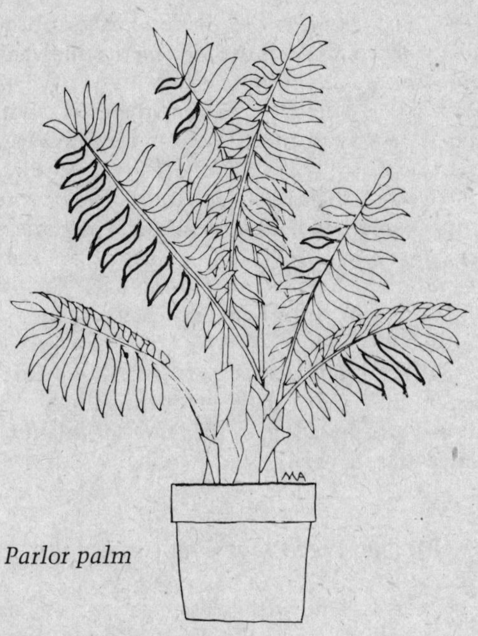

Parlor palm

Light and sun: Palms are good plants for locations without much light. They do not like direct sun light.

Water and Humidity: During the active growing season, between March and October, the palm needs moist soil but it will not tolerate soggy soil. In the winter months, allow the soil to dry on the surface before rewatering. If the foliage shows signs of browning and drying on the tips, it needs more humidity. Misting regularly is recommended to keep the foliage healthy.

Soil: The palm needs well-drained soil of equal parts rich garden loam, peat moss and sand. It will need repotting only every two or three years. It prefers being a bit potbound.

Philodendron (*Philodendron oxycardium*)

By nature, the common philodendron is a climbing plant, but it also trails. It looks best on a bracket beside the window frame, and for good effect must be kept strongly pinched back so that the plant is full of bushy young growth and does not deteriorate into two or three stringlike stems.

Temperature: Normal house or office temperatures are fine.

Light and sun: The philodendron is quite hardy and robust and will grow almost anywhere. However, it will fare better in a well-lighted area.

Water and humidity: The plant should be kept evenly moist and never be allowed to dry out. Be certain water does not remain in the saucer after watering. The foliage should be misted daily and the leaves cleaned of accumulated dust.

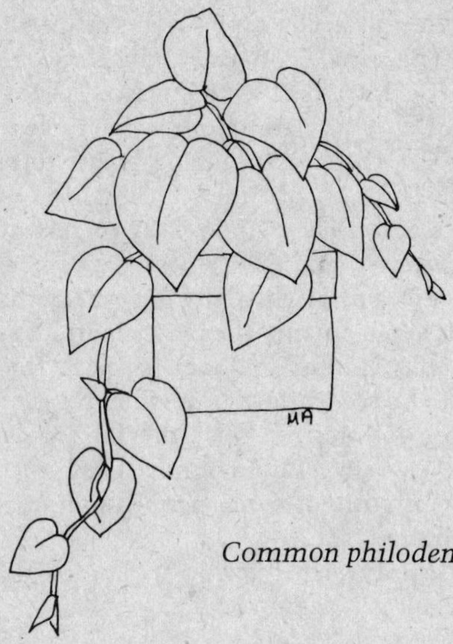

Common philodendron

Soil: Potting soil mixed with perlite, vermiculite, or sand and peat moss is recommended.

How to start new plants: Tip cuttings can be easily rooted in water and then potted in good potting soil.

Philodendron, Windowleaf
(*Monstera deliciosa, Philodendron pertusum*)

Windowleaf philodendron has large heart-shaped leaves that are slashed irregularly. It is an enthusias-

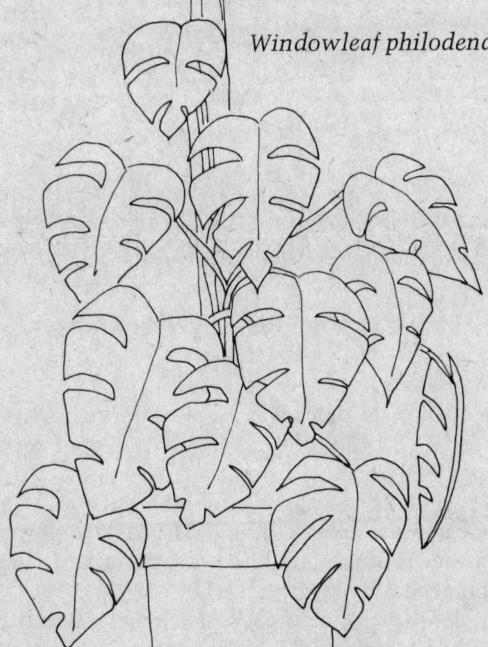

Windowleaf philodendron

tic climber and needs a piece of bark or totem for support. The aerial roots can be inserted in the soil or encouraged to attach to the totem. There does not seem to be an explanation for why some leaves split and why some do not. Splitting seems to occur erratically.

Temperature: The windowleaf prefers temperatures between 65 and 70 degrees.

Light and sun: Bright light is best for this plant. However, avoid putting the plant in direct sunlight.

Water and humidity: Soak the plant thoroughly and allow the soil surface to remain dry for a day or two before rewatering. Mist the foliage daily and wash the leaves weekly to remove dust.

Soil: A mixture of equal parts garden loam, peat moss, and sand is fine.

Special care: Keep growing tips pinched back so plant doesn't get leggy.

Purple passion plant—Velvet plant

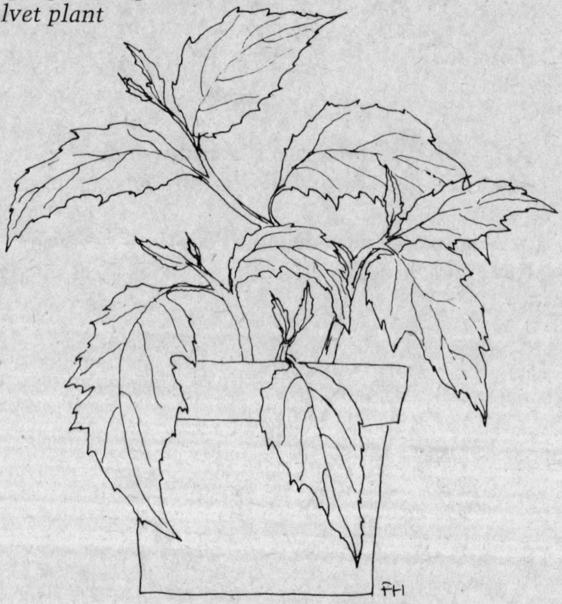

Purple Passion Plant, Velvet Plant (*Gynura aurantica*)

The strikingly rich royal purple coloring and velvety texture of the foliage and stems attract many growers. The leaves and stems are covered with tiny purple hairs. The straggly growth habit is best kept in check by frequent pruning. The yellow flowers sometimes produced are rather unattractive and are best pinched off.

Temperature: The purple passion plant likes temperatures in the 65 to 70 degree range.

Light and sun: Direct or partial sun will intensify the purple color.

Water and humidity: It is important that the plant not dry out. Keep the soil evenly moist at all times. A humid atmosphere is important to keep the brilliant color. Mist the foliage frequently and place the pot in a tray of moistened pebbles to raise the humidity.

Soil: Use potting soil of equal parts garden loam, peat moss and sand. This plant will also grow in water.

Special care: Regularly pinching back the stems will force the plant to branch. It has a tendency to get leggy.

How to start new plants: Set 6-inch stem cuttings in water; they root easily. Frequent taking of new cuttings will help keep the mother plant well trimmed and shapely.

Rubber Tree Plant (*Ficus elastica*)

This house plant with glossy dark-green leaves can grow to be 4 feet high with a little care and not too much water.

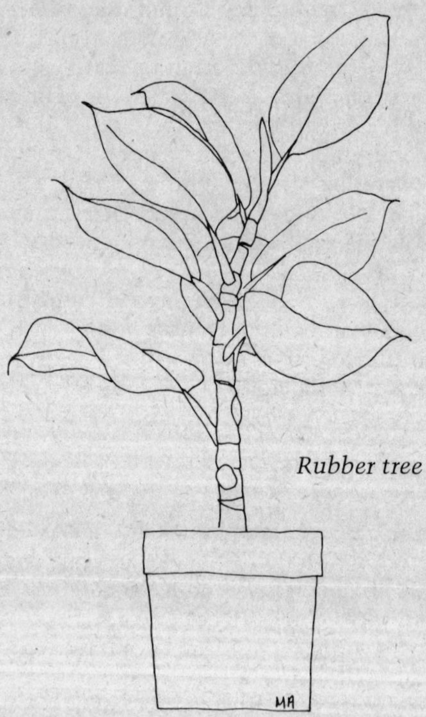

Rubber tree plant

Temperature: Due to its hardy nature, the plant does well in any normal household temperature.

Light and sun: It will grow in almost any light, but a well-lighted area is best for the rich green foliage characteristic of the rubber tree plant.

Water and humidity: Water only when the soil is completely dry all through the pot. You should set the entire pot in a bucket when watering, so that moisture can penetrate the deepest roots. Clean the leaves every two weeks or so with a damp cloth. Do not artificially shine the leaves as this clogs the plant's pores and does not allow it to breathe!

Soil: Soil should be a well-drained mixture of equal parts of sand, peat moss and garden loam. If pot is plastic or ceramic be sure to provide plenty of drainage material in the bottom.

How to start new plants: This is usually done by professionals. However, you can try the air-layering process by following the details outlined in a gardening encyclopedia.

Schefflera, Umbrella Tree (*Schefflera actinophylla*)

If you are looking for a tree for your indoor garden, a schefflera is a good choice. It has handsome deep-green leaves that radiate out from a long slender stalk rather like the ribs of an umbrella.

Temperature: The umbrella tree does well in a room where the temperature ranges from 55 to 75 degrees.

Light and sun: The schefflera does not like direct sunlight. It grows best in good light from a shaded window.

Water and humidity: When watering your schefflera, soak the pot thoroughly and then allow the soil to dry before rewatering. The plant likes a humid atmosphere and responds well to daily misting with warm water. This is essential if the plant is in a room with forced hot-air heat. This plant needs a pebble tray.

Soil: The soil mixture should be equal parts of peat moss, garden soil and sand. A layer of gravel or bits of broken pots should be placed underneath the soil to ensure good drainage.

Special care: Weekly washing of the foliage will keep dust from building up and suffocating the plant. Poor drainage or too much water will cause the leaves to drop.

Snake Plant (*Sansevieria trifasciata*)

Seen in many homes and offices, this spikey banded plant will take almost any abuse.

Temperature: Normal household temperatures are best, *but* do not allow the plant to become suddenly chilled!

Light and sun: The snake plant is a good low-light plant but needs sun in order to bloom.

Water: The plant likes the dryness of the usual home and should never be overwatered. The leaves should be cleaned with clear water every two weeks.

Soil: Garden loam, peat moss and sand mixed together provide the best soil for the snake plant.

How to start new plants: There are several common varieties of the snake plant and they are distin-

Schefflera—Umbrella tree

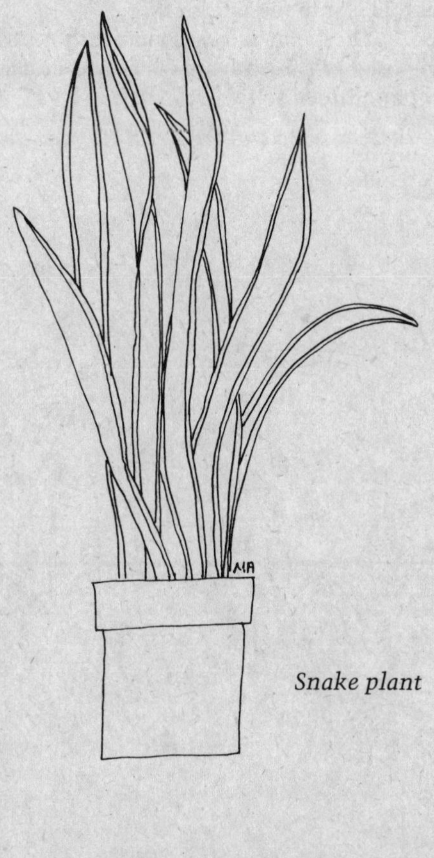

Snake plant

guished by their coloring and shape. In order to maintain these distinctions, it is necessary that the cultivation of each variety remain distinct. Among them are:

Zeylonica: distinguished by bands that vary from light green to white. Cut the leaves into two or three sections and root them in sandy soil.

Laurentii: recognizable by its yellow bands. You should divide the leaves of the plant and repot. It is possible to cut the leaves into sections and plant, but the yellow coloration would not be maintained.

'Haknii': a sport of *Laurentii*; relatively small and grows in circular clusters. Propagation is by division of the "creeping" root stock.

Spider Plant (*Chlorophytum elatum vittatum*)

With its green-and-white foliage and trailing habit, the spider plant makes one of the best hanging plants. The graceful trailing runners sprout plantlets and white star-shaped flowers. There are some all-green varieties but the green-and-white-striped one is more commonly seen.

Temperature: The plant thrives best in a warm location.

Light and sun: This lovely plant does very well hanging in indirect sun or a moderately lighted area.

Water and humidity: Spider plant should be allowed to dry out before rewatering. Brown leaf tips usually indicate lack of humidity. To tidy up the plant, just snip these tips off.

Soil: The plant grows contentedly in a rich soil composed of garden loam, sand and peat moss, but ordinary garden soil will do.

How to start new plants: New plantlets will appear on the ends of runners (long slender trailing stems) sent out from the parent. When the plantlets have six or seven leaves they can be cut from the parent and potted separately or rooted in water. Or pin down a plantlet in a different pot and sever the runner when new growth appears.

Wandering Jew
(*Zebrina pendula, Tradescantia* varieties)

This is a particularly attractive hanging plant. It is hardy and easy to grow, with one special requirement—regular pinching to keep it full and bushy. There are several plants called Wandering Jew, distinguished from each other by their different colorings and markings. The illustration is a *Zebrina pendula.* The leaf, is a pointed oval with a deep purple underside, and the upperside is dark green striped with pale silvery-green. *Tradescantia fluminensis* has small oval green leaves marked with white, silver and white, or yellow.

Temperature: These plants prefer warm temperatures.

Light and sun: Bright indirect sunlight keeps the foliage brilliant. Avoid direct sunlight as plants are susceptible to sunburn.

Water and humidity: Water generously, keeping the soil moist at all times. During the winter months it will not need quite so much water.

Soil: Grows in a well-drained potting soil or in water.

How to start new plants: Root 4-inch cuttings in moist soil or water.

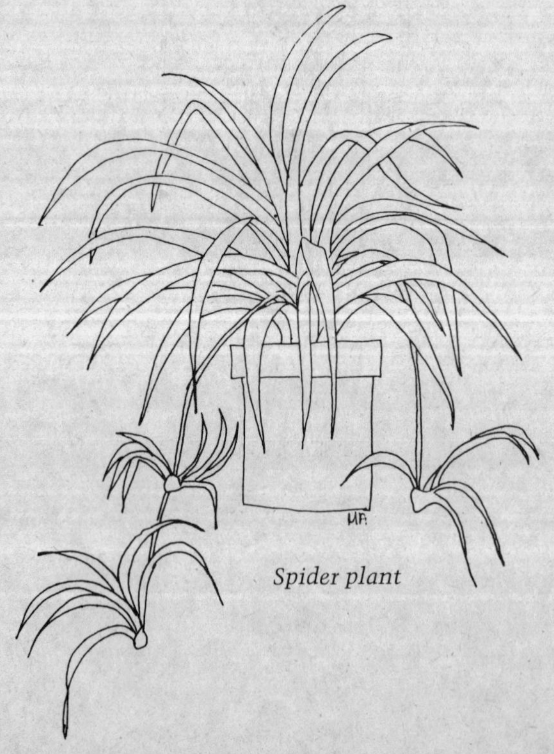

Spider plant

Wandering Jew

II

GROWING ANNUALS

CHAPTER 4

Flowering Annuals

GARDEN ANNUALS ARE EASY to grow and they do well in all parts of the United States. Among the most popular of the garden annuals are zinnias, marigolds, petunias, and ageratums. Many other kinds also are available.

You can sow annual seeds directly in the beds where the plants are to bloom or you can start plants early from seed indoors and set them out in beds after the weather warms.

You also can buy started plants of many annuals from your local nursery or garden shop. These started plants usually are in bloom when they are offered for sale, which allows you to select the colors you want for your garden. It is an easy task to prepare beds and set out these started plants. The plants provide color from the time they are set out until they are killed by fall frosts.

To grow annuals successfully:

- Start with vigorous plants or seeds. The best plan is to buy started plants. Next best is to sow fresh seed where the plants are to grow. Usually, the least satisfactory plan is to start your own plants from seed indoors.
- Prepare soil in the flower beds thoroughly.
- Set out plants or sow seed at the recommended times. Plants set out too early may be killed by frost. Seed sown too early will not germinate until the soil warms—and by that time it may rot.
- Provide the recommended distances between plants when thinning seedlings or setting out started plants. Proper spacing is necessary for fullest development of the plants.

SELECTING ANNUALS

You probably already have decided which kind of annuals you want to grow; annuals are high on everyone's list of favorite flowers. If you have not decided, however, a good plan is to visit other gardens in your area to see which annuals are doing well there and which are most attractive to you.

Perhaps you have a specific purpose in mind for annuals—to provide a mass of color for brightening the dark foliage of background shrubs, to fill in beds until shrubs grow large enough to be decorative in their own right, or to overplant bulb beds to provide color after spring-flowering bulbs have passed. If so, you can choose annuals for your garden by considering their characteristics—shown in Table 1—and deciding which of the flowers meet your requirements.

Some annuals are best for use as bedding plants, grouped to give large masses of color in the garden. Some are best as border plants. Some are best for low edging around beds and walks. And some—the tall ones—are best used as quick-growing screens.

Most of the annuals are sources of cut flowers. Some of them also are sources of plants for drying—to be used indoors during the winter.

Whatever your requirements for garden flowers, you probably can find an annual flowering plant that is suitable.

BUYING SEED

To get a good start toward raising vigorous plants, buy good seed.

Be sure your seed is fresh. Do not buy it too far in advance of planting time; for best results, allow no more than a three-month interval.

Old seed saved from previous years may lose much of its vitality under household conditions. It tends to germinate slowly and to produce poor seedlings.

Keep the seed dry and cool until you plant it. Special instructions for storage are printed on some seed packets. Follow these instructions.

When buying seed, look for new varieties listed as F_1 hybrids. Seed for these hybrids costs more than the seed of the usual inbred varieties, but its superiority makes it worth the extra price.

These F_1 hybrids are produced by crossing selected inbred parents. Plants of F_1 varieties are more uniform in size and more vigorous than plants of less

TABLE 1
Characteristics of Selected Garden Annuals

PLANT	HEIGHT	BEST USE	REMARKS
	Inches		
Ageratum	6 to 20	Edging	Tall varieties grown for cut flowers. Good rock-garden plant. Pot and bring in house for winter bloom.
Babysbreath	12 to 18	Borders	Source of cut flowers and plants for drying. Filler material in arrangements. Grows well on alkaline soils.
Balsam	20 to 28	Bedding	Good window-garden plant. Will not tolerate wet or cold weather.
Calendula	14 to 18	Bedding	Source of cut flowers; good window-garden plant.
Calliopsis	18 to 24	Bedding, edging	Source of cut flowers. Blooms quickly, lasts all summer.
Candytuft	9 to 12	Edging, bedding	Rock-garden plant. Filler. Select dwarf ones for bedding.
China-aster	12 to 24	Bedding	Source of cut flowers.
Cockscomb	16 to 40	Bedding	Source of cut flowers and plants for drying.
Coleus	20 to 24	Bedding	Perennial grown for decorative foliage. Good plant for window gardens.
Cornflower	16 to 36	Bedding	Source of cut flowers.
Cosmos	30 to 48	Screen bedding	Source of cut flowers. Background.
Dahlia	18 to 40	Bedding, edging	Source of cut flowers. Blooms early.
Forget-me-not	8 to 12	Bedding, borders	Source of cut flowers. Does not withstand heat.
Four-o'clock	20 to 24	Bedding	
Gaillardia	12 to 18	Borders	Source of cut flowers and plants for drying.
Globe-amaranth	18 to 24	Borders	Source of cut flowers, plants for drying.
Impatiens	10 to 12	Bedding	Perennial grown as annual. Good plant for window gardens. Deep-shade plant.
Larkspur	18 to 48	Screen	Source of cut flowers and plants for drying. Make successive sowings for cut flowers.
Lupine	18 to 24	Borders	Source of cut flowers.
Marigold	6 to 30	Bedding	Source of cut flowers; good window-garden plant.
Morning-glory	See Remarks	Screen	Vine; grows 8 to 12 feet tall.
Nasturtium	12	Bedding, edging	Blooms 1 month after sowing. Needs well-drained soil

select inbred varieties and they produce more flowers.

Seed of F_2 petunia varieties also is available. These hybrids are not as vigorous as the F_1 hybrids but usually are better than the inbred varieties. This seed costs less than that for F_1 hybrids.

PREPARING THE SOIL

Satisfactory results in growing annuals depend, to a large extent, on thorough preparation of the soil where the plants are to grow.

You can make a scratch in the soil and plant seeds

TABLE 1
Characteristics of Selected Garden Annuals—Continued

PLANT	HEIGHT	BEST USE	REMARKS
	Inches		
Pansy	6 to 10	Bedding, edging	Source of cut flowers. Pot plants after bloom, protect for over winter. Replace with petunia for summer bloom.
Petunia	8 to 24	Bedding	Good plant for window gardens. Long blooming period.
Phlox	6 to 12	Bedding	Withstands heat. More compact than petunias.
Pink	6 to 16	Edging, borders	Source of cut flowers.
Poppy	12 to 16	Borders	Source of cut flowers. Successive sowings.
Portulaca	6 to 9	Bedding, edging	Good plant for rock gardens. Withstands heat.
Rudbeckia	20 to 24	Borders, bedding	Source of cut flowers. Heat-loving.
Salpiglossis	24 to 30	Bedding	Source of cut flowers. Does not withstand heat.
Scabiosa	18 to 36	Borders	Source of cut flowers. Remove dead flowers.
Scarlet sage	14 to 36	Borders, bedding	Short varieties bloom early; tall varieties bloom late.
Snapdragon	10 to 36	Bedding	Source of cut flowers, good plant for window gardens (dwarf).
Spider plant	30 to 36	Borders, hedges	Long blooming period.
Stock	24 to 30	Bedding	Source of cut flowers; good plant for window gardens. Overwinters in protected areas.
Strawflower	30 to 40	Bedding	Source of cut flowers and plants for drying.
Summer-cypress	30 to 36	Screen	Grown for foliage.
Sunflower	48 to 84	Screen	Source of cut flowers.
Sweet alyssum	6 to 10	Edging, borders	Grow in well-drained soil. Damps off easily. Neat and free-flowering. Long blooming period.
Sweetpea	See Remarks	Screen	Vine, grows 4 to 8 feet long. Source of cut flowers.
Verbena	9 to 12	Bedding	Source of cut flowers. Covers spots left by spring-flowering bulbs.
Vinca	15 to 18	Bedding	Perennial grown as annual. Good plant for window gardens.
Zinnia	18 to 36	Bedding	Source of cut flowers. Endures heat. Foliage frequently mildews.

in the scratch and you will probably have flowers growing there before the season is over. But the plants will be spindly and the flowers sparse.

On the other hand, if you prepare beds for annuals as carefully as you would for bulbs or shrubs—by spading deeply, providing adequate drainage, and lightening heavy soil with sand and organic matter—the flowers grown there are almost certain to be outstanding. Water can enter well-prepared soil easily. Seed germinates readily; the plants grow deep, healthy roots, strong stems and large and abundant flowers. And the benefits of careful soil

TABLE 2
Planting and Culture of Selected Garden Annuals

PLANT	WHEN TO PLANT SEED	EXPOSURE	GERMINATION TIME	PLANT SPACING	REMARKS
			Days	*Inches*	
Ageratum	After last frost	Semishade or full sun	5	10 to 12	Pinch tips of plants to encourage branching. Remove dead flowers.
Babysbreath	Early spring or summer	Sun	10	10 to 12	Make successive sowings for prolonged blooming period. Shade summer plantings.
Balsam	After last frost	Sun	10	12 to 14	
Calendula	Early spring or late fall	Shade or sun	10	8 to 10	
Calliopsis	After last frost	Shade or sun	8	10 to 14	
Candytuft	Early spring or late fall	Shade or sun	20	8 to 12	
China-aster	After last frost	Shade or sun	8	10 to 12	For best plants start early, grow in coldframe. Make successive sowings for prolonged bloom.
Cockscomb			10	10 to 12	
Coleus	Sow indoors anytime; outdoors after last frost	Sun or partial shade	10	10 to 12	
Cornflower	Early spring	Partial shade	5	12 to 14	
Cosmos	After last frost	Sun	5	10 to 12	
Dahlia	After last frost	Sun	5	12 to 14	For maximum bloom, sow several weeks before other annuals.
Forget-me-not	Spring or summer; shade in summer	Partial shade	10	10 to 12	
Four-o'clock	After last frost	Sun	5	12 to 14	Store roots, plant next year.
Gaillardia	Early spring through summer; shade in summer	Sun	20	10 to 12	
Globe-amaranth	Early spring	Sun	15	10 to 12	
Impatiens	Indoors anytime. Set out after last frost	Partial shade or deep shade	15	10 to 12	
Larkspur	Late fall in South, early spring in North	Sun	20	6 to 8	Difficult to transplant; grow in peat pots.
Lupine	Early spring or late fall		20	6 to 8	Soak seed before planting. Guard against damping-off.
Marigold	After last frost	Sun	5	10 to 14	High fertility delays bloom.
Morning-glory	After last frost	Sun	5	24 to 36	Reseeds itself.
Nasturtium	After last frost	Sun	8	8 to 12	For best flowers, grow in soil of low fertility.

TABLE 2

Planting and Culture of Selected Garden Annuals—Continued

PLANT	WHEN TO PLANT SEED	EXPOSURE	GERMINATION TIME	PLANT SPACING	REMARKS
Pansy	Spring or summer; shade in summer.	Sun or shade	10	6 to 8	Does best in cool season.
Petunia	Late fall (in South)	Sun	10	12 to 14	Start early in spring indoors. Keep cool.
Phlox	Early spring	Sun	10	6 to 8	Make successive plantings for prolonged bloom.
Pink	Early spring, spring or summer; shade in summer.	Sun	5	8 to 12	Start early in spring indoors. Keep cool. Remove dead flowers.
Poppy	Early spring through summer; shade in summer.	Sun	10	6 to 10	Difficult to transplant; start in peat pots. Make successive plantings.
Portulaca	After last frost or in late fall.	Sun	10	10 to 12	
Rudbeckia	Spring or summer; shade in summer.	Sun or partial shade	20	10 to 14	Perennial grown as annual. Blooms first year.
Salpiglossis	Early spring	Sun	15	10 to 12	Needs support. Avoid cold, heavy soil.
Scabiosa	Spring or summer; shade in summer.	Sun	10	12 to 14	Keep old flowers removed.
Scarlet sage	Spring or summer; shade in summer	Sun	15	8 to 12	
Snapdragon	Spring or late fall	Sun	15	6 to 10	Start cool, pinch tips to encourage branching.
Spider plant	Early spring; spring, or fall.	Sun	10	12 to 14	Reseeds freely. Pinch to keep plant short. Water and fertilize freely.
Stock		Sun	5	6 to 10	
Strawflower	Early spring	Sun	5	10 to 12	
Summer-cypress	Early spring	Sun	15	18 to 24	
Sunflower	After last frost	Sun	5	12 to 14	
Sweet alyssum	Early spring	Sun	5	10 to 12	Damps off easily. Sow in hills, do not thin.
Sweetpea	Early spring or late summer through late fall.	Sun	15	6 to 8	Select heat-resistant types.
Verbena	After last frost	Sun	20	18 to 24	Pinch tips often to encourage branching.
Vinca	After last frost	Sun	15	10 to 12	Avoid overwatering.
Zinnia	After last frost	Sun	5	8 to 12	Thin after plants begin to bloom; remove poor-flowering plants.

preparation carry over from season to season. It is better to grow a small bed of flowers in well-prepared soil than to attempt to grow great masses of flowers in poorly prepared soil.

If you want to plant annuals in bulb beds after the bulbs have bloomed or in shrub beds for decoration while the shrubs are small, little soil preparation will be needed; bulb beds or shrub beds already should be well prepared. Just scratch a half-inch of peat moss into the soil surface before planting annuals.

If you must prepare new beds, begin soil preparation the fall before planting time.

Before preparing new beds, test the soil to see that it is capable of absorbing water from rainfall. Dig a hole about 10 inches deep and fill the hole with water. The next day, fill the hole with water again and see how long the water remains in the hole. If the water drains away in eight to ten hours, the permeability of the soil is sufficient for good growth of annuals.

If an appreciable amount of water remains in the hole after ten hours, it will be necessary to improve the drainage of the planting site; otherwise, water will collect in your prepared flower bed and prevent proper development of roots on your annuals.

To improve drainage, bed up the soil. Dig furrows along the sides of the bed and add the soil from the furrows to the bed. This raises the level of the bed above the general level of the soil. Excess water can seep from the bed into the furrows.

Raised beds are subject to formation of gullies during heavy rains. You can prevent gullying by surrounding the beds with wooden or masonry walls, making, in effect, raised planters of the beds.

Also, raised beds are more subject to drying than flat beds; little moisture moves up into the bed from the soil below. Therefore, be sure to water beds frequently.

After forming the beds, or determining that drainage is satisfactory without raising bedding, spade the soil to a depth of 8 to 10 inches. Turn the soil over completely. In this spading remove boards, large stones and building trash, but turn under all leaves, grass, stems, roots, and anything else that will decay easily.

Respade three or four times at weekly intervals. If the soil tends to dry between spadings, water it. If weeds grow, pull them before they set seed.

In spring, just before planting, spade again. At this spading, work peat moss, sand and fertilizer into the soil. Soils east of the Mississippi River may need to be limed.

For an ordinary garden soil, use a 1- to 2-inch layer of peat moss and a 1-inch layer of unwashed sand—the latter available from building-supply yards.

If your soil is heavy clay, use twice this amount of peat and sand. By adding peat and sand to the soil each year, you can eventually improve even poor subsoil to make a good garden soil.

Add a complete fertilizer at this last spading. Use grade 5–10–5 at a rate of 1½ pounds per 100 square feet. Add ground limestone at a rate of 5 pounds per 100 square feet if needed.

Rake the soil surface smooth. After raking, the soil is ready for seeding or planting with already started plants.

PLANTING TIMES

Do not be in a rush to start seeds or to set out started plants. As a general rule, delay sowing seed outdoors or setting out started plants until after the last frost.

Most seeds will not germinate well until the soil warms to about 60°. If they are sowed in soil that is cooler than this, they will remain dormant until the soil warms and may rot before they germinate.

Exceptions to this rule are babysbreath, cornflower, gaillardia, globe-amaranth, phlox, poppy, salpiglossis, cleome, stock, strawflower, summer-cypress, sweet alyssum, and sweetpea. Seeds of these annuals can be sowed in early spring, as soon as the soil can be worked.

Many annuals can be seeded throughout the growing season for a prolonged display of color. Proper times for seeding most of the common annuals are listed in Table 2.

Start seed indoors no sooner than 8 weeks before the average date for the last killing frost in your area. If you start seed earlier than this, the plants will be too large for satisfactory transplanting by the time the weather is warm enough for them to be set outside.

SETTING STARTED PLANTS

By setting started plants in your garden you can have a display of flowers several weeks earlier than if you sow seeds of the plants. Use of started plants is especially helpful for annuals that are slow to germinate or that need several months to bloom. Examples of these slow-to-bloom annuals: candytuft, gaillardia, lupine, rudbeckia, verbena and scarlet sage.

You can buy plants of these and many other annuals, or you can start your own. (See "Starting Plants Indoors," p. 47.)

When the time comes to set plants out in the garden, remove them from flats by slicing downward in the soil between the plants. Lift out each plant with a block of soil surrounding its roots and set the soil block in a planting hole.

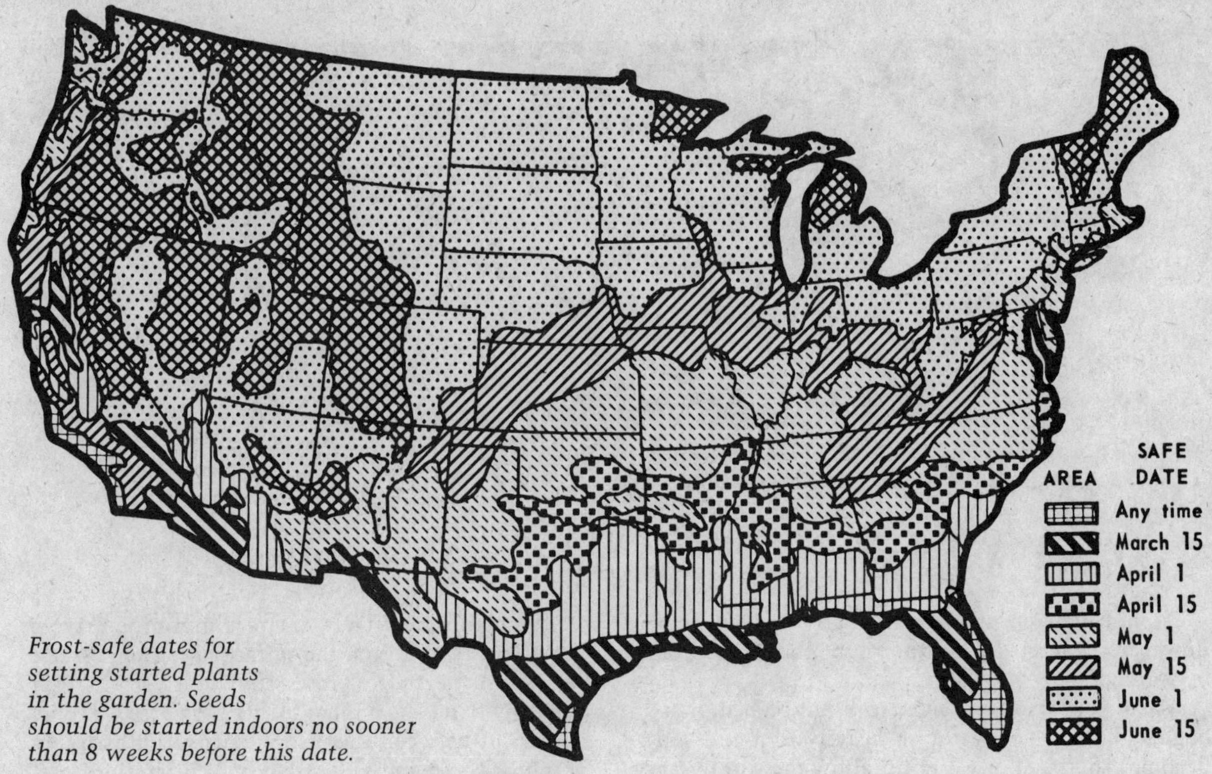

Frost-safe dates for setting started plants in the garden. Seeds should be started indoors no sooner than 8 weeks before this date.

If the plants are in fiber pots, remove the paper from the outside of the root mass and set the plant in a prepared planting hole.

When setting out plants in peat pots, set the entire pot in the planting hole. The pot will break down in the soil and improve the soil around the plant.

After setting the plants, water them with a starter solution made from 1 tablespoon of high-phosphate fertilizer—grade 10–52–17—in 1 gallon of water.

SOWING SEED OUTDOORS

Annuals seeded in the garden frequently fail to germinate properly because the surface of the soil cakes and prevents entry of water. To aoid this, sow the seed in vermiculite-filled furrows.

Make the furrows in the soil about ½ inch deep. After filling them with fine vermiculite, sprinkle them with water.

Then make another shallow furrow in the vermiculite and sow the seed in this furrow. Sow it at the rate recommended on the packet.

Cover the seed with a layer of vermiculite and, using a nozzle adjusted for a fine mist, water the seeded area thoroughly.

To retard water evaporation, cover the seeded area with sheets of newspaper. Support the newspaper on blocks or sticks 1 to 2 inches above the surface of the bed. Remove the paper when seedlings appear.

THINNING

When annuals grown outdoors develop two true leaves, most kinds should be thinned to the recommended spacing (see "Plant Spacing," Table 2). This recommended spacing allows the plants to have enough light, water, nutrients, and space for them to develop fully. If they have been seeded in vermiculite-filled furrows, the excess seedlings can be transplanted to another spot without injury.

Zinnias are an exception to this rule of thinning. In every variety of zinnias will appear plants with undesirable flowers of the "Mexican-hat" type. The only way to avoid having these undesirable flowers in your garden is to wait until the plants have bloomed for the first time before you thin them to their final spacing.

The recommended spacing for zinnias is 8 to 12 inches. When the plants develop two true leaves, thin them merely to 4 to 6 inches, transplanting the extra plants.

Then when they bloom—they will still be quite small—pull and destroy plants having the undesirable flowers. Now thin the remaining plants to the 8- to 12-inch spacing.

Another exception to the usual rules for thinning is sweet alyssum. This annual is particularly susceptible to damping-off. To ensure a good stand of plants, sow the seed in hills and do not bother to thin the seedlings.

Zinnia flowers: left, *desirable type of fully double flowers;* right, *semidouble "Mexican-hat" flowers*

WATERING

Do not rely on summer rainfall to keep your flower beds watered. Plan to irrigate them from the beginning.

When you water, moisten the entire bed thoroughly, but do not water so heavily that the soil becomes soggy. After watering, allow the soil to dry moderately before watering again.

A canvas soaker hose is excellent for watering beds. Water from the soaker hose seeps directly into the soil without waste. The slow-moving water does not disturb the soil or reduce its capacity to absorb water.

Sprinklers are not as effective as soaker hoses. Water from sprinklers wets the flowers and foliage, making them susceptible to diseases. The structure of the soil may be destroyed by the impact of water drops as they fall on its surface; the soil may puddle or crust, preventing free entry of water.

The least effective method for watering is with a hand-held nozzle. Watering with a nozzle has all the disadvantages of watering with a sprinkler. In addition, gardeners seldom are patient enough to do a thorough job of watering with a nozzle; not enough water is applied, and the water usually is poorly distributed over the bed.

MULCHING

Mulches help to keep the soil surface from crusting, aid in preventing growth of weeds, and add organic matter to the soil. Grass clippings make a good mulch for annuals.

Sheet plastics or aluminum foil also may be spread over the soil surface to retard evaporation of water and to prevent growth of weeds. However, these materials are unsightly for use in the flower garden.

CULTIVATING

After plants are set out, or after thinning, cultivate only to break crusts on the surface of the soil. When the plants begin to grow, stop cultivating. Pull weeds by hand. As annual plants grow, feeder roots spread out between the plants; cultivation is likely to injure these roots. In addition, cultivation stirs the soil and uncovers more weed seeds, which then germinate.

REMOVING OLD FLOWERS

To maintain vigorous growth of plants, remove mature flowers and seed pods. This step is particularly desirable if you are growing ageratum, calendula, cosmos, marigold, pansy, rudbeckia, scabiosa or zinnia.

INSECT PESTS

Do not apply an insecticide unless it is necessary to prevent damage to your flowers or shrubs. Most of the insect pests in your garden will not cause appreciable damage if you protect their predators and parasites by avoiding unnecessary applications of insecticides. However, if you have a pest that usually causes serious damage unless an insecticide is used, apply the insecticide when the infestation first appears.

Watch for such insect pests as spider mites, aphids, Japanese weevils and other weevils, lacebugs and thrips; these are some of the insects most likely to need prompt treatment with insecticides. Do not treat for soil insects unless you find numbers of cutworms, white grubs, or wireworms when preparing the soil for planting.

For aid in identifying insect pests consult your

county agricultural agent, the agricultural college or experiment station, or your local garden-supply store.

When using a pesticide, be certain that the specific pest and the flower or shrub for which this pesticide is intended are indicated on the label. Read and follow all directions for use, including precautions, shown on the label. If pesticides are handled, applied or disposed of improperly, they may be injurious to human beings, desirable plants, or flowers and beneficial insects. Use pesticides only when needed and handle them with care.

CUTTING FLOWERS

Grow plants for cut flowers in a section of the garden by themselves. Do not mix them with border plants.

Early in the season, when the plants first begin to bloom, whole plants can be removed and used in flower arrangements. Let the remaining plants in the beds develop. Remove all old flowers and promote formation of new shoots and flowers by watering and fertilizing.

DRYING FLOWERS

As for cut flowers, grow plants for drying in a section of the garden by themselves. Remove whole plants for drying at the following times:

Plant	*Time to Cut*
Babysbreath	When flowers are well formed
Cockscomb	When in color but before seed sheds
Gaillardia	When in full color but before petals dry
Globe-amaranth	When mature
Larkspur	When oldest floret matures; plant forms a spike
Strawflower	When buds begin to open
Zinnia	When in full color but before petals begin to dry

After cutting, hang the plants upside down in a shady place to dry. Use them in flower arrangements during the winter.

STARTING PLANTS INDOORS

Unless you are willing to invest in special lighting equipment and to devote considerable care to starting plants indoors, it usually is best to buy plants or to sow seed of annuals directly in the garden, as we have said earlier. Home-started plants seldom are as satisfactory for setting out as those bought from nurserymen. And they seldom grow as well or bloom as prolifically as those planted directly in the garden.

Home-started seedlings frequently are attacked by a fungus disease called damping-off. Those seedlings that escape the disease usually are weak and spindling and never become good garden plants; conditions of light, temperature and humidity normally found in the home are not favorable for growth of garden annuals.

Preventing Damping-Off

Damping-off causes seeds to rot and seedlings to collapse and die. The disease is carried in soil and may be present on planting containers and tools. Soil moisture and temperature necessary for germination of seeds also are ideal for development of damping-off.

Once the disease appears in a seed flat, it may travel quickly through the flat and kill all seedlings planted there.

This can be prevented if, before planting, you treat the seed with a fungicide, sterilize the soil, and use sterile containers.

Treat the seed with thiram. Tear off the corner of the seed packet and, through the hole in the packet, insert about as much fungicide dust as you can pick up on the tip of the small blade of a penknife. Close the hole by folding over the corner of the packet; then shake the seed thoroughly to coat it with the fungicide dust.

Sterilize the soil in an oven. Fill a container—a pan or metal tray—with moist, but not wet, soil, bury a raw potato in the center of the soil and bake in a medium oven.

When the potato is cooked, the soil should be sterile.

A good way to avoid introducing the damping-off organism on containers is to use fiber seed flats or peat pots. These containers are sterile, inexpensive and easily obtainable from garden shops.

Fiber flats are light and strong. They cost so little that they can be thrown away after one use.

Peat pots can be set out in the garden along with the plants they contain; roots of the plants grow through the walls of the pots. Plants grown in peat pots suffer no setback when they are transplanted to the garden. Larkspur and poppy, which ordinarily do not tolerate transplanting, can be grown in peat pots satisfactorily.

If you use wooden boxes or clay flower pots for soil containers, clean them well. Soak clay pots in water and scrub them well to remove all of the white fertilizer crust from the outside.

STARTING SEEDS

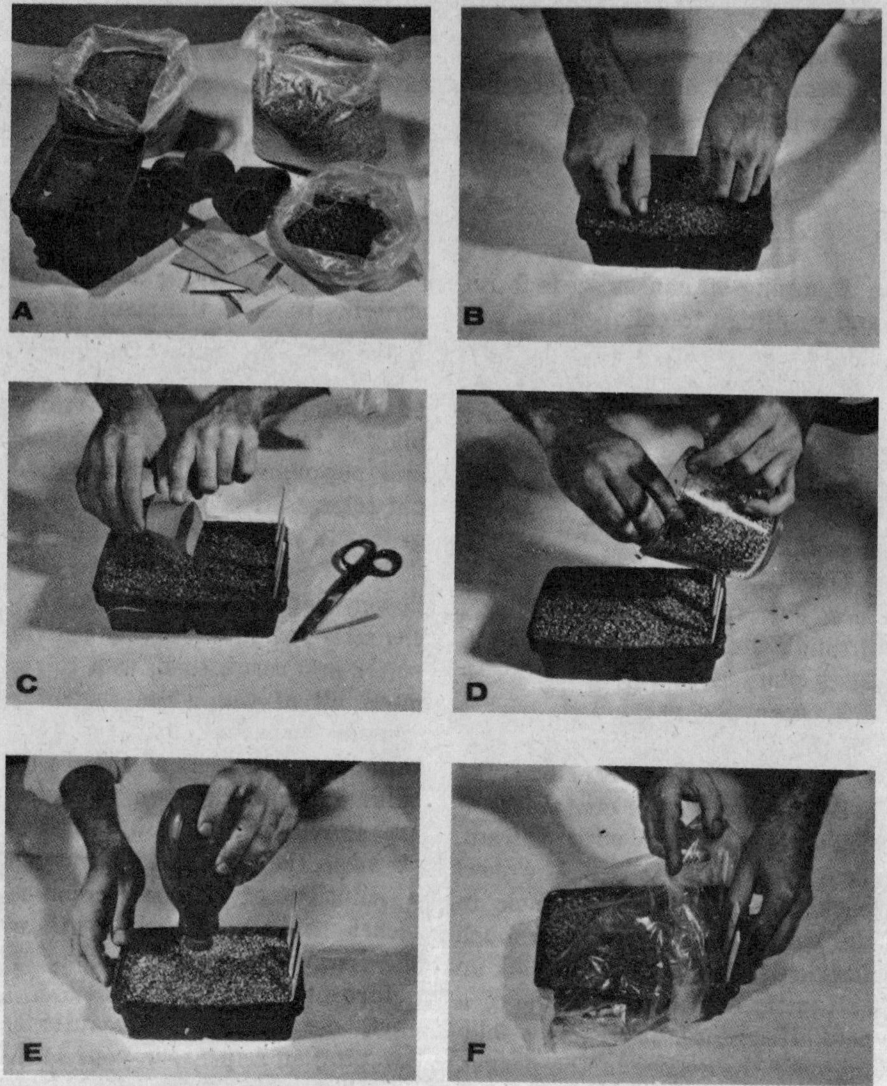

A. Use sterile containers and planting medium—sterilized soil or vermiculite. B. Press the moist planting medium firmly in the container. C. Tap the seed packet with your forefinger to distribute the seed at the rate recommended on the label. D. Cover large seeds with a layer of fine vermiculite (leave small seeds uncovered). E. Wet the seeded container until water runs out of the bottom. F. Place the seeded container in a polyethylene bag and keep it in a warm place until the seeds germinate. Then remove the bag and begin watering and fertilizing the seedlings.

Sterilize clay pots and boxes by baking them in the oven when you are sterilizing the soil mixture. Or swab the pots and boxes with a solution of 1 part chlorine bleach to 10 parts water. Allow the containers to dry thoroughly before filling them with soil.

If, despite your precautions, damping-off appears in your seedlings, it is best to discard the containers and soil and start over.

Starting Seeds

The best soil for starting seeds is loose, well drained, fine-textured and low in nutrients. To pre-

TRANSPLANTING

A. When seedlings have developed two true leaves (left), transplant them to another container. The plants on the right have been allowed to get too large before transplanting. B. Using a knife blade, carefully lift seedlings from the planting container. C. Make a slit with the knife blade in the vermiculite and set the seedling in the slit. Firm the vermiculite around the roots with your forefingers, taking care not to crush the seedling. D. Fertilize seedlings twice a week. Seedlings on the left were not fertilized; those on the right, the same age, were fertilized twice weekly. E. Seedlings, 8 weeks old, ready to be transplanted to the garden. Note roots growing through the walls of the peat pot. F. The petunia seedling on the left is about the right size for setting in the garden. The plant on the right is too large.

pare a soil having these properties, mix equal parts of garden soil, sand, and sphagnum peat moss.

Fill soil containers about ⅔ full with this mixture. Level the soil and soak it thoroughly. Then sift more of the soil mixture through window screening to form a layer that fills ¼ to ½ of the remaining depth of the container.

Make a furrow ¼ inch deep in the fine soil. Sow large-seeded plants—cosmos, zinnia, marigold, nasturtium, cornflower, sweetpea, morning-glory, or four-o'clock—directly in the bottom of the furrow. Before sowing small-seeded plants, fill the furrow with vermiculite; sow small seeds on the surface of the vermiculite.

Sow seeds in flats at the rate recommended on the seed packet. If you are growing large-seeded plants in peat pots, sow two to four seeds in each pot.

After you have sowed the seeds, cover all furrows with a thin layer of vermiculite, then water with a fine mist.

Place a sheet of polyethylene plastic over the seeded containers and set them in the basement or some other location where they can be kept at a temperature between 60° and 75° F.

The containers need no further water until after the seeds have germinated. Nor do they need light. Under no circumstances should the plastic-covered containers be placed in sunlight; heat buildup under the plastic could kill emerging seedlings.

Raising Seedlings

Supplying light: As soon as the seed has germinated, remove the plastic sheeting and place the seedlings in the light.

Many gardeners supply light to the seedlings by placing the containers on a windowsill. This practice usually is unsatisfactory; light on a windowsill usually is diffused, it comes from only one direction, and the period of strong daylight varies from day to day. In addition, the air surrounding plants on a windowsill is too dry and the temperature is too high.

For best results, seedlings should be raised under lighting conditions that can be closely controlled as to intensity and duration.

Use a fluorescent tube as the light source. For proper intensity, place the containers 6 inches below the tube. Control the duration of lighting by connecting the fluorescent fixture to a timer such as is used for controlling refrigerators or air conditioners.

Some plants develop best for setting out if they are grown under short-day conditions—10 to 12 hours of light each day. Under these conditions they produce compact plants that flower only after they are set outside. These plants usually do best also if the temperature is kept between 60° and 65° F. Grow the following seedlings on short days:

Calliopsis	Poppy
China-aster	Portulaca
Cornflower	Rudbeckia
Gaillardia	Salpiglossis
Glove-amaranth	Scabiosa
Petunia	Snapdragon
Phlox	Verbena

Most plants need longer days—18 hours of light each day. If they are started on short days they soon begin to form flowers, and they never produce good bedding plants. Grow the following seedlings with a day length of 18 hours and a temperature of 65° F.

Cockscomb	Morning-glory
Cosmos	Scarlet sage
Dahlia	Sunflower
Marigold	Zinnia

If your plants are on neither of these lists, grow them with a day length of 18 to 20 hours.

Day length is not important for plants grown at temperatures of 50° to 55° F. However, seedlings grown at these low temperatures develop more slowly than those grown at 60° F.

Watering and fertilizing: After the plastic is removed from the container, the new plants must be watered frequently, and they must be fertilized. You can do both of these jobs at one time by using a solution made by mixing 1 tablespoon of soluble fertilizer in 1 gallon of water.

When you use this solution, moisten the soil thoroughly; but be careful not to wash out the seedlings when you water them. To avoid this, use a rubber-bulb syringe—available from garden stores—to apply the solution as a fine mist.

If you do not have a syringe, you can place the solution in a container that is somewhat larger than the seed containers and submerge the pots or flats up to their rims in the solution. This waters the plants from the bottom. Remove the pots or flats from the solution as soon as the soil is thoroughly moistened.

You also can water flats without disturbing the soil if you sink a small flower pot in the center of the flat and pour the water in the pot.

Transplanting

When seedlings develop two true leaves, thin those in peat pots to one seedling per pot.

Transplant seedlings in flats to other flats. Using a knife or spatula, dig deeply under the seedlings in the flats, lifting a group of the seedlings. Let the group of seedlings fall apart and pick out individual plants from the group. Handle the seedlings as little as necessary. Don't pinch them.

Set the seedlings in new flats that contain the same soil mixtures as was used for starting the seed. Space the seedlings about 1½ inches apart in the new flats.

Water thoroughly and replace the seedlings under the fluorescent lights. Continue watering and fertilizing the plants until time for setting them out.

If you must hold seedlings indoors longer than eight weeks after sowing, transplant them to a flat containing pure sphagnum moss. Do not fertilize them. For best results, however, plan ahead so that it is unnecessary to hold seedlings longer than eight weeks.

IIII

GROWING PERENNIALS

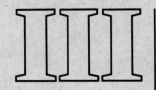

CHAPTER 5

Flowering Perennials

PERENNIALS ARE FLOWERING or foliage plants whose roots live from year to year. Their tops may or may not die back in the winter.

Perennials give color to the garden in a shady spot and in front of shrubs. They are colorful in spring and throughout the growing season.

Some perennials flower the first year. You can grow them as annuals and eliminate the problem of protecting them in the winter.

Usually perennials will not flower unless they develop to a certain size and are then exposed to low temperature for a number of weeks, then exposed to increasing day lengths and increasing temperatures. Their flowering time is the result of this sequence of day length and temperature.

Although perennials require constant care, they do well in most parts of the United States.

Among the most popular of the garden perennials are delphinium, alyssum, hollyhock, columbine, candytuft, carnation, and primrose.

To grow perennials successfully:

- Prepare soil in the flower beds thoroughly.
- Start with vigorous plants or seeds. The best plan is to buy started plants. Next best is to sow fresh seed where the plants are to grow. Usually, as with annuals, the least satisfactory plan is to start your own plants indoors.
- Set out plants or sow seed at the recommended times. Plants set out too early may be killed by frost. Seeds will not germinate until the soil warms—and, if sown too early, they may rot. However, early spring growth is important for the survival of many perennials.
- Provide the recommended distances between plants when thinning seedlings or setting out started plants. Proper spacing is necessary for fullest development of the plants.
- Do not grow annuals that crowd and grow wildly in the same bed with perennials; they will crowd the perennials.
- Let the perennials stand out. Give them a background to show them off. Evergreens or wooden fences make good backgrounds.
- Do not consider perennials as permanent plants. Replanting, dividing old plants, and preparing the soil are essential for vigorous, flowering plants.

PLANNING YOUR GARDEN

Preparing the Soil

Preparing the soil is extremely important to perennials. Annuals can grow and flower in poorly prepared soil, but perennials seldom survive more than one year if the soil is not properly prepared.

Properly prepared soil will have:

- Good drainage.
- Protection from drying winds.
- Adequate water in the summer.

If you prepare beds carefully—by spading deeply, providing adequate drainage and lightening heavy soil with sand and organic matter—the flowers grown there are almost certain to be outstanding. Water can enter well-prepared soil easily. Seed germinates readily; the plants grow deep, healthy roots, strong stems, and large and abundant flowers. And the benefits of careful soil preparation carry over from season to season.

It is better to grow a small bed of flowers in well-prepared soil than to attempt to grow great masses of flowers in poorly prepared soil.

For new beds, begin preparing the soil in the fall before planting time.

Before preparing new beds, test the soil to see that it is capable of absorbing water from rainfall. The soil must have water-holding capacity so that the plants will never be under stress. Dig a hole about 10 inches deep and fill with water. The next day, fill the hole with water again and see how long the water remains in the hole. If the water drains away in eight to ten hours, the permeability of the soil is sufficient for good growth.

If an appreciable amount of water remains in the hole after ten hours, it will be necessary to improve the drainage of the planting site; otherwise, water will collect in your prepared flower bed and prevent proper development of roots.

To improve drainage, bed up the soil. Dig furrows along the sides of the bed and add the soil from the furrows to the bed. This raises the level of the bed above the general level of the soil. Excess water can seep from the bed into the furrows.

You may find gullies in raised beds after heavy rains. You can prevent gullying by surrounding the beds with wooden or masonry walls, making, in effect, raised planters of the beds.

Also, raised beds dry out more quickly than flat beds; little moisture moves up into the bed from the soil below. Be sure to water beds frequently during the summer.

After forming the beds, or determining that drainage is satisfactory without raised bedding, spade the soil to a depth of 8 to 10 inches. Turn the soil over completely. In this spading remove boards, large stones and building trash, but turn under all leaves, grass, stems, roots and anything else that will decay easily.

Respade three or four times at weekly intervals. If the soil tends to dry between spadings, water it. If weeds grow, pull them before they set seed.

In spring, just before planting, spade again. At this spading, work peat moss, sand, fertilizer and lime into the soil.

For ordinary garden soil, use a 1- to 2-inch layer of peat moss and a 1-inch layer of unwashed sand—available from building-supply yards.

If your soil is heavy clay, use twice this amount of peat and sand. By adding peat and sand to the soil each time you reset the plants, you can eventually improve even poor subsoil to make a good garden soil. You can use well-rotted compost instead of peat moss.

Have your soil tested. Your state experiment station will do this, and it will make recommendations for adding fertilizer and lime. Allow sufficient time between sending your sample to the experiment station and need for the information. State clearly that you are planning to grow flowers in the soil.

Add a complete fertilizer such as 5–10–5 at the last spading. Use at a rate of 1½ pounds (3 rounded cups) per 100 square feet. Add ground limestone at a rate of 5 pounds (7 rounded cups) per 100 square feet.

Rake the soil surface smooth. After raking, the soil is ready for seeding or planting with started plants.

Add organic matter to the beds each year—peat moss or compost.

Selecting Perennials

Select perennials for your particular area. Notice what grows well in local gardens. Also consult nurserymen and check with your state experiment station. Then choose those plants that are most attractive to you. The plants discussed in the listing beginning below do well in most areas of the United States.

Perhaps you have a specific purpose in mind for perennials—you can plant them as flowering edging plants, for accents in an evergreen planting, to achieve masses of bloom by covering a single area with one species, as rock garden specimens, or to provide a screen of color. With this specific purpose, you can choose perennials for your garden by considering their characteristics and deciding which of the flowers meet your requirements.

For a good display from a limited number of plants in a limited amount of space, select named varieties.

Observe the flowering times of perennials in your area. That way you will be able to choose plants that will flower together and plants that will flower when nothing else is in bloom. The flowering time may vary as much as six weeks from year to year, but plants of the same kind usually flower at the same time.

The list of plants given does not include all perennials. It is only a selection of the more commonly grown ones. These are the perennials that support and fill out a garden. You can obtain details on particular plants from plant societies and specialty books.

Many popular magazines and books are devoted to garden design. Consult them for ideas and ways to display perennials.

ACHILLEA

Achillea millefolium (Yarrow) grows about 2 feet high. It looks best in borders that bloom from June to September. Achillea is grown also for cut flowers. Plant seed in early spring or late fall. Choose a sunny spot in your garden. Space plants 36 inches apart. Seed germinates in seven to 14 days. Because seed is very small, water with a mist. Achillea is easy to grow.

ALYSSUM

Alyssum saxatile (Golddust) grows 9 to 12 inches high. It is used in rock gardens and for edging and cut flowers. It blooms in early spring. Alyssum is excellent in dry or sandy soil. Plant seed in early

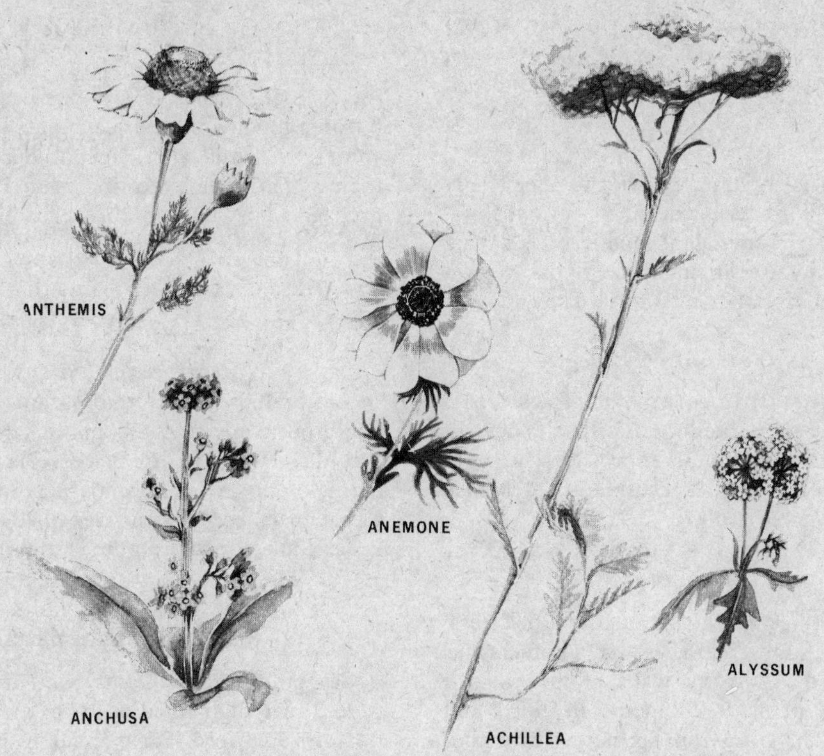

spring in a sunny spot. Space plants 24 inches apart. Seed germinates in 21 to 28 days.

ANCHUSA

Anchusa italica and *A. myosotidiflora* (Alkanet) grow 4 to 5 feet high. They are used for borders and backgrounds, as well as a source of cut flowers. Anchusa blooms in June and July. Refrigerate seed for 72 hours before sowing. Plant seed any time from spring to September in a semishaded part of your garden. Shade summer plantings. Space plants 24 inches apart. Seed germinates in 21 to 28 days.

ANEMONE

Anemone pulsatilla (Windflower) grows about 12 inches high. It is grown in borders, rock gardens and pots. Anemone blooms in May and June and is a source of cut flowers. Plant seed in early spring or late fall in a sunny part of your garden. Plant tuberous-rooted anemones in well-drained soil in September. Cover with straw over winter. Space plants 35 to 42 inches apart. Seed germinates in four days. Anemone is not hardy north of Washington, D.C.

ANTHEMIS

Anthemis tinctoria (Golden Daisy) grows about 2 feet high. It looks best in borders that bloom from midsummer to frost. Anthemis is grown also for cut flowers, which are slightly aromatic. Plants can be started indoors eight weeks before planting outdoors. Or you can plant seeds outdoors after soil has warmed in the spring. Anthemis grows well in dry or sandy soil. Plant in a sunny spot. Space plants 24 inches apart. Seeds germinate in 21 to 28 days.

ARABIS

Arabis alpina (Rockcress) grows 8 to 12 inches high. It is used for edging and in rock gardens. Arabis blooms in early spring. Plant seed in well-drained soil any time from spring to September. It grows best in light shade. Shade summer plantings. Space plants about 12 inches apart. Seed germinates in about five days.

ARMERIA

Armeria alpina (Sea Pink) grows 18 to 24 inches high. It is used in rock gardens, edgings and borders. Armeria blooms in May and June. The dwarf tufted plants are also used as cut flowers. Plant seed in dry, sandy soil any time between spring and September. Space plants 12 inches apart in a sunny part of your garden. Shade the seedbed until plants are sturdy. Seed germinates in about ten days.

ARTEMISIA

Artemisia stelleriana (Wormwood, Dusty Miller) grows about 2 feet high. It is used in flowerbeds, as a border and in rock gardens. Artemisia blooms in late summer. Plant seed in full sun from late spring to late summer. It grows even in poor and dry soils. Space plants 9 to 12 inches apart.

ASTER

Aster alpinus (Hardy Aster) grows 1 to 5 feet high. It is used in rock gardens, borders, and for cut flowers. Aster blooms in June. Plant seed in early spring in a sunny spot in your garden. Space plants about 3 feet apart. Seed germinates in 14 to 21 days.

ASTILBE

Astilbe japonica (Japanese Astilbe) grows 1 to 3 feet high. It is used in borders. Astilbe blooms in masses of color in summer. Plant seed in early spring in rich, loamy soil. Space plants 24 inches apart. Seed germinates in 14 to 21 days.

AUBRIETA

Aubrieta deltoidea graeca (Rainbow Rockcress) grows about 6 inches high. It is grown in borders and rock gardens and along dry walls. Aubrieta is a dwarf, spreading plant that blooms in April and May. Plant seed any time from spring to September in light shade. Space plants about 12 inches apart. Seed will germinate in about 20 days. Shade plants in summer. To propagate, divide mature plants in late summer.

BEGONIA

Begonia evansiana (Hardy Begonia) grows 12 inches high. It is used in flower beds in shady areas. Begonia blooms in late summer. Plant seed in early summer in a shady, moist spot. Space plants 9 to 12 inches apart. Seed germinates in 12 days. You can propagate begonia by planting the bulblets that grow in the axils of the leaves.

CANDYTUFT

Candytuft (*Iberis sempervirens*) grows about 10 inches high. It is used in rock gardens and for edging and ground cover. It blooms in late spring. Candytuft does well in dry places. Plant seed in early spring or late fall in a sunny spot. Space plants about a foot apart. Seed germinates in 20 days. Shear flowers as they fade to promote branching of plants.

CANTERBURY BELLS

Canterbury Bells (*Campanula medium*) grows 2 to 2½ feet high. It is used in borders and for cut flowers. Sow seed thinly about 15 inches apart, any time between spring and September. Plant in partial shade; do not cover. Seed germinates in about 20 days. Shade seedbed in summer. Divide mature plants of perennial forms every other year.

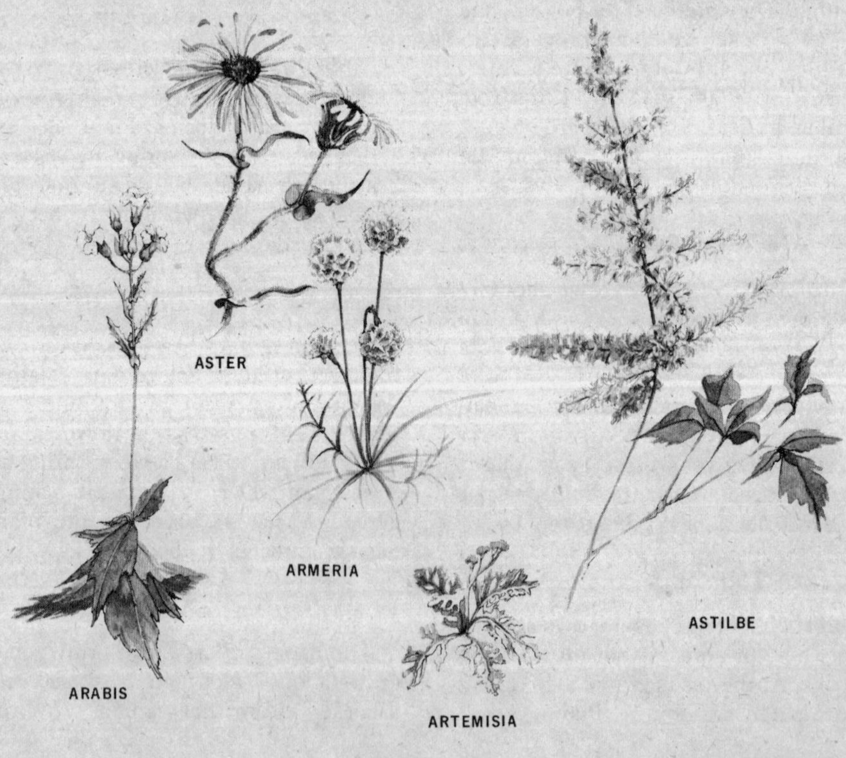

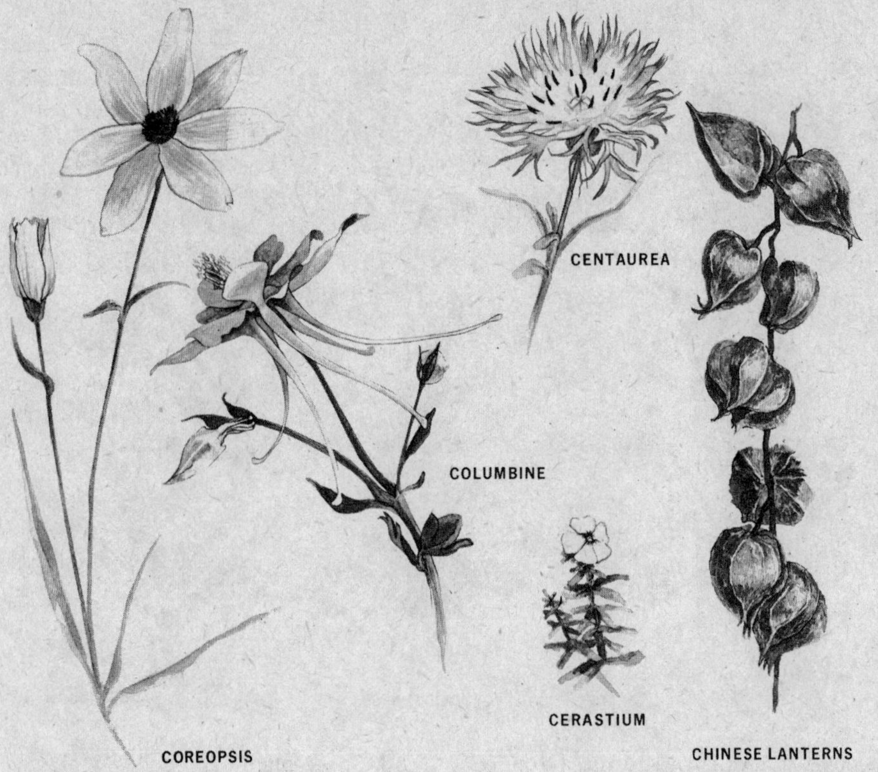

CARNATION

Carnation, Clove Pink, Hardy Garden Carnation (*Dianthus caryophyllus*) grows 18 to 24 inches high. It is used for beds, borders, edging, pots and rock gardens. Carnation blooms in late summer. Plant seed in late spring in a sunny spot. Space plants 12 inches apart. Seed germinates in about 20 days. Cut plants back in late fall, pot them and hold them over winter in a coldframe.

CENTAUREA

Centaurea montana (Centaurea, Cornflower) grows about 2 feet high. It is used in borders and for cut flowers. Centaurea blooms from June to September. Plant seed in early spring in a sunny spot. Space plants about 12 inches apart. Seed germinates in 21 to 28 days. Remove flowers as they fade to prolong time of display.

CERASTIUM

Cerastium tomentosum (Cerastium, Snow-in-Summer) grows about 6 inches high. It is used in rock gardens and for ground cover. Plants form a creeping mat that blooms in May and June. Cerastium does well in dry sunny spots. Plant seed in early spring. Space plants about 18 inches apart. Seed germinates in 14 to 28 days. Cerastium is a hard, tough plant, a rampant grower. Do not allow it to cover other plants.

CHINESE LANTERN

Chinese Lantern (*Physalis alkekengi*) grows about 2 feet high. It is used in borders and for specimens. The "lantern" is borne the second year, in September and October; it lasts several weeks for winter bouquets. Plant seed in late fall or early winter. You can plant Chinese lanterns in spring if you keep seed in the refrigerator over winter. Plant seeds in a sunny spot. Space plants about 3 feet apart. Seed germinates in about 15 days.

COLUMBINE

Columbine hybrids (*Aquilegia*) grow 2½ to 3 feet high. They are used for borders and for cut flowers. Columbine blooms in late spring or early summer. It needs fairly rich, well-drained soil. Plant seed any time from spring to September in sun or partial shade. Space plants 2 to 18 inches apart. Seed germinates in about 30 days; germination is irregular. Grown as a biennial to avoid leaf miner and rotting of crown.

COREOPSIS

Coreopis grandiflora (Bigflower Coreopsis) grows 2 to 3 feet high. It is used in borders. Coreopsis blooms from May to fall, if old flowers are removed. Plant seed in a light loam in early spring or late fall. Choose a sunny spot in your garden. Space plants about 10 inches apart. Seed takes about 5 days to

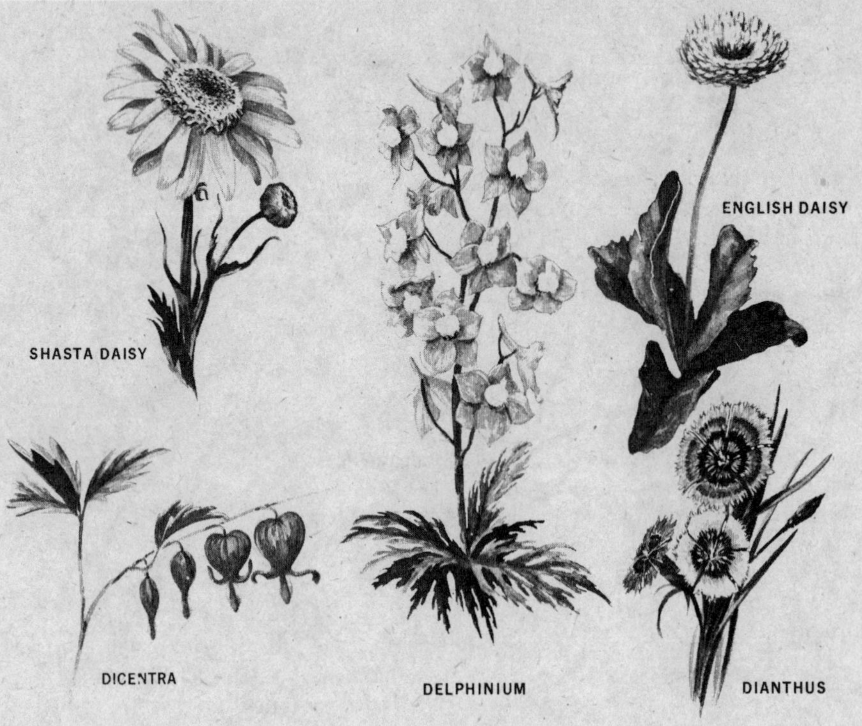

germinate. Coreopsis is drought-resistant. Grow it as a biennial.

DAISY, ENGLISH

English Daisy (*Bellis perennis*) grows about 6 inches high. It is used in beds, borders and rock gardens. In cool climates, it blooms all summer; also in early spring or late fall. Choose a spot in partial shade that has moist, well-drained soil. Space plants about 6 inches apart. Seed germinates in about eight days. English daisy needs plenty of water during summer. Protect rosetting plants in winter with cut branches of conifers.

DAISY, SHASTA

Shasta Daisy (*Chrysanthemum maximum*) grows 2 to 2½ feet high. It is used for borders and for cut flowers. It blooms in June and July. Plant seed any time from early spring to September in a sunny spot. Space plants about 30 inches apart. Seed germinates in about 10 days, Shasta daisy is best grown as a biennial. It is winter-killed by a wet location or a heavy winter cover.

DELPHINIUM

Delphinium elatum (Candle Larkspur) grows 4 to 5 feet high. It is used for borders, background and cut flowers. Delphinium blooms in June; if you remove old flowers, it will bloom twice more. Plant seed any time from spring to September in a well-drained sunny spot. Plants tend to rot in wet, heavy soil. Space plants 24 inches apart. Seed germinates in about 20 days. Shade summer plantings. Foliage tends to mildew. Stake plants and protect them from the wind.

DIANTHUS

Dianthus deltoides and *D. plumarius* (Pinks) grow 12 inches high. They are used for borders, rock gardens, edging and cut flowers. Dianthus blooms in May and June. Plant seed any time from spring to September in a sunny spot. Space plants 12 inches apart. Seed germinates in 5 days. Dianthus is best when grown as a biennial. It is winter-killed in a wet location. It is very susceptible to rotting at the soil line.

DICENTRA

Dicentra spectabilis (Bleeding Heart) grows 2 to 4 feet high and *D. cucullaria* (Dutchman's Breeches) grows 1 foot tall. They are used for borders, in front of shrubbery and as pot plants. Dicentra blooms in late spring. Plant seed in late autumn. Space plants 12 to 18 inches apart. Seed takes 50 days or longer to germinate.

FOXGLOVE

Foxglove (*Digitalis purpurea*) grows 4 to 6 feet high. It is used in borders and for cut flowers. Foxglove blooms in June and July. Plant seed any time from spring to September in sun or partial shade. Space plants 12 inches apart. Seed germinates in about 20 days. Shade summer plantings. Select—and propagate—strains that bear flowers at right angles to stem. Discard plants with drooping flowers.

GAILLARDIA

Gaillardia grandiflora (Blanketflower) grows 12 to 30 inches high. It is used in borders and for cut flowers. It blooms from midsummer to frost. Gaillardia is easily grown from seed, which you can plant in early spring or late summer. Choose a sunny spot in your garden. Space plants 24 inches apart. Seed germinates in about 20 days.

GEUM

Geum chiloense (Chilian Avens) grows 6 to 24 inches high. It is used in borders and rock gardens and for cut flowers. Most geum plants bloom in June and July; some, however, bloom from May to October. Geum will grow in many different locations. You can plant seed in spring or summer in a sunny spot. Space plants about 18 inches apart. Seed germinates in 25 days. Geum is winter hardy if you give it some protection.

GYPSOPHILA

Gypsophila paniculata (Babysbreath) grows 2 to 4 feet high. It is used for borders and as a source of cut flowers and flowers for drying. Perennial gypsophila blooms from early summer to early autumn. It does best in a deeply prepared soil that is high in lime content (alkaline). Plant seeds any time from early spring to September, in a sunny spot. Space plants about 4 feet apart. Seed germinates in about ten days.

HELIANTHEMUM

Helianthemum nummularium (Sun Rose) grows about 12 inches high. It is used in borders. Plants are evergreen, and bloom from June to September. Helianthemum will grow in dry soil. Plant seed any time from spring to September in a spot that gets full sun all day, but shade seedbed. Space plants 12 inches apart. Seed germinates in about 15 days.

HELLEBORUS

Helleborus niger (Christmas Rose) grows to about 15 inches high. It is used for borders and specimen plants. Helleborus blooms in early spring. Plant seed in the late fall or early winter. For spring planting, refrigerate seeds for 2 months before sowing. Germination is very slow; it usually takes 30 days. Plant in a sunny spot. Space plants about 24 inches apart. Do not disturb after planting. Do not transplant. Helleborus requires three to four years to bloom.

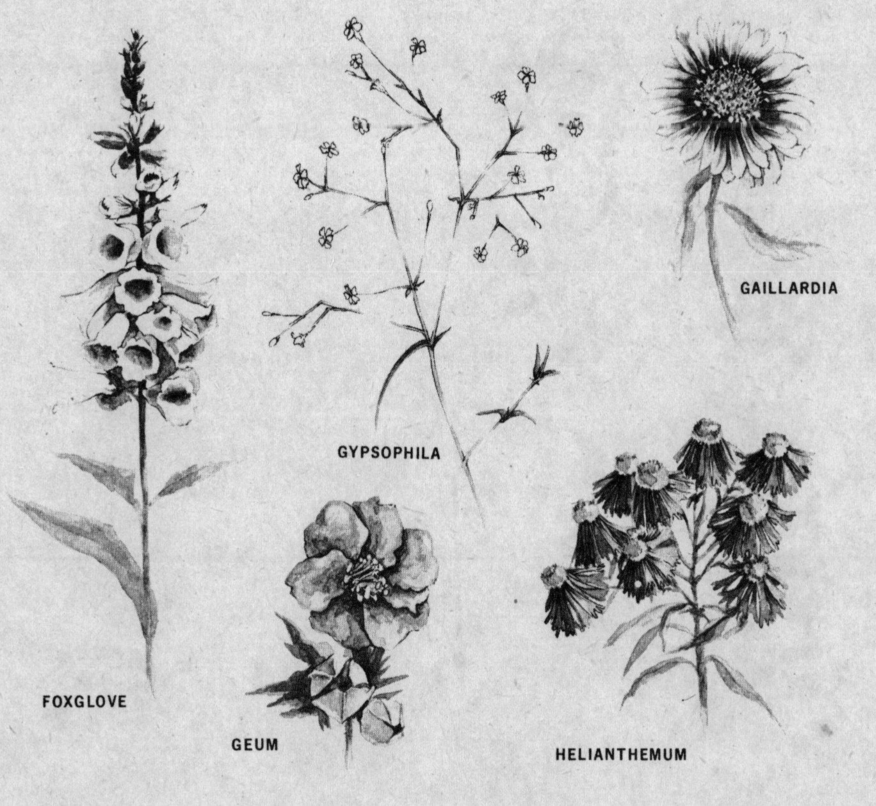

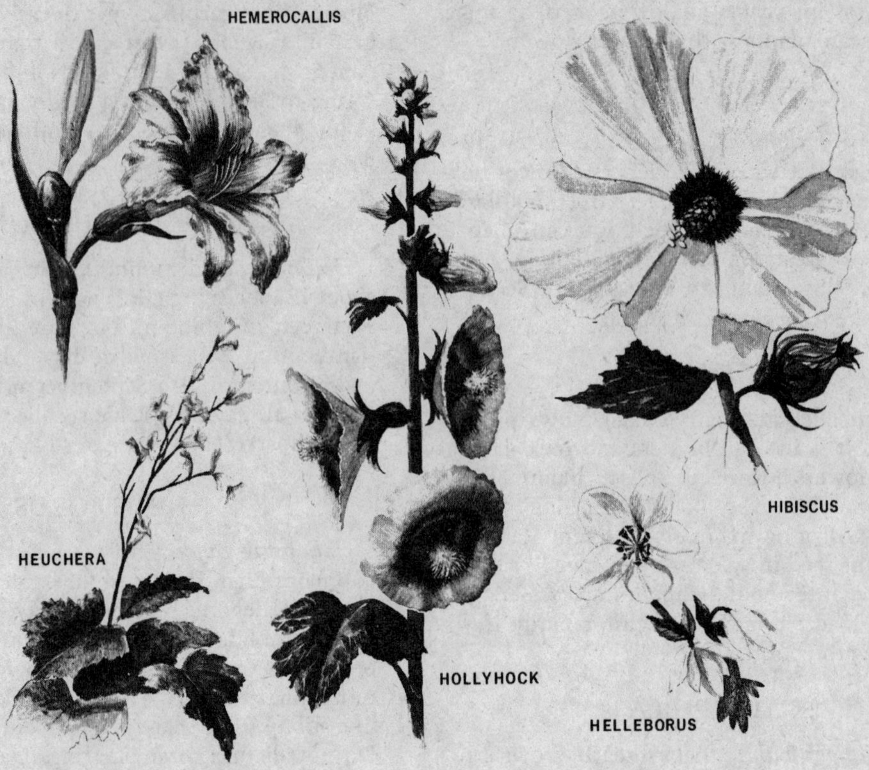
HEMEROCALLIS
HIBISCUS
HEUCHERA
HOLLYHOCK
HELLEBORUS

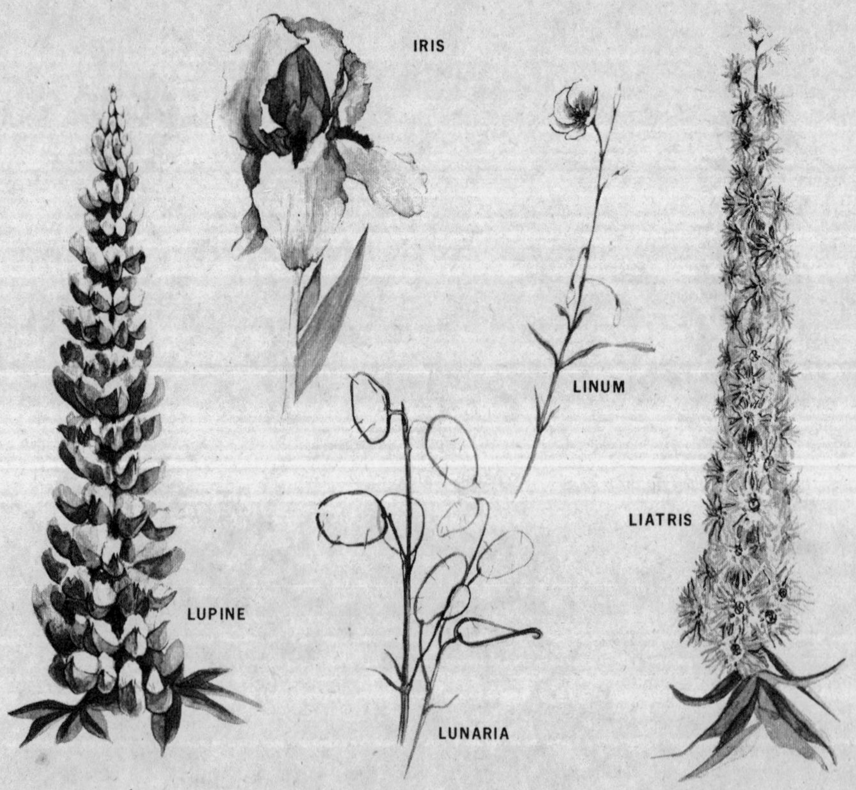
IRIS
LINUM
LIATRIS
LUPINE
LUNARIA

HEMEROCALLIS

Hemerocallis (Daylily) grows 1 to 4 feet high. To have daylily flowers throughout the growing season, plant various species of this perennial. Hemerocallis is used in borders and among shrubbery. Plant seed in late fall or early spring in full sunlight or partial shade. Space plants 24 to 30 inches apart. Seed germinates in 15 days.

HEUCHERA

Heuchera sanguinea (Coral Bells) grows up to 2 feet high. It is used for rock gardens, borders and cut flowers. Heuchera blooms from June to September. It grows best in a limed (alkaline) soil. Plant seed in early spring or late fall in partial shade. Space plants about 18 inches apart. Seed germinates in about ten days. Propagate by division.

HIBISCUS

Hibiscus moscheutos and *H. oculiroseus* (Mallow) grow 3 to 8 feet high. They are used in flower beds or as background plants. Hibiscus blooms from July to September. Plant seed in spring or summer, in sunlight or partial shade, and in moist or dry soil. Space plants at least 2 feet apart. Seed usually germinates in 15 days, but may take much longer.

HOLLYHOCK

Hollyhock (*Althea rosea*) grows to 6 feet tall. It is used for background screening. Hollyhock blooms from late spring to midsummer. It does best in deep, rich, well-drained soil. Plant seed any time from spring to September in a sunny spot. Space plants about 3 feet apart. Seed germinates in ten days. Stake plants to protect them from the wind.

IRIS

The kinds of iris commonly grown are German, Japanese, Siberian and dwarf. Iris grows from 3 inches to 2½ feet high. Use iris in borders and as cut flowers. Different kinds of iris can be grown so that you will have flowers throughout spring and summer. Plant bulbs or rhizomes in late fall. They germinate the following spring. Space plants 18 to 24 inches apart.

LIATRIS

Liatris pycnostachya (Gayfeather) grows 2 to 6 feet high. It is used in borders and for cut flowers. It blooms from summer to early autumn. Liatris is easily started from seed. Plant seed in early spring or late fall in a sunny spot. Space plants about 18 inches apart. Seed germinates in 20 days. You can propagate new plants by cutting thick, fleshy roots into pieces.

LINUM

Linum perenne (Flax) grows about 2 feet high. It is used for bedding and in rock gardens. Linum blooms through the summer. You can plant seed any time from spring to September in a sunny spot. Shade summer plantings. Space plants 18 inches apart. Seed germinates in about 25 days.

LUNARIA

Lunaria biennis (Money Plant) grows to about 4 feet high. It is used in a cutting garden and as a source of seed pods for drying to use in winter bouquets. Lunaria blooms in summer. It is easy to grow. Plant seeds in early spring in a sunny spot. Space plants about 2 feet apart. Seed germinates in ten days.

LUPINE

Lupine polyphyllus grows to about 3 feet high. It is used in borders and for cut flowers. Lupine blooms in summer. Plant seed in early spring or late fall in a sunny spot that has perfect drainage. Soak seeds before planting; inoculate with legume aid. Plant seed where lupine is to flower—it does not transplant well. Space plants about 36 inches apart. Seed germinates in about 20 days.

LYTHRUM

Lythrum (Blackblood) grows 4 to 6 feet high. It blooms in July and August. Use lythrum scattered in gardens and yards or among trees and shrubs. Plant seed in late fall or early spring in a moist, lightly shaded area. Space plants 18 to 24 inches apart. Seed germinates in 15 days.

MONARDA

Monarda didyma (Bee-balm) and *M. fistulosa* (Wild Bergamot, Horsemint) grow 2 to 3 feet high. They are used in borders and for masses of color. Monarda blooms all summer. Plant seed in spring or summer. Space plants 12 to 18 inches apart. Cut plants back after flowering and they will bloom again the same season. Seed germinates in 15 days.

PENSTEMON

Penstemon murrayanus grandiflorus (Beardlip, Pagoda Flower) grows 1½ to 2 feet high. It is used in borders and for cut flowers. If it is planted early, penstemon blooms throughout the season. It grows best in well-drained soil and does well in rather dry soil. Plant seed in early spring or late fall in a sunny

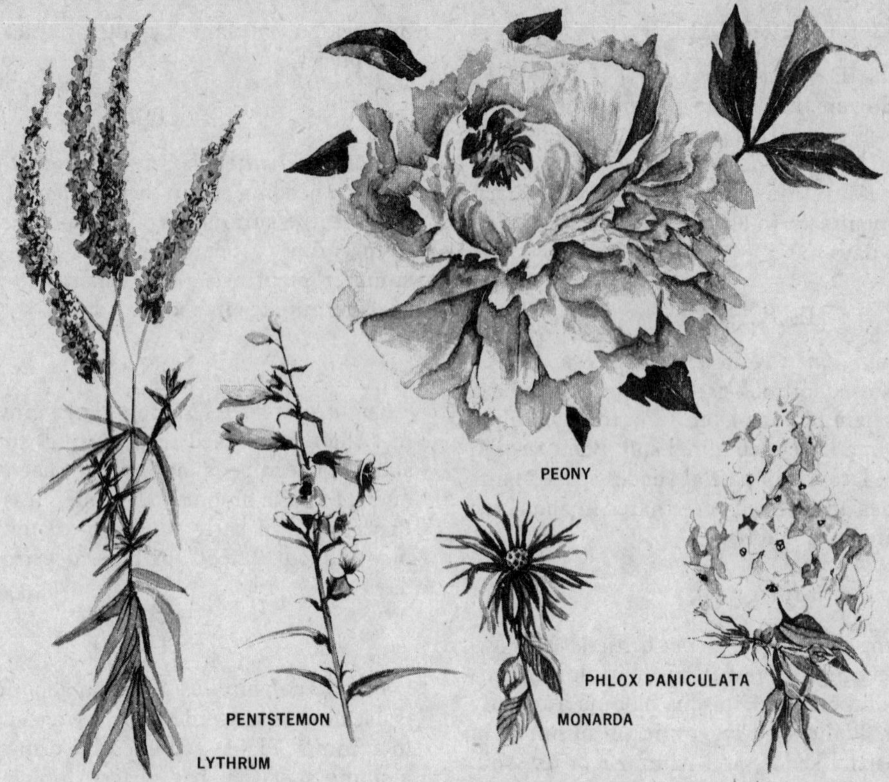

spot that is sheltered in winter. Space plants 18 inches apart. Seed germinates in about ten days.

PEONY

Peony (*Paeonia*) grows 2 to 4 feet tall. It is used in borders and for cut flowers. Peony blooms in late spring and early summer. It is difficult to grow from seed; plant tubers in late fall at least 3 feet apart and 2 to 3 inches deep.

PHLOX

Phlox paniculata (Summer Phlox) grows to about 3 feet high. It is used in borders and for cut flowers. It blooms in early summer. Plant seed in late fall or early winter in a sunny spot. Keep seed in refrigerator one month before seeding. Space plants about 2 feet apart. Keep soil moist. Germination takes about 25 days and is very irregular. Plants grown from seed are very variable in color and form.

Phlox subulata (Moss Phlox) grows 4 to 5 inches high and is used in borders. It blooms in the spring. *P. subulata* is normally grown from stolons. Plant in a sunny spot. Space plants about 8 inches apart. *P. subulata* is drought-resistant.

PLATYCODON

Platycodon grandiflorum (Balloonflower) grows about 2 feet high. It is used for borders and cut flowers. Platycodon blooms from spring until frost. Plant seed any time between spring and September in a sunny spot. Space plants about 12 inches apart. Seed germinates in ten days. In the fall, dig root and store in moist sand in a cool (but frost-free) coldframe. Replant in early spring.

POPPY

Iceland Poppy (*Papaver nudicaule*) grows 15 to 18 inches high. The Oriental Poppy *(P. orientale)* grows 3 feet high. Both are used in borders and for cut flowers. Poppies bloom in summer. Plant seed in early spring in a permanent location; poppies do not transplant well. Choose a sunny spot. Space plants 2 feet apart. Seed germinates in about 10 days.

PRIMROSE

Primula polyantha (Polyantha Primrose) grows 6 to 9 inches high; *P. veris* grows 6 inches high. Primrose is used in rock gardens. It blooms in April and May. Early in year, sow seed on soil surface in pots; water with a mister; cover with glass; place outside to freeze; bring inside to germinate. Seed also can be planted outside in spring if it is first frozen in ice cubes. Usually seed is planted outside in late autumn or early winter. Choose a spot in partial shade. Space plants about a foot apart. Seed germinates in about 25 days, but germination is very irregular.

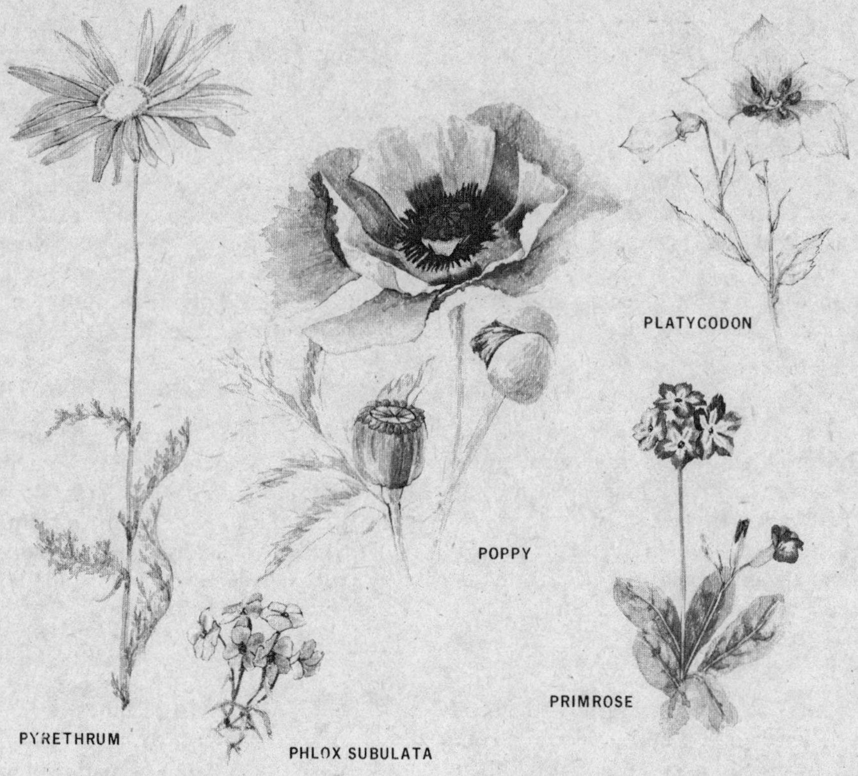

PYRETHRUM

Pyrethrum roseum (Chrysanthemum, Painted Daisy) grows about 2 feet high. It is used in borders and for cut flowers. Pyrethrum blooms in May and June. Plant seed any time from spring to September in a sunny spot. In wet soil, plants are winterkilled. Space plants about 18 inches apart. Seed germinates in 20 days.

RUDBECKIA

Echinacea purpurea (Rudbeckia, Coneflower) grows 2½ to 3 feet high. It is used in borders and bedding and for cut flowers. It blooms midsummer to fall. Plant seed any time from spring to September in a sunny spot. Shade summer plantings. Space plants about 30 inches apart. Seed germinates in 20 days.

SALVIA

Salvia azurea grandiflora and *S. crinacea* (Sage) grow 3 to 4 feet tall and bloom from August until frost. Use salvia in borders. Plant seed in spring in a sunny spot. Space plants 18 to 24 inches apart. Seed germinates in 15 days.

SEA-LAVENDER

Sea-lavender, perennial Blue Statice (*Limonium latifolia*) grows 2 to 3 feet high. It is used for bedding, cut flowers and flowers for drying. Sea-lavender blooms in July and August. Plant seed in early spring while the soil is cool. Choose a sunny spot. Space plants about 30 inches apart. Seed germinates in 15 days.

SIBERIAN WALLFLOWER

Siberian Wallflower (*Cheiranthus cheiri*) grows 12 to 18 inches high. It is used in rock gardens and for cut flowers. It blooms in May and June. Siberian wallflower does very well in cool climates. Plant seed in early spring while the soil is cool. Choose a sunny spot. Space plants about a foot apart. Seed germinates in five days.

STOKESIA

Stokesia cyanea (Stokes' Aster) grows 15 inches high. It is used for borders and cut flowers. If started early, it blooms in the first season—in September. Plant seed any time from spring to September in a sunny spot. Shade summer plantings. Space plants 18 inches apart. Seed germinates in about 20 days.

SWEETPEA

Everlasting Sweetpea (*Lathyrus latifolius*) grows 5 to 6 feet high. It is used as a background vine, on a fence or trellis or for cut flowers. Sweetpea blooms June to September. It succeeds almost anywhere without care. Plant seed in early spring in a sunny spot. Space plants about 2 feet apart. Seed germinates in 20 days.

SWEETWILLIAM

Sweetwilliam (*Dianthus barbatus*) grows 12 to 18 inches high. A dwarf form also is available. It is used for borders, edging and cut flowers. Sweetwilliam blooms in May and June. It is very hardy, but grows best in well-drained soil. Plant seed any time from spring to September in a sunny spot. Space plants about a foot apart. Seed germinates in five days.

TRITOMA

Tritoma, Red Hot Poker (*Kniphofia uvaria*) grows 3 to 4 feet high. It is used in borders and for cut flowers. Tritoma blooms from August to October. Plant seed in early spring or late fall in a sunny spot. Space plants about 18 inches apart. Seed germinates in 20 days. In the North, dig and store roots.

TROLLIUS

Trollius ledebouri (Globe Flower) grows about 20 inches high. It is used in borders. It blooms from May to July. Trollius requires extra moisture. Plant seed in late fall. Allow seed to remain outdoors over winter for germination. If you want to plant seed in early spring, soak it in hot water 30 minutes before sowing. Space plants about a foot apart. Seed germinates in something over 50 days.

VERONICA

Veronica spicata (Speedwell) grows about 18 inches high. It is used in borders and rock gardens and for cut flowers. Veronica blooms in June and July. It is easily grown. Plant seed any time from spring to September in a sunny spot. Space plants 18 inches apart. Seed germinates in about 15 days.

VIOLA CORNUTA

Viola cornuta (Tufted Pansy) grows about 6 inches high. It is used for bedding, edging and window boxes. It blooms all summer if you remove old flowers. *V. cornuta* is easily grown from seed and is very hardy. Plant seed any time from spring to September in partial shade. Space plants about 12 inches apart. Seed germinates in ten days.

Buying Plants or Seed

You can buy plants of many perennials from your local nursery or garden shop. These plants usually are in bloom when they are offered for sale, which

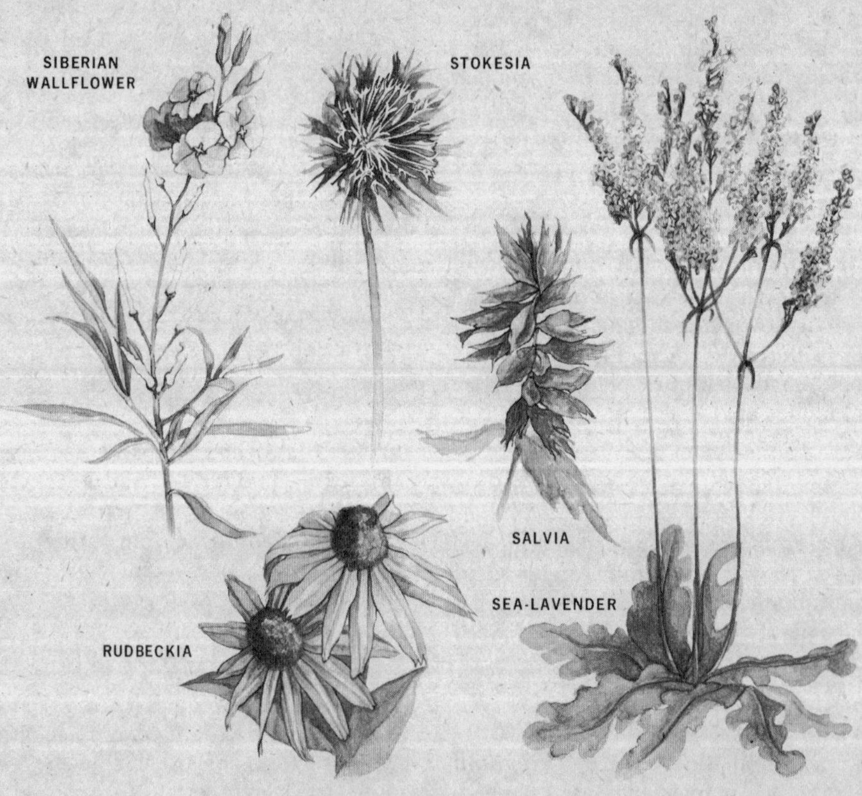

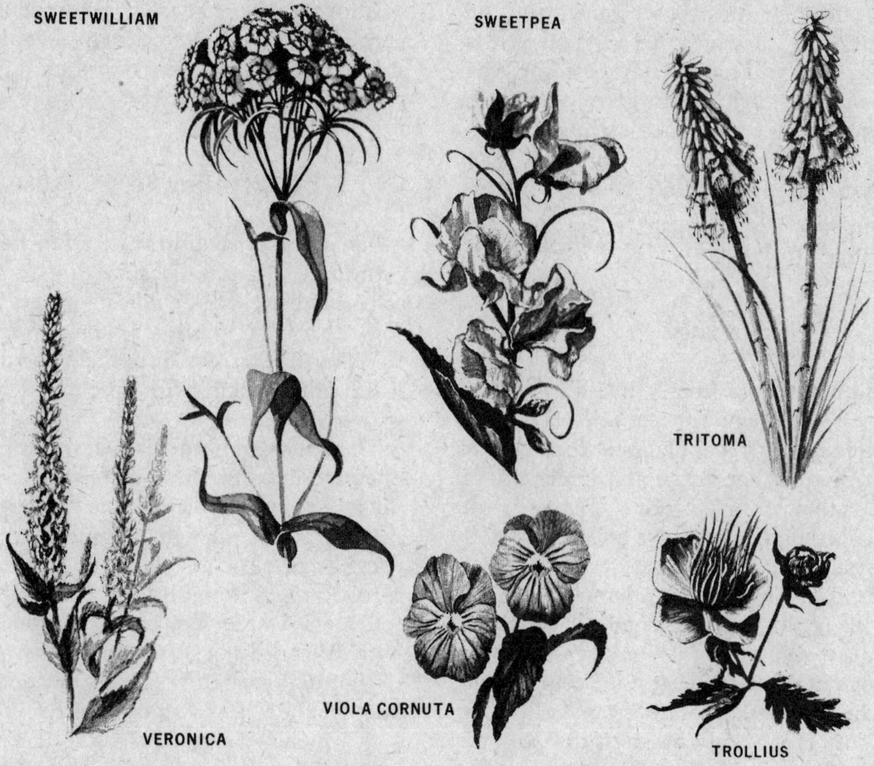

allows you to select the colors you want for your garden.

Buy perennial plants that are compact and dark green. Plants sold in warm shopping areas are seldom vigorous. You can detect plants held in warm areas too long by the thin pale yellow stems and leaves. Avoid buying these plants.

Named varieties are most useful in the garden—useful because we know their disease resistance, their heat and cold resistance, and their plant habit (height and branching). They are the backbone of a good perennial garden. Named varieties are available everywhere in the United States.

Select plants of named varieties for special colors or growing habits. Propagate these by cuttings or clump divisions. Colors are definite from cuttings or divisions.

Many perennials do not grow true to type from seed. If you plant seed, many off-types as to color, flower form and plant habit are produced.

You can sow perennial seeds directly in the beds where the plants are to bloom or you can start early plants indoors and set them out in beds after the weather warms. (See "Starting Plants Indoors," page 72.)

Many perennials are best grown from seed each year. Many of the so-called biennials—plants that flower the second year—are grown only from seed: columbine, foxglove, canterbury bells, sweetwilliam and delphinium.

To get a good start toward raising vigorous plants, buy good seed.

Be sure your seed is fresh. Do not buy it too far in advance of planting time; for best results, allow no more than a three-month interval.

Old seed saved from previous years may lose much of its vitality under household conditions. It tends to germinate slowly and to produce poor seedlings.

Keep the seed dry and cool until you plant it. Special instructions for storage are printed on some seed packets. Follow these instructions.

When buying seed, look for new varieties listed as F_1 hybrids—widely available in annuals and now beginning to show up in perennials. Seed for these hybrids costs more than the seed of the usual inbred varieties, but its superiority makes it worth the extra price.

These F_1 hybrids are produced by crossing selected inbred parents. Plants of F_1 varieties are more uniform in size and more vigorous than plants of inbred varieties and they produce more flowers.

PLANTING YOUR PERENNIAL GARDEN

Do not be in a rush to start seeds or to set out started plants. As a general rule, delay sowing seed outdoors or setting out plants until after the last frost.

Most seeds will not germinate well until the soil warms to about 60°. If they are sowed in soil that is cooler than this, they will remain dormant until the soil warms and may rot before they germinate.

Start seed indoors no sooner than eight weeks before the average date for the last killing frost in your area. If you start seed earlier than this, the plants will be too large for satisfactory transplanting by the time the weather is warm enough for them to be set outside.

Setting Plants

Whether you buy plants from a nursery or start your own indoors, set them out the same way.

When the time comes to set plants out in the garden, remove them from flats by slicing downward in the soil between the plants. Lift out each plant with a block of soil surrounding its roots and set the soil block in a planting hole.

If the plants are in fiber pots, remove the paper from the outside of the root mass and set the plant in a prepared planting hole.

When setting out plants in peat pots, remove the top edge of the pot to keep rain from collecting around the plant. Thoroughly moisten the pot and its contents to help the roots develop properly.

Drench the soil around the planting hole with a liquid fertilizer—16–52–10 or 20–20–20—mixed 1 tablespoon per gallon of water, to stimulate root growth.

Set the moistened pot in the planting hole and press the soil up around it. The pot will break down in the soil and improve the soil around the plant.

Allow plenty of space between plants because perennials need room to develop. Perennials usually show up best when planted in clumps or groups of plants of the same variety.

Planting Seed Outdoors

Perennials seeded in the garden frequently fail to germinate properly because the surface of the soil cakes and prevents entry of water. To avoid this, sow the seed in vermiculite-filled furrows.

Make the furrows in the soil about ½ inch deep. After filling them with fine vermiculite, sprinkle with water.

Then make another shallow furrow in the vermiculite and sow the seed in this furrow. Sow it at the rate recommended on the packet.

Cover the seed with a layer of vermiculite and, using a nozzle adjusted for a fine mist, water the seeded area thoroughly.

To retard water evaporation, cover the seeded area with sheets of newspaper or polyethylene film (plastic garment bags from the dry cleaner are excellent). Support the newspaper or plastic on blocks or sticks 1 or 2 inches above the surface of the bed. Remove the paper or plastic when seedlings appear.

When most outdoor-grown perennials develop two true leaves, they should be thinned to the recommended spacing. This allows the plants to have enough light, water, nutrients and space for them to develop fully. If they have been seeded in vermiculite-filled furrows, the excess seedlings can be transplanted to another spot without injury.

Lift out each plant with a block of soil surrounding its roots.

Watering

Do not rely on summer rainfall keep your flower beds watered. Plan to irrigate them from the beginning.

Correct watering can make the difference between a good flower display and a poor one.

Water on a regular schedule. Water perennials throughout the growing season, particularly during dry weather. Allow the water to penetrate deeply into the soil. Never water by hand—it requires too much time to do a thorough job and it always tears up the soil structure and washes the beds.

When you water, moisten the entire bed thoroughly, but do not water so heavily that the soil becomes soggy. Water again when the soil is dry to touch and the tips of the plants wilt slightly at midday.

A canvas soaker hose is excellent for watering beds, but it is difficult to maintain because the canvas rots quickly. Water from the soaker hose seeps directly into the soil without waste. The slow-moving water does not disturb the soil or reduce its capacity to absorb water.

If you water with a sprinkler, use an oscillating sprinkler. This type covers a large area and produces rainlike drops of water. Do not use a rotating sprinkler—it tends to tear up the surface of the soil and covers only a small area.

Run the sprinkler at least 4 hours in each place. This deep watering will allow a longer interval between waterings.

The least effective method for watering is with a hand-held nozzle. Watering with a nozzle has all the objections of watering with a rotating sprinkler. In addition, gardeners seldom are patient enough to do a thorough job of watering with a nozzle, not enough water is applied, and the water that is applied usually is poorly distributed over the bed.

It is difficult to water plants in bloom. The flowers tend to rot if they catch and hold water, so if possible avoid wetting blossoms.

If possible water in the early part of the day; this will allow plenty of time for the flowers and foliage to dry before night—but any time during the day is satisfactory. Night watering, however, increases the chances of disease.

Mulching

Mulch gives an orderly look to the garden, cuts down weeds and weeding labor and adds organic matter to the soil.

Trim the plants of excess foliage and stems before mulching.

Mulch with buckwheat hulls, peat moss, salt hay, pine bark, pine needles, or wood chips. Select an organic material that will decompose slowly, that will allow water to penetrate to the soil below, and that adds a neutral color to the soil.

Spread mulch over the whole bed, 2 inches deep. Spread before the plants have made a great deal of growth. Water the mulch into place (dry mulches prevent water penetration). All mulches require care to keep them attractive—litter is very noticeable.

Mulch during both summer and winter.

Mulch during the summer to:

- Retard water loss.
- Prevent soil baking and cracking.
- Hold down weeds.
- Prevent soil splashing when watering.

Mulch during the winter to:

- Protect newly planted perennials.
- Protect less hardy plants.

Be careful with winter mulching; it can do more harm than good. Apply mulch around the plants only after the soil temperature has gone down—usually in the late fall, after several killing frosts. If the winter mulch is applied too early, the warmth from the soil will cause new growth to start. Severe damage to the plant can result from new growth being frozen back.

The best winter mulch is snow—if the bed has good drainage.

A thin layer of peat moss is sufficient for a winter mulch. Keep winter mulch loose. It must be well drained and have good air circulation to keep the plants from rotting.

Screen winter-mulched plants from the wind.

Remove the winter mulch as soon as growth starts in the spring. If you don't, the new growth will develop abnormally, with long, gangly stems and insufficient chlorophyll.

If you have trouble carrying a particular plant over the winter, a mulch can help. But remember, a mulch is not a substitute for a coldframe. It may be better to grow the plant as a biennial, carry it over the winter in a coldframe, and move it to the flower bed in the second spring.

In many of the colder areas of the United States, spring planting from coldframe-held plants is the only way to have a particular perennial in the garden.

Fertilizing

You must fertilize the planting bed regularly to keep it fertile. The long growing times that perennials require rob the soil of its natural fertility.

Do not fertilize perennials heavily with inorganic

POLYETHYLENE AND PERENNIALS

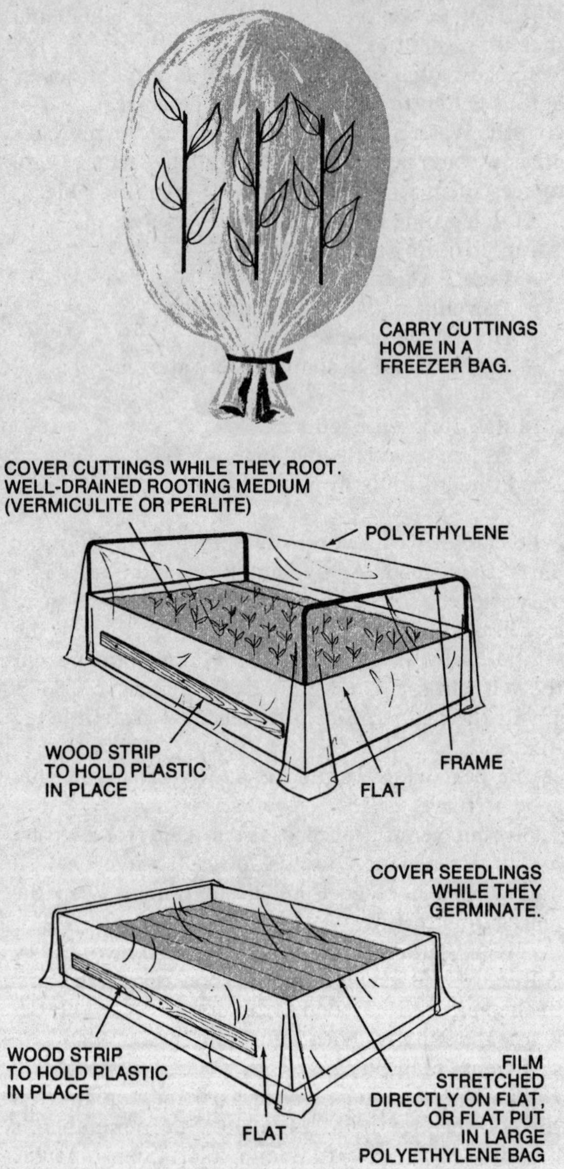

fertilizers. A light fertilization program gives a continuous supply of nutrients to produce plants that are easier to train or support on stakes, and plants that do not have foliage so dense it interferes with air circulation and has difficulty drying. (Air circulation is helped by proper spacing of plants, also.)

If your soil is highly organic—has lots of peat moss or compost in it—you can fertilize with 5–10–5. Put little rings of fertilizer around each plant in early spring (March). Repeat about six weeks later, and again six weeks after that. This should be enough to carry plants through the summer. Apply another treatment of fertilizer to late-blooming plants in late summer or early fall.

Always water the bed after applying fertilizer. This will wash the fertilizer off the foliage and prevent fertilizer burn. It will also make the fertilizer available to the plant immediately. Until the fertilizer enters the soil—regardless of how long it has been on the surface of the soil—it is not available to the plant.

Establish a fertilization program and fertilize right along, a little at a time.

Cultivating

After plants are set out or after they are thinned, cultivate only to break crusts on the surface of the soil. When the plants begin to grow, stop cultivating. Pull weeds by hand in limited areas, and frequently. As plants grow, feeder roots spread out between them; cultivation is likely to injure these roots. In addition, cultivation stirs the soil and uncovers other weed seeds that then germinate.

Staking

Most perennials are top-heavy; all of them need staking.

If plants fall over, the stem will function poorly where it has been bent. If the stem is cracked, rot organisms can penetrate the break.

Stake plants when you first set them out so that:

- They will grow to cover the stakes.
- They can be oriented; turn them to face the front of the bed.
- They can better withstand hard, driving rain and wind.

You can use stakes made of twigs, wood dowels, bamboo, wire or even plastic.

STAKING PLANTS

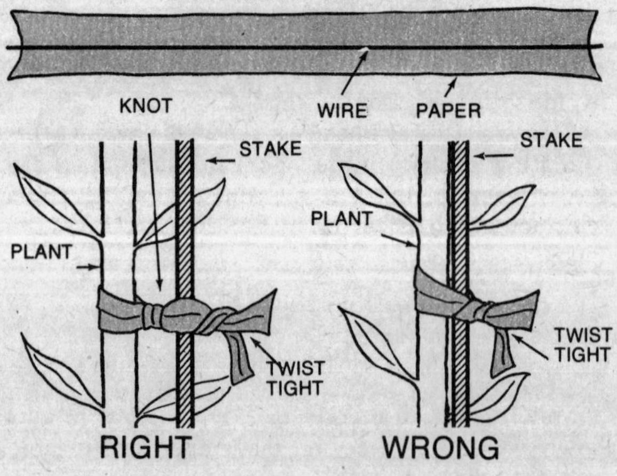

Tie the plant to the stake; never use wire, it breaks the stem; never use string, it shows and eventually rots in the garden; use green plastic strips or wire covered with green paper strips.

WHEN AND HOW TO DIVIDE PERENNIALS

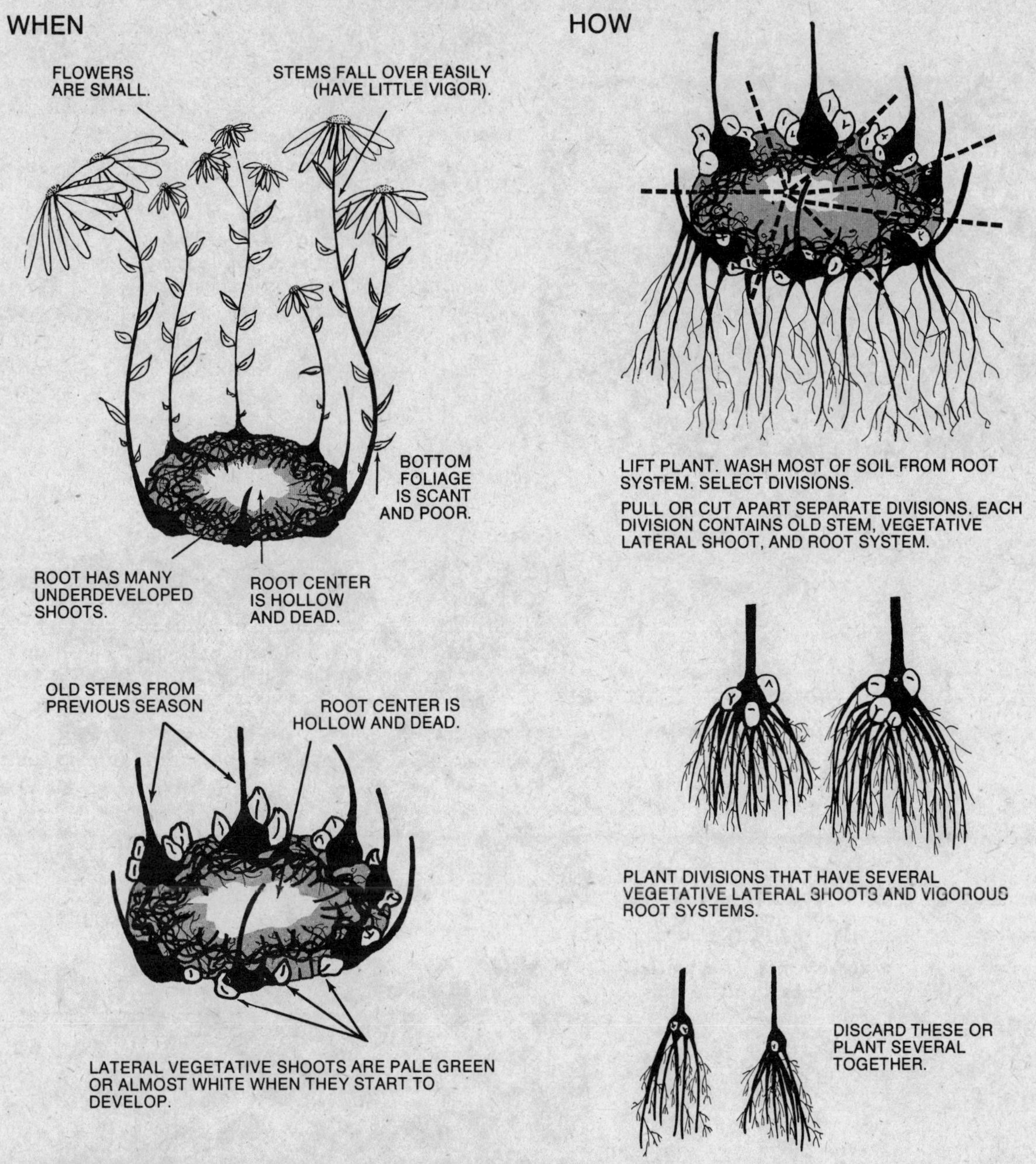
WHEN
FLOWERS ARE SMALL.
STEMS FALL OVER EASILY (HAVE LITTLE VIGOR).
BOTTOM FOLIAGE IS SCANT AND POOR.
ROOT HAS MANY UNDERDEVELOPED SHOOTS.
ROOT CENTER IS HOLLOW AND DEAD.
OLD STEMS FROM PREVIOUS SEASON
ROOT CENTER IS HOLLOW AND DEAD.
LATERAL VEGETATIVE SHOOTS ARE PALE GREEN OR ALMOST WHITE WHEN THEY START TO DEVELOP.
HOW
LIFT PLANT. WASH MOST OF SOIL FROM ROOT SYSTEM. SELECT DIVISIONS.
PULL OR CUT APART SEPARATE DIVISIONS. EACH DIVISION CONTAINS OLD STEM, VEGETATIVE LATERAL SHOOT, AND ROOT SYSTEM.
PLANT DIVISIONS THAT HAVE SEVERAL VEGETATIVE LATERAL SHOOTS AND VIGOROUS ROOT SYSTEMS.
DISCARD THESE OR PLANT SEVERAL TOGETHER.

Select stakes that will be 6 to 12 inches shorter than the height of the grown plant.

Place the stakes behind the plants. Sink the stakes into the ground far enough to be firm.

Loosely tie plants to the stakes. Use wire covered with a layer of paper or plastic to tie the plants. Do not use string; string rots and is unsightly.

Tie the plant, making a double loop of the wire with one loop around the plant and the other around the stake. Never loop the wire in a single loop around both stake and plant—the plant will hang to one side and the wire may girdle the stem.

Dividing

Never leave a perennial planted in the same place for more than three years. The center of the clump will grow poorly, and the flowers will be sparse. The clump will deplete the fertility of the soil in which it is grown. The plant will crowd itself.

Divide mature clumps of perennials. Select only vigorous side shoots, the outer part of the clump. This is the part that will grow best. Discard the center of the clump.

STARTING SEEDS

Gather your materials—wooden or fiber flat potting strips or peat pots, potting soil (equal parts of garden soil, vermiculite, and sphagnum peat moss—or bagged soil mix from garden or variety store), vermiculite, watering can, polyethylene film for cover, and seeds.

Clean the flat; allow to dry thoroughly before putting in pots. Fill pots with soil mix, and water thoroughly.

Put seeds on top of soil; plant two or three large seeds or a pinch of small seeds in each pot. Firm the soil (you can press lightly with an empty pot without disturbing the seed).

Cover the seeds with fine vermiculite and firm it. Water thoroughly and allow to drain.

Cover the flat with polyethylene film and put it in warm (65° to 75°F.) place. The flat needs no further water until after the seeds have germinated; nor does it need light. Do not place the plastic-covered flat in sunlight; heat buildup under plastic could kill emerging seedlings.

Divide the plant into clumps of three to five shoots each. Be careful not to overdivide; too small a clump will not give much color the first year after replanting.

Divide perennials in the fall in southern areas and in the spring in northern areas.

Stagger plant division so that the whole garden will not be done over at the same time; a good rotation will give you a display of flowers each year.

Do not put all the divisions back into the same area that the original plant came out of. That would be too many plants in a given area; there would be poor air circulation around them.

Give extra plants to friends or plant them elsewhere in your yard—or discard them.

Removing Old Flowers

To maintain vigorous growth of plants, remove mature flowers.

Do not allow perennials to go to seed, By not allowing them to seed you will promote the growth of side shoots.

Remove dead foliage and stems in the fall. Keep dead foliage and stems out of the garden area.

Making Cuttings

Many plants can be propagated from either tip of root cuttings. Generally, tip cuttings are easier to propagate.

Select second growth of dianthus, candytuft, and phlox for cutting.

Make tip cuttings 3 to 6 inches long. Treat the base of the cutting with a root stimulant. Leave all foliage on the cutting except the part that will be below the soil line. Insert one cutting in each peat pot.

Make root cuttings of phlox, babysbreath, and oriental poppy. Dig the plants in late summer, after they have bloomed. Select pencil-size roots; cut them into 4-inch sections. Put each piece in a peat pot.

Prepare a tray of peat pots as for seeds, except the soil mix should be 2 parts sand, 1 part soil, and 1 part peat moss. Water thoroughly.

Put peat pots of root cuttings in a coldframe. Transplant them the next spring.

Place the tray of tip cuttings in a lightly shaded place. Cover with a sheet of plastic. Check regularly to make sure the cuttings do not dry out.

When the cuttings do not pull easily out of the soil, they have begun to root. Make holes in the plastic sheet to let air in and to increase the exposure of the cuttings to the air. This will harden the cuttings. Every few days make new holes, or make the holes larger.

Finally, remove the cover. Allow the cuttings to grow. Pinch back their tips ten days after the cover is removed—this will promote branching. Transplant the rooted cuttings to a freshly prepared bed in midsummer.

STARTING PLANTS INDOORS

Unless you are willing to invest in special lighting equipment and to devote considerable care to starting plants from seed indoors, it usually is best to buy young plants or to sow seed of perennials directly in the garden. Home-started plants seldom are as satisfactory for setting out as those bought from nurserymen. And they seldom grow as well or bloom as prolifically as those planted directly in the garden.

Damping-off Disease

Home-started seedlings frequently are attacked by a fungus disease—damping-off. Those seedlings that escape the disease usually are weak and spindly and never become good garden plants; conditions of light, temperature, and humidity normally found in the home are not favorable for plant growth.

Damping-off organisms cause seeds to rot and seedlings to collapse and die. The disease is carried in soil and may be present on planting containers and tools. Soil moisture and temperature necessary for germination of seeds also are ideal for development of damping-off.

Once the disease appears in a seed flat, it may travel quickly through the flat and kill all the seedlings planted there.

It can be prevented.

Before planting, treat the seed with a fungicide. Sterilize the soil, and use sterile containers.

Treat the seed with thiram, chloranil, dichlone, or captan. Tear off one corner of the seed packet and, through the hole in the packet, insert about as much fungicide dust as you can pick up on the tip of the small blade of a penknife. Close the hole by folding over the corner of the packet, then shake the seed thoroughly to coat it with the fungicide dust.

Sterilize the soil in an oven. Fill a container—a pan or metal tray—with moist—but not wet—soil, bury a raw potato in the center of the soil, and bake in a medium oven. When the potato is cooked, the soil should be sterile.

To avoid introducing the damping-off organism on containers, use fiber seed flats or peat pots. These containers are sterile, inexpensive, and easily obtainable from garden shops.

Fiber flats are light and strong. They cost so little that they can be thrown away after one use.

Peat pots can be set out in the garden along with the plants they contain; roots of the plants grow through the walls of the pots. Plants grown in peat pots suffer no setback when they are transplanted to the garden. Larkspur and poppy, which ordinarily do not tolerate transplanting, can be grown in peat pots satisfactorily.

If you use wooden boxes or clay flower pots for soil containers, clean them well. Soak clay pots in water and scrub them well to remove all of the white fertilizer crust from the outside.

Sterilize clay pots and boxes by baking them in the over when you are sterilizing the soil mixture. Or swab the pots and boxes with a solution of 1 part chlorine bleach to 10 parts water. Allow the containers to dry thoroughly before filling them with soil.

If, despite your precautions, damping-off appears in your seedlings, it is best to discard the containers and soil and start over.

Caution: If fungicides are handled, applied, or disposed of improperly, they may be injurious to human beings, domestic animals, desirable plants, and pollinating insects, fish, or other wildlife, and may contaminate water supplies. Use fungicides only when needed and handle them with care. Follow the directions on the container label.

Raising Seedlings

Supplying light: As soon as the seeds have germinated (in about 5 days to 3 weeks), remove the plastic covering and move the tray outside to a lightly shaded area.

Protect the plants during bright weather with light shade. Shade the trays with a single layer of cheese cloth, inexpensive muslin, or part of an old sheet.

Make a frame to support the shading material. Make the frame of wire; attach the shading material to the frame with shower-curtain rings so that the cover can be opened on dull days and closed on bright days.

Watering and fertilizing: The new plants must be watered frequently, and they must be fertilized. You can do both of these jobs at one time by using a solution made by mixing 1 tablespoon of soluble fertilizer (20–20–20) in 1 gallon of water.

MAKE A SHADE FOR YOUR SEEDLINGS

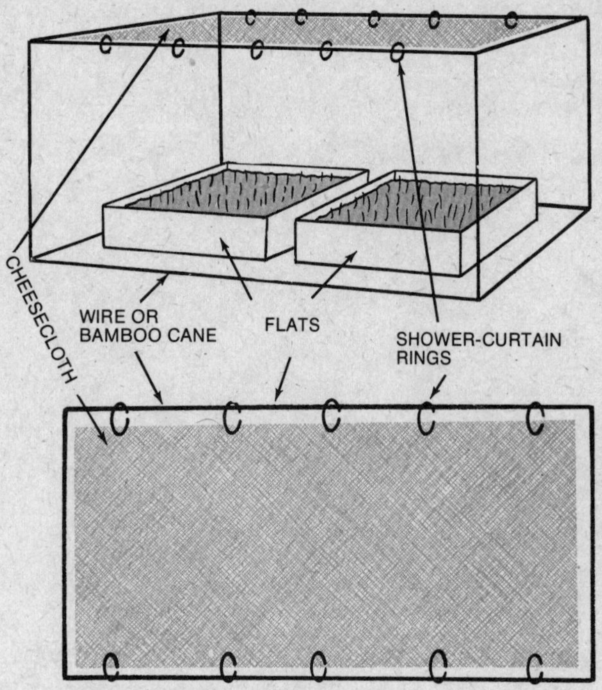

Moisten the soil thoroughly but be careful not to wash out the seedlings when you water them. To avoid this, use a rubber-bulb syringe—available from garden stores—to apply the solution as a fine mist. Or place the solution in a container that is somewhat larger than the pots and submerge them up to their rims in the solution. This waters the plants from the bottom. Remove the pots from the solution as soon as the soil is thoroughly moistened.

Transplanting

When seedlings develop two true leaves, thin those in peat pots to one seedling per pot. A pair of tweezers is a good tool for thinning. The plants that are thinned out can be transferred to other pots if you wish to save them. Handle the seedlings as little as necessary. Don't pinch them.

Continue watering and fertilizing the plants.

In late summer, plant the pots in a permanent garden location.

IV

GROWING BULBS

CHAPTER 6

Spring-flowering Bulbs

SPRING-FLOWERING BULBS ARE hardy plants that require little care. They provide early color in your garden or yard at a time when few other plants are in bloom.

Among the more popular spring-flowering bulbs are tulip, narcissus, hyacinth, iris and crocus. Some that are not so well known are scilla, chionodoxa, muscari and galanthus.

You can use bulbs anywhere in your garden. Some are best as border plants. Others are best when grouped in large masses of color. And many kinds can be scattered in lawns or planted among shrubs as ground cover.

To grow spring-flowering bulbs successfully:

- Select healthy, mature bulbs and store them in a cool, dry place until planting time.
- Prepare the soil in the planting beds thoroughly.
- Plant at depths, distances apart and planting times recommended for each kind of bulb.
- Maintain a winter mulch to prevent damage from alternate freezing and thawing.

The following list gives a brief description of how to plant and manage the more commonly grown spring-flowering bulbs.

ALLIUM

Allium (Flowering Onion) varies in height from 9 inches to 5 feet. It lives many years and grows well throughout the United States. Many varieties are grown. Allium blooms in May, June and July. Flowers are white, yellow, red or pink.

Some commonly grown kinds of spring-flowering allium and their characteristics are as follows:

Allium christophi—Purple flowers, 12 inches in diameter; grows 2 feet tall; blooms in June.

Allium cowanii—White flowers; grows 2 feet tall; blooms in early spring.

Allium moly—Yellow flowers, 12 inches in diameter; blooms in June.

Allium ostrowskianum—Reddish-pink flowers, 6 inches in diameter; blooms in June.

Plant bulbs 2 or 3 inches deep in late fall. Space them 6 to 15 inches apart in clumps of six to 12 bulbs. The distance between bulbs depends on the height of the plant at flowering time.

You can leave the bulbs in place for many years. Dig, separate and replant them when they become crowded or produce small flowers.

AMARYLLIS

Amaryllis (*Hippeastrum*) is grown as a potted plant indoors for spring flowering. It blooms from February to April. Flowers are red, pink, rose, white or salmon. The plants grow about 3 feet tall.

Plant bulbs in early December in an 8-inch pot. Use a mixture of sandy soil and peat moss with an inch of small gravel in the bottom of the pot. Plant only half of the bulb beneath the soil. Water thoroughly after planting, and each time the soil becomes moderately dry.

When the flower begins to form, water and fertilize at weekly intervals; continue for three months after flowering. Fertilize with a mixture of 1 teaspoon of 20–20–20 soluble fertilizer per gallon of water.

Keep the potted bulb in a cool room (60° to 65° F.) and away from direct sunlight until May, when it may be put outside.

When the leaves turn yellow, decrease watering until the soil becomes very dry. Store the potted plant on its side in a cool, dry place (40° to 55° F.). Begin watering again when it shows signs of regrowth the following season. Leave the bulb in the same pot for three years.

ANEMONE

Anemone (Windflower) varies in height from 5 to 12 inches. It grows from tubers and blooms in March

MINOR BULB PLANTING GUIDE

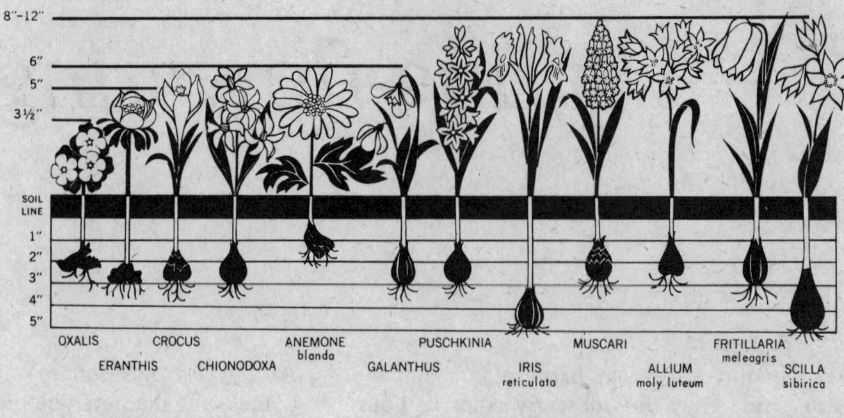

or April. Flowers are purple, red, blue, white, or pink. Anemone is a good source of cut flowers.

Select a planting site that is sheltered from the wind and lightly shaded. Soak tubers in water for 48 hours before planting. Plant them in October, 2 inches deep and 4 inches apart in clumps of 12 tubers. Leave tubers in place two to three years.

CHIONODOXA

Chionodoxa (Glory-of-the-Snow) grows 3 or 4 inches tall. It blooms very early, as the snow is melting. Flowers are silvery pink, or blue and white. Use chionodoxa in groups under deciduous trees or in lawns.

Plant bulbs 3 inches deep in the fall. Space them 2 inches apart in clumps of 12 to 25 bulbs. Leave bulbs in place until they become crowded, often five to eight years.

CROCUS

Many varieties of crocus are grown. Bulbs are usually sold by variety and graded by size. The largest bulbs produce the largest flowers.

The varieties generally recommended for planting are Yellow Mammoth (yellow); Snowstorm, Remembrance, Mont Blanc (white); King of the Striped (white, striped blue); and *Purpurea grandiflora* (purple).

Crocus grows 4 or 5 inches high from corms planted in October or early November. It blooms in late February or early March. Use crocus in a rock garden, border, or scattered in the garden.

Select a planting site that is sheltered from the wind for early flowering. Plant in an exposed area for late flowering. Plant corms 3 inches deep and 3 to 6 inches apart in clumps of 25. Leave them in place for many years.

ERANTHIS

Eranthis (Winter Aconite) grows 2 to 8 inches high. It blooms in early spring and produces a yellow flower cushioned on green leaves. Use eranthis in rock gardens.

Plant tubers 2 inches deep in the fall. Space them 2 to 6 inches apart in clumps of 12 tubers. Leave them in place for many years. They are too small to dig.

FRITILLARIA

Fritillaria includes both *meleagris* (Snakeshead Fritillaria) and *imperialis* (Crown Imperial).

Meleagris produces bell-shaped flowers in April and May. They are white, grayish purple or pink. Use *meleagris* in rock gardens, as borders, or scattered as ground cover.

Plant the bulbs 3 or 4 inches deep, and put a handful of sand around each bulb. Space them 3 or 4 inches apart in clumps of 12 bulbs. Plant them in the fall. Leave the bulbs in place for many years; they are too small to dig.

Imperialis produces large flowers that hang in a circle from the top of the stem. Flowers are coppery red, orange or yellow. Use *imperialis* in borders.

Plant these bulbs 6 to 8 inches deep and 12 inches apart in the fall. Use at least three bulbs in each clump. Plant the bulbs on their sides to keep water from settling in the centers of the bulbs and rotting them.

Fertilize the plants three or four times during the growing season with a mixture of 1 teaspoon of 20–20–20 fertilizer per gallon of water. Leave the bulbs in place for many years.

GALANTHUS

Galanthus (Snowdrop) grows 6 inches tall. It blooms at the end of January. Flowers are snow-white. Use galanthus in flower beds, as borders, or scattered in lawns and gardens.

Select a planting site that is shaded. Plant bulbs 6 inches deep in light sandy soil and 4 inches deep in heavy clay soil. If you wish, you may plant galanthus with other small bulbs such as muscari or chionodoxa.

Plant galanthus in September or October in clumps of at least 25 bulbs. Plant bulbs so they almost touch each other. Leave them in place until they become crowded.

HYACINTH

Hyacinth is showy and formal. It produces many small flowers close together along the stem.

These bulbs are sold by variety and usually are graded by size. Size of bulb indicates size of flower. Top-grade bulbs produce the largest flowers.

Hyacinth

Some well-known and dependable varieties are:

City of Haarlem (yellow), L'Innocence (white), Gertrude (rose), and Bismarck, King of the Blues (blue).

You can buy hyacinth plants that are specially grown and potted for indoor flowering at Christmas.

Hyacinth grows 6 to 12 inches high. It usually blooms in April when narcissi fade and before tall tulips blossom. Flowers are all colors. Use hyacinth in formal plantings among shrubs and as borders.

The bulbs of some varieties are larger than others. Plant small bulbs 3 or 4 inches deep and 4 to 6 inches apart; plant large bulbs 5 or 6 inches deep and 6 to 8 inches apart. Plant bulbs in October.

Handle these bulbs carefully because they bruise easily. Leave them in place for several years. Flowers become smaller each year; dig and discard the bulbs when flowers become too small for good display.

IRIS

Two kinds of iris are grown. Tall iris grows 2 to 2½ feet high. Dwarf iris varies in height from 3 to 12 inches.

Some varieties of both kinds of iris are grown from bulbs and some from rhizomes (underground stems). Both bulbs and rhizomes are called "bulbs" here.

Tall iris produces flowers that are erect on firm, straight stems. The most common types are Dutch, Spanish and English. Blooming time varies among the types, but the difference is slight.

Some commonly grown varieties are Golden Harvest, Pacific Gold, Yellow Queen (yellow); White Excelsior, White Superior (white); Wedgewood (light blue); and Imperator (dark blue).

Tall iris blooms in May, June and July. Flowers make excellent indoor arrangements; cut when a blue or yellow slit appears down the side of the opening flower.

Plant bulbs 3 inches deep and 6 to 8 inches apart in October. If flowers appear before the danger of freezing has passed in the spring, protect them by placing cut branches over the plants. Leave bulbs in place two or three years.

Dwarf iris produces small flowers; some, as *Iris reticulata,* are very fragrant. Dwarf iris should be planted in masses for best display.

Dwarf iris blooms from January to March. Flowers are yellow, purple, violet or blue. Use dwarf iris in rock gardens. Select a planting site in the rock garden that is protected from the wind. Plant 2 to 4 inches deep in October or November. Space 1 or 2 inches apart in drifts of 25 to 50 bulbs. Leave bulbs in place for many years. They are too small to dig and replant.

LEUCOJUM

Leucojum (Snowflake) grows 16 inches tall. It blooms in April and May. Flowers are white like those of galanthus, but much larger.

Select a planting site that is well drained and lightly shaded. Plant bulbs 4 inches deep in the fall. Space them 4 inches apart in clumps of 12 bulbs. Leave them in place for many years.

LILY-OF-THE-VALLEY

Lily-of-the-Valley grows 12 to 15 inches high from pips (underground stems). It produces white, bell-shaped flowers in May. Use lily-of-the-valley as bedding plants in lightly shaded areas, among shrubs as ground cover, and in rock gardens.

Plant pips in late summer. Plant them so their tops are level with the ground. Space them 6 to 12 inches apart in clumps of 12 pips. Leave them in place for many years. Dig and divide pips only when they become crowded.

MUSCARI

Muscari (Grape Hyacinth) grows 6 to 8 inches tall. It blooms in mid-April. Its flowers generally are shades of blue or white. Starch muscari, however, has large, almost black flowers, 5 inches in diameter; Ostrich Feather produces violet-blue flowers in a feathery plume.

Use muscari in rock gardens or scattered among shrubs as ground cover.

Plant the bulbs 3 or 4 inches deep and 3 or 4 inches apart in October. Leave them in place until they become crowded. These bulbs seldom are dug and replanted because they are too small to handle.

NARCISSUS

The Narcissus family includes the Narcissus and the Daffodil. They are classified by the length of the crown—the center of the flower that forms either a cup or a trumpet. Flowers are white, cream, yellow, orange, red or peach.

Narcissi grow 3 to 20 inches high. They bloom in March and April. Use them in flower beds or scatter them in lawns and gardens. Narcissi make good cut flowers.

Bulb size determines the number of flowers. Double-nose bulbs produce two flowers and smaller, round bulbs produce one flower. Bulbs with old and new growth on them may produce three or four flowers.

Plant bulbs 4 to 6 inches deep and 4 to 8 inches apart in September and October. If you plant them scattered in lawns, you may replace the sod over them. Leave the grass uncut at least until July.

Narcissus bulbs may be left in place until they become crowded, usually three or four years.

ORNITHOGALUM

Ornithogalum (Star of Bethlehem) grows 8 to 18 inches tall. It blooms in May and June; flowers are white or silvery gray. You may scatter ornithogalum wherever you like throughout the garden. Cut flowers last a long time.

Plant bulbs 3 inches deep and 4 inches apart from September to November. Leave them in place for many years. Do not dig and replant the old bulbs; use new ones.

OXALIS

Oxalis grows 3 to 4 inches high. Flowers are lilac pink or coppery red. Lilac-pink oxalis blooms from May to July and coppery-red oxalis in mid-August.

In warm climates, use oxalis in rock gardens. Plant the bulbs in October, 3 inches deep and 3 to 6 inches apart in clumps of 12 bulbs.

Oxalis will not grow outdoors in cold climates; use it indoors as a potted plant. Plant eight or nine bulbs ½ inch deep in a 5-inch pot in October. Keep the potted bulbs in a cool, dark place until buds appear; then move them to a bright room for flowering.

PUSCHKINIA

Puschkinia (Lebanon Squill) grows 6 inches high. It blooms in March and April. Flowers are pale blue or white. Use puschkinia in clumps in rock gardens, and in drifts or clumps in lightly shaded areas.

Plant the bulbs 3 inches deep and 3 inches apart in the fall. Use 12 to 25 bulbs in each clump or drift. Leave them in place for many years. The bulbs are too small to dig and replant.

RANUNCULUS

Ranunculus grows 10 to 14 inches high. It produces flowers of all colors from May to July. Use ranunculus as color masses in gardens and as cut flowers.

Select a sunny, well-drained planting site. Plant the bulbs 2 inches deep and put a handful of sand around each bulb. Space them 6 to 8 inches apart in clumps of 12 bulbs. Mulch the ground with 2 or 3 inches of peat moss to keep the soil and bulbs from drying.

In warm climates, plant the bulbs any time from December until mid-April. In cold climates, plant them after the danger of freezing has passed in spring. These bulbs will not overwinter.

SCILLA

Scilla includes Squill and Bluebells. Squill grows 3 to 6 inches high and bluebells grow 12 inches high. Use either kind in beds, as borders, in rock gardens or scattered in lawns.

Squill blooms in March and April and bluebells bloom in May and June. Flowers are blue, white or pink.

Plant squill bulbs three times their diameter in depth and bluebell bulbs 3 or 4 inches deep. Space both kinds 3 or 4 inches apart in clumps of 12 bulbs. Plant them in October and November. Leave the bulbs in place for many years. Do not dig these bulbs for replanting; use new ones.

TULIP

Tulips are sold by type, variety or species. Common types of tulips and some of their characteristics are as follows:

Breeder—Bronzed, almost muddy appearance; colors are not bright and clear.

Cottage—Bloom later than other tulips; petals form a deep cup.

Darwin—Tallest tulips; flower is as wide as it is deep.

Lily-flowered—Petals curve outward and form a bell-shaped flower.

Parrot—Twisted, ruffled petals.

Double—Two or more rows of petals.

TULIP PLANTING GUIDE

Many new types of tulips are being developed. Some have ruffled petals with lace edges. Others have mottled petals and foliage. Most of the new forms are similar to the varieties from which they were developed.

Tulips that do not belong to the common types are sold by species. Some well known species are *greigii, kaufmanniana, fosteriana, tarda, praestans* and *eichleri.*

Tulips vary in height from 3 inches to almost 3½ feet. Most varieites have one cup-shaped flower to a stem. Tulips bloom in April and May. Flowers are red, pink, yellow, white or blue. Use tulips for landscaping and as cut flowers.

Plant tulip bulbs 4 to 6 inches deep in late October or early November. Space them 6 to 12 inches apart in clumps of at least eight to ten bulbs.

Flowers become smaller each year. Dig and discard bulbs after about three years, or when flowers become too small for good display. Use new bulbs for replanting. Bulbs that you dig from the garden and replant often fail to bloom.

SELECTING BULBS

Bulbs are sold in nurseries, variety stores, garden shops and through florists' or nursery catalogs. Buy from a dealer who sells good bulbs. Cheap bulbs are usually of poor quality.

Make sure bulbs are not diseased. Diseased bulbs are moldy, discolored, or soft and rotted. Bulbs should be firm and have an unblemished skin.

Know types, colors and sizes of bulbs, and the places they grow best. Choose either domestic or imported bulbs. They are equally good.

Select varieties and colors that will blend with the rest of your garden. You can get ideas from local garden clubs, public parks and botanical gardens.

Buy bulbs of named varieties that flower together and grow to about the same height. Be sure to buy enough of each color and type for a good display in your garden. You can buy mixtures of colors and types, but they are often unsatisfactory because they fail to give enough of each color.

If you buy bulbs before planting time, keep them in a cool, dry area. A temperature of 60° to 65° F. is cool enough to prevent bulbs from drying out until you plant them. Temperatures higher than 70° F. will damage the flower buds inside the bulbs.

Although spring-flowering bulbs are primarily cold-weather plants, some will grow and produce flowers in warm areas. Tulip, hyacinth, crocus and narcissus grow well in the deep South and other hot areas.

When you buy bulbs in hot climates, be sure the bulbs have been stored in reliable commercial storage at 40° F. and are kept at that temperature until planting time in mid-January. When bulbs are left in the ground in hot climates or stored in warm temperatures, they will not produce good flowers.

PLANTING

In most areas, spring-flowering bulbs should be planted in the fall so that roots can develop before the ground freezes. Specific planting times are given in the list of bulbs beginning on page 77.

In states south of a line from South Carolina to southern California, bulbs should be planted in mid-January. Bulbs bloom in these warm areas in eight to ten weeks after planting.

Most bulbs need full sunshine. Try to select a planting site that will provide at least five or six hours of direct sunlight a day. Bulbs that you leave in the ground year after year should have eight to ten hours of daily sunlight for good flowering.

If you plant bulbs in a southern exposure near a building or wall, they will bloom earlier than bulbs you plant in a northern exposure.

To look their best, bulbs should be planted in groups or clumps; in general, avoid planting in rows. You can plant them in front of evergreens, among perennials and flowering shrubs, or preceding annuals. Satisfactory results depend on good drainage and thorough preparation of the soil in the planting site.

Before preparing new flower beds test the drainage of the soil. Dig a hole about a foot deep and fill it with water. The next day, fill the hole with water again and see how long the water remains. If the water drains away in eight to ten hours, the soil is sufficiently well drained.

If water remains in the hole after ten hours, it will be necessary to improve the drainage of the planting site. Dig furrows along the sides of the bed and add soil from the furrows to the bed. This raises the level of the bed above the level of the ground.

Dig and plant your bulb beds when the soil is fairly dry. Wet soil packs tightly and retards plant growth. If you can crumble the soil between your fingers, it is dry enough for digging and planting.

Spade the soil 8 to 12 inches deep. As you dig, remove large stones and building trash, but turn under all leaves, grass, stems, roots, and anything else that will decay easily.

Add fertilizer, sand and coarse peat moss to the soil. Use 1 pound (2 rounded cups) of 5–10–10 fertilizer for a 5- by 10-foot area, or a small handful for a cluster of bulbs. Place a 1-inch layer of sand and a 1- to 2-inch layer of peat moss over the bed. Thoroughly mix the fertilizer, sand and peat moss with the soil.

Plant bulbs upright, and press the soil firmly over them to prevent air pockets underneath. Water the planted beds thoroughly to help settle the bulbs in the soil.

In loose, sandy soil, plant bulbs 3 or 4 inches deeper than the depths recommended in the bulb list on page 78.

Be sure to plant bulbs at recommended distances apart because many of them need room to develop new offshoots.

You may allow space for overplantings of pansy, alyssum, saxatile, viola, wallflower, phlox, forget-me-not or English daisy. These annuals provide excellent color contrast and flower display with your bulbs.

CARE OF BULBS

In areas where the ground freezes in winter, mulch your bulbs with 2 to 4 inches of straw, pine bark, hay or ground leaves. Do not use large leaves; they pack too tightly on the ground. A winter mulch prevents alternate freezing and thawing, which damages bulbs and plant roots.

Apply the mulch after cold weather arrives. You may damage the bulbs if you mulch while the soil temperature is still high.

Remove the mulch as soon as the danger of freezing has passed in early spring. If you leave the mulch on the ground after new growth starts, the tops of new shoots will be pale green or colorless, and new stems and foliage may be broken.

Some bulbs sprout leaves in the fall. If the tips of the leaves turn yellow after exposure to sunlight, they have been damaged by alternate freezing and thawing. This damage often cannot be avoided; it occurs when the leaves sprout too early in the fall. Leave the bulbs in place.

When plants bloom, fertilize them lightly with 5–10–10 fertilizer. Use no more than 1 pound for a 5- by 10-foot flowerbed. Many flowerbeds will be fertile enough from fertilizer used on other plants grown in the bed. Avoid high-nitrogen fertilizer.

Be sure to keep fertilizer off the leaves and away from roots; it will burn them.

In addition to 5–10–10 fertilizer, you can use bonemeal as an extra source of nitrogen to promote plant growth for the next year. Bulbs decay when too much nitrogen is used at one time. But decay is unlikely when you use bonemeal because it releases nitrogen slowly.

Apply bonemeal at flowering time. Use nor more than 3 pounds for a 5- by 10-foot bed. Mix it thoroughly into the soil.

Normal rainfall usually provides enough moisture for bulbs. But, during dry weather, you should water the plants at weekly intervals. When you water, soak the ground thoroughly.

It weeds grow in your flowerbeds, you can usually pull them by hand. Be careful when you use a hoe or other weeding tool; they can injure plant stems and bulbs.

When flowers fade, cut them off to prevent seed formation, Seeds take stored food from the bulbs.

If you want to leave bulbs in place for blooms the next year, do not cut the leaves after flowering. Green leaves produce food for plant growth the next year. When you cut flowers for indoor arrangements, leave as much green foliage on the stalks as possible.

After the leaves turn yellow, cut and destroy the stems and foliage of the plants. Dead foliage left on the ground may carry disease to new growth the next year. If disease is severe, plant bulbs in a new location.

You may want to remove the bulbs from your garden after they bloom each spring, especially if you have limited space. Also, foliage is unsightly after flowers fade.

Bulbs you dig before the leaves turn yellow are useless. But if you wish, you may dig and discard bulbs after flowering, plant summer annuals in the empty space, and replant new bulbs in the fall.

Division and Storage

Although bulbs, corms, and tubers are all referred to as bulbs, they differ in appearance.

A bulb is composed of layers of flesh, or scales, that overlap each other like the layers of an onion. A complete flowering plant develops inside the bulb. Each year, the growing plant replaces the bulb entirely, the way a tulip does, or it replaces the bulb partially the way a narcissus does.

A corm is a swollen underground stem that grows upright. Each year, the growing plant produces a new corm on top of the old one. The plant grows from the top of the corm.

A tuber is the swollen end of an underground side shoot that has eyes, or growing points. Each eye produces a separate plant.

Tubers multiply from year to year and may be cut apart, or divided, to increase the number of plants you can have in your garden. When tubers are divided for replanting, each division must have eyes on it. Tubers without eyes will not grow.

In cold areas you can leave most kinds of bulbs in the ground for several years. When bulbs become crowded, you can dig, store, and replant them.

In warm areas, you should dig and discard bulbs each year after the blooms have faded. Bulbs seldom flower well in hot climates after the first year.

Make sure your bulbs have matured before you dig them for replanting in the fall. When the leaves on the plants turn yellow, uncover a few bulbs without disturbing them. If the bulb coats are tan to brown, the bulbs are ready to be dug. The coat of an immature bulb is white.

Use a spading fork to lift the bulbs from the ground. Very little soil will cling to them. Wash off any soil that remains on the bulbs and remove any old, dry scales.

Inspect your bulbs for signs of disease. Keep only large, healthy bulbs that are firm and free of spots. Discard undersized bulbs because they require one or two years' growth before they bloom and many never bloom at all.

Spread the bulbs you keep in a shaded place to dry. When the outer scales have dried, store the bulbs away from sunlight in a cool, dry basement, cellar, garage or shed at 60° to 65° F. Avoid temperatures below 50° or above 70° F.

If you have only a few bulbs, you can keep them in paper bags hung by strings from the ceiling or wall. You should store large numbers of bulbs on trays with screen bottoms. Separate your bulbs by species or variety when you store them.

Be sure that air can circulate around your stored bulbs. Never store bulbs more than two or three layers deep. Deep piles of bulbs generate heat and the bulbs decay.

Inspect bulbs in storage several times during the summer. Remove any that are decaying as soon as possible. A musty odor may indicate that trouble is brewing.

FORCING BULBS

Bulbs can be forced to bloom indoors earlier than they normally would outdoors in the garden or yard. The easiest bulbs to force are crocus, galanthus, hyacinth, narcissus, scilla and tulip. A nurseryman can tell you the varieties that are best suited for forcing.

Forcing bulbs includes two phases. The bulbs develop buds and roots in the first phase and bloom in the second.

You should begin the first phase in October or early November. Plant the bulbs in pots and keep them at a temperature of 40° F. for eight to 12 weeks. During this phase, you can keep the potted bulbs outdoors or in a cold room indoors.

If you keep your bulbs indoors, the room must be dark and kept at 40° F. Do not let the soil in the pots dry out; water the bulbs every day.

The second phase begins about mid-January, after shoots have appeared on the bulbs. When the shoots are well out of the necks of the bulbs, bring the bulbs into a cool, bright room that can be kept at 55° F. They will bloom in about one month.

You may refrigerate crocus, hyacinth, narcissus, and tulip bulbs at 40° F. for two months instead of planting them in pots. At the end of two months, plant the bulbs in bowls and start them in the second phase of development.

After they bloom, you should discard the forced bulbs. They seldom grow and flower well when replanted in the garden.

FLOWERING BULBS INDOORS

Many spring-flowering bulbs make excellent flowers for indoor arrangements. You may use the whole plants of tulips and other small bulbs, or you may use cut flowers of all kinds of bulbs. If you dig the whole plant, the flower will last much longer.

Dig the plants when flowers appear, wash the soil from the roots, and plant the bulbs in coarse sphagnum moss or vermiculite in waterproof containers. Water lightly to keep the plants alive. When the flowers fade, discard the plants.

Cut flowers last only a few days. After you cut the flowers, put them in water. Be sure to wash containers with soap and water before you use them.

CHAPTER 7

Summer-flowering Bulbs

SUMMER-FLOWERING BULBS ARE EASY to grow, and do well in all parts of the United States. Most of them are grown for their flowers, some for their foliage.

Among the more popular summer-flowering bulbs are tuberous rooted begonia, canna, dahlia, gladiolus and lily; caladium, too, is prized, not for its flowers (buds should be removed when and if they appear) but for its striking foliage.

Some bulbs may be grown as pot plants, some as pot or garden plants, and others as garden plants only. In the garden, various kinds of bulbs may be used as foundation plantings, as borders, in front of shrubs or in groups for masses of color.

To grow summer-flowering bulbs successfully:

- Select healthy, mature bulbs and store them in a cool, dry place until planting time.
- Prepare the soil in the planting site thoroughly.
- Plant at depths, distances apart and planting times recommended for each kind of bulb.
- Water the plants at regular intervals.

The following list gives a brief description of how to plant and manage the more commonly grown summer-flowering bulbs.

ACHIMENES

Achimenes (Nut Orchid) grows 8 to 12 inches high and blooms in summer. The flowers are almost every color. Use achimenes in shady flower beds, as borders or as pot plants.

Plant the tubers in 4-inch pots in early spring. Use a mixture of equal parts of peat moss, sand and garden soil. Keep the tubers indoors at 65° F. until after the last killing frost; then replant them in the garden or leave them in the pots. Grow the plants in a lightly shaded area away from direct sunlight.

Water and fertilize the plants at monthly intervals throughout the growing season. Use a mixture of 1 teaspoon of 20–20–20 soluble fertilizer per gallon of water.

When the leaves turn yellow in the fall, dig the tubers in the garden and let them dry. Store them in a cool, dry area at a minimum of 50° F. with the soil still clinging to them. In the spring, wash the soil from the tubers and start the growing cycle again.

Store potted tubers in the pots in a cool, dry area at 50° F. Dig, wash, and replant them in the spring.

ALLIUM

Allium (Flowering Onion) varies in height from 9 inches to 5 feet. Many varieties are grown. Summer-flowering varieties bloom in June and July. Flowers are white, red, yellow, blue or pink. Use allium in borders.

Some commonly grown kinds of summer-flowering allium and their characteristics are as follows:

Allium azureum—Deep-blue flowers; grows 2 feet tall; blooms in July.

Allium giganteum—Blue flowers, 9 inches in diameter; grows 5 feet tall; blooms in July.

Allium unifolium—Pink flowers; grows 15 inches tall; blooms in July.

Plant bulbs 2 or 3 inches deep in early spring. Space them 6 to 15 inches apart in clumps of six to 12 bulbs. The planting distance between bulbs depends on the height of the plant at flowering time.

Leave the bulbs in place for many years. Dig, separate and replant them when they become crowded or are producing small flowers.

AMARYLLIS

Amaryllis (Hippeastrum) grows about 3 feet tall. As an outdoor plant it blooms in June and July. Flowers are red, pink, rose, white or salmon. Use amaryllis in borders or as pot plants.

Plant the bulbs in May, after the soil has warmed. Space them 12 to 18 inches apart in clumps of three to five bulbs. Plant only half of the bulb beneath the soil. Water thoroughly after planting and each time the soil becomes moderately dry.

When flowers begin to form, water and fertilize the plants every other week until late fall when the leaves turn yellow. Fertilize with a mixture of 1 teaspoon of 20–20–20 soluble fertilizer per gallon of water. Avoid getting fertilizer directly on the bulbs.

Dig and store the bulbs each fall. It is important to retain the roots on the bulbs from year to year. Keep roots moist by storing bulbs in moistened peat moss or vermiculite. Amaryllis can be forced to flower indoors as a pot plant in the winter.

BEGONIA

Begonia that is grown for summer and fall flowering is tuberous-rooted. It grows 1 to 2 feet tall. Flowers are red, pink, orange, salmon, yellow or white and they grow up to 4 inches in diameter. Use begonia as a pot plant, for cut flowers, and in lightly shaded flower beds. It blooms throughout the summer.

Plant the tubers in February or March in flats (shallow boxes) indoors, using a mixture of equal parts of peat moss and coarse sand. Press the tubers into the mixture; make sure the "growing eyes" are upward. Space tubers 2 to 3 inches apart.

Keep the flats in a dark room at 65° F. Water the tubers often enough to keep the sand and peat-moss mixture damp. When pink shoots appear, add ½ inch of the mixture over the tubers and move them to a lighted room that is kept at a minimum of 65° F.

Six weeks after you put the plants in a lighted room, transfer them to 5- to 6-inch pots or outdoors in the garden. Use a mixture of equal parts of garden soil, sand and leaf mold. Grow the plants in a cool, lightly shaded area.

If you put pot plants under fluorescent lamps for 16 hours a day, they will continue blooming throughout the winter. Keep the room temperature at a minimum of 65° F.

Fertilize begonias at least every other week after you replant them in pots or in the garden. Use a mixture of 1 teaspoon of 20–20–20 soluble fertilizer per gallon of water.

Water often enough to keep the soil moist. Water early in the day so the flowers and leaves will dry quickly; they rot easily.

When the leaves turn yellow in the late summer or early fall, dig the tubers in the garden. Store potted tubers in their pots and dug tubers, with the soil that clings to them, in a cool, dry place away from frost. Start the growing cycle again in February or March.

CALADIUM

Caladium is grown for its showy, colorful leaves. The flower buds should be removed as soon as they appear so the leaves can develop fully.

Many varieties of caladium are grown. Dwarf varieties grow up to 9 inches. Ordinary tall varieties grow up to 18 inches, and elephant's-ear grows up to 6 feet. Use caladium in front of shrubs, as foundation plantings around the home, and as pot plants.

Plant the tubers close together in a flat from January to mid-May. Use a mixture of peat moss and coarse sand. Cover the planted tubers with a 1-inch layer of peat moss.

Water the tubers often enough to keep the soil mixture damp. Roots grow from the tops of the tubers; they must be kept moist and covered with peat moss. Keep the room temperature no lower than 70° F. Tubers often rot in cool soil.

Replant tubers of the elephant's-ear variety outdoors in the ground or in tubs or boxes as soon as roots develop; replant the tubers of other varieties outdoors or in 6-inch pots. Use a mixture of equal parts of garden soil and peat moss. Grow the plants in a lightly shaded area, never in direct sunlight, as the leaves burn easily.

Try to balance the light and shade to get the most color in the leaves. When plants are grown in deep shade, the leaves will have more green coloring and less pink or red.

Water and fertilize caladium at least every other week. Do not allow the soil to become dry. Fertilize with a mixture of 1 teaspoon of 20–20–20 soluble fertilizer per gallon of water.

When the leaves turn yellow in the fall, dig the tubers from the garden and store them with the soil around them. Store potted tubers in their pots. Keep the storage area dry and at no less than 60° F. Start the growing cycle again the next year.

CALLA

Calla is a large plant and may grow 4 to 5 feet tall. It blooms at almost any time. Flowers are white, red, pink and yellow. Use calla as a pot plant.

Plant tubers in 6-inch clay pots in October. Use a mixture of equal parts of garden soil, peat moss and sand. Barely cover the tubers with the mixture.

Grow the plants in a temperature of 50° to 60° F. Water heavily every day during the growing season. Fertilize calla every other week. Use a mixture of 1 teaspoon of 20–20–20 soluble fertilizer per gallon of water. Reduce watering gradually after bloom and let the tubers dry.

Store the potted tubers in a cool, dry area. The tubers can remain in the same pots for many years.

CANNA

Many types of canna are grown. Tall types grow 5 to 7 feet high and dwarf types, 18 to 30 inches. Canna blooms for many weeks in summer. Flowers are red, pink, orange, yellow and cream. Use canna in flower beds.

Plant rhizomes (underground stems) from March to May in flats filled with peat moss. Cover the rhizomes with 1 inch of peat moss and water them often enough to keep the peat moss damp.

When shoots appear, replant the rhizomes in 4-inch pots. Use a mixture of equal parts of garden soil, peat moss and sand. Leave the pot plants indoors until all danger of frost has passed. Then plant them outside in full sunshine.

Dig the planting site thoroughly and mix well-rotted cow manure into the soil. Plant the rhizomes just below the soil surface. Space them 12 to 18 inches apart.

Water and fertilize the plants at two-week intervals throughout the growing season. Apply a light ring of 5–10–5 or 10–6–4 fertilizer around each plant. Stake the tall varieties; they fall over easily.

After the first light frost, cut off the stems of the plants. Then dig the rhizome clumps and let them dry. Store them, with the soil around them, away from frost. If your storage conditions are dry, embed the rhizomes in flats of dried peat moss for the winter. The next spring, clean the rhizomes and start the growing cycle again.

DAHLIA

Dahlia varies in height from less than 1 foot to more than 6 feet. It blooms in summer and fall. The flowers are white, yellow, red, orange or purple. Use dahlia in borders and flower beds, or as cut flowers.

DAYLILY

Daylily (Hemerocallis) varies in height from 6 inches to 6 feet. By selecting varieties that bloom at different times, you can have flowers all summer. The flowers are red, pink, orange, yellow or cream. Use daylily in borders and flower beds, or as foundation plants.

Plant tubers just below the surface of the soil, preferably in early spring or late summer; but they may be planted at almost any time of year. Space the plants 18 to 24 inches apart.

Apply a light ring of 10–6–4 fertilizer around each plant three or four times during the growing season. Water often enough to keep the soil moist.

Remove seed pods when they appear; they use food needed by the plant. Leave the tubers in the ground until they become crowded, usually 3 or 4 years.

GLADIOLUS

Gladiolus grows 2 to 4 feet high. It blooms in summer and fall and produces flowers of all colors. The kinds of gladiolus that are commonly grown are *grandiflora, primulinus, primulinus* hybrids, and *colvilleii.* Use gladiolus for cut flowers or in flower beds.

Plant gladiolus bulbs in rows 36 inches wide or in flower beds. Prepare the beds the year before you plant, applying 1 pound of 10–6–4 fertilizer for each 100 square feet of planting space. Thoroughly mix the fertilizer with the soil.

Start planting as soon as the soil is dry enough to work in the spring. Plant the bulbs 4 to 7 inches deep and 6 to 8 inches apart. Continue planting every 7 to 10 days until early July; this assures a continuous supply of flowers.

When shoots are 6 to 10 inches tall, fertilize the plants with 1 pound of 10–6–4 fertilizer per 100 square feet of space. Water the soil around the plants every ten days in dry weather.

In the North, dig the bulbs every year about 6 weeks after the plants have bloomed. Wash the soil off the bulbs and spread them in a shaded area to dry for several weeks. In the South, gladiolus are left in the ground for several years before they are dug.

When the bulbs are dry, separate them by size and keep only those that are more than 1 inch in diameter. Store them in a well-ventilated area at 35° to 45° F.

GLOXINIA

Gloxinia grows 12 inches tall. It produces both single and double flowers in many colors. Use gloxinia as a pot plant.

Plant the bulbs in 5- to 6-inch pots in late winter or spring. Use a mixture of equal parts of peat moss, sand and garden soil. Keep the bulbs indoors at 65° F. until after the last killing frost; grow the plants in a lightly shaded area away from direct sunlight.

Water often enough to keep the soil mixture damp throughout the growing season. Fertilize every other week with a mixture of 1 teaspoon of 20–20–20 soluble fertilizer per gallon of water.

When the leaves turn yellow in the fall, gradually withhold water and allow the bulbs to dry. Store the potted bulbs in a cool, dry area at 50° F. Repot the bulbs in the spring and start the growing cycle again.

Gloxinia also may be grown from seed, but this is not recommended because it requires at least six months to grow a flowering plant.

IRIS

Iris grows in both tall and dwarf forms. Some tall iris are summer-flowering; these grow 2 to 2½ feet high and have white, blue, purple, orange or yellow flowers. (Dwarf iris blooms in early spring.)

ISMENE

Ismene (Peruvian Daffodil) grows 2 feet high and produces large, funnel-shaped white flowers with green stripes down the funnel. Use ismene in front of shrubs, as foundation plantings around the home, and as pot plants.

Plant the tubers close together in a flat from January to mid-May. Use a mixture of peat moss and coarse sand. Cover the planted tubers with a 1-inch layer of peat moss.

Water the tubers often enough to keep the soil mixture damp. Roots grow from the tops of the tubers; they must be kept moist and covered with peat moss. Keep the room temperature no lower than 70° F.—tubers often rot in cool soil.

As soon as roots develop, replant the tubers in 6-inch pots or outdoors. Use a mixture of equal parts of garden soil and peat moss. Grow the plants in a lightly shaded area, never in direct sunlight.

Water and fertilize ismene at two-week intervals. Do not allow the soil to become dry. Fertilize with a mixture of 1 teaspoon of 20–20–20 soluble fertilizer per gallon of water.

When the leaves turn yellow in the fall, dig the tubers from the garden and store them with soil around them. Store potted tubers in their pots. Keep the storage area dry and at no less than 60° F. Start the growing cycle again the next year.

LILIUM HYBRIDS

Lilium hybrids are among the most beautiful plants grown from bulbs. They have many forms, heights, colors and flowering times.

The most common types of lilium hybrids and some of their characteristics are as follows:

Lilium candidum (White Madonna Lily): Blooms in June; grows 3 to 4 feet tall; fragrant flowers; plant in September.

Lilium excelsum (*testaceum*): Blooms in June; grows 5 to 6 feet tall; apricot flowers; plant in light shade.

Lilium regale: Blooms in July; grows 3 to 5 feet tall; white or yellow flowers.

Lilium speciosum and *auratum:* Blooms in August and September; grows 4 to 6 feet tall; many hybrids between these two types.

Upright lily: Blooms in June; grows 2½ feet tall; many hybrids in this group.

Except as indicated in the descriptions of the types above, plant the bulbs in October and November in a sunny, well-drained area. Plant them at a depth that is three times the height of the bulb. Space the bulbs 6 to 18 inches apart according to the height of the plants.

Water and fertilize the plants at frequent intervals during the growing season. Use a light ring of 5–10–5 or 10–6–4 fertilizer around each plant. Do not use high rates of high nitrogen fertilizers.

Remove the seed pods when they appear on the plants in the fall; seeds use up plant food needed for growth the next year. When the leaves turn yellow, cut and destroy the stems and foliage.

Leave the bulbs in place for 2 to 4 years. Dig the bulbs in late summer or fall and replant them as soon as possible; they will not grow successfully if allowed to dry out excessively in storage.

LYCORIS

Lycoris (Spider Lily) grows 15 to 18 inches tall. It blooms from late July to October, depending on season and variety. Flowers are creamy white or red. Use lycoris as a pot plant in areas where the ground freezes in winter. In warm areas, it may be grown in the garden and used in flower beds in light shade.

The two main types are *Lycoris squamagera* and *L. radiata. Squamagera* blooms from late July to October; foliage is produced in early spring and dies in early summer. *Radiata* blooms from late July to October; foliage is produced in the fall, remains green all winter and dies in the spring.

Outdoors, plant the bulbs 4 inches deep and 8 inches apart, in August. Indoors, plant the bulbs in 5- to 6-inch pots in a mixture of equal parts of garden soil, peat moss and sand.

Water and fertilize the plants at weekly intervals. Use a light ring of 5–10–5 or 10–6–4 fertilizer around each plant.

Leaves continue to grow on the plant after it flowers, and they stay green all winter. When the leaves turn yellow in spring, dig the bulbs and store them during the summer.

MONTBRETIA

Montbretia grows 3 feet tall. It blooms in August and September and produces flowers 4 inches in diameter. Colors of the flowers are orange, gold, red or yellow. Use montbretia in borders and as cut flowers.

Plant montbretia bulbs in rows 36 inches wide. Prepare the rows the year before you plant, applying 1 pound of 10–6–4 fertilizer for each 100 square feet of planting space. Thoroughly mix the fertilizer with the soil.

Start planting as soon as the soil is dry enough to work in the spring. Plant the bulbs 4 to 7 inches deep and 6 to 8 inches apart. Continue planting every seven to ten days until early July; this assures a continuous supply of flowers.

When shoots are 6 to 10 inches tall, fertilize the plants with 1 pound of 10–6–4 fertilizer per 100 square feet of space. Water the soil around the plants every ten days in dry weather.

Weeds should be removed by hand. Digging around the plants will injure the corms, which are just below the surface of the soil.

In areas where the ground freezes in winter, dig the bulbs every year about six to eight weeks after the plants have bloomed. Wash the soil off the bulbs and spread them in a shaded area to dry for several weeks.

When the bulbs are dry, separate them by size and keep only those that are more than 1 inch in diameter. Handle bulbs carefully to avoid damaging them. Store them in a well-ventilated area at 35° to 45° F.

In areas where the ground does not freeze in winter you may leave the bulbs in the ground for several years.

PEONY

Peony grows 2 to 4 feet tall. It blooms in late spring and early summer. The flowers are white, yellow, cream, pink and red. Use peony in borders and for cut flowers. Plant tubers in late fall at least 3 feet apart and 2 to 3 inches deep.

TIGRIDIA

Tigridia (Mexican Shell Flower) grows 2 feet tall and blooms in midsummer. The tri-petaled flowers are a mixture of white, red, yellow and rose colors.

Plant tigridia bulbs in rows 36 inches wide or in clumps of 12 bulbs 8 to 12 inches apart. Prepare the rows or beds the year before you plant, applying 1 pound of 10–6–4 fertilizer for each 100 square feet of planting space. Thoroughly mix the fertilizer with the soil.

Start planting as soon as the soil is dry enough to work in the spring. Plant the bulbs 3 inches deep and 4 to 8 inches apart. Continue planting every seven to ten days until early July; this assures a continuous supply of flowers.

Mulch the bulbs with 2 inches of pine bark, ground leaves, peat moss or hay to keep the soil from drying. Remove the mulch in the fall.

When shoots are 6 to 10 inches tall, fertilize the plants with 1 pound of 10–6–4 fertilizer per 100 square feet of space. Water the soil around the plants every ten days in dry weather.

Dig the bulbs every year about six to eight weeks after the plants have bloomed. Wash the soil off the bulbs and spread them in a shaded area to dry for several weeks.

When the bulbs are dry, separate them by size and keep only those that are more than 1 inch in diameter. Handle bulbs carefully to avoid damaging them. Store them in a well-ventilated area at 35° to 45° F.

TUBEROSE

Tuberose (*Polianthes tuberosa*) grows 2 feet high and blooms in late fall. Its waxy white double flowers are very fragrant. Use tuberose in flower beds and as cut flowers.

Plant the tubers 2 to 3 inches deep in a sunny, well-drained area in May. Space them 8 to 12 inches apart in clumps of six to eight tubers.

You also may grow tuberose in pots. Use 5- to 6-inch pots and plant the tubers in a mixture of equal parts of garden soil, peat moss and sand.

Water tuberose plants every day. Fertilize every other week with a mixture of 1 teaspoon of 20–20–20 soluble fertilizer per gallon of water.

Dig the tubers from the pots and from outdoor flower beds in the fall and store them; they will not overwinter in temperatures that fall below 40° F.

SELECTING BULBS

The same advice applies to summer-flowering bulbs as to those that flower in spring. See page 81.

SELECTING BULBS

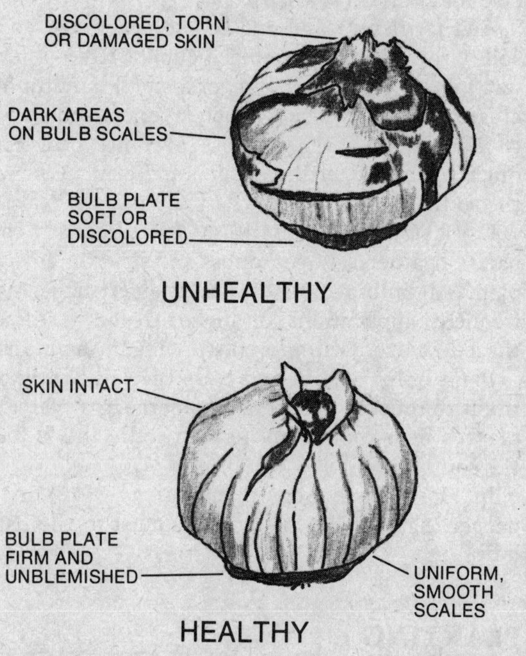

PLANTING

Some kinds of summer-flowering bulbs are grown in the garden outdoors and others in pots indoors. You can start many bulbs in flats or pots indoors in winter or early spring and replant them outdoors when the danger of frost has passed in the spring. Specific planting times are given in the list beginning on page 85.

Most bulbs need full sunshine. Try to select a planting site that will provide at least six to ten hours of direct sunlight a day. Bulbs planted in a southern exposure near a building or wall bloom earlier than bulbs planted in a northern exposure.

Before preparing new flower beds, test the drainage of the soil. Dig a hole about a foot deep and fill it with water. The next day, fill the hole with water again and see how long it remains. If the water drains away in eight to ten hours, the soil is sufficiently well drained.

If water remains in the hole after ten hours, it will be necessary to improve the drainage of the planting site. Dig furrows along the sides of the bed and add soil from the furrows to the bed. This raises the level of the bed above the level of the ground.

Dig and plant your bulb beds when the soil is fairly dry. Wet soil packs tightly and retards plant growth. If you can crumble the soil between your fingers, it is dry enough for digging and planting.

Spade the soil 8 to 12 inches deep. As you dig, remove large stones and building trash, but turn under all leaves, grass, stems, roots and anything else that will decay easily.

Add fertilizer, sand and coarse peat moss to the soil. Use ½ pound (1 rounded cup) of 10–6–4 fertilizer for a 5- by 10-foot area, or a small handful for a cluster of bulbs. Place a 1-inch layer of sand and a 1- to 2-inch layer of peat moss over the bed. Thoroughly mix the fertilizer, sand and peat moss with the soil.

Use a small handful of 10–6–4 fertilizer and equal parts of garden soil, peat moss and sand for each pot plant. All bulbs require low levels of fertilizer. Avoid frequent applications of high-nitrogen fertilizers; these fertilizers will promote rotting in the bulbs.

Plant bulbs upright and press the soil firmly over them to prevent air pockets underneath. Water the planted beds thoroughly to help settle the bulbs in the soil.

In loose, sandy soil, plant bulbs 3 to 4 inches deeper than the depths recommended in the list of bulbs.

Be sure to plant bulbs at recommended distances apart because many of them need room to develop new offshoots.

You may allow space for overplantings of dwarf marigold, petunia, ageratum, alyssum, coleus or verbena. These annuals provide excellent color contrast and flower display with your bulbs.

CARE OF BULBS

If weeds grow in your flower beds, you can usually pull them by hand. Be careful when you use a hoe or other weeding tool; these implements may injure plant stems and surface roots.

Normal rainfall usually provides enough moisture for summer-flowering bulbs. But during dry weather, you should water the plants at weekly intervals. When you water, soak the ground thoroughly.

When plants bloom, fertilize them lightly with 5–10–5 fertilizer. Use no more than ½ pound for a 5- by 10-foot flower bed or a light ring around each plant. Many flower beds will be fertile enough from fertilizer used on other plants grown in the bed. Avoid high-nitrogen fertilizers.

Be sure to keep fertilizer off the leaves and away from bulbs and roots; it will burn them.

In addition to 5–10–5 fertilizer, you can use bonemeal as an extra source of nitrogen to promote plant growth for the next year. Bulbs decay when too much nitrogen is used at one time. But decay is unlikely when you use bonemeal because it releases nitrogen slowly.

Apply bonemeal at flowering time. Use no more than 3 pounds for a 5- by 10-foot bed. Mix it thoroughly into the soil. Do not use bonemeal on pot plants.

PLANTING BULBS

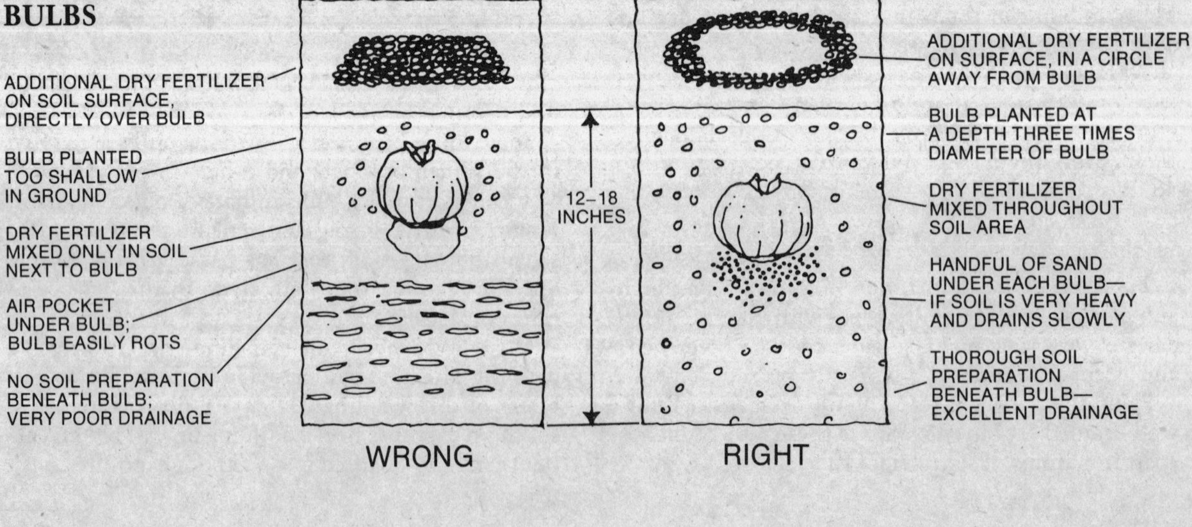

CUTTING FLOWERS

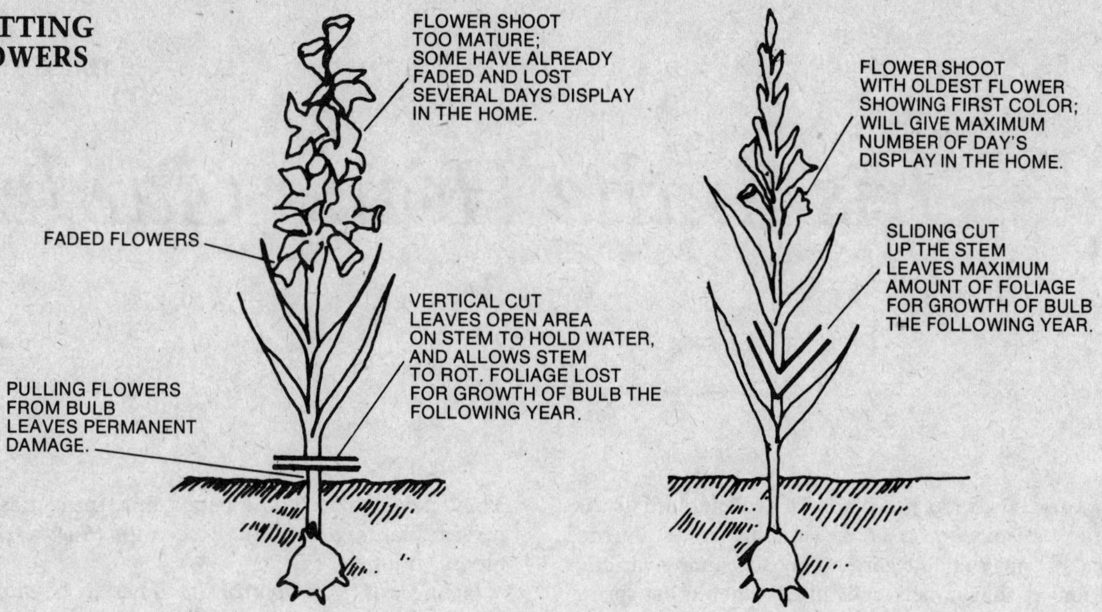
FLOWER SHOOT
TOO MATURE;
SOME HAVE ALREADY
FADED AND LOST
SEVERAL DAYS DISPLAY
IN THE HOME.
FADED FLOWERS
VERTICAL CUT
LEAVES OPEN AREA
ON STEM TO HOLD WATER,
AND ALLOWS STEM
TO ROT. FOLIAGE LOST
FOR GROWTH OF BULB THE
FOLLOWING YEAR.
PULLING FLOWERS
FROM BULB
LEAVES PERMANENT
DAMAGE.
WRONG
FLOWER SHOOT
WITH OLDEST FLOWER
SHOWING FIRST COLOR;
WILL GIVE MAXIMUM
NUMBER OF DAY'S
DISPLAY IN THE HOME.
SLIDING CUT
UP THE STEM
LEAVES MAXIMUM
AMOUNT OF FOLIAGE
FOR GROWTH OF BULB
THE FOLLOWING YEAR.
RIGHT

When flowers fade, cut them off to prevent seed formation. Seeds take stored food from the bulbs.

After the leaves turn yellow, dig the bulbs and store them for replanting the next year. Destroy the dead stems and foliage of the plants. Foliage left on the ground may carry disease to new growth the next year. If disease is severe, plant bulbs in a new location.

Besides the general instructions given here for the care of bulbs, be sure to follow the special instructions given for each plant. If the general instructions conflict with the special instructions, follow the special instructions.

Division and Storage

Tubers * multiply from year to year and may be cut apart, or divided, to increase the number of plants you can have in your garden. When tubers are divided for replanting, each division must have eyes on it. Tubers without eyes will not grow.

Most summer-flowering bulbs should be dug and stored when the leaves on the plants turn yellow. Use a spading fork to lift the bulbs from the ground. Wash off any soil that clings to the bulbs, except for bulbs that are stored in pots or with the soil around them.

Leave the soil on achimenes, begonia, canna, caladium, dahlia and ismene bulbs. Store these bulbs in clumps on a slightly moistened layer of peat moss or sawdust in a cool place. Wash and separate them just before planting.

Spread the washed bulbs in a shaded place to dry. When dry store them away from sunlight in a cool, dry basement, cellar, garage or shed at 60° to 65° F. Avoid temperatures below 50° or above 70° F. unless different instructions are given for a particular bulb.

Inspect your bulbs for signs of disease. Keep only large, healthy bulbs that are firm and free of spots. Discard undersized bulbs.

If you have only a few bulbs, you can keep them in paper bags hung by strings from the ceiling or wall. Store large numbers of bulbs on trays with screen bottoms. Separate your bulbs by species or variety before storing them.

Be sure that air can circulate around your stored bulbs. Never store bulbs more than two or three layers deep. Deep piles of bulbs generate heat and decay.

---

* For definitions of, and distinctions between, bulbs, corms and tubers, see page 83.

CHAPTER 8

Iris in the Home Garden

GARDEN IRISES ARE HARDY, long-lived perennials that need a minimum of care. They are an established "backbone" of home gardens because many varieties bloom at that in-between time—when most spring-flowering bulbs are past their prime and before the peonies, delphinium and phlox.

Easy-to-grow iris varieties adapted to every region of the United States are available. They produce graceful flowers in a wide range of shapes, sizes and colors.

DESCRIPTION

Iris flowers have six petals. The three upright petals are called standards; the three that hang down are called falls. Flowers may be white, yellow, pink, purple, blue, reddish or bicolored.

Principal typs of irises are bearded, beardless, crested and bulb.

Bearded irises have a fuzzy line, or beard, that runs down the middle of the falls. They are called German Iris, or Pogoniris. *Iris germanica* is the most commonly grown bearded species.

Bearded irises live through severe droughts and cold. The sword-shaped leaves are evergreen in warm climates and remain green until late fall in cold climates.

Most bearded iris plants grow 2 to 3 feet tall. Because they are easy to grow, tall bearded irises are recommended for beginning gardeners.

Tall bearded irises usually bloom in May and June. Several varieties bloom in both spring and fall.

A group of bearded irises that naturally grow 4 to 9 inches tall is called dwarf iris. The two most common species are *I. pumila* and *I. chamaeiris.* Both are well adapted to rock gardens because they spread quickly and form dense mats of foliage. They bloom in March, April, and May.

Beardless irises are called Apogoniris or Apogons. They have smooth fall petals and thin, grasslike leaves. Plants grow 1 to 4 feet tall. Most varieties bloom in June.

Japanese (*I. kaempferi*) and Siberian (*I. sibirica*) irises are the most commonly grown beardless species. Japanese irises have soft, drooping standards and wide falls. Plants grow 2 to 4 feet tall. Flowers are borne on long stems. Siberian irises have stiff narrow falls and narrow upright standards. Stems grow 18 inches to 2 feet tall. Beardless types, which thrive in moist soil, frequently are planted on stream and lake banks.

Crested irises have a small raised area, or crest, on the middle of each fall. Often, the color of these crests contrasts with petal colors. One of the more popular crested irises is a dwarf species, *I cristata.*

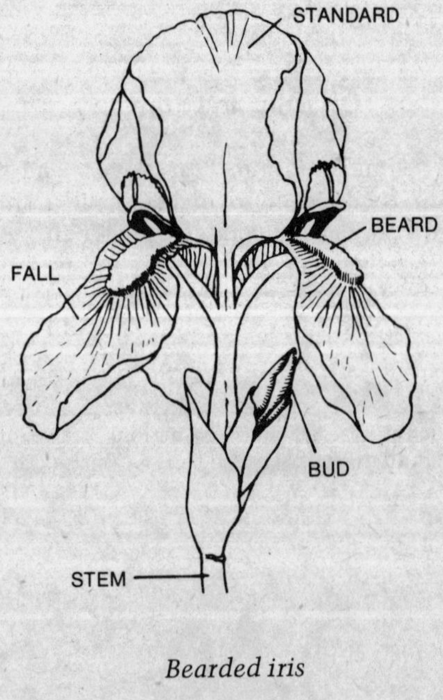

Bearded iris

HOW IRISES GROW

Bearded, beardless and crested irises grow from thick, underground stems, called rhizomes, that store food produced by the leaves.

Rhizomes grow slightly below the surface of the ground or at ground level. Many small roots penetrate the soil deeply.

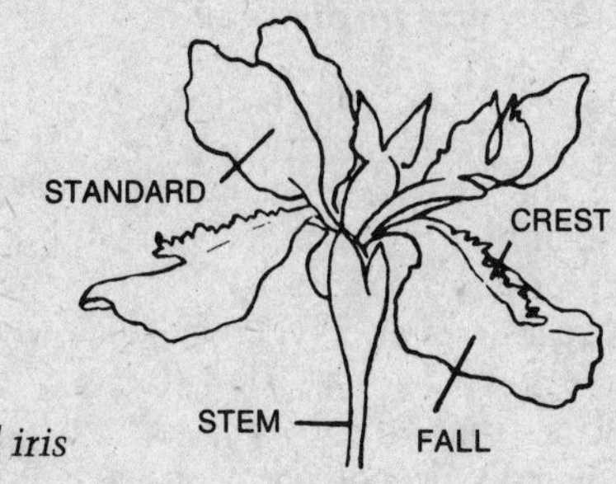

Crested iris

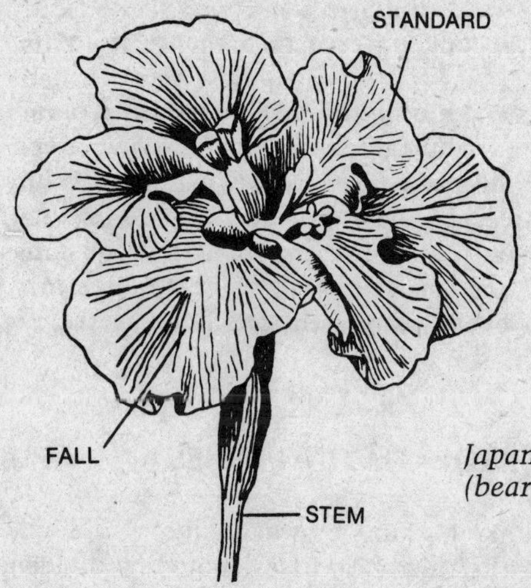

Japanese iris (beardless)

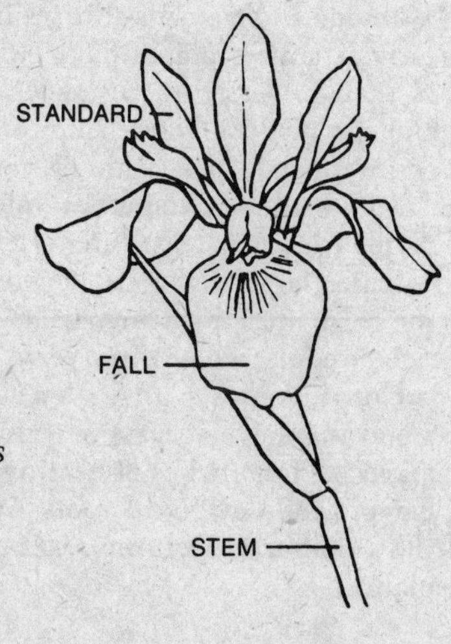

Siberian iris (beardless)

Each year, underground offshoots develop from the original rhizome. Offshoots may be divided and transplanted to grow new irises.

A rhizome that will produce a plant has at least one bud or growing point. Each bud produces a large fan of leaves and a flower stalk. Irises grown from rhizomes should bloom the next spring after planting.

Irises also may be grown from seed. A seed pod may develop below a pollinated flower that is left on the stalk after blossoming. Most seedlings do not bloom for two or three years after planting.

The slow process of growing plants from seed is used chiefly by breeders to develop new varieties. Because irises are hybrids, flowers of seedlings rarely look like flowers of parent plants.

From the several thousand varieties of irises available, select varieties that will provide the colors you want in your garden.

Many new varieties are introduced each year. Growers' and breeders' catalogs and garden magazines describe and picture many popular irises.

PLANTING IRISES

Irises may be planted in triangles, clumps, or borders or in beds with other garden flowers.

When and Where to Plant

The best time to plant irises is in late summer or early autumn. They should be established in the soil before winter. Most garden-supply stores sell rhizomes only during the planting season. If you order irises by mail, usually you will receive rhizomes at the planting time recommended for your locality. Plant rhizomes as soon as practical after you receive them.

Irises need full sunshine. Select a site with southern exposure and good air circulation. Bearded and crested irises need lime soil with good drainage; rhizomes may rot in soil that holds water around them. Beardless types need moist, slightly acid soil.

Preparing the Soil

Prepare the bed one to two weeks before planting irises, to allow the soil time to settle. Dig and loosen the soil at least 18 inches deep. Thoroughly break up all lumps.

Use commercial fertilizer to enrich poor soil in the iris bed; use organic matter to improve soil structure and productivity. For poor soil, add ½ pound of a 5–10–5 fertilizer for each 5- by 10-foot

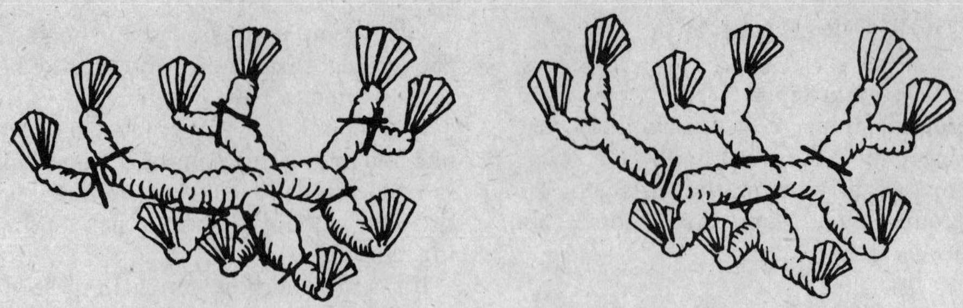

Left, *small rhizome divisions;* right, *large rhizome divisions*

area, or ½ cup for every 6 or 7 rhizomes. Thoroughly mix fertilizer into the soil so that lumps of it do not touch iris roots. Spading organic matter—compost, well-rotted manure or peat moss—into relatively heavy soil may improve drainage.

How to Plant

In a well-prepared bed, dig a shallow hole large enough to receive the rhizome or clump of rhizomes you are planting. Form a cone of earth in the center of the hole for the planting base. The height of the cone—or planting depth—is determined by the type of garden soil.

In medium soil, make the cone high enough so that the planted rhizome is just below ground level.

In light or well-drained soil, build a low cone. The top of the planted rhizome could be 2 inches below ground level.

In heavy soil, build a cone even with the ground surface. The top of the planted rhizome should be slightly above ground.

Place the rhizome on the cone, parallel with the ground surface. Carefully spread the roots around the cone. Do not wad roots together.

Fill the cone with soil and press it firmly in place around the rhizome. Water immediately; thoroughly soak soil around roots.

To obtain a good display of iris color, use at least 3 rhizomes of the same variety in a triangle or a pattern that alternates plants in rows. Plant rhizomes about 18 inches apart. Point each fan of leaves away from other plants in the group.

If you want to produce masses of flowers quickly, plant undivided rhizome clumps or set 3 individual rhizomes 8 to 10 inches apart.

Before replanting a full-grown iris, cut leaves to ⅓ their full height.

CARE OF IRISES

Water plants often enough before blooming time to keep soil moist but not wet. Remove weeds and grass around the rhizomes.

Before plants bloom, loosen the surface soil with a hoe or hand cultivator. Be careful not to injure the rhizomes or the roots.

Cut flowers as soon as they fade, unless you want to obtain seeds.

Plants that are growing well with good green foliage usually do not need fertilizer. If you use fertilizer, apply it immediately after plants bloom. Work it into the soil around plant bases. Use about ½ cup of 5–10–5 fertilizer for six small plants or about 1 cup for a large iris clump.

In early fall, cut leaves 6 to 8 inches from the ground.

All irises need mulch the first season after planting. Apply a light mulch of straw or evergreen boughs after the ground first freezes. Mulch prevents roots from freezing and stops the alternate freezing and thawing of the soil that harms plants by pushing them out of the soil. Irises in northern states may need mulch every year, even after they are established.

PROPAGATING IRISES

When plants become crowded, divide the offshoots from the rhizomes. Irises should be divided two to five years after planting.

Divide and transplant irises in the late summer or early fall, after plants have bloomed. Cut leaves to ⅓ their full height. Dig under a clump of rhizomes and lift out the whole clump at once. Wash away soil with a steady stream of water.

Make small divisions if you do not want to redivide iris for at least three—perhaps five—years.

Make large divisions if you want many flowers the year after planting. Large divisions should be separated in two or three years.

Cut rhizomes apart with a sharp knife. Each division must have at least one growing point (or fan of leaves), a few inches of healthy rhizome and a number of well-developed roots. When separated from the original iris clump, each division is ready to plant.

IRIS DISEASES

Iris diseases reduce the number of flowers, disfigure the leaves and sometimes kill the plant.

Prevent diseases by giving plants plenty of space, sunlight and good drainage. Clean up dead material quickly. Do not plant irises in crowded or completely shaded areas.

Bacterial Soft Rot

Bacterial soft rot is the most destructive iris disease. Bacteria enter the plant through breaks in the rhizome. Leaf bases and rhizomes begin rotting, and the plant soon dies,

Control: Dig up the diseased rhizomes. If rot is extensive, destroy iris. Cut out and discard diseased parts on less seriously affected plants.

Fungus Rots

Sclerotic rot, or southern blight, attacks irises in warm, humid areas. A fungus affects plants at or near the soil surface. The leaves turn yellow and dry prematurely or rot off at the base. Small yellowish-brown seedlike structures appear.

Another fungus disease, Botrytis rhizome rot, occurs in cool areas. The fungus produces small black seedlike structures on the rhizomes and in the soil. A dry pithy gray rot develops in the leaf bases and rhizomes.

Control: Dig and burn plants that are seriously infected with either kind of fungus rot. Remove soil from the surrounding area; replace it with new soil, sterilized, if possible. Cut out the rotted areas of slightly damaged rhizomes.

Iris Leaf Spot

Iris leaf spot disfigures leaves and weakens plants. About flowering time, infected leaves become dotted with small brown spots. Water-soaked margins around the spots turn yellow. Spots later develop a grayish center with black fruiting tufts. The leaf spot fungus overwinters in old leaves and produces new spores in the spring.

Control: If iris leaf spot has been a problem in your area, spray or dust the plants every two weeks from the time leaves emerge until they stop growing. Use a copper fungicide spray or zineb dust. Follow label directions.

In mild climates, cut and burn leaves of infected plants in the fall. If leaves are not removed, the fungus may remain active throughout the winter.

In cold areas, remove dead foliage before shoots appear in spring.

Rust and Bacterial Leaf Spot

Rust and bacterial leaf spot weaken, but seldom kill, iris plants.

Rust produces small raised dark-red dots on iris leaves.

Bacterial leaf spot causes dark-green watery spots and streaks. The spots later turn yellow and become translucent.

Control: Remove and burn all leaves that show signs of rust or bacterial leaf spot. Do not let any diseased leaves remain around plants. Infected leaves harbor spores that spread both rust and leaf spot.

Nematode Infection

Root-knot nematodes and lesion nematodes are microscopic worms that attack irises and a wide range of other plants.

Root-knot nematodes cause distinct knots or galls on the roots. These knobby swellings on a root look like beads on a string.

When lesion nematodes attack iris, the roots discolor and decay. In advanced stages of infestation, many roots rot off. Small lateral roots that replace the rotted ones give the root system a matted or turfed appearance. Younger, newer roots are dotted with small reddish-brown spots.

Control: Remove and burn plants with knotted roots or unthrifty plants with extensive root decay. Do not replant irises in the same place until nematodes have been eliminated.

Treat infested soil with a nematicide or soil fumigant such as methyl bromide, metham, or DD. Use according to manufacturer's directions.

Mosaic

Iris mosaic, the most widespread disease of irises, is caused by a virus transmitted by aphids.

Diseased flowers may be mottled or striped. Light-green streaks appear on the leaves of some plants.

Many infected plants do not show signs of disease. Individual plants may have typical symptoms at one season of the year and appear disease-free at another season.

Control: Dig up and burn irises that show severe mosaic damage. Reduce the spread of iris mosaic by controlling aphids.

IRIS INSECTS

Iris Borer

The iris borer causes more damage to iris than all other insects.

The pink caterpillarlike larvae have rows of black spots along their sides. They are about 1½ inches long when full-grown. Iris-borer adults are large brown moths with black markings.

First symptoms of borers are stains and chewed leaf edges that appear on leaves in early spring. Irises later develop loose, rotted bases and holes in rhizomes.

Borer larvae hatch in early spring from overwintering eggs. These caterpillars pierce leaves and tunnel into the stem. Then they bore into the rhizome, where they remain to feed and grow. At maturity, larvae leave the rhizome and pupate in the soil.

Bacterial rhizome rot readily attacks borer-infested plants.

Control: To eliminate overwintering eggs, clean up and destroy old leaves, stems and debris in fall or winter. To kill young, hatching larvae, apply dimethoate spray or a lindane spray to the iris beds at two-week intervals from time first growth starts until June 1. To kill older larvae in fans and rhizomes, spray with dimethoate. Read the directions and heed all precautions on the container label. With aid of a pointed stick or pencil, locate and destroy borers in young leaf sheaths that escape dust treatment. Transplant infested iris after it flowers; destroy larvae and infested rhizomes and chestnut-brown pupae in soil before replanting. Community effort is important in iris-borer control.

Aphids

Aphids, or plant lice, are small green, pink or mealy-white insects that attack many plants.

Aphids may appear on iris plants in early spring. They pierce leaves and suck the juices. When they feed, they may transmit the virus that causes iris mosaic.

Control: To kill aphids, spray plants with malathion. Repeat if aphids reappear. Read the directions and heed all precautions on the container label.

Verbena Bud Moth

Larvae of the verbena bud moth tunnel into new iris shoots and buds. Larvae are about ½ inch long. They have greenish-yellow, wormlike bodies and black heads. Mature moths do not attack irises.

Control: Cut and burn infested shoots and buds.

Iris Thrips

Larvae and adults of the iris thrips pierce the surfaces of young leaves and leaf sheaths. They suck juices that ooze from the wounds. Dry wounds become small straw-colored spots. Flower buds blacken; plant tops weaken. Iris thrips are especially injurious to Japanese iris.

Larvae of iris thrips are milky white. The black-bodied adults usually are wingless; they are about 1/25 inch long when mature.

Control: Spray plants with dimethoate four times at weekly intervals during May and June. Do not spray during flowering.

V

GROWING ORNAMENTALS

CHAPTER 9

Ornamentals in Urban Gardens

SOCIETY IS CHANGING RAPIDLY. In many areas, space and resources are scarce commodities. People live in crowded conditions where wastes often pollute both the air and soil. Green, growing things have a difficult life. They are needed, however, to brighten and soften the environment—even to help purify the air we breathe.

All the skills and techniques urban gardeners can muster are needed to help plants adapt to this urban environment. For urban gardeners to learn the required skills, they must depend on horticulturists and other plant experts for information on how to propagate, grow and protect plants. The urban gardener needs specific information on the kinds of plants that will grow in an urban environment, the methods and techniques used to grow them, and the protection plants need to survive.

GROWING AREA

The growing area for your urban garden can be a yard, terrace, patio, balcony, roof, window box, tub or hanging basket—or a combination of these.

Containers can be made of plastic, fiber glass, metal or clay. Ordinary lumber and plywood are not, as a rule, recommended for planter boxes because these materials rapidly rot, lose their shape, are difficult to make waterproof and need frequent replacement.

Portable, readymade containers are so widely available that it is not worthwhile for you to build your own. Many that are not designed especially for growing plants can easily be modified, particularly pails and tubs. The exteriors of these containers can be covered or painted to blend in with the surrounding area. When you use improvised containers of such waterproof materials as plastic or metal, make sure to provide for proper drainage. Drill ½-inch holes at least 12 inches apart at the base of the containers. Otherwise water will accumulate in the containers and rapidly decay them.

You can buy prebuilt planter boxes in various sizes to fit almost any space. If you do get wooden boxes, paint both inside and outside with wood preservative and then paint the inside with tar asphalt paint. Finish the outside with marine paint of any color you prefer, but do not use mildew-proof paints because they contain chemicals toxic to plants.

Dark-colored surfaces absorb heat and are best for cool shady areas. Light-colored surfaces reflect heat and are best for warm, bright areas.

If you wish, you can construct permanently built-in planter boxes of cement block, brick, stones, cement forms and other material. Be sure to install drainpipes or small holes in the planters so excess water can drain away. You can varnish the outside surfaces of such material as stone or brick, or you can leave them in their natural condition.

The disadvantages of built-in planter boxes are that they take a great deal of work to build and their weight may cause too much stress on balconies, floors and other parts of the house. Permission to install them is required from the landlord if the property is rented. Also, they can be expensive.

Portable containers are attractive, sturdy and lightweight. They also are easily replaced and can be moved to any area you wish. They are preferred to built-in containers.

Hanging baskets are containers that provide a place to grow vines and other plants for a different kind of effect in the garden. They permit you to display plants in space and view them from all sides.

Old-style hanging baskets were made of wire frames lined with moss. They dripped water, were hard to handle, and could be used only on porches and patios. New types are made of plastic, have a flat bottom with a drainage area and can be used anywhere. A plant can be started with the basket on the floor and then hung when the plant becomes

PREPARING CONTAINERS FOR PLANTING

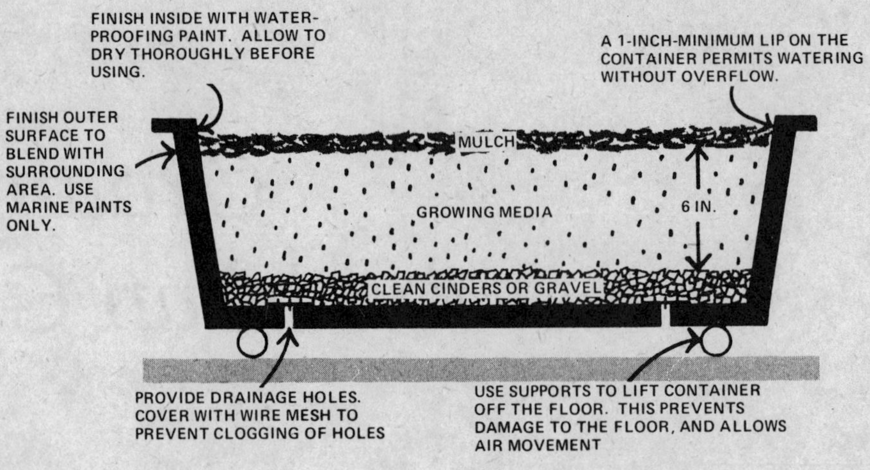
FINISH INSIDE WITH WATER-PROOFING PAINT. ALLOW TO DRY THOROUGHLY BEFORE USING.
A 1-INCH-MINIMUM LIP ON THE CONTAINER PERMITS WATERING WITHOUT OVERFLOW.
FINISH OUTER SURFACE TO BLEND WITH SURROUNDING AREA. USE MARINE PAINTS ONLY.
MULCH
GROWING MEDIA
6 IN.
CLEAN CINDERS OR GRAVEL
PROVIDE DRAINAGE HOLES. COVER WITH WIRE MESH TO PREVENT CLOGGING OF HOLES
USE SUPPORTS TO LIFT CONTAINER OFF THE FLOOR. THIS PREVENTS DAMAGE TO THE FLOOR, AND ALLOWS AIR MOVEMENT

established. Hanging baskets can be hung from horizontal bars or from walls.

Algae and mosses often grow on clay containers that are used for growing plants. You can buy a disinfectant that contains quaternary ammonium compound to control algae. Dilute the compound with water as directed on the package. Then dip new clay pots in the solution for two minutes and let them dry. Use these treated containers as you would any other container; the compound is harmless to plants. You also can wash down walks, walls or used containers to prevent the growth of algae and mosses without damaging fabrics or surfaces.

PREPARATION OF GROWING MEDIA

If all or part of your garden is in the yard, inspect the soil very carefully before planting. You can expect it to contain little or no organic matter and to be poorly drained. It also may contain debris from construction—nails, bricks, pieces of wood—and such toxic substances as oil and cleaning fluids. Do not try to grow plants in this kind of soil.

If the soil is too poor to grow plants, get new growing media. You can (1) use garden loam; (2) prepare a soil mix of topsoil, sand and peat moss; or (3) buy or prepare an artificial growing medium. The three types of growing media are collectively referred to as "soil" in this book.

The type of soil you use depends on your preference, the size of your planting area and the availability of materials. Any of these soils can be used in window boxes and other containers, as well as outdoors in the yard.

Garden loam is expensive and heavy to handle but may be used when only small amounts are needed. When used in the yard, dig out the planting area 3 feet deep. Put a 4-inch layer of cinders or coarse gravel in the bottom of the dug-out area to help excess water drain away. If possible, run a drainpipe from the bottom of the planting area to a lower ground level to provide better drainage. Then put a layer of coarse sand or perlite over the drainage material to keep the soil from sinking into it. Fill the rest of the planting area with garden loam.

When garden loam is used in containers, make sure the containers have one or more drainage holes in the bottom. Put in a layer of cinders or coarse gravel and a layer of sand or perlite on top of the cinders. Then fill the containers with garden loam. The amount of drainage material you need depends on the size of the containers.

If you prefer, you can prepare a soil mix of 2 parts sand, 1 part topsoil, and 1 part coarse peat moss. Prepare as much as you need. Add to these materials 1 pound (3 rounded cups) of 5–10–5 fertilizer for each 5- by 10-foot area to be planted. Thoroughly mix all ingredients. Prepare for drainage the same as when you use garden loam.

An artificial growing medium is more convenient and simpler to use in urban gardens than garden loam or soil mix. It is lightweight and relatively lightweight even when water is added, clean and easy to move and store. It also is free of weeds and other pests, and can be used in the yard and in all kinds of containers—either indoors or outdoors.

If you prepare your own artificial growing medium, thoroughly mix the ingredients in the following proportions: ½ bushel of perlite or vermiculite, ½ bushel of ground peat moss, 4 ounces of 20 percent superphosphate, 4 ounces of dolomitic limestone, and 2 ounces of 5–10–5 fertilizer. Use an artificial growing medium in your yard or in containers the same way you use loam or soil mix.

Regardless of the kind of soil you use, be sure to prepare it properly. Otherwise, drainage will be poor and your plants will not thrive. Some plants will

PLANTING LARGE CANNED SHRUBS IN THE GROUND

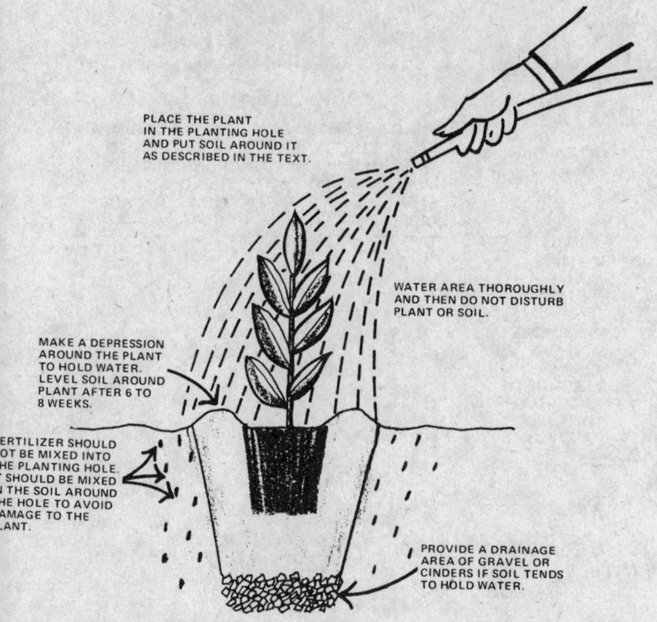
PLACE THE PLANT
IN THE PLANTING HOLE
AND PUT SOIL AROUND IT
AS DESCRIBED IN THE TEXT.
WATER AREA THOROUGHLY
AND THEN DO NOT DISTURB
PLANT OR SOIL.
MAKE A DEPRESSION
AROUND THE PLANT
TO HOLD WATER.
LEVEL SOIL AROUND
PLANT AFTER 6 TO
8 WEEKS.
PROVIDE A DRAINAGE
AREA OF GRAVEL OR
CINDERS IF SOIL TENDS
TO HOLD WATER.

PLANTING LARGE BALLED AND BURLAPPED TREES IN THE GROUND

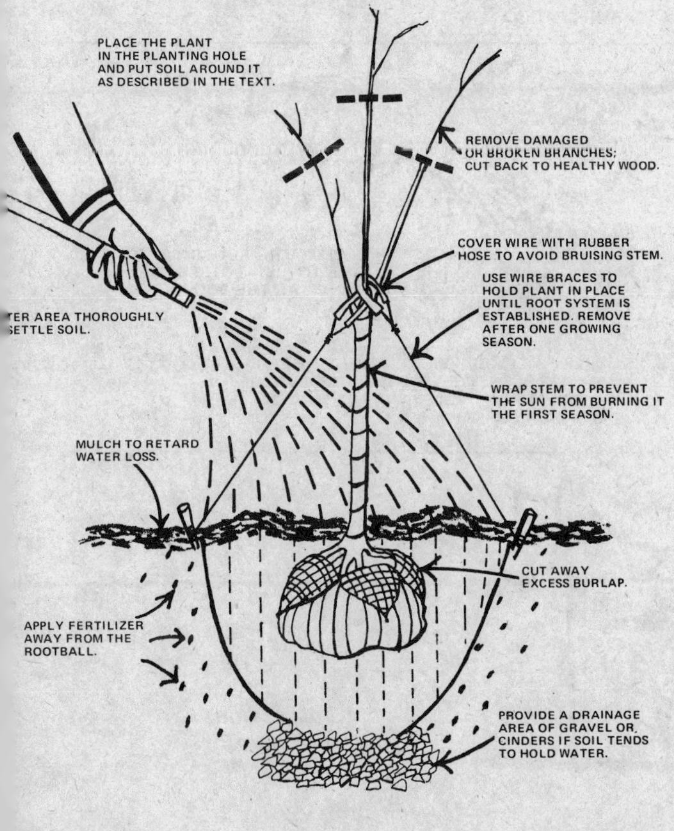
PLACE THE PLANT
IN THE PLANTING HOLE
AND PUT SOIL AROUND IT
AS DESCRIBED IN THE TEXT.
REMOVE DAMAGED
OR BROKEN BRANCHES;
CUT BACK TO HEALTHY WOOD.
COVER WIRE WITH RUBBER
HOSE TO AVOID BRUISING STEM.
USE WIRE BRACES TO
HOLD PLANT IN PLACE
UNTIL ROOT SYSTEM IS
ESTABLISHED. REMOVE
AFTER ONE GROWING
SEASON.
WRAP STEM TO PREVENT
THE SUN FROM BURNING IT
THE FIRST SEASON.
MULCH TO RETARD
WATER LOSS.
CUT AWAY
EXCESS BURLAP.
APPLY FERTILIZER
AWAY FROM THE
ROOTBALL.
PROVIDE A DRAINAGE
AREA OF GRAVEL OR
CINDERS IF SOIL TENDS
TO HOLD WATER.

grow without any drainage material if the soil is properly prepared. But do not depend on drainage material to compensate for poorly prepared soil.

The best time to prepare your soil is in late summer or early fall. This gives you time to plant spring-flowering bulbs and allows time for fall-planted shrubs and evergreens to root before winter.

PLANTING

You can grow your plants from seed or you can set out started plants. Delay sowing seed or setting plants outdoors until after the last frost in spring.

If you plant seed, follow the planting directions on the package label. You should start seed indoors no sooner than eight weeks before the average date for the last killing frost in your area. Then, when the weather is warm enough, you can transplant the plants outdoors either in containers or in the yard.

When you buy the larger, established plants, they usually come in plastic or metal cans or with the roots balled and wrapped in burlap (balled and burlapped). Plants in cans are more convenient to use because they are easy to move and do not have to be planted immediately. Balled and burlapped plants should be planted immediately.

Some cans are ridged so the plants can be removed easily. Test by gently pulling on the plant. The rootball should slide out, but if it resists removal, cut the sides of the can in four sections with metal shears and remove the rootball carefully. Avoid any stress on the stem and roots of the plant. If you force the plant from the can, you may break off the matted roots and cause the root system to die.

Examine the rootball. If a white net of roots is on the surface, make four cuts ½ inch long down the sides of the rootball. This will loosen the rootball and allow the roots to grow into the soil. If you find a mass of roots and drainage material such as stones or cinders at the base of the rootball, remove drainage material from the roots.

When the roots of the plant are balled and burlapped, you need not remove the burlap before setting the plant in the planting hole or container. After the plant is set, you can cut the twine around the top of the rootball and fold back or cut off exposed parts of the burlap.

Dig the planting hole twice as wide and slightly deeper than the size of the rootball, or set the plant in a container that provides an equal amount of space. Refill the hole ½ its depth with garden loam, soil mix or artificial growing medium. If garden loam is used, mix in additional peat moss. Tamp the soil to provide a firm base for the plant and water thoroughly.

Then place the plant in the hole or container and

TRANSPLANTING SMALL PLANTS

1. *Care of Plants Before Planting*

Ⓐ

THOROUGHLY WATER PLANTS. ALL SURFACES MUST BE MOIST.

Ⓑ

SHADE PLANTS FROM DIRECT SUNLIGHT UNTIL THEY ARE TRANSPLANTED. DO NOT HOLD PLANTS ANY LONGER THAN NECESSARY SO ROOT DEVELOPMENT AND TIME OF GROWTH AND FLOWERING ARE NOT DELAYED.

2. *Preparation of Plants for Planting*

TEAR UPPER LIP OFF THE POT.

REMOVE BOTTOM OF POT OR INSERT A STICK TO OPEN BOTTOM. KEEP POTS MOIST.

Ⓐ

PLANTS IN PEAT POTS OR PEAT PELLETS

KNOCK PLANTS OUT. DO NOT PULL ON STEM.

MAKE FINE CUTS 1/4 IN. DEEP IN SURFACE OF SOIL BALL IF ROOTS ARE MATTED.

REMOVE ALL DRAINAGE MATERIAL FROM BOTTOM.

Ⓑ

PLANTS IN CLAY OR PLASTIC POTS

KEEP BURLAP MOIST AT ALL TIMES. DO NOT PULL ON STEM MORE THAN NECESSARY. BALLED AND BURLAPPED PLANTS HAVE MANY FINE ROOT SYSTEMS THAT ARE EASILY DAMAGED.

Ⓒ

PLANTS BALLED AND BURLAPPED

3. *Inserting Plants in Soil*

DO NOT MAKE A POCKET OR DEPRESSION AROUND THE PLANT. A DEPRESSION ALLOWS EXCESS WATER TO STAND.

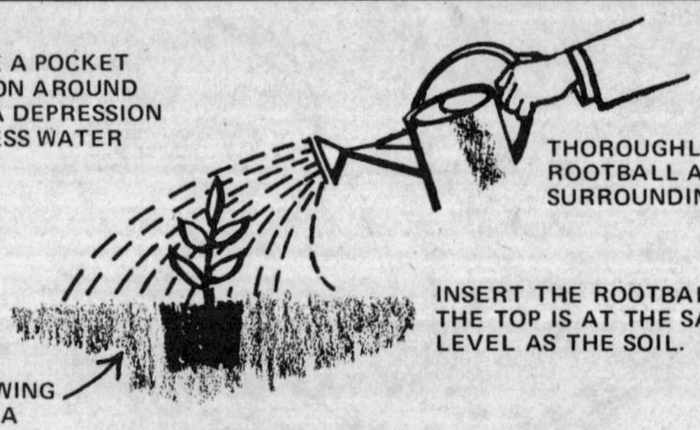

THOROUGHLY WATER ROOTBALL AND SURROUNDING SOIL.

INSERT THE ROOTBALL SO THE TOP IS AT THE SAME LEVEL AS THE SOIL.

GROWING MEDIA

APPLY A LIQUID FERTILIZER AT TIME OF PLANTING TO HELP THE PLANTS DEVELOP ROOTS. USE 1 TABLESPOON OF 16-52-10 PER GALLON OF WATER.

4. *Care of Plants After Planting*

Ⓐ

HAND PINCH 1/2 IN. OFF THE TIPS OF THE PLANTS WHEN THEY START TO GROW. DO NOT REMOVE LEAVES.

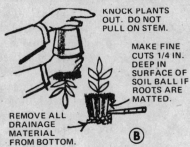

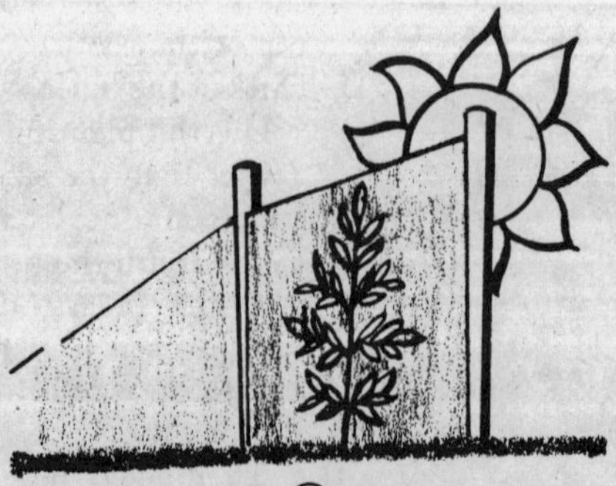

Ⓑ

SHADE PLANTS FOR THE FIRST SEVERAL DAYS IF THEY ARE EXPOSED TO DIRECT SUNLIGHT. REMOVE COVER IN THE AFTERNOON TO HELP PLANTS ADJUST TO THE NEW ENVIRONMENT.

pack enough soil under the roots to allow the top of the rootball to sit slightly above the level of the ground or the point where the top of the soil will be in the container. Then fill the rest of the hole or container with soil.

Pack the soil tightly around the rootball. Then water the plant thoroughly to settle the soil around the roots.

Prune the plant so it will not get too large for the container or planting area. Continue to prune the plant as needed to slow its growth. Otherwise the plant will get too large and top-heavy

FERTILIZING

The best way to fertilize your plants is with liquid fertilizer because the plants can use it immediately and no fertilizer residue is left to burn the plant roots. Liquid fertilizer is available in a neutral formulation for most plants as azaleas, rhododendrons, hollies, and others that grow best in an acid soil.

You can apply liquid fertilizer when you water the plants. If you water your plants by hand, mix the fertilizer with the water as specified on the container label. You also can use automatic watering equipment that will mix the fertilizer and water in the right proportions.

If you apply dry fertilizer, use 5–10–5. Spread it on the planting area in early spring and mix it thoroughly with the soil. During the growing season, apply little rings of dry fertilizer around the plants at 6-week intervals. Apply fertilizer as evenly as possible and rake it into the soil.

Do not use such fertilizers as manure, bonemeal, tankage or dried blood. They are not practical for small, urban planting areas. These fertilizers are hard to handle, have a disagreeable odor, often contain weed seeds and some of them do not contain all the nutrients essential for plant growth.

WATERING

Water your plants on a regular schedule, either by hand or with automatic watering equipment.

When you water by hand, moisten the soil thoroughly but not so heavily that the soil becomes soggy. Water again when the soil is dry to the touch and when the tips of the plants wilt slightly at midday. Pour the water directly on the soil. Do not spray your plants with a sprinkler in your urban garden. The repeated use of spray will raise the humidity, cause algae and mosses to grow, and do little to aid the development of the plants.

If you have only a few plants in small containers, you can water them with a plastic funnel. This method is slow but it allows only the right amount of water to enter the soil. You also can use a funnel to learn how much water you need to apply to a plant growing in a container of a specific size.

Use a funnel this way:

- Insert the neck of the funnel into the soil.
- Fill the funnel with water. When it empties, fill it again.
- When water no longer drains from the funnel, stick your finger in the neck so the water will not run out, and remove the funnel.

AUTOMATIC WATERING SYSTEM

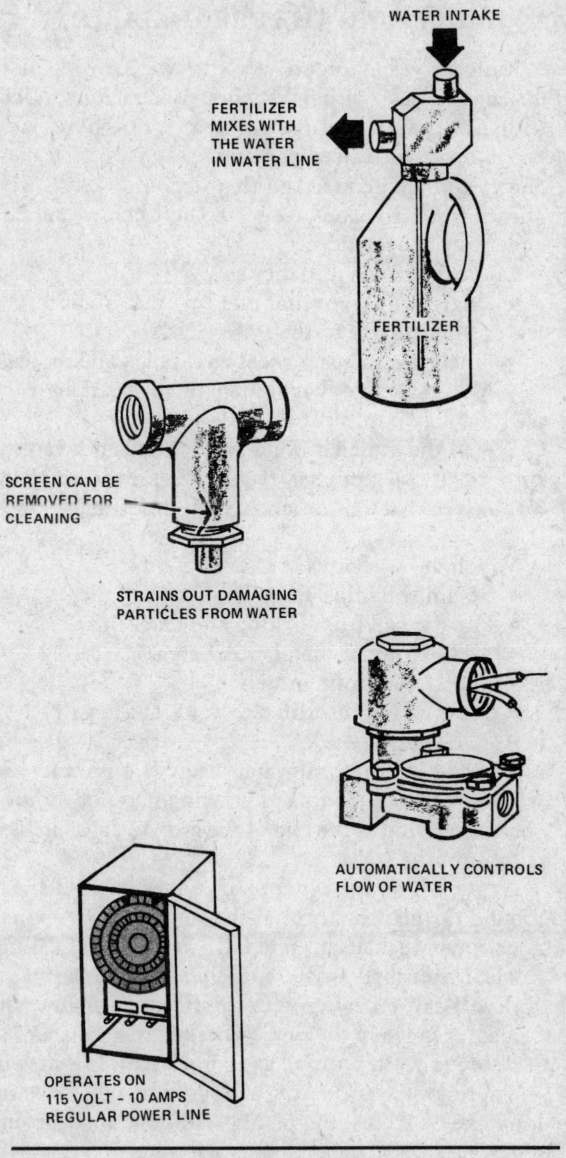
WATER INTAKE
FERTILIZER MIXES WITH THE WATER IN WATER LINE
FERTILIZER
SCREEN CAN BE REMOVED FOR CLEANING
STRAINS OUT DAMAGING PARTICLES FROM WATER
AUTOMATICALLY CONTROLS FLOW OF WATER
OPERATES ON 115 VOLT - 10 AMPS REGULAR POWER LINE

The most efficient way to water your plants is with an automatic waterer. This allows you to leave your plants unattended for longer periods of time than is possible when you water by hand.

An automatic waterer includes:

(1) A proportioner to mix the water with liquid fertilizer. It is attached to the water faucet. All moving parts should be stainless steel or plastic.

(2) A solenoid valve to control the flow of water automatically. It operates electrically.

(3) A line strainer to clean the water. It protects nozzles, solenoids and pumps from damaging particles. The screen must be removed and cleaned periodically.

(4) A 24-hour electric timer to control the time of watering and fertilizing.

MULCHING THE URBAN GARDEN

Mulch gives an orderly look to the urban garden, among its many other benefits. When you mulch, use such materials as coarse peat moss, pine bark, cocoa hulls, pine needles or coarsely ground leaves. Select an organic material that decomposes slowly, allows water to penetrate to the soil below and has a pleasing appearance.

Do not use such mulches as:

- Unground leaves that mat together and prevent water from getting to the soil.
- Finely ground peat moss that plugs all surfaces.
- Materials that have such large particles they will not stay in place.

Spread the mulch around your plants and water it into place. All mulches require care to keep them attractive. Litter in mulch is very noticeable.

Mulch during both summer and winter to:

- Retard water loss.
- Prevent soil from baking and cracking.
- Add texture to the planting area.
- Keep weeds from growing.
- Tie together the different parts of the garden.

Apply summer mulch about 1 or 2 inches deep in late spring or early summer, after the ground has warmed and the plants are growing. Do not remove summer mulch at the end of the growing season. Let it rot into the soil.

Apply winter mulch several inches deep. Place it around the plants only after the soil temperature has gone down, usually in late fall, after several killing frosts. If you apply winter mulch too early, the warm soil will cause new growth to start and plants will be damaged when the new growth is frozen back.

Remove winter mulch as soon as growth starts in the spring. If you do not, new growth will develop long gangly stems, the plants will have insufficient chlorophyll, and many shoots will die.

A special decorative gravel or sand is available from garden-supply stores for mulching. It comes in all colors, sizes and textures, and gives special accents to the garden. Spread this mulch about 2 inches thick, except when stones are used. Stones should be in a thicker layer of up to 4 or 5 inches.

When a large open area is covered with decorative mulch, underline the mulch with plastic to help keep weeds from growing. You must provide a grade or trench for water to drain off the plastic. Otherwise, algae and mosses will cover the mulch.

Decorative mulch requires daily care to keep it attractive. Litter accumulates rapidly. Be sure to keep some extra mulch on hand because mulch slowly disappears from compaction and handling.

DAYTIME LIGHTING

The amount of light in your garden will determine the kind of plants you can grow. Most plants need full sunlight but some plants will grow in partial sunlight and others in shade. You should observe other gardens in your community to see what plants grow well under conditions similar to those in your garden.

The degrees of sunlight and shade and the types of plants that will grow in them are described as follows.

Full sunlight is the absence of any shade from morning until night. All kinds of flowering, fruiting and foliage plants will grow in full sunlight.

Partial sunlight is the presence of dense shadow or shade for part of the day. Some flowering plants will grow but only a few fruiting plants will survive. The growth of all plants is slowed in partial sunlight.

Light shade is light shadow from distant buildings or the filtering of sunlight through leaves or screens. Green foliage plants will grow in light shade but few flowering plants survive.

Dense shade is deep shadow everywhere and no direct sunlight. The best solution is to grow foliage and flowering annuals in sunlight and then move them into densely shaded areas when they are fully developed.

Besides observing other gardens to determine the degrees of sunlight and shade in your area, you can measure the amount of sunlight with a light meter. Light is measured in foot candles (FC) and a light meter will show you the number of FC of light in different parts of your garden.

When you measure the light, do it on a day when the sun is shining brightly, and check all parts of your garden from deep shade to full sunlight. The number of FC that are comparable to the various degrees of light and shade are as follows:

- 100 FC or less: Not enough light for plants to survive.
- 100 to 500 FC: Dense shade.
- 500 to 1200 FC: Light shade.
- 1200 to 3000 FC: Partial sunlight.
- 3000 FC or more: Full sunlight.

If you do not measure the light with a meter, you should observe the amount and kind of shade you have in your garden each day. You can expect your plants to grow slowly and need replacement every few years in shady areas. Most flowering plants in shady areas should be discarded each year and new ones planted.

When you have shady areas in your garden, select shade-tolerant plants. Some plants that will grow in shade are listed below.

Shade-Tolerant Plants

Deciduous Shrubs

Abelia grandiflora (Glossy Abelia)
Amelanchier (Juneberry)
Berberis thunbergii (Japanese Barberry)
Calycanthus floridus (Carolina Allspice)
Cercis canadensis (Redbud)
Cornus (Dogwood)
Hydrangea quercifolia (Oakleaf Hydrangea)
Ilex verticillata (Winterberry)
Ligustrum (Privet)
Symphoricarpos (Snowberry)
Viburnum

Evergreen Shrubs

Aucuba japonica (Gold Dust Tree)
Berberis julianae (Barberry)
Buxus (Boxwood)
Camellia japonica (Camellia)
Euonymus fortunei vegetus
Fatsia japonica
Ilex (Holly)
Kalmia latifolia (Mountain Laurel)
Leucothoë
Mahonia aquifolium (Holly Mahonia)
Nandina domestica
Photinia serrulata
Pieris (Andromeda)
Taxus (Yew)

Vines

Aristolochia durier (Dutchman's Pipe)
Gelsemium sempervirens (Carolina Yellow Jessamine)
Hedera canariensis (Algerian Ivy)
Hedera helix (English Ivy)
Lonicera (Honeysuckle)
Pathenocissus (Boston Ivy)
Vitis labrusca (Fox Grape)

Flowering Annuals

Begonia semperflorens (Wax Begonia)
Coleus
Impatiens holstii
Lobelia ermus
Nicotiana (Flowering Tobacco)
Torenia fournieri (Wishbone Flower)
Vinca rosea (Madagascar Periwinkle)

Flowering Perennials

Ajuga (Bugleweed)
Anemone japonica
Aquilegia (Columbine)
Astilbe (Spirea)
Campanula (Bellflower)
Convallaria majalis (Lily of the Valley)
Dicentra (Bleeding Heart)
Digitalis (Foxglove)
Helleborus (Christmas-rose)
Heuchera (Coralbells)
Hosta (Plantain Lily)
Hypericum calycinum (St. Johnswort)
Lunaria biennis (Honesty)
Mertensia virginica (Virginia Bluebell)
Myosotis (Forget-Me-Not)
Trollius (Globeflower)
Viola (Violet)

Bulbs

Begonia
Caladium
Chionodoxa luciliae (Glory-of-the-Snow)
Colchicum (Autumn Crocus)
Colocasia antiquorum (Elephant's Ear)
Galanthus nivalis (Snowdrop)
Leucojum aestivum (Summer Snowflake)
Lilium (Lily)
Muscari (Grape Hyacinth)
Narcissus
Ornithogalum (Star of Bethlehem)
Scilla hispanica (Spanish Bluebell)

NIGHTTIME LIGHTING

Several kinds of lamps may be used for lighting gardens at night, including ordinary incandescent lamps, incandescent flood lamps, mercury lamps and high-pressure sodium lamps. All of these lamps emit blue light except high-pressure sodium lamps and amber or yellow ceramic-coated incandescent lamps. Blue light attracts insects. Also, incandescent lamps of all kinds will alter plant growth if they are used for too many hours each day.

If you use incandescent lamps, light your plants only in the early evening. If you keep the light on later than 9:30 or 10:00 P.M., the extra light will

CHARACTERISTICS OF ARTIFICIAL LIGHTING

LAMP LAMPS OF VARIOUS SHAPES ARE AVAILABLE		COLOR OF LIGHT	ALTERS PLANT GROWTH	ATTRACTS INSECTS
INCANDESCENT  FLOOD ORDINARY	WHITE AND FROSTED	WHITE	YES	YES
	YELLOW	YELLOW	YES	NO
MERCURY 	ORDINARY	PALE BLUE	SLIGHTLY	YES
	COLOR IMPROVED	PALE PINK	YES	YES
HIGH PRESSURE SODIUM 		PALE YELLOW	NO	NO

cause the plants to grow and flower later in the season. Serious cold damage may result when plants continue to grow into the fall.

Ordinary white-frosted incandescent lamps are efficient light sources and are the most commonly used lamps in gardens. Many people object to amber-coated incandescent lamps because they make warm colors appear dull and cool colors appear gray. Amber-coated lamps will not attract insects; however, they cause plants to continue growing into the fall the same as white-frosted lamps.

Ordinary mercury lamps and high-pressure sodium lamps are extremely efficient light sources and they do not cause plants to grow and flower longer than the regular growing season. Mercury lamps attract moths and other insects, as ordinary incandescents do. High-pressure sodium lamps, however, appear amber to the eye and do not attract insects.

Both mercury and high-pressure sodium lamps require special installation. They cannot be used in ordinary incandescent light fixtures.

CONTROLLING HEAT, WIND, DUST AND NOISE

The environment of the urban garden is abnormal because it contains many objects of potential damage to plants. For example, many surfaces radiate heat, and the walls of buildings set up canyons that cause rapid changes in air circulation. Under these conditions plants are soon damaged, especially if they are in direct sunlight.

You can use screens in your garden to help protect the plants against heat and wind damage. Screens can be made of reeds, wood, cloth or plastic. Observe where your plants wilt rapidly and screen these areas from strong drafts and direct sunlight. You must arrange the screens so they permit some air flow. Otherwise the area will lack air circulation and become overheated, and plants and soil will become covered with mildew, algae and mosses.

Water your plants frequently but only enough to keep the soil moist. If you give your plants more water than they need to grow, they will not be trained to survive in the urban environment.

Because the frequent watering keeps the soil pliable, many plants may need staking. You can use stakes made of wood, bamboo, wire or stiff plastic. Use stakes that are shorter than the plants so the stakes will not be seen. Drive the stakes into the soil behind the plants.

Loosely tie the plants to the stakes with plastic- or rubber-covered wire. Bare wire will cut the plants and string will rot and break. Make a double loop of the wire with one loop around the plant and the other around the stake. Tie a knot between the loops. Never make a single loop around both stake and plant. The plant will hang to one side and the wire may girdle the stem.

You can reduce damage from heat, wind and cold by covering your plants with a waterproofing spray made of latex, wax or plastic. These antitranspirant sprays are available from garden-supply stores.

Apply the antitranspirant spray to the leaves and stems in spring and summer when the plants are growing rapidly; again at the beginning of winter; and when plants are transplanted. The spray covers the plants with a clear, flexible film that prevents too-rapid drying and protects against air pollutants.

Spray on several thin coatings at frequent intervals instead of only one heavy coat. In this way you can keep the growing plant tips covered and prevent the spray from caking on the foliage.

Do not spray on a bright, hot day; the plant foliage may be damaged from the film. Once the film is on the plants, it has no effect on growth.

In the urban garden, plants soon become covered with dust and dirt. This grime dulls the foliage and shuts out light from the plants. Removal of dust is difficult and requires a great deal of time. Also, if you are not careful, you can damage the leaves and flood the soil with water.

To clean your plants, use soapy water heated to about bath temperature. Use only soap that is mild enough for a baby's skin. Do not use laundry powders or liquids because they may damage the soil and plant roots.

Apply the soapy solution to the plants with a hand sprinkler similar to the kind used for sprinkling clothes before they are pressed. Sprinkle only enough to moisten the foliage but not enough for the solution to drip. Wait five to ten minutes for the soapy water to dissolve the dirt. Then use a water hose with a fine-particles nozzle to wash away the dirt and soapy water.

Very little information is available on how to control noise in the urban garden. Noises come from passing vehicles, industrial plants and mechanical equipment. Fairly large growing plants or screens in the garden may help to deflect and rechannel some noises.

One major source of noise in the garden is the air conditioner. Screens 3 or 4 feet from the air-conditioner compressor will redirect much of this noise. However, a better solution is to install the compressor away from the outdoor living area if possible.

WINTER CARE

In early fall, start training your plants to withstand cold weather. The first step in cold-hardiness training is to stop using nighttime lights in September so your plants will get natural, short days. This will permit the plants to go dormant for winter.

Continue to water your plants in fall but stop fertilizing them. Never prune in late summer or fall because new growth will start, and this soft wood is extremely sensitive to freezing.

Leave your plants exposed to the first several frosts of fall. These frosts are not as severe as those later on, but they let your plants develop maximum cold hardiness. During this period, the soil temperature will be cold at night and warm in the day.

In late fall, after the soil temperature goes down

PROTECTING PLANTS FROM DAMAGE

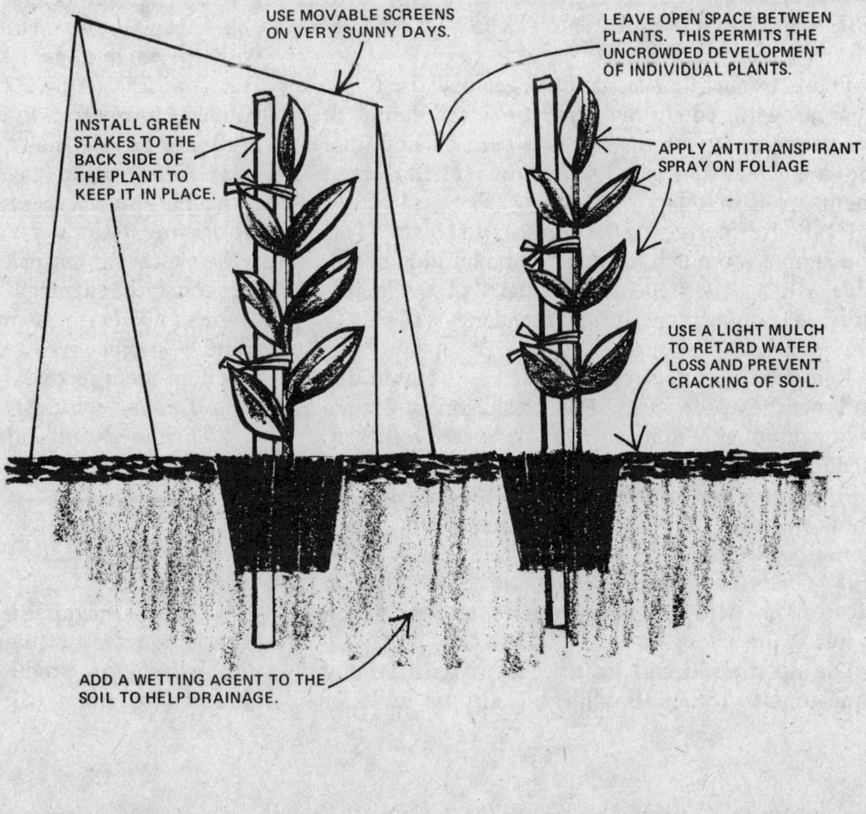
USE MOVABLE SCREENS ON VERY SUNNY DAYS.
LEAVE OPEN SPACE BETWEEN PLANTS. THIS PERMITS THE UNCROWDED DEVELOPMENT OF INDIVIDUAL PLANTS.
INSTALL GREEN STAKES TO THE BACK SIDE OF THE PLANT TO KEEP IT IN PLACE.
APPLY ANTITRANSPIRANT SPRAY ON FOLIAGE
USE A LIGHT MULCH TO RETARD WATER LOSS AND PREVENT CRACKING OF SOIL.
ADD A WETTING AGENT TO THE SOIL TO HELP DRAINAGE.

and stays down, take steps to winterize your plants. The aim is to protect the soil from freezing and the tops of the plants from losing moisture.

To winterize your plants, mulch them as explained under "Mulching," on page 104. Tie evergreen branches around the plants and cover deciduous plants with black polyethylene sheeting to keep off direct sunlight. Do not cover evergreen plants with polyethylene because they need sunlight in winter to keep their green color.

Move plants in containers to a shady location that is not windy and where water from snow or rain will not collect. Dig drainage furrows for your plants in the yard so water will not collect around them. Spray all plants with antitranspirant spray.

Most flowering plants should be replaced each year, but a few kinds of flowering perennials in containers can be kept over the winter—such plants as fuchsias, roses, cannas and dahlias. When the plants are dormant, let the soil dry out. Then turn the containers on their sides in a dry cool place and cover the plants and containers with moss, leaves or plastic until spring.

Many potted house plants can be used from year to year. Keep them in the garden during summer, return them to the house in winter, and put them out in the garden again the next spring.

Cuttings of many plants such as coleus, impatiens, geranium or ivy may be started in late summer or early fall to provide new plants for the next year.

SIGNS OF POOR GROWING CONDITIONS

Plants frequently become damaged because of the poor growing conditions that are often found in urban areas. Symptoms of plant damage and poor growing conditions, and what you can do about them, are as follows:

(1) *White coating on the surface of the soil.* This is a sign of too much fertilizer and a buildup of soluble salts. This prevents root hairs of the plants from developing properly, and the plants will slowly die.

Remove the surface crust of the soil without disturbing the plant roots. Add fresh soil and then water thoroughly to leach away all excess fertilizer. Reduce the amount of fertilizer you use or switch to a liquid or water-soluble fertilizer. These fertilizers contain only the essential elements for plant growth.

(2) *Green slime on containers and soil.* This indicates very acid soil, poor drainage, and too much water and fertilizer.

Dig up the soil and lightly dust it with ground limestone to reduce its acidity. Continue to water the plants thoroughly each time you water, but water less frequently.

(3) *Leaves that turn gray-green, wilt, and fall from the plants.* Roots are deficient in oxygen because of poor soil aeration. The plants do not get enough water and nutrients. Often, root rot kills the roots after they are weakened or damaged from poor aeration.

Replace the soil every four to five years when it becomes heavy and compacted. Add extra perlite and peat moss to the soil from time to time to provide good aeration. At garden-supply stores you can get an organic, nonionic wetting agent to pour on the soil. This liquid increases the water-holding ability of the soil and thoroughly wets the peat moss, which is often dry. It also permits easy movement of nutrients through the soil and allows excess water to flow easily out of the soil. Use the wetting agent according to the directions on the container label.

(4) *Retarded plant growth.* If the soil appears to be satisfactory, and proper cultural practices have been followed, slow plant growth may mean that the water is too hard (contains too much calcium) or that it contains other impurities.

You can strain out some of these impurities by using a strainer on a hose or by having a strainer installed in the water line of an automatic waterer. The strainer should be removed from the waterer and cleaned periodically.

Do not use water softeners in the water; these substitute sodium for calcium, and sodium damages plants more than calcium does. Deionizers are available that will chemically purify water but they are very expensive to use.

Rainwater is a safe source of water for plants if you have a way to collect and store it. It can be kept in tubs or barrels and used as needed.

(5) *Young leaves become twisted and flowers fall early.* This means that herbicides or other chemicals are drifting onto the plants from nearby areas.

Prune the abnormal foliage and let the plants overcome the damage if they are strong enough. There is no chemical treatment to help plants overcome pesticide damage. Only time and regrowth will help them recover.

(6) *Tan and white spots on leaves and rapid wilting.* This condition indicates air-pollution damage. Air pollution is discussed below.

AIR-POLLUTION PROBLEMS

Air pollution comes from many sources, and most of these sources are concentrated in urban areas. Automobile engines produce such gases as carbon monoxide, hydrocarbons, nitrogen dioxide and lead compounds. Electric generators and industrial plants contribute sulphur dioxide, hydrogen fluoride and hydrocarbons. Refuse-burning, heating plants and forest fires emit tons of smoke into the air. All the pollutants in the air are known collectively as smog.

The two pollutants that cause the most damage to growing plants are produced by the chemical action of sunlight on smog. These pollutants are ozone and peroxyacetyl nitrate, better known as PAN. Ozone and PAN are known as photochemical pollutants.

Some of the most common pollutants and the damage they cause to plants are as follows:

- Ozone and PAN: Spotted, streaked and bleached foliage; retarded plant growth; leaves drop early.
- Nitrogen dioxide: Tan or white, irregular lesions near leaf margins.
- Sulphur dioxide: Bleached spots between leaf veins; retarded plant growth.
- Hydrogen fluoride: Bleached leaf tips and margins; dwarfed plant growth.
- Ethylene: Withered and twisted leaves; flowers drop early.

Pollution damage comes and goes, but more damage occurs in spring and fall than in other seasons. In spring and fall, stationary layers of warm and cold air create barriers to the movement of gases in the atmosphere. When this happens, smog collects beneath these barriers and damages plants.

Some plants can tolerate smog, particularly photochemical smog, better than others. Plants that are especially resistant to photochemical smog are in the first of the two lists below; plants acutely sensitive to photochemical smog are in the second.

Plants Resistant to Photochemical Smog

Shrubs and Trees

Acacia
Acanthopanax sieboldianus (Aralia)
Arbutus
Buxus (Boxwood)
Camellia japonica (Camellia)
Cedrus
Cistus
Cotoneaster
Cupressus (Cypress)
Fraxinus (Ash)
Ginkgo biloba (Ginkgo, Maidenhair Tree)
Prunus (many species—Ornamental Cherry, Peach, Plum, etc.)
Pittosporum tobira, (Japanese Pittosporum)
Pyracantha (Pyracantha Firethorn)
Quercus (Oak)
Spiraea (Bridal Wreath)
Syringa (Lilac)
Viburnum
Yucca

House Plants

Dieffenbachia
Dracaena
Fatsia
Philodendron
Pittosporum

Plants Sensitive to Photochemical Smog

Shrubs and Trees

Acer (Maple)
Alnus (Alder)
Calycanthus (Carolina Allspice)
Ficus (Fig)
Gleditsia (Locust)
Hibiscus
Juglans (Walnut)
Mentha (Mint)
Petunia
Persea (Avocado)
Pinus (Pine)
Platanus (Sycamore)
Rhododendron
Robinia (Locust, Rose-acacia)
Salix (Willow)
Salvia (Salvia, Sage)
Ulmus (Elm)

Within a given species of plant, some forms will be more resistant or sensitive than others. For example, common white petunias are extremely sensitive to smog, but purple, blue and red ones are more smog-resistant. Besides color, size is a factor. Small-flowered petunias (multiflora) are generally more resistant than large-flowered ones (grandiflora). And small-leaved plants are more resistant than large-leaved types.

The extent of air-pollution damage depends greatly on what stage of development a plant is in. Young leaves and old leaves usually are more resistant to pollutants than recently matured leaves. Slow-growing plants are more resistant than soft, rapidly growing plants. Before you select plants for your garden, visit other gardens in the area and see what kinds of plants are growing best.

If your plants show signs of pollution damage, reduce the amount of nitrogen fertilizer and the frequency of watering. High levels of nitrogen and water stimulate plant growth and increase sensitivity to air pollution. Moderate fertilizer and watering will slow growth and help plants survive. There are no practical chemical treatments available that can be used on plants to increase their tolerance of the polluted environment.

CHAPTER 10

Selecting Shrubs for Shady Areas

MANY KINDS OF SHRUBS are easy to grow in shady areas, and once established they require little care. Regular watering during dry periods and some fertilizing during the growing season will satisfy the needs of most of these shrubs.

To grow shrubs in shady areas:

- Start with nursery-grown stock adapted to your area.
- Plant during the winter or early spring in well-prepared soil.
- Maintain a mulch around shrubs.
- Water regularly.

KINDS OF SHADE

Shrubs in the list beginning on this page do well in at least one of the four kinds of shade described here—full shade, open shade, half shade, and light shade.

Full shade under trees: Areas of full shade occur under low-branching trees with heavy foliage; therefore, shrubs in these areas get practically no direct sunlight during the growing season. Also, these areas may be unfavorable for shrub growth because the shrub roots are constantly competing with the tree roots for the available soil moisture.

Open shade: This kind of shade can be found in areas next to the north side of high walls, buildings or trees. These areas are in full shade but are open to the sky.

Half shade: Areas of half shade get direct sunlight either in the morning or the afternoon. This kind of shade is similar to open shade and is caused by a high wall or building facing east or west.

Light shade: Areas of light shade get a broken flow of sunlight. This is caused by sunlight filtering through the leaves of high-branched trees.

SELECTING SHRUBS

When you select a shrub, consider whether you want to:

- Beautify an area by planting masses of colorful flowers, berries or foliage.
- Screen a particular view.
- Accent the lines of a building.

A single kind of shrub may satisfy all these needs.

Low-growing shrubs are best used for ground cover or borders; the tall ones make excellent screens; and the most colorful ones are best used for ornamental groupings.

Before selecting a shrub for your garden, make sure it will grow well in your hardiness zone. Hardiness is the plant's tolerance to high or low temperatures. Other factors such as wind velocity, soil conditions, humidity and availability of moisture also play an important role. Temperature is one of the most important factors in determining where a plant may be grown. (The numbers at the end of each shrub's description in the following list indicate the climatic zones in which that shrub will normally grow.) You can find out which zone you are in by looking at the plant hardiness map on page 14.

Visit local gardens—see what grows well in your area. You can get advice about selecting shrubs from your nurseryman, county agricultural agent or state extension horticulturist.

Shrubs growing wild in the woods are generally harder to transplant and need more initial care than shrubs you buy from a nursery.

The following list contains descriptions of some of the more common shrubs that will do well in shady areas. Others may be found among shrubs listed in Chapter 11.

*ANDROMEDA, JAPANESE

Japanese Andromeda (*Pieris japonica*) is an evergreen shrub that grows 5 to 8 feet under cultivation.

* Plants marked with an asterisk require acid soil. They should not be selected for areas having neutral or alkaline soil unless the planting site is specially prepared in advance to provide an acid, well-drained soil.

Japanese andromeda

It is valued for its shiny dark-green foliage and early flowers similar to lily of the valley. The young foliage is a rich reddish-bronze. Japanese andromeda is used as a background or specimen plant. (A specimen plant is one that can be grown alone for display purposes.) Plant in light shade. Zones 6 to 9.

ARALIA

Five-leaf Aralia (*Acanthopanax sieboldianus*) is a deciduous shrub that grows 6 to 9 feet. It is valued for its shiny foliage and because it withstands city conditions. Five-leaf aralia is used as a background or screen. Plant in light to full shade. Zones 5 to 8.

ARROWWOOD

Arrowwood (*Viburnum dentatum*) is a deciduous shrub that grows 8 to 15 feet. It is valued for its white flowers in late spring and its shiny red foliage in autumn. Arrowwood is used in shrub borders or massed for general foliage effects. Plant in any kind of shade. Zones 3 to 8.

AUCUBA

Japanese Aucuba (*Aucuba japonica*) is an evergreen shrub that grows as high as 15 feet, but generally 5 to 7 feet in cultivation. It is valued for its thick shiny foliage. There are male and female plants. Only the female bears bright-red berries, but both sexes must be in the same vicinity before these berries are produced. Japanese aucuba is a vigorous shrub, used in the garden as a specimen plant. Plant in light to full shade. Zones 7 to 10.

AZALEA, FLAME

Flame Azalea (*Rhododendron calendulaceum*) is a deciduous shrub that grows 6 to 8 feet. It is valued for its large, brilliant blossoms in May and June. The flowers grow in clusters of 5 to 25 and range in color from orange-red to a clear yellow. Flame azalea is native to the mountains of Eastern U.S. Plant in light to open shade. Zones 5 to 8.

BARBERRY, WARTY

Warty Barberry (*Berberis verruculosa*) is an evergreen shrub that grows to 4 feet. It is valued for its golden-yellow flowers in May and its shiny evergreen foliage that is white underneath. Warty barberry is used chiefly as a specimen plant or in hedges. Plant in light shade. Zones 4 to 9.

*CAMELLIA, COMMON

Common Camellia (*Camellia japonica*) is an evergreen shrub that grows 15 to 30 feet, 6 to 12 feet in cultivation. It is valued for its early single or double flowers that range from white to deep red and its shiny dark-green foliage. Common camellia is used primarily as a specimen shrub. Plant in light to open shade; it will not flower in dense shade. Zones 7 to 9.

*CAMELLIA, SASANQUA

Sasanqua Camellia (*Camellia sasanqua*) is an evergreen shrub that grows 8 to 15 feet. It is valued for its single and semi-double flowers that range from white to pink and bloom in autumn. Sasanqua camellia is used as a specimen plant, in shrub borders and as a flowering hedge; it can also be trained to grow on a trellis. Plant in light to open shade; little flowering will occur in dense shade. Zones 7 to 9.

DOGWOOD, GRAY

Gray Dogwood (*Cornus racemosa*) is a deciduous shrub that grows 6 to 15 feet. It is valued for its white flowers in June and its white berries on pink stems. Gray dogwood is used in shrub borders and as a screen. Plant in light to half shade. Zones 4 to 8.

FOTHERGILLA, ALABAMA

Alabama Fothergilla (*Fothergilla monticola*) is a deciduous shrub that grows 4 to 6 feet. It is valued for its white flowers in May and its bright-yellow-and-red autumn foliage. Alabama fothergilla is effective when used in foundation plantings, especially in front of evergreens. Plant in moist soil in half shade. Zones 5 to 8.

*FRINGETREE

Fringetree or White Fringe (*Chionanthus virginicus*) is a deciduous shrub that grows 15 to 30 feet. It is valued for its fragrant white flowers in early spring. Fringetree is used chiefly as a specimen plant or as a background in shrub borders. Plant in moist soil in light shade. Zones 4 to 8.

*HOLLY, JAPANESE

Japanese Holly (*Ilex crenata*) is an evergreen shrub that grows 5 to 15 feet. It is valued for its shiny dark-green foliage and because it withstands city conditions. Japanese holly is used as a specimen plant, a hedge, or a screen. Light shade is best, but plant will tolerate dense shade. Zones 6 to 9.

HOLLYGRAPE, OREGON

Oregon Hollygrape (*Mahonia aquifolium*) is an evergreen shrub that grows 3 to 4 feet. It is valued for its yellow flowers in early spring, its shiny foliage that turns bronze-red when exposed to winter sun, and its bluish-black grapelike fruits. Oregon hollygrape is used chiefly as a specimen plant. Protect from winds and plant in light to half shade. Zones 5 to 9.

IVY, ENGLISH

English Ivy (*Hedera helix*) is a creeping, trailing evergreen vine. It is valued because it grows almost anywhere. English ivy is used as a ground cover and for clinging to walls and tree trunks. Plant in any shade. Zones 5 to 10.

JETBEAD

Jetbead (*Rhodotypos scandens*) is a deciduous shrub that grows 4 to 6 feet. It is valued for its white flowers in late spring, its bright-green foliage and its shiny black berries. Jetbead can be used as a specimen plant or in a shrub border. Plant in any soil in light shade. Zones 5 to 9.

*LEUCOTHOË, DROOPING

Drooping Leucothoë (*Leucothoë fontanesiana* also called *L. catesbaei*) is an evergreen shrub that grows 4 to 6 feet. It is valued for its white flowers in early spring and for its shiny dark-green foliage, which turns bronze in winter sun. Drooping leucothoë is used in shrub borders or is mixed in with other evergreens. Prune away older branches to keep shrub in vigorous condition. Plant in moist peaty soil in any shade. Zones 5 to 9.

*MOUNTAIN-LAUREL

Mountain-Laurel (*Kalmia latifolia*) is an evergreen shrub that grows 8 to 20 feet. It is valued for its large clusters of pink-and-white flowers in early summer. Mountain-laurel is used chiefly in woodland plantings and as a foundation planting. Plant in moist, acid soil an any shade; but flowering is sparse in dense shade. Zones 5 to 9.

NANDINA

Nandina (*Nandina domestica*) is an evergreen shrub that grows 6 to 8 feet. It is valued for its large clusters of white flowers in midsummer, its fine-textured foliage and its red berries in autumn and winter. Nandina is used in shrub borders and as an ornamental in front of taller evergreen plants. Plant in light to open shade. Zones 7 to 9.

PERIWINKLE

Periwinkle or Myrtle (*Vinca minor*) is a trailing evergreen perennial that grows 6 to 8 inches. It is valued because it is easy to grow almost anywhere. Periwinkle is used chiefly as a ground cover. Plant in any soil and any shade. Zones 5 to 10.

PITTOSPORUM

Japanese Pittosporum (*Pittosporum tobira*) is an evergreen shrub that grows 6 to 10 feet. It is valued for its white flowers in late spring and its shiny dark-green foliage. Japanese pittosporum is used as a specimen plant or as a hedge. Plant in light shade. Zones 8 to 10.

PRIVET, GLOSSY

Glossy Privet (*Ligustrum lucidum*) is an evergreen shrub or small tree that grows 30 to 35 feet. It is valued for its evergreen foliage and ease of care. Glossy privet is used in shrub borders or as a hedge. Plant in light to open shade. Zones 7 to 10.

*RHODODENDRON, ROSEBAY

Rosebay Rhododendron (*Rhododendron maximum*) is an evergreen shrub that grows 15 to 20 feet. It is valued for its white to purplish-pink flowers in June and July, and because it is probably the hardiest evergreen rhododendron. Rosebay rhododendron is used as a screen or as an evergreen background for more ornamental shrubs. Plant in almost any shade. Zones 4 to 8.

*SALAL

Salal or Shallon (*Gaultheria shallon*) is an evergreen woody trailer that grows to 1½ feet. It is valued for its white to pink flowers in early summer and its dark-green leathery foliage. Salal is used in evergreen borders throughout much of the Pacific Coast region. Plant in moist soil in light to open shade. Zones 6 to 9.

SARCOCOCCA, FRAGRANT

Fragrant Sarcococca (*Sarcococca hookeriana* var. *humilis*) is an evergreen shrub that grows 1½ feet. It is valued for its glossy foliage. Fragrant sarcococca is used as a tall spreading ground cover, as a foreground for evergreen shrubs or as a low edging. Plant in almost any shade. Zones 6 to 9.

*SKIMMIA, JAPANESE

Japanese Skimmia (*Skimmia japonica*) is an evergreen shrub that grows 2 to 4 feet. It is valued for its bright-red berries in autumn and its rich green foliage. Japanese skimmia is used as an evergreen hedge or as a specimen plant. Plant in any shade. Zones 7 to 9.

*SUMMERSWEET

Summersweet or Sweet Pepperbush (*Clethra alnifolia*) is a deciduous shrub that grows to 9 feet. It is valued for its very fragrant white flowers in late July, and because it is easy to grow. Summersweet is used in shrub borders and tends to grow in clumps. Plant in moist soil in any except dense shade. Zones 3 to 9.

*SWEETBAY

Sweetbay (*Magnolia virginiana*) is an evergreen shrub or small tree that grows 30 to 50 feet. It is valued for its fragrant white flowers in early summer and for its foliage, which is green above and white below. Sweetbay is used alone or as a background for ornamental evergreens. In the deep South, sweetbay grows into a tree and is nearly evergreen, but in New England it is much more shrubby and deciduous. Plant in slightly acid, moist soil in open shade. Zones 5 to 10.

*VIBURNUM, MAPLELEAF

Mapleleaf Viburnum (*Viburnum acerifolium*) is a deciduous shrub that grows 4 to 6 feet. It is valued for its ability to grow in the shade and its pale-pink color in the fall. Mapleleaf viburnum is used as a specimen or in woodland plantings. Plant in light to full shade. Zones 3 to 9.

WINTERCREEPER

Wintercreeper (*Euonymus fortunei*) is an evergreen shrub that grows 8 to 10 inches. The cultivar '*Coloratus*' is valued for its foliage, which turns purple in the winter sun. The cultivar '*Gracilis*' is valued for its variegated leaves. Wintercreeper is used chiefly as a ground cover. Plant in any shade. Zones 6 to 10.

*YELLOWROOT

Yellowroot (*Xanthorhiza simplicissima*) is a deciduous shrub that grows 1½ to 2 feet. It is valued for its ability to thrive on moist shady slopes. Yellowroot is used as a tall ground cover or in borders. Plant in moist soil in light to full shade. Zones 4 to 10.

PREPARING THE SOIL

The benefits of careful soil preparation carry over from year to year. Satisfactory results depend largely on properly prepared soil.

Properly prepared soil has good drainage; allows shrub roots to grow deep and extensively; provides proper nutrients for growth.

To test whether the soil has good drainage, see page 18.

If water remains in the hole after ten hours, the drainage is poor and should be improved. If it is not improved, water may begin to collect and rot the roots.

One of the simplest ways to improve slow drainage is to dig a hole about a foot deeper than that needed to plant the shrub. Fill this deeper part with stones, crushed rock, or gravel. For too-rapid drainage, add loam, clay or organic material to your soil.

TESTING FOR ACID SOIL

Most shade-tolerant shrubs grow best in acid soil. To find out if you have acid soil, consult either your county agricultural agent or your local nurseryman. If necessary, get directions for changing the acidity of your soil.

Be sure to tell the person testing your soil which shrubs you want to grow there.

PLANTING AND CARE

The best time to plant shrubs is in late winter or early spring, before growth begins.

For shrubs having a rootball, dig planting holes about twice the width and depth of the rootball. For those without a rootball, dig planting holes wide enough to allow the roots to be spread out and deep enough for the shrubs to stand at the same height they stood in the nursery.

After the shrub is set, tamp soil around the roots and water thoroughly.

Mulching: After planting, cover the soil around the shrub with a mulch—peat moss, pine bark, or wood chips. Mulches help prevent:

- Soil from drying.
- Soil surface from crusting.
- Weeds from growing.

In addition, mulched beds have an orderly look that will beautify your yard.

Apply a layer of mulch 2 or 3 inches deep. For continuing effectiveness, add new mulch regularly. (For additional information on mulching, see Index.)

Weeding: If you keep a mulch around your shrubs, few weeds will grow. Be careful when you use a hoe or dig around shrubs; the shallow roots are easily injured.

Watering: Watering is essential during the first two years after planting. In only a few places is summer rainfall adequate enough to keep shrubs healthy.

Water your shrubs regularly; they should have the equivalent of 1 inch of rain every ten days. Be careful not to overwater and drown your shrubs.

Moisten the entire area around the shrub thoroughly, but do not water so heavily that soil becomes soggy. After watering, let the soil dry out a little before watering again.

Fertilizing: Shrubs planted in rich soil seldom need fertilizing. Shrubs growing in shade, however, may be competing for nutrients with established trees or other plants. These shrubs require annual fertilizing, preferably in late winter or early spring. Also, you may want to use fertilizers if your shrubs show signs that the soil is not adequate for their specific needs. Signs of low soil fertility are small pale leaves and short twig growth.

Pruning: Some shrubs grow well with little or no pruning. But most shrubs do require pruning to remove dead branches, to shape plants or reduce their size, or to check disease. Shrubs that bloom in early spring should be pruned after they flower. Summer-flowering types and those grown for foliage alone should be pruned in early spring. Make pruning cuts back to a bud or a larger branch. (For further information on pruning see Chapter 12.)

CHAPTER 11

Shrubs, Vines and Trees for Summer Color

COLOR IN MOST GARDENS is a springtime thing. In the heat of the summer, color in the garden is usually limited to shades of green. But by planting just a few of the great variety of colorful shrubs, vines and trees available, you can relieve this monotony and have a lively and beautiful garden all summer long.

When you stop to consider the small amount of care required, flowering shrubs, vines and trees can be just as rewarding in your garden as annuals or perennials.

Will the plants described in the list below grow in your garden? You can find out by referring to the plant hardiness map on page 14. From the map, determine what zone you live in. The zone range in which the plant will grow is indicated at the end of its description in the following list.

If the plant is suitable for your geographic area, next consider whether you have a suitable location for it in your garden. That is, can you provide shade or sun, acid or neutral soil, protection from wind and air pollution, or any other special requirement that the plant might have?

SHRUBS

BEAUTYBERRY

Beautyberry (*Callicarpa japonica*—purple berries; *C. japonica 'Leucocarpa'* — white berries) is a graceful medium-size shrub that grows 5 to 7 feet tall. It dies back to the ground in severe winters, but sends up new shoots the following spring. This shrub blooms in the late summer, usually August, bearing small pink flowers in short clusters. The flowers are followed by purple or white berries that last a few weeks in autumn.

Plant beautyberry in the early spring or fall in a place sheltered from high winds. Beautyberry thrives in the sun, but will tolerate partial shade. Zones 6 to 9.

BLUEBEARD

Bluebeard (*Caryopteris incana*) is usually small, growing 3 to 6 feet tall. The wispy flowers are violet blue to powder blue, or sometimes white, lasting from August until the first frost.

Bluebeard needs lots of sunshine and should be set out in well-drained soil. In the winter, protect the plants with a light mulch, and prune them to the ground every spring. Zones 5 to 10.

BOTTLEBRUSH BUCKEYE

Bottlebrush Buckeye (*Aesculus parviflora*) is a coarse, widespreading shrub. It grows 8 to 12 feet tall and up to 20 feet broad, spreading by underground suckers. The small white flowers appear in

Beautyberry

July and August. They form erect cylindrical clusters or spikes about one foot long on the end of each branch.

Bottlebrush buckeye thrives and shows its flowers to best advantage in full sunlight; however, it will tolerate partial shade. Zones 5 to 10.

BUTTERFLYBUSH

Butterflybush, sometimes called Summer Lilac or Orange-eye Butterflybush (*Buddleia davidii*) is a compact shrub that grows 6 to 8 feet tall. It begins blooming in July and continues until the first heavy frost. The stems of the plant bear fragrant clusters of flowers 12 to 18 inches long. Four colors are available from most nurseries: pink, white, blue, and a deep reddish purple. the butterflybush is good for cut flowers and the blooms attract butterflies. It is hardy throughout most of the United States.

Set your plants out in the spring. If you plant them in the sun, they will grow well in practically any soil. It is a good idea to leave plenty of room when you plant this shrub because it often grows to be as broad as it is tall.

Butterflybush is a "die-back" shrub; in a hard winter it is likely to die back all the way to the ground. But it will grow again the next spring, flowering on the new growth. Prune out the dead wood each spring. Zones 5 to 9.

BUTTONBUSH

A native shrub, the Buttonbush (*Cephalanthus occidentalis*) grows well over most of the United States. The flowers look like creamy-white pincushions. They appear in early July and continue until late August. They are about an inch in diameter and are pleasantly fragrant. This shrub grows about 15 feet tall.

Plant in the spring. A moist soil and partial shade are the best conditions for growth. It is especially valued for its ability to grow in swampy land. Zones 4 to 10.

CAROLINA-ALLSPICE

Carolina-Allspice, sometimes called Sweetshrub (*Calycanthus floridus*), grows quickly to a height of 4 to 6 feet. The blossoms, borne from May until July are reddish brown, have a spicy, fragrant scent and are nearly 2 inches in diameter. This shrub is hardy as far north as the Great Lakes region.

Set plants out in the early spring or fall. This shrub grows vigorously in almost any well-drained soil and requires little care once established. Zones 5 to 10.

CHASTE-TREE

In the South, the Chaste-tree (*Vitex agnus-castus f. latifolia*) grows to a considerable height and width, increasing about 3 to 5 feet each year. It blooms from July until September. The flowers are small and fragrant, borne in terminal clusters 5 to 7 inches long. Colors are lilac, pale violet or white. The gray foliage of the plant is pleasantly aromatic. You will find this shrub especially useful at the back of a perennial border as a filler.

Spring is the best time for planting. Be sure to keep the roots from drying out. The chaste-tree thrives in light sandy soil and full sunlight. If you have difficulty with this plant, add some peat moss or leaf mold to the soil.

North of Philadelphia the chaste-tree is a die-back shrub and should be pruned back within 6 or 8 inches of the soil each spring and mulched with loose straw or evergreen branches to protect it during the winter. Zones 5 to 9.

CRAPEMYRTLE

Crapemyrtle (*Lagerstroemia indica*) requires little care. It is easily grown in either tree or shrub form. It grows taller in zones 9 and 10 than it does farther

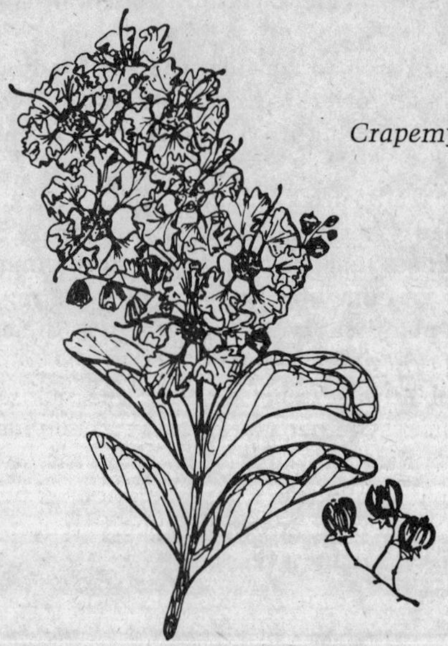

Crapemyrtle

north, often reaching a height of 20 feet. The flowers begin appearing in July and continue through September; they form crinkly clusters 4 to 9 inches long. Exact time of bloom depends on variety and location. Crapemyrtle usually has one heavy flush of bloom followed by sporadic blooming during the rest of the growing season. Colors available are white, pink, red or lavender. This shrub often blooms in the first year.

Set the plants out in late fall or early spring. Plant them bare-rooted in any ordinary garden soil at the same depth as they were in the nursery. For best blooming, set the plants in full sunlight. Zones 7 to 10.

DEVILS-WALKINGSTICK

Also known as Hercules-Club, Devils-Walkingstick (*Aralia spinosa*) is planted to best advantage as a specimen on a large open lawn. It takes up too much space for a small garden. It ordinarily reaches a height of 12 to 16 feet, but will sometimes grow to 25 feet and higher. The whitish flowers appear in August. They are extremely small, but form large clusters 2 to 3 feet long and nearly a foot across.

Transplant bare-rooted in the spring. Devils-walkingstick favors a moist, rich soil; it will grow well in sun or partial shade. Zones 5 to 9.

FLOWERING RASPBERRY

Flowering Raspberry (*Rubus odoratus*) grows quickly to a height of 3 to 6 feet. It blooms from June until September. The flowers are purple, fragrant, and about 2 inches in diameter. They form in multiflowered clusters at the tips of the stems.

Plant in the early spring. Try to select a spot with moist soil where the plants will receive some shade during the day. Zones 3 to 4.

GERMANDER

Germander (*Teucrium chamaedrys*) is a good substitute for boxwood in hedges and borders. It grows about a foot high, and its rosy-purple spikes of flowers begin to bloom in July. This plant is a good source of cut flowers.

Plant in early spring or fall. Set the plants in the sun in a well-drained place. If you want a hedge, set plants out in early spring about 6 inches apart. Zones 6 to 10.

GLORY BOWER

Glory Bower (*Clerodendrum trichotomum*) is a tall-growing shrub. It almost always reaches a height of 20 feet. The flowers appear in August. They are white, very fragrant, and nearly 2 inches in diameter. They are borne in clusters at the ends of the branches, and are followed by blue berries in a red, star-shaped calyx. And the berries remain on the shrub for several weeks. The calyx is attractive even after the berries have dropped. Glory bower does best in partial shade.

Plant glory bower in the spring, especially in cold climates. It is best planted alone as a specimen tree.

It is not particular about soil but it needs partial shade. Zones 6 to 9.

GLOSSY ABELIA

Glossy Abelia (*Abelia grandiflora*) is a dense, spreading plant with long, arching branches This shrub flowers freely in August and September. The small pink flowers are borne in clusters. Glossy abelia is attractive even after the petals have fallen because of the bronze, star-shaped calyx that remains on the plant for a long time. The foliage is semi-evergreen, and the color in autumn is bronze.

Glossy abelia will grow almost anywhere but does best in a sunny place in well-drained soil. It is excellent for either natural or pruned hedges. Plant 2 to 3 feet apart. Zones 6 to 10.

HEATH

Heath (*Erica vagans*) is native to southwest Europe. It grows about one foot tall, flowering from July until October. The pinkish-purple flowers are small, very bright, and bloom in pairs.

Set the plants out in the spring or fall in well-drained, sandy soil. Pick a sunny location and place the plants about 12 inches apart. Heath does best in poor soil, so don't add any fertilizer. Keep well watered through the hot weather until the plants are firmly established. Though heath needs plenty of water, large quantities applied at a single watering will damage the plants. It is better to give them frequent light waterings.

The plants will grow thicker if you cut them back to the ground just after the flowering season. Zones 6 to 10.

HEATHER

Heather (*Calluna vulgaris*) is good for rock gardens and other places where space is limited. It grows only a foot or so tall, but forms a dense ground cover. Heather is one of the few shrubs that thrives in and actually requires poor soil. Heather blooms in the summer. The flowers are small upright spikes 6 to 8 inches long. Colors are pink, white, red and lavender.

Set the plants out in the spring or fall in a damp place. Space them about 12 inches apart. Heather requires an acid soil; peat moss or leaf mold will make the soil sufficiently acid for good growth. Don't use fertilizer. Set the plants in full sunlight for more effective flowering.

In zone 5 provide some winter protection with a loose covering of straw or evergreen branches. To make the plants thicker, cut them back to the ground in early spring. Zones 5 to 10.

HYDRANGEA

The four popular varieties of Hydrangea that bloom through the summer are House Hydrangea, Peegee Hydrangea, Snowhill Hydrangea and Oakleaf Hydrangea. Each of these has individual characteristics that make it more or less desirable for use in your garden. Some are hardier than others, some bloom early in the summer, some bloom late, some have better-looking foliage. However, all hydrangeas have certain virtues that make them excellent choices for summer color in most gardens. They are very hardy shrubs; the blooms are large, colorful and long lasting; and they are very easy to plant and care for.

House Hydrangea (*Hydrangea macrophylla*): Flowers of house hydrangea can be made to vary in color by changing the soil condition. You can change the color of the blooms to pink by adding lime to the soil. You can intensify their normally blue color by adding alum or forms of iron. These chemicals are available at most nurseries. House hydrangea is dense and round, and grows to a height of 8 feet except north of zone 6 where it freezes back to about 3 feet. It does very well near the seashore. Some good cultivars are 'Ami Pasquier'—a rich, purple-flowered hydrangea, and 'Amethyst'—the latest of all to flower. These varieties grow 3 to 4 feet tall and are suitable for formal plantings near the house.

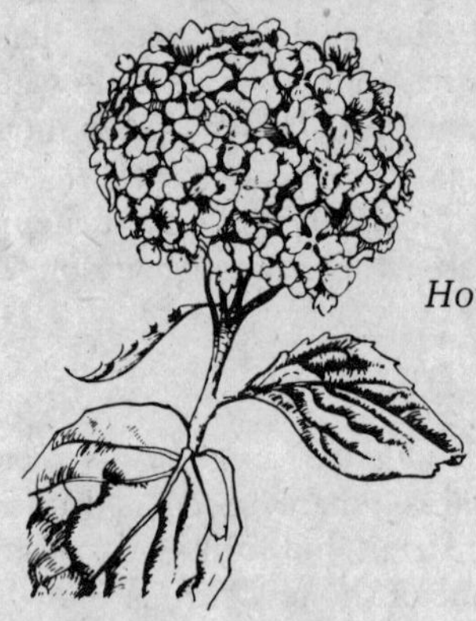

House hydrangea

Set plants out in early spring or early fall. House hydrangea does best in full sunlight, although it will tolerate partial shade. The soil should be moist, well-drained and rich in humus. Zones 6 to 10.

Peegee Hydrangea (*Hydrangea paniculata f. grandiflora*): Many nurserymen consider peegee to be the best all-around variety of hydrangea. It is by far the most striking of the group, it grows quickly, and is very hardy. It begins blooming in August and continues until frost. The huge white cone-shaped clusters of flowers are very handsome. A versatile plant, it can be grown either as bush or a tree. You can let all of the shoots develop to form a bush about 8 feet tall, or you can remove all shoots except one to form a miniature tree.

Set your plants out in the spring, or fall. They will do best in full sun, but are tolerant of partial shade. Zones 4 to 10.

Snowhill Hydrangea (*Hydrangea arborescens f. grandiflora*): Snowhill is a very hardy, compact, low-growing variety. The blooms are creamy-white large rounded clusters that begin appearing in July and continue until frost. This shrub grows about 4 feet tall and is suitable for foundation plantings.

Set your plants out in early spring or fall in full sunlight. This shrub does best in a moist well-drained soil and a place sheltered from high winds. Zones 4 to 10.

Oakleaf Hydrangea (*Hydrangea quercifolia*): Oakleaf, a slow-growing shrub, looks good whether planted as a single specimen or used in mass plantings. It grows 4 to 6 feet tall. The flowers are pinkish white, turning purple, and are borne in narrow upright clusters. They appear in June and last well into autumn.

Set plants out in early spring. This variety thrives in rich soil and partial shade. Zones 5 to 10.

KASHMIR FALSE-SPIREA

False-Spirea (*Sorbaria aitchisonii*) is a very decorative shrub with large showy flowers. It grows about 9 feet tall, flowering in July and August. The flowers are broad, erect clusters 10 to 12 inches long, white or creamy white in color. When setting out this shrub, allow plenty of room for it to spread. False-spirea is generally broader than it is tall.

Set your plant out in spring or fall, in full sun or partial shade. Zones 6 to 10.

LEATHERWOOD

Also called American Cyrilla, Leatherwood (*Cyrilla racemiflora*) grows well in most parts of the United States. You can use it as a border shrub or as a specimen tree in partially shaded places. It generally reaches a height of 25 feet. The white flowers resemble lily-of-the valley and appear on slender clusters through June and July. This plant is not hardy above the Great Lakes region.

Plant in spring or fall, in sun or partial shade. This plant will grow best in a sandy loam. Zones 6 to 10.

NANDINA

Nandina (*Nandina domestica*) sometimes called Heavenly Bamboo and Chinese Sacred Bamboo, is a slow-growing shrub that reaches a height of 7 or 8 feet. It begins blooming in July. White flowers are produced in great profusion on large erect clusters.

Plant nandina in the spring. Add some peat moss or leaf mold to the soil. In the South this plant thrives in either sun or shade. Zones 7 to 10.

NEW JERSEY-TEA

New Jersey-Tea (*Ceanothus americanus*) is an excellent shrub to plant in poorer soil where other shrubs will not grow. From July on, it produces fragrant white flowers in upright oblong clusters. The leaves are said to have been used as a substitute for tea during the American Revolution. This shrub grows about 4 feet tall.

New Jersey-tea is difficult to transplant. Set plants out very carefully in spring. They will do well in full sun or partial shade. Zones 4 to 10.

OCEAN-SPRAY

Ocean-Spray (*Holodiscus discolor var. ariaefolius*) is a spirea-like shrub that produces large drooping plumes of white to creamy-white flowers in July and early August. Its blooming period is short but impressive. This shrub grows from 6 to 10 feet tall. It is useful as a background for perennial borders.

Plant in early spring or fall. Ocean-spray will grow best in sunny or lightly shaded places.

Thin the plants out when they get too crowded to flower effectively. Zones 4 to 10.

POTENTILLA

Bush Cinquefoil (*Potentilla fruticosa*): Bush cinquefoil has a fine texture and grows about 3 feet tall. The flowers resemble tiny roses and range from yellow to white. This shrub blooms freely all summer long, from late May until the first killing frost, making it an excellent choice for summer color. It can be used to advantage as an informal hedge. Some of the better cultivars are *'Grandiflora,'* noted for its large golden-yellow flowers nearly 2 inches across, and *'Veitchii,'* which has large white flowers.

Set plants out in the early spring or fall. Bush cinquefoil prefers a lime soil and a sunny place; however, it will withstand partial shade. If you want a hedge, space the plants about 12 inches apart. Zones 1 to 10.

Golddrop (*Potentilla fruticosa 'Farreri'*): Golddrop is a compact shrub that grows about 2 feet tall. It is useful as a border or hedge. Golddrop blooms from early June until late October. The small yellow flowers resemble buttercups.

Plant in early spring or fall in either sun or partial shade. If you are planting a hedge, set the plants 18 inches apart; for a border, 2 feet apart. Zones 4 to 10.

ROSE-OF-SHARON

Rose-of-Sharon (*Hibiscus syriacus*) can be grown either as a large shrub or a small tree. It is useful in boundary plantings, screens and hedgerows, or as a background for smaller shrubs. One of the easiest shrubs to grow, it quickly reaches a height of 6 to 10 feet and is vigorous and free flowering from July until September. The large flowers always stand out. Colors are white, pink, red, blue or purple, according to variety. This shrub will withstand poor soil and neglect.

Set plants out in the spring. Plant them in full sun for more effective flowering.

Prune in late winter or early spring. Zones 5 to 10.

ROSES

Roses (*Rosa* species and hybrids) are probably the most popular of all summer garden flowers. They can be grown in any part of the country, and can be adapted to many garden needs.

There are thousands of varieties of roses. New hybrids are introduced all the time as old ones are dropped from the catalogs. You can choose from a tremendous variety of sizes and colors. The major groups of roses are climbers, ramblers, teas, floribunda, grandiflora and polyantha.

The many varieties of roses can be used for many different purposes. There are varieties for planting on lawns and borders and for growing on arbors and trellisses. There are specimen tree roses and roses for use as bedding plants and hedges.

Roses are sold three ways: potted, packaged and bare-rooted. Buying them in pots is least preferred—the major drawback of buying potted roses is that the roots may have become potbound; and once roots have grown around in circles inside the pot, they will never straighten out again. Therefore the plant will never be really healthy even after it is planted in the garden.

The best way to buy roses is bare-rooted—from the grower. But when you buy bare-root plants, make sure they are dormant.

Roses that come in packages may have a small amount of soil around the roots, and it is all right to buy those if they are dormant.

When planting either the bare-root or the packaged roses, make sure that the roots are spread out. Don't wind them around in the bottom of the hole. This is almost as bad as buying potbound roses.

Roses will grow best where they have sunshine all day. The proper time to plant roses depends on the severity of the winter temperatures in your region. In colder regions, set the plants out in early spring; either fall or spring planting is satisfactory in all other areas. Set the plants in full sunlight about 2 feet apart. Roses need at least 6 hours of sun a day and a great deal of water. Roses are not particular about the pH (degree of acidity or alkalinity) of the soil. When you fertilize them, use a 5–10–5 fertilizer.

Winter protection will vary a great deal between the far northern states and the southern states. In the North, soil is mounded over the entire plant during the winter; in medium latitudes, say around Washington, D.C., a very light mulch is put on; and in the South roses remain evergreen. Zones 1 to 10.

SHRUBBY BUSHCLOVER

Shrubby Bushclover (*Lespedeza bicolor*) blooms in late July. The rosy-purple pealike flowers appear in loose, thin-stalked clusters near the ends of the stems. The best use of this shrub is for specimen planting. It is very easy to grow and it quickly reaches a height of 6 to 9 feet.

Set out plants in the spring or fall. They will thrive in a light sandy soil and a sunny place. They can be cut to the ground in the fall without seriously affecting the bloom. Zones 4 to 10.

SPIREA

Japanese White Spirea (*Spiraea albiflora*): Japanese white spirea is a medium-size shrub, useful as a filler in a shrub border. It generally grows less than 2 feet tall. White flowers appear in rounded clusters in July. This shrub requires very little care.

Set your plants out in the spring or fall. Plant them in full sun for best blooming. Zones 4 to 10.

Froebel Spirea (*Spiraea bumalda f. froebelii*): Froebel spirea grows very quickly. Like the Japanese white spirea, it is best used in open or very lightly shaded places. The flowers are deep rose-red and will appear continuously throughout the late summer if you prune the shrub back after the first blooming. Its best use is a foundation plant or border.

Set plants out in the early spring or fall. Plant them in full sun if possible, in ordinary garden soil. Zones 4 to 10.

STEWARTIA

Stewartia is a very good choice to add summer color to your garden. The four varieties presented here range from 10 to 30 feet tall.

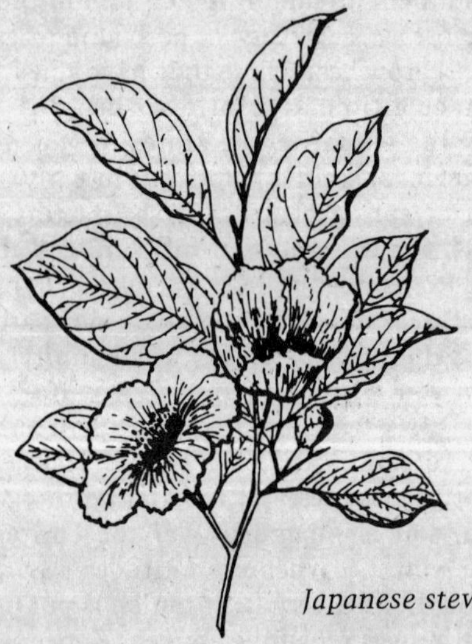
Japanese stewartia

Set plants out in the early spring or fall. They grow best in partial shade and require an organically rich, moist, slightly acid soil.

Plant all stewartias in a place sheltered from high winds. Allow a space about 10 feet square for each plant. During the winter keep the plants mulched with fallen leaves.

Japanese Stewartia (*Stewartia pseudo-camellia*): Japanese stewartia blooms in early July. The flowers are large, cup-shaped and white. The species often grows 30 feet tall. Zones 5 to 10.

Mountain Camellia (*Stewartia pentagyna*): Mountain camellia grows to 15 feet tall and blooms through July and August. The flowers are white with touches of orange and are about 3 inches across. Zones 5 to 10.

Showy Stewartia (*Stewartia ovata var. grandiflora*): Sometimes called Mountain Stewartia, showy stewartia grows from 15 to 20 feet tall. The flowers appear in early summer. They are large, white and very beautiful. Zones 6 to 9.

Silky Camellia (*Stewartia malachodendron*): Silky camellia grows to 12 feet. The flowers mostly appear in June but continue in sporadic production through July and August. They are white with touches of red and purple at the base of the petals. Zones 5 to 10.

ST. JOHNS-WORT

All varieties of St. Johns-wort are yellow-flowered and useful at the front of a border or as a low hedge. The flowers are cup-shaped and are produced in profusion for many weeks through most of the summer. The species included here are Aarons-Beard, Golden, Goldflower, Kalm, and Shrubby.

Plant in the spring or fall. For a hedge or ground cover, allow about 18 inches between the plants.

Aarons-Beard (*Hypericum calycinum*): Aaronsbeard blooms in late July. The flowers are solitary, bright yellow, about 3 inches in diameter. This species makes an excellent ground cover in sandy soil. It grows 12 to 18 inches tall and does well in light shade. Zones 6 to 10.

Golden St. Johns-wort (*Hypericum frondosum*): Golden St. Johns-wort, sometimes called Areum is the preferred species when a small shrub is needed. It grows well in partial shade, reaching a height of about 3 feet. It blooms from July until October. The solitary yellow flowers are about 2 inches in diameter. Zones 6 to 8.

Goldflower St. Johns-wort (*Hypericum moserianum*): Goldflower St. Johns-wort does well in partial shade. It varies in size from 1 to 3 feet and spreads out to become as broad as it is tall. The flowers appear in June and continue until first frost. The golden-yellow flowers have a waxy texture and are pleasantly fragrant. This shrub will die back during a severe winter, but will grow and flower much better the following spring.

Unlike other species of St. Johns-wort, goldflower should be set out only in the spring. Zones 7 to 10.

Kalm St. Johns-wort (*Hypericum kalmianum*):

Kalm St. Johns-wort is very useful for small lawns and gardens. It is a spreading bush that grows 2 to 4 feet tall and its diameter is often greater than its height. The small flowers appear in August and are very numerous. Zones 5 to 8.

Shrubby St. Johns-wort (*Hypericum prolificum*): Shrubby St. Johns-wort grows taller than the others, usually 4 to 6 feet high. The flowers are about ½ inch across and are produced in large, showy clusters. The flowering period is July through September. Zones 4 to 8.

SUMMERSWEET

Sometimes called Pepperbush, Summersweet (*Clethra alnifolia*) is a highly ornamental shrub that generally reaches a height of about 5 feet. This is an excellent shrub for a border, and, since it is resistant to the effects of salt spray, it does well at the seashore. The fragrant white flowers grow in narrow spikes 4 to 6 inches long. They appear from late July through September.

Summersweet is a difficult shrub to transplant. Set plants out carefully in either fall or spring in a moist, acid soil. Mix peat moss or leaf mold with ordinary garden soil and pack a 3-inch layer of the mixture firmly around the roots. Like azaleas, summersweet will thrive in shady, damp places. Zones 3 to 9.

SWAMP AZALEA

Sometimes called Swamp Honeysuckle, Swamp Azalea (*Rhododendron viscosum*) generally grows 4 to 7 feet tall. From late June to July and early August it produces pale purplish-pink or white flowers that are fragrant and sticky. Swamp azalea will tolerate sun, but the flowering season is prolonged if the plants are set in partial shade. This shrub will thrive in moist places from Maine to South Carolina.

In cold climates, set plants out in the spring. In the South, winter is preferable. Set the plants 2 to 6 feet apart in soil that is slightly acid. You can increase the acidity of the soil by adding peat moss or leaf mold. Zones 4 to 8.

TAMARISK

Tamarisk (*Tamarix pentandra*) is a tall-growing shrub, occasionally reaching a height of 15 feet. The whole plant has a light, airy texture. The flowers are small and pink, and are borne along almost the entire length of the branch. This shrub flowers in July.

Tamarisk should be pruned heavily to keep it within bounds. Since it blooms on the current season's wood, cut it back early in the spring while it is still dormant. This shrub does fairly well in dry soil and is useful at the seashore.

Plant in sandy or alkaline soil in full sun. Tamarisk is most appropriate in informal gardens. Set the plants a foot or so apart to form a clump. Zones 2 to 9.

VINES

Vines are versatile. You will find the solution to many landscape problems through the thoughtful use of vines. Vines serve as screens, ground covers and hiders of unsightly walls and fences. They may be an excellent source of cut flowers, and best of all, they provide plenty of summer color. And most of them don't take up much ground space.

As screens, they give needed privacy; as ground covers, they help stabilize loose banks and hide unsightly bare spots; as coverers of walls and fences, they soften and lessen the ugly intrusion of woven steel, aluminum and concrete into the natural surroundings of your home; as sources of cut flowers, they provide fragrance and beauty for your home; and as for summer color . . . well, that's what you're after in the first place.

BITTERSWEET

Bittersweet (*Celastrus orbiculatus*) is a good choice for bank planting. It will also climb walls and other supports and it thrives in ordinary garden soil. It often reaches a height of 35 feet. Small yellow flowers appear in the summer, followed by orange-colored fruits in the fall.

Bittersweet has male and female flowers that are borne on separate plants. You must have the female plant to bear fruit and the male for pollination. American bittersweet and oriental bittersweet are the most used and are readily available at nurseries.

Plant in the early spring or fall. Mix some peat moss or leaf mold with the soil and pack it firmly around the plants. Zones 4 to 10.

CLEMATIS

Clematis can be a difficult vine to grow. However, its beauty makes it well worth the effort. If you decide to grow clematis, get expert advice from your nurseryman or some other qualified person. A book on the subject of vines will also be of some help. In some areas gardeners have trouble with clematis because it requires a limestone alkaline soil.

The flowers range from wine red to pure white, and come in many shapes—bells, urns, saucers and stars. Some are as small as 1 inch, others are as large as 10 inches across. The plants vary in size from 5 to 50 feet, according to variety. Some species bloom on last year's wood and some bloom on the current season's growth. If you plant the former, prune the plants only after they flower; if the latter, you can prune them (severely if you wish) early in the spring. The species presented here are those that will add color to our summer garden.

Sweet Autumn Clematis (*Clematis paniculata*): Sweet autumn clematis bears small white flowers in late August. It blooms on the current year's growth and is by far the most common and vigorous clematis. It has very dark foliage and fragrant flowers, is very easy to grow, and it is excellent for use as a screen. It usually grows 10 to 15 feet tall, but will often reach 30 feet on a warm wall. Zones 5 to 10.

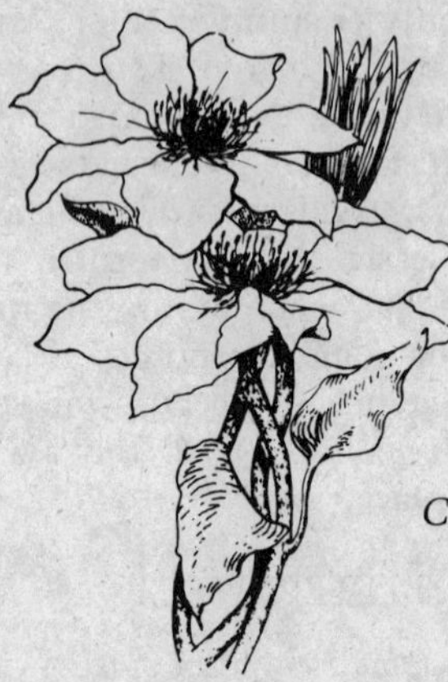

Clematis

Anemone-flowered Clematis (*Clematis montana*): Anemone-flowered clematis is a hybrid with medium-size flowers that appear in June and July. Colors are white, pink or red. It blooms on the previous year's wood. Zones 6 to 10.

Scarlet Clematis (*Clematis texensis*): This distinctive Texas species bears urn-shaped flowers in July. It grows about 6 feet tall. Its main period of bloom is in July, but it will flower sporadically until frost. Scarlet clematis frequently dies back to ground in winter, but sprouts again the following spring. It blooms on current year's growth. Zones 4 to 8.

Jackman Clematis (*Clematis jackmanii*): Jackman clematis is one of the most popular. It blooms in mid-July and the flowers are violet-purple, 5 to 7 inches in diameter. Since it blooms on the current year's wood, it can be heavily pruned early in the spring.

Plant in spring in alkaline soil or a light, loamy soil to which lime has been added. The plant should be in a spot where the top portion receives sun or dappled shade, but where the roots can remain cool. String or other narrow support is necessary because the vine climbs by twisting its leaf stalks around the support.

Many large flowering hybrid clematis (of *jackmanii* and others) are available. A few plants of each variety will provide lasting summer color.

Variety	*Color*
'Prins Hendric'	Azure Blue
'Crimson Star'	Dark Red
'Lord Neville'	Dark Plum
'Comtesse de Bouchaud'	Rose
'Duchess of Edinburgh'	White

Set the plants out in early spring or fall. Plant in a moist, rich, alkaline soil that is well drained. The roots need a cool, shady spot. If winters are severe, it is safer to plant only in the spring. Set the collar of the plant about 2 inches below the surface. Guide the new stems with string until they reach the wall or trellis. When starting young clematis, it is a good idea to train them to grow fanwise. If you don't, you'll end up with a tangled mass of unmanageable foliage. Screen the main stem of each plant from pets. A hungry puppy can quickly do a great deal of damage. Zones 5 to 10.

HONEYSUCKLE

There are many varieties of honeysuckle, but only a few are suitable for adding summer color to your garden. While the two species presented here are not the only ones suitable, they have been chosen because they are relatively easy to grow, they bloom over a long period, and are hardy over most of the United States. Honeysuckle is very ornamental, and grows 15 to 20 feet tall.

Set your plants out in the early spring or fall. Honeysuckle does best in full sun, but will withstand partial shade. For a fence, screen or trellis, set the plants about 2 feet apart.

Halls Honeysuckle (*Lonicera japonica var. halliana*): Halls honeysuckle grows taller than the everblooming variety, often as high as 20 feet. It makes a very good ground cover. The flowers appear in midsummer and continue until fall. They are deep yellow and white and are very fragrant. This species can often be seen growing in the woods in zones 6 and 7, where it is a nuisance. Zones 5 to 9.

Sweet Honeysuckle (*Lonicera caprifolium*): Sweet honeysuckle is the most fragrant species. The flowers appear in early June and are white to pale yellow, trumpet-shaped, about 2 inches long. Zones 6 to 9.

SILVER FLEECE VINE

Silver Fleece Vine (*Polygonum auberti*) is sometimes called the Silver Lace Vine. The flowers appear in August. They form dense clusters and are white, pale green or pink. This vine often reaches a height of 20 to 30 feet. Zones 5 to 10.

TRUMPET VINE

Trumpet Vine (*Campsis radicans*) flowers in July. The flowers are orange to scarlet, trumpet-shaped, and about 2 inches in diameter. Trumpet vine has large leaves, and it will reach a height of 30 feet on a warm wall.

Trumpet vine clings by small rootlike holdfasts. It is rampant and soon becomes very heavy. Trumpet vine grows in almost any soil in full sun. Plant only where there is plenty of room for the vine to spread. Zones 4 to 10.

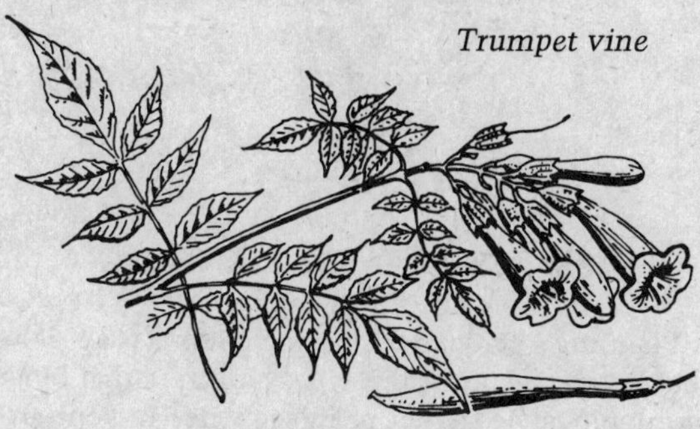

Trumpet vine

A WORD OF CAUTION CONCERNING VINES

A word of caution is necessary concerning vines. Masonry walls are good for vines; wooden walls are easily damaged by the weight of the vine and the moisture held in the foliage.

Do not allow your vines to grow above the rain gutters of your house. Once they become established on rooftops, they are extremely difficult to remove, and if they are not removed, they will cause a great deal of damage to shingles.

Vines that cling, such as the trumpet vine, should be planted close to their supporting wall. The shoots of a clinging vine may need to be held in place until they can establish their own contact. You can do this with waterproof tape.

TREES

Selection of the right kinds of ornamental flowering trees can add summer color to your garden, too. Some suggestions follow.

FRANKLIN TREE

A slow-growing tree, the Franklin Tree (*Franklinia alatamaha*) is a good choice for a shady location and can be planted successfully under a canopy of larger trees. It seldom grows as high as 20 feet. The flowers first appear in August and open continuously for several weeks. They are cup-shaped, white and pleasantly fragrant.

Transplant in the early spring. This tree requires an acid soil and a fairly moist location. Zones 6 to 9.

GOLDEN-RAIN TREE

The Golden-rain Tree (*Koelreuteria paniculata*) is a small but rapidly growing tree that does well in light sandy soils. It grows 15 or 20 feet tall and forms a broad, irregular umbrella of foliage. This tree produces many clusters of deep-yellow flowers in July, which are followed by conspicuous yellow-green fruits that remain on the tree for several weeks.

Transplant in the early spring. This tree will grow in practically any garden soil, but it flowers most freely if planted in a warm sunny place. Zones 6 to 8.

Golden-rain tree

JAPANESE PAGODA TREE

The Japanese Pagoda Tree (*Sophora japonica*) is often called the Chinese Scholar Tree. This graceful and wide-spreading tree does well in a variety of conditions. It grows 40 to 60 feet tall and makes a striking lawn specimen. The flowers appear in August and are followed by clusters of pale-green beanlike pods that often remain on the tree all winter. The flowers are about ½ inch long, yellowish white, pealike, and borne on loose clusters 10 to 15 inches long.

Transplant in early spring. Plant in ordinary garden soil in a well-drained place. Zones 5 to 10.

Japanese pagoda tree

MAACKIA

Maackia (*Maackia amurensis*) is a medium-size tree. The *M. amurensis* grows 40 to 45 feet tall; another species, *M. chinensis,* eventually reaches a height of nearly 70 feet. Other than height, there is little difference between the two species. Both bloom in July and August. The white, pealike flowers appear in erect clusters 4 to 6 inches long.

Plant in the spring or fall. For best blooming, set your plant in a sunny place. Maackia will thrive in practically any soil. Zones 4 to 10.

MIMOSA

Mimosa (*Albizia julibrissin*) is also known as Silk Tree. It blooms in July and August. The flowers are masses of pink stamens on rounded heads. Mimosa will do well in poor, dry, gravelly soil. It blooms on current season's wood, so you should prune it early in the spring while still dormant.

Mimosa

To get the best out of your mimosa, give it winter protection in cooler areas of the country for the first two or three years until it is well established. Mimosa is susceptible to a fungus wilt. The fungus is in the soil, and it kills the tree rapidly and for no cause that is apparent above the ground. There are, however, some wilt-resistant varieties. These are 'Tyron' and 'Charlotte.' Mimosa can reach a height of 36 feet, but heights of 15 to 20 feet are most common. It has several trunks, and the branches are horizontal. It has large, lacy, compound levels. Zones 7 to 10.

SORREL TREE

Sorrel Tree (*Oxydendrum arboreum*) sometimes called Sourwood, may be planted as a lawn or border specimen. This is one of the more beautiful ornamental trees. The flowers appear in July. They are small, white or off-white, and are arranged in loose, drooping clusters about 10 inches long. Its fall foliage is noted for its scarlet brilliance, and it makes an attractive background for the seed clusters, which remain on the tree well into the winter.

Transplant in the spring with a good-size ball of earth. This tree prefers a moist, somewhat acid soil, but will adapt readily to neutral soils if they are not too dry. Zones 5 to 8.

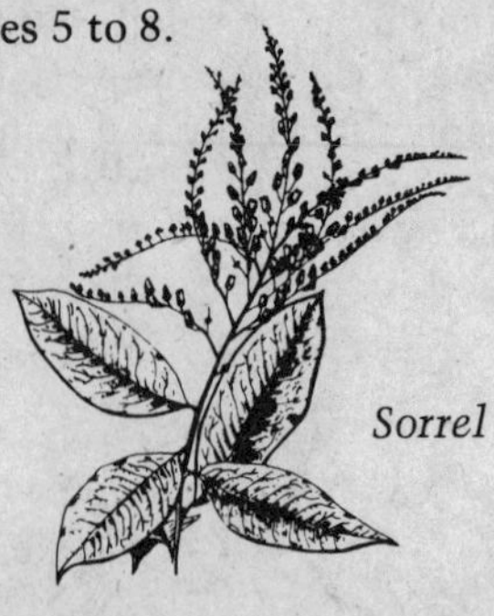

Sorrel tree

SELECTION AND PLANNING

Planning a garden for summer color is easy. Select those varieties of shrubs, vines and trees that bloom harmoniously together or in sequence in your area. Members of local garden clubs are usually good sources of this type of information as well as more specific information concerning those varieties of plants that do well in your locality. Your nurseryman can also help you.

When you have made your decision as to what plants you want to try, the next step is to prepare plant beds. It is important that you set new plants out as soon as you get them so that the roots don't dry out.

Planting shrubs, vines and trees is not difficult. First, loosen up the soil with a shovel or spade. Then mix the loose soil with some peat moss or other organic matter. Before setting the plant in the hole, trim off broken roots and cut back excessively long ones. This is better than winding the roots around in the bottom of the hole.

Set the plants at about the same depth in your garden as they were in the nursery, pack the soil around them and water them thoroughly. Remove weak and broken branches on the plant. Wait until the plant has about 2 inches of new growth before fertilizing.

The instructions given here for planting shrubs, vines and trees are general. Where they differ from the specific instructions given for plants in the list, the specific instructions should be followed.

Follow these simple rules for success in growing vines, shrubs and trees:

- Buy vigorous plants from reputable dealers.
- Set your plants in well-prepared beds.
- Water your plants frequently.
- Prune the plants every year (shrubs and trees).
- Protect your plants from winter injury.
- Spray for insects and disease.
- When cutting flowers from the plant, do so without damaging the remaining part of the plant.

CHAPTER 12

Pruning Ornamental Shrubs and Vines

PRUNING SHOULD START when you plant your shrubs and vines and should be part of a regular maintenance program. You should prune to improve the health of your plants, control size and shape, increase the flower display and remove overcrowded stems or branches.

To improve the health of your plants, cut out dead, diseased or damaged wood and remove old wood that interferes with new growth. Prune your shrubs so they keep their natural shape, unless you use them as formal hedges. Vines need pruning to limit growth and remove old wood. When you prune, avoid damaging shoots and branches that are to remain on the plant.

DECIDUOUS SHRUBS

Deciduous shrubs shed their leaves in the fall. You should prune them to control their size, shape and flowering and to remove dead, diseased or damaged wood. Individual shrubs that keep their natural size and shape need less pruning than hedges that are trimmed to a specific, "designed" size and shape.

You can train an individual shrub to keep its natural shape by thinning branches and stems and by pruning branches back to a bud to control the direction of growth.

The new shoot will grow in the direction the bud points. Before you cut branches or stems, think ahead to how the plant will look when new shoots appear. Then prune the plant the way you want it to grow.

When you prune back to a bud, make the cut on a slant about even with the top of the bud. When removing an entire branch, make the pruning cut flush with the stem. When you cut out dead wood, cut into live wood an inch or two below the dead wood.

Control the size of your shrubs by thinning out disorderly branches and stems. Cut the branches back to larger branches or to the stems. Thin the stems by cutting them back to the ground.

Thinning allows room for the growth of side branches, which make the plant bushier. When you thin the stems, cut out the older, taller stems first.

Do not try to remove all the old stems in one year. Cut out about ⅓ of the stems each year for three years so you will always have a flower display.

Hedges usually need more pruning than other shrubs to give them the shape you want them to have. Cut hedges back about 6 to 8 inches from the ground. Cut the new shoots back 6 to 8 inches from the old growth. Continue this until the hedges reach the desired thickness and height. Then, as new shoots appear, cut them back to a single bud. Prune your hedges as often as necessary during the growing season.

Branches that are diseased, dead or damaged should be pruned as the need arises. Most of this

PROPER PRUNING ANGLE

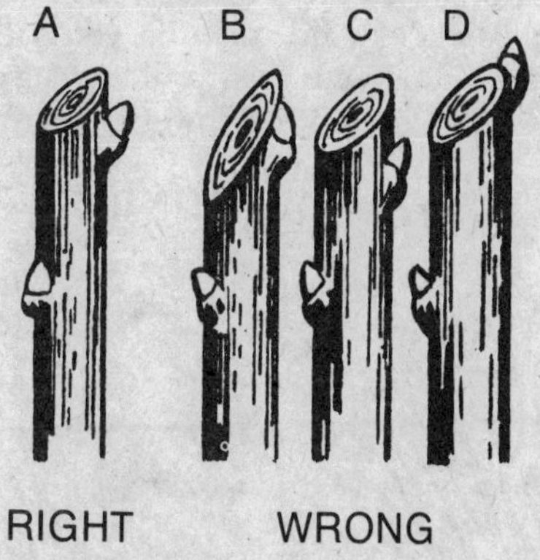

When possible, cut back to a side bud and make the cut at a slant. A is cut correctly. B is too slanting. C is too far from the bud. D is too close to the bud.

PRUNING OVERGROWN PLANTS

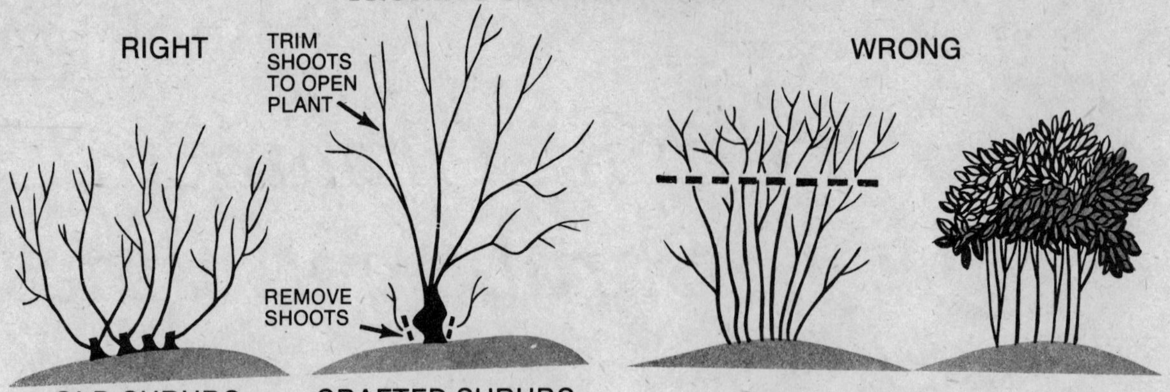

OLD SHRUBS

To prune old shrubs, cut the old stems back to the point at which the branches originate, near the ground.

GRAFTED SHRUBS

When pruning shrubs that have been grafted, always remove new twigs that start below the graft knuckle.

When shrubs are beheaded, as at left, new growth comes only from the top of the plant, resulting in the leggy, bushy-topped shrub shown at the right.

pruning can be done, however, in early spring before growth starts.

You can increase the number and size of flowers for the next year by removing seed pods as soon as they form. And if you prune as little as possible, your shrubs will have more flowers. Some pruning is necessary, but light pruning usually is best; heavy pruning reduces the number of blooms.

Some deciduous shrubs bloom in spring and others in summer. Spring-flowering shrubs bloom until mid-June; summer-flowering shrubs bloom from mid-June into fall. They are pruned at different times of the year and are discussed below.

Spring-flowering Shrubs

The blooms of spring-flowering shrubs are formed on growth produced the previous year. If you prune these shrubs in the winter months, you will remove many of the flower buds that would produce blooms the following spring. Spring-flowering shrubs should be *pruned as soon as the flowers fade* in the spring, before new growth starts. Pruned plants will have larger flowers than unpruned ones.

Some common spring-flowering shrubs and their pruning requirements are as follows:

Almond, Flowering (*Prunus*): Prune branches to shape the plant.

Azalea: Prune branches to promote new growth. Remove sucker shoots from the base of the plant.

Beautybush (*Kolkwitzia*): Prune old wood as necessary to promote new growth.

Barberry (*Berberis*): Prune to shape the plant and to remove old branches so new growth can develop.

Blueberry (*Vaccinium*): Prune small, weak twigs to promote growth of vigorous shoots that will provide more foliage color in the fall.

Broom (*Cytisus*): Prune to control size.

Burningbush (*Euonymus*): Prune to control shape and size when used as a hedge. Remove crowded branches of single plants.

Crab Apple (*Malus*): Prune to shape the plant and to remove old wood so new growth can develop.

Currant (*Ribes*): Remove three-year-old wood to promote new growth.

Deutzia: Remove three-year-old wood to promote new growth.

Dogwood (*Cornus florida* and *C. mas*): Prune three-year-old stems of shrubs to promote new growth. Trees may be grown to their natural shape without pruning.

Elder (*Sambucus nigra*): Prune to shape the plant.

Enkianthus, Redvein (*Enkianthus campanulatus*): Prune to shape the plant. Only slight pruning is needed.

Firethorn (*Pyracantha*): Prune lightly to control size

TYPES OF PRUNING

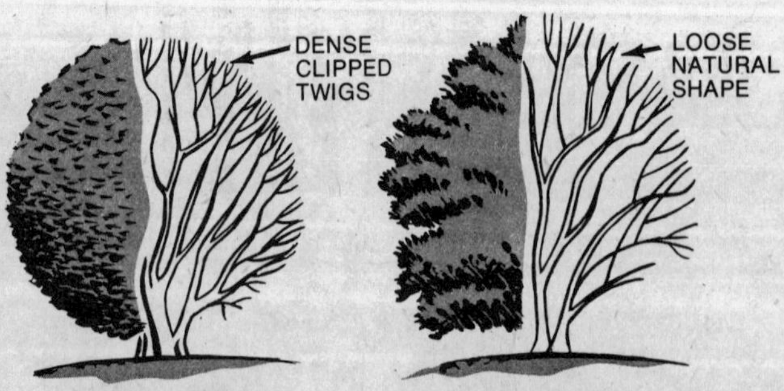

FORMAL INFORMAL

CONTROLLING SHAPE

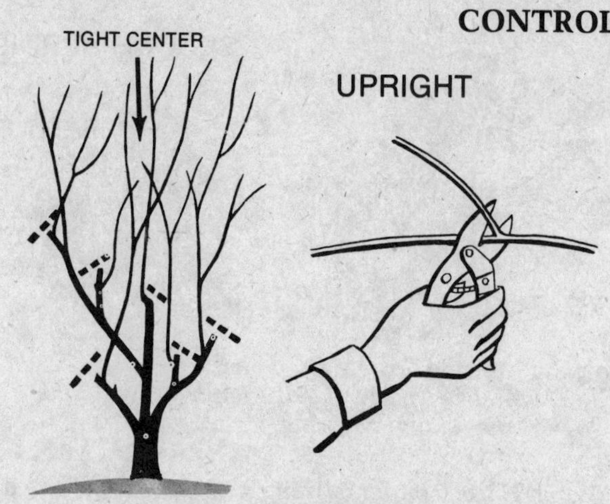

To change the shape of a plant, cut it back to where a branch or twig grows in the direction you want the plant to grow.

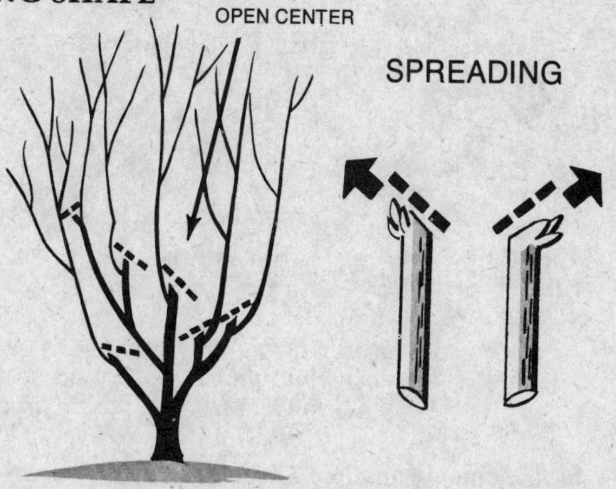

You can control the direction of the new growth by cutting back to a side bud that points in the direction you want the branch to grow. New growth will follow the dotted line.

and shape. Severe pruning reduces the number of berries on the plant.

Forsythia: Cut old stems to the ground as necessary to promote new growth.

Fringetree (*Chionanthus virginicus*): Prune old stems and branches as necessary to control size.

Garlandflower (*Daphne cneorum*): Prune to control size and shape. Severe pruning may be needed to keep the plant from becoming ragged.

Heath (*Erica*): Prune to promote new growth. Severe pruning may be needed.

Honeysuckle (*Lonicera*): Prune old stems and branches as necessary to control size and promote new growth.

Hydrangea (*Hydrangea macrophylla hortensis*): Prune after flowering to promote new growth. Winter damage to flower buds may cause plants to produce only foliage and no flowers. When this happens, prune in summer after plants would have flowered; do not prune in winter or early spring.

Kerria: Prune old wood to promote new growth.

Lilac (*Syringa*): Remove suckers and old flowers.

Magnolia (*Magnolia stellata*): Remove seed pods and, when necessary, prune branches to shape the plant.

Mockorange (*Philadelphus*): Prune three-year-old wood to promote new growth.

Ninebark (*Physocarpus*): Prune crowded stems as necessary to thin them and to promote new growth.

Pearlbush (*Exochorda*): Thin branches to promote new growth and to make the plant bushier and less leggy.

Privet (*Ligustrum*): Cut four-year-old wood to the ground to promote new growth. Clip several times in summer to shape the plants when used as a hedge.

Quince, Flowering (*Chaenomeles*): Cut out old wood as necessary to promote new growth.

Rockspray (*Cotoneaster*): Prune branches to control size and shape.

Rose (*Rosa*): Prune shrub roses to shape the plant and thin crowded branches; cut stems back to a

HEDGE PRUNING

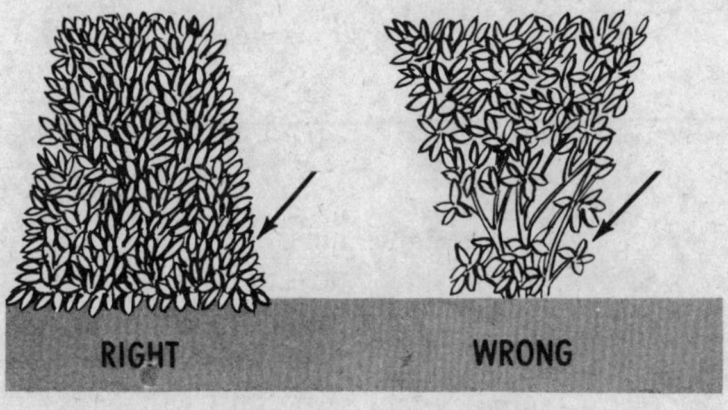

BEST WOOD TO PRUNE FOR RAPID REGROWTH

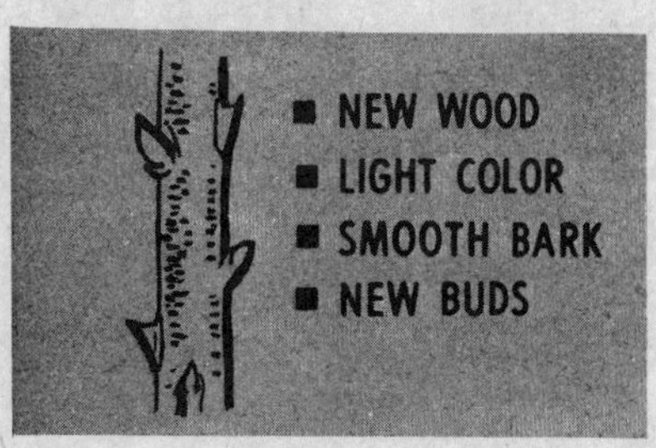

SPRING-FLOWERING SHRUBS

Prune only before vegetative buds begin to grow. Cutting flowers from plants is a good way to prune. Do not prune in fall or winter because this will remove flower buds that would produce flowers the following spring.

healthy bud. Cut some of the old stems of rambling and climbing roses back to young shoots every year to thin the plants and promote new growth and larger flowers.

Shadbush (*Amelanchier*): Prune old stems and branches as necessary to control size.

Snowball (*Styrax*): Prune to shape the plant and to remove crowded branches. To grow plant as a tree, cut out all stems except one; to grow as a shrub, leave several stems.

Spirea (*Spiraea*): Some common early flowering types are Bridal-wreath, Garland, Reeves, Thunberg, and Vanhoutte. Remove three-year-old wood and prune branches to shape the plant.

Sweetshrub (*Calycanthus floridus*): Prune old stems and branches as necessary to control size.

Tamarisk (*Tamarix parviflora, T. tetrandra,* and *T. juniperina*): Prune stems and branches to control size and shape. Cut old stems to the ground if they become leggy and tall.

Viburnum: Many kinds of viburnum are grown for flowers and fruit. Some of the more common kinds are *Viburnum burkwoodi, V. carlesi, V. fragrans, V. opulus, V. macrocephalum, V. sieboldi,* and *V. tomentosum mariesi.* Prune to control shape and height.

Weigela: Prune old branches and thin new growth as necessary to prevent crowding.

Witch Hazel (*Hamamelis mollis*): Cut out old wood to control size and promote new growth.

Summer-flowering Shrubs

The blooms of summer-flowering shrubs grow on wood produced the same season. These shrubs should be *pruned in the dormant season,* usually in early spring before growth begins.

Some common summer-flowering shrubs and their pruning requirements are as follows:

Abelia: Prune to control size and shape, and cut out crowded branches and stems to promote new growth. To keep the plant compact, remove wild shoots when they appear.

Beautyberry (*Callicarpa japonica*): Cut stems about 12 inches from the ground every year to promote new growth.

Bladder Senna (*Colutea*): Cut stems to the ground every year to promote new growth.

Bluebeard (*Caryopteris*): Cut stems to the ground every year to promote new growth.

Bushclover (*Lespedeza*): Prune to shape the plant; cut top growth to control the height.

Butterflybush (*Buddleia davidii*): Cut stems to the ground every year to promote new growth and produce large flower stalks.

SUMMER-FLOWERING SHRUBS

Prune in late fall to early spring before growth starts. Pruning after growth starts removes flower buds that would form blooms.

Chaste-tree (*Vitex*): Cut stems about 6 to 12 inches from the ground to promote new growth.

Coralberry (*Symphoricarpos*): Prune stems back to three or four buds. Cut out crowded stems and branches as necessary.

Crapemyrtle (*Lagerstroemia*): Prune to control shape and produce flowers. Lack of pruning will cause plant to produce small flowers or none; heavy pruning is needed for vivid flower displays. Plant may be grown as a compact shrub or as a tree.

Elder, Red Berry (*Sambucus pubens*): Prune to shape the plant.

Elaeagnus: Every few years, prune to shape the plant and promote new growth.

Heather (*Calluna*): Cut stems to the ground to promote new growth and more flowers. Do not prune in summer or winter because plants will die; prune only in early spring before new growth starts.

Hibiscus (*Hibiscus rosa-sinensis*): Prune stems, leaving two buds, to shape the plant and promote flowering.

Honeysuckle, Bush (*Diervilla*): Prune to the ground to control spreading growth and to retain compact appearance.

Hydrangea (*Hydrangea paniculata* and *H. arborescens*): Prune back to a few buds to promote new growth, and cut out crowded stems as necessary.

Indigobush (*Amorpha*): Prune out old wood as necessary to promote new growth.

Magnolia (*Magnolia virginiana*): Cut back tips to new shoots when necessary to shape the plant. Do not prune branches except when a badly shaped plant must be reshaped.

Mintshrub (*Elsholtzia*): Cut stems to the ground every year to promote new growth.

New Jersey-tea (*Ceanothus*): Cut stems about 6 inches from the ground every year to promote new growth.

Raspberry, Flowering (*Rubus*): Cut back stems after flowering to promote new growth.

Rose (*Rosa*): Prune all types of roses in summer when the flowers fade. Follow the instructions given for pruning spring-flowering roses (see page 127).

St. Johns-wort (*Hypericum*): Cut out crowded branches, and cut other branches back, leaving about two buds on each branch to promote new growth.

Snowberry (*Symphoricarpos*): Prune stems back to a few buds. Cut out crowded stems and branches as necessary.

Spirea (*Spiraea*): Some common summer-flowering types are 'Anthony Waterer,' *bumalda*, Japanese and Billiard. Cut out crowded stems as necessary, and cut other stems back to a few buds. Remove seed pods when they form.

Spirea, False (*Sorbaria*): Prune heavily every three or four years to control rapid growth; remove seed pods each year.

Stephanandra: Prune out small, cold-damaged twigs.

Sumac (*Rhus*): The common types are staghorn and smooth sumac. Prune the stems to the ground to promote new growth. Sumac can be trained to grow as a tree when only one stem is allowed to grow.

SPECIAL PRUNING PROBLEMS

SHAPING PLANTS

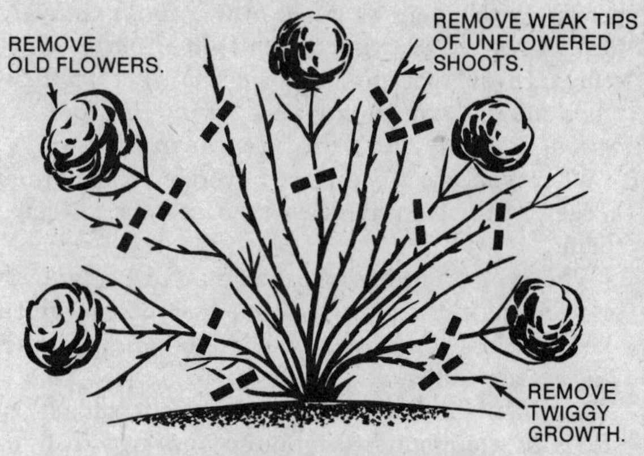
REMOVE OLD FLOWERS.
REMOVE WEAK TIPS OF UNFLOWERED SHOOTS.
REMOVE TWIGGY GROWTH.

REMOVING SEED PODS

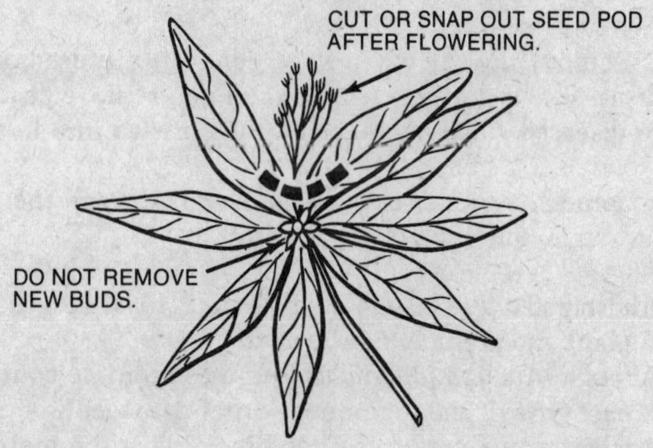
CUT OR SNAP OUT SEED POD AFTER FLOWERING.
DO NOT REMOVE NEW BUDS.

Summersweet (*Clethra*): Prune to control shape and spreading growth.

Tamarisk (*Tamarix hispida, T. pentandra,* and *T. odessana*): Remove seed pods when they form. If plants become ragged and unattractive, cut them back to the ground to promote new growth.

EVERGREEN SHRUBS

Evergreen shrubs are plants that have leaves on them throughout the year. They do not shed all their leaves at one time and their branches are not bare in winter.

Evergreens should be pruned to control their shape and size, to remove dead, diseased or damaged wood, and to remove old branches to allow for new growth. Usually evergreens need less pruning than deciduous shrubs.

Some evergreens are broad-leaved and some are coniferous, or narrow-leaved. The pruning requirements of the two types are different.

Broad-leaved Evergreens

Broad-leaved evergreens that go into the dormant period with their *swelled flower buds already formed should be pruned immediately after flowering.* Those that produce their *flowers on new wood may be pruned any time during the dormant period, or if they bear fruit, after the fruit ripens.*

When you use broad-leaved evergreens as formal hedges, trim them as often as necessary to shape them.

When you prune branches to promote new growth or to shape the plant, cut back to a bud or green shoot. Unless you leave a bud or shoot, new growth will not appear.

If a plant has several stems, cut the old, leggy stems to the ground to promote new growth from the base of the plant. Do not cut back all the old stems in one year. Cut some of them each year for two or three years.

Remove flowers when they fade. Cut out dead or diseased wood at any time. When you remove dead or diseased wood, cut back an inch or two into live wood or to a bud.

Some common broad-leaved evergreens and their pruning requirements are as follows:

Andromeda (*Pieris japonica*): Prune to shape the plant and promote new growth.

Aucuba (*Aucuba japonica*): Prune to promote compact growth and to remove winter-damaged wood.

Azalea: Prune branches after flowering to promote new growth; cut back leggy stems.

Blueberry, Box (*Vaccinium*): Prune to promote new growth.

Box (*Buxus*): Cut branches and stems to keep the plant compact.

Camellia (*Camellia japonica* and *C. sasanqua*): Cut out old wood to promote new growth and improve flowering.

Cherry Laurel (*Prunus*): Cut back old stems and branches to control size and shape.

Holly (*Ilex*): Prune to control size and shape.

Hollygrape (*Mahonia*): Cut back the stems to keep them from becoming leggy.

Holly Osmanthus (*Osmanthus*): Prune to shape the plant.

Inkberry (*Ilex*): Prune to control size and shape.

Leucothoë (*Leucothoë catesbaei*): Cut out old stems when they become crowded.

Mountain Laurel (*Kalmia*): When plants get too large, cut some of the old stems to the ground to promote new growth.

Nandina (*Nandina domestica*): Prune out old stems to promote new growth.

Oleander (*Nerium oleander*): Prune top and branches to control size.

Privet (*Ligustrum*): Japanese and glossy privets are evergreen. Prune to control size and shape.

Rhododendron: Prune branches after flowering to promote new growth. Cut leggy stems in early spring.

Skimmia (*Skimmia japonica*): Prune to shape the plant.

Coniferous Evergreens

Many coniferous evergreens can become large trees. If you want to slow their growth, prune the roots in early spring before growth starts. Cut the ends of the roots by digging around the plant about ⅓ of the way in from the tips of the branches. The plants that may need root pruning are fir, spruce, red cedar, pine and juniper.

It is best to prune coniferous evergreens in May or June when the buds and shoots are newly formed. If the plants are pruned every year, pruning usually can be limited to cutting back part or all of the new growth. When branches need more severe pruning, cut them back to a growing shoot shortly before or just as growth starts in the spring. Trim formal hedges as often as necessary to shape them and to thin out the shoots.

You can remove the top leaders of coniferous evergreens to keep the plants shorter and more dense. If you leave the top leader, the plant will grow taller and more open. If two leaders develop, cut out the weaker one.

Some common coniferous evergreens and their pruning requirements are as follows:

Arborvitae (*Thuja*): Prune both American and Oriental arborvitae before growth starts in early spring and again in June. Clip ragged branches in early spring to shape the plant; prune new growth in June to control size and shape.

False Cypress (*Chamaecyparis*): Prune new growth to control size and shape.

Fir (*Abies*): Cut back new shoots (candles) about halfway to promote new side growth.

Hemlock (*Tsuga*): Prune new growth to control size and shape.

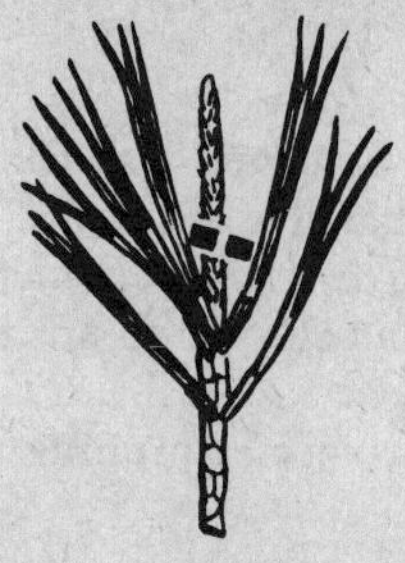

Prune pines in late spring by removing one-half of the candle, or new shoot. Do not damage needle tips because the tips of cut needles tend to turn brown.

You can reduce open spaces on spruces by cutting off one-half of the leader, or terminal shoot, in the spring when the new needles are about half developed.

Keep side branches from growing out of bounds by removing the terminal bud. This not only slows outward growth but also helps to make the plants more bushy.

You can replace a lost leader by tying one of the branches in the top whorl to a vertical brace.

Trees that have already grown too wide can be narrowed by cutting the branches back to an inner bud.

If the tree develops two leaders, remove the less desirable one in early spring. Trees with more than one leader are weaker and less attractive than trees that have a single, strong, central leader.

Juniper (*Juniperus*): Prune ragged branches in early spring and clip new growth in June to control size and shape. You may need to cut out some branches completely if they become overcrowded.

Pine (*Pinus*): Cut back candles about halfway to promote new side growth.

Red Cedar (*Juniperus*): Prune ragged branches in early spring and clip new growth in June to control size and shape.

Spruce (*Picea*): Cut back candles about halfway to promote new side growth.

Yew (*Taxus*): Prune ragged branches in early spring and clip new growth in June to control size and shape.

VINES

Vines usually need pruning to limit growth, to thin the stems and branches, and to remove dead wood. Some vines grow so thick and fast that considerable pruning is necessary. Others need little pruning.

Prune spring-flowering clematis after flowering. Prune all other vines in the dormant season. Thin crowded stems by cutting them to the ground. To limit growth, cut tops and branches back as far as necessary. Cut dead or diseased branches back to healthy wood.

Some common vines and their pruning requirements are as follows:

Bittersweet (*Celastrus*): Prune stems each year, leaving three or four buds, to promote new growth. Cut back the top to make the plant branch.

Clematis: Thin stems and branches to promote new growth. Use care when pruning because the stems are very brittle and easily damaged.

Dutchman's Pipe (*Aristolochia*): Cut back the top to control size and make the plant branch. Thin the stems to promote new growth.

Honeysuckle (*Lonicera*): Thin stems and branches to promote new growth.

Silverfleece Vine (*Polygonum*): Cut stems back to the ground each year to promote all new growth.

Trumpet Creeper (*Campsis*): Prune stems each year, leaving three or four buds, to promote new growth. Cut back the top to make the plant branch.

Wintercreeper (*Euonymus*): When used as ground cover, prune the top growth to keep it close to the ground. When used as a wall cover, clip branches to control spreading.

Winter Jasmine (*Jasminum*): Thin stems and branches to promote new growth.

Wisteria: Prune back to three or four buds each year to promote new growth and to produce flowers. Cut back the top to make the plant branch.

Woodbine (*Parthenocissus*): Prune branches to control spreading.

PRUNING TOOLS

The basic tools for pruning are hand shears, pruning saw and lopping shears.

Hand shears are used to cut twigs, small branches and vines. When you use this tool, cut straight through the wood. If you twist the blade as you cut, the wound will be ragged and take longer to heal.

A pruning saw is used to cut branches and stems that are too large for shears. A saw with a narrow curved blade and coarse teeth set wide is best for pruning shrubs that have branches growing close together.

Lopping shears have long handles and are used to prune larger and tougher branches than hand shears will cut. Also, the long handles are useful to reach high branches and to reach through branches with spiny leaves. As with hand shears, do not twist the blade when you cut.

You may need to rent special pruning tools for difficult pruning jobs.

Keep your pruning tools sharp so they will make smooth, clean cuts. To help prevent disease and decay, disinfect all tools with denatured alcohol after pruning diseased parts of plants.

PRUNING EQUIPMENT

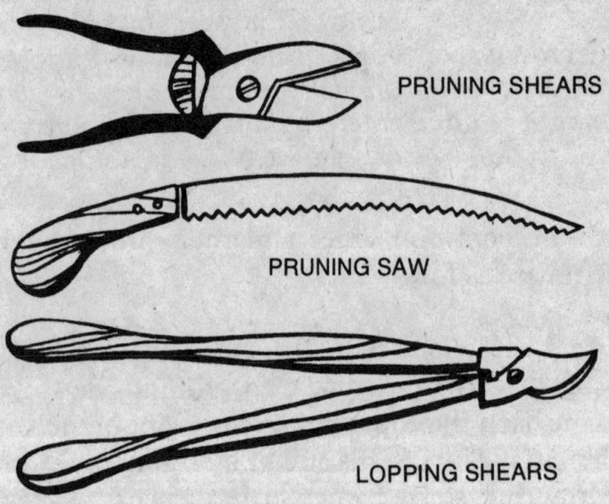

These are essential pruning tools. They should be kept sharp, or they will make a ragged, slow-healing cut.

TREATING WOUNDS

Small pruning cuts of less than 1 inch in diameter usually heal quickly if they are smooth and at an angle so water does not stand in them. But you should treat wounds over 1 inch in diameter to prevent decay, disease and penetration by insects while the wound is healing.

The best wound dressing is asphalt varnish containing an antispetic. An antiseptic prevents the spread of harmful organisms that may contaminate the treating material. Asphalt varnish containing an antiseptic is available at most garden-supply stores.

If you cannot get a dressing containing antiseptic, use ordinary asphalt varnish. Before applying plain asphalt varnish, swab the wound with alcohol or coat it with shellac.

Apply the dressing as soon as the wound is dry. Asphalt varnish will not stick if the wound is wet.

One coat of dressing will last two to three years. This usually is long enough for the wound to heal. Inspect wounds periodically and apply additional dressing if the coating is cracked or peeling.

Coniferous evergreens usually seal small wounds with natural resin. If no resin forms, treat the wounds with asphalt dressing.

VI

GROWING TREES

CHAPTER 13

Selecting and Growing Shade Trees

SHADE TREES MAY BE DIVIDED into two main groups: deciduous and evergreen. Deciduous trees produce new leaves in spring. These leaves die and drop at the end of the growing season. Evergreen trees hold their leaves for one or more years.

Both deciduous and evergreen trees may be either broadleaf or needle leaf. Broadleaf trees bear leaves that have broadly expanded blades. Maples, oaks and magnolias are broadleaf trees. Needle-leaf trees have narrow, linear, needlelike leaves. Pine, larch and spruce are needle-leaf trees.

Some kinds of trees have no leaves but have green twigs that function as leaves. Casuarina is a leafless tree. Scale-leaf trees have flattened, scalelike leaves that lie flat against the twigs. Arborvitae is a scale-leaf tree.

The size and form of different kinds of shade trees vary greatly, and individual trees may deviate widely from the standard. The size and form of some common shade trees compared to the size of a house are shown in the illustration on page 136.

Branching habits also differ among the many species. Some of the general branching habits of shade trees are shown in the illustration on page 137.

Deciduous trees generally grow faster than evergreens, but the growth rate varies among all kinds of trees. Also, the rate of growth depends on soil fertility, rainfall and temperature.

The life of a shade tree varies with species, climate and soil. In densely populated cities, and especially in some industrial areas, the lives of many trees are much shorter than in suburban or rural areas. Diseases, insects, improper care and air pollution also can shorten a shade tree's life.

Cold hardiness is the primary requirement to consider when you select a shade tree. Some species are intolerant of high temperatures. Heat and drought resistance usually are linked. By watering, however, you can grow some species in hot, dry climates where they would not otherwise survive. In areas of low rainfall, drought-resistant species require less care than trees that must be watered.

You should consider the rate of growth of different kinds of trees. In general, trees that grow rapidly have weak wood that is easily damaged by storms and decay. Slower-growing trees have stronger wood. However, if you want quick shade, the use of fast-growing trees may be desirable.

Also consider the size and shape of trees at maturity. A tree 35 feet tall at maturity is acceptable on the average city lot with a one-story house, but a tree 50 to 100 feet high would be too tall. However, large trees may be suitable for large yards.

A few suggestions may help you avoid certain problems. Roots of elms, willows, poplars and maples, for example, can clog sewers. Do not plant these trees near drainage pipes. Avoid planting trees beneath telephone and power lines. Trees that grow over the roof of a house can fill the gutters with leaves; but these trees also shade the house from the hot summer sun.

In general, you should not select a young tree with a divided lower trunk because it might split.

Some trees such as horsechestnut produce hard, poisonous fruits. The thorny fruits of sweetgum and some other trees can be a nuisance in lawns. Fruits of ginkgo smell bad when they decay. Plant only male ginkgo to avoid producing smelly fruits.

Trees such as Siberian elm, poplar, red maple, and mimosa produce abundant fruits, seeds and seedlings that can become a nuisance in lawns and gardens. Some trees, such as the black locust, sprout from the roots and the sprouts often interfere with lawn mowing. One species of eucalyptus harbors rats in its old foliage. Dry foliage hanging on the trunks of palm trees can be a fire hazard.

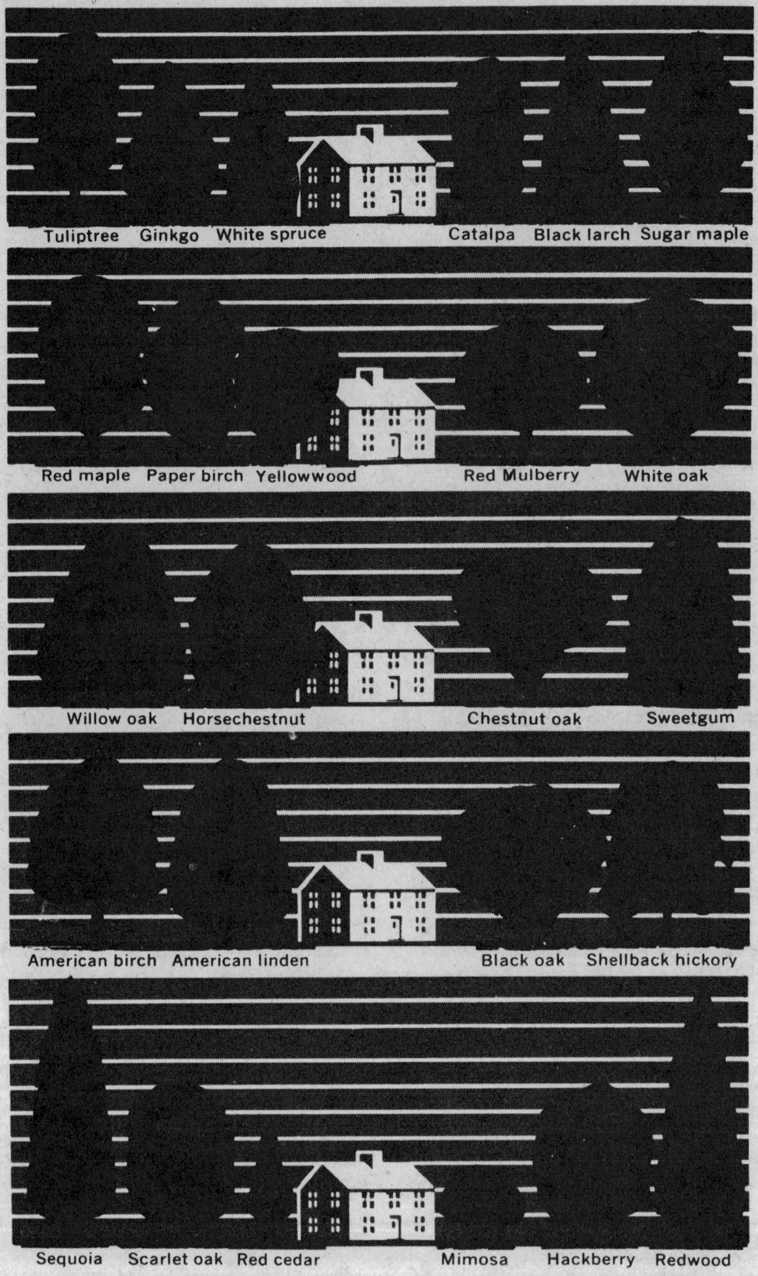

Size of mature shade trees in relation to the height of a 2-story house. Each horizontal line represents 10 feet.

It is difficult to find a species with no faults. Balance the faults of trees against their good qualities in deciding what kind to plant.

BUYING AND PLANTING SHADE TREES

You can obtain shade trees with the soil held around their roots by burlap, wire or plastic. These are known as balled and burlapped trees. Trees that are sold in containers are commonly known as container-grown trees, and those without soil on the roots are called bare-rooted trees.

The chances of survival usually are high for balled and burlapped and container-grown trees. Balled and burlapped trees should have a rootball of 1 foot in diameter for each inch of diameter of the tree trunk.

Nursery-grown trees are more likely to survive than trees dug from the woods. Root systems of nursery-grown trees usually are compact and less likely to be injured seriously when they are dug. Many arborists, nurserymen and landscape contractors guarantee their trees for at least 1 year after they plant them.

Trees with a trunk diameter of 1.5 to 3 inches may be planted with bare roots. Larger trees should be balled and burlapped; when transplanted, the roots should be disturbed as little as possible. Generally, as trees get larger, they cost more to buy and transplant. Get a professional tree mover to move large trees.

Planting Seasons

The most favorable planting season for shade trees varies with the region, kind of tree, soil, source of planting stock and method of handling. Method of handling refers to the way that trees are grown, dug, stored and transported.

Deciduous Trees

In general, you should plant bare-rooted deciduous trees in autumn after their leaves change color and before the ground freezes; you can also plant them in late winter, or early spring after the ground has thawed, but before buds start to grow.

Spring is considered the best time to plant in areas where the ground freezes deeply, where strong winds prevail or where soil moisture is deficient. The drying effects of strong winds can be reduced if you water the trees and wrap their trunks and larger limbs with burlap or special protective paper.

Evergreen Trees

In cold regions, needle-leaf evergreens such as pine, spruce, juniper and arborvitae usually are planted early in the fall or in spring after the ground has thawed. However, you may plant needle-leaf evergreens that are balled and burlapped or in containers any time the ground in cold regions is workable, but you must mulch and water them after planting.

In warm regions, you may plant needle-leaf evergreens at any time if you water them regularly after planting. Small needle-leaf evergreens will live in warm regions if planted bare-rooted but large ones will survive better if they are balled and burlapped.

Spring is the best season to plant such broadleaf evergreens as magnolia and holly; but you can plant them in autumn if you allow time for the roots to grow before the ground freezes.

The best time to plant palms is during warm, wet months; but you can plant them any time if you keep them watered after planting.

Temporary Storage

Trees should be planted as soon as possible after they are dug. If you must hold them for several days, keep the roots moist. Roots die if they dry out.

Sprinkle the roots of balled and burlapped trees as often as needed to keep the soil from drying out. Sprinkle the tops on windy or hot days. You may cover the tops and roots of balled and burlapped trees with plastic or canvas, or with plastic over wet burlap. *Do not let the roots dry out.*

Bare-rooted trees that cannot be planted immediately after they are delivered may be heeled-in. To heel-in a tree, dig a trench with one sloping side. Spread the roots in the trench with the trunk resting against the sloping side. Then cover the roots with soil or a loose, moist mulch of straw, peat moss or similar material. Keep the mulch moist until the trees are planted. Protect the tops of heeled-in trees as much as possible from drying winds. Locate the heeling-in bed in a shady place if possible.

BRANCHING HABITS OF TREES

TRUNK SINGLE,
BRANCHES HORIZONTAL
WHITE PINE

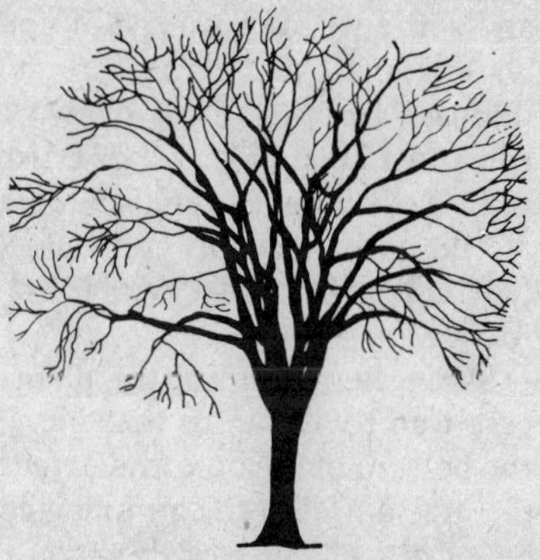

TRUNK DIVIDING,
BRANCHES SPREADING
ELM

BRANCHES PENDULANT
WILLOW

BRANCHES ASCENDING
WHITE OAK

Spacing

Plant shade trees as far apart as their mature limb spread is expected to be so they can develop fully without crowding each other. You should plant most trees at least 30 feet from a house. On narrow streets and in congested areas, use trees that are relatively small at maturity.

Preparing the Planting Hole

Dig the planting hole for bare-rooted trees wide enough to spread the roots in their natural position. Do not double back the roots. The planting hole for a balled and burlapped or container-grown tree should be about 2 feet wider than the diameter of the rootball or container so fertile soil can be put around the roots.

The hole should be deep enough for the tree to be planted as deep as it was originally. However, if the soil is poorly drained, the hole should be at least a foot deeper than required for planting so a drainage system can be installed.

Planting holes must be well drained for most trees to grow satisfactorily. Most trees will not grow well and some will not survive if you plant them where water stands for even a short time. You can provide drainage by putting one or two lines of 3- or 4-inch tile and a layer of gravel or crushed rock in the bottom of the hole. For holes 5 to 6 feet across, one line of tile usually is sufficient. For holes more than 6 feet across, at least two lines of tile are recommended.

Slope the bottom of the planting hole so that excess water will run to the side. Place the tile across the bottom of the hole and extend it beyond the hole to a free outlet. If the ground is level, the outlet may be a dry well filled with gravel or a storm sewer. If the ground is sloping, the tile may be extended from the bottom of the planting hole to the surface of the ground farther down the slope. Never connect the tile to a sanitary sewer because the tree roots can grow into sanitary sewers and clog them.

After you lay the tile, carefully spread enough gravel or crushed rock over the bottom of the hole to hold the tile in place and cover it. Put glass cloth or roofing paper over the tile to help keep soil out of the drainage system. Then spread 2 to 3 inches of fertile soil over the cloth or paper.

If the soil is low in fertility, mix fertilizer with the soil. Well-decayed leaf mold, steamed bonemeal or similar organic material may be used. For trees 6 to 10 feet tall, mix about ½ pound of 5–10–5, 4–12–4, or a similar complete fertilizer with each 4 bushels of filling soil. The fertilizer will help stimulate early growth.

Most shade trees tolerate a considerable range of soil acidity but for best growth, some require an acid soil, some a nearly neutral soil and some an alkaline soil. Usually, county agricultural agents, state agricultural experiment stations or state agricultural colleges will test soil to determine acidity and the need for fertilizer. Some states charge a fee for the service.

Setting the Tree

A tree with a trunk 6 inches or more in diameter should be set with the trunk facing the same direction it was in at its original site. You may plant smaller trees without regard to orientation.

When you plant a tree with bare roots, hold it in place while you adjust the roots to their natural position in the hole and cover them with soil. If you removed fertile loam from the hole, use it to cover the roots. Loam usually is sufficiently permeable to air and water for good growth of shade trees.

Heavy clay soil has poor permeability. You can make it more permeable by mixing it with as much sand as necessary to obtain good percolation of water. You can make sandy soil less permeable by mixing it with loam, clay and organic material such as peat moss. Do not use fresh manure or fresh green plant material in the planting hole because when these materials decay they release compounds that are toxic to tree roots.

Work the soil around the roots and pack it with a blunt tool. Gently sway and shake small trees in all directions to settle the soil around the roots and to eliminate air pockets. Continue to tamp and pack the soil as you add it. When the roots are covered, tamp the soil so that it is settled firmly around the roots. Do not tamp wet soil.

Before you fill the hole completely, add water to settle the soil. When the water has soaked into the soil, add enough soil to complete the backfill. Do not pack this soil. Then put a ridge of soil around the rim to form a low basin to hold water over the root area.

Set balled and burlapped trees in the hole with the burlap around the rootball. If the hole is too deep, lift small trees and add soil to raise the ball to the proper level. If the tree is too heavy to lift, rock it back and forth in all directions and ram soil beneath the ball until it is at the proper height. Loosen the burlap and drop it from the side of the ball. Burlap does not have to be removed from beneath the ball.

A hard crust sometimes forms on the surface of the ball. Break the crust before filling the planting hole. Pack the filling soil as it is added. Settle it with water the same as for bare-rooted trees.

If the tree is in a container, cut away the sides of the container with metal shears and remove the rootball carefully. After you remove the tree from the container, plant it the same way you plant a balled and burlapped tree.

Newly planted trees usually need support to hold them in position and to keep the roots from loosening and the crowns from breaking. Unsupported trees often lean permanently away from prevailing winds. To prevent this, install bracing stakes before you cover the roots.

One to three wooden stakes usually will support trees that have a trunk diameter of no more than 2 inches. The wooden stakes should be 6 to 9 feet long and 2 to 2½ inches square. The stakes should be strong enough to hold the trunk rigidly in place.

Set the stakes 3 to 18 inches from the trunk before you fill the planting hole. Fasten the trunk to the stakes with canvas tape or loops of wire passed through a section of rubber or plastic hose or similar material. Bare wire will scrape or cut the bark.

A tree with a trunk diameter of more than 2 inches usually needs three guy wires to hold it securely in place. Fix the guy wires so they can be tightened as needed. Fasten one wire to a stake driven securely in the ground on the side of the tree that is against the prevailing winds. Fasten the other two wires to stakes driven into the ground so that all three stakes form an equilateral triangle.

The stakes should slope away from the tree at approximately a right angle to the slope of the guy wires. You may use a heavy log or beam (deadman) instead of a stake to anchor the guy wires. Fasten the guy wires about ⅔ of the way up the trunk of the tree. Remove the stakes and wires as soon as the tree roots are firmly established in the ground—usually in about a year.

Steps in Planting

The steps in planting shade trees follow:

- Select the tree and decide when and where to plant it.
- Protect the roots from drying.
- Dig a hole large enough to hold the entire root system.
- Make certain that drainage from the hole is good.
- Prune the top of the tree as needed to compensate for roots lost in digging and moving.
- Put some fertile soil in the hole.
- Set the tree in the hole no deeper than it was at its original site.
- Install supporting stakes.
- Cover the roots with fertile soil, tamping it or settling it with water.
- Wrap the trunk and large limbs with a protective covering such as a burlap or paper.
- Install guy wires.
- Care for the tree after planting.

CARE AFTER PLANTING

Water trees as needed during the first and second growing seasons after you plant them. Watering thoroughly once a week is better than light daily watering. Do not saturate the soil so much that you can squeeze water from it by hand.

Frequent light misting of the tops of newly planted evergreens in early morning or late afternoon will help the leaves. Evergreens planted in autumn should be watered frequently to provide them

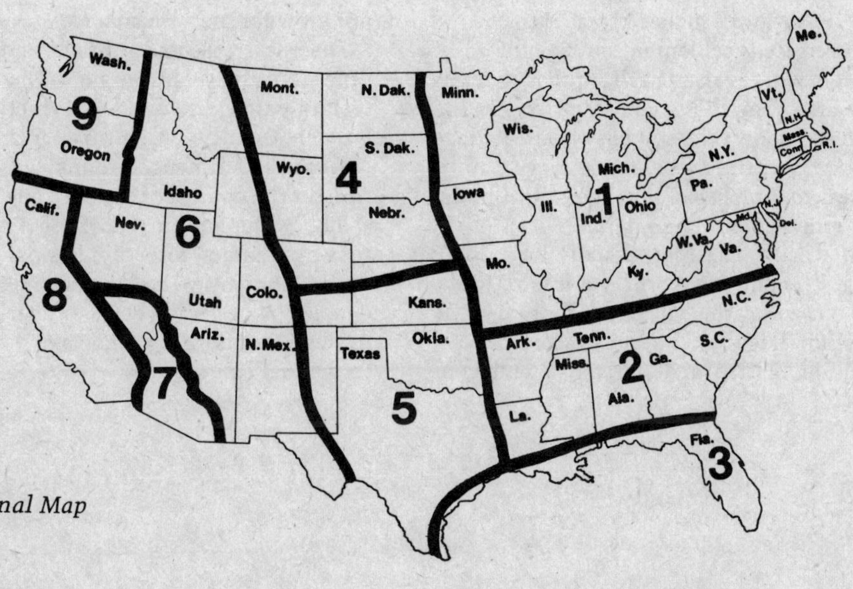

Regional Map

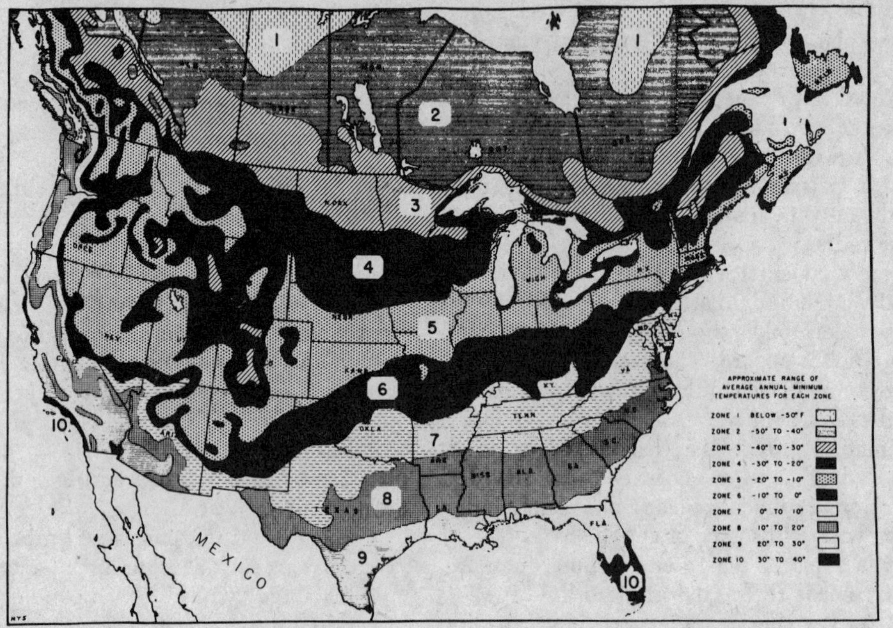

Plant Hardiness Zone Map

with plenty of soil moisture before the ground freezes.

To protect the trunk of a newly planted deciduous tree from drying and from pests, wrap it spirally with strips of burlap or specially prepared paper. You can use strips of kraft paper but special crepe paper is easier to handle. Some wraps are treated to increase protection against trunk-boring insects.

Overlap each turn of paper half the width of the strip. Reinforce the wrapping with stout cord wrapped spirally in the direction opposite to that of the paper. Tie the cord at intervals as necessary to hold the paper in place. Leave the wrap on the trunk for 2 years. If it rots away sooner, replace it.

Trunks of evergreens seldom need wrapping.

When you plant trees in the fall, mulch them as soon as you plant them. When you plant trees in the spring, mulch them after the soil has warmed. Place the mulch over the entire root area and leave it until it decays. Use 2 to 3 inches of peat moss, leaf mold, pine needles, straw or similar material.

Trees planted with bare roots usually have some roots missing. To compensate for the loss of roots, prune out about ⅓ of the top. New roots usually will grow within a few weeks and restore normal water absorption. Balled and burlapped and container-grown trees usually need no pruning when planted. Pruning at this time is not necessary in humid areas.

After trees are established, you should prune them to shape them and to remove dead, diseased or mutilated parts. Reduce top growth by pruning whole branches, if possible, unless the tree has few branches and would be mutilated if whole branches were removed. Cut close to the trunk or a branch fork so that you do not leave short stubs. Do not prune the central leader of trees that normally have only one. If the central leader of these trees is removed, they will be disfigured and a new leader will not grow for many years.

Diseases, insects, animals and lawnmowers or other tools may damage trees. Use an antiseptic tree wound paint on wounds 1½ inches or more in diameter. County agricultural agents and state agricultural experiment stations can provide information on the control of diseases and insects.

The wrapping on trunks of newly planted trees may give some protection against rodents and dogs. Stakes and guy wires around trees will help reduce damage by lawnmowers and other small mechanical devices. Sometimes a fence may be necessary to protect a small tree.

CHAPTER 14

Trees for Use and Beauty

TREES PLANTED AROUND HOMES and along city and village streets fill a need. They fill a need for shade, a need for screening, a need for softening the harsh and stark lines of buildings, a need for adding beauty and graciousness and a feeling of welcome to streets that otherwise are purely functional.

For trees to do their intended job satisfactorily—and continue to do it—they must be selected carefully, then watched over until they become established. Once they are established, carefully selected trees require less attention.

SELECTING THE RIGHT TREE

When you plant a tree you also plant shade, or shape, or background, or screening or color. The use that you intend for your tree and the location in which you will plant it should guide you in its selection.

In selecting a shade or ornamental tree:

- Limit selection to trees of reliable hardiness in your area.
- Select the form that is best for the intended use.
- Determine the mature size that is desirable; consider whether *growth rate and longevity* are limiting factors.
- Avoid trees having undesirable characteristics for the intended use.
- Determine availability of suitable trees.

Hardiness

Start with a list of trees that are reliably hardy to the environment they they must grow in. Consider the total environment: the climate, the soil type, the available moisture, the contaminants in the atmosphere and the competition from the activities of human society.

When you consider hardiness to the climate of your area, remember the summer's heat as well as the winter's cold. Trees native to northern climates easily withstand southern winters but may be scorched beyond use by heat of a southern summer.

And be sure trees are *reliably* hardy in your area; trees planted north of their adapted range may grow satisfactorily through a series of milder-than-normal winters, but when an especially severe winter comes along they will be killed. Then the person who planted them will have lost money and labor and—most precious of all—time.

Soils in the city tend to be compacted and poorly drained. If you are selecting trees for city planting, therefore, you must either select trees that are tolerant of soil compaction or be prepared to invest time and labor in preventing these conditions.

Available moisture, too, can limit a tree's usefulness. In park plantings or specimen plantings in a yard, trees native to the area are not likely to suffer from lack of water during periods of normal rainfall. Near a street, however, trees can never receive their fair share of water. Rain flows off into gutters and storm drains and is carried away. For city plantings, select trees that can grow in reasonably dry soil, then see that they get enough water to keep them growing until their root systems adjust to the continuous subnormal soil moisture.

City air is filled with smoke and fumes and dust and soot. Some trees can grow successfully in this environment, others cannot. For example, ginkgo and London plane trees do well in downtown fumes and dirt; sugar maple does not.

Trees planted in the open—in parks or large yards—usually have less competition from the activities of human society than street trees. But many city trees must compete with automobiles and foot traffic, with lawnmowers, with sewer lines underground and with utility lines overhead. To compete with human society successfully, a tree must be tough.

Form

Consider whether the mature form of a tree is appropriate to its intended use. A broad-spreading and low-hanging tree may be ideal as a park or yard tree, but it would be unsatisfactory along a driveway. A slim, upright tree may be perfect for lining driveways, but of little use for shading a patio.

If you are not familiar with the mature form of trees under consideration, study illustrations of them in books or nursery catalogs.

Size

Many homeowners have learned by experience that Norway spruce is not a suitable tree for foundation plantings. The 6-foot-tall evergreens that look so attractive beside the front steps can eventually grow to a height of 70 feet and a spread of 40 feet. And they seem to get out of hand before the homeowner does anything about it.

Size of Mature Trees

SMALL (UP TO 40 FEET)	MEDIUM (40 TO 75 FEET)	LARGE (MORE THAN 75 FEET)
Arborvitae	American holly	American beech
Brazilian pepper	Blue spruce	Pecan
Cherry laurel	Goldenrain tree	Southern magnolia
Desert willow	Hackberry	Sugar maple
Green ash	Honeylocust	Tulip tree
Hemlock	Live oak	White oak
Jacaranda	Norway maple	Willow oak
Mimosa	Red maple	
Wax myrtle	Scotch pine	
	Valley oak	

Growth rate of a potentially large tree, however, may be slow enough to allow the tree's use for many years before it gets too large. Tulip trees, for example may grow to a height of 100 feet or more, which makes it much too large for a yard tree on the usual city or suburban lot. But a tulip tree takes more than 100 years to mature. The tree may be of acceptable size for 40 or 50 years after planting. You must decide whether you care what happens 40 years hence.

Longevity also is a matter for thought. Some trees grow rapidly, giving shade and screening soon after they are planted. They reach maturity quickly, then decline. How soon will they decline? Will their decline—and need for removal—affect you? If, when you are twenty-five years old, you plant a tree with a 40-year life expectancy, you may have to cut it down just as you are planning to spend some of your retirement time sitting under it. But if you plant the same tree when you are forty-five, you can sit under it in retirement years and you are not likely to care when it begins to decline. You have to decide whether you are planting trees for posterity or for yourself.

Useful Life Expectancy

SHORT (TO 50 YEARS)	MEDIUM (TO 75–100 YEARS)	LONG (100 PLUS YEARS)
Arborvitae	American holly	American beech
Brazilian pepper	Blue spruce	Live oak
Desert willow	Goldenrain tree	Pecan
Mimosa	Green ash	Southern magnolia
Redbud	Hackberry	Tulip tree
Sydney wattle (Acacia)	Honeylocust	White ash
Chinaberry tree	Jacaranda	White oak
	Norway maple	Willow oak
	Red maple	
	Scotch pine	
	Valley oak	

Undesirable Characteristics

It is difficult to find a tree that has no undesirable characteristics. Some traits make a tree unsuited for any use. For example, the American elm—one of our favorite trees—is susceptible to Dutch elm disease, which makes the tree a poor risk in areas where the disease occurs. Thornless honeylocust is subject to attack by the mimosa webworm, which ruins the appearance of the tree unless it is sprayed every year. White mulberry and the female ginkgo produce fruits that are so objectionable that these species may be considered garbage trees.

Some trees have traits that are nuisances, but the tree still may be tolerable. Oaks, hickorys, horsechestnuts, crabapples—all produce fruits that attract children who may use them for missiles. Sweetgum fruits—gum balls—are covered with thorny protuberances that make the fruits a nuisance in lawns. Poplars and mimosa produce an abundance of seeds that sprout in lawns and flower beds. If you like these trees otherwise, you may choose to overlook their undesirable characteristics.

Some trees have characteristics that are intolerable in one situation but not in another. Some maples, for example, have a tendency to raise and crack pavement with their roots. If they are planted where there is no nearby pavement, this is no problem. Some trees—red and silver maples, elm, willow and poplar—are notorious sewer cloggers. If they are planted away from sewer lines, again this is no problem.

You must match the tree's characteristics with its intended use; decide if they are compatible.

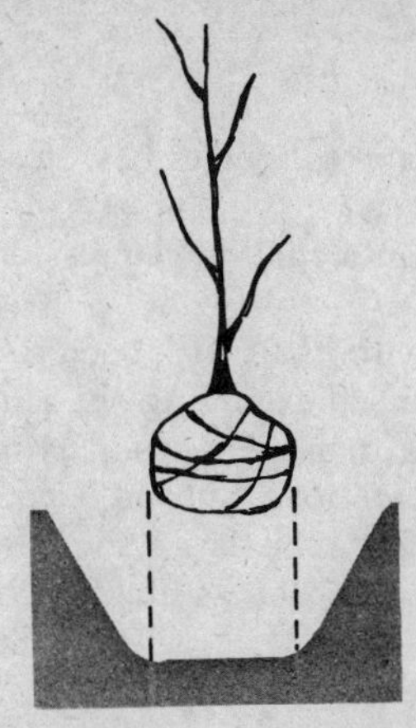

Dig the planting hole large enough for the roots plus plenty of good soil.

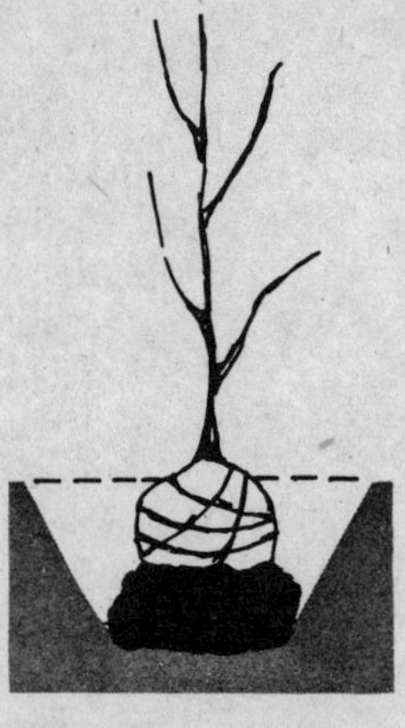

Fill hole until top of rootball is even with soil surface.

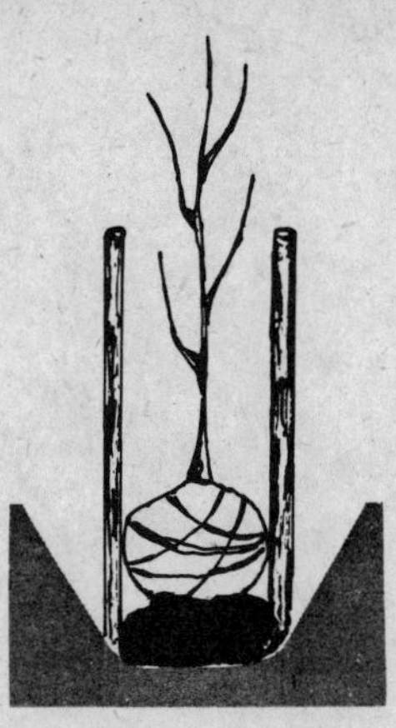

Drive supporting stakes next to the rootball.

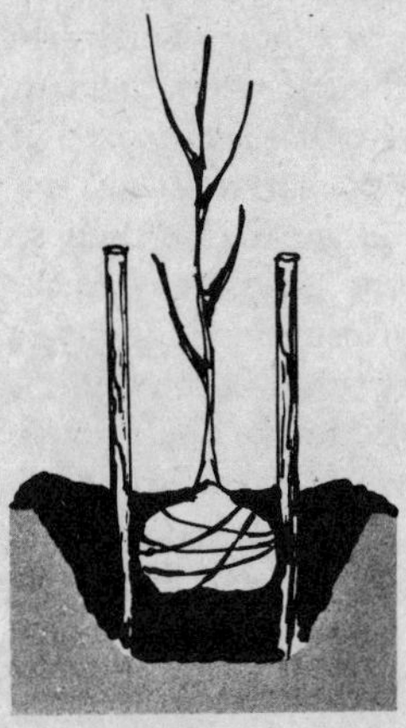

Fill hole with good soil, tamping it firmly. Ridge soil to form shallow basin.

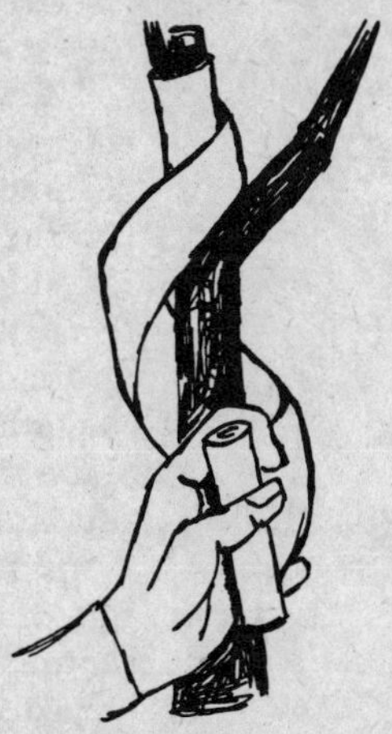

Wrap the trunk with burlap strip. Tie wrapping every 18 inches with stout cord.

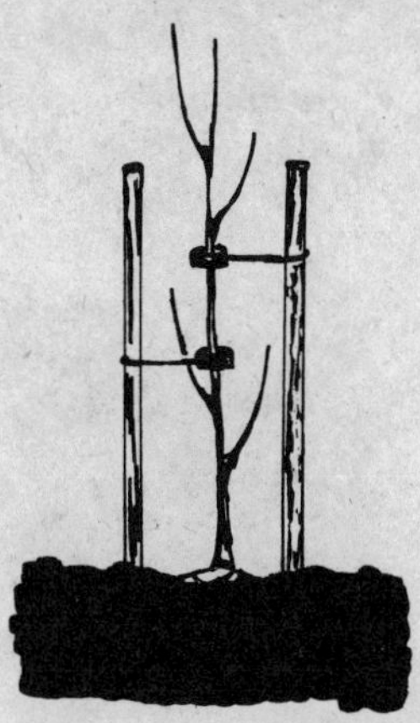

Attach tree to supporting stakes with hose-covered wire. Water well, and . . .
STAND BACK AND BE PROUD

Availability

When you have narrowed your list down to a few acceptable trees, you must find which of them are available. There is a good chance that the best tree for the purpose may be in such demand that it is not available locally. Then you must either settle for second best or shop around by mail to find the tree you want.

Many reputable nurseries do business by mail. You can feel secure in dealing with any of the old-line firms. But beware of firms that make fantastic claims for their nursery stock or promote common trees by giving them unusual names.

CARING FOR TREES IN THE CITY

The city is a difficult, often hostile, environment for shade trees. Success in growing shade trees in the city depends most on selection of a tree that can survive in this unfavorable environment. Then the tree must be cared for until it has a chance to become established.

Planting; fertilizing; watering; mulching; pruning; protecting from insects, diseases, and mechanical injury—these are the steps in preparing a tree for survival in the city.

Planting

The key to good tree planting is generosity. Be generous in digging a planting hole, in replacing poor soil with good, in expending energy to do the job right.

The right way to do the job depends on how good the soil is on the planting site.

In good soil:

• Dig planting holes for bare-root trees large enough to receive the roots when they are spread in a natural position.

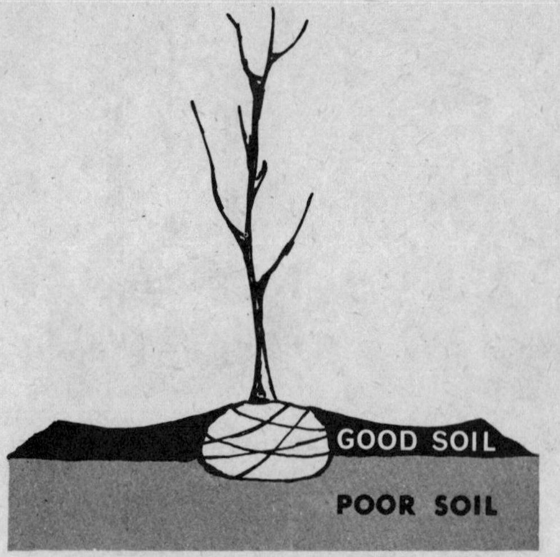

In soil where drainage is poor or nonexistent, trees can be planted on the "high side" and the area around the rootball bedded with good soil.

Dig holes for fertilizer under the dripline of the tree—about 15 inches deep and 18 to 24 inches apart.

• Dig planting holes for balled and burlapped trees 2 feet wider than the rootball.

• Dig holes deep enough so you can set the trees at the same level at which they grew in the nursery.

In poor soil:

• Dig holes for all trees as wide and deep as you can conveniently make them.

• Replace the poor soil from the hole with good soil when you fill in around the newly set tree.

In soil with impossibly poor drainage:

• Take all practical measures to improve drainage (see Index).

• Limit tree selection to species having a mature height less than 50 feet.

• Set the rootball in a shallow depression in the soil.

• Fill in around the rootball with good soil, forming a slightly concave bed extending out as far from the trunk as you can manage. Topsoil is often removed in building operations. Subsoil is commonly unfavorable for trees. In such cases, the best procedure is to use as much topsoil as practicable in the planting hole.

Pack soil under the newly set tree until it sets at the level at which it grew in the nursery.

Before filling around the rootball, stake or guy the tree. If the trunk diameter of the tree is 3 inches or less, use one or two 6-foot poles or steel fenceposts to stake the tree. Set the poles vertically into the soil next to the rootball. Fasten the trunk to the poles with a loop of wire that is enclosed in a section of garden hose to prevent bark cutting.

If the tree trunk is larger than 3 inches in diameter, support it with three hose-covered guy wires. Loop the wires around the trunk about ⅔ the way up the main stem or trunk. Stake one guy wire to the ground in the direction of the prevailing wind. Stake the other two wires to the ground to form an equilateral triangle.

After the tree is set and the hole is filled with good soil, settle the soil around the roots by watering thoroughly. Then wrap the trunk with burlap or creped kraft paper to prevent sunscald. Start wrapping at the top and wrap toward the ground. Tie the wrapping material with stout cord, knotting it about every 18 inches. The wrapping should remain for one to two years.

Fertilizing

If you use plenty of good soil for backfilling newly planted trees, the trees are not likely to need fertilizer for the first year after planting. However, street trees, planted in the narrow parking between sidewalk and curb, may need earlier feeding.

If you think your trees need fertilizer—if the leaves are paler then normal and if growth is slower than normal—you can apply it in spring this way:

• Measure the diameter of the trunk 3 feet above the ground; use 2 pounds of 5–10–5 for each inch of diameter (a 1-pound coffee can holds about 2 pounds of fertilizer).

• Using a soil auger, if one is available, or a crowbar or posthole digger, make holes 15 to 24 inches deep and about 18 to 24 inches apart around the drip line of the tree (the area beneath the ends of the longest branches).

• Distribute the fertilizer equally among the holes, then fill the holes with good soil. A mixture of equal parts topsoil, sand and peat moss is good for filling the holes; it provides aeration and water access as well as filling the space.

Watering

City trees often get too little water. Many trees grow in places where the area of soil exposed to rainfall is small. Lawn trees have to compete with grass and other plants for water. Drainpipes honeycomb the city and remove thousands of gallons of water every day.

Trees can become conditioned to this constantly low amount of water. But they have to be kept alive until they can adjust.

Water trees for the first two seasons after planting them. Water about once a week and let the water run for several hours.

Pruning

Inspect your shade trees regularly and prune them when needed. By following this procedure, you can imporve their appearance, guard their health and make them stronger. And by pruning as soon as the need becomes apparent, you can easily correct defects that would require major surgery if allowed to wait.

By following a program of regular and frequent pruning, you can correct defects while they are minor, rather than wait until they require major surgery.

In your program of scheduled pruning, try to eliminate undesirable branches or shoots while they are small. Drastic, difficult or expensive pruning may be avoided by early corrective pruning.

Here is a list of things to look for and prune:

- Dead, dying or unsightly parts of trees.
- Sprouts growing at or near the base of the tree trunk.
- Branches that grow toward the center of the tree.
- Crossed branches. If branches cross and rub together, disease and decay fungi can enter the tree through the abraded parts.
- V crotches. If it is possible to do so without ruining the appearance of the tree, remove one of the members forming a V crotch. V crotches split easily; their removal helps to prevent storm damage to the tree.
- Multiple leaders. If several leaders develop on a tree that normally has only a single stem and you wish the tree to develop its typical shape, cut out all but one leader. This restores dominance to the remaining stem.
- "Nuisance" growth. Cut out branches that are likely to interfere with electric or telephone wires. Remove branches that shade street lights or block the view in streets so as to constitute a traffic hazard. Prune out branches that shut off breezes. Cut off lower limbs that shade the lawn excessively.

Do not leave stubs when you prune. Stubs usually die. They are points at which decay fungi can enter the tree.

Small pruning cuts heal quickly. Large cuts—more than 1 inch in diameter—should be treated with antiseptic tree dressing to prevent entrance of decay or disease while the wound is healing.

Protecting from Insects, Diseases and Mechanical Injury

Most insects and diseases can be controlled by spraying. Your county agricultural agent, extension landscape specialist or state agricultural experiment station can tell you what spray schedules to follow in protecting your trees from insects and diseases. When trees are small, you can spray them yourself. As they grow larger, however, spraying becomes a job for professional arborists, who have the equipment and knowledge required to do a thorough job.

Danger from mechanical injury by lawnmowers, bicycles and foot traffic is reduced when stakes and guy wires are installed. If needed for protection, tree boxes can be made from snow fencing and placed around trees.

CHAPTER 15

Dwarf Fruit Trees: Selection and Care

DWARF APPLE AND PEAR TREES have several advantages over larger trees. They utilize sunshine much better and produce better fruit. Dwarf trees are easier to spray, prune and harvest. They begin to produce fruit earlier than semidwarf and standard-size trees. They require less space per tree than standard trees. The production per acre is higher with dwarf trees, even though dwarf trees produce less fruit per tree. In general, although dwarf trees require more care, they repay that extra care with earlier and higher production.

A dwarf tree is expected to develop not taller than about 6 to 8 feet. Semidwarf trees are 10 to 12 feet tall, and standard trees may grow as high as 20 feet.

Dwarf apple and pear trees are widely available. But dwarf peach, plum, cherry, apricot and nectarine trees are generally unsatisfactory. The standard trees of these stone fruits, except sweet cherries, are smaller than standard apple trees and can be restricted in size by pruning.

The size of the tree is determined by the rootstock, the richness of the soil, the size of the variety, the pruning technique and the earliness of production.

ROOTSTOCKS AND INTERSTOCKS

Apples

All apple trees are grafted. Standard trees are produced by planting seeds, growing the seedlings for two years, and grafting the desired variety on them. Dwarfing rootstocks must be propagated vegetatively by rooting the shoots of specific rootstocks in stoolbeds. The East Malling Research Station, East Malling, Kent, England, played a leading role in selecting dwarfing rootstocks from wild small-growing apple species. Therefore, most of the common dwarfing rootstocks carry the designation M (Malling) and a number.

The rootstock with the greatest dwarfing effect that is in common use is M 9. Trees on this rootstock rarely grow larger than 8 feet. However, M 9 has a poor root system which requires good soil and frequent irrigation, and the trees on this rootstock must be staked or grown beside a trellis. Free-standing trees grown on M 9 rootstock without support are often toppled over by the heavy weight of fruit or by high winds.

The next most dwarfing rootstock is M 26. Trees on this rootstock are somewhat larger than trees on M 9. The root system of this rootstock is stronger than that of M 9, but the trees still require staking.

M 7 and M 106 both produce semidwarf trees. Although trees on these rootstocks do not require staking, trees on M 7 rootstock have poor anchorage and may be pushed over by heavy winds. M 2 and M 111 rootstocks produce more vigorous semidwarf trees than M 7 and M 106, and their root systems are less sensitive to diseases. Trees on M 106, M 2, and M 111 are relatively large and require a more laborious training method during their early years.

Trees dwarfed by the interstem method are usually grafted twice. First, a piece of dwarfing rootstock (equivalent to M 9) is grafted on a larger root system of a semidwarf rootstock. The variety is then grafted on the top of the stem piece, which becomes a so-called interstem.

The length of the interstem determines the degree of dwarfing. Such trees are produced to take advantage of the larger root and the dwarfing effect of the interstem. However, it takes one year longer to produce double-grafted trees than to produce single-grafted ones. We consider M 9, M 26 and M 9 interstem to be the only rootstocks that produce truly dwarf trees.

Pears

Pear trees are dwarfed by using quince root as rootstock. Some varieties, including Bartlett, do not unite well with quince. In these cases, a compatible variety is first grafted on quince. The desired variety is then grafted on the stem. In fact, most dwarf pear trees are interstem-type trees. However, in this interstem combination the root is dwarfing and the interstem is used only to overcome incompatibility.

The quince is a shallow-rooted tree and requires very good soil with even soil moisture. On poor soils or with inadequate soil moisture, pears and quince do not produce well.

SIZE OF THE VARIETY

Apple trees vary in size regardless of the rootstock they are planted on. For example, Golden Delicious and Jonathan are small trees whereas McIntosh and Delicious are large trees. This means that if Golden Delicious and McIntosh are grafted on the same rootstock the McIntosh tree will be much larger than the Golden Delicious tree.

Fruit growers of the Northwest were the first to notice that some Delicious trees are less vigorous than others. The stems on such trees elongate less and the leaves are closer together on the stem. Such trees produce more spurs on which the fruit is produced. They are called spur-type trees. Various experiment stations have produced spur types of other varieties by artificially induced mutations.

Today, there are spur types of Delicious, Golden Delicious, Rome, McIntosh and some other varieties. The spur-type tree of a given variety is much smaller than the non-spur type of the same variety.

Pear trees also differ in size. Magness is the largest of the pear varieties. Bartlett, Moonglow and many others are considerably smaller. There are no spur-type pears.

Delicious on M 26 on poor soil with branches pulled down (3 years old)

MODIFYING EFFECT OF SOIL

Trees grow better on rich soil than on poor soil. Therefore, on good soil one must use a dwarfing rootstock in combination with a small variety. It may even be necessary to use the spur type of a small variety to get a truly dwarf tree.

A Golden Delicious/M 9 or Jonathan/M 9 combination is considered to produce the most dwarf tree. In contrast, a McIntosh/M 9-Delicious/M 9 combination may be too large on good soils and may require the use of the spur type of these varieties or additional pruning as described below. On poor soils, M 9 may produce too small a tree even with Delicious grafted on it. Therefore, M 26 or M 106 with a spur-type variety should be chosen if the soil is poor.

MODIFYING EFFECT OF EARLY FRUIT PRODUCTION

Early fruiting is the most powerful dwarfing agent we know to date. Some people believe that the dwarfing rootstock produces a dwarf tree because it forces early fruit production and not because it somehow interferes with the growth of the tree. Before fruiting begins, trees on dwarfing rootstock grow about as much as trees on standard roots. They slow down in growth only after the third year when they begin to produce fruit.

On rich soils, or on semidwarf roots, the additional effect of forced early production is needed to produce dwarf trees. Flower buds develop during June and July in the year previous to flowering. Therefore, all manipulation needed to enhance flowering should be done during early summer in order to successfully influence fruiting the next year.

EFFECT OF PRUNING ON DWARFING

For the development of flower buds, the tree needs carbohydrates. Severe pruning early in the life of the

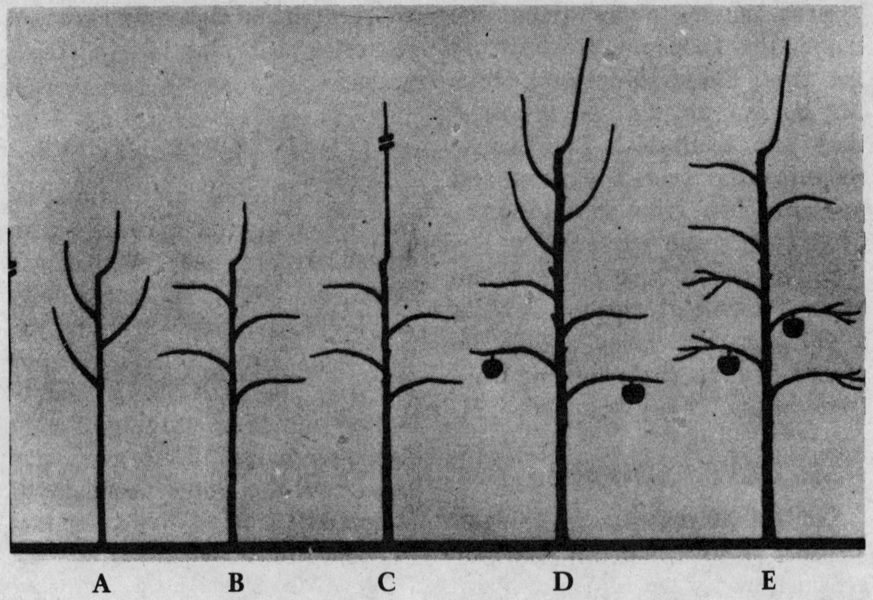

Development of a dwarf tree. First year: A, after planting is pruned back at the mark; B, the side shoots are developed; C, side shoots pulled down. Second year: D, leader is cut back; E, second tier of branches developed.

tree will restrict the leaf area and consequently reduce carbohydrate production. This will delay fruiting and increase tree size. However, occasional pruning is still needed to shape the tree and ensure good light penetration to the inside branches and leaves.

The terminal bud of a shoot produces a hormone which keeps the lateral buds from growing. When this terminal bud is removed, the four to six buds below the cut will grow and produce shoots. Therefore, every such heading cut will produce four to six shoots. Sometimes this is desirable; other times it is not.

During the first two years of the life of the tree, heading cuts are desirable. During the later years, there is greater need for thinning cuts. These thinning cuts remove the entire shoot at its base where a visible ring is located. If thinning cuts are made in August they have a strong dwarfing effect on the tree. In contrast, heading cuts, especially when applied during the winter, strongly promote growth.

Pulling or bending the branches down to near horizontal position strongly promotes the formation of flower buds. Pulling the branches down can be done in various ways. A string can be tied to the end of the shoot and then to the base of the tree. A Styrofoam block can be placed in the crotch angle between the main stem and the side shoot, forcing the shoot into the right position. A clothespin can be used to attach a weight to the end of the shoot, pulling it into the right position.

Any of the above methods will work. If the side shoot was pulled down or bent below the horizontal level it should be released from this position about three weeks later. The shoot will not go back to its original position—but if it is left too long in bent position it will produce strong shoots at the top of the bow, which is undesirable.

If the trees are grown along a trellis, bending the shoots to the wire and tying them there will also promote flowers buds.

PLANTING AND TRAINING OF DWARF TREES

When purchased, dwarf trees may have only a single stem or may have two or three branches along the main stem. Plant them in early spring in areas where the winters are severe; in late fall or early spring in areas where the climate is milder.

Place trees 6 to 8 feet apart depending on soil type, variety, and rootstock.

Trees must be planted in soil with good drainage. In poorly drained soils, dwarf trees soon die. If you are not sure about the drainage capacity of the soil, dig the hole for a tree and fill it with water. If the water drains within 24 hours the soil is drained well enough for dwarf trees. If the water remains in the hole after 24 hours, dwarf trees should not be planted at that location.

Plant the trees at the depth at which they stood in the nursery. You can see the change of color of the bark near the root below the graft union. Usually the color of the bark changes at the soil line. Be sure that the graft union is above the ground when you plant the tree. It is better to plant the tree too high than too deep.

At the time of planting place a metal stake (fence stake) or a 2- to 3-inch diameter redwood or treated wood post into the hole about 6 inches from the stem. The pole should extend 5 feet above the ground. Pack good topsoil firmly around the roots and water the plant well. Do not apply fertilizer at the time of planting.

After planting, head the tree back about 30 inches above the ground. If the tree has strong side branches, head back the leader about 12 inches above the side branches. The buds below the heading will grow.

When the side shoots are about 12 inches long, pull them into horizontal position. If the tree had side branches at the time of planting, pull these down. In the latter case, Styrofoam blocks or clothespins are easier to apply than strings.

During the following spring, head back the leader about 12 inches above the first tier of branches. Develop the second tier of branches the same way as you did a year before for the first tier. The first-tier branches should give you a few apples this year.

From this point on you should not need heading cuts. If the tree is too full, use thinning cuts in July or August. If the tree is too high and you want to cut it back, make sure that your heading cut is made in such a way that a pencil-size shoot remains on the top. The terminal bud of this small shoot will produce enough hormone to keep the other buds from growing.

FERTILIZING

Dwarf trees require a well-limed soil. Liming can be done successfully only at the time of planting. Mix about 10 pounds of dolomitic limestone into the soil dug out from the hole. Make sure that the lime is thoroughly mixed with the soil.

Do not apply fertilizer in the year of planting. From the second year on, apply fertilizer only when shoots make less than 12 to 18 inches of growth and the leaves are light green. The only exception is Golden Delicious, which normally has pale-green leaves.

When fertilizer is needed, the ideal choice is 10–4–10 at a rate of ½ pound per year of age of the tree. If this fertilizer is not available, apply the available mixture at the same calculated rate for nitrogen. For example, if you have a 20–6–4 fertilizer, use half the recommended rate. (The first number is the one that indicates the percentage of nitrogen in the mixture.)

MULCHING

Mulching is an excellent practice for growing dwarf trees. Mulch provides a better uptake of nutrients, ensures a more even supply of moisture, and prevents the overheating of soil around the roots.

Keep mulch away from the trunk: this keeps mice away from the tree. Sharp bluestone chips can be put around the trunk if they are available. This keeps rodents away from the trunk and prevents them from damaging the bark during the winter.

Rabbits may also damage the bark. To protect against rabbits a chicken-wire mesh should be placed around the trunk of each tree.

CHAPTER 16

Flowering Crabapples

FLOWERING CRABAPPLES ARE deciduous (leaf-shedding) trees or shrubs. Their flowers range from white to brilliant pink and purple. Fruits, which are pea-size to 2 inches in diameter, are green, yellow or red. Fruits on some varieties drop in the fall; fruits on others cling through winter.

Some flowering crabapples are suited to one-story houses and small yards as well as to large estates, parks and highway plantings.

Since flowering crabapples require about 50 cumulative days of under 45° F. to break their dormancy, many of them do not grow well in areas where winters are mild.

Flowering crabapples grow well in most kinds of soil and often do well on very poor soil. They need good soil drainage, however, and watering during periods of drought.

You can grow flowering crabapples successfully if you:

- Buy nursery-grown trees.
- Plant them in late winter or early spring.
- Prepare planting holes carefully; be sure the planting site is well drained.
- Maintain a mulch around the trees or shrubs.
- Water them during dry periods.

VARIETIES

You can ask a reputable nurseryman in your area to recommend species or varieties; the plants he has for sale generally are adapted to your area. You also can ask neighbors which kinds have done well for them. Or you can ask your county agricultural agent or your state agricultural college to recommend varieties suitable to your area.

Some of the more commonly grown varieties of crabapples are described below. Crabapple flowers are single, semidouble or double. Single flowers have five petals. Semidouble flowers have six to 11 petals. Double flowers have 12 or more petals.

ALDENHAM

Aldenham (*Malus* x *purpurea* 'Aldenhamensis') is a spreading shrub or small tree that grows 10 to 15 feet tall. Its flowers are single and semidouble, red to purplish red, and 1 to 1½ inches across. They bloom annually, except in extreme southern areas. Its leaves first are reddish or purplish bronze; they turn green. Fruits are purple to brownish purple and about ¾ inch across.

Single *Semidouble* *Double*

ARNOLD

Arnold (*Malus* x *arnoldiana*) is an upright, spreading shrub or small tree that grows 10 to 15 feet tall. Its flowers are single, pinkish white to white, and about 2 inches across. They blossom more profusely in alternate years. Fruits are yellow with a reddish tint, and up to ½ inch across.

BECHTEL

Bechtel (*Malus ioensis* 'Plena') is an upright, spreading tree that grows 10 to 15 feet tall. Its flowers are double, pink or rose pink, and about 2 inches across. They bloom annually, except in extreme southern areas. Bechtel rarely produces fruits.

CARMINE

Carmine (*Malus* x *atrosanguinea*) is an upright, spreading shrub or tree that grows 10 to 15 feet tall. Its flowers are single, rose or rose pink, and up to 1 inch across. They bloom annually. Its leaves are glossy dark green. Fruits are usually yellow to red, and up to ½ inch across.

DOLGO

Dolgo (*Malus 'Dolgo'*) is an upright, spreading, roundheaded tree that grows 10 to 20 feet tall. Its flowers are single, white, and about 2 inches across. They bloom more profusely in alternate years. Fruits are red, cone-shaped, and 1 to 1½ inches across.

DOROTHEA

Dorothea (*Malus 'Dorothea'*) is an upright, spreading shrub or small tree. It is 10 to 15 feet tall when fully grown. Its flowers are semidouble or double, rose pink, and about 2 inches across. They bloom annually. Fruits are yellow to orange-yellow, and ½ inch across.

ELEYI

Eleyi (*Malus* x *purpurea* 'Eleyi') is an upright, spreading, roundheaded tree that grows 10 to 20 feet tall. Its flowers are single, red to purplish red, and about 1½ inches across. They bloom more profusely in alternate years. Fruits are red to purple, and ½ to 1 inch across. Leaves turn from reddish or purplish bronze to green.

JAPANESE (FLOWERING)

Japanese (*Malus floribunda*) is an upright, spreading shrub or tree that grows 10 to 15 feet tall.

Its flowers are single, red to pinkish white, and 1 to 1½ inches across. Blooming is good in southern areas. Fruits are yellow, brownish or reddish, and about ½ inch across.

KATHERINE

Katherine (*Malus* 'Katherine') is an upright, spreading shrub that grows 10 to 15 feet tall.

Its flowers are semidouble or double, pink to pinkish white, and about 2 inches across. They bloom more profusely in alternate years. Fruits are greenish yellow, and up to ½ inch across.

LEMOINEI

Lemoinei (*Malus* x *purpurea* 'Lemoinei') is an upright, spreading shrub or small tree that grows 10 to 15 feet tall.

Its flowers are single and semidouble, red or purplish red, and about 1½ inches across. They bloom annually, except in the lower South. Fruits are dark red and ½ to 1 inch across. Reddish or purple-bronze leaves turn green.

MIDGET

Midget (*Malus* x *micromalus*) is an upright, spreading shrub, or small tree that grows 10 to 15 feet tall.

Its flowers are single, pink, and 1½ to 2 inches across. They bloom more profusely in alternate years; and poorly in lower southern areas. Fruits are yellow, and ½ and 1 inch across.

PARKMAN

Parkman (*M. halliana* var. *Parkmanii*) is a slow-growing shrub or small tree that grows 6 to 7 feet tall. Its flowers are double, pink to rose pink, and about 1 inch across. They bloom annually. Fruits are reddish brown and less than ½ inch across.

PINK WEEPER

Pink Weeper (*Malus* 'Oekonomierat Echtermeyer') is a weeping shrub or small tree that grows 10 to 15 feet tall. Its flowers are single, purplish red, and about 1½ inches across. They bloom annually. Fruits are purple to purplish brown and about 1 inch across. Leaves turn from reddish or purplish bronze to green.

PRINCE GEORGES

Prince Georges (*Malus* 'Prince Georges') is an upright, dense, roundheaded shrub or small tree that grows 10 to 15 feet tall. Its flowers are double, rose pink, and about 2 inches across. Prince Georges does not bear fruit.

REDBUD (CRABAPPLE)

Redbud (*Malus* x *zumi* 'Calocarpa') is an upright, spreading tree that grows 10 to 15 feet tall. Its flowers are single, pinkish to white, and about 1 inch across. In northern areas blossoms are more profuse in alternate years; blossoming is poor in southern areas. Fruits are red, and up to ½ inch across.

SARGENT

Sargent (*Malus sargentii*) is a spreading shrub that rarely grows over 7 feet tall. Its flowers are single, white, and about 1 inch across. They bloom more profusely in alternate years. Fruits are red or purplish red, and about ⅓ inch across.

SCHEIDECKER

Scheidecker (*Malus* x *scheideckeri*) is an upright shrub or small tree that grows 10 to 15 feet tall. Its flowers are semidouble or double, pink, and 1 to 1½ inches across. They bloom more profusely in alternate years. Fruits are yellow and about ½ inch across.

TEA

Tea (*Malus hupehensis*) is an upright, spreading, V-shaped tree that grows 10 to 15 feet tall. Its flowers are single, pink to white, and about 1½ inches across. The bloom is more profuse in alternate years. Fruits are greenish yellow with a reddish tint, and about ⅜ inch across.

VAN ESELTINE

Van Eseltine (*Malus* 'Van Eseltine') is an upright, V-shaped tree that grows 10 to 15 feet tall. Its flowers are double, pale pink to rose pink, and 1½ to 2 inches across. They bloom more profusely in alternate years. Fruits are yellow or red, and ½ to 1 inch across.

PLANTING

The best time to plant flowering crabapples is in late winter or early spring, before growth begins.

The planting site should be well drained and provide sufficient growing space—at least 150 square feet for the small species and 300 to 500 square feet for larger species.

Dig a planting hole at least 18 inches deep and twice the diameter of the rootball or spread of the roots.

Crabapples usually are sold bare-rooted. If you buy them balled and burlapped, do not remove the burlap before setting the tree or shrub in the hole. After the plant is in place, cut the twine around the top of the rootball and fold back or cut off exposed parts of the burlap.

Plant the tree or shrub so that the roots are slightly higher than they were in the nursery. Then refill the hole with topsoil and press the soil firmly around the roots. Finally, water the plant thoroughly.

After the plant has settled, it should be about the same depth as it was before transplanting.

Stake and brace crabapple trees at planting time (for staking and bracing see pages 138 and 139). This prevents root damage that often occurs if you drive stakes later.

CARE OF TREES

Mulching

After planting, cover the soil under the branches with a mulching material—peat moss, bark or leaves. Apply a layer about 3 inches deep, and add new mulching material annually to maintain the mulch.

Mulching helps keep the soil moist; and as the mulching material decays, it releases some nutrients for use by the crabapple tree or shrub.

Weeding

If you maintain an adequate mulch around crabapple trees or shrubs, few weeds will grow. Those that do can be pulled easily by hand. Be careful if you use a hoe or other weeding tool around crabapples; you may harm the shallow roots.

Watering

Crabapples are fairly drought-resistant, and 12 to 15 inches of rain during the growing season usually is adequate for good growth. During droughts, however, the plants should be watered at weekly intervals. When you water, soak the root area thoroughly. Be careful that you do not drown trees or shrubs growing in poorly drained soil.

Fertilizing

If crabapples are planted in reasonably fertile soil that is well supplied with organic matter, they seldom need fertilizing.

If you want to stimulate growth of crabapples after they have recovered from transplanting, or if they show signs that the soil is infertile (small, pale leaves and annual twig growth of less than 5 inches), apply the same fertilizer that you use for your lawn or garden. Apply it once between late winter and early summer.

Use 2 pounds of fertilizer per inch of trunk diameter. Spread the fertilizer in a band 2 or 3 feet wide under the ends of the branches. (Do not let the fer-

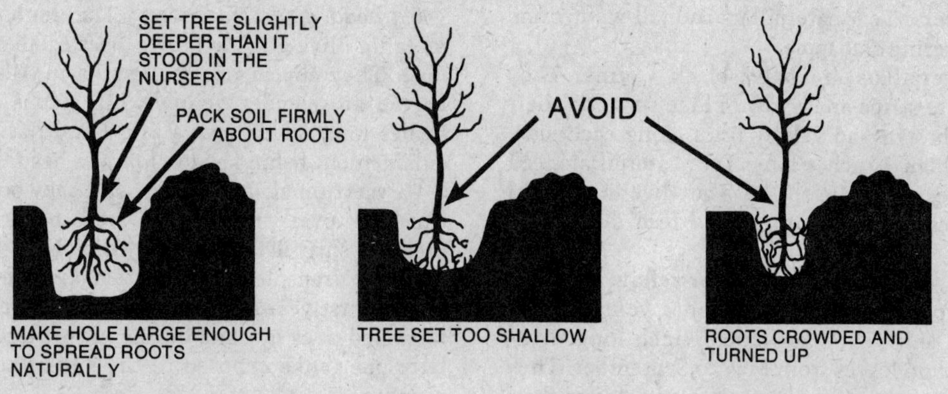
SET TREE SLIGHTLY DEEPER THAN IT STOOD IN THE NURSERY
PACK SOIL FIRMLY ABOUT ROOTS
AVOID
MAKE HOLE LARGE ENOUGH TO SPREAD ROOTS NATURALLY
TREE SET TOO SHALLOW
ROOTS CROWDED AND TURNED UP

tilizer touch the trunk.) Then thoroughly soak the fertilizer into the ground.

Pruning

Heavy pruning of crabapples can ruin their natural appearance and result in an excessive number of shoots. The only pruning normally needed is to remove (1) shoots at the base of the trunk; (2) shoots at the top of the plant; and (3) branches that are dead, diseased or broken. The best time to prune crabapples is in winter.

Coat all pruning cuts that are an inch or more across with white lead paint or tree-wound dressing.

DISEASES AND INSECTS

Few diseases and insects attack flowering crabapples but those that do can seriously disfigure or kill the trees. Inspect your crabapple trees frequently for signs of diseases and insects described below. See your county agricultural agent or state agricultural experiment station for information on how to control diseases and insects.

Diseases

Powdery mildew: Powdery mildew is a common fungus disease, particularly in humid areas. Crabapples usually survive it without much damage. The disease is characterized by a white moldy growth that disfigures the leaves and stems.

Cedar apple rust: Cedar apple rust is a fungus disease that originates on cedar trees and infects flowering crabapples.

The disease appears first as yellow spots on the upper surfaces of leaves. These spots enlarge, turn orange, and develop small black specks in their centers. Blisters form in the leaf tissue under the spots. Severely infected leaves become distorted and fall from the plant.

Fire blight: Fire blight is a bacterial disease that may severely damage susceptible varieties of flowering crabapple. Some varieties are immune to fire blight.

Infected leaves turn brown or black and eventually dry up; they remain attached to the branch. The bark on infected twigs becomes dark and sunken. A milky or brownish ooze may form on the infection.

Cankers form where the disease enters a large branch or a trunk. The bacteria overwinter in these cankers and are a source of infection the following year.

Apple scab: Apple scab is a fungus disease that infects the leaves and twigs. The disease appears on leaves as dark-green velvety spots. The fungus overwinters in fallen leaves and reinfects trees during rainy weather in the spring.

Insects

Aphids: Aphids, or plant lice, are usually green but may be brown or black. Their presence is frequently accompanied by large numbers of ants.

Usually aphids attack the leaves of flowering crabapple. They suck juice from the leaves and make them crinkle or curl downward. Sometimes aphids attack shoots that develop late in the season and water sprouts that grow from the base of the trunk or from below ground. The wooly apple aphid, which is bluish black and has a white waxy covering, sometimes is found in cracks or pruning wounds.

Spider mites: Spider mites are red or greenish-red pests that feed on the underside of leaves. They are barely visible to the naked eye, but their presence can be detected by fine webs on the undersides of leaves.

Infested leaves become yellow, gray or brownish and flowers become discolored or faded. Severely infested trees become stunted. Spider mites frequently attack severely during dry years.

Caterpillars: Tent caterpillars and fall webworms attack flowering crabapple.

Tent caterpillars are hairy black worms. They have a white stripe and a row of blue spots on their back, and brown and yellow lines along each side. They are about 2 inches long. Tent caterpillars feed on young leaves in the spring. They live in webs in the crotches of trees at night and feed during the day.

Fall webworms are pale green or yellow and have a dark stripe down their back and a yellow stripe along each side. They are about 1 inch long. Webworms feed on leaves from May to September. They form loose, unsightly webs at the ends of branches.

Flathead apple tree borer: The adult borers are metallic olive-gray or brown beetles about ½ inch long. They appear on tree trunks in May or June. Larvae are slender yellow-white grubs about 1¼ inches long. They have a broad and flattened body enlargement behind a small brown head.

Larvae tunnel in the bark and sapwood of trees. The bark over the tunneled areas becomes discolored and shriveled, and finally dies.

Newly transplanted trees that are infested often die the first year after transplanting. Damage to established trees is worst during dry weather, particularly on trunks exposed to the sun after excessive pruning.

CHAPTER 17

Flowering Dogwood

THE FLOWERING DOGWOOD (*Cornus florida*) is native to much of the eastern half of the United States. It can be grown wherever the winter temperature does not normally go below −15° F.

Dogwood is a versatile little ornamental tree. As a landscaping plant it is as suited to one-story houses and small yards as it is to mansions and large estates. It is adaptable to several types of soil, though it grows best in a moist, fertile loam that is slightly acid. Its primary demands within its area of climatic adaptation are good soil drainage and protection from drought.

When dogwood grows in the open in full sunlight, it normally reaches a mature height of 12 to 15 feet. In shade, or when crowded by other trees, it grows somewhat taller and does not flower as freely as it does in full sun.

For success in growing flowering dogwood:

- Buy nursery-grown trees.
- Plant them in late winter or early spring.
- Prepare planting holes carefully; be sure the planting site is well drained.
- Maintain a mulch around the tree.
- Water frequently during dry weather.
- Protect the bark from mechanical injury.
- Prevent borer attack by wrapping the bark of newly planted trees and by spraying the trunk and branches with endosulfan.

CULTIVARS (CULTIVATED VARIETIES)

Most of the flowering dogwoods that are sold are either the white-bracted wild form, *Cornus florida*, or the pink-bracted form, *C. florida 'Rubra'*. Several other cultivars are sometimes available: *'Cherokee Chief', 'Cherokee Princess', 'DeKalb Red', 'Belmont Pink', 'Welchii', 'Weaver', 'White Cloud'*, among others. *C. florida 'Pendula'* has weeping branches, *'Pluribracteata'* has double flowers, and *'Xanthocarpa'* has yellow fruits. All varieties of flowering dogwood are similar in their hardiness and cultural requirements.

The special forms of dogwood are propagated by grafting them onto the wild form. If shoots grow from below the graft, the shoots will exhibit characteristics of the wild form of dogwood. For example, a pink dogwood would have white-bracted flowers on growth originating below the bud or graft union. To prevent this "turning white," prune off all shoots that arise below the bud or graft.

OBTAINING PLANTS

Wild trees are difficult to transplant successfully and they often are poorly shaped.

Nursery trees have usually been grown in the sun. As a rule their tops are pruned and trained to a desirable shape, and they have been root-pruned frequently; they can be transplanted with most of the roots intact.

Nursery-grown trees usually are sold with a burlap-wrapped ball of soil surrounding the roots. They recover from transplanting shock more quickly than bare-rooted trees or trees dug from the woods.

PLANTING

The best time to plant dogwoods is in late winter or spring, before growth begins.

Dig a planting hole twice the diameter of the rootball and at least 18 inches deep. Refill the hole to the depth of the rootball with the loosened soil. Tamp the soil to provide a firm base for the tree.

If the roots of the dogwood are balled and burlapped, you need not remove the burlap before setting the tree in the hole. After the tree is set, you can cut the twine around the top of the rootball and fold back or cut off exposed parts of the burlap.

Place the dogwood in the hole and pack soil under

the rootball until the tree sits slightly higher than it grew in the nursery. Then refill the hole with a mixture consisting of equal parts of soil and organic matter—peat moss, well-decayed manure or leaf mulch. Press the soil mixture firmly around the rootball and water thoroughly.

After the plant has settled, its depth should be about the same as it was before transplanting. Avoid planting too deeply.

CARE

Mulching

After planting, cover the soil beneath the branches with a mulching material—peat moss, oak leaves or forest litter. Apply a layer about 3 inches deep. Add new mulching material periodically to maintain the mulch.

A mulch helps to keep the soil moist near the surface, where dogwood roots are most active. It helps to prevent the growth of weeds. And as the mulching material decays it releases nutrients for use by the dogwood tree.

Weeding

If you maintain an adequate mulch around dogwood trees, few weeds should grow there. Those that do can easily be pulled out by hand. Be careful if you use a hoe or other weeding tool around dogwoods; these implements may harm the shallow roots of the tree.

Watering

Normal rainfall ordinarily provides enough moisture for mulched dogwoods. During droughts, however, the trees should be watered at weekly intervals. When you water, soak the root area thoroughly. Be careful, however, that you do not drown trees growing in soil with poor drainage.

Fertilizing

If dogwoods are planted in reasonably fertile soil that is well supplied with organic matter, they seldom need fertilizing. Free blooming is promoted by moderate rather than quick growth.

If you want to stimulate growth of your trees after they have recovered from transplanting, or if they show signs that the soil is infertile, you can apply the same fertilizers that you use for your lawn or garden. Apply them from late winter through early summer. (Signs of low soil fertility are small, sparse, pale leaves and short twig growth.) Use 2 pounds of fertilizer per inch of trunk diameter. Broadcast the fertilizer in a band 2 to 3 feet wide under the ends of the branches. Do not place fertilizer near the trunk.

The flowering dogwood is a versatile ornamental tree, suited for planting in natural settings or in formal gardens.

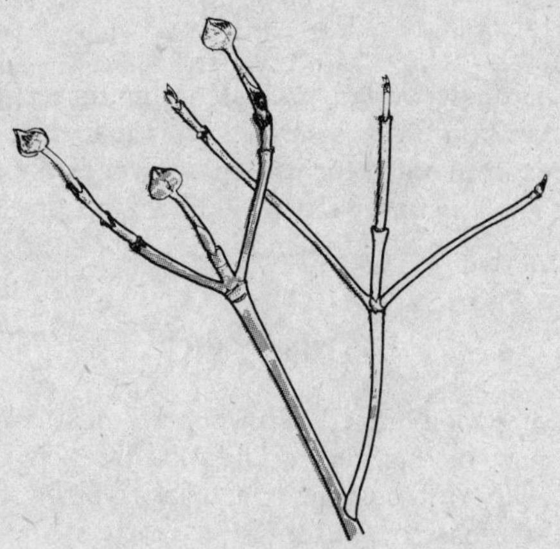

Dogwood branch in winter. Twigs on the left are tipped by buds for next season's flowers. The other twigs end in leaf buds.

Pruning

Dogwoods seldom need pruning, except for removal of dead, injured, diseased or insect-infested parts. Make pruning cuts back to a crotch. Treat all cuts over ½ inch in diameter by coating them with a tree-wound dressing; this helps to prevent harmful fungi and borers from invading the tree. Generally, pruning should be done during the dormant season to prevent bleeding of the pruning cut.

Transplanting

The best time to transplant dogwoods is in late winter or spring, as soon as the soil thaws and before the leaves begin to unfold.

Dogwoods growing around the home are not easy to transplant, but you can avoid transplanting losses by digging carefully to preserve most of the roots from drying while they are out of the ground.

If you are collecting wild trees, you are most likely to be successful if you choose only small trees—not over 3 feet tall. After you replant them, cut the branches back severely to compensate for loss of roots in digging.

DISEASES

Poor appearance of dogwood trees often is due to factors other than disease—poor planting site, low soil fertility, heat or drought. A few diseases do affect dogwood, however. Some of them are temporarily disfiguring but have no lasting effect on the trees. One disease—trunk canker—frequently is fatal to the tree.

Trunk Canker

Trees with low vitality, particularly those growing on poor or wet sites, often are the victims of this disease, but vigorous trees also may be attacked.

Cankers sometimes start at injuries, such as those resulting from bumping the trunk with a lawn mower. A fungus (*Phytophthora cactorum*) attacks the bark, cambium and outer sapwood. The infected tissues are discolored and often a black fluid exudes from the lesion and runs down the trunk.

Cankers may enlarge slowly for several years. The bark falls from older parts of the lesion but covers the advancing margin of the lesion. Diseased trees often bear large crops of flowers and fruits for several years prior to their death. Affected trees often decline slowly over a period of years; but sometimes they die within a year or two after infection. In late stages of the disease, tops of affected trees may become lopsided. When the canker finally encircles the trunk, the tree dies.

There is no certain control for the disease. Sometimes small lesions can be cured by cutting away all diseased bark, sterilizing the exposed wood and bark at the edge of the wound with shellac, and painting the wound with tree-wound dressing. Attempts to save trees by cutting out large lesions have been unsuccessful.

Trunk Decay

Wood-decay fungi may enter the tree through wounds made by bumping the trunk with the lawn mower. Be careful when mowing around dogwoods. As soon as possible after injuring the bark, paint the exposed wood with tree-wound dressing.

Decay in the lower part of the trunk sometimes can be cut out. After removing all the decayed wood, sterilize the cavity by painting with shellac. Then coat the cavity with tree-wound dressing.

Leaf and Flower Spots

Several diseases can infect dogwood leaves and flowers and cause spotting and dying. These diseases often mar the appearance of the tree and can cause defoliation at times. Usually they do no permanent harm to the tree. One disease that seriously disfigures flowers and leaves is called spot anthracnose.

If your trees are attacked by spot anthracnose or the other leaf and flower spots and you want to prevent their recurrence, spray with a garden fungicide—zineb, or maneb—mixed and applied as directed on the package label. Apply the spray as the flowers open. For best control of leaf and flower diseases, spray every three or four weeks during spring and summer.

Powdery Mildew

In late summer or early fall, mildew often develops on dogwood leaves. The leaves are covered with a thin, cottony growth and may appear to have been powdered. The disease usually appears too late in the season to do much damage. If you want to control it, apply a sulfur dust or spray when the mildew first becomes apparent. More than one application may be needed. For best results, keep the leaves covered with the sulfur.

Twig Dieback

The fungus *Myxosporium nitidum* causes twigs of dogwood to die back. This dying back sometimes may become conspicuous on the tree and make the tree unsightly. To control the disease, prune the dead twigs back to sound wood. Fertilize the tree and water it during dry weather.

HEAT AND DROUGHT INJURY

During hot, dry weather dogwood leaves often curl or cup and change color. The leaves fold upward on the midrib and at the same time the midrib curls downward at the tip. Because of the closing of the leaves, the tree appears to have less foliage than normal. The leaves may turn red or reddish purple. Some leaves may drop. Dogwoods growing in the open are more likely to develop these symptoms than dogwoods growing in shade.

Usually the affected tree gradually returns to a normal appearance in fall when the weather cools and fall rains begin. If hot, dry weather continues too long, however, severe dieback of the top may follow. To prevent this, keep the tree well mulched and water it weekly during the dry period.

HERBICIDE DAMAGE

Dogwoods are extremely sensitive to weed-killing chemicals. The trees can be severely injured or killed by wind-carried droplets of the herbicides, fumes from nearby applications, or traces of the herbicides in equipment used for applying insecticides or fungicides.

Do not use these materials around dogwoods. Do not apply insecticides or fungicides to dogwoods with sprayers that you have used for applying weed killers.

INSECTS

Unless dogwoods are protected from insect attack, they may be killed or seriously disfigured. Insecticides recommended for use on dogwoods are available at garden-supply stores. Follow label directions for dilution and care in handling.

Dogwood Borer

The dogwood borer is probably the most common insect pest of established dogwood trees. It makes irregular burrows under the bark on the trunk, around the base of limbs, or frequently at the edges of wounds or scars on the trees. Small trees or the base of branches may be girdled. Healthy trees may also be attacked.

To prevent borer attack, spray the trunk and lower branches of the tree with endosulfan. Begin spraying about May 15. Spray once a month through September 15.

If borers attack your trees, these pests can be cut out. Inspect the trunks and branches in late summer for evidence of injured bark or of fine boring dust being pushed from the burrows. Cut the borers out with a sharp knife, trim the edges of the wound back to green bark, and paint the wound with tree-wound dressing.

Flathead Borers

Flathead borers often attack newly transplanted dogwoods or dogwoods seriously weakened from other causes. They bore under the bark and may cause death of the tree.

Swollen twigs infested with dogwood club gall. These swellings should be pruned and burned in summer.

The best preventive for flathead borer attack is to keep the trees growing vigorously. Wrap trunks of newly transplanted trees with burlap strips or kraft paper wrapping, available from garden-supply stores.

Dogwood Twig Borer

The wilting of leaves on individual twigs or the dropping of girdled tips usually indicates infestation by the dogwood twig borer. The borer tunnels down the center of the twig, expelling boring dust through a row of small holes in the bark.

The dogwood twig borer usually does not infest trees in large numbers. To control the borer, prune out and destroy infested twigs. This can be done any time after the injury becomes apparent in summer.

Dogwood Club-gall Midge

The dogwood club-gall midge causes spindle-shaped or tubular swellings from ½ to 1 inch long at the tips or along the stems of dogwood twigs. Some of the twigs may be killed above the swollen part and the tree may be deformed if the infestation is heavy.

To prevent heavy infestation of midges, spray the tree with lindane once a week for three to five weeks. Begin treatment around May 15, after the leaves have started to grow. To destroy emerging adults, spray the ground beneath the tree as well. During summer, prune galls before the larvae have completed their development.

Scales

Several kinds of scale insects sometimes become serious on dogwoods. These insects attach themselves to twigs and branches of the dogwood, giving these parts a crusty appearance. They suck juices from the tree. If they are numerous, scale insects can weaken the trees or kill heavily infested branches.

For controlling scales, spray in early spring, before growth starts, with white-oil emulsion or lime-sulfur diluted for dormant spraying. To kill the young insects before they attach themselves to the bark and develop a protective coating, spray with malathion. Apply two sprays, the first when the leaves are about ½ inch long and the second about ten days or two weeks later.

Other Insects

Other insects—aphids, leafhoppers and whiteflies—sometimes are an annoyance, but they seldom are injurious. If they become numerous, spray with malathion.

CHAPTER 18

Magnolias

MAGNOLIAS ARE TREES OR SHRUBS that are grown principally for their showy flowers. They grow well where temperatures do not usually go below 10° F. They do best in soil that is slightly acid and well drained.

You can grow magnolias successfully if you:

- Buy species and varieties that are adapted to your area.
- Get balled and burlapped plants or plants growing in a can.
- Plant in early spring, in mildly acid soil that is high in organic-matter content.
- Maintain a mulch around them during the growing season.
- Water them during dry periods.
- Brace the trees until the root system has become well established.
- Protect the bark from mechanical injury.

VARIETIES

Magnolias commonly grown in the United States are of two kinds—native and Asian. Native magnolias bloom from late spring to summer; they have white, yellowish or green flowers. Asian magnolias bloom in early to late spring; they have white, pink or reddish-purple to purple flowers.

Native magnolias are evergreen or deciduous (leaf-shedding); Asian magnolias grown in cultivation are deciduous.

Some of the more commonly grown varieties of magnolias follow.

Native

Southern magnolia (*Magnolia grandiflora*) is an evergreen tree that grows 30 to 50 feet tall. It is hardy to the warmer parts of zone D (see hardiness zone map for magnolias). Southern magnolia is the most popular of all native varieties. Its fragrant white flowers are 6 to 10 inches across. Its leaves are shiny and 3 to 5 inches wide.

Cucumber tree (*M. acuminata*) is a deciduous tree that grows 40 to 60 feet tall. It is hardy to zone F. Its flowers are about 2 inches across and have three sets of petals—yellow, greenish yellow, and green. Its leaves are 6 to 10 inches long and 3 to 5 inches wide. Cucumber tree grows rapidly and is used as a shade tree.

Yellow cucumber tree (*M. cordata*) is a deciduous tree that grows 20 to 30 feet tall. It is hardy to zone E. Its flowers are bright canary yellow and about 2 inches across. Its leaves are 4 to 6 inches long and 3 to 4 inches wide.

Sweetbay (*M. virginiana*) is a deciduous shrub or tree that grows 30 to 50 feet tall. It is hardy to zone E. It grows as a semi-evergreen in zone C. Sweetbay leaves are shiny green, 3 to 6 inches long, and 1 to 3 inches wide. Its fragrant flowers are waxy white and 2 to 3 inches across.

Asian

Lily magnolia (*M. liliflora*) is a shrubby species that is hardy to the warmer parts of zone E. It has red-purple flowers, 4 to 5 inches long, which grow erect on slender stems. Its leaves are about 3½ inches long and 2 inches wide. This species can grow up to 12 feet high.

A variety of this species is purple lily magnolia (*M. liliflora* 'Nigra'). It has dark-purple flowers, 4 to 5 inches across.

Yulan magnolia (*M. denudata*) is a tree that is hardy in zone E. It has white flowers that bloom before the leaves appear. The flowers are 6 to 8 inches across and are saucerlike when fully open.

When fully grown, yulan is about 40 feet tall and has a widely spread and rounded top.

Star magnolia (*M. stellata*) is a large shrub or small

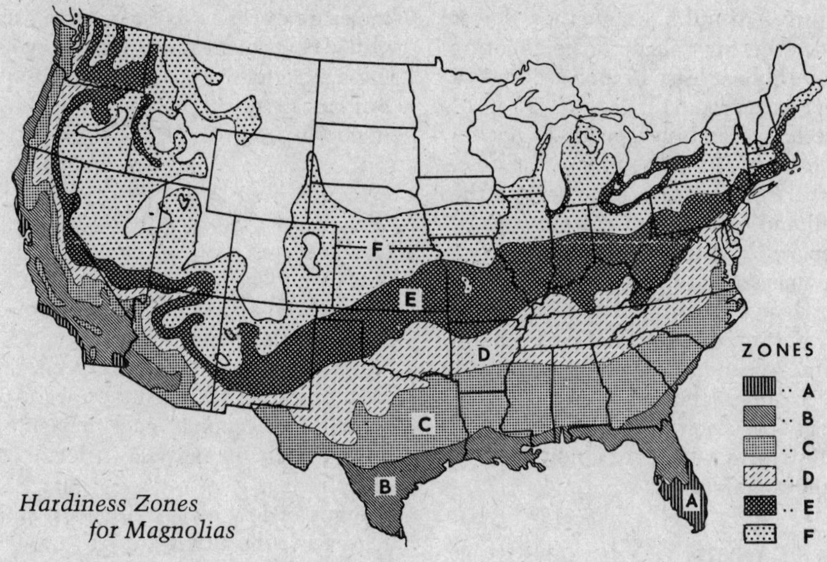

Hardiness Zones for Magnolias

tree that has white flowers. Its height and top spread are 10 to 20 feet. Star magnolia is hardy to zone E. Its flowers are about 3 inches across. The pink variety of the star magnolia is *M. stellata* 'Rosea'; the red is *M. stellata* 'Rubra'.

Sprenger magnolia (*M. sprengeri* Diva') is a tree that grows 35 feet tall and has a top spread of 25 feet. It is hardy to warmer parts of zone D. Its crimson flowers are often 8 inches across.

Saucer magnolia (*Magnolia* x *soulangiana*) is a small tree or a large shrub, hardy to zone E. Its height and top spread are 15 to 25 feet. Its flowers are 4 to 6 inches across.

Some varieties of saucer magnolia are:

'Lennei', a large, vigorous shrub. Its saucer-shaped flowers are deep reddish purple.

'Rustica', a large, vigorous spreading shrub. Its saucer-shaped flowers are rosy red.

'Verbanica', a small tree. Its chalice-shaped flowers are lavender pink.

'Alba', a small tree. Its saucer-shaped flowers are white and purple.

'Lilliputian', a small shrub with pink flowers.

BUYING MAGNOLIAS

Some magnolias do not survive cold temperatures. When buying magnolias, therefore, be sure to select varieties adapted to your area.

You can ask a reputable nurseryman in your locality to recommend species or varieties; generally the plants he has for sale are adapted to your area. You also can ask neighbors which kinds have done well for them. Or you can ask your county agricultural agent or your state agricultural college to recommend species that are adapted to your area.

Ordinarily you can buy two-year-old trees planted in cans or older trees that are balled and burlapped. If fat woolly buds are visible on the older trees, you can expect a few blooms the year you plant. Magnolias that have a ball of soil around the roots do not dry out readily, and they are easily established. Do not buy bare-root magnolias.

PLANTING

The best time to plant magnolias is in early spring, before new leaves start to grow.

The planting site should be about 12 feet on each

Southern magnolia

side. Magnolias thrive in full sun, but they flower satisfactorily under the high shade of neighboring trees. Dig a planting hole at least 18 inches deep and twice the diameter of the rootball.

If the roots are balled and burlapped, do not remove the burlap before setting the tree in the hole. After you plant the tree, cut the twine around the top of the rootball and fold back or cut off exposed parts of the burlap.

Plant the magnolias so that the top of the rootball is slightly higher than it was in the nursery. Then refill the hole with a mixture of equal parts of soil and organic matter—peat moss, well-decayed manure or leaf mulch. Press the soil mixture firmly around the rootball and scoop loose soil away from the top of rootball to form a basin for holding water. Water the plant thoroughly.

CARE

Mulching

After planting, cover the soil under the branches with a mulching material—peat moss, oak leaves or forest litter. Apply a layer about 3 inches deep. Add new mulching material periodically to maintain the mulch.

A mulch helps to keep the soil moist near the surface, where magnolia roots are most active. It also helps to prevent the growth of weeds. And as the mulching material decays, it releases nutrients for use by the magnolia tree.

If you use a hoe or other weeding tool around magnolias, be careful to avoid harming the shallow roots.

Watering

Rainfall ordinarily provides enough moisture for mulched magnolias. They need about 1 inch of moisture every 14 days. In some areas, rainfall will provide sufficient moisture. In dryer areas, and during dry periods, soak the roots at weekly intervals. But be careful that you do not drown trees growing in poorly drained soil.

Fertilizing

If magnolias are planted in reasonably fertile soil that is well supplied with organic matter, they seldom need fertilizing.

Trees growing in lawns benefit from fertilizers used on the lawn. But if you want to stimulate the growth of magnolias, or if they show signs that the soil is infertile, apply lawn fertilizer in late fall or early spring.

Signs of low soil fertility are small, sparse, pale leaves and short twig growth.

Use 2 pounds of fertilizer per inch of trunk diameter. Spread the fertilizer in a band 2 to 3 feet wide under the ends of the branches. Do not let the fertilizer touch the trunk. After applying fertilizer, water it into the soil.

Pruning

The best time to prune magnolias is in late spring, so that the pruning wounds will have time to heal during the growing season. Coat the wounds that are 1 inch or more in diameter with a good grade of asphalt paint or with tree-wound dressing.

DISEASES AND INSECTS

Magnolias seldom suffer serious damage from diseases and insects. A few diseases and insects affect these plants, however. Inspect magnolias frequently for signs of diseases and insects described in this

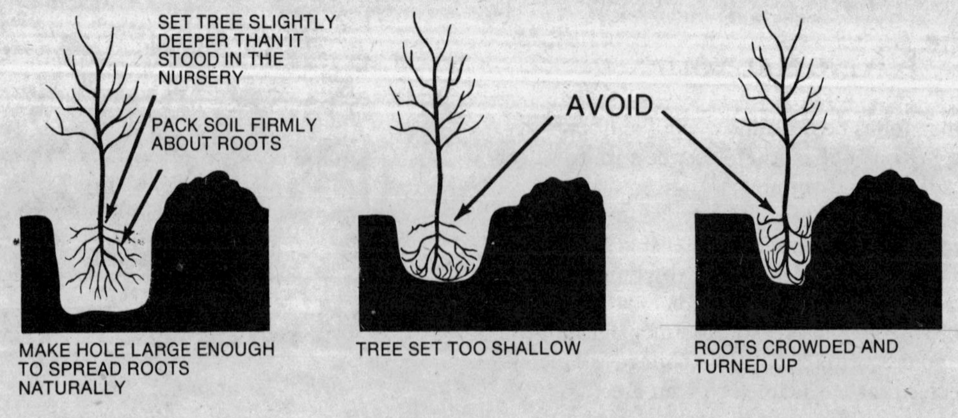
SET TREE SLIGHTLY DEEPER THAN IT STOOD IN THE NURSERY
PACK SOIL FIRMLY ABOUT ROOTS
AVOID
MAKE HOLE LARGE ENOUGH TO SPREAD ROOTS NATURALLY
TREE SET TOO SHALLOW
ROOTS CROWDED AND TURNED UP

section. See your county agricultural agent or state agricultural experiment station for information on how to control diseases and insects.

Diseases

Nectria canker: Nectria canker (European canker) ordinarily does not kill magnolias, but it disfigures them. A few cankers on the branches do little harm.

Cut out diseased bark and apply shellac to the wound. Then coat the wound with a tree-wound dressing.

Dieback: Freezing injury may cause dieback at the tops of magnolia trees. Late-season growth is especially susceptible to dieback. Prune dead branches and twigs back to healthy wood. Treat cuts with a tree-wound dressing.

Trunk decay: Fungi that cause trunk decay can enter magnolia trees through wounds made by bumping the trunk with a lawnmower. If damaged trees have multiple stems, remove the damaged stems and then select young shoots to replace them. Paint cuts with a tree-wound dressing.

If you find decay in the trunk, cut out the diseased wood. Slope the bottom of the cut downward so water can drain away, and apply shellac to the wound.

Leaf spots: Several leaf-spot diseases attack magnolias. These diseases often mar their appearance and at times can cause defoliation.

Glomerella leaf spot is common in the South; the spots are dark brown and have pale-yellow borders around them. Another leaf-spot disease is magnolia scab, which mottles the leaves a pale gray.

Powdery mildew: Powdery mildew sometimes develops on leaves of some magnolia varieties. Infected leaves are covered with a thin, cottony growth and have a powdery appearance.

Insects

Magnolia scale: The adult magnolia scale is 1½ inch in diameter, nearly round in shape, and varnish brown in color. Secreted wax often covers the scales, giving them a white, dusty appearance. Infested trees have reduced vigor and poor growth. The foliage and twigs appear sooty because of fungus on the honeydew secreted by the scales.

Immature scales overwinter on the twigs. During August, the females mature and produce eggs beneath their bodies. Crawlers hatch from these eggs, exit from under the mother scale during late August and September and settle on the twigs. There is one generation each year.

Wax scale: Wax scales have a thick, white, waxy covering on their reddish-brown bodies; they sometimes are tinted pink. Scales are about ³⁄₁₆ inch wide. They live on the stems of magnolias. Infested plants become stunted; heavily infested branches die. The insect has only one generation a year; the young scales hatch from eggs about July 1 and settle on new growth.

Tulip tree scale: Adult tulip tree scales are oval, dark-brown insects about ⅓ inch across the back. They usually crowd together on young stems, often near the ground. Their eggs hatch in August or September. Young scales are dull brown; they overwinter on the bark of magnolia trees.

Scales suck the sap from the trees and thus cause branches to die and sometimes kill trees. The insects often coat the leaves with a clear sirupy liquid called honeydew. A black sooty mold then grows on the coating and the leaves thus become unsightly.

Japanese beetles: Magnolia grandiflora and other summer-flowering species may attract Japanese beetles. Adult beetles have shiny, metallic-green bodies and coppery-brown wings. They are about ½ inch long.

Japanese beetles attack magnolia flowers in June and July. They feed on the petals and stamens. The edges of the petals first become ragged, then the flowers turn brown and curl.

Control

To control scales apply a spray containing malathion when scales are in the crawler stage. Malathion will also control the Japanese beetle. Follow the directions and heed are precautions on the insecticide label.

Contact a commercial pest control operator for effective treatment of large trees.

CHAPTER 19

Growing Apricots for Home Use

YOU CAN GROW APRICOT TREES in your yard or garden. They are adapted to a wide range of soil types. Apricots are attractive, symmetrical lawn trees that require only routine care. They produce fruit, however, only on sites that are relatively free of frosts during early spring. The fruit can be eaten fresh, preserved or dried.

ADAPTATION

Apricots produce fruit on favorable sites in most parts of the country, except in very cold and very warm areas. Blooms appear early and are easily damaged by spring frost. The blossoms and small fruits are as cold-tender as peaches and other stone fruits.

The frost hazard is primarily responsible for the concentration of commercial production in California (97 percent), Washington and Utah. There is also a little commercial growing in Colorado, Idaho, Michigan and Oregon.

High winter temperatures also limit apricot production in the very warm sections of the country. Apricot buds must be winter-chilled to break their rest period and start rapid growth. If minimum temperatures are high during winter, many fruit buds drop before flowering.

PLANTING SITES

Apricot trees are adapted to a variety of soils and climatic conditions, but the growing site must be relatively frost-free for the trees to produce fruit. The most frost-free sites are near large lakes, on the tops or sides of hills, or near the base of high hills or mountains. In valleys, there is little air movement and the coldest air settles in the lowest places where damaging temperatures occur more frequently and for longer periods than on sites with good air drainage.

Apricot trees grow best in deep, fertile, well-drained soil but they also grow well in light sandy soil when adequately fertilized and watered. Avoid heavy, poorly drained soil. Also avoid sites where tomatoes, cotton or brambles have grown; these crops harbor the verticillium wilt fungus that causes "black heart" of apricot.

Adequate soil moisture until harvest is necessary to produce large fruit. Trees need water after harvest for forming the next year's fruit buds. Supplemental irrigation may be required during long dry periods.

Temperatures of 102° F. or more just prior to fruit maturity cause pit burn. Pit burn is darkening of the flesh around the pit. High humidity and heavy rainfall increase brown rot infection.

VARIETIES

Fruit characteristics of the common varieties of apricots follow.

'Royal' and 'Blenheim': These are very similar and represent nearly ⅔ the apricot acreage in the United States. They have excellent flavor, small- to medium-size, and medium firmness; they are subject to pit burn when nearing maturity.

'Tilton': Tilton represents nearly ¼ the acreage in the United States. It is larger, lighter-colored, and firmer-fleshed than 'Royal' but the flavor is not as desirable. It is less subject to pit burn than 'Royal', which makes it better adapted to warm areas. It bears heavy crops but has a tendency to produce fruit only every other year.

Other varieties that may be available locally include 'Derby', 'Wenatchee' ('Moorpark'), 'Modesto', 'Goldcot', 'Moongold', 'Sungold', 'Manchu', 'Reliable' and 'Superb'. Varieties that are not self-fruitful and require another variety for pollination are 'Earliril', 'Riland' and 'Perfection'.

PLANTING

A year-old tree 4 to 6 feet tall and ½ to ¾ inch in diameter at the base is the ideal size. This may be a June-budded or August-budded tree, but in either case, it will have produced only one season's growth of the bud. Larger, or two-year-old, trees may be used but they generally are more expensive. Although smaller trees often are satisfactory, they require extra care during the first year. Nursery trees usually are straight whips; however, they may be branched.

When you receive trees from the nursery and cannot plant them immediately, bury the roots temporarily in moist, well-drained soil to keep them from drying. Pack soil around them to the same depth they were in at the nursery.

Another way to keep the roots moist temporarily is to place moist packing material such as sawdust, old straw or peat moss around them. Keep the trees in a cool, shaded place and keep the packing material moist.

Plant apricot trees 24 to 30 feet from houses and other trees, if possible. At these distances, trees are more easily held to the desired height and shape by pruning.

In cold climates, plant trees while they are dormant in late winter or early spring. In moderate climates you may plant them in late fall or winter so that roots can become established before top growth starts.

Thoroughly spade or plow the planting site to loosen the soil and remove weeds. Loose soil encourages root growth. The soil must not be too wet to cultivate at time of planting, but it should be moist. Prepare the planting hole large enough to hold the roots without bending them.

Cut off broken or diseased roots and shorten any unusually long ones. Plant the tree at the same depth it was at the nursery. Sift the soil in around the roots and pack it. Fill the hole until level with the ground surface. Water the soil to settle it around the roots.

Newly planted trees need nitrogen fertilizer. Apply ⅛ to ¼ pound of nitrogen fertilizer evenly over a 3-foot circle around the tree at planting. Repeat this two or three times in early summer, if needed to maintain good growth. Do not fertilize after midsummer. This will allow normal hardening of the tree before winter.

PRUNING

The purpose of pruning is to shape the tree, limit the crop when necessary (see "Thinning the Fruit," page 166) and maintain vigor. Young trees just developing their fruit-bearing branches should be pruned lightly because pruning dwarfs them and delays bearing. Prune the top at planting time by cutting back the main stem 18 to 30 inches from the ground.

Cut off all lateral branches that are within 12 inches of the ground close to the trunk. Large lateral branches that are attached higher on the trunk and are distributed around the tree at different heights should be cut back to 4 to 6 inches in length. You may use three or four of these later as scaffold branches that will control the shape of the tree. Remove all other laterals, but leave short stubs to produce new buds.

In the spring, when new growth is 3 to 4 inches long, the three or four scaffold branches may be selected by their position on the trunk. Pinch back the tips of new shoots on all other growth. Remove only the tip of each shoot; removal of the entire shoot will cause a drastic setback in growth. Additional pinching back later will also help in directing tree growth into the scaffold branches.

After the first growing season, the three or four branches selected to form a uniformly shaped tree should be headed back 2 or 3 feet from the trunk to form the primary scaffolds. Make the cut just above an outside lateral branch on each scaffold branch.

Remove branches other than the scaffolds from the trunk of the tree. Leave the lateral branches on the scaffolds that do not cross each other. Lightly pruned trees will bear earlier and heavier than heavily pruned ones.

In the second dormant-season pruning, leave the short spur-type branches on the tree. Remove laterals forming on the scaffolds near the trunk. Select five to seven secondary scaffolds from laterals growing on the primary scaffolds. The secondary scaffolds should arise 4 to 5 feet from the ground. Nor-

Newly planted apricot tree headed back at about 28 inches (arrow). Union is at ground line.

One-year-old apricot tree with well-placed scaffold branches selected and headed back

Ten-year-old apricot tree with strong framework of three scaffold branches and strong secondary branching

mally these grow where the main scaffolds were headed the previous season. They should be well spaced around the tree because they will form the main framework.

Remove other secondary branches and keep the center of the tree open. Some heading back and balancing of scaffolds may be needed. The topmost scaffold should be the largest to prevent it from being crowded out by lower branches.

The dormant-season pruning is also a shaping and thinning process. Severe heading back is not necessary until the tree grows to the desired height.

After the growing tree has been trained and shaped the first three or four years, the mature tree is pruned to control height, maintain vigor and renew the short branches or spurs.

Most apricot varieties bear principally on the spurs, which are short-lived. A common practice is to replace about one third of the spurs each year. You can encourage their formation by spacing branches for exposure to sunlight, cutting back vigorous growth to weaker laterals, and thinning out upper branches to prevent excessive shading. The tree should produce from 15 to 30 inches of new growth each year.

THINNING THE FRUIT

Apricot trees tend to produce more fruit than they should bear. Thinning the fruit reduces the load, produces larger fruit, encourages regular bearing and promotes earlier maturity. Thin the fruit during the pit-hardening stage when growth of the fruit has temporarily slowed (six to eight weeks after bloom).

Twelve-year-old orchard after pruning

Remove smaller fruits first and break up clusters. The amount of thinning needed depends on the number of fruits set on the tree and the ultimate size of fruit desired.

FERTILIZING

Nitrogen is needed more than any other fertilizer by most apricot trees. Nitrogen deficiency causes yellow foliage, lower production, and smaller, firmer fruit that matures early. The proper amount of nitrogen to apply is best determined by trial or from previous experience. You may apply nitrogen in fall or early spring.

Apricots need additional potash when the soil is low in potassium. Land scraped in leveling or leached by rain is most likely to be low in potassium. Two to 4 pounds of muriate or sulfate of potash per tree applied in early spring is usually adequate.

CULTIVATING AND HARVESTING

Apricot trees are generally cultivated in late winter or early spring to kill grass and other weeds, which should not be permitted to compete with the trees during the period of most active growth. Later, you may allow grass or weeds to grow. A ground cover of grass, weeds or mulch at harvest helps prevent pit burn by keeping temperatures lower, but it also encourages brown rot infection.

Allow fruit harvested for canning to become firm-ripe on the tree but not fully mature. Harvest fruit for drying when it is fully mature.

PEST CONTROL

Fungus and Bacterial Diseases

The most serious fungus and bacterial diseases that attack apricots are brown rot, shot-hole, bacterial canker, cytosporina and crown gall.

Brown rot: Brown rot attacks both blossoms and fruits. Infected blossoms wither and die. The fungus then moves into the twigs at the base of the blossoms and causes cankers. Masses of ash-gray powdery spores appear and these may cause new infection throughout the season and the following year.

To control blossom infection, remove infected twigs at pruning time before blossoms develop. Spray with benomyl, captan or bordeaux mixture between the redbud stage and full bloom. Do not use a sulfur spray on apricots because it seriously injures them.

Brown rot can be controlled on ripening fruit by preharvest sprays of captan or benomyl. Destroy all mummies, or rotted fruits, on the tree or ground.

Shot-hole: Shot-hole fungus causes defoliation of trees and malformation of fruit. In the spring, reddish spots appear on the leaves and fruits. Affected parts of the leaves fall out, causing holes. Infected buds die during the winter.

To control the disease, spray with ziram or captan at redbud stage, early bloom and full bloom, and spray with bordeaux mixture, ziram, or ferbam just after leaf fall.

Bacterial canker: Young apricot trees are highly susceptible to bacterial canker, which usually affects buds and spurs. However, the disease may produce large dead areas or cankers on large limbs and the trunk. Infected branches or the whole tree may die.

There is no satisfactory control for bacterial canker. A spray of 10–10–100 bordeaux mixture just as leaves begin to fall and again when most of the leaves are off may be of some benefit, but is not always effective.

Cytosporina: Cytosporina is a fungus disease that occurs almost entirely at pruning wounds and causes dieback of small branches, large limbs, and even entire trees. The infection produces cankers, discolored wood, gum exudation as the disease advances, and weak growth.

Sanitation is the best control. Remove and burn all infected parts, cutting at least 6 inches below a canker. Seal large pruning wounds with grafting wax or an oil-base paint. Sterilize pruning tools with formalin after cutting through a canker.

Crown gall: This bacterial disease infects large roots or crowns of apricot trees. It produces irregular gall enlargements and growths that may girdle the tree.

Crown gall bacteria are widely distributed in soils and enter trees through wounds. Care should be taken in planting trees and during cultivation to avoid injuring the trunks and large roots. You can control the infection by cleaning the soil away from the diseased area and painting the gall with metacresol.

Virus Diseases

Many virus diseases are capable of infecting apricot trees, but few do serious damage. Ring pox and ring spot are the most common.

Ring pox: Ring pox causes the leaves of apricot trees to develop irregular rings and angular spots, or yellowed areas. Fruits develop surface bumps and may drop. Infected trees should be destroyed.

Ring spot: Ring spot symptoms are rare on most apricot varieties. Rings and yellowed patterns on leaves may develop in the initial acute stage of the disease but disappear later. The disease reduces growth. No control has been developed.

Insects

Many species of insects attack apricot trees. Some

of the more common ones, and the insecticides for their control, follow:

Pest	*Insecticide*
Aphids	malathion
Borers	endosulfan
Japanese beetles	carbaryl or malathion
Mites	dicofol
Oriental fruit moth	carbaryl
Plum curculio	malathion or methoxychlor
Scales	malathion

Follow all directions and heed all precautions on the insecticide package labels. For further information on insect control, see your county agricultural agent or state extension service.

VII

GROWING PLANT SPECIALTIES

CHAPTER 20

Azaleas and Rhododendrons

AZALEAS AND RHODODENDRONS ARE at their best in climates that are fairly mild and humid. They grow well throughout the Appalachian Mountains and in the states along the Atlantic and Gulf coasts. They do well around Lake Erie, in the southern Mississippi Valley and along the Pacific coast from Puget Sound to San Francisco Bay.

Soils or climate in the rest of the United States may be unfavorable for azaleas. Azaleas can be grown in unfavorable regions, but they need more attention than in favorable regions.

You can grow azaleas successfully if you follow these rules in planting and caring for them:

- Buy species and varieties that are adapted to your area.
- Get plants that are at least 8 to 16 inches tall.
- Plant them in well-drained, acid soil that is high in organic matter.
- Set plants no deeper than they were in the nursery.
- Maintain a mulch around them during the growing season.
- Guard against drought; be sure that young or freshly moved plants receive adequate water, particularly the first two years after transplanting. Do not overwater in areas where drainage is poor.
- Protect azaleas from insect attack.

BUYING AZALEAS

Some kinds of azaleas will survive colder winter temperatures than other kinds. Some will withstand hotter summer temperatures than others. Before you buy azalea plants, be sure they are adapted to your area. You can ask a reputable nurseryman in your locality to recommend species or varieties; generally, plants that have been propagated and grown by the nursery are adapted to your area. You also can ask neighbors which kinds have done well for them. Or you can ask your county agricultural agent or your state agricultural experiment station for species and variety recommendations.

Buy plants that are sturdy and well branched and at least 8 to 16 inches tall. Small plants are easily injured in winter. If you get plants less than 8 inches tall, grow them in a coldframe for a year or two before you set them out. Plants more than 16 inches tall are satisfactory, but they are more expensive than the smaller sizes.

Get balled and burlapped plants—plants that have a burlap-wrapped ball of soil around the roots. These do not dry as easily as bare-root plants, and they are more easily established.

PLANTING AZALEAS

You can plant azaleas most successfully when they are dormant.

In their northern range, the best time to plant them is early spring, before new leaves start to grow. In the South they can be planted from fall to early spring, at any time the ground is unfrozen.

You also can plant or move azaleas while they are growing, though with more risk than while they are dormant. Many azaleas are sold in the spring while they are in bloom. These can be established successfully in the garden if they are protected carefully from drying after they are planted.

Planting Sites

Azaleas do not grow well in dense shade; they become spindly and bloom only sparsely. They will grow satisfactorily, however, either in full sunlight or in moderate shade.

They grow best where they have alternating sunshine and shade and are protected from the wind. A good place to plant azaleas is under tall, deep-rooted trees such as oaks and pines. There, the mixture of sunshine and shade is good.

Do not plant azaleas under shallow-rooted trees such as elms and maples, however. These trees will use water and plant food needed by the azaleas.

Evergreen trees with low branches make good windbreaks and attractive backgrounds for azaleas. Closely planted shrubs are good also, if they do not encroach on the space needed for the azalea plants.

If you are planting azaleas around a building, they will do best on the north and east sides of the building, where they are protected from the hot afternoon sun. You can plant them on other sides of the building, but you will have to give them more attention to protect them from drying.

Spacing the Plants

Spacing of azalea and rhododendron plants depends on the variety you plant and the effect you want.

Mature rhododendrons spread to 6 or 8 feet in diameter. Mature azaleas need 4 to 6 feet of space per plant.

Spacing is no problem for single plants; plant them far enough from other plants or from buildings so they will not be crowded when mature.

If you want a mass of blooms, set plants close together while they are young, then transplant them as they become crowded.

A good plan is to space small azaleas 2 feet apart. After three or four years, when they start crowding each other, remove alternate plants and replant them in another location. This will give remaining plants room to develop.

Preparing the Soil

Prepare the planting site several weeks in advance of planting. Prepare beds to spade depth or dig individual holes at least 18 inches in diameter and 12 inches deep.

Azaleas need acid soil that holds moisture and is well drained. Adding organic matter of the right type—peat moss, one- to two-year-old oak leaves, or forest leaf mold—increases soil acidity and improves water-holding capacity of sandy soils and drainage of clay soils.

If your soil is neutral or alkaline, organic matter may not add enough acidity. Then it is necessary to make the soil acid with chemicals or grow the plants in tubs or planters that contain suitable soil.

Press soil firmly under the rootball to set the plant at the proper level and to keep it from settling.

If you are preparing planting beds, spread a layer of organic matter 4 or 5 inches deep over the surface of the spaded bed. Mix the organic matter with the upper 6 inches of soil.

If you are preparing separate planting holes, mix the soil from the hole with an equal volume of organic matter.

After you have added organic matter to the soil, the surface of the bed or planting hole will be higher than the surrounding soil. If the soil is heavy and your area has frequent hard rains, leave the surface mounded; it will help drain away excess water and keep the beds from getting waterlogged. Under normal conditions, level the beds or planting holes.

Setting the Plants

Dig planting holes larger than the rootballs of the azalea plants. If the roots of the plant are balled and burlapped, it is not necessary to remove the burlap before setting the plant in the hole. Cut the twine around the top of the rootball and fold back or cut off exposed parts of the burlap after placing the plant in the hole. If other materials are used for wrapping the rootball, remove them.

Press soil around the rootball. Pack it firmly under the plant. While you are doing this, set the plant so it is no deeper than it was in the nursery. If the roots are planted too deeply, they will not get enough air, and the plant will die.

After you fill the hole, soak the soil thoroughly. This helps to bring the soil into close contact with the roots.

CARE

Mulching

As soon as you have the plants set, mulch the soil around them with oak leaves, peat moss, pine needles or leaf mold.

Use at least 2 inches of peat moss or pine needles or 2 to 5 inches of leaves or leaf mold. Spread the mulch so all the soil is covered beneath the branches.

If the plants are not sheltered by nearby buildings, shrubs or trees, remove the mulch at the onset of cold weather and replace again after the ground freezes. If they are growing in sheltered locations, the mulch can remain in place. Add additional mulching material every spring.

Watering

Water plants thoroughly when weather conditions make it necessary. The amount needed will vary, depending on amount of rainfall, temperature, humidity and wind velocity. However, be sure the plants get enough water.

Watering is essential during the first two years after planting. After azaleas become well established, they usually will survive with normal rainfall.

If you plant azaleas under overhanging eaves or where rain does not reach them, you will have to supply all their water. If this is the case, continue watering through the winter whenever the ground is not frozen.

Fertilizing

Azaleas may need light fertilizing soon after planting. Apply fertilizer in early spring. After the first season, organic matter usually furnishes enough nutrients to the plants. If the plants need fertilizer, their leaves begin to turn light green. Garden stores sell fertilizer formulated especially for azaleas. Apply it according to the directions on the package.

Do not apply fertilizer after July 1. Do not use special lawn fertilizers on azaleas. These fertilizers often are alkaline and may contain herbicides that could kill the azaleas.

Pruning

Azaleas grow well without pruning. You may want to prune them, however, to remove dead or injured branches, to shape the plants or to reduce their size.

If you want your plants to be bushier, cut growing twigs halfway back after they elongate.

Plants that have grown too tall or are crowded can be pruned back severely to the size and shape you want. Prune after blossoming to reduce flower loss. The plants will not have many flowers the season after pruning, but in following years the flowers will be more abundant.

Weeding

A heavy mulch prevents weeds from growing readily around plants. Hand-pull those weeds that do manage to grow. Do not cultivate with a hoe or other garden implements. Azalea roots grow close to the surface and will be injured if the soil is disturbed.

INSECTS AND DISEASES

If your azaleas or rhododendrons are damaged by insects or related pests (for example, spider mites) or diseases, determine the kind of pest or disease responsible for the damage, then apply an appropriate remedy. Without protection against insects, the plants will not thrive.

Insects

The azalea lacebug and spider mites are particularly troublesome, and are discussed below. The insecticides recommended for controlling them are available at garden-supply stores.

Azalea lacebug: Adults are about ⅛ inch long and have lacy wings and brown-and-black markings. The young, called nymphs, are spiny; they are colorless at first, then become black.

Adults and nymphs suck sap from the underside of leaves. This causes the upper surface to have a gray, blanched or coarse-stippled appearance, and reduces plant vitality. The undersides of leaves become discolored by excrement and cast skins. Plants in the sun are more severely damaged than those in the shade.

Control: Apply a spray containing malathion. The first application should be made about June 1 in the North, and earlier in the year in the South. Repeat application every ten days until control is obtained.

Spider mites: Adults and young of these tiny mites—they are barely visible to the naked eye—are found on the undersides of leaves. They are red or greenish red.

First signs of infestation are yellow, stippled areas on leaves and fine webs on leaves and flowers. Entire leaves become yellowed, gray or brownish. Flowers are discolored and faded. Injury usually appears in June or later.

Control: Apply a spray containing dicofol. Follow directions and heed all precautions on the insecticide labels.

To keep spider mites from occurring in damaging numbers every year, keep area weed-free and avoid planting overwintering mite hosts such as foxglove, hollyhock and violets among the azaleas.

For further information on control of insects on azaleas and rhododendrons, contact your county agricultural agent.

Diseases

Many troubles with azaleas and rhododendrons are caused by planting varieties that are not adapted to the particular environment or by taking improper care of the plants. However, the diseases discussed below may affect plants that have been well cared for.

Petal blight: Flowers become spotted, then limp. All flowers on the plant are quickly destroyed. Spray with zineb, prepared as directed by the manufacturer, two or three times a week during the flowering season.

Tip blight or dieback: Starts with light-brown blotches on the leaves. May spread down the leaf stalk into the branch. Branch dies. Cut off diseased branches below brown discoloration. Remove faded flower clusters. Spray the plant with 6 to 7 ounces of dry bordeaux mixture in 10 gallons of water immediately after the flowers fade.

Leaf gall: Pale-green or whitish fleshy galls grow on leaves or flowers. Hand-pick the galls. Spray with zineb prepared as directed on the package.

Leaf scorch: Leaves have yellowish spots with brown centers and reddish borders. Leaves drop off and plant is weakened. Apply zineb in spring and fall.

Iron chlorosis: Leaves turn light green or yellow between the veins, but the veins remain green. Plants lack iron, usually because the soils are not acid enough. If acid-forming fertilizer does not make your soil acid enough, spread 1 teaspoonful of aluminum sulfate crystals in the plant's "drip area." Do not apply lime or too much phosphate.

Rain washes lime from masonry walls into azalea plantings nearby and lowers soil acidity. This can be checked temporarily by spraying the foliage with 1 ounce of ferrous sulfate in 1 gallon of water; or by using iron chelates on soil, or sprays on foliage, as recommended on the manufacturer's label.

Soil acidity must be changed for longer-lasting control. Consult your county agricultural agent or your state agricultural experiment station for control recommendations.

CHAPTER 21

Bonsai

BONSAI ARE MINIATURE TREES grown in pots. The aim of bonsai culture is to develop a tiny tree that has all the elements of a large tree growing in a natural setting. This look is achieved principally by branch and root pruning and shaping, but other factors are also important. The texture of the trunk, its look of age, the moss and underplantings in the container—all contribute to the illusion of a miniature tree as it is seen in nature.

A presentable bonsai can be created in a few seasons. Cultivating these miniature potted trees is both an intriguing hobby and a means of adapting a wide range of plants to specialized and decorative uses. Bonsai require daily watering during their growing season and, because the plants are rooted in shallow pots, careful pruning.

Bonsai are kept outdoors most of the year, but from time to time these miniaturized versions of nature are brought indoors for display. Only certain tropical trees, shrubs and vines can be continuously kept indoors full time as bonsai.

Bonsai, as an art form, stems from ancient Oriental culture. It originated in China and was developed by the Japanese. In the thirteenth century the Japanese collected and potted wild trees that had been dwarfed by nature. These naturally formed miniatures were the first bonsai.

When demand for the small trees outgrew the supply, Japanese gardeners began to train bonsai from native trees. They shaped the trees to give them the illusion of age and naturalness. Over the years, the Japanese devised standards of shape and form which gradually became the classic bonsai styles.

American bonsai are much freer in concept and style than Japanese bonsai. American bonsai growers have recognized that the horticultural and aesthetic rules are important, but that these are specifically aimed at Japanese culture. Americans have taken Oriental styles and applied them to plants never grown by the Japanese. Therefore, the rigid procedures and names used by the Japanese are not used here.

PRINCIPLES OF BONSAI

Not all plants are equally effective as bonsai. To produce a realistic illusion of a mature tree, look for plants with the following characteristics:

- Small leaves or needles.
- Short internodes, or distances between leaves.
- Attractive bark or roots.
- Branching characteristics for good twig forms.

All parts of the ideal bonsai—trunk, branches, twigs, leaves, flowers, fruits, buds, roots—should be in perfect scale with the size of the tree. Plants used for bonsai should have small leaves, or leaves that become small under bonsai culture. Plants with overly large leaves, such as the avocado, will look out of proportion if chosen for bonsai. Sycamores also develop leaves that are too large. Certain species of both maple and oak trees usually respond well to bonsai culture and develop leaves that are in proportion.

Among the plants with small leaves and needles are spruce, pine, zelkova, pomegranate and certain oaks and maples.

Plants chosen for bonsai should have attractive bark, and the trunk must give the illusion of maturity. The trunk should have girth, but must remain in proportion to the entire tree. The trunk should taper gradually toward the top of the tree. Sometimes one or two of the main branches must be shortened to emphasize the vertical line of the trunk and give the trunk a balanced appearance.

To give the appearance of age, the upper third of the root structure of a mature bonsai is often exposed. This is especially effective if the roots have good girth and form. Twisted and tangled roots should be straightened before potting or repotting a tree to achieve an aged appearance.

Both bonsai from nursery stock and trees collected from the wild should have a root system that will, when exposed, add to the appearance of the finished bonsai.

Plants have a "best profile," just as people do. Decide on where the front of the tree will be at the very beginning, because planting and shaping are done with the front of the tree in mind. However, you may change your ideas about the plant's ultimate shape as you clip and prune.

The front of a bonsai should offer a good view of the main trunk, which must be clearly visible from the base to the first branch, typically about one third the way up. Everywhere on the tree, but mostly from the front, the branches should look balanced and appear to be floating in space; they should not appear lopsided or top-heavy. The branches should not be opposite one another with their lines cutting horizontally across the trunk. The branches give the bonsai dimension and establish the tree's basic form.

A bonsai should have a harmonious arrangement of branches without unsightly gaps. Flaws can be spotted by looking down on a bonsai. Upper branches should not overshadow lower branches.

Before deciding on the shape of your bonsai, study the tree carefully and take into account the natural form of the species. Observe the way mature trees of the same kind grow in their natural setting, so that you can achieve an impression of age and reality.

Decide on the final shape and size of your bonsai before starting. Make a rough sketch of what you wish to create and use it as a guide.

CHOOSING A STYLE

Bonsai can be classified into five basic styles: *formal upright, informal upright, slanting, cascade,* and *semicascade.* These classifications are based on the overall shape of the tree, and how much the trunk slants away from an imaginary vertical axis.

The numerous Japanese bonsai styles are principally variations of these five basic styles. The styles discussed here apply to trees with single trunks. The single-trunk style is a basic design that is simplest to shape because the one trunk determines the overall composition.

The *formal upright style* has classic proportions and is the basis for all bonsai. It is the easiest for a beginner to develop because it requires the least experimentation, avoids the problem of selective pruning and should almost immediately become a displayable bonsai.

In this style, the form is conical or sometimes rounded, and the tree has an erect leader and horizontal branches. One of the branches is lower and extends a little farther from the trunk than the others.

Note the off-center placement of this mugo pine in its rectangular container. This tree was trained in the formal upright style.

Also, the two lowest branches are trained to come forward on the front side of the tree, one slightly higher than the other. The third branch of this style extends out in back of the tree at a level between the two side branches to give the plant depth.

Plants in the formal upright style look best in oval or rectangular containers. Do not center the plant

The formal upright style is considered the easiest for the novice bonsai grower. This style features a straight trunk and a bottom branch that is lower and extends further from the trunk than its opposite.

when placing it in the container. Plant it about a third of the distance from one end.

In choosing a nursery plant for this style make sure the trunk rises from the ground in a fairly straight line. The trunk should be straight and should not fork or branch out for the total height of the tree. Trim off the small branches or twigs that are too close to the base and near the main stem. These branches detract from the overall composition.

The *informal upright style* has much the same branch arrangement as the formal upright style, but the top, instead of being erect as in the formal upright style, bends slightly to the front. This bend makes the tree's branches appear to be in motion and enhances the look of informality.

Many nursery trees are naturally slanted. This makes them well suited to the informal upright style. Check the tree's slant by looking down at the trunk from above; from this angle the top should slant to the front. If this view is not attractive, you may move the rootball to slant the tree in another direction.

If you choose a vertical tree at the nursery and want to train it in the informal upright style, simply tilt the plant when potting it. When you do this, trim the branches and foliage so they are scaled to the size of the tree.

The informal upright style looks best in an oval or rectangular container. It should be planted, not in the center of the container, but a third of the distance from one end.

In the *slanting style,* the trunk has a more acute angle than in the previous styles. The lowest branch

Flowering plum bonsai, trained in the informal upright style, is set on a rock; this setting enhances the illusion of a tree growing in the wild.

Lodgepole pine was 67 years old when it was collected from the Sierra Nevada mountains of California; it was trained in the slanting style of bonsai.

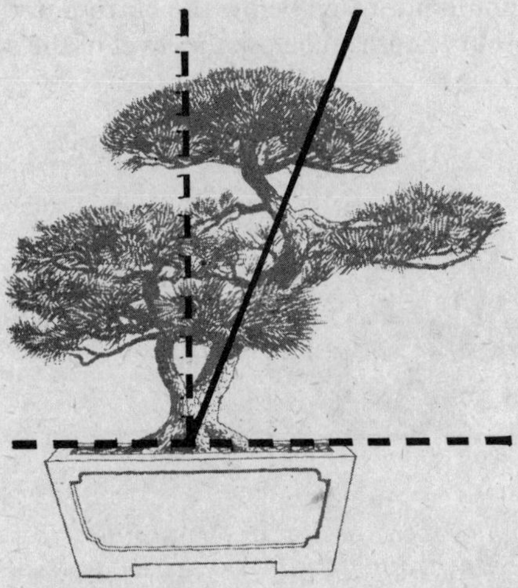

The trunk in the informal upright style bends slightly to the front. This bend helps to give the style its look of informality.

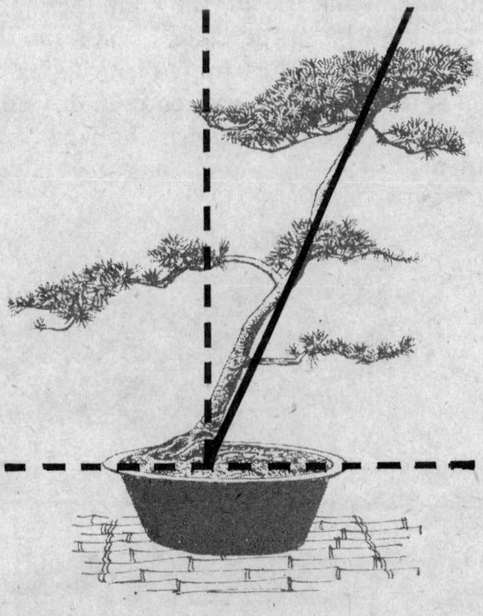

In the slanting style the trunk has a more acute angle than in the informal upright style. The lowest branch spreads in a direction opposite to that in which the tree slants.

Firethorn bonsai, trained in the cascade style, has a characteristic leader that descends below the bottom edge of the container.

The cascade style of bonsai represents a natural tree growing down the face of an embankment. A cascaded planting usually looks best in a round or hexagonal container.

should spread in the direction opposite that in which the tree slants. The top of the tree is bent slightly toward the front. The lower branches are arranged in groups of three, starting about one third the way up the trunk.

Slanting trees in nature are called "leaners"—trees that have been forced by the wind and gravity into nonvertical growth. The attitude of the slanting style falls between the upright and the cascade styles. This style looks best planted in the center of a round or square container.

In the *cascade style* the trunk starts by growing upward from the soil, then turns downward abruptly and reaches a point below the bottom edge of the container. For this reason, the container should be placed on the edge of the table, or on a small stand.

The cascade style has most of its foliage *below* the soil surface. This style is representative of a natural tree that is growing down the face of an embankment.

Training a tree in the cascade style takes longer than in the slanting style. Choose a low-growing species instead of forcing a tree that normally grows upright into an unnatural form. Bend the whole tree forward so one back branch is vertical and the side branches fall naturally.

A cascaded planting usually looks best in a round or hexagonal container that is higher than it is wide. The tree should be planted off-center from the cascading side.

The *semicascade style* has a trunk that is allowed to grow straight for a certain distance and then is cascaded down at *a less abrupt angle* than in the cascade style.

The cascading branches are thought of as the front of the tree, and the back branches are trained closer to the trunk than in the other styles. The semicascade should not reach below the bottom of the container, but should go below the level of the soil surface.

Cotoneaster in round container was trained in the semicascade style.

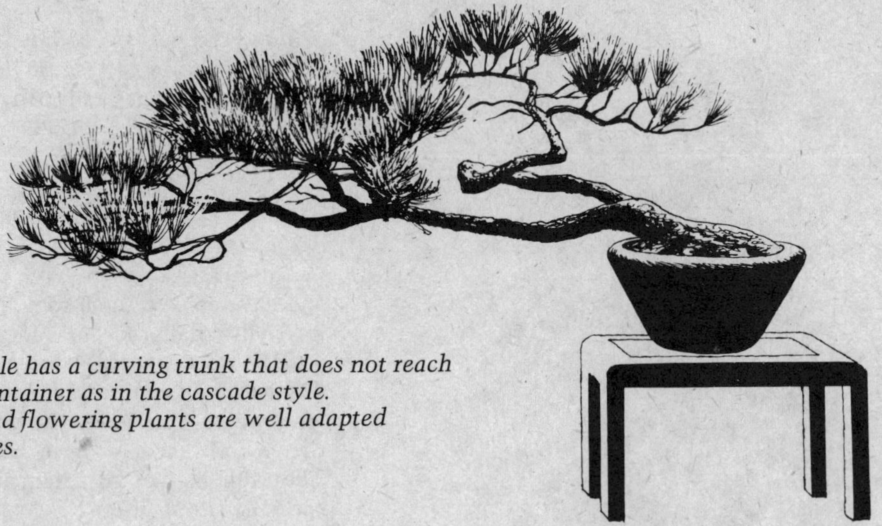

The semicascade style has a curving trunk that does not reach the bottom of the container as in the cascade style. Prostrate junipers and flowering plants are well adapted to both of these styles.

Plants that are well adapted to the cascade and semicascade styles are prostrate junipers and flowering plants such as chrysanthemums, wisteria, willows and star jasmine.

Before potting a tree for bonsai in any of the five styles, keep in mind the image of how the tree will stand in the container. Don't plant a tree one way and then uproot it to make a change.

Keep your overall theme in mind when planting bonsai. Upright trees should have a stabilized look in the container; slanted and cascaded styles often have their upper root surfaces exposed to imitate plants that grow this way in nature.

No matter what style of bonsai you choose—whether single trunk specimens or groups of trees from single roots—everything depends on your selection of plant material and your ability to visualize the bonsai's final form.

BONSAI GUIDE

Trees and Shrubs

The following list of plants includes trees and shrubs suitable for traditional bonsai. This is not intended to be a complete list. Specialty nurseries often have a wide selection of dwarf and semidwarf varieties of many of these species. Dwarf plants, however, do not always convey the same impression as their full-size counterparts because their growth habit is quite different.

Apricot (*Prunus* species)
Arborvitae:
  American (*Thuja occidentalis*)
  Oriental (*Thuja orientalis*)
Azalea:
  Hiryu (*Rhododendron obtusum*)
  Indica (*Rhododendron indicum*)
  Kurume (*Rhododendron* hybrids)
Beech:
  American (*Fagus grandifolia*)
  European (*Fagus sylvatica*)
Birch, White (*Betula alba*)
Box (*Buxus* species)
Burningbush (*Euonymus nana*)
Cedar:
  Atlas (*Cedrus atlantica*)
  Deodar (*Cedrus deodara*)
Cherry (*Prunus* species)
Cotoneaster (*Cotoneaster* species)
Crabapple (*Malus* species)
Cryptomeria (*Cryptomeria japonica* and cultivars)
Cypress:
  Bald (*Taxodium distichum*)
  Dwarf hinoki (*Chamaecyparis obtusa* var. *'Compacta'*)
Elm:
  American (*Ulmus americana*)
  Chinese (*Ulmus parvifolia*)
  Siberian (*Ulmus pumila*)
Fir (*Abies* species)
Firethorn (*Pyracantha* species)
Ginkgo (*Ginkgo biloba*)
Goldenrain Tree (*Koelreuteria paniculata*)
Hawthorn:
  English (*Crataegus oxyacantha*)
  Washington (*Crataegus phaenopyrum*)
Heather (*Calluna vulgaris*)
Hemlock, Canadian (*Tsuga canadensis* and cultivars)
Hornbeam:
  American (*Carpinus caroliniana*)
  Japanese (*Carpinus japonica*)

A group planting in any of the bonsai styles makes use of only one species of tree. Cryptomeria is shown here.

Ivy (*Hedera helix* and cultivars)
Jasmine, Winter (*Jasminum nudiflorum*)
Juniper (*Juniperus* species and cultivars)
Locust, Black (*Robinia pseudoacacia*)
Maple:
  Amur (*Acer ginnala*)
  Hedge (*Acer campestre*)
  Trident (*Acer buergerianum*)
Oak:
  English (*Quercus robur*)
  Pin (*Quercus palustris*)
  Scarlet (*Quercus coccinea*)
  White (*Quercus alba*)
Peach (*Prunus* species)
Pine:
  Bristlecone (*Pinus aristata*)
  Japanese black (*Pinus thunbergii*)
  Japanese white (*Pinus parviflora*)
  Mugo (*Pinus mugo mughus*)
  Swiss Stone (*Pinus cembra*)
  White (*Pinus strobus*)
Plum (*Prunus* species)
Pomergranate, dwarf (*Punica granatum nana*)
Quince, Japanese (*Chaenomeles japonica*)
Snowbell, Japanese (*Styrax japonica*)
Spruce (*Picea* species and cultivars)
Sweet Gum (*Liquidambar styraciflua*)
Willow, Weeping (*Salix blanda*)
Wisteria, Japanese (*Wisteria floribunda*)
Yew (*Taxus* species and cultivars)
Zelkova, graybark elm (*Zelkova serrata*)

Bonsai as House Plants

American gardeners have taken bonsai concepts and have applied them to house plants. By combining traditional procedures for handling house plants with bonsai concepts of design, growers have created different bonsai styles. The following list consists of woody plants (native to the tropics and subtropics of the world) that have been grown as indoor bonsai. These plants can be obtained from either local or specialized nurseries.

Acacia (*Acacia baileyana*)
Aralia:
  (*Polyscias balfouriana*)
  (*Polyscias fruticosa*)
  (*Polyscias guilfoylei*)
Bird's Eye Bush (*Ochna multiflora*)
Camellia (*Camellia japonica, C. sasanqua*)
Cape-Jasmine (*Gardenia jasminoides, G. jasminoides radicans*)
Citrus (*Citrus* species: calamondin, kumquat, lemon, lime, orange, and tangerine)
Cherry, Surinam (*Eugenia uniflora*)
Cypress:
  Arizona (*Cupressus arizonica*)
  Monterey (*Cupressus macrocarpa*)
Elfin Herb (*Cuphea hyssopifolia*)
Fig, Mistletoe (*Ficus diversifolia*)
Hibiscus (*Hibiscus rosa-sinensis 'Cooperi'*)
Holly, miniature (*Malpighia coccigera*)
Jacaranda (*Jacaranda acutifolia*)
Jade Tree (*Crassula* species)
Jasmine:
  (*Jasminum parkeri*)
  Orange (*Murraea exotica*)
  Star (*Trachelospermum jasminoides*)
Laurel, Indian (*Ficus retusa*)
Myrtle, classic (*Myrtus communis*)
Natal Plum (*Carissa grandiflora*)
Oak:
  Cork (*Quercus suber*)
  Indoor (*Nicodemia diversifolia*)
  Silk (*Grevillea robusta*)
Orchid Tree (*Bauhinia variegata*)
Olive, common (*Olea europaea*)
Oxera pulchella
Pepper Tree, California (*Schinus molle*)
Pistachio, Chinese (*Pistacia chinensis*)
Poinciana, Royal (*Delonix regia*)
Pomegranate, dwarf (*Punica granatum nana*)

Popinac, White (*Leucaena glauca*)
Powderpuff Tree (*Calliandra surinamensis*)
Shower Tree (*Cassia eremophila*)
Yellow-rim (*Serissa foetida variegata*)

OBTAINING THE PLANTS

There are many ways to obtain bonsai. At the beginning it is best to work with the more common plants, those obtainable at local nurseries. Plants that are native to the area where you live often make fine subjects for bonsai. But make sure these plants meet the bonsai requirements of size, leaf, trunk and scale.

Some old favorites grown as bonsai because of their classical good looks are: Sargent juniper (*Juniperus chinensis sargentii*); Japanese black pine (*Pinus thunbergii*); wisteria (*Wisteria floribunda, Wisteria sinensis*); flowering cherries (*Prunus subhirtella, Prunus yedoensis*); and graybark elm or sawleaf zelkova (*Zelkova serrata*).

Among the plants recommended for the beginner are: firethorn (*Pyracantha coccinea* or *Pyracantha fortuneana*) which is an evergreen with small leaves; cotoneaster (*Cotoneaster dammeri*), which has characteristics similar to those of firethorn; dwarf pomegranate (*Punica granatum nana*), which is deciduous and has tiny green leaves; and juniper (*Juniperus scopulorum* or *Juniperus virginiana*), which is a hardy evergreen with heavy foliage that takes well to pruning.

In addition to buying nursery stock, you can collect plants for bonsai from the wild or propagate them from plants in your garden. (See discussion of propagation on page 186).

Growers can now purchase mature bonsai created in this country; these plants have recently become available at selected nurseries. Mature bonsai plants also can be imported from Japan, but only deciduous varieties ship well.

Collecting Plants from the Wild

The job of finding plants in the wild that adapt well to bonsai is difficult for the beginner. Traveling in wild terrain where such specimens are found can be hazardous. Also, at least a year must pass before a plant collected this way can be containerized, and much care is necessary to ensure survival during this period. Wild plants, however, often look older than they actually are and make handsome specimens.

The best time for collecting plants in the wild is during March or early April, when new growth or leaves have not yet begun to sprout. But the collector must recognize when the wild plant is in its dormant period.

On a collecting trip the following items will be helpful: a small collapsible shovel; polyethylene sheeting and string for wrapping rootballs; sphagnum moss for packing around the rootball; a container of water for wetting leaves and rootball; and a small crowbar for getting roots out of rocks.

Remember the following points when taking plants from the wild:

1. Get permission to dig from the owner of the property.
2. Do not randomly dig wild plants. Make sure that the plant you are removing is not on your state conservation list. Remember that nothing can be removed from national parks and similarly conserved areas.
3. When digging the plant you want, try not to injure the taproots. Dig the plant with as much soil around the roots as possible. Older trees will require greater care and a slower training schedule.
4. After you cover the roots and soil with wet sphagnum, wrap the rootball in polyethylene film or in burlap. Wet the branches with water frequently.
5. At home, unwrap the rootball carefully. (It is not necessary to unwrap the rootball if it is wrapped in burlap.) Plant the tree in loose garden soil in a location that is protected from the sun and wind.
6. Water; examine the roots of the new plant from time to time for several months. Feed the plant sparingly.
7. After at least a year, the plant can be dug up and placed in a container. (Large trees may have to go into a succession of smaller containers before they are ready.) Trim the roots around the base carefully so the plant will fit into its container.
8. If shaping is necessary when potting a collected tree, prune the branches lightly.
9. Two years after the plant has been collected from the wild, start it on a regular training program.

Importing Mature Plants

If you are going to import bonsai trees from Japan, it is best to do so during their dormant period. Such plants are subject to severe fumigation before they are allowed to enter this country and thus are likely to be harmed by fumigation.

Bonsai plants that have been trained in the United States are now available. These plants do not have import restrictions and have the advantage of being acclimated to various areas of the country.

The Nursery Plant

The easiest and best method for the beginner to obtain bonsai is to buy nursery stock and develop his own. These plants come in 1- to 5-gallon cans and their root systems have become adapted to cramped conditions.

Buy only young, healthy plants when purchasing nursery stock. When searching for potential bonsai among nursery stock, do the following:

- Look for plants that are well rooted and well branched. The plant must be able to withstand severe initial pruning.
- Inspect the overall plant and then push back the foliage and examine the base from all sides. See if the foliage is full enough to be shaped into an interesting bonsai. Check to see if branches are where you will need them.
- Do not purchase a plant that cannot be easily transplanted to a pot.

Do not thin the root system excessively all at once when placing the plant in a smaller container. By thinning the roots gradually and reducing the root system safely over a period of years, you will not damage the plant. If you prune and shape first and neglect thinning the roots, some plants may die.

SHAPING YOUR BONSAI

Strive for flowing form when shaping bonsai. Visualize the overall theme and try to get a three-dimensional effect. Remember to select the front, back and sides of your bonsai before pruning, and don't forget to examine the roots that will influence the growth of these areas.

For overall design the "Rule of Thirds" is a simple concept to use as a basis for obtaining a pleasing form for your bonsai. The "Rule of Thirds" assures you of getting the proper division of space. In this aid to design, the total space is divided into thirds—both horizontally and vertically.

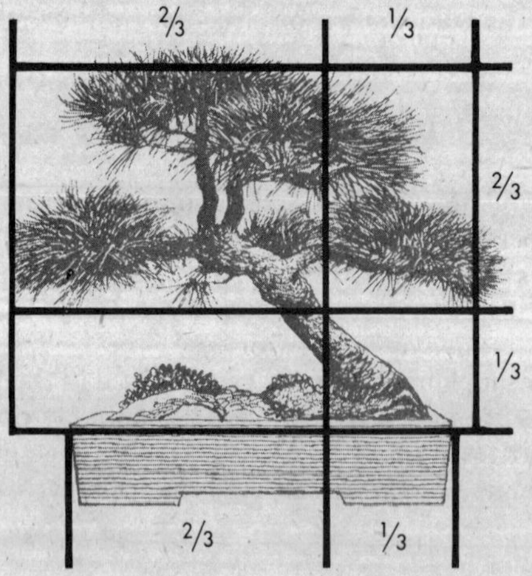

The "Rule of Thirds" is a useful design aid when planning the overall form of your bonsai. The total space of plant and container is divided into thirds, both horizontally and vertically.

Use your pruning shears judiciously to make changes that benefit your bonsai. Fine adjustments are made by wiring and bending and thinning (removal of branches). Remember that a badly designed bonsai will not grow well.

Before shaping a plant into a bonsai, decide whether the best attitude of the tree is upright, slanted, cascaded or semicascaded. Examine the general form of the tree and note whether it is straight or twisted. Match the potential of a tree to the style that fits it best. Decide whether the base will rise from the soil level or whether you will expose bare roots.

Three basic operations are necessary to establish the basic form in bonsai culture: pruning, nipping and wiring.

You will need the following basic tools: a pair of sharp hook-and-blade pruning shears; a garden trowel; blunt sticks; a pair of sturdy wire cutters; copper wire of various lengths; and a sprinkling can. Also useful are scissors for trimming leaves, tweezers for nipping, and brushes for cleaning top soil.

Pruning

Nursery plants are often overgrown and need much pruning to establish their best form. Through pruning, you control growth and form by removing excess foliage and ugly limbs.

Some points to remember when pruning are:

- Make all cuts above a bud, a side branch or a main fork of the tree. Remove all buds except those on the outside of the trunk to force the growth outward and upward.
- Leave stubs flush with stem; long stubs serve as an entry for insects.
- Avoid cutting back so far that you weaken the main branches.

When pruning, keep branches growing toward an open space instead of toward each other or the trunk. Do not shear bonsai as you would cut a hedge; shearing makes the plant look artificial.

After deciding on the foliage form for your bonsai, remove all crossed branches and any dead branches. Then thin other branches until the tree takes on the form you selected.

If you want to slant a tree that has been growing in an upright position and ensure that branches take a normal shape, prune it in an upright attitude, and then tip it to where it should be and work on it that way.

Next, cut back new growth and thin out excess branches. When pruning an upright style, remove unneeded side branches and leave the center ones that will fill out as they grow.

Space out your pruning schedule, even if the plant has heavy foliage. Plants must have a certain number of leaves for photosynthesis.

Protect pruning scars when removing heavy wood from thick branches or from the trunk. Cut the wood as close to the trunk as possible, pare the stump flush, then scoop it out with a chisel, making a shallow wound that will heal without looking unsightly. Treat these wounds with grafting compound and they will be unnoticeable after healing. Several years must pass before bark will grow over these cut surfaces and replace the scar tissue.

Nipping

A tree usually requires only one heavy pruning in its life to establish its basic form. After this initial pruning, shaping is done by nipping. Nipping, or pinching back, is done to shape and develop the trunk and to control the overall size of the plant. Nipping controls new growth before it becomes so dense that it must be pruned.

A twiggy plant can be made more dense when it is nipped. When all terminal buds on a branch have been pinched, several side shoots develop. In this way side growth is stimulated. This will give the plant a bushier appearance.

Nipping is done not only to shape a plant but to develop more luxuriant foliage. As the new growth tips show up, nip them with your fingers, twisting rather than cutting or pulling. Also nip off tiny spurs that appear on the trunk or along heavy branches. These may develop into unsightly suckers that will leave scars when removed. Do not overdo this removal; be careful not to damage the foliage you leave on the plant.

After the top of a bonsai is pruned, trim the roots. Try to keep all fibrous roots and maintain a balance, if possible, of one branch for one root. Remove any roots that were damaged in digging. Leave the surface root system intact and make it appear as if the roots cling to the soil surface. Prune roots with sharp, sloping cuts to avoid damaging them.

Wiring

The wiring and bending of branches that give a bonsai its shape are unique to the art. Wiring is done after pruning when the tree has been thinned to essential branches.

Copper wire is usually used for shaping bonsai because it is flexible. The sizes of copper wire that are best for bonsai work are 10, 12, 14, 16 and 18. (No. 8 wire is heavy and should be used only for the trunk.) Wire as light as No. 16 should be used for very thin branches, and for tying rather than bending.

Wire evergreen trees only during their dormant period, when the branches can be shaped without damaging growth. Wire deciduous trees only during their growing season.

The day before you wire a plant do not water it; this will make the branches more flexible. Once a branch has taken on its trained form, remove the wire, straighten out its twists, and flatten it with a mallet for reuse.

Wiring and shaping should begin at the lowest point on the tree, working upward. Do the following when wiring:

1. Anchor the end of the wire at the base of the tree before winding it. Push the end of the wire deep into the soil.
2. Wire from the trunk to the main branch. Use a foam pad under the wire to prevent damaging the bark. Keep the turns about ¼ inch apart and spiral upward at a 45 degree angle. Do not wire too tightly so as not to damage leaves or stems.

One length of wire can serve for two branches by anchoring the center of the wire at the trunk.

After wiring, the plant is shaped or bent by hand. The trunk and main branches are gradually bent in the planned direction. Never try to straighten a branch that has been bent; this may split the bark.

Branches sometimes snap, even when carefully wired and bent. If the branch is not completely broken, rejoin the broken ends and wind some garden tape around the break. These fractures often heal quickly. If a branch snaps off, prune back cleanly at the first side branch.

Wire should be kept on the plant for not more than a year. Remove the wire before the bark becomes constricted; ridges will form if the wire is left on too long. When removing a wire, start at the outermost end of branches, taking care not to harm leaves, twigs or bark.

CONTAINERS FOR BONSAI

Most plant material for bonsai has long roots that will not fit into a bonsai container. For this reason a training pot is used. The training pot is larger than a bonsai container and holds the heavy roots, which are gradually cut back, for a period of years, until small, fibrous roots develop.

All kinds of containers are used for training pots: clay saucers, plastic containers and wooden boxes of many different sizes. Many of these clay and plastic pots are available at garden centers. The azalea pot and the bulb pan are especially suitable. The pot

The trunk of this bonsai plant (Berchemia paucifolia) *has cracks and scaly ridges that give it a look of age. Note the off-center placement of tree in round container.*

should be just large enough to accommodate the tree's root system. It should be similar in shape to the bonsai pot which will eventually replace it.

For example, an upright tree destined for a low, flat container should be grown in a fairly low training pot. A cascading tree, to be planted later in a high bonsai pot, should be trained in an ordinary flowerpot. Make sure that all containers you use have drain holes at least ½ inch in diameter.

Choose a pot in which to display your bonsai when its training is sufficiently advanced. The size and shape of this pot will depend on the size and shape of the tree.

Trees trained in the cascade and semicascade styles look best in round or rectangular pots. Plant the trunk in the center of the pot with the branches sweeping down over the side.

Place upright trees slightly off-center (one third the distance from one end) in oval or rectanglular pots. Place trees with thick trunks and dense foliage in deep, heavy pots.

Branches of a bonsai should harmonize with the shape of a pot. If the branches are longer at one side then the other, place the trunk off-center in the pot.

The color of the pot should contrast with the tree's foliage. Use white, tan or green pots for trees with brightly colored flowers or fruits. Use unglazed pots for pines and deciduous trees.

Generally, bonsai containers come in five shapes: round, oval, square, rectangular and hexagonal. In each shape there is a wide variety of sizes.

Bonsai containers can be obtained from some of the larger nurseries. Chinese or Japanese stores and other stores that specialize in imported items also offer containers.

Bonsai plants must be anchored to their containers until the roots take hold. One method used to anchor the plant is to tie it down with wires leading up through the screens that are placed over the drainage holes in the container. After tying the plant to the container, adjust the plant's elevation.

POTTING

At the end of the first year, the tree is usually transplanted from its training pot (or from the ground) into a pot suitable to its dimensions. Retain some of the original soil and trim the roots if necessary. Cut away any abundant growth of new roots at the base of the trunk before repotting.

If only a few roots have formed around the taproot, prune these roots slightly. Prune the taproot again at the end of the second year, and cut it short at the end of the third year. This final cutting should be done when new roots have appeared at the base.

Repotting

Repotting of bonsai plants is usually needed when soil insects damage the plants, when the pot breaks, or when the soil is in poor condition. Sometimes, however, a soil condition can be corrected without repotting and disturbing the roots of the plant. This is done by adding new soil around the outer surface, or by removing plugs of soil and replacing them with a free-draining soil mix.

The health of trees grown as bonsai depends largely on the care taken in changing the soil in the pots and the proper pruning of surface roots.

A healthy bonsai puts out new surface roots every year. The growth of these roots makes it difficult for water and air to penetrate the soil beneath. The surface roots will be nourished but the main root near the trunk will die if no air and water reach it. Therefore, periodically cut back the main root and thin out the surface roots.

A tree's rate of growth determines the frequency of repotting. Pines and spruces, for example, need repotting only once every three to five years; flowering and fruiting trees, every year or, depending on the variety, every second year. Repot quick-growing species, such as willow and crape myrtle, at least twice a year. These intervals apply to healthy trees that have received proper care.

Repot your plants in the early spring when the first new buds appear. A secondary season occurs in late summer or early autumn when, for a short time, the roots check their growth. It is dangerous to repot in late spring and early summer when the leaves are just open and still tender.

When the tree is in a dormant state it is unable to establish itself in the new soil, and root diseases are likely. For this reason, bonsai must never be repotted in winter, except when kept in greenhouse culture.

GROWTH MEDIA

Soil mixtures vary a great deal depending on geographical area and personal preferences. There are many conflicting ideas on the type of mix to use.

Many growers find that bagged potting soil is satisfactory for potting bonsai plants. If you use bagged soils, make sure they contain sphagnum peat moss and coarse perlite in equal quantities. Bagged soils are available in most garden-supply houses.

Generally, the soil mixture should have rapid drainage, a structure that permits fine roots to develop, and should contain decaying humus and mineral nutrients. It should also be free of root rot and have a pH similar to the tree's native soil. Try to avoid high levels of dry fertilizers in the soil mix. Screen bagged soil to remove the fine clay particles.

A good basic mix consists of ⅓ clay, ⅓ humus and ⅓ sand. If you live in an area where humus is not available, obtaining an artificial soil mix from your garden store or nursery is the only answer. River or quarry sand can be purchased from lumber yards and variety stores, where it is sold under the name of white aquarium sand.

SEASONAL CARE

Bonsai from miniature forest trees must live outdoors all the time. They are brought into the house for short periods on special occasions. Bonsai from forest trees will die if kept too long indoors, particularly in overheated rooms. These bonsai may be brought inside once or twice a week for two or three hours—during winter, spring, and autumn. They should not be brought inside in summer unless the room is well ventilated.

Summer Care

Bonsai are very sensitive and thrive best in localities that offer cool nights, sunny days and mist or rain almost daily. Most of the United States does not have this climate, so special provisions must be made to compensate for the lack of desired climatic conditions. Extremes in temperature, light, rain and wind are to be avoided.

Place your bonsai on a platform or table in your garden where the plants can receive three to five hours of direct sunlight a day. The site should be shaded, preferably in the afternoon. If the area is subject to drying winds, put up screening around the plants to protect them. Screening also serves to provide the plants with shade.

Water the entire bonsai—plant and soil—daily. If you skip even one day you can permanently damage the plant. Make sure your plants are located where rain can fall on them. However, plants should not remain wet or waterlogged for long periods.

Fertilizer

To maintain plant growth use fertilizer to supply nutrients. Maintain the nutrient level in the soil mix throughout active growth with monthly applications of a diluted liquid fertilizer. Apply fertilizer only before and during active growth. For liquid fertilizer you can use a house-plant fertilizer (20–20–20 or its equivalent) diluted to ¼ to ½ the strength recommended on the label.

Fall Care

During this period bonsai must be prepared to endure the approaching cold. Plant growth must be slowed. Water plants less frequently to slow growth and, when growth slows, reduce applications of fertilizers.

Do not prune or cut any branches after mid-August. Do not use artificial night lighting (incandescent filament lamps) on plants after August 1. To reduce winter dieback of flowering trees and maples, make light applications of 0–10–10 fertilizer.

Winter Care

A major problem in winter is to protect bonsai against low temperatures and drying winds. Bonsai can only be left outdoors in climates where temperatures drop no lower than 28° F. This is not the case throughout most of the United States, so a greenhouse, pit or coldframe is necessary.

Winter frosts will seldom bother bonsai that are sheltered under the foliage of a spreading tree. Watch out, however, during the frost period for drying soil.

Coldframes

It is easy to construct a simple coldframe for bonsai. Before the ground is frozen, dig a hole at least 1½ feet in the soil. Make the hole as long and as wide as you need for all your plants. Line the sides of this hole with exterior-grade plywood which extends 6 inches above the surface. Put 4 to 6 inches of gravel in the bottom of the hole, set your plant containers on this gravel, and spread straw around and over them. Put a loose-fitting cover on the frame made of polyethylene sheeting or any similar material.

Be sure the top of your coldframe is strong enough to withstand a heavy load of snow. Ventilate on days when the air temperature is above 40° F. to keep the plants cool and dormant.

To purchase a coldframe kit, check your local nurseries or see catalogs of mail-order garden-supply houses.

Spring Care

Spring is the time when new bonsai are started. It is the time for any pruning and training of last season's bonsai. The plants then have a whole growing season to readjust to these changes.

Watering

In the summer, during hot weather when the temperatures are over 90 degrees, water the bonsai plants one or more times a day. If the plants are in an unusually sandy soil they will require watering three or more times a day.

In early autumn, follow the watering directions for late spring. In late autumn, follow the watering directions for early spring.

In winter, keep the trees in a coldframe and ventilate the plants on one or more sides to keep them dormant. Check for dryness every two weeks. Water the plants every second day, or less, as required. Keep in mind that far more bonsai are killed by overwatering than by a lack of water.

PROPAGATING YOUR OWN BONSAI

Seedlings

Growing bonsai from seed is a slow process, unless you intend to grow plants whose maximum height will be six inches. A more nearly perfect tree can be grown from seed because the trunk can be shaped from the beginning to suit the grower.

To develop the trunk rapidly, plant seedlings in the ground outdoors; seedlings are kept outside from 2 to 5 years, depending on the type of material planted and its rate of growth. Each spring dig up the plant and prune its roots just as if it were in a pot.

When you choose a seedling, select one that has small leaves to begin with. For example, silk oak and cherimoya seedlings have been successfully grown indoors.

Cuttings

Starting bonsai from cuttings is faster than starting them from seed. Make cuttings in the late spring and early summer, just before the buds open or after the new growth has hardened. Plants that propagate easily from cuttings are olive, willow, cotoneaster, firethorn, azaleas and boxwood.

Layering

This is a simple and convenient method of rooting branches in the soil while they are still attached to the parent plant. The branches immediately have a well-established form and branch structure. Layering often results in good, balanced root systems.

Midspring is the best time to do soil layering. Choose a branch that has good form. Make sure the branch is low enough to reach the ground. Mark a point about 1 foot from the end of the branch and dig a hole in the ground 4 inches deep. In the soil, mix equal parts of sand and peat moss made from ground bark.

Make a slanting cut on the underside of the branch. Insert a pebble in this cut. Bend the branch back in the hole, taking care not to crack the branch. Anchor the bent branch in the hole with a wire loop, and stake the end of the branch in a vertical position. Then cover it with the prepared soil, and water it.

In 9 months to a year the branch (layer) should have rooted. When this occurs, it is ready for transfer to a bonsai pot. (Remember to cut the stem just below the original cut when removing it for transfer.)

Softwood plants that are layered will root in six to eight weeks. When they have rooted, be sure to cut them from the parent plant and pot them. Pinch off new buds until the layered stem develops a mature root system. Remember to keep the layered area moist so that root systems will develop quickly.

Among the plants that propagate well by the layering method are rhododendrons, maples, pomegranate and cryptomeria.

Grafting

Grafting is complex and requires patience and practice. It is not as successful as the other methods

Bonsai tables for garden display are high enough to prevent cascaded plants from touching the ground. The lath overhead provides shade for the plants.

of propagation. One of the drawbacks of propagating bonsai by this method is that even after a graft has taken an ugly scar remains. The "side" or "notch" grafting methods have the advantage of hiding the scar.

Grafting is usually done in the winter or early spring when the buds are dormant. There are numerous methods of grafting, but the most popular among bonsai enthusiasts are "cleft" and "whip" grafting. If you wish to try your skill at grafting consult a book specifically devoted to bonsai.

DISPLAYING YOUR BONSAI

Indoor Display

Before you bring your bonsai indoors to display them, water them first and let them drain well. Wipe all dirt and dampness from the container.

Bonsai look well placed in front of a plain wall on a raised stand. The Japanese display bonsai on a platform raised a few inches above the floor in one corner of the living room. Paintings and scrolls are hung against the wall at the back. Other objects, such as ceramic ware and flower arrangements, are grouped with bonsai on the platform.

If you set bonsai on a low stand or table, try using a small Japanese folding screen behind it. These stands can be purchased in Oriental stores. It's a good idea to contrast the shape of the stand with the bonsai container; the height of the stand should harmonize with the height of the tree.

Bonsai in the Garden

Display bonsai in the garden on simple shelves set on concrete blocks. Place the shelves against an outside wall away from trees, and protect them from the sun. Other good locations for bonsai are slat benches and decks, either in the garden or adjoining the house. Bonsai in large containers look better displayed alone. Place them on some kind of stand, rather than setting them on the ground.

CHAPTER 22

Boxwoods

BOXWOODS HAVE BEEN CULTIVATED in the Middle Atlantic states from colonial times. The center of climatic adaptation for boxwoods is the Chesapeake Bay region and the foothills of the Blue Ridge in Virginia and North Carolina. Fine specimens are also found in the Piedmont of South Carolina, in Tennessee and Kentucky, in the vicinity of Delaware Bay, on Long Island, N.Y., and on the Pacific coast.

SPECIES AND VARIETIES

The two most widely cultivated boxwood varieties are the English box and the common box. Both are members of the botanical species *Buxus sempervirens.* The English box, or *B.s. suffruticosa,* is a dwarf shrub, often less than 3 feet tall at maturity. The common box, or *B.s. arborescens,* is larger, usually attaining the height of a small tree. Both have standard boxwood characteristics: dense foliage and full, rounded shapes.

Some other forms of the species *B. sempervirens* are:

- Weeping Box is a tall boxwood with drooping branches and wispy foliage. Example: *B.s. pendula.*
- Fastigiate Box is a narrow, upright type particularly suitable for hedges. Example: *B.s. fastigiata.*
- Variegated Box is a shrub with leaves that are mottled or bordered with white or light yellow. Example: *B.s. argenteo-variegata.*

Other species of boxwood, in addition to *B. sempervirens,* include *B. balearica, B. harlandii,* and *B. microphylla.* Two hardy plants, the Japanese box and the Korean box, are members of the species *B. microphylla. B. balearica* plants are somewhat scarce, but the other species are available from nurserymen.

HARDINESS

Boxwood varieties differ in their ability to resist cold weather (see hardiness zone map opposite). Boxwood culture is almost impossible in areas where temperatures drop to −10° F. or lower. The dry, cold winters of the Midwest are unsuitable for boxwood growth.

SITES AND SOIL

Boxwoods are tolerant of shade and are often planted in heavy shade adjacent to walls or under tall trees. They also do well in full sunlight. An ideal site would provide full sunlight during part of the day and mottled shade at other times.

A wide range of soil types, from sandy loam to heavy clay, are suitable for boxwoods. Soil texture is important only as it influences moisture-holding capacity. Best growth is made in fairly heavy clay that is well supplied with organic matter.

Boxwood soil must be well drained and aerated. If the planting site has no natural drainage, boxwoods can be "planted high"; that is, the hole for the rootball can be made shallower than the depth of the rootball. Earth can then be built up around the protruding rootball to provide a sloping surface. This improves drainage around the base of the plant.

Acid soils and lime-rich soils are both satisfactory for boxwoods; the plants thrive in either.

If the planting site is suitable for boxwood culture, little preparation of soil is necessary before planting. Make a hole big enough to accommodate the rootball. If the excavated soil is stiff and lumpy, put it aside and use woods soil or topsoil. If good topsoil is not available, mix bonemeal or commercial fertilizer with the excavated soil.

CARE OF BOXWOODS

Fertilizing

The boxwood is a heavy-feeding plant and will grow rapidly if liberally fertilized. If its root system is well established, it will make some growth even if soil is of low fertility.

The USDA plant hardiness zone map. English box and common box can be grown best in zone 7. Japanese box can be grown in zone 6, and the even hardier Korean box can be grown in the southernmost portions of zone 5. Many varieties can be grown in the warm climates of zones 7, 8, and 9, but zones 4 and lower are too cold for any of the boxwood varieties.

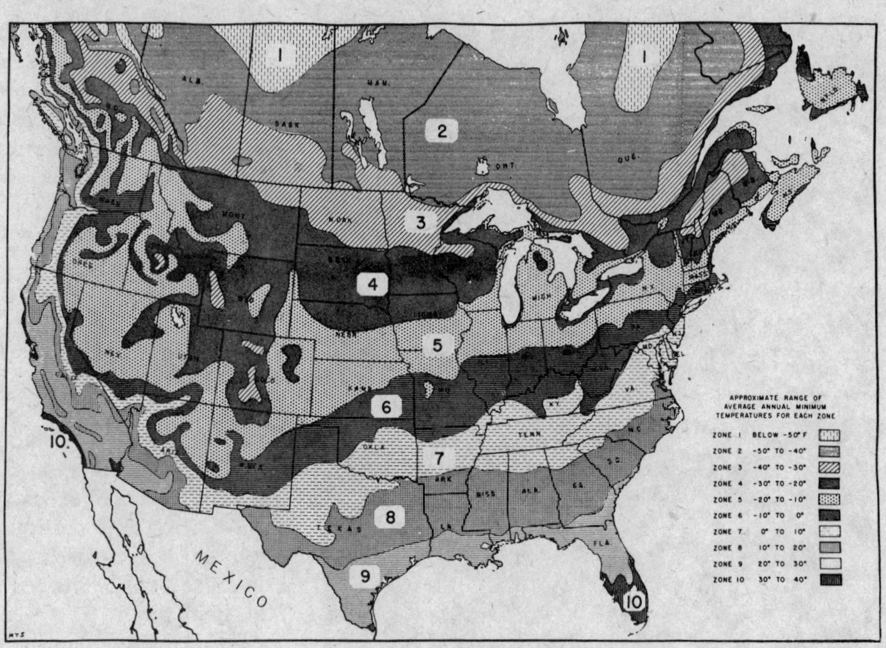

Do not rely on winter mulches to supply all of the nutrients needed by boxwoods. Some boxwoods—particularly trees and large shrubs—may lack vigor if fed entirely by surface mulch. You can prevent this lack of vigor by sprinkling commercial fertilizer around the base of each plant. Use fertilizer grade 10–6–4. Apply 1 to 2 pounds per 100 square feet of soil surface.

A full, billowing shape characterizes mature boxwood plantings.

Apply fertilizer in late fall just before the ground freezes, or as soon as the ground thaws in the spring. Fertilizing in early fall may delay the maturing of the shoots and may promote second growth, which will be subject to winterkill.

Watering

Boxwoods need the equivalent of about 1 inch of rainfall every ten days. Water plants thoroughly every ten days from spring to midsummer. Omit watering for ten days after heavy or prolonged rains.

From midsummer on, water sparingly—every two to three weeks. If fall weather is dry, water the plants heavily just before the first freezing weather is expected.

If drought persists into winter, water the plants every two to three weeks during the winter, whenever the ground is not frozen.

Pruning

Boxwood foliage is very dense. Outer shoots should be pruned so that inner shoots can get light and air.

Small shoots should be pruned at their juncture with larger branches. If large branches must be removed, standard precautions should be observed: The cut should be close and clean; the bark should be bruised as little as possible; and cut surfaces of a

Some of the variation in boxwood leaves: Top, variegated box; bottom left, common box; bottom right, English box

square inch or more should be promptly coated with shellac followed by tree paint.

At least once a year, remove debris (leaves, twigs, etc.) that has accumulated in your boxwoods. Much of it will come out if you shake the bushes vigorously. Pick out the rest. Debris that has been allowed to remain may promote fungus growth.

Transplanting

Boxwoods can be transplanted at any time except when they are in active growth or when the ground is frozen. Rootballs should be large and solid. Dwarf boxwoods require a rootball with a diameter at least half the diameter of the top of the plant. Tree boxwoods should have a rootball with a diameter at least ⅓ the height of the top.

Plants 2 to 3 feet high or broad should be shaded for a year after transplanting. A lattice that cuts off about half the light should be used. Shading is especially important if the plants are moved from a partly shaded to an exposed site. The lattice should clear the foliage by 10 to 18 inches and should protect at least the sunny sides as well as the top of the plant.

Newly transplanted boxwoods must be watered thoroughly and regularly. Direct a slow flow of water underneath the crown to the trunk. Continue watering until the rootball is wet all the way through. Build a low ridge of soil around the rootball to prevent wasting water and to allow thorough wetting.

Winter Protection

In areas ideally suited for boxwood culture, a mulch of wood chips, leaf mold or similar material provides adequate protection to boxwood plants during the winter. A mulch protects by preventing rapid temperature change at the soil surface, deep penetration of frost, and excessive loss of surface water.

Additional protection is needed in areas where the winter temperature is likely to be colder than 20° F. In these areas, some covering is necessary for the top of the plant.

The covering can be made of burlap, a section of snow fence or any other material that will protect the top, yet permit air circulation around the plant. The foliage should not rub against the covering.

Boxwoods may need winter covers. In mild climates, pine branches placed along the north side of hedges will provide adequate protection.

Do not put the cover on until the ground surface freezes; take it off as soon as the risk of temperatures colder than 20° F. is past. Mild frosts after removal of covers do little harm.

DISEASES

Diseases of boxwoods can be divided into three classes: those that attack the leaves, those that attack the stems and branches, and those that attack the roots. All of these diseases are caused by fungi.

Leaf diseases result in spotted or discolored leaves. Fungus pustules usually appear on the leaves. Leaf diseases can be controlled by spraying from one to four times with bordeaux mixture. The first spray application should be made in the spring, before plant growth begins; the second, when new growth is about half completed; the third, about three weeks after the second; and the fourth, in the fall after growth has ceased.

Some symptoms of stem disease are loss of color in the leaves, development of spore pustules in the bark, and loosening and peeling of bark. Most stem diseases can be controlled by pruning the diseased parts or gouging out the diseased areas. Pruning should be done before humid summer weather arrives and promotes further growth of fungus spores. As a preventive measure, remove all debris from the interior of the plant. Shake bushes vigorously and go over them with a broom or vacuum cleaner.

Root rot affects many plants in addition to boxwood; it is very difficult to control once it becomes established. Good cultural practices will help prevent infection. Good drainage around the roots is especially important. If boxwoods die of root rot, the roots should be dug up and the soil sterilized before new trees are planted.

INSECTS AND RELATED PESTS

The principal pests of boxwoods are the boxwood leaf miner, the boxwood psyllid, the boxwood mite and the oyster-shell scale. Pesticides suggested in this section kill pests present in old foliage and protect new foliage from infestation. Local conditions may influence spraying requirements; if you want advice about spraying, get in touch with your county agricultural agent.

Boxwood Leaf Miner

The boxwood leaf miner is the larva of a small gnatlike fly. In spring, the flies inject their eggs into the young boxwood leaves. Larvae from the eggs develop slowly during the summer, hollowing out areas inside the leaves as they feed. They winter inside the leaves.

The larval, or feeding, stage of the life cycle is completed late in April or early in May. The pupal stage follows; it lasts about 10 days. During this stage the larvae turn to pupae. The pupae break through the surfaces of the leaves and work themselves partway out. The adult flies then emerge from the pupae.

Adults of this insect are easily controlled with properly timed applications of carbaryl. To determine the right time to apply carbaryl, watch the development of the pupae. Every two or three days during the pupal period, break open a leaf and examine the pupae. A pupa's head and wing pads turn dark brown near the end of the pupal period—just before the adult fly emerges from the leaf. This is the time to apply carbaryl.

To control the leaf miner when in the young larvae stage, spray with carbaryl about June 15, just after they hatch. Spraying later in the summer or autumn also controls the larvae, but their mines will remain as yellow spots in the leaves.

Dimethoate sprays will control mature larvae if applied in early spring as plants resume growth.

Boxwood Psyllid

The adult boxwood psyllid is a grayish-green sucking insect about ⅛ inch long. In its preadult (nymph) stage, the psyllid feeds on leaves and causes the characteristic leaf-cupping deformity on young spring growth. The nymph also excretes a white waxy substance. In late May and early June the nymphs become adults. The adults feed for six to seven weeks, then deposit their eggs at the base of overwintering buds. The eggs hatch between August and October.

The newly hatched nymphs are oval, legless and scalelike in appearance. They feed by inserting their thin, hairlike mouth parts into the live tissues of the plant, and they hibernate in this stage under the bud cover. In spring, usually about mid-April, they molt, grow legs and crawl to new leaves to feed. To control nymphs, spray with malathion in early spring when new plant growth starts and again about May 15. Spray again about June 15 to control adults.

Boxwood Mite

The boxwood mite is found in most boxwood plantings. The adults are yellowish green to reddish brown and about 1/64 inch long. Eight or more generations may be hatched during the spring, summer, and fall. The last generation to mature in the fall lays eggs that remain dormant during the winter and hatch in mid-April.

Newly hatched mites feed first on adjacent leaf tissue, then move from leaf to leaf. The adult mites feed mostly on tender shoots and on the upper surfaces of leaves. Leaves at first show tiny scratchlike markings; later they become bronzed and withered and sometimes drop to the ground. Dicofol and dimethoate, applied about May 15 and again June 15, will control most mite infestations. If infestations are extremely heavy, spray once every two weeks.

Oyster-shell Scale

Oyster-shell scale attacks many kinds of plants besides boxwoods. This scale has a covering shaped like an oyster. The covering is brownish gray, ⅛ inch long, and 1/16 inch wide. The scale itself is yellow and soft-bodied.

Scale eggs pass the winter under the coverings of female scales. The eggs hatch in May or June, and the nymphs become adult scales by mid-July.

If large numbers of scales build up, severe stunting or death of infested branches may result. Prune heavily encrusted branches before spraying. Apply dimethoate about June 15 to control young scales. In addition, apply a summer oil emulsion before plant growth begins in the spring. Follow the directions on the container label.

Nematodes Affecting Boxwoods

Boxwoods are attacked by several species of plant-parasitic nematodes, the most common of which are root-knot nematodes, root-lesion nematodes and spiral nematodes.

Root-knot nematodes enter the roots and cause the root swellings, or galls, that are usually called root-knot. When infections are severe, plants become stunted, foliage turns yellow, and leaves fall. The plants may eventually die.

Root-lesion nematodes enter the root cortex and kill the cells on which they feed. The damaged tissue is invaded by bacteria and fungi, and the roots rot. This stimulates formation of new lateral rootlets above the dead area, which in turn are invaded by the nematodes. The result is an excessively branched root system with the individual roots rotted or partly rotted.

Spiral nematodes feed with their heads imbedded in the root tissue. Cells of the root cortex are killed and adjacent cells are affected by a substance secreted by the nematodes. The result is an open wound that may be invaded by bacteria and fungi.

If the roots are seriously damaged by nematodes the plant will be unable to get food and water and will appear sickly even when heavily watered and fertilized.

Because nematodes are too small to be seen without magnification, and because a number of other ailments cause similar symptoms, nematode infestation is difficult to determine.

Treating infested plants: The chemical 1,2-dibromo-3-chloropropane (DBCP) has been used with some success. *Caution:* This chemical may kill boxwoods if too much is applied. Follow the manufacturer's directions carefully.

Emulsifiable formulations of DBCP are the most convenient. Bank up the earth to form a basin around the plant, then pour the chemical, mixed with water, into the basin. Use enough water to distribute the chemical evenly over the area of the basin. Add enough water to fill the basin to a depth of at least 3 inches. The chemical is effective only if enough water is used. The water carries the chemical down around the roots.

Do not apply DBCP when plants are in active growth. The best time of year for application is spring or early fall. Soil temperature at a depth of 6 inches should be between 40° and 80° F. during application.

One treatment does not kill all nematodes. Repeat the treatment as nematode populations rebuild, but do not repeat it more frequently than once a year.

Before replacing a nematode-damaged plant, treat the soil with DBCP or some other nematode killer. Examine the roots of the replacement plant for nematode damage. Do not buy nematode-infested plants. Such plants seldom thrive, even in fumigated soil.

Precautions

Pesticides used improperly can be injurious to man, animals, and plants. Follow the directions and heed all precautions on the labels. Store pesticides in original containers—out of reach of children and pets—and away from foodstuff. Apply pesticides selectively and carefully. Do not apply a pesticide when there is danger of drift to other areas. Avoid prolonged inhalation of a pesticide spray or dust. When applying a pesticide it is advisable that you be fully clothed. After handling a pesticide, do not eat, drink, or smoke until you have washed. In case a pesticide is swallowed or gets in the eyes, follow the first aid treatment given on the label and get prompt medical attention. If a pesticide is spilled on your skin or clothing, remove clothing immediately and wash skin thoroughly.

Dispose of empty pesticide containers by wrapping them in several layers of newspaper and placing them in your trash can. It is difficult to remove all traces of a herbicide (weed killer) from equipment. Therefore, to prevent injury to desirable plants, do not use the same equipment for insecticides and fungicides that you use for a herbicide.

CHAPTER 23

Camellias

CAMELLIAS BLOOM WHEN few other plants do—in late fall, winter and early spring. These evergreen shrubs will grow and bloom best in light shade.

Though camellias are primarily plants of the deep South, their area of adaptation extends as far north as Long Island, N.Y. In general, camellias can withstand winter temperatures as low as 10° F. You can grow camellias anywhere if you protect them from temperatures lower than 10° F. and keep their roots from freezing.

Like most other shrubs that grow in shade, camellias are shallow-rooted. They grow best in loose, fertile soil that is slightly acid. They will not tolerate poor drainage.

KINDS OF CAMELLIAS

Three species of camellias are in general cultivation in the United States—*Camellia japonica, C. sasanqua,* and *C. reticulata.* Varieties of these species have flowers that are red, pink or white, or combinations of these colors.

Camellia japonica is the hardiest of the three species. It is the best species for planting along the Atlantic coast north of the District of Columbia. This species has glossy leaves. It blooms from late winter through spring.

Camellia sasanqua is almost as hardy as *C. japonica;* its northern limit of hardiness along the Atlantic coast is the District of Columbia. *C. sasanqua* also has glossy leaves. It blooms in October and November.

The tenderest of the camellias commonly grown in the United States is *Camellia reticulata.* It can be grown outdoors in southern California or in the deep South, but in other areas it needs indoor protection during the winter. This species has dull-green leaves. It blooms in spring.

BUYING CAMELLIAS

Before buying plants, be sure you know which varieties are adapted to your area. For a list of varieties that are adapted to your area, write to the National Arboretum, USDA, 24th and R Streets, N.E., Washington, D.C. 20002. Nurserymen and members of local garden clubs or camellia societies can tell you which of the adapted varieties are available in your area.

Most nurseries offering camellias for local sale sell them planted in a container or with a burlap-wrapped ball of soil around the roots. Most mail-order nurseries sell camellias bare-rooted, to save shipping charges. Buy container-grown or balled and burlapped plants if you can; they are easier to establish successfully than are bare-rooted plants. Buy plants that are at least two years old; plants of this age are 18 to 24 inches tall.

Be sure they are healthy. Inspect plants for wounds or scars near the base of the main stem. Wounded areas may become cankerous and cause the plant to die. Note: Grafted plants may have a swollen area near the base of the main stem; this is not a sign of poor health.

If you are selecting plants from a group, select plants that are well branched from the ground up. Choose those that have the best shape and the freshest, greenest foliage. If you select the plants with the greatest number of healthy leaves, you probably will get those with the best root systems.

Do not be misled by the size of the containers. A vigorous plant growing in a gallon can is better than a poor plant in a 5-gallon can; the vigorous plant will probably outgrow the poor one in a single season.

PLANTING

In general, fall is the best time for planting camellias. However, in Virginia, Maryland and states to the north, spring planting is best.

Try to select a planting site that provides alternating sunshine and shade in summer, complete shade in winter, and protection from winter winds. A planting site under tall pine trees or on the north side of a building can provide these conditions.

Mature camellias spread to 8 or 10 feet in diame-

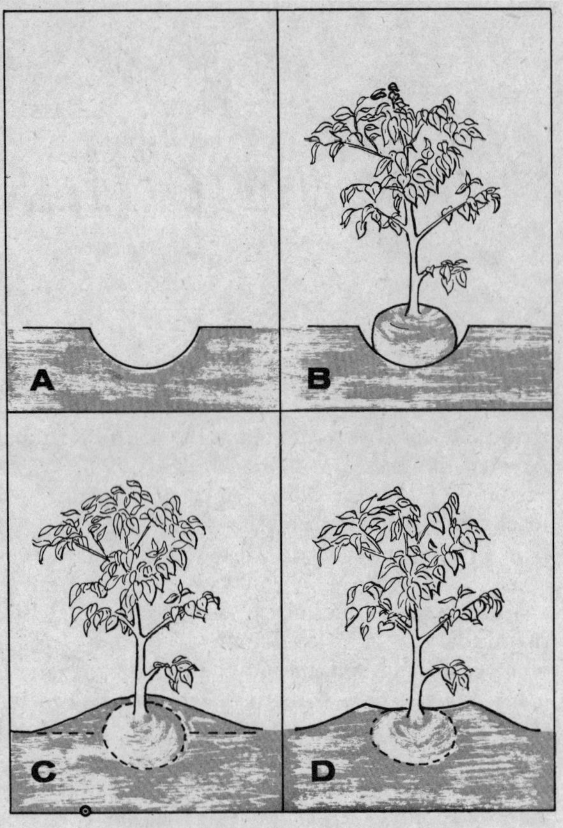

MOUND PLANTING

A. Dig a hole the same diameter as the rootball and about one-half its depth.
B. Set the rootball in the hole.
C. Cover the rootball with a mixture of soil and organic matter; slope the soil away from the plant.
D. Form a basin around the stem for watering, and water thoroughly to settle the soil.

ter. To allow for future growth without crowding, set plants at least 3 feet away from buildings. When using them as hedge plants, set camellias 5 to 7 feet apart; this will provide a compact hedge when the plants are fully grown.

Setting Plants

If your soil is well drained, dig planting holes for your camellias. If your soil is heavy and poorly drained, set the plants in mounds.

Planting holes: Dig planting holes about twice the width and depth of the rootball. Refill the hole slightly more than half full with good soil. Tamp the soil to provide a firm base for the plant.

If the roots of the plant are balled and burlapped you may remove the burlap before setting the plant in the hole. If the rootball is broken or if the removal of the burlap will cause the soil to fall apart, you can simply cut the twine and fold back or cut off exposed parts of the burlap after setting the plant, with burlap covering, in the hole.

If the plant is in a container, cut away the side of the container with metal shears and remove the rootball carefully. Do not knock the rootball from the can; you are likely to injure the roots if you do.

Place the plant in the hole and pack soil under the rootball until the plant sits slightly higher than it grew in the container or nursery soil. Then refill the rest of the hole with a mixture consisting of equal parts soil and organic matter—peat moss, weathered sawdust or muck from freshwater ponds. Press the soil firmly around the rootball and water thoroughly.

After the plant has settled, its depth should be the same as it was before transplanting. Avoid planting too deep; this is the most common cause of plant failure.

Mounds: If you are setting the plant in a mound, first dig a hole in the soil about ¼ to ½ the depth of the rootball and the same diameter as the rootball. Set the plant in the hole and build a mound around it with a half-and-half mixture of topsoil and peat moss.

Cover the rootball with soil mixture to a height several inches above the original soil level of the plant. Slope the soil away from the plant so it extends 2 to 3 feet from the rootball.

Then scoop the loose soil away from the base of the main stem to form a basin for holding water. Fill the basin with water and soak the mound thoroughly to settle the soil around the plant's roots.

CARE

Mulching

Apply a mulch after planting and maintain it continuously. Mulching reduces fluctuations in soil temperatures, conserves soil moisture and helps to prevent weeds from growing.

For mulching materials use granulated peat, pine needles or weathered sawdust; apply it 2 to 3 inches deep over the root zone. Oak leaves, forest debris, bagasse and other similar coarse materials also are satisfactory if kept at a depth of 2 to 4 inches.

Watering

Normal rainfall in humid areas ordinarily provides enough moisture for mulched camellias. During droughts, however, the plants should be watered at weekly intervals. When you water, soak the ground thoroughly. Particular attention should be given to providing adequate water during the time of bud set.

Fertilizing

Camellias may need light fertilizing during the first growing season. Apply in spring when the plants are beginning growth.

After the first growing season, organic matter usually furnishes enough nutrients to the plants. If the plants are making 6 to 8 inches of new growth a year, no fertilizer is needed. Overfertilizing—a common practice—promotes loose, open growth that spoils the compact habit of the plant. Overfertilizing also increases the susceptibility of the plants to winter injury.

If fertilizer is needed, broadcast cottonseed meal over the root area at a rate of 8 to 16 ounces per plant. Or use a fertilizer formulated especially for camellias. These special formulations are available at garden-supply stores. Apply them according to the directions on the package.

Do not fertilize after July 1. Do not use lawn fertilizers on camellias; these fertilizers are often alkaline.

Adjusting Soil Acidity

Camellias grow best in acid soil. The soils in most areas where camellias can be grown are acid enough for good growth. In some areas, however, the soil is too alkaline, and the acidity must be increased.

If the soil is not acid enough for camellias, the leaves turn yellow and the plant grows slowly, even though it has been adequately fertilized and watered. Your county agricultural agent can arrange to have your soil tested.

To increase acidity, apply powdered sulfur to the soil. Use 1 pound of sulfur per 100 square feet in sandy or loamy soils or 2 pounds per 100 square feet in clay soils. Water the sulfur into the soil. Repeat the application in 1 or 2 months if the plant fails to regain its normal color and growth.

Pruning

Camellias grow well without pruning. You may want to prune your plants, however, to remove dead, injured or diseased branches, or to reduce the size of the plants.

The best time to prune is after the plants have bloomed. Make pruning cuts back to a bud or a larger branch.

Treat pruning wounds larger than ½ inch in diameter with a tree-wound dressing to prevent harmful fungi from invading the branches.

Weeding

Pull weeds out by hand. Do not use hoes or other tools; they may injure the surface roots of the plants.

Container-grown camellias can be transplanted in the garden or can be grown as potted plants.

Transplanting

Transplant camellias when they are dormant. In North Carolina and states to the south, move the plants in fall, winter or spring. In states to the north, move them only in the spring.

Dig a good-sized ball of earth along with the roots to protect the roots from drying. The ball should be about 13 inches in diameter for a 2- to 3-foot plant. Add 2 inches to the diameter for each foot of height greater than 2 to 3 feet. Make the depth of the ball about ¾ its diameter—9 or 10 inches for a 13-inch ball, 10 to 12 inches for a 15-inch ball. Follow instructions on page 193 for replanting the camellia.

Camellias can be moved in warm weather but at greater risk than when the plants are dormant. If you move them in warm weather and the plants wilt, spray the leaves with water several times a day.

Preventing Winter Injury

The first step in preventing winter injury to camellias is selection of varieties that are adapted to your area. The second step is selection of a planting site that protects plants from winter sun and wind.

Even after you have selected a hardy variety and have planted it in a favorable location, your plants may be winter-injured by sudden cold weather or by freezing of the soil.

Though camellias are hardy to 10° F. when they are dormant, a sudden drop to below-freezing temperatures after warm fall weather may injure new growth and buds. If a sudden cold snap is forecast after warm weather, you can protect your camellias to some extent by covering them at night with cloth, plastic or paper tents. Support the covering above the plants so it does not touch the plants. Remove the covering material as soon as the weather warms to normal.

When the soil freezes, leaves and stems of the camellia cannot get water from the roots, and the top of the plant may become dehydrated. However, if you maintain a good mulch on the soil surface, it will keep the soil from freezing too deeply.

POTTED PLANTS

Camellias can be grown in containers indefinitely if they are given the proper care. Their requirements are essentially the same as for plants grown outdoors—partial shade, adequate moisture, rich soil and good drainage.

If the plant you buy from the nursery is container-grown, you need not transplant it unless you want a more attractive container. Nursery plants are usually potted in good soil. If your plant outgrows its container, you can transplant it at any time of the year.

Use a potting soil made of ¼ woods mold, ¼ sand, and ½ peat moss. Place a 1-inch layer of gravel at the bottom of the new container to provide drainage.

Water the plants heavily, then allow the soil to dry moderately before watering again. The crucial period in watering occurs in spring when the plants are growing rapidly. They need much more water then than at any other time of the year.

During the hot summer months, spray the leaves with water every afternoon. Spraying keeps the air humid around the plants.

Fertilize potted plants monthly throughout the year. For monthly feedings from March through July, use a liquid fertilizer, analysis 15–5–5. In August through February, use a 7–6–19 liquid fertilizer. Do not overfertilize; it is better to feed too little than too much. Never fertilize a dry plant.

Potted camellias may be pruned any time of the year to control their size and maintain their shape. When cutting a bloom, take two or three leaves with it. This will help to maintain the shape of the plant.

You may want to disbud your plant to obtain large specimen blooms. The best time to disbud is when you are able to distinguish the flower bud from the growth bud. For early blooming varieties this may be as early as midsummer. For mid- or late-blooming varieties, disbudding is best done in September or October.

To disbud, use a large pin or a shingle nail to pierce a hole from the tip of the bud downward. This allows air to enter the bud so it will dry and fall off naturally, thus eliminating possible injury to the adjoining bud that you want to keep.

In some parts of southern California, southern Texas and Florida, potted camellias can be left outdoors all winter. In other areas it is best to move them in winter to someplace where their roots will be protected from freezing.

They can be taken indoors and will bloom there if the room temperatures can be kept between 35° and 50° F. and the humidity held reasonably high.

DISEASES

Inspect your plants frequently for the signs of camellia diseases described below. Treat these diseases promptly.

Dieback and Canker

Dieback and canker is a fungus disease that forms cankers on twigs and causes branches to die back. Young succulent shoots suddenly wilt and die when attacked by this fungus. The leaves turn dark brown but may remain attached to the shoot for some time. Where the dead and living tissues join, a small area of bark and woody tissue may turn brown.

Cankers are usually present. Often, however, they are inconspicuous, slightly depressed dark areas in the bark at the base of the dead portion of the twig or branch.

To control this disease:

- Remove dead twigs or branches well below any visible cankers, and paint wounds with wound dressing.
- Burn all infected debris.
- Spray pruning wounds or scars left where infected leaves fell off with bordeaux mixture of captan during the growing season.
- Dip graft scions and grafting or pruning tools in ferbam or captan (8 teaspoons per gallon of water) to prevent transfer of the fungus to new wounds.

Flower Blights

Sclerotinia flower blight: Sclerotinia is the main fungus causing flower blight. It invades the flower as soon as the tips of the petals are visible. The first signs of this infestation are small, irregular brownish specks on the expanding flowers. Where spring is warm and humid, the specks enlarge and unite until the whole petal is destroyed. Then the entire flower becomes dull brown and falls from the plant.

The fungus continues to develop in the fallen flower and eventually forms hard, irregularly shaped, dark-brown-to-black bodies called sclerotia. These sclerotia endure through the winter and spores from them infect new flowers the following spring.

To control this disease, gather and destroy all fallen flowers for at least two seasons. Drench the soil with ferbam or captan (8 teaspoons per gallon of water) to reduce the number of sclerotia surviving in the soil.

New flower infections can often be prevented by placing a 3-inch mulch of wood chips around the base of each plant. This provides a barrier that prevents the spores from the sclerotia from blowing onto the leaves or flowers.

Botrytis flower blight: Plants that have been damaged by frost may be attacked by the fungus botrytis. This fungus invades weakened tissue during cool, humid weather. It causes brown, discolored areas on the petals or leaves. Often a "cloud" of spores can be seen coming from infected tissue with the slightest air movement. The only control for this disease is to prevent tissue injury.

Leaf Gall

Leaf gall is caused by a fungus that invades new leaf tissue in the spring. Infected tissues swell and appear fleshy. Extreme swelling results in a whitish, fleshy gall on the leaf by summer.

To control this disease, prune out and burn these galls, and spray the foliage with bordeaux mixture (2–2–50), zineb, or captan (4 teaspoons per gallon of water).

Leaf Scorch

Leaf scorch normally occurs when the leaves dry out during freezing winter weather, and the plant cannot get enough moisture from the soil. Protect plants exposed to freezing wind with burlap windbreaks. Water plants during winter. Heavy mulching helps to keep the subsoil from freezing.

The scorch appearance of leaves may also result from too much sun, too much or too little fertilizer, or deep planting.

Chlorosis

Yellow leaves or areas on leaves often appear on camellias. This disorder is often caused by deficiency of some elements in the soil, especially iron. Normally it can be corrected by application of iron chelate to the foliage or to the soil, or to both.

Bud Drop

Bud drop causes the tips of young buds and edges of petals to turn brown and decay, or to drop completely from the plant. This disorder results from growing camellias in an unfavorable environment.

Bud drop on indoor plants is usually due to overwatering, insufficient light, high temperatures or potbound roots. Outdoor plants may drop buds during severe frost in the fall or severe freezing in the winter. In dry climates, bud drop may result from lack of adequate water.

INSECTS

Camellias may be severely damaged by insects unless they are protected by prompt application of insecticides. No one insecticide will control all pests on camellias. To select an effective insecticide you must first identify the insect or its characteristic plant injuries. Recommended insecticides are available at garden-supply stores. Follow label directions for dilution and care in handling.

Scales

The leaves or bark of camellias frequently become encrusted with hard-shelled insects known as scales. The insects feed on plant juices and cause injury or death to the plant.

The most common species of scales found on camellias are tea scale, peony scale, and wax scales.

The young insects of all species are tiny, flat and yellow; they can be seen crawling on leaves in summer.

Some characteristics of the adult scales are as follows:

Tea scale: Brownish shell, about 1/16 inch long. Causes yellow blotches on upper leaf surfaces; infested leaves drop off prematurely.

Peony scale: Grayish brown; grows to about 1/10 inch long. Burrows beneath bark of twigs and stems and feeds on plant juices; infested areas swell, later sink; smaller stems die quickly. Produces one generation of young a season; other species, several generations.

Wax scale: Reddish-brown body with thick, white or slightly pink waxy coating. Grows to about ⅓ inch long. Causes stunting or dying of plants.

Control: When the scales are in the crawler stage, spray leaves and twigs with malathion or dimethoate three times or more at ten- to 15-day intervals. Begin spraying in May or June in the South, and June or July in the North. Use 2 teaspoons of either 57 percent malathion emulsifiable concentrate or 23.4 percent dimethoate emulsifiable concentrate per gallon of water.

Some species of scales, such as the tea scale and the peony scale, can be controlled with summer oil emulsion. Apply it only in early spring before plant growth starts. Use 5 tablespoons of summer oil emulsion in 1 gallon of water. Summer oil emulsion does not give satisfactory control of wax scales.

Whiteflies

Adult whiteflies are very tiny; they have pale-yellow bodies and white-powdered wings. The scalelike young feed on underleaf surfaces and cause black, sooty deposits on the leaves.

To destroy overwintering young, spray foliage with a summer oil emulsion in early spring before plant growth starts. Use 5 tablespoons of summer oil emulsion in 1 gallon of water.

For summer infestation spray with malathion or lindane. Make two or three applications at weekly intervals. Use either 2 teaspoons of 57 percent malathion emulsifiable concentrate or 1 teaspoon of 25 percent lindane emulsifiable concentrate per gallon of water.

Mealybugs

Adult mealybugs are oval or elongated about ⅕ inch long, with a white, waxy or mealy covering. Black sooty molds on leaves followed by wilting and dying of the leaves are signs of infestation by mealybugs.

Mealybugs are usually found in clusters along the veins and undersides of leaves or in crotches of twigs. They secrete a sticky honeydew that attracts ants; the ants feed on the honeydew and spread the mealybugs to other plants.

The first step in controlling mealybugs is to eliminate ants in the garden. Soak the soil with a mixture of 2 level teaspoons of 40 percent chlordane wettable powder per 3 gallons of water for 30 square feet.

The second step is to kill the mealybugs. Spray with malathion as for whiteflies when they are first observed. Spray two or three more times at ten-day intervals.

Fuller Rose Beetle

The fuller rose beetle leaves black excrement on leaves and eats notches in the leaf margins. This pest is common on camellias in the South.

The adult beetle has a brown or grayish body. It is about ⅜ inch long and has a white diagonal stripe across each side.

Spray or dust plants with lindane about July 1 and repeat 2 weeks later. Use 2 percent lindane dust or spray with 1 teaspoon of 25 percent lindane emulsifiable concentrate per gallon of water.

Leaf-feeding Beetles

Several kinds of beetles sometimes feed on the foliage or flowers. Beetles such as flea beetles can be controlled with diazinon. Use 2 teaspoons of 50 percent diazinon wettable powder or 1 teaspoon of 50 percent diazinon emulsifiable concentrate per gallon of water.

Mites

Speckled leaves that later turn rusty brown are a sign of the southern red mite. This dark-red pest is common on camellias throughout the South. It attacks both upper leaf and lower leaf surfaces. It lays shiny eggs that resemble red pepper.

Feeding injury starts in April and continues until fall. Injured leaves do not recover, but control measures will prevent injury to new growth.

When injury is noted, spray foliage with dicofol. Use 1 teaspoon of 18.5 percent dicofol emulsifiable concentrate in 1 gallon of water. Repeat spraying in ten days.

CHAPTER 24

Chrysanthemums

CHRYSANTHEMUMS CAN BRING a variety of bold colors to your garden from mid-July until killing frost. Flowers may be shades of yellow, orange, red, purple, bronze, pink or white. They range in form and size from clusters of small, round pompons to individual 4-inch decoratives.

Chrysanthemums are customarily planted in masses or in small groups. Almost every garden setting is suitable for them. Because of their long-lasting flowers, mums are popular in indoor arrangements as well as in gardens.

The plants are easy to grow and can be grown throughout the United States. Even without care, they usually produce flowers. However, neglected mums may have weak branches, yellowish leaves, and only a few small flowers.

SELECTING PLANTS

Mums are sold in the spring as cuttings, in spring and fall as packaged plants, and the year round as potted plants.

Well-rooted cuttings quickly establish themselves in the soil; they bloom the same year they are planted.

Packaged plants are sold with their roots wrapped in burlap. They bloom at the normal time for the individual variety. If you do not want to spend time growing cuttings, buy packaged plants with well-developed buds.

Although potted chrysanthemums purchased from florists may be transplanted into the home garden, most of these plants do not survive the first winter.

Hardiness

Hardy varieties produce underground shoots, or stolons, which enable these mums to persist from year to year without replanting. Hardy varieties usually thrive in home gardens.

Nonhardy varieties do not persist from year to year. They produce few or no stolons; they are winterkilled by the alternate freezing and thawing of the soil; or they bloom so late in the season that flowers are killed by frost. For these reasons, commercial florists grow nonhardy varieties in greenhouses or under cloth-covered frames.

You can grow some of the nonhardy varieties in your garden if you give them extra protection.

Types

Chrysanthemums are classified according to shape and arrangement of petals. Following are the major types and their characteristics:

Single: Daisylike flowers, with 1 to 5 rows of long

Single type

Pompon type

Anemone type

Decorative type

petals radiating from a flat, central "eye"; nearly all varieties hardy.

Pompon: Small, stiff, almost globular flowers; some hardy varieties.

Cushion: Sometimes called "azalea" mums; early flowering; grow on low, bushy plants; nearly all varieties hardy.

Anemone: Flowers like single mums, but with a rounded crest of deeper colored petals; nearly all varieties hardy.

Decorative: Flowers "incurved" (close, regular petals curving toward flower center), "incurving" (loose, irregular petals curving toward flower center), or "reflexed" (all petals curving away from flower center); many hardy varieties.

Spoon: Petals spoon-shaped; some hardy varieties.

Spider: Petals long and tubular with hooked ends; few hardy varieties.

Quill: Petals straight, long and tubular; few hardy varieties.

Single, pompon, cushion and anemone types normally are small-flowered—or garden—mums. These varieties are selected to bloom before killing frost.

Mums that have blossoms over 3 inches in diameter are large-flowered. Usually these are grown under greenhouse conditions; they may be single, anemone or decorative types.

PLANTING

Plant chrysanthemums in fertile, well-drained soil. Plants should be in full sunshine all day.

When you buy packaged mums in the fall, plant them early enough for the roots to become established before winter—about six weeks. Wait until after killing frosts are over to plant those you buy in the spring.

Ten days to two weeks before planting chrysanthemums, prepare a soilbed. Dig and loosen the soil to a depth of 6 inches; break up all lumps. Spade organic matter—peat moss, compost or well-rotted manure—into the soil. If the soil is very poor, use 5–10–5, 7–6–5 or similar garden fertilizer. Apply 1 to 1½ pounds per 100 square feet and work it into the soil.

Just before planting mums, respade the soilbed to kill weed seeds that have germinated.

To grow chrysanthemums in extremely heavy soils, you may have to install underground drainage. For information about soils and drainage, see your county agent.

How to Plant

Dig a hole large enough to accommodate the chrysanthemum plant or cutting. As you plant, press soil firmly around roots to prevent air pockets between roots and soil. Water thoroughly to settle the plant.

Plant low-growing, bushy varieties 2 to 2½ feet apart; plant other mums 1 to 1½ feet apart.

Place a coarse mulch (1 to 2 inches of straw or tobacco stems, or a layer of evergreen boughs) on

Take cuttings when new shoots from base of the plant are 3 to 5 inches high. Use a sharp knife to cut off the top 2 to 3 inches of the shoots.

Dip bottom half-inch of cuttings in hormone powder that stimulates root growth. Insert cuttings up to leaves and press rooting material tightly around them. Space 1 inch apart. Water immediately; thereafter, water lightly but often.

After 2 weeks, gently pull up a few cuttings. If they have few roots, reset and wait a week. If roots are well developed (above), dig up cuttings and plant them.

soil around plants. Use an extra inch of mulch if you plant mums in the fall.

PROPAGATING

Chrysanthemums become crowded quickly. Divide them or take cuttings from them every two years.

Dividing

After the last killing frost in spring, lift plants out of the soil. Wash some of the soil from the roots. You will find that several smaller plants—each with its own roots—surround the old plant. Separate plants carefully. Plant the small ones outdoors in newly prepared soil. Discard the old plants.

Taking Cuttings

In the spring, take cuttings from plants already established in the garden.

Fill shallow pots or wooden boxes with clean sand or sterile rooting material such as perlite or vermiculite. Wet rooting material thoroughly. Make a cut in it 1½ inches deep to receive each mum.

Follow directions for taking cuttings given in the pictures on page 200. Do not take cuttings from diseased plants.

Keep cuttings where the temperature is about 65° F. Protect new cuttings from strong sunlight by covering them with newspapers for a day or two.

GROWING

Watering and Fertilizing

In most areas, rainfall gives chrysanthemums enough water. Water plants if they seem to need it; never let them wilt.

About 4 weeks after planting, apply 1 to 1½ pounds of 5–10–5, 7–6–5 or similar garden fertilizer per 100 square feet. Cultivate and water in.

Fertilize again at the same rate later in the season, if plants are not growing vigorously.

Pinching and Disbudding

When small-flowered varieties are 6 to 8 inches high, pinch off the light-green growing tips to encourage branching. Unless the growing tips are pinched, plants may develop tall, weak stems that produce only a few flowers. After you pinch, new branches will develop along the stem. Pinch all shoots every two weeks until June 10 for early varieties, June 20 for mid-season varieties, and July 1 for late varieties. Flowers will not form if you continue to pinch later than these dates.

Pinching blooms

Disbud large-flowered mums. Concentrate growth in a few flowers by taking off side buds. When plants are 5 to 6 inches high, pinch out the growing tip. New shoots will develop along the stem. Break off all but two or three of these new shoots. Let those that remain grow into branches. Every two weeks, remove all side shoots that grow from these branches. When flower buds show, remove all except those on the top 3 inches of the branch.

As these top buds develop, notice the first, or crown, bud. When you are sure it is healthy and well developed, pinch off all other buds. Do this by carefully bending the stem of the bud downward and sideward with your thumb. The stem should snap off easily at the point where it joins the branch.

If the terminal flower bud is injured, or looks as if it will not develop, pinch it off and leave the second flower bud from the tip. Take care not to damage or break off the one flower bud that is left. A new one will not develop after you have taken all the others off. Continue to remove side branches until flowering time.

Disbudding small-flowered varieties does not make them produce large flowers.

Staking

Stake tall or weak plants. Each branch of large-flowered varieties needs support.

If heavy, pounding rains or hailstorms are common in your area, protect large-flowered chrysanthemums with a frame covered with cheesecloth or soft plastic sheeting.

Care After Blooming

When plant tops die after blooming, cut them to the ground. Clean up fallen leaves. Remove the mulch you applied at planting. Burn all refuse.

New shoots begin to grow late in the fall. Protect them from frost; put down a new mulch.

DISEASES

Many diseases attack chrysanthemums. Although diseases rarely kill, they damage and often disfigure plants.

Prevention

You can prevent many diseases by following these suggestions:

- Don't plant in wet, shady places.
- Don't crowd plants. Leave room for air to circulate.
- Water early in the day so leaves can dry before nightfall. Fungus diseases thrive on wet leaves.
- Stake plants. Keep branches off the ground.
- Remove and burn dead or diseased leaves, stems, and flowers.
- As soon as plants become well established, apply a disease-preventive spray every seven to ten days and after heavy rains. Apply a spray containing zineb or bordeaux mixture; follow mixing instructions on the label of the spray-material container. To make the spray spread evenly over leaf surfaces, add ⅓ teaspoon of synthetic detergent or mild soap to each gallon.
- Be sure to spray under surfaces of leaves.
- Stop spraying when buds show color.

In the following discussion, diseases are grouped according to the kind of injury they produce.

Disfigured leaves: Mildew, rust, bud rot and septoria leaf spot disfigure chrysanthemum leaves. Each of these diseases is caused by a fungus that lives on the plant. All can be controlled with dusts or sprays.

Mildew causes grayish-white powdery patches on leaves; later, leaves turn yellow and wither.

Control: As soon as you notice the disease, dust plant with finely ground sulfur. Repeat once a week until buds show color.

Rust causes small, brown blisters on under surfaces of leaves. Areas around blisters turn light green. Leaves curl and die.

Control: Spray plant with ferbam or dust with sulfur as soon as you notice the disease. Spray or dust once a week until buds show color.

Bud rot causes growing tips and buds to soften and turn brown. Affected buds do not open.

Control: Apply a spray containing zineb, bordeaux mixture or fermate every seven days until just before the plant flowers.

Septoria leaf spot causes leaves to turn brown, yellow or reddish. Then black spots develop. Infection starts at the bottom of the plant and spreads upward.

Control: Spray plants with ferbam or bordeaux mixture every seven to ten days; continue until buds show color.

Wilting: Verticillium wilt is caused by a fungus that lives in the soil. Diseased plants usually wilt, turn brown, become stunted and produce poor flowers. If the plants do not wilt, areas between veins of the leaves turn yellow.

Control: Remove and burn infected plants.

Before planting chrysanthemums where verticillium wilt has occurred, fumigate the soil with vapam or methyl bromide. Follow directions on the container label. Vapam can be applied with a sprinkling can; however, it is not as effective as methyl bromide. A plastic covering is required to fumigate with gaseous methyl bromide.

Stunting: Chrysanthemum stunt, aster yellows and leaf nematode infection prevent normal growth. They are not easily controlled.

Control: Pull up severely stunted plants and burn them immediately.

Chrysanthemum stunt is caused by a virus. Diseased plants are stunted; often they bloom earlier than healthy plants. Leaves fade to light green or turn a reddish color.

The virus may be carried to uninfected plants on a knife used to take cuttings or on your hands when you pinch plants. Prevent spread by thoroughly washing your hands and the cutting knife after touching any stunted plant.

Aster yellows is caused by a virus that is carried to chrysanthemums by leafhoppers. Diseased plants develop distorted flowers and many small, weak shoots.

Leaf nematodes are microscopic parasitic worms that feed on many garden plants. Nematode-infected chrysanthemums have dark spots on the under surfaces of the leaves. They often have brown areas between leaf veins. Leaves wither and dry, but they hang on the stems after they die. Plants are stunted and buds do not develop.

Leaf nematodes can live three or more years in dead chrysanthemum leaves. They also can live a long time in the soil. Do not plant healthy mums in soil where infected plants have grown. Wait at least three years or use a soil fumigant such as methyl bromide or DD.

INSECTS

Many species of insects attack chrysanthemums. Aphids, lace bugs, leaf miners, thrips and plant bugs may be controlled with malathion. Spittle bugs may be controlled with methoxychlor. Follow directions on the insecticide label.

CHAPTER 25

Dahlias

DAHLIAS ARE POPULAR ADDITIONS to many gardens because they display a variety of sizes, shapes and colors. They are also an excellent source of cut flowers for indoor arrangements.

Dahlias are native to the Western Hemisphere; they grow with relatively little care in all parts of the United States. They do well even in dry areas, if sufficient water is provided. They are hardy plants and, depending on the length of the growing season in your locale, will provide colorful blooms from July until they are killed by frost in autumn.

Fully grown dahlia plants range from less than 1 to more than 6 feet in height. They may be bushy and filled with clusters of miniature or medium-sized flowers, or they may have two to four stalks bearing one to several very large blooms on each.

The flowers measure from less than 2 to more than 8 inches in diameter. Colors range from pure white to pastel tints to brighter shades of yellow, red and orange, and to deeper hues of red and purple.

You may decide to raise dahlias for show or simply to beautify your yard. In either case you can choose from thousands of named varieties.

Dahlias as Cut Flowers

Cut dahlias can last a week or more if properly treated. Always cut dahlias early in the morning or after sunset. Place the flower in the container in which it will remain and cut off a small portion of the stem *under water.* Or you may scrape the bottom 3 or 4 inches of stem before placing the flower in water.

You can also prolong the life of cut dahlias by passing the end of the stem quickly over a flame or by dipping the stem in boiling water for several seconds before placing the flower in cool water.

CLASSES OF DAHLIAS

Dahlias are primarily classified according to the shape and arrangement of their petals. Single-flowering dahlias have no more than a few rows of petals, and they show a central disc. Double-flowering dahlias have multiple rows of petals and display no central disc. Dahlias of any variety that grow on a low, bush-type plant are referred to as dwarf dahlias.

Single-flowering dahlia plants are generally about 3 feet tall with flowers 4 inches or less in diameter. Double-flowering plants are usually taller and have larger blooms. But, because dahlias vary so in height and blossom size, be sure to select varieties that will suit your purposes. Height and flower size are given in most garden catalogs, or you can ask your nurseryman.

Single-flowering Dahlias

These include single, orchid-flowering, anemone, collarette and peony dahlias.

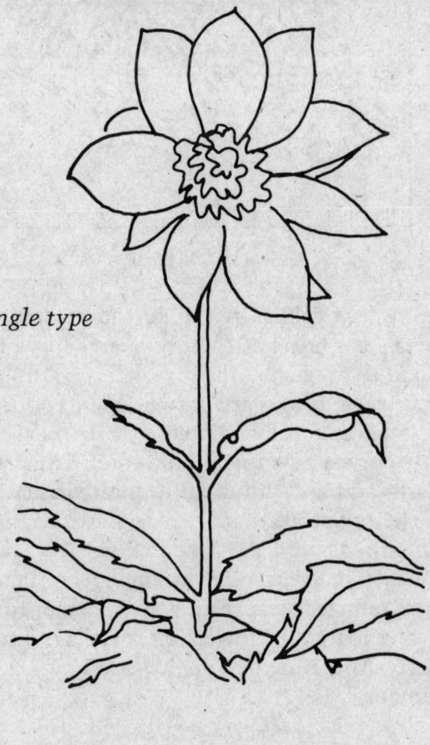

Single type

Singles are daisylike in appearance with one row of petals surrounding a central disc.

Orchid-flowering dahlias are like singles, but the petals turn inward along their length and are somewhat tubular in shape.

Anemone dahlias have a ring of petals surrounding a central disc, which itself is made up of smaller, tubular petals.

Collarettes have a single row of petals around a central disc, plus one or more rows of smaller petals. These smaller petals are usually of a different color and form a collar around the disc.

Peony dahlias have two to five rows of petals surrounding a central disc.

Double-flowering Dahlias

Double-flowering dahlias include cactus, semicactus, decorative, ball and pompon types.

Cactus dahlias have petals that curve backward for more than half their length. Petals are somewhat tubular.

Cactus type

Semicactus dahlias resemble cactus dahlias, but the petals are broad at their base and curve for less than half their length.

Decorative dahlias are of two types. Formal decoratives have broad pointed or rounded petals, slightly curved back toward the stem. The petals are regularly arranged. Informal decoratives have long, often twisted petals that are irregularly arranged.

Ball dahlias are ball-shaped or slightly flattened, having petals in a spiral arrangement. Petals are blunt or rounded at the tips, and quilled or turned in along the margins. Flowers are over 3½ inches in diameter. Miniature ball dahlias are 2 to 3½ inches in diameter.

Pompons have the same characteristics as ball dahlias, but are under 2 inches in diameter.

Cactus, semicactus, and decorative dahlia flowers are also classified into four groups, based on the diameter of the flower: Large, over 8 inches; medium, 6 to 8 inches; florist, 4 to 6 inches; and miniature, under 4 inches.

PLANTING

Depending on the varieties and types you select, you may plant dahlias in low borders, along fences or walls, in clumps and beds, or simply in rows.

Where to Plant

Dahlias do best in a sandy loam that is slightly acid, but they will grow successfully in most garden soils that are well drained. Select a planting site that gets at least six hours of sun a day. Dahlias should have good air circulation and protection from strong winds.

Dahlias need room to develop. Large flowering dahlias should be placed about 3 or 4 feet apart in rows that are also separated by 3 or 4 feet. You can plant smaller dahlias about 2 feet apart.

What to Plant

You can buy dahlias as seeds, rooted cuttings or dormant roots.

Because dahlias are hybrids, seeds won't always produce plants with flowers like those from which the seeds were taken. Rooted cuttings are simply immature plants. Most gardeners prefer to buy dormant roots or to plant dormant roots saved from the previous year.

When to Plant

Ordinarily you should start seeds indoors in boxes of sandy-loam soil not more than a month before the last spring frost is anticipated. Keep the soil moist. Then transplant the seedlings outside when frost is no longer a danger. Where the frost-free season is long enough, you may broadcast seeds or sow them in rows directly outdoors in a sunny location. About 12 to 14 weeks are needed for blooms to appear.

Whether you sow seeds indoors or outdoors, cover them with only ½ inch of soil. It is also a good idea to treat seed with a seed fungicide before planting.

Do not plant rooted cuttings until after the last spring frost. If necessary, keep them in a coldframe or a greenhouse until they can be transplanted to the garden.

Plant roots or cuttings outdoors as soon as the danger of spring frost is past. If the soil needs enriching, spade in well-rotted manure at least two or three weeks before planting. A 5–10–5 commercial fertilizer can also be used for this purpose at a rate of about 2 or 3 pounds per 100 square feet.

How to Plant

When planting roots, dig a hole 6 to 8 inches deep and large enough to accommodate the root. Put the root in the hole and place a stake directly alongside. All dahlias should be staked, except for dwarf varieties. You should place stakes at planting time, because driving a stake later on could injure developing root systems. Stakes should be 3 to 6 feet above ground, the height depending on the variety of dahlia grown.

Cover the root with 2 or 3 inches of soil. As growth develops, add soil around the plant until the surface is level or slightly mounded.

Soil should be kept loose over the root, since crusting can prevent the sprout from emerging.

When planting rooted cuttings outdoors, dig a hole about 1 inch deeper than the rootball. Place the plant in the hole and fill in with soil to ground level.

CARING FOR DAHLIAS

Watering and Fertilizing

Dahlias should be watered often enough to prevent the soil from drying out. To help prevent mildew, always soak the soil thoroughly around the base of the plant in preference to sprinkling the foliage.

Fertilizer may be used to condition the soil before planting, as described earlier. Soon after sprouts emerge, you may add a top dressing of 5–10–10 or 2–12–12. The fertilizer you use will depend on the amount of nitrogen already in the soil. A third of a cup to a cup of fertilizer per plant should be raked into the soil. Keep the fertilizer away from the base of each plant.

Cultivating

Early in the growing season, apply a mulch to control weeds and to keep the soil cool. Then cultivate dahlias only as much as is needed to control any weeds that may grow through the mulch. After about mid-July, avoid working the soil more than an inch deep within 18 inches of the plants; dahlia roots are shallow and can be injured.

Pinching

When plants reach about a foot in height and display three or four pairs of leaves, break off the center stem above the top pair. This encourages strong side-branching. One pinching is enough for larger dahlias; an additional pinching will be necessary for smaller plants.

Tying

When the plant is tall enough to need support—more than a foot—tie it loosely to the stake you placed at planting time. This will ensure an upright plant with straight branches.

Disbudding

You can increase the size of blossoms by removing lateral buds from large-flowered varieties. When the three buds that form at the end of each branch reach the size of small peas, remove the two side buds. The center bud will then develop into a larger blossom. Small-flowered dahlia plants should not be disbudded. Dead flowers should be removed from all dahlia plants.

PROPAGATING DAHLIAS

You can propagate dahlias by growing seeds, taking cuttings or dividing the roots of plants that you grew the previous year.

Seeds

Propagating dahlias from seeds is a relatively easy process and is a way to produce new dahlia varieties. Single varieties generally provide abundant seeds; doubles produce considerably fewer. Grow dahlias from seed as described under "When to Plant," page 204.

Cuttings

Propagating dahlias from cuttings is a popular way to produce more plant stock of a particularly desirable variety. Here's how it's done:

About March 1, place the root in a flat or pot and cover it with sand or loam soil, but leave the crown exposed. Place the flat or pot in a warm, light place and keep the soil slightly moist. When the sprout forms a shoot with two pairs of leaves, cut the shoot off with a razor blade to make about a 2-inch cutting. Dip the shoot in a rooting medium and pot it. When it is strong enough, and the weather is warm enough, plant it outdoors in a well-prepared bed.

Where the shoot was cut, two or more additional shoots will begin to grow. These can also be cut and potted, and still more sprouts will develop. By spring planting time, six or eight plants can usually be obtained in this manner.

Root Division

By far the easiest and most popular method of propagation is root division. By the end of the growing season the single root that was planted in the spring will have developed into a clump of roots. Lift these clumps gently in the fall and store them during the winter in a cool, dry place, such as an attic in which the temperature does not drop to 32° F.

Then, as the next spring planting time approaches, divide these clumps carefully with a sharp knife. Be sure that a piece of the crown with an eye is connected to each root. Roots without an eye will not grow and should be thrown away. If it is difficult to distinguish the eyes on the root clumps, keep them moist in a warm place, such as a furnace room, for a short time before you try to divide them. Sprouts will form. Divide the clumps as soon as eyes are visible.

After you have made the division, brush the wounds with a sulphur dust, obtainable from your garden-supply store. The dust will help protect the roots from fungus attack through the wound.

DISEASES

Of several diseases that affect dahlias, two virus diseases are the most destructive. One is dahlia mosaic, which stunts plant growth and produces yellow or pale green bands along the veins of affected leaves. The leaves may be smaller than normal, wrinkled, or blistered.

The other major disease is ringspot, so called because of the yellow circles produced on the leaves. As time passes these may merge into larger yellow or pale-green areas, and the centers of the rings may turn brown.

Both diseases are carried in roots and cuttings from diseased plants, and new plants produced from them will also be infected. Therefore, if disease symptoms should appear, your safest course is to pull the affected plant out and destroy it.

Dahlia mosaic and ringspot are transmitted by insects from infected to healthy plants. You should, therefore, spray or dust with a general-purpose insecticide for good insect control, which may reduce but will not prevent virus disease spread.

Insects

Aphids spread dahlia mosaic, and thrips transmit ringspot virus. A number of other insects also attack dahlias. The corn earworm, the blister beetle and the European corn borer may be controlled with carbaryl; spider mites with dicofol; and cucumber beetles, plant bugs, aphids and thrips with malathion.

Follow directions and precautions on the insecticide label.

CHAPTER 26

Ground Covers

GROUND COVERS INCLUDE a wide range of low-growing plants. They can be used to:

- Cover bare areas of ground.
- Prevent erosion of the soil.
- Give variety in the yard or garden.
- Regulate foot traffic in the yard or garden when used as edging for pathways.
- Tie together unrelated shrubs and flower beds in the landscape.

Many kinds of annuals or perennials may serve as ground covers. Broad-leaved evergreens are the best, but conifers and deciduous plants also are suitable.

Plants can be propagated at home, but home propagation is slow. Usually plants that you buy from a nursery grow better than home-propagated plants. Nursery plants are already established in containers and ready for planting.

Ground covers range in size from plants as short as grass to shrubs 3 or more feet high. Creeping and dwarf lilyturf, for example, cover the ground like grass, but cotoneaster and juniper depend on the matting of stems and leaves or the interlocking of branches to cover the ground. Ground covers usually maintain themselves with a minimum of care once they become established.

Because the thick, spreading growth of ground covers helps to delay the alternate freezing and thawing of the soil, these plants may grow better in cold climates than most upright plants. This is especially true in areas where snow covers the ground in winter or the planting is mulched with pine needles, straw or branches.

Ground covers are least adapted to areas of low rainfall and low humidity. For example, in the dry areas of the Southwest, they are usually grown only where they can be sprinkler-irrigated.

Plants described in this chapter are keyed to numbered hardiness zones shown on the map on page 140. The temperatures shown for each zone are based on average minimum temperatures taken from long-term weather records. Soil type, rainfall, summer temperatures, day length and other conditions also govern whether a plant can thrive without unusual attention. But a plant hardiness map is the most useful single guide to plant adaptability.

The following list gives a brief description of the most commonly grown ground covers.

Barrenwort (*Epimedium alpinum, E. grandiflorum,* and *E. pinnatum*): Barrenwort grows to 12 inches tall and maintains a uniform height throughout the season. The foliage is dense and often lasts well into the winter. The flowers are white, yellow or lavender. Barrenwort grows well in semishade, tolerates almost any soil, and is particularly useful as an underplanting for evergreens and shrubs. Propagate by dividing the plant. Zones 4 to 8.

Bearberry (*Arctostaphylos uva ursi*): Bearberry is a fine-textured, broad-leaved evergreen 6 to 10 inches high, with trailing stems, dark, lustrous foliage, and bright-red fruit. It is excellent for stony, sandy or acid soils and is particularly suited to sandy banks. Because of its hardiness, bearberry grows well along the northern tier of states where soils are acid. It is hard to transplant and should be obtained as a sod or as a pot-grown plant. Zones 2 to 9.

Bugleweed (*Ajuga reptans*): Bugleweed is a creeping perennial 4 to 8 inches tall, bearing blue or purple flowers. It thrives in either sun or shade, is a rapid grower and tolerates most soil conditions. Bugleweed can be used alone or in combination with other small plants. Propagate by planting seed or by dividing. Zones 5 to 9.

Capeweed (*Lippia nodiflora*): Capeweed is a creeping perennial 2 to 4 inches tall, often used in sand dunes and waste areas. The leaves are greenish to purple and the flowers are light pink. Because it is low-growing, spreads rapidly and thrives in sun or shade, capeweed is often used as a grass substitute. It withstands trampling, can be mowed like grass, and is more drought-resistant than common warm-season lawn grasses. Propagate by planting sod pieces or making stem cuttings. Zones 9 and 10.

Coralberry (*Symphoricarpos orbiculatus* and *S. chenaultii*): Coralberry is a deciduous shrub that grows to 3 feet tall. It spreads rapidly by underground stems and thrives in poor soil in full sun or partial shade. The foliage is fine-textured, and the plants form neat mats where a tall cover is acceptable. Propagate by dividing or by making cuttings. *S. orbiculatis*, Zones 3 to 9; *S. chenaultii*, Zones 5 to 9.

Cotoneaster (*Cotoneaster adpressa, C. apiculata, C. dammeri, C. horizontalis* and *C. microphylla*): The cotoneasters are flat, horizontal plants 6 to 30 inches high that bear bright-red berries. They make excellent ground covers, especially on banks and in rough areas. Most of the cotoneasters are subject to fire blight, red spider and lace bug. *C. apiculata* appears to be the hardiest of the group. All do best in full sun and are often used as accent plants in combination with other ground covers. Cotoneasters are self-seeding, and you may grow them from seedlings that appear in the area, or you may propagate them by making cuttings. *C. adpressa, C. apiculata,* Zones 5 to 9; *C. dammeri, C. horizontalis,* Zones 6 to 10; *C. microphylla,* Zones 7 to 10.

Cowberry (*Vaccinium vitis-idaea*): Cowberry is a small evergreen shrub that grows to 12 inches tall and makes excellent ground cover in acid soils. It bears small pink flowers and dark-red berries. Cowberry will not tolerate summer heat and is limited to regions with cool, moist climate. Propagate by dividing, making cuttings, or layering (rooting a branch by burying it in the soil with only the tip protruding). Zones 5 to 9.

Creeping Lilyturf (*Liriope spicata*): This grasslike evergreen perennial grows to 12 inches tall and does well in heat, dryness, intense sun or deep shade. The leaves are dark green and the flowers are purple. It grows in almost any kind of soil and can stand exposure to salt spray without injury. Once established, creeping lilyturf forms a dense mat from which small divisions can be removed for propagation. Zones 5 to 10.

Creeping Thyme (*Thymus serpyllum*): Creeping thyme is an evergreen that bears purplish flowers and is used as edging or between stepping stones. It rarely exceeds 3 inches in height, it tolerates dry soils and full sun, and it is excellent in small areas as a substitute for grass. Propagate by dividing. Zones 5 to 10.

Crownvetch (*Coronilla varia*): Crownvetch is used frequently to cover dry, steep slopes. It grows 1 to 2 feet tall and bears small pink flowers. Crownvetch spreads by underground stems, and a single plant can cover up to 6 feet of ground in all directions. It grows best in neutral soil but tolerates slightly acid conditions. Propagate by making cuttings or by seeding at the rate of 20 pounds per acre. Buy seed that has been scarified (hulls cut) to improve germination and inoculated to introduce bacteria for nitrogen fixation. Zones 3 to 7.

Daylily (*Hemerocallis*): Daylily thrives along banks in both dry and boggy soil. It blooms throughout the growing season and is seldom attacked by insects or diseases. Propagate by dividing. Zones 3 to 10.

Dichondra (*Dichondra repens*): Dichondra has runnerlike stems that spread rapidly. It seldom grows more than 1 to 2 inches tall and rarely needs clipping. Dichondra grows well in either sunny or shady locations. Do not dig around the plants; if weeds appear, pull them by hand. Poor drainage and winter cold may cause alternaria root rot. Propagate by replanting small clumps. Zones 9 and 10.

Dwarf Bamboo (*Sasa pumila, Sasa veitchii* and *Shibataea kumasaca*): The dwarf bamboos are excellent grass substitutes and can be mowed and treated like warm-season grasses. The foliage turns brown in winter and new growth does not start until late spring. Propagate by dividing or by replanting small clumps. Zones 6 to 10.

Dwarf Hollygrape (*Mahonia repens*): Dwarf hollygrape is an evergreen shrub that grows to 10 inches tall and makes a good ground cover in sun or shade. It grows rapidly in any kind of soil. The flowers are yellow. Propagate by dividing. Zones 6 to 9.

Dwarf Lilyturf (*Ophiopogon japonicus*): Dwarf lilyturf grows to 10 inches tall and is similar to creeping lilyturf in most characteristics, except that dwarf lilyturf is not as hardy in the North. Propagate by dividing. Zones 7 to 10.

Dwarf Polygonum (*Polygonum reynoutria*): Dwarf polygonum is a deciduous plant 1 to 2 feet high that grows in full sun, is extremely hardy and spreads rapidly. It grows well in rocky or gravelly soil. The foliage turns red in autumn. Propagate by dividing. Zones 4 to 10.

English Ivy (*Hedera helix*): English ivy is an evergreen 6 to 8 inches tall. It has coarse foliage, forms a dense cover, and is often used where it can spread on the ground and then climb adjacent walls. It grows in either shade or full sun. Propagate by pulling vines free and rooting them in a new site. Zones 5 to 9.

Germander, (*Teucrium chamaedrys*): Germander is a small woody perennial that grows to 10 inches tall. It is excellent as a border for walks. Germander grows well in sun or partial shade. A winter mulch may be needed in areas where the ground freezes. Propagate by dividing or making cuttings. Zones 6 to 10.

Goldmoss Stonecrop (*Sedum acre*): Goldmoss

stonecrop is good ground cover for dry areas. It grows only 4 inches tall. It spreads by creeping and forms mats of tiny foliage, making it particularly useful between stepping stones and in rocky places. Propagate by dividing or making cuttings. Zones 4 to 10.

Ground-ivy (*Nepeta hederacea*): Ground-ivy is a creeping perennial that grows to 3 inches tall and forms a low mat. It does well in either sun or shade. It is considered a weed in lawns and may become a pest if not confined. Propagate by dividing. Zones 3 to 9.

Heartleaf Bergenia (*Bergenia cordifolia*): Heartleaf bergenia is a creeping, clumpy perennial that grows to 12 inches tall and has thick, heavy foliage. It grows well in sun or partial shade and produces pink flowers in May. Propagate by dividing or planting seed. Zones 5 to 10.

Honeysuckle (*Lonicera japonica*): Honeysuckle is a climbing, twisting, fragrant vine with evergreen to semi-evergreen foliage and flowers that are at first white, and then turn yellow. It grows well in sun or partial shade, but it can get out of bounds and may become a serious pest, covering trees and shrubs. It must be pruned yearly for control. Propagate by dividing or making cuttings. Zones 5 to 9.

Iceplant (*Cephalophyllum, Carpobrotus, Delosperma, Drosanthemum, Malephora,* and *Lampranthus*): Iceplant is excellent evergreen ground cover for banks and roadsides. It produces brilliant flowers that open only in full sunlight. In cold climates, iceplant makes good temporary summer ground cover for newly prepared sloping banks until grass can be planted. Propagate by planting seed. Zone 10.

Japanese Holly (*Ilex crenata*): Japanese holly is a low-growing evergreen that can be kept down to 2 feet tall. When planted in mass, it makes a good medium-height ground cover for small banks and semishaded areas. Because Japanese holly is slow-growing and requires special equipment for propagation, it is established best from nursery plants Zones 6 to 10.

Japanese Spurge, Pachysandra (*Pachysandra terminalis*): Japanese spurge is an evergreen that grows to 6 inches tall. It spreads by underground stems, covers quickly and is excellent cover under trees and in other semishade. It should not be planted in full sun. Japanese spurge is sometimes attacked by scale. Propagate by dividing or making cuttings. Zones 5 to 8.

Juniper (*Juniperus horizontalis, J. sabina, J. procumbens, J. chinensis* and *J. conferta*: Juniper is an excellent evergreen ground cover that usually grows 1 to 2 feet tall. The growth varies from low and spreading to upright, but the plants rarely get more than 3 feet tall. The various species have foliage that ranges from light green to steel blue, and foliage often turns purple in winter. Juniper grows well on slopes and banks and in other sunny, dry areas. Propagate by making cuttings. *J. horizontalis, J. sabina,* Zones 3 to 9; *J. procumbens,* Zones 4 to 9; *J. chinensis, J. conferta,* Zones 4 to 10.

Memorial Rose (*Rosa wichuraiana*): Memorial rose is a low-growing, trailing plant 6 to 12 inches high with semi-evergreen foliage and white flowers 2 inches in diameter. It grows well on banks and sand dunes and is highly tolerant to salt spray. The stems will root wherever they touch the soil. Propagate by planting seed or making cuttings. Zones 5 to 9.

Moss Sandwort (*Arenaria verna*): Moss sandwort is a low-growing mosslike perennial 3 inches high that is particularly suited to small areas and between flagstones. It requires fertile soil, moist partial shade and some winter protection in cold, exposed sites. Propagate by dividing or by planting seed. Zones 2 to 9.

Periwinkle (*Vinca minor* and *V. major*): Periwinkle is an evergreen trailing plant that has dark-green foliage and purple, blue or white flowers. *Vinca minor* grows 6 inches tall and has small leaves; *V. major* grows 8 inches tall and has large leaves. Periwinkle grows well in full sun or partial shade, is especially useful on rocky banks, spreads in all directions and is easily propagated. Avoid high-nitrogen fertilizer and poorly drained soil; plants easily rot at soil line. Bulbs may be interplanted to give spring color. Propagate by dividing or by making root cuttings. Zones 5 to 10.

St. Johns-wort (*Hypericum calycinum*): This semi-evergreen shrub grows well in semishade and sandy soil. It grows 9 to 12 inches tall and its bright-yellow flowers appear in midsummer and continue until frost. The foliage turns red in autumn. Propagate by planting seed, dividing, or making cuttings. Zones 6 to 10.

Sand Strawberry (*Fragaria chiloensis*): Sand strawberry spreads rapidly and is similar in appearance to strawberry plants that are cultivated for fruit. It grows in most soils, particularly sandy types. Propagate by dividing. Zones 6 to 10.

Sarcococca (*Sarcococca hookeriana humilis*): Sarcococca is a shrubby evergreen to 3 feet tall, with glossy, leathery leaves 1 to 2 inches long, and small, white flowers. This ground cover grows in shade, spreads by underground stems, and is used as edging for large plants and around the base of trees. It must be sheared to control its height. Propagate by dividing or by making cuttings. Zones 6 to 10.

South African Daisy (*Gazania rigens*): The South African daisy grows 6 to 9 inches tall and has light-green foliage and orange flowers. It blooms continually during spring and summer. Once established, it will thrive for the entire season with little water. No serious pests or diseases attack the South African daisy in dry climates. Avoid high-nitrogen fertilizer and poorly drained soil; plants rot easily. Propagate by planting seed. Zones 9 and 10.

Strawberry Geranium (*Saxifraga sarmentosa*): Strawberry geranium is a perennial that grows to 15 inches tall and spreads by runners. It grows best in partial shade and may be used around the base of other plants, in rock gardens and in areas of heavy clay or loam. Propagate by making cuttings. Zones 7 to 9.

Wandering Jew (*Zebrina pendula*): Wandering Jew is a perennial 6 to 9 inches high that grows easily in the shade and roots readily. It is a tender plant but is excellent ground cover in both acid and alkaline soils. Propagate by dividing or by making cuttings. Zones 9 to 10.

Weeping Lantana (*Lantana sellowiana* and *L. montevidensis*): Weeping lantana is a trailing shrub that has hairy branches up to 3 feet long. Many kinds are available in a wide range of colors. Lantana grows best in sunny sites, is highly salt-tolerant, and does well regardless of soil quality. It is frequently mixed with junipers or used as a hanging cover for walls. Propagate by making cuttings or by planting seed. Zones 8 to 10.

Wintercreeper (*Euonymus fortunei*): Wintercreeper is a clinging evergreen vine with uniform leaves and a rapid, almost flat growth. It is a good cover for banks and slopes because it keeps its leaves through the winter. Scale insects may become a serious pest on wintercreeper. Propagate by dividing or by making cuttings. Zones 5 to 10.

Wintergreen (*Gaultheria procumbens*): Wintergreen is an evergreen ground cover that grows well in acid soils and moist shady areas. It is a creeping plant that grows 4 inches tall. Propagate by dividing. Zones 5 to 7.

PLANTING

The selection of ground covers and methods of planting vary from region to region. Ground covers normally are used in areas where conditions are bad for plant growth, such as steep slopes, dense shade, dryness, poor drainage or exposure to wind. Once ground covers are established, they usually need little care. But the site must be prepared thoroughly before it is planted.

Dig the soil at least 6 inches deep. Spread 2 to 3 inches of organic material such as peat, well-rotted manure or leaf mold over the ground and spade it into the soil.

On uneven ground where the entire area cannot be worked, dig individual planting holes. Dig these deep enough so you can backfill partially with soil mixed with organic material before you set the plants. Use topsoil for the rest of the refill.

You can plant most slopes and banks in ground covers. Low banks 2 to 4 feet high can be planted without any additional preparation, but you should build retaining walls at the foot of steep slopes to reduce the slope and help prevent erosion. Sloping areas are usually dry, so you must select plants that will tolerate periodic drought. Large, vigorous plants such as junipers or cotoneasters usually are grown on slopes.

Use a fertilizer on the soil when you prepare the planting site. Follow recommendations generally used in your area. Fertilizer needs vary according to soil types. Spade the fertilizer into the soil.

Except under extreme conditions, you should not alter the soil pH (the degree to which the soil is acid or alkaline) for specific plants. Generally you should choose plants adapted to existing pH conditions. But when soils are extremely acid, you can improve

DRY STONE RETAINING WALL

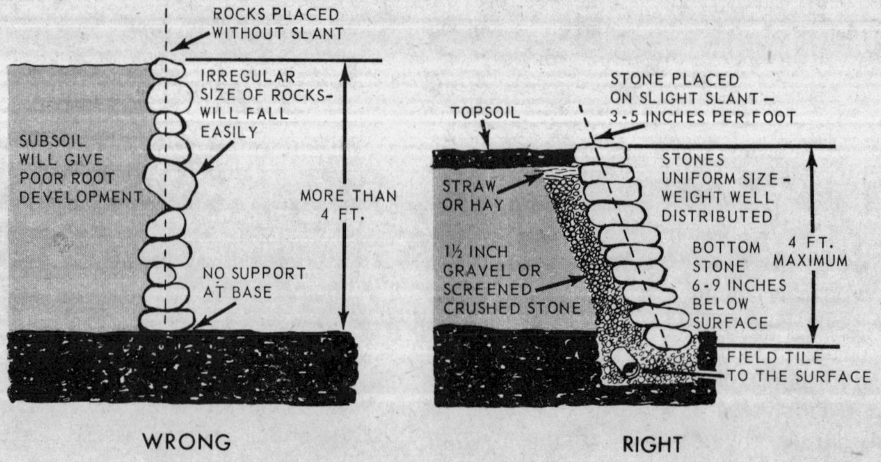

STEPS IN PLANTING

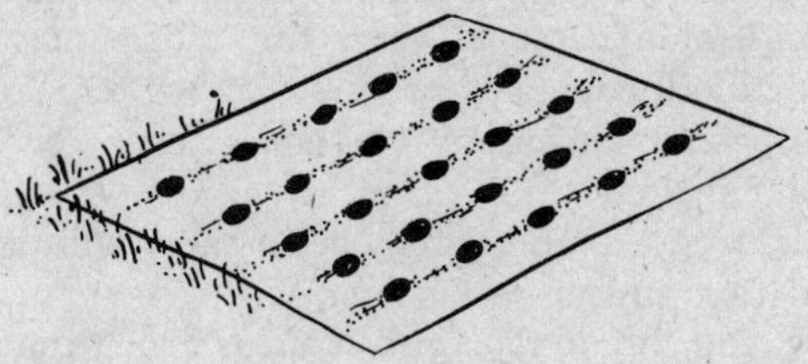

1. Prepare the planting site in the fall. Dig planting holes 4 to 6 inches wider and deeper than the plant rootball. Mix peat moss and organic matter in the planting holes. Space plants evenly over the site.

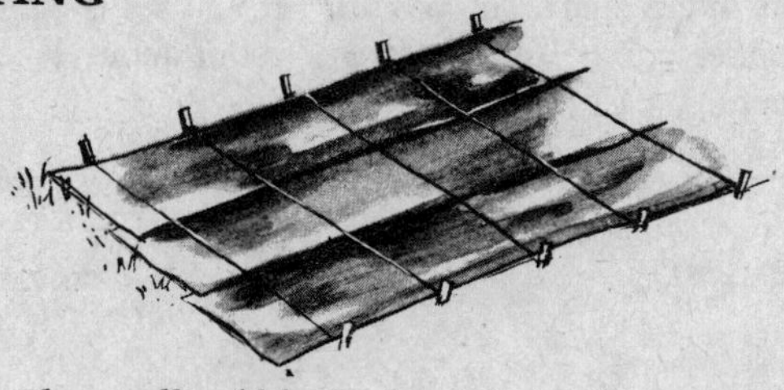

2. Place rolls of black plastic over the area to shade out weeds and retard water loss. Use three or four wide strips slightly overlapping. Tie down the plastic with rocks, wires, or stakes. You may cover the area with a mulch of organic matter instead of using plastic if you wish. Keep the mulch moist to keep it in place.

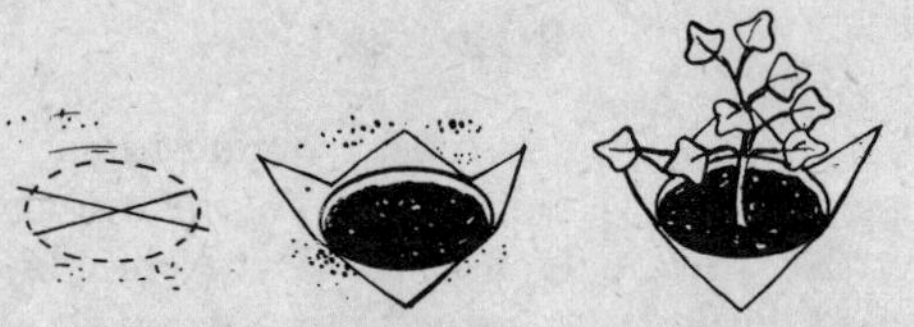

3. Cut an X slit in the plastic over each planting hole. Enlarge the slits to the proper size hole and set the plants through them.

4. Set the plants at the same level they were growing before they were transplanted. Fill the hole with good soil and pack the soil firmly around the roots. Leave a slight basin at the top to hold water. Water thoroughly after planting.

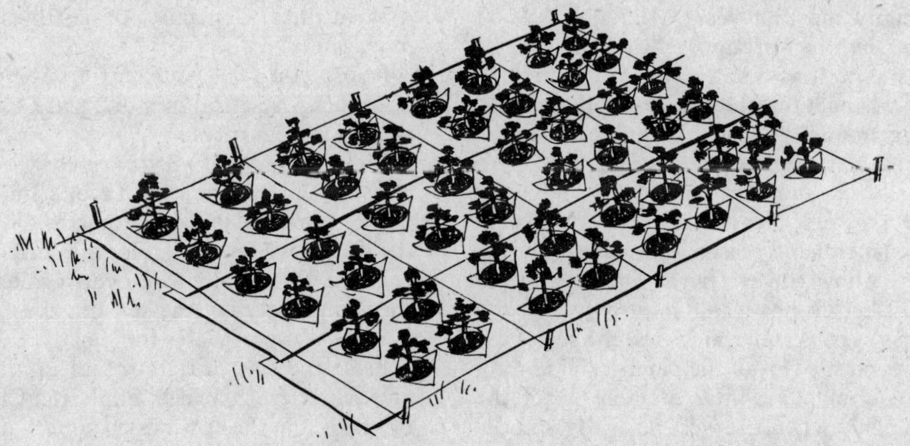

5. Keep the plants in place with an organic mulch over the plastic until the plants are established. Use a mulch of pine boark, wood chips, or hulls. Pull weeds by hand if they grow.

them by using 10 to 25 pounds of dolomitic limestone per 100 square feet.

Although you can plant ground covers any time during the growing season, early spring is the best time in most localities. This allows the plants to become well established during a long growing period before winter.

When you plant ground covers, space them so they will cover the site as quickly as possible. You may put small plants like bugleweed as close as 4 to 6 inches apart. Set such large plants as juniper or cotoneaster as much as 4 feet apart. Closer planting will cover the ground more rapidly but the cost of additional plants may be prohibitive.

The following chart shows the area that approximately 100 plants will cover when set at various distances apart. For example, if you set the plants 4 inches apart, 100 plants will cover about 11 square feet.

Planting Distance (inches)	*Area Covered (square feet)*
4	11
6	25
8	44
10	70
12	100
18	225
24	400
36	900
48	1600

CARE OF PLANTS

A well-established ground-cover planting usually needs little maintenance. Fertilizing, mulching, weeding and watering are the main requirements.

Fertilize the plants in winter and again in early spring. To avoid burning the foliage, scatter a pelleted form of commercial fertilizer over the planting when the foliage is dry.

Ground covers are slower than grass in covering bare ground. Consequently, weeds are likely to grow, especially the first year. A mulch of wood chips, straw or other organic refuse will control most weeds, as well as retain moisture in the soil. Pull weeds by hand if they break through the mulch.

Do not dig around the plants. Digging breaks the roots and promotes germination of weed seeds.

Do not rely on summer rainfall to keep your ground covers watered. Water on a regular schedule throughout the growing season, particularly during dry weather. Allow the water to penetrate deeply into the soil, but do not water so heavily that the soil becomes soggy. Water again when the soil is dry to the touch and the tips of the plants wilt slightly at midday. During the winter months, water the plants thoroughly when the weather is dry and the temperature is above freezing.

In cold climates with no permanent snow cover, plantings in direct sunlight may need protection during the winter months to prevent thawing of plant tissues. Direct sunlight can cause permanent damage. Place conifer branches or burlap over the beds to protect the plants. If the plants heave out of the soil in cold weather, push them back immediately. Do not wait until spring.

Ground covers usually need pruning only to remove dead wood and keep the planting in bounds. You can mow some plants that are grown on level ground.

Ground covers will show winter injury just as other plants do. Evergreen plants, for example, suffer considerable damage when the foliage has been burned following an extremely dry winter. You can shear such plantings or individually prune out damaged branches.

Plantings of juniper may be so badly winter damaged that soil areas become bare. When this happens, you should replant bare areas rather than wait until the old planting fills in the gaps.

You can reduce winter damage by covering the plants with a waterproofing spray. These sprays are available at garden-supply stores. If you spray plants in the fall, they will retain the waterproof cover for most of the winter months. You also should spray plants when you transplant them.

PROPAGATION

The propagation of most ground covers is simple. Making cuttings and dividing are the most common methods. Annuals and some perennials can be seeded outdoors or seeded in flats and transplanted outdoors. Most of the larger plants, such as junipers or cotoneasters, are established from plants purchased from a nursery.

Making Cuttings

Many plants can be propagated from either tip or root cuttings. Generally, tip cuttings are easier to propagate.

Before you take your cuttings, prepare a tray of peat pots. Use a soil mix of 2 parts sand, 1 part soil and 1 part peat moss.

Make tip cuttings 3 to 6 inches long. Treat the base of each cutting with a root stimulant. Rooting powders are sold in three strengths. Be sure to follow the directions on the can for the correct dosage.

Leave all foliage on the cuttings except the part that you put below the soil line. Insert one cutting in each peat pot. Water thoroughly.

Place the tray of tip cuttings in a lightly shaded area. Cover with a sheet of plastic. Check regularly to make sure the cuttings do not dry out.

The cuttings should start rooting in ten to 30 days. You can test them by pulling gently to see if they are secure. When rooting starts, make holes in the plastic sheet to let air in and to increase the exposure of the cuttings to the air. This will harden the cuttings. Every few days make new holes, or make the holes larger.

Finally, remove the cover. Allow the cuttings to grow. Pinch back their tips ten days after the cover is removed to promote branching. Transplant the rooted cuttings to a freshly prepared bed in midsummer.

Dig root cuttings in late summer. Select pencil-size roots and cut them into 4-inch sections. Put each piece in a peat pot. Water thoroughly. Keep the peat pots of root cuttings in a coldframe. Transplant them the next spring.

Dividing

Divide mature clumps of ground covers. Select only vigorous side shoots, the outer part of the clump. This is the part that will grow best. Discard the center of the clump.

Divide the plant into clumps of three to five shoots each. Be careful not to overdivide, because too small a clump will not give much cover the first year after replanting.

The best time to divide ground covers is late summer or fall in southern areas, and in spring in northern areas.

When you divide ground covers, do not put all the divisions back into the same areas from which they came. That would crowd the area and air circulation around them would be poor.

CHAPTER 27

Hollies

HOLLIES ARE AMONG the most popular ornamental trees and shrubs. Nineteen species are native to the United States; about 37 species are grown in two major areas. The eastern area extends from the Atlantic coast to central Texas and Oklahoma, and south of a line from Boston to central Illinois and Missouri. The western area is the coastal region of Washington, Oregon and California.

Hollies will not grow in most parts of the Southwest, the Rocky Mountains or the Plains states.

Although hollies will grow in various kinds of soils, they grow best in neutral to slightly acid, well-drained loam that is fairly light and sandy.

For success in growing hollies:

- Buy nursery-grown plants.
- Plant them in early spring.
- Select a well-drained planting site and prepare planting holes carefully.
- Maintain a mulch around the plants.
- Water frequently during dry weather.

KINDS OF HOLLIES

From the many species of hollies, you can get any shape or size plant you need. Shrubs range from 1 foot to 20 feet in height, and full-grown trees are 20 to 60 feet tall. Hollies are evergreen or deciduous (leaf-shedding). Leaves may be spiny or spineless.

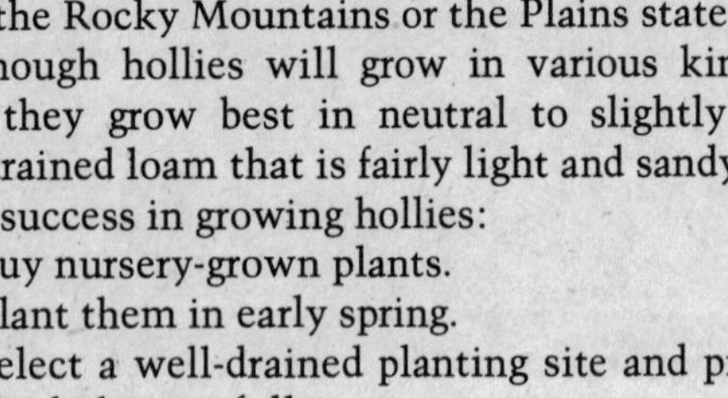

Holly flowers: left, *female;* right, *male*

Hollies can be grown from seed or cuttings. When grown from seed, they may take from 3 to 20 years to flower; the number of years depends on the species. Most hollies are grown from cuttings; these bloom in 2 to 3 years and produce berries in 6 to 8 years. Male and female flowers are borne on separate plants.

Female hollies produce berries after insects transfer pollen from male to female flowers. Berries are red, yellow or black; the color depends on the species and variety. Male hollies produce no berries.

Hollies may be roughly classified into six principal groups: American, English, Chinese, Japanese, miscellaneous evergreen species, and deciduous.

American holly, *Ilex opaca,* is a broad pyramidal tree with dull olive-green leaves. Most varieties have spiny leaves and red berries, but some forms have spineless leaves and red or yellow berries.

English holly has glossy foliage, and several of its forms have variegated leaves. You can get varieties that produce either yellow or red berries. *Ilex aquifolium* and hybrids between it and *Ilex perado* make up the group. The Oregon hollies of the Christmas trade are in this classification.

Chinese holly, *Ilex cornuta,* has glossy foliage and large red berries. It may have sharply spined leaves, but it is best known in its spineless-leaved form, *Ilex cornuta* 'Burford'.

Japanese holly, *Ilex crenata,* includes many forms and is the most widely grown of all the hollies. Because of its small spineless leaves, like those of the box plant, and its black fruit, most people do not recognize it as a holly. The dwarf form, *Ilex crenata* 'Helleri', is one of several that are widely grown.

The miscellaneous evergreen hollies include the native black-fruited inkberry, *Ilex glabra,* which is the hardiest of all evergreen hollies; two Asiatic species, *Ilex pedunculosa,* which has red berries suspended on long stalks, and *Ilex pernyi,* a slow-growing species with spiny leaves; *Ilex aquipernyi,* a hybrid of *Ilex pernyi* and *Ilex aquifolium;* and *Ilex*

'Foster', a hybrid between *Ilex opaca* and *Ilex cassine,* which can be used as a hedge.

The only deciduous holly usually available from nurseries is the native winterberry, *Ilex verticillata,* which is also called black alder. It normally grows in swamplands but will adapt itself to drier garden soils. The winterberry produces many red berries at Christmas time.

SELECTING TREES

Some kinds of hollies will grow in colder temperatures than others. Ask a reliable nurseryman, your county agricultural agent, or the horticultural department of your state agricultural college to recommend species or varieties best suited to your area.

Buy the plants from a nursery. Most dealers sell hollies planted in a can or in a ball of soil wrapped in burlap.

Transplanting hollies from the woods is usually unsuccessful. They are hard to keep alive because most of the roots are cut off when the plants are dug. Also, you have no way of knowing the sex of wild hollies when they are small enough to dig. Male and female hollies look alike until they reach flowering age. When you buy nursery-grown stock, the sex of the plants is known.

PLANTING

The best time to plant hollies is in early spring before growth starts. However, fall planting has been successful in warm regions.

Select a well-drained site that will provide sufficient room for the full-grown plant. Hollies need space if they are to retain their lower branches.

Dig the planting hole twice as wide and slightly deeper than the size of the rootball. Refill the hole ½ its depth with good soil. If the soil is heavy, mix it with sand and organic matter such as leaf mold or well-decayed manure. Tamp the soil to provide a firm base for the tree.

If the roots of the holly are wrapped in burlap, you need not remove the burlap before setting the plant in the hole. After the plant is set, you can cut the twine around or cut off exposed parts of the burlap.

If the holly is in a can, cut away the side of the container with metal shears and remove the rootball carefully. Do not pull or knock the rootball from the can.

Place the holly in the hole and pack soil under the roots until the top of the rootball sits slightly above the level of the ground. Then fill the rest of the hole with soil.

Pack the soil tightly around the rootball. Leave a slight basin at the top to hold water. Then water the plant thoroughly to settle the soil around the roots.

CARE

Mulching

After planting, mulch the soil beneath the branches with a 3-inch layer of peat moss, leaf mold or forest litter. Spread the mulch so that it extends beyond the tips of the branches. To reduce damage by mice and decay, place the mulch about a foot away from the trunk of the plant.

Maintain the mulch continuously. It protects the shallow roots from alternate freezing and thawing, reduces weed growth, and holds moisture in the soil.

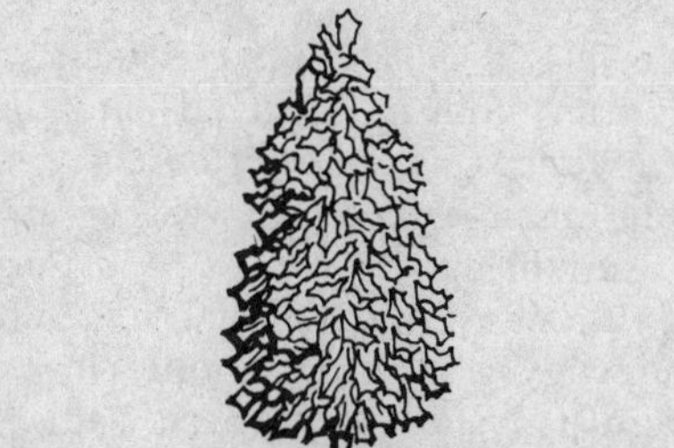

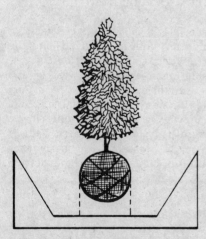

Dig the planting hole twice as wide and slightly deeper than the size of the rootball.

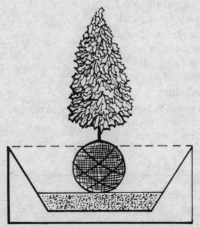

Place the tree in the hole and pack soil under the roots until the top of the rootball is slightly above the level of the ground.

Fill the hole with good soil and pack the soil firmly around the rootball. Leave a slight basin at the top to hold water.

Watering

Normal rainfall usually provides enough moisture for hollies except in areas where irrigation is necessary throughout the growing season. During dry weather, soak the root area thoroughly at weekly intervals. Be careful not to drown trees growing in poorly drained soil.

Weeding

Ordinarily, a mulch will keep weeds from growing. But if they do grow, pull them by hand or remove them with a hoe. If you use a hoe, be careful not to injure the shallow roots.

Fertilizing

Fertilize hollies in mid-March or late fall. The kind of fertilizer you use will vary with the type of soil. Generally, a fertilizer specially prepared for acid-loving broadleaf evergreens is satisfactory.

Spread the fertilizer on the soil around the tree to about 1½ feet beyond the tips of the branches. Do not let the fertilizer touch the trunk. Normally you will need ½ pound of fertilizer for a tree that has a trunk diameter of ½ inch or less at the base. For larger trees, use 1 to 2 pounds of fertilizer for each inch of trunk diameter.

After applying fertilizer, water it thoroughly into the soil.

Pruning

Hollies usually need little pruning except to train a leader or to remove dead, diseased or damaged branches. You may prune hollies any time during the dormant season. A good time to prune is at Christmas when you remove branches for decorations, or just before new growth starts in the spring.

If several stems develop where you want only one leader (main stem), remove the rest. If part of a leader is dead or injured, cut it back to healthy wood just above a bud or leaf. If the entire leader is dead, cut it back to the nearest whorl of branches.

You can control the direction of a branch by pruning it back to the proper bud. The bud points the direction that the new shoot will grow.

Prune hollies only to shape the plant and to remove dead or injured parts. If you cut a branch completely back to the trunk, or cut a twig back to a branch, a new growth may not appear. Unless you want to remove an entire branch or twig, cut it back only to a bud.

Coat pruning cuts over ½ inch in diameter with an asphalt-base tree-wound dressing. Treatment of smaller wounds usually is unnecessary.

FAILURE TO FRUIT

Most hollies must be pollinated before they will produce berries. The only commonly grown holly that will produce berries without pollination is *Ilex cornuta.*

If your hollies fail to produce berries, the reason may be:

- The plant is male.
- The plant is too young to flower.
- The plant is female and has no nearby flowering male to pollinate it.
- The plant is female, but nearby male plants do not blossom at the same time as the female. A male plant of the same species as the female is the best pollinator.
- Late spring frosts or cold weather injured the flowers.
- Cold, rainy weather prevented insects from spreading pollen effectively.

DISEASES AND INSECTS

Only a few diseases and insects attack hollies in the United States. Poor appearance of trees is often caused by improper planting, dry weather, alternate freezing and thawing of the roots, and planting varieties that are not adapted to the area.

You can prevent much damage from diseases and insects by giving hollies plenty of growing space and pruning out crowded twigs and branches. You should see your county agricultural agent or state agricultural experiment station for information on how to control diseases and insects.

Diseases in the East

Tar spot: Tar, or black, spot causes considerable damage to American hollies, especially in the Southern states. A fungus, *Phacidium curtisii,* attacks the plants during prolonged wet weather, and leaves and berries turn black.

Root and twig diseases: Fusarium dieback and a few other root and twig diseases attack hollies in the East, but damage usually is slight. These diseases cause canker in the bark and dieback of new twig growth. Cut out the damaged parts and destroy them.

Diseases in the West

Phytophthora leaf and twig blight: This is the most widespread disease of hollies in the West. During cool, rainy weather, dark spots appear on leaves and black cankers form on branches. Later, the infected leaves fall off and the black cankers turn brown. Young trees may die.

Sooty mold: Sooty mold fungi form a dark-green or black layer of mold on the upper surfaces of the leaves. The fungi grow on the honeydew that scale insects deposit on the leaves. You can prevent sooty mold by keeping trees free of insects.

Leaf spots: Several kinds of fungus leaf spots can damage hollies.

Small, circular swellings or large, reddish swellings sometimes form on the undersides of leaves. The cause is unknown.

Large, purple-red spots may appear on the upper surfaces of leaves. Frost damage or insect and spine punctures cause these spots.

Plant-food shortages may turn leaves yellow or white. This disease is common in spring when new growth starts and in late summer after berries have formed.

Insects in the East

Holly leaf miners: Holly leaf miners attack English and American hollies. Adults are black flies about 1/16 inch long. They lay their eggs on the undersides of young leaves in May. The larvae are greenish yellow and grow to about 1/8 inch long.

Adults puncture the young, tender leaves as they feed, causing brown puncture marks and distortion of the leaves. Larvae tunnel and feed in the leaves during summer and fall and overwinter in the leaves as larvae or pupae. Blotches or serpentine mines appear on the upper surfaces of infested leaves.

Southern red mite: Southern red mites damage many holly shrubs in the South. The adult females are spiny, nearly black, and about 1/50 inch long. Eggs and young mites are red.

Mites feed on both the upper and lower surfaces of the leaves. They are most abundant in spring and fall. Infested leaves turn gray or brown and fall from the plants.

Insects in the West

Holly leaf miners: These insects are discussed under "Insects in the East."

Soft scale: Soft scales are flat, soft, yellowish-green or greenish-brown insects about 1/8 inch long. They live on the stems and leaves of hollies throughout the year. Infested plants become weakened and stunted. Honeydew and sooty mold appear on the leaves.

Holly bud moth: Adult holly bud moths are grayish insects mottled with brown and have a 1/2-inch wing spread. They lay their eggs in July and August on leaves and twigs. Larvae hatch in the spring. They are yellowish to greenish gray and are about 1/2 inch long. Leaves infested by the larvae turn brown. The larvae pupate in leaves on the ground; rake and destroy the leaves of infested plants.

CHAPTER 28

Lilacs

LILACS ARE VERSATILE flowering shrubs that have a wide range of uses in the home garden. They can serve as border plants with smaller shrubs, as corner plantings, as windscreens. or as flowering hedges. Both plants and flowers are very attractive.

Although lilacs display flowers that are among the most delicate of the ornamentals, the plants are among the most hardy. Some varieties can survive winter temperatures of −60° F. They are therefore suited to all parts of the United States except the South, where winters are too mild to provide the plants with the seasonal rest period they need.

Lilac plants often grow and continue to flower for many years even if totally neglected. Normally the only care they need is pruning to keep them within bounds.

The plants range from 3 feet to as much as 30 feet in height, depending on the age or type grown. Most, however, remain under 10 feet.

Lilac flowers can be white, violet, blue, true lilac, pink, magenta, purple or variations of these colors. Depending on where you live, and the lilac varieties you choose, lilacs can provide color and fragrance from April through June.

TYPES OF LILACS

There are many species and kinds of lilacs. Extensive cross-breeding, however, has made these species very much alike. Even botanical experts sometimes find them difficult to identify.

All lilacs belong to the genus *Syringa.* Common to most kinds are unlobed leaves and flowers that grow in clusters. Among the best known are the following:

Common Lilac (*Syringa vulgaris*), as the name implies, is the best known of all the lilacs in the United States. This shrub can be as tall as 20 feet, and the flowers are fragrant and usually lilac-colored, although they can be of other hues. Leaves are somewhat heart-shaped and smooth.

Persian Lilac (*Syringa persica*) can grow to a height of 10 feet. The fragrant flowers are a pale lilac color and are about half the size of those of the common lilac. The leaves are narrow on drooping branches. This plant makes a good hedge.

Chinese or Rouen Lilac (*Syringa chinensis*) is a cross between the Persian and the common lilac. It is somewhat taller than the Persian. The fragrant lilac-purple flowers are about the same as common lilacs, but appear in greater profusion. The leaves are smaller than those of the common lilac.

Late or Himalayan Lilac (*Syringa villosa*) blooms later than other lilacs. It grows to a maximum of about 10 feet and produces fragrant clusters of rose-lilac blossoms. The leaves are pointed and have hairy veins.

Hungarian Lilac (*Syringa josikaea*) resembles the late lilac in many ways, but the fragrant flowers are darker and the leaf veins are smooth, not hairy.

Largeleaf Lilac (*Syringa oblata*) is among the very first lilacs to bloom in the spring. It grows to a height of about 12 feet and has fragrant flowers. Its relatively big, broad leaves are tinged with red when young, and turn red in autumn.

Littleleaf Lilac (*Syringa microphylla*) is a round, low, bushlike plant that seldom grows more than 5 feet tall. It produces small, late-blooming, fragrant lilac flowers. Both leaves and flowers of this species are small.

Dwarf Korean Lilac (*Syringa palebinina*) is an even shorter bush than the littleleaf lilac and seldom grows more than 4 feet tall. Its lilac flowers are fragrant.

Tree Lilacs (*Syringa amurensis*) resemble small trees, and can reach a height of 30 feet. In early summer, tree lilacs produce spectacular clusters of off-white, privetlike blooms. A common variety is the Japanese Tree Lilac (*Syringa amurensis japonica*), which produces huge clusters of yellow-white flowers late in the season. It grows 25 to 30 feet tall.

Other fairly well-known types of lilacs are: *Syringa pekinensis,* an attractive shrub with long, yellow-white, nonfragrant flowers; *Syringa reflexa,* the "nodding" lilac, so named because its pink flowers hang somewhat limply on the 10- to 12-foot bush; *Syringa prestoniae,* a very hardy species that results from crossing the nodding lilac and the late lilac; and *Syringa pubescens,* a 6- to 12-foot shrub with pale flowers that are among the most fragrant of all varieties.

A new free-flowering lilac named Cheyenne will withstand the extra-cold temperatures and severe winters of the northern states. Cheyenne grows to a height and spread of about 8 feet, and has dense symmetrical growth. The highly fragrant flowers are a distinctive and delicate shade of light blue—different from most other lilacs.

When selecting lilacs, keep in mind how you want to use them, and choose varieties accordingly. Your nurseryman can suggest the best types for your particular needs.

PLANTING LILACS

It is best to buy nursery-grown plants for plantings around the house and garden. They should be 2 to 4 feet tall—big enough to stand transplanting. You can also buy larger plants that are balled and burlapped.

The best time to plant lilacs is in the fall, after the leaves have dropped but before the ground freezes. You can also plant lilacs in the spring before the buds start to unfold. Spring periods are very short, however, and transplanting at this time is recommended only in areas where winters are very severe. Lilacs planted in the fall usually have a better chance to survive, because new roots get a head start in spring before the shrub leafs out.

Lilacs grow best in an open area that offers good drainage. They need room, and they thrive where exposed to sun and wind. A hillside or slope in full sun is perfect. But they will grow in most garden settings.

The ideal soil for growing lilacs is a loam that is not too rich, and that is neutral or slightly alkaline. But lilacs will grow well in all types of soil, except for acid soil. If the soil is low in fertility, mix in cow manure or a fertilizer low in nitrogen and high in phosphate and potash. Bonemeal is a good fertilizer for lilacs, and it contains the lime that will sweeten acid soil.

How to Plant

Dig a hole big enough to accommodate the roots without bending or breaking them. Work a bucket of peat moss and a cup of 5–10–5 fertilizer into the hole. This will promote the development of a good root system and hasten the establishment of the plant. Mix peat moss and fertilizer with the soil throughout the area. Good soil preparation will aid in producing a good-looking, profusely flowering plant.

Set the plant 2 or 3 inches deeper than it grew in the nursery and work topsoil in around the roots. Setting the plant deeper can kill it. Pour in water and let it drain away. Then fill in the hole to ground level with more topsoil.

Use a 3- to 4-inch mulch of leaves or hay around the plant in the fall to keep moisture in and to prevent heaving—the alternate freezing and thawing of soil. Heaving can kill the plant. After the soil settles, the level around the plant should be even with the surrounding soil. Allow 6 feet or more between most lilac plantings.

CARING FOR LILACS

Lilacs require a minimum of care. They seldom need supplemental water—only in drought conditions. If weeds grow around the plant, pull them out by hand; then apply mulch. Do not cultivate around the base of the plant.

Do not overprune lilacs. Let the plant develop several branches from the base, instead of only one or two. This allows you to remove stems that have grown too tall, or have been attacked by diseases or insects, and still have flowering wood.

Pruning is unnecessary for the first three or four years. Thereafter, limit pruning to the removal of weaker wood from the center of the bush. This prevents a thicket from developing. You should do this soon after flowers have fallen. Do not prune in late summer, fall or winter; late pruning often results in removal of flower buds.

Old bushes with runaway growth will need severe pruning. In such cases, remove about ⅓ the height of the plant each year for three years until the old wood has been cut to about level.

Remove dead flowers soon after they wither. This helps ensure vigorous growth for the rest of the season and abundant blooming the following year.

PROPAGATING LILACS

Lilacs can be propagated from root sprouts, by layering, by cuttings and by cleft and bud grafts. Each method has its advantages and disadvantages in time and degree of difficulty. The easiest methods for the home gardener are root sprouts and layering, using a named variety.

OLD OVERGROWN PLANT

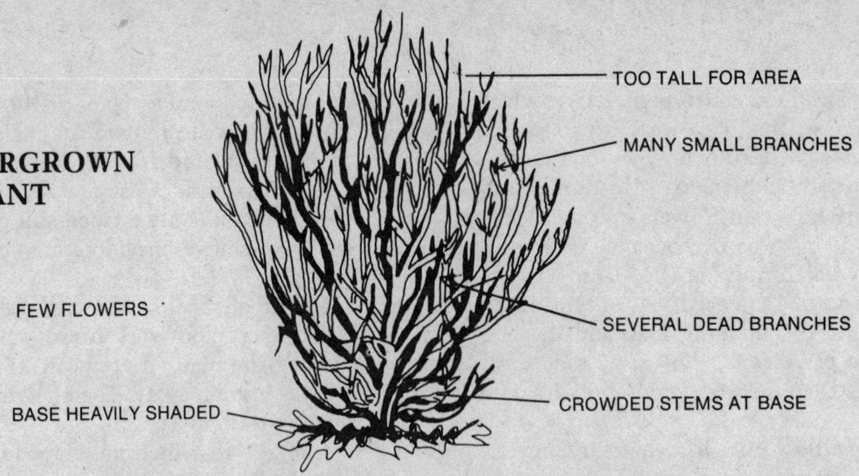

WRONG

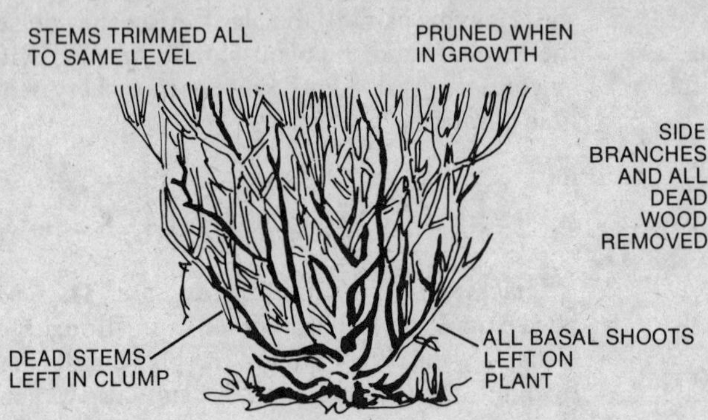

RIGHT

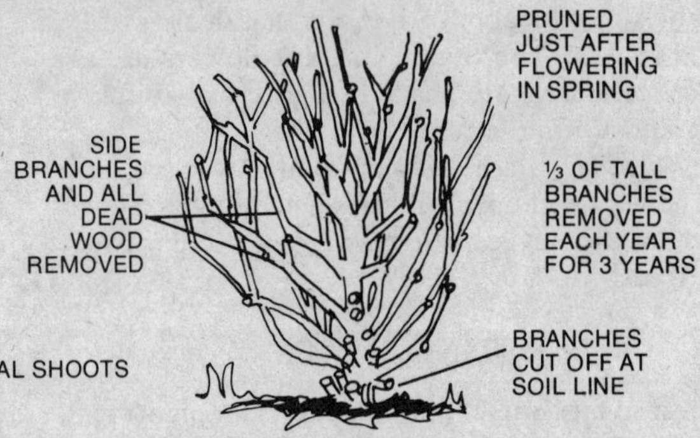

THREE-YEAR PLAN

REMOVE ⅓ OF TALL BRANCHES EACH YEAR FOR 3 YEARS

1 YEAR LATER

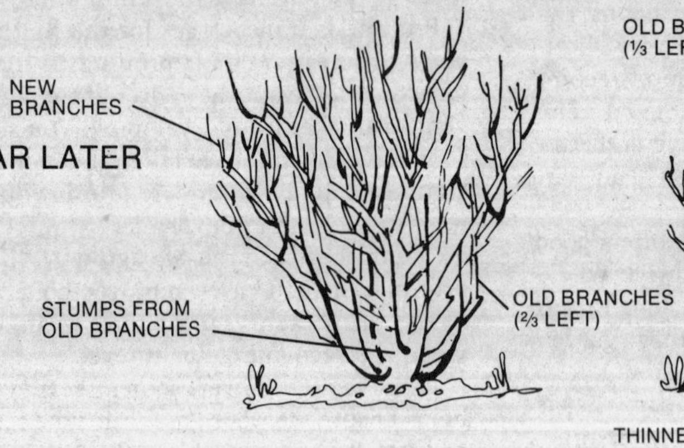

2 YEARS LATER

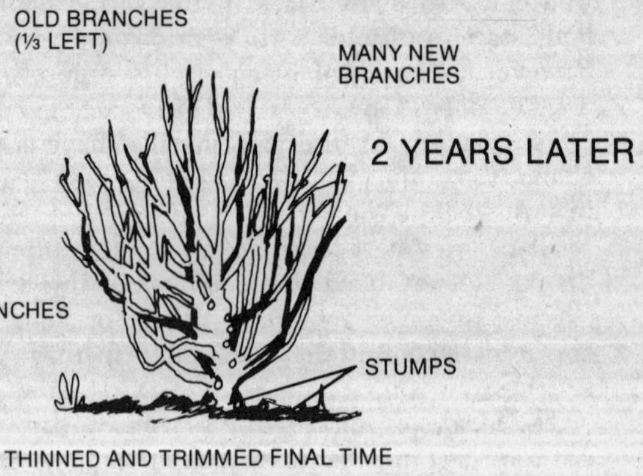

3 YEARS LATER

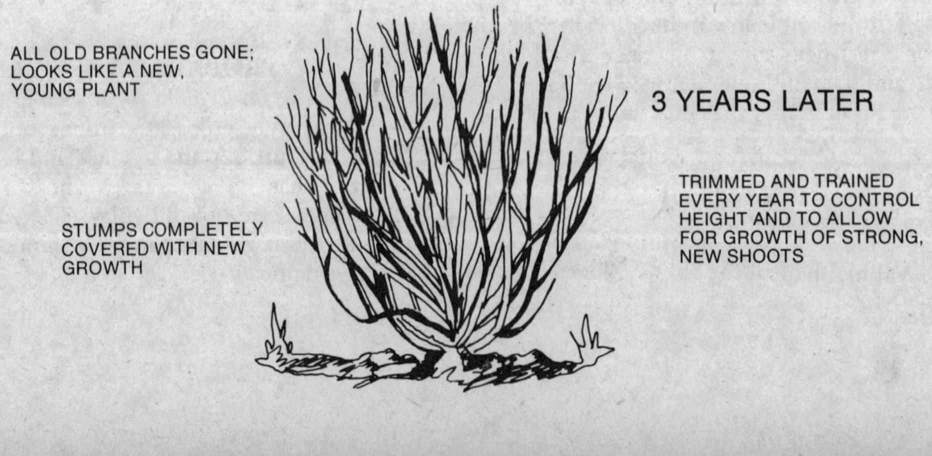

Growing lilacs from seed is not recommended. Because most lilacs are hybrids, plants grown from seed will not produce plants just like the parent plant. Few seedlings are worthy of a place in the home garden.

Root Sprouts

Root sprouts provide the simplest and most usual way of propagating the common lilac. Some lilacs send out suckers near the base of the plant. Dig up these new sprouts in the fall and transplant them elsewhere in the garden or in a nursery. They often develop into satisfactory plants in about three years. This method, however, will not be satisfactory for grafted plants, because the suckers will not be like the tops of the plants. Look for a graft union near the soil line to determine if a plant is grafted.

Layering

Layering is an easy but slow process for increasing lilac plants in the home garden. The new plants are identical to the parent, even if the parent plant was grafted. It is a satisfactory method of propagation for the home gardener with limited equipment and time. Layering is most successful in spring or early fall, since cool weather is an aid to rooting.

Start layering by working peat or leaf mold and sand into the soil where the branch is to be layered. Next, make a slanting 2-inch cut (but don't cut all the way) on the upper side of the branch about a foot from the tip. Dust rooting stimulant on the cut. Bend the branch down, and fasten it to the ground at a point between the trunk and the wound. Use a wooden peg or wire wicket, or simply weigh it down securely with a stone. Bend the tip upright at the wound, and as you do, twist the tip a half-turn to open it. Then place another peg or pin over the branch at the point of the wound, and mound 3 or 4 inches of firmly packed soil over the wound. Place straw or leaf mulch on the mound, and water frequently.

If you layer in the spring, the branch should develop roots by the following spring. If you layer in the fall, roots will develop by the second spring. When roots have developed, you can cut the new plant free from the parent. Leave the new plant in place for three weeks to recover from the shock of being cut. Then transplant it to a nursery bed and tend it for a year or more.

To prevent water loss that can kill the newly rooted layers, prune ⅓ their original length from all side branches of these rooted layers as soon as you plant them in the nursery bed. As a further measure to prevent water loss, screen the new plants to shade them from the sun. A makeshift screen will do—burlap or other porous material on a simple wood frame, for example. You can remove the screen after the first winter. By then, plants should be strong enough to transplant from the nursery to their permanent locations.

Cuttings, Cleft and Bud Grafts

Cuttings, cleft grafts and bud grafts are still other methods of propagating lilacs. You can root lilac cuttings from suckers at the base of an older plant for use as understock. Cuttings from terminal growth of new wood can be grafted onto these. This method produces high-quality plants. The process requires a great deal of knowledge, however, and takes several months in a greenhouse or a glass-covered frame where the air can be kept moist continuously. Cleft grafting is the most common way of propagating the named varieties of lilacs on a commercial basis. And bud grafting is an especially economical and very rapid method if you want to grow many new plants.

PESTS

A number of insects and diseases attack lilacs, but only a few cause serious injury.

Powdery mildew is the most common disease. It appears on foliage in late summer and gives leaves a whitish, dusty appearance. You can control it by dusting with sulfur as soon as you notice the disease.

Oyster-shell scale and San Jose scale pierce the bark and suck sap from the plant, thus weakening flower-bearing stems. To control scale insects, use either carbaryl or malathion.

Lilac borers, as the name suggests, burrow into the wood of the plant, sometimes leaving small amounts of sawdust as evidence of their presence. Larvae are creamy-white caterpillars about ¾ inch long. These larvae usually concentrate on old branches, but they may also go after healthy new wood. They are especially damaging to grafted plants. A heavy, uncontrolled infestation can affect the entire bush, causing leaves to wilt and stems to break off. You may have to remove seriously riddled branches. You can dig borers from the stems with a knife, or kill them by probing their burrows with a wire.

CHAPTER 29

Pansies

PANSIES ARE AMONG the most popular garden flowers today. They exhibit a wide range of colors, markings and sizes.

Although pansies are handy biennials, they are also grown as annuals. The ideal temperature range for growing pansies is from about 40° F. at night to 60° F. during the day. They will grow in all parts of the United States. They produce their best flowers in the spring when the weather is mild, then fade and are usually discarded when really hot weather arrives. In areas where long periods without frost are common, strong pansy plants will bloom in the fall and even in the winter.

KINDS OF PANSIES

We read about pansies in the poetry of sixteenth- and seventeenth-century England, but the flowers described are hardly like the ones we know today. In many cases they were the *Viola tricolor,* known since ancient Greek times, a relatively small and simple ancestor of the large and fancy blooms we grow now.

The *Viola tricolor,* so named because it is generally a combination of three colors—white, yellow and either blue or purple—is still grown in some gardens, but with decreasing frequency.

The modern pansy probably represents crosses among the *Viola tricolor* and other members of the *Viola* family. Shortly after 1800, British growers began to breed the now familiar "faces" into pansy flowers, and to improve color and markings generally. Later, French, Belgian, Swiss and American breeders developed the larger, brighter-colored, fancier varieties that are now available.

Pansies come in named varieties of pure colors and mixtures, as well as first-generation hybrids that are becoming increasingly popular because of plant vigor, uniform color and a wider color range, increased flower size and greater resistance to hot weather.

Pansies nowadays display scores of hues. They range in color from white and pastel shades, rich gold and burnished orange, to deep rose, violet and blue, and even deeper maroons and browns. They may be single-colored, streaked or blotched.

Certain types have petals with crinkled fluffy edges; others do not. Flower size may range from about 1 to 3 inches in diameter, depending on culture.

PLANTING

Where to Plant

Pansies are excellent choices for low borders and for bedding. You may place them among other flowers too, especially tulips and other spring bulbs.

Growing pansies

They will start to bloom soon after the earliest bulbs and will continue until summer flowers take over. Pansies are also colorful in planters and window boxes.

Place pansies where they will receive full sun or partial shade. The new types thrive in full sun. Too much shade reduces the number of flowers and flower size and makes pansies spindly.

Space plants for bedding about 7 to 12 inches apart. Do not plant pansies more than three years in a row in the same location, because a fungus disease (*Pythium*) builds up in the soil.

When and What to Plant

If you decide to plant seed, and you want plants to bloom as early as possible in the spring, plant the seed in July or August. If you live in the North, where summers are relatively short and cool, plant seed in early July. This is also the time to start seedlings that are to bloom under glass in the winter. Plants will require protection in the North. They are often overwintered in coldframes, then transplanted in the spring to their permanent locations outside.

If you live farther south, sow seeds a little later in July, or in August. In hot weather it usually takes six weeks for seeds to become pansy seedlings of a size suitable for transplanting to their permanent locations. Then they should have another month or six weeks to become established in their permanent site and to approach blooming size before cold weather arrives. In this way they will winter well and will be ready for early spring bloom.

Instead of planting seed, you can buy pansy seedlings in late summer or fall and set them out about six weeks before killing frost. Choose short, stocky pansy seedlings with at least four or five strong leaves.

You can also buy plants of blooming size in spring and set them out at that time. These seedlings are usually quite satisfactory and provide many flowers quickly but you will get stockier plants from seedlings bedded in the fall.

Still another possibility is to start seed in a greenhouse in January or February. Then transfer seedlings to a coldframe in early spring for summer blossoming. In the greenhouse, keep the night temperature about 55° F. and day temperature from 60° to 65° F.

How to Plant

SOWING SEED

Pansies thrive in rich, well-drained soil. So, before you plant seeds, add manure, peat moss and a 5–10–5 commercial fertilizer to the soil. If the soil is heavy, dig in some sand. Spade the soil to a depth of 6 to 8 inches. Make sure it is fine and free of lumps, stones and other coarse materials.

Pansies in bloom

If you plant seed in boxes or frames, you can either broadcast the seed or plant it in rows. Select boxes 9 to 12 inches deep and fill them with rich, sandy loam soil.

If you plant in open beds, it is always better to sow seeds in rows about 4 to 6 inches apart, instead of broadcasting. This makes it easier for you to identify the seedlings when they emerge and permits you to cultivate and weed more readily.

Whether you plant indoors or out, in frames or in open beds, water the seedbed first. Then, when the water has drained away, sow the seeds thinly. Cover the seeds with only ⅛ inch of soil or coarse, washed sand, and press down with a flat board. Water the bed again, but not so much as to wash the seeds away.

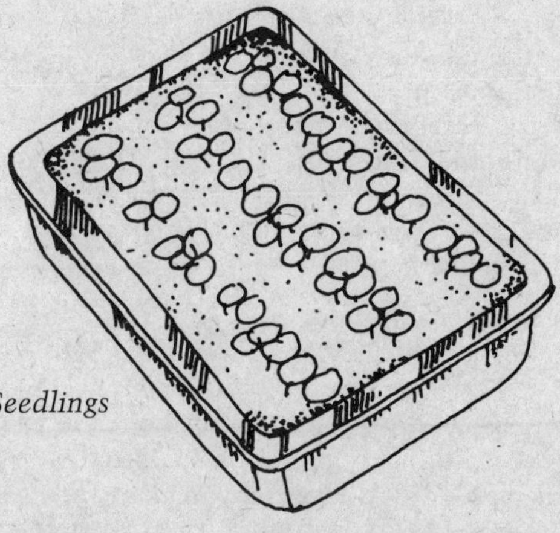

Seedlings

White plastic film, aluminum foil or a piece of moist burlap placed on the seedbed will help keep moisture in. This should be removed as soon as the seeds begin to sprout, in about five to eight days.

Shade the seedlings with a canopy for a few days until they have developed their first leaves. They can usually stand direct sunlight by that time. The canopy (and it can be a makeshift one) should be a foot or more above the bed to let air circulate.

Water frequently, but lightly, in the morning. Seedlings should be neither too dry nor too wet. If seed dries out after it begins to sprout, it will die. But if you keep it too moist, it may rot. Raise the level of bedded soil 2 to 4 inches if necessary to keep water from standing in puddles.

After the seedlings have emerged, thin them to an inch or more apart. You can plant the seedlings you remove in another bed prepared like the one in which you sowed the seeds.

After the seedlings develop six or eight leaves, move them to their permanent locations. Place them 7 to 12 inches apart. In transplanting, try to disturb the roots as little as possible. And be sure to set the plants at the same level in the ground as they were before.

When the ground freezes, apply pine boughs, straw mulch or a lattice frame to minimize temperature variations. Repeated freezing and thawing is harmful to the plants.

In the North, transplant by early September. Where winters are mild—as in the Washington, D.C., area—transplant later in September or early in October. If you're not sure, ask your garden supplier, your county agricultural agent, or your state experiment station about the best times to plant and transplant in your area.

PLANTING SEEDLINGS

The planting procedure for seedlings you buy is the same as that for seedlings you have grown from seed. But there are additional steps to follow. When you first get your seedlings, sprinkle them with water and let them stand a short while to restore lost moisture before planting. When you replant them, carefully separate and spread the roots, and water the soil. Press the soil firmly around the plants so that good contact is made with the roots—but don't press soil so tightly that it cakes when it begins to dry.

PROPAGATING PANSIES

In general it is better for the home gardener to buy seed, seedlings or plants than to attempt to grow his own seed stock. Especially in areas where summers are quite hot and dry, it is best to start with new seedlings each year.

But if you wish to propagate your own pansies you may grow seeds or divide old plants. Taking cuttings is not recommended.

Although you can obtain seed from your own plants, it usually will not produce flowers exactly like the ones on the plant it came from. Moreover, if you allow seed to form, your plants will probably produce fewer and smaller flowers. Some seedlings will volunteer (grow from self-sown seed) in the garden.

Pansy plants from the previous spring that have been cut back in late summer or early autumn can then be divided into several small clumps as a means of propagation. Here again, this propagation method is recommended only as a means of increasing stock of a favorite variety, and is not recommended for pansies in general.

Lift these old plants carefully 6 weeks before first fall frost and break them into clumps. Each plant should retain some new growth and a portion of the roots. Place the clumps in a coldframe to strengthen for three or four weeks; then plant them in their permanent locations.

Although this method is relatively easy, plants propagated in this way are seldom as vigorous as those grown from good seed.

Again, the best and most successful method for home gardeners is to buy high quality seeds, seedlings or plants from a reputable dealer.

PANSY CARE

Watering and Fertilizing

The way to succeed in providing moisture for pansies is to water thoroughly once a week with about 1 inch of water during the growing season. Never water in the late afternoon or evening, as this encourages disease development. After transplanting pansy seedlings to their permanent locations in the fall, water plants only after dry periods and when you fertilize.

You should use manure and a 5–10–5 fertilizer to condition the soil prior to planting, as described under "How to Plant." Apply the fertilizer about a week after fall transplanting, then once more in late fall or early winter, and again in March. Avoid high levels of nitrogen—it can cause plants to produce soft foliage and to rot easily. Many gardeners use an organic fertilizer, which gives a slow release over many months.

During the growing season, application of 5–10–5 every 3 or 4 weeks will help give you bigger, brighter flowers on sturdy plants. An average rate is about 1 pound per 50 square feet of pansy bed. Liquid fertilizer in the same proportions (5–10–5) can also be used.

Always check the application directions on the

fertilizer label, and, if they appear there, also on the label from the package your pansy seed or plants came in. Follow these directions carefully when applying fertilizer. And always water pansies before applying any kind of fertilizer.

Cultivating

The day after planting seedlings in their permanent locations, work the ground around them, but only to a depth of about ½ inch. You can use a hand cultivator and work right up to the base of the plant. Thereafter, work the ground around plants as soon as the soil is dry enough after every watering or after every rain.

During the growing season, be sure to keep weeds down. Weeds will rob pansies of food and moisture and may cause pansies to become spindly.

Remove fading flowers to encourage more blooms. This prevents seed pods from forming, and extends considerably the period of flowering.

DISEASES AND INSECTS

Diseases

Pansies are subject to attack from several fungus diseases.

Anthracnose shows up on the leaves as brown areas with black margins. Petals may develop abnormally. If not treated, the disease can kill pansy plants.

Gray mold may appear under conditions of sustained moisture. It is particularly noticeable on flowers, where it may produce a soft, slimy decay.

Leaf spot, as the name implies, produces spots on the leaves which are small at first, but grow to cover leaves completely. Spots may also appear on flowers.

Rust causes red-brown pustules on the upper sides of leaves. On the undersides you can see light green spots where the pustules form.

Yellows (*aster yellows*), takes its name from the chief symptom it produces—it turns leaves a yellow-green shade. It also causes stunting of plants. The disease is spread by a leafhopper.

Beet curlytop disease, which attacks pansies as well as beets, causes leaf curl and a reduction of flower size. It is transmitted by the beet leafhopper.

Sprays or dusts containing zineb are effective against anthracnose and leaf spot. Maneb is effective against gray mold. Plants affected by yellows or beet curlytop must be pulled up and destroyed or the disease will spread. In fact, it is always safer to destroy diseased plants to prevent disease spread. Do this also if the zineb or maneb treatments are ineffective. Ask your garden supplier for sprays or dusts with zineb or maneb, and follow directions on the label carefully.

In addition to the diseases already mentioned, a fungus disease caused by a species of *Pythium* builds up in soils if you plant pansies in the same spot year after year. The disease causes wilting and can kill the plant. Because of this, change the location of pansies every year or every other year. *Never plant pansies in the same soil more than three years in succession.*

Insects

Along with the leafhoppers that transmit disease, aphids and spider mites also attack pansies. To control leafhoppers and aphids, apply malathion as a dust or spray. Spider mites may be controlled with dicofol. You can buy sprays and dusts at your garden-supply store, and at many drug and variety stores. Follow the directions on the label carefully.

You may obtain information on insects and diseases from your county agricultural agent or your state experiment station.

Precautions

Pesticides used improperly can be injurious to man, animals, and plants. Follow the directions and heed all precautions on the labels.

Store pesticides in original containers—out of reach of children and pets—and away from food.

Apply pesticides selectively and carefully. Do not apply a pesticide when there is danger of drift to other areas. Avoid prolonged inhalation of a pesticide spray or dust. When applying a pesticide it is advisable that you be fully clothed.

After handling a pesticide, do not eat, drink or smoke until you have washed. In case a pesticide is swallowed or gets in the eyes, follow the first aid treatment given on the label, and get prompt medical attention. If a pesticide is spilled on your skin or clothing, remove clothing immediately and wash skin thoroughly.

Dispose of empty pesticide containers by wrapping them in several layers of newspaper and placing them in your trash can.

It is difficult to remove all traces of a herbicide (weed killer) from equipment. Therefore, to prevent injury to desirable plants, do not use the same equipment for insecticides and fungicides that you use for a herbicide.

NOTE: Some states have restrictions on the use of certain pesticides. Check your state and local regulations.

CHAPTER 30

Peonies

PEONIES ARE HARDY perennial plants. They need little care and live through severe winters. After they become established in a garden, peonies bloom each spring for many years. They are the backbone of the perennial border and make good cut flowers.

Plant peonies in clumps of three, in masses, or among other plants. Planted singly, they contribute little to good landscaping. Like iris, daylily and chrysanthemum, their leaves make an excellent background for small plants; grow them in beds at least 4 feet wide. Group them with phlox and plantain lily for contrast of foliage and time of blooming.

Most peonies are grown in states north of South Carolina and Texas. Some varieties will grow farther south, but they seldom bloom because winter temperatures are not low enough for flower buds to develop properly.

KINDS OF PEONIES

Two kinds of peonies are grown. Garden, or herbaceous, varieties have full, bushy stems that grow 2 to 4 feet tall. Tree peonies often grow to eye-level height on woody stems with few branches.

Garden Peonies

Garden peonies are grouped into five types according to the shape of the petals. These types are single, semidouble, double, Japanese and anemone. Each type includes many varieties.

Single, or Chinese, peonies have one row of broad petals that surround a cluster of yellow, pollen-bearing stamens. Other flower types have central petals in the place of stamens. Semidouble peonies have broad central petals; double peonies have central petals that are as wide as the outer ones; Japanese peonies have long, thin central petals; and anemone peonies have broad central petals.

Peonies bloom in May and June. Colors are white, yellow, cream, pink, rose and deep red.

Some popular, dependable varieties of garden peonies are: Early blooming: 'Festiva Maxima' (white); midseason blooming: 'Mary Brand' (red) and 'Mikado' (red); late blooming: 'Myrtle Gentry' (pink) and 'Sarah Bernhardt' (mauve rose).

Tree Peonies

Tree peonies produce many flowers on a single shrublike plant. Colors are yellow, pink, white, rose, crimson, scarlet, black and purple. The centers of the flowers are yellow, pink or red. Petals are mottled at the base.

The stems of these peonies stay alive all winter. They are less common than garden types.

Many varieties of tree peonies have been developed. Some of the dependable ones are 'Argosy', 'Flambeau', 'Flora', 'La Lorraine', 'Souvenir de Ducher', and 'Yeso-no-mine'. All of these bloom early.

HOW PEONIES GROW

Peonies grow from tubers, or underground stems, that store food produced by the leaves. New growth develops from buds, or eyes, on the tuber. A single tuber may have many eyes, but it must have at least three to thrive.

Plants grown from tubers with less than three eyes may take three to five years to produce more than a few small blooms. But peonies grown from tubers with three to five eyes may flower well the second year after planting.

Immature shoots are bright red, succulent and easy to damage; mature leaves are dark green and shiny.

Peonies develop a taproot and many short, thin

roots. The taproot is a straight, thick, central root that extends farther into the soil than other roots. Often it grows 12 to 15 inches deep.

You can buy hybrid tree peonies. They produce larger flowers than regular tree peonies.

Both hybrid and regular tree peonies have a serious fault. The stems are weak at the top.

Tree peonies grow either from seed or from grafts. When grown from seed, they take at least six years to bloom. Plants grown from grafted tubers usually bloom the third year after planting. Because grafting is difficult, the average gardener should buy tubers that already have grafts on them.

BUYING PEONIES

Buy peony tubers that have three to five eyes. Tubers without eyes, or with only one or two eyes, often rot in the ground. And tubers with more than five eyes often fail to produce large flowers.

Tubers are sold in late summer and fall. Some dealers sell fully grown peonies in the spring, but these plants are expensive, and few of them live through the dry weather of summer. It is better to buy and plant tubers in the fall.

Select peonies whose colors will harmonize with your garden. Selection for color combinations depends on personal taste. See the flowering plants at neighborhood gardens, nurseries or botanical gardens before choosing colors.

PLANTING PEONIES

Plant tubers of both garden and tree peonies in September or early October so they will have time to become established in the soil before winter.

Although, as stated above, you can plant fully grown peonies in the spring, they are much harder to keep alive than are tubers planted in the fall because they are already growing when you plant them.

Peonies need well-drained soil. They grow best in slightly raised beds that provide good drainage. Roots quickly rot in soil that holds water around them. Peonies thrive in deep, fertile clay loam, although they will survive in any good garden soil.

Although peonies will grow in spots that are shaded two or three hours each day, they will not produce large flowers when they grow beneath trees or shrubs because the roots of these plants take up water that peonies need.

Plant peonies where they will be sheltered from strong winds. However, good air circulation helps control fungus diseases.

TYPES OF PEONIES

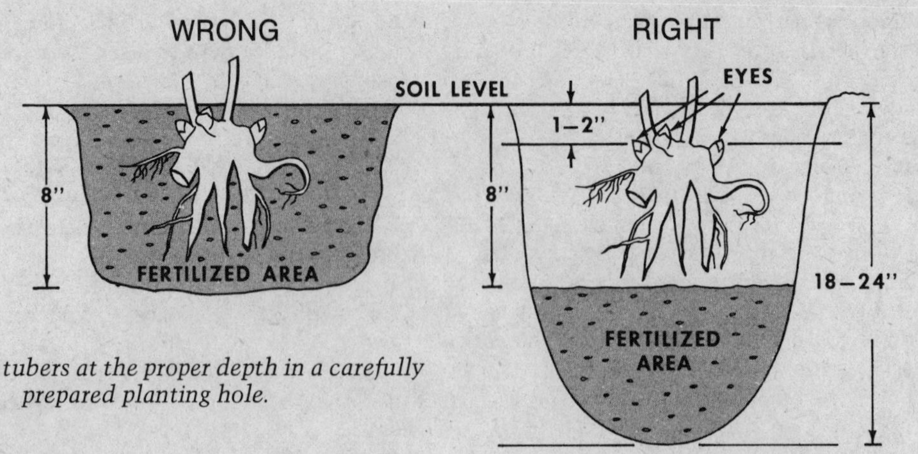

Plant peony tubers at the proper depth in a carefully prepared planting hole.

Peonies need carefully prepared beds because they remain in place for many years. They will not grow well in poorly prepared soil.

Prepare the soil two to four weeks before planting time, so that it will settle thoroughly by the time you plant.

Spade organic matter—compost, well-rotted manure or peat moss—into the soil.

Dig a hole 18 inches across and 18 inches deep for each tuber. Space the holes so that plants will be at least 3 feet apart. Pile loose soil at the side of the hole and break up all lumps.

Fill the hole about half full of soil mixed with a handful of 10–6–4 fertilizer. Leave the rest of the soil at the side until planting time.

Plant a garden-peony tuber with the uppermost eye not more than 2 inches below the ground surface. Put a little soil around the tuber and water thoroughly. Then fill the hole with the remaining soil, and press it down firmly. Water again to settle the tuber.

Plant a tree peony tuber with 4 or 5 inches of soil covering the graft. You can recognize the graft by the ridging on the stem and the different texture of the bark. Deep planting allows the grafted section to establish its own roots in the soil. Add soil and water in the planting hole the same way you would for a garden peony.

CARING FOR PLANTS

Mulching

Mulch peonies in both winter and summer. Winter mulch prevents the alternate freezing and thawing that pushes plants out of the soil. Summer mulch keeps the soil from drying out and prevents weed growth.

Immediately after the ground first freezes, cover the clumps with 1 to 2 inches of straw or peat moss and a layer of evergreen boughs.

In the spring, when the danger of freezing has passed, remove and burn the winter mulch and spread a summer mulch of straw or peat moss 1 to 2 inches thick around the plants. In the fall, remove and burn the summer mulch before you spread a winter mulch.

Weeding

Weeds use water, fertilizer and space that peonies need. Ordinarily a summer mulch will keep weeds from growing. But if you must remove weeds, hoe only deep enough to cut them off. Do not disturb the peony roots.

In early spring, and again in midsummer, dig up a strip of ground between your peony beds and any nearby trees or shrubs to limit the growth of tree

and shrub roots. Dig at least 3 feet from the peony clumps.

Watering

Water peonies frequently after tubers are planted in the fall and again during the spring and summer of the first growing season. Frequent watering is needed the first season to establish the roots in the soil.

After the first year, normal rainfall usually provides enough water except during long dry periods. In dry weather, water peonies often enough to keep the soil slightly damp, but not wet. Allow the soil to dry between waterings.

Fertilizing

Fertilize peonies moderately if you want them to produce large flowers. The first spring after planting, apply a handful of 10–6–4 fertilizer to the soil around each clump before the shoots emerge.

Be careful not to get fertilizer directly on the roots, stems or leaves of the plants. It will burn them.

In the spring of subsequent years, apply fertilizer to the soil when the flower buds are pea size. For maximum flower production, drench the soil with a liquid fertilizer (20–20–20, or similar proportions), 1 teaspoon in a gallon of water—or with a solution prepared from 1 cup of dried sheep manure in a gallon of water. Repeat the application once or twice during the growing season.

If you fertilize your plants well, you can leave them in place for ten to 15 years before they become too crowded.

Staking

Stake plants when they grow tall. Specially made stakes are available in garden-supply stores, but you may improvise with sticks, wood dowels, bamboo or wire. Select stakes that will be 6 to 12 inches shorter than the grown plant.

Sink the stakes behind the plants where they will be out of sight. Never put stakes in the center of the clump. Loosely tie the plants to the stakes, using wire covered with green paper or plastic. Do not use string or uncovered wire. String is unsightly, and uncovered wire breaks the stems.

Tie the plant, making a double loop of the wire with one loop around the plant and the other around the stake. Never loop the wire around both stake and plant—the plant will hang to one side and the wire may girdle the stem.

Disbudding

Remove the side buds on each stem as soon as they are visible. If you remove them later, the stump will be unsightly. Roll the buds out with your finger to keep from leaving scars on the stem.

Leave the terminal bud on each stem tip. Each will develop a large, showy bloom.

Disbud peonies by rolling the buds out with your finger.

Cutting

Cut flowers as soon as they fade so that seeds will not develop. Seeds use up needed plant food. Leave all foliage on the stems; the plants need green foliage for flowering the next year.

When the foliage of garden peonies turns brown in the fall, cut the plants back to ground level. Burn the cut leaves and stems.

Tree peonies usually are grafted on garden, or herbaceous, peonies; they will not overwinter if cut back to ground level. However, you must remove all shoots that grow from below the soil line. Otherwise the plants will grow like garden varieties. Allow flowers to develop only on the woody stems.

FLOWERS

A few flowers appear two or three years after planting. When plants are well cared for, blooms increase in number and quality each season for several years.

Peonies will bloom earlier in the season if you plant them where they have a southern exposure and if you place a protective screen around the beds. They will bloom later if the beds are covered with snow during winter.

If you want flowers for indoor arrangements, cut the stems when buds begin to unfold. Often they can be kept in a refrigerator for one to three weeks. When cut flowers are handled, the stems may crack and fall over. Attach each stem to a florist wire to support the flower.

Pale-pink flowers are at their best when they open in shade. Put a plastic or cheesecloth screen over the plants, or cut the budding stems and let them open indoors.

When you cut flowers for indoor arrangements, try to leave ⅔ of each cut stem. And, where possible, leave three leaves on the stump of each stem you cut. The leaves store food in the roots for next year's growth.

FAILURE TO BLOOM

Often, peonies fail to bloom although roots and tops appear healthy. If your plants do not bloom, look for signs of disease, and examine the growing site. Too much shade—especially in dry soil under trees—and poor drainage may prevent blooming.

Peonies will not bloom if you plant tubers too deep in the soil or cut back the plants in the fall before the foliage turns brown.

Other causes of failure to bloom are lack of growing space because of tree or shrub roots and late frosts that kill flower buds in the spring.

DIVIDING PEONIES

If peonies are originally planted in a favorable site with adequate spacing, they should grow well for years without dividing.

Divide and replant peonies only when they become crowded, usually in ten to fifteen years. Never divide a plant that is less than three years old because transplanting upsets the plants and retards flowering for several years.

Divide plants in early fall. Carefully dig around and under the plants. As you dig up the clumps, be careful not to break off the roots, especially taproots.

With a heavy stream of water, wash off any soil that clings to the clumps. Strip off the leaves.

Cut tubers apart with a sharp knife that you have sterilized over a flame or in alcohol. Each section should have three to five eyes. Be sure to leave a taproot attached to each tuber that has eyes on it. As you cut, look for signs of disease. To keep cuts free of disease organisms, dust them with zineb; you can buy it in large garden-supply shops.

Replant tubers immediately in a new area. Follow planting directions given on page 227.

DISEASES AND INSECTS

Peony diseases disfigure foliage, reduce flowering and rot roots. Buy disease-free stock from a reliable nursery. Plant resistant varieties if available. To prevent spread of foliage diseases, water plants early enough in the day for foliage to dry before dark.

Most fungus diseases can be controlled by fungicides applied before the disease appears or at first signs of infection, repeating the application every seven to ten days and after rains. More frequent applications may be needed during periods of damp weather.

Fungus Diseases

Botrytis blight: Botrytis blight is caused by a fungus that overwinters in dead peony leaves, stems and roots. The disease usually appears in midsummer. It is most damaging in cool, rainy weather.

Early in spring, infected shoots turn gray-brown. Mature stems rot at ground level. A mass of gray-brown feltlike spores appear on leaves and stems. Young buds dry up, and shoots and mature buds and flowers soften and rot. Infected petals drop onto healthy leaves and spread the disease.

Control: Remove diseased parts as soon as you notice them. Pull out and burn badly infected plants. Cut plants to the ground after the foliage turns brown in the fall. Burn dead material.

As a preventive aid, spray just as the new shoots emerge in very early spring. Repeat two to three times at ten-day intervals and during prolonged periods of wet or humid weather. Use 1½ to 2 tablespoons of 65 to 76 percent zineb or ferbam; two tablespoons of basic copper sulfate (containing 53 percent of metallic copper equivalent); or ⅛ pound of dry bordeaux mixture (containing 12.75 percent metallic copper equivalent) per gallon of water. Do not apply during blooming period.

Select varieties that are resistant to botrytis blight.

Phytophthora blight: Phytophthora blight is less common than botrytis blight, but it causes more damage to individual plants. Infection spreads down the stem from the buds. Stems dry up and turn dark brown and leathery. Plants rot at the ground line, or crown, of the plant.

Control: Remove diseased parts as soon as you notice them and pull out and burn badly infected plants. Cut plants back to the ground in the fall. Burn dead material.

Spray new shoots with zineb. Use 1 to 1½ tablespoons of 65 to 75 percent zineb for 1 gallon of water. Repeat at seven- to ten-day intervals.

Wilt: Wilt is caused by a fungus that lives in water-conducting tubes of stems. Infected plants wither and die quickly.

Control: Dig plants out immediately. Do not replant peonies in the same spot until at least three years after wilted plants have been removed.

Leaf blotch: Leaf blotch, or measles, is a disease that usually occurs after plants bloom. Leaf blotch fungus overwinters in dead plants. Infected plants have small red or reddish-brown spots on stems, leaves and flowers. The spots on the leaves later enlarge into purplish-brown blotches on the upper surfaces. Dull brown blotches appear on lower surfaces.

Control: Cut plants to the ground in the fall. Remove diseased leaves as they appear in the spring and summer. Spray foliage with 1½ tablespoons of 50 percent captan in 1 gallon of water every seven to ten days, beginning when leaves unfold.

Other leaf spot diseases: One type of leaf spot produces circular spots with grayish-white centers and reddish-brown borders. The spots appear on leaves and stems. Another disease produces long, reddish spots on the leaves. Later the centers of the spots turn gray; sometimes edges of leaves pucker.

Control: In the fall, cut plants to the ground. In the spring, remove diseased leaves as they appear. Spray foliage with 1½ tablespoons of 50 percent captan in 1 gallon of water every seven to ten days, beginning when leaves unfold.

Crown and stem rots: Crown rot is caused by an unidentified fungus that rots the area where roots join stems. Sometimes small, circular spots appear on the roots of infected plants.

Two stem rot diseases—each caused by a fungus—attack peonies. The diseases rot shoots and full-grown stems. They cause white molds on the surfaces of stems and leaves. Both fungi produce sclerotia—small brown or black bodies about the size of a mustard seed. Sclerotia overwinter in stems or on roots. They reinfect new shoots in the spring.

Control: In the fall, dig up infected plants. Cut away decayed areas. Burn badly damaged plants.

Replant peonies in a different spot in your garden. If you want to put plants back in the same place, remove a few shovels of the contaminated soil and replace with new soil.

If you use manure in peony beds, mix it thoroughly with the soil around the clumps. Do not use it on top of the crown; used this way, manure fosters development of crown rot.

Lemoine disease: Lemoine disease is a root disease whose cause is not known. Infected plants do not produce flowers. Shoots are weak. Small knobby swellings appear on the small roots, and soft yellow areas appear on the large roots.

Control: Dig up and burn infected plants.

Root knot: Root knot, or root gall, is caused by nematodes. Nematodes are tiny worms that feed on many kinds of plants. They are most damaging where winters are mild, where the growing season is warm and where the soil is light.

Nematode-infected plants lack vigor. They produce only a few small flowers. Stems are short and thin. Leaves are light green. Large roots become swollen and stubby. Small roots develop knobby outgrowths.

Control: Dig out and burn heavily infected plants. If possible, plant lawn grass on the infested soil and let it grow two years before you replant peonies. Or, if you wish to replant peonies within a few weeks, you can sterilize the infested soil with a nematocide.

Virus Diseases

Mosaic is the most common virus disease of peonies. It produces yellowish blotches and rings on leaves but it does not cause much damage. Infected plants are not dwarfed or deformed.

Crown elongation, another virus disease, causes many long branched crowns to develop from the tubers. Plants develop many slender, weak shoots. These dwarfed shoots produce no flower buds.

Leaf curl, or curly leaf, virus causes plants to become dwarfed. Leaves grow close together on the stem and curl up. Leaf surfaces crinkle. No flower buds form.

Control: Dig up and burn plants infected with any of the virus diseases.

Insects

Insects seldom attack peonies. Those most likely to damage the plants and flowers are rose chafers, scale insects and flower thrips. Use carbaryl to control the rose chafer, and malathion and dimethoate to control scale insects and flower thrips. Follow directions on container labels.

VIII

GROWING BERRIES

CHAPTER 31

Blackberries

BLACKBERRIES GROW BEST in temperate climates. They are not well adapted to areas in the Plains states or mountain states where summers are hot and dry and winters are severe.

If properly managed, a blackberry plantation should yield at least 6,000 pounds of berries per acre. To get the greatest yield and longest productive life from the plantation:

- Choose types and varieties that are adapted to your area.
- Prepare the soil thoroughly.
- Plant only highest-quality stock.
- Cultivate frequently.
- Apply fertilizer every year.
- Thin out all weak canes and suckers.
- Protect plants from insects, diseases and winter injury.

TYPES OF BLACKBERRIES

The two types of blackberries—erect and trailing—differ primarily in the character of their canes. Erect blackberries have arched self-supporting canes. Trailing blackberries, also called dewberries, ground blackberries, or running blackberries, have canes that are not self-supporting; the canes must be tied to poles or trellises in cultivation.

The two types also differ in fruit characteristics. Fruit clusters of the trailing blackberry are more open than those of the erect blackberry. Trailing blackberries generally ripen earlier and are often larger and sweeter than the erect type.

Some varieties have canes that trail the first year after planting. Canes developed in subsequent years are more erect. These are called semitrailing blackberries, but they are essentially erect varieties.

PLANTING SITES

Availability of soil moisture is the most important factor to consider in choosing a planting site for blackberries. While the fruit is growing and ripening, blackberries need a large supply of moisture.

Blackberries

During the winter, however, the plants are harmed if water stands around their roots.

Almost any soil type except very sandy soil is suitable for blackberries, as long as the drainage is good.

In areas where winters are severe, the slope of the planting site is important. Blackberries planted on hillsides are in less danger of winter injury and damage from late spring frosts than those planted in valleys.

In areas where drying winds occur frequently, the plantation should be sheltered by surrounding hills, trees or shrubs.

PLANTING

Plant blackberries as soon as you can prepare the soil—in early spring in the North, in late winter or early spring in the South.

Preparing the Soil

Prepare the soil for blackberries as thoroughly as you would for a garden. For best results, plow to a depth of 9 inches as soon as the soil is in workable condition. Disk and harrow the soil just before setting the plants.

Before establishing a new plantation, it is a good idea to seed and plow under one or two green-manure crops of cowpeas or rye and vetch. This thorough working gets the soil in good condition for planting, and the added organic matter and nitrogen help the plantation to produce an early fruit crop.

Spacing the Plants

Plant erect varieties of blackberries 5 feet apart in rows 8 feet apart. Space vigorous varieties of trailing or semitrailing blackberries, such as Thornless Evergreen, 8 to 12 feet apart in rows 10 feet apart. Space other trailing varieties 4 to 6 feet apart in rows 8 feet apart.

In the Central states, set erect varieties 2 feet apart in rows 9 to 10 feet apart. Let the plants grow into hedgerows.

Setting the Plants

Do not let planting stock dry out. If you cannot plant the stock as soon as you receive it, protect the roots from drying by heeling-in the plants.

To heel-in, dig a trench deep enough to contain the roots. Spread the plants along the trench, roots down, and cover the roots with moist soil.

If the plants are dry when you receive them, soak the roots in water for several hours before you plant them or heel them in.

When you are ready to set the plants in the field, dip the roots in a thin mud made with clay and water (or keep the plants in polyethylene bags until you actually set them in the ground). This coating helps to protect the roots from rapid drying while the plants are being set.

Before setting the plants, cut the tops back so they are about 6 inches long. The 6-inch top is useful as a handle when setting the plants and will serve to show the location of the plants.

To make a planting hole, cut a slit in the soil with the blade of a mattock or shovel. Press the handle of the tool forward to open the slit.

Put the root of the blackberry plant in the hole. Set it so it is about the same depth as it was in the nursery.

Withdraw the blade of the mattock or shovel and pack the soil firmly around the root with your heel.

INTERCROPPING

During the first summer after the blackberry plants are set, vegetables can be grown between the rows. Intercropping is not used in the Northwest and is used much less elsewhere now than formerly.

Good crops for intercropping are cabbage, cauliflower, beans, peas and summer squash. Do not grow grain crops; they are not cultivated and they take too much of the moisture and nutrients needed by the blackberry plants.

Do not grow intercrops after the first year; blackberry plants of bearing size need all the nutrients and moisture for satisfactory production.

FERTILIZING

To get maximum yields from your blackberry plantation, apply fertilizer each year at blossoming time. In Southeastern and South Central United States, make a second application after fruiting.

Use commercial 5–10–5 fertilizer for the first application. Apply it as a top dressing at a rate of 500 to 1,000 pounds per acre or 5 to 10 pounds per 50-foot row. Use nitrate of soda or ammonium nitrate after fruiting. Apply nitrate of soda at the rate of 200 to 300 pounds per acre and ammonium nitrate at the rate of 80 to 100 pounds per acre.

TRAINING

Train blackberry plants to trellises. Erect blackberry plants can be grown without support, but many of the canes may be broken during cultivation

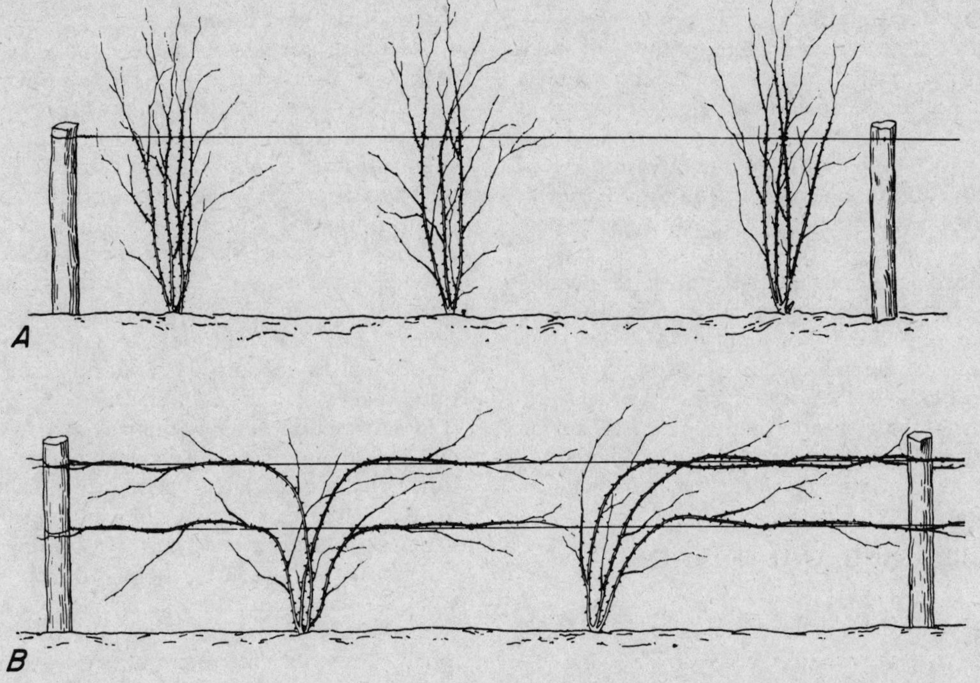

Trellises for blackberries: A. Train erect plants to a one-wire trellis. B. Train trailing plants to a two-wire trellis.

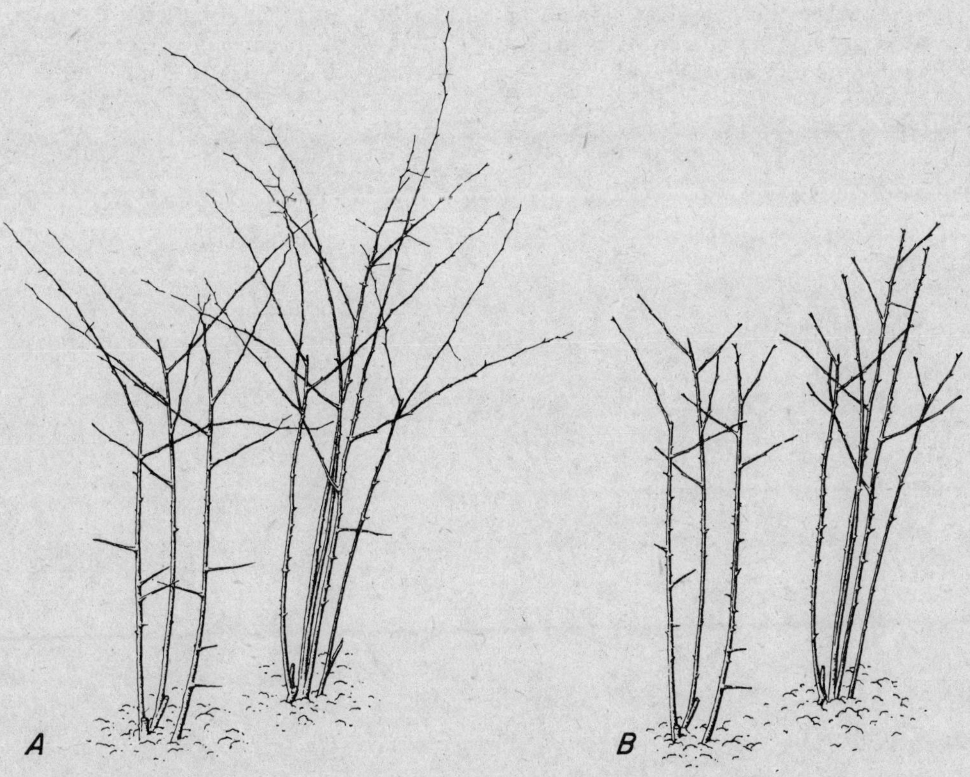

An erect blackberry plant: A. Before pruning. B. After pruning.

and picking. Trellises will pay for themselves by reducing this damage.

Many trellis arrangements and methods of training are in use by blackberry growers. The simplest methods of trellis construction and of training are as follows:

- Construct trellises by stretching wire between posts set 15 to 20 feet apart in the row. For erect blackberries, use a single wire attached to the post about 30 inches from the ground. For semitrailing and trailing blackberries, use two wires, one about 3 feet from the ground and the other about 5 feet from the ground. (See illustration on page 237.)
- Tie the canes to the wires with soft string. Tie erect varieties where the canes cross the wire. Tie trailing canes horizontally along the wires, or fan them out from the ground and tie them where they cross each wire. Avoid tying the canes in bundles.

PRUNING AND THINNING

The crowns of blackberry plants are perennial; new canes arise from them every year. The canes are biennial; they live for only 2 years. During the first year they grow and send out laterals (side branches). The second year, small branches grow from buds on the laterals. Fruit is borne on these buds. After the laterals fruit, the canes die.

The laterals should be pruned back in spring. Fruit from pruned laterals is larger and of better market quality than fruit from unpruned laterals.

Before growth starts, cut the laterals back to a length of about 12 inches.

Erect blackberries send up root suckers in addition to the new canes that arise from the crown. If all the root suckers were allowed to grow they would soon turn the blackberry plantation into a thicket.

During the growing season, remove all suckers that appear between the rows. Pull the suckers out of the ground. Suckers that are pulled do not regrow as quickly as suckers that are cut down.

When canes of erect blackberries reach a height of 30 to 36 inches, cut off the tips. This makes the canes branch. Tipped canes also grow stout and are better able to support a heavy fruit crop than untipped canes.

In summer, as soon as the last berries have been picked, cut out all the old canes and burn them. Also thin out the new canes, leaving three or four canes of erect varieties, four to eight canes of semitrailing varieties, and eight to 12 canes of trailing varieties.

In areas of the South where anthracnose and rosette are serious diseases on blackberries, cut out all the canes—both old and new—after fruiting. Then fertilize and cultivate to promote growth of replacement canes for the next year's fruit crop.

If you let suckers form within rows of erect blackberries, thin the suckers to about five or six canes per lineal foot of row.

Note: For information on cultivating, harvesting, disease and insect control, see Chapter 32, "Thornless Blackberries for the Home Garden."

CHAPTER 32

Thornless Blackberries for the Home Garden

FOR YEARS HOME GARDENERS hesitated to grow blackberries in their backyards because of the annoyance of the thorns. Then two thornless blackberry varieties—'Smoothstem' and 'Thornfree'—were developed by the U.S. Department of Agriculture. Popular with home gardeners and proprietors of "you-pick" enterprises, these productive blackberries are easy to handle and require little summer pruning. The fruits are firm and highly flavored.

THORNLESS BLACKBERRY VARIETIES

Both 'Smoothstem' and 'Thornfree' are genetically thornless blackberries—all the cells have the thornless character. When new canes develop they retain this thornless characteristic.

Other thornless blackberries, such as 'Thornless Young', 'Thornless Logan' and 'Thornless Evergreen', have a thornless character only in the outer cell layer of their canes. New canes originating below the crown have thorns.

Thornless blackberries have trailing or semitrailing canes that are not self-supporting. They can be grown along the ground in their first season, but thereafter must be trained on trellises.

Blackberries are planted in early spring in the North; in late winter or early spring in the South.

Blackberries vary in their ability to withstand cold, but none should be grown where temperatures drop to 0° F. and below.

PLANTING

Planting sites for thornless blackberries, as well as soil type and soil preparation, are similar to those for other types of blackberries (see Chapter 31).

Spacing the Plants

Leave plenty of space between rows when planting thornless blackberries, or severe competition for soil nutrients and moisture will result.

'Smoothstem' and 'Thornfree' are vigorous varieties and should be set 6 to 8 feet apart in rows that are at least 8 feet apart.

Less vigorous varieties, such as 'Thornless Young' and 'Thornless Logan', should be set 4 to 6 feet apart in rows that are at least 8 feet apart.

Align plants carefully in the row to accommodate a trellis which will be constructed. (See below.)

Setting the Plants

Take the same precautions against drying out that were advised in Chapter 31 and set plants in the same way.

INTERCROPPING

During the first summer after setting the blackberries, vegetables such as beans, peas or cabbage can be grown in the spaces between rows. Their cultivation will benefit the blackberry plants and put the unused portion of your garden to good use.

Intercropping should not be done after the first year of planting; when the blackberry plants are of bearing size they will need all available moisture and nutrients.

TRELLIS CONSTRUCTION

After the first season, thornless blackberries should be trained on trellises. This will assure clean fruit and ease of picking, and will help in disease control.

Many trellis arrangements and training methods are satisfactory. To construct a simple and effective trellis:

- Stretch two wires (gauge size 12 or 14) between heavy end posts set 15 to 25 feet apart in the row. String one wire 2½ feet from the ground and the other about 5 feet from the ground.
- Staple the wires loosely to all posts between the end posts. (Wires must be loose enough to allow for contraction in cold weather.)
- Tie trailing canes horizontally along the wires or fan them out from the ground and tie them where they cross each wire. Avoid tying the canes in large bundles.

TRAINING

During the first year, blackberry canes grow vegetatively and send out side branches. In the second year, these canes bear fruit, and then the canes die. (The canes arising from the crown are biennial; they live for only two years. The roots and crowns are perennial.)

Methods of training blackberries largely depend on the length of the growing season and the degree of winter cold.

In northern areas, leave trailing varieties of thornless blackberry canes on the ground, under the trellis, until their second season. Then, before the buds swell, bring the canes up to the trellis wires, wrap them in groups of three or four, and tie.

Tie semitrailing blackberry varieties to the wires in their first year.

In the South, tie new canes of both trailing and semitrailing varieties to the trellis as soon as harvest is over. The old canes should be cut out immediately.

PRUNING

After harvest, prune away old canes and destroy them as a sanitation measure. In certain areas of the South anthracnose and rosette, both serious diseases of blackberries, threaten crops. In these areas, all the canes should be cut out after harvest.

Before tying canes to the trellis wire, remove any that are weak, spindly or broken.

Thin out to leave 12 to 16 new canes. Tie these to wires or, depending on the management plan being used, leave them under the trellis for the rest of the season.

'Thornfree' and 'Smoothstem' varieties require little summer pruning; they do not tend to branch freely and usually will not develop more than three or four canes.

Before growth starts in spring, prune all side branches back to 12 inches. Side branches that are pruned will produce larger fruit than those that are not pruned.

FERTILIZING AND WATERING

Mixed fertilizers are satisfactory for blackberries. For best results, apply fertilizer in early spring when growth starts and again in summer just after harvest. Use a 10–10–10 fertilizer mix or a 10–6–4 mix, at the rate of 5 pounds per 100-foot row.

For late-ripening varieties, such as 'Smoothstem' and 'Thornfree', apply the fertilizer mix no later than July. This is to avoid forcing a late-season growth that will be subject to winter injury.

For the first year or two, before the root systems of the plants develop fully, spread 3 or 4 ounces of the fertilizer mix in a 12-inch radius around the base of each plant.

Blackberry plants require plenty of moisture while the berries are growing and ripening. The amount of the water needed is roughly equivalent to 1 inch of rainfall per week. Irrigate sufficiently to meet this requirement.

Mulching reduces the frequency of watering. Good mulch materials include seed-free straw or prairie hay, pine needles, corncob, wood chips, or cotton hulls. Lawn clippings are not satisfactory.

CULTIVATION

Blackberry plants need thorough and frequent cultivation; weeds and grasses compete for moisture and are difficult to control.

Cultivate thornless blackberries during the summer, and as often as necessary to keep the weeds down. To avoid harming shallow roots of the plants, cultivate only 2 or 3 inches deep near the rows. Unnecessary pruning of roots stunts plant growth.

Discontinue cultivation at least a month before freezing weather begins.

Cover Crops

Winter cover crops planted between the rows help to maintain the structure of the soil, and reduce erosion. If a legume cover crop is planted, valuable nitrogen will be added to the soil.

Sow cover crops during the fall. The following cover crops are adapted to thornless blackberries: field rye, vetch (a legume) and rye, and spring oats.

Drill or broadcast the seed by hand between rows. Plant at least 18 inches away from either side of the row to allow air circulation for the blackberry canes on the ground.

Herbicides

Herbicides can be useful, especially in large plantings. Control recommendations depend on soil types and weed species in various areas. Contact your county agricultural agent or state agricultural experiment station for local recommendations.

HARVESTING

Blackberries that are picked at the proper time, handled carefully, and stored in a cool place will stay in good condition for several days. Overripe or injured berries spoil quickly.

Harvest thornless blackberries at least twice a week, but do *not* pick thornless blackberries as soon as they turn black. It is better to wait three or four days and pick when the color has a dull appearance. This will assure a better flavor, color and wholeness, especially if you are canning the berries.

Remember the following when harvesting the berries:

- Pick berries in the morning while the temperature is still cool. Blackberries picked in the morning do not spoil as easily as those picked in the afternoon.
- Pick carefully and do not crush or bruise the fruits when placing them in berry baskets.
- Pick when the berries are fully ripened but still firm.

PREVENTING WINTER INJURY

Winter protection is needed for blackberries in areas where winter temperatures are expected to go below 10° F. Cold-hardy varieties, however, need no special protection in the winter.

In areas with low winter temperatures and cold, drying winds, cover the canes with a layer of soil, straw or coarse manure. This should be done after the canes have become dormant, but before the onset of severe cold weather. Remove this protective layer before growth starts in spring.

Where winters are mild and moist, such as in western Oregon, canes of trailing varieties left lying on the ground will be damaged. It is best, in areas with similar conditions, to tie the canes to the trellis in early fall and allow them to stay up through the winter. However, in areas with severe drying winds, canes tied to trellises are subject to winter injury.

DISEASES AND INSECTS

Diseases and insects vary in kind and severity from area to area. For information suited to your local conditions contact your county agricultural agent or state agricultural experiment station.

To keep disease and insect damage to a minimum:

- Choose disease-resistant varieties adapted to your area.
- Burn diseased plants or canes.
- Remove old canes soon after harvest.
- Remove all wild blackberry plants in the vicinity of your garden.
- Prune out and burn canes that have been infested with insects.
- Keep the garden free of weeds and fallen leaves.

THORNLESS BLACKBERRY VARIETIES

The thornless blackberry varieties that follow are listed in their approximate order of ripening. Specific ripening dates will vary with location and season. All the varieties are partly susceptible to winter damage.

The variety descriptions include: the degree of hardiness (four degrees are given: hardy, moderately hardy, less hardy, and tender); the duration of harvest; the characteristics of the plant; and the area of special adaptation.

For local variety recommendations consult your county agricultural agent or your state agricultural experiment station.

Thornless Logan: Less hardy; harvest period is ten to 15 days; berry large, long, reddish, acid, high flavor; plant is vigorous, very productive. Grown on Pacific coast. Not adapted to East.

Austin Thornless: Moderately hardy; harvest period is ten to 15 days; genetically thornless, berry is large, round, black, good flavor; plant is vigorous but only moderately productive. Widely grown in the South.

Thornless Young: Moderately hardy; harvest period is ten to 15 days; berry large, soft, wine-colored, very sweet; plant is vigorous and fairly productive. Adapted in the South and Pacific states.

Cory Thornless: Less hardy; harvest period is ten to 15 days; berry large, black, sweet, soft; plant is vigorous and fairly productive. Grown on the Pacific coast.

Thornless Boysen: Moderately hardy; harvest period is ten to 15 days; berry large, soft, wine-colored, very sweet; plant is vigorous and fairly productive. Adapted in the South and on Pacific coast.

Black Satin: Hardier than Thornfree and 12 to 14 days earlier. Harvest period lasts three to four weeks; slightly more vigorous and productive than Dirksen Thornless (see below) but otherwise very similar in fruit and plant habits and in area of adaptation.

Dirksen Thornless: Hardier than Thornfree and about three weeks earlier. Harvest period lasts three weeks; genetically thornless; berry medium-large, firm, black, slightly dull at full maturity, good flavor, very little astringency; plant is vigorous, healthy and very productive. Winter-hardy south of a line from Kansas City to Urbana, Illinois, to central Ohio to New Jersey, and in the Pacific Northwest.

Thornfree: Hardy, harvest period lasts for about one month; genetically thornless, berry medium, firm, black, good flavor; plant is notably healthy and very productive. Grown in central New Jersey, southern Pennsylvania, southern Ohio southward to North Carolina and west to Arkansas, and in the Pacific Northwest.

Smoothstem: Moderately hardy; harvest period lasts for about one month; genetically thornless, berry medium-large, black, good flavor; plant is extremely healthy and vigorous, very productive. Adapted from southern Maryland to North Carolina along Atlantic coast.

Thornless Evergreen: Hardy; harvest period lasts for about one month; berry is large, exceptionally firm, sweet, black; plant is vigorous, productive and healthy. Best adapted to Pacific Northwest.

CHAPTER 33

Raspberries

RASPBERRIES GROW BEST in cool climates. They are not well adapted south of Virginia, Tennessee or Missouri, nor are they well adapted to areas in the Plains states or mountain states where summers are hot and dry and winters are severe.

TYPES OF RASPBERRIES

Three main types of raspberries—red, black and purple—are grown in the U.S. They differ in several ways other than the color of their fruit.

Red raspberries have erect canes. They usually are propagated by suckers, which grow from the roots of the parent plant. Red raspberries are grown most extensively in the West.

Black raspberries (blackcaps) have arched canes that root at the tips. They are propagated by the plants that grow at the tips of the canes. Blackcaps are grown mostly in the eastern half of the country and in Oregon.

Purple raspberries are hybrids of red raspberries and blackcaps. They have the same growth characteristics as blackcaps and are propagated in the same way. They are grown extensively only in western New York, though the area where they are adapted is about the same as the area where blackcaps are grown.

Some raspberries have yellow fruit. Yellow raspberries are variations of red raspberries and, except for fruit color, have all the characteristics of red raspberries. They are grown chiefly in home gardens.

PLANTING SITE

A wide range of soil types, from sandy loam to clay, are satisfactory for growing raspberries. The character of the subsoil is more important than the type of surface soil. The subsoil should be deep and well drained.

If the subsoil is underlaid by a shallow hardpan or water table, the root system of the raspberry plant will be restricted in its development. Plants with restricted root systems may be damaged during a drought because raspberries need an abundant supply of moisture at all times.

The slope and exposure of the planting site may be important. In areas where winters are severe, raspberries planted on hillsides are in less danger of winter injury than raspberries planted in valleys. In the southern part of the raspberry-growing area, sites with a northern or northeastern exposure retain humus and moisture longer and are better suited to raspberries than sites with a southern exposure.

PLANTING

In the East, plant raspberries in the spring. On the Pacific Coast, plant them in the spring or during the rainy season.

Plant only the highest quality stock from a nursery that is certified disease-free. If you propagate your own stock, plant only the most vigorous tip plants or suckers.

Preparing the Soil

For the best results, prepare the soil for raspberries as follows:

- Plow, in early spring, to a depth of at least 6 inches.
- Treat the soil with chlordane to control soil insects. Apply 10 pounds of actual chlordane per acre.
- Disk and harrow the soil just before setting the plants.

Prepare the soil for raspberries as thoroughly as you would for corn.

A good plan is to seed and plow under one or two

green-manure crops of oats or barley with vetch before you establish a raspberry plantation. This thorough working gets the soil in good condition for planting, and the added organic matter and nitrogen help the plantation to produce an early fruit crop.

Most land that has been in cultivated crops is in good condition for growing raspberries.

Raspberries should not follow potatoes, tomatoes or eggplant; wilt diseases that affect these crops also affect raspberries. The fungus causing wilt may remain in the soil and damage the raspberry plants.

After plowing, treat the soil with chlordane spray of dust at a rate of 10 pounds of actual chlordane per acre. This is the amount of chlordane contained in 20 pounds of 50 percent chlordane wettable powder or 100 pounds of 10 percent chlordane dust.

Chlordane treatment controls insects in the soil. It is especially needed for controlling grubs in land that has just been in sod.

Immediately before setting the plants, disk and harrow the soil.

Spacing the Plants

Spacing for raspberry plants depends on the system of training you plan to use and on the type of cultivating equipment you own.

Raspberry plants can be set in hills and cultivated on all four sides or set in rows and cultivated on two sides.

For planting in hills, space the plants far enough apart each way so you can cultivate between them. Align the plants in each direction.

For planting in rows, space the rows far enough apart to cultivate with the equipment you will be using. Set red raspberry plants 2 to 3 feet apart in the rows and black raspberry plants 4 to 5 feet apart.

If you plan to cultivate with a garden tractor or wheel hoe, 5 feet is enough distance between hills or rows.

If you plan to use a farm tractor, leave 7 to 10 feet between rows.

Setting the Plants

Do not let planting stock dry out. If you cannot plant the stock as soon as you receive it, protect the roots from drying by heeling-in the plants.

To heel-in, dig a trench deep enough to contain the roots. Spread the plants along the trench, roots down, and cover the roots with moist soil.

If the plants are dry when you receive them, soak the roots in water for several hours before you plant them or heel them in.

When you are ready to set the plants out in the field, keep them moist by covering the bundles or lots of plants with wet burlap or canvas, or with plastic film, until they are planted.

Before setting the plants, cut the tops back so they are about 6 inches long. The 6-inch top is useful as a handle when setting the plants and will serve to show the location of the plants and aid in aligning them.

To make a planting hole, cut a slit in the soil with a mattock blade or shovel. Press the handle of the tool forward to open the slit.

Put the root of the raspberry plant into this opening. Set red raspberry plants so they are 2 to 3 inches deeper than they were in the nursery. Set black or purple raspberries the same depth as they were in the nursery or no more than 1 inch deeper.

Firming the soil around the roots of a newly set plant.

Withdraw the blade of the mattock or shovel from the soil and firm the soil around the roots of the plant with your foot.

After the planting has been set, the protruding canes or red raspberries can be left in place. To help control disease on purple or black raspberries, however, go over the planting again and cut off all protruding canes.

TRAINING AND PRUNING

Raspberries are easier to cultivate if they are planted in hills than if they are planted in rows. This increased ease of cultivation more than compensates for lower per acre yield of hill-planted raspberries. Hill culture may not always be practical, however. Some red raspberry varieties have long, slender canes that must be tied. If stakes are not available at reasonable cost, the plants are more profitably set in rows and the canes trained to wire trellises. The wires to which the canes are tied are strung between posts set 15 to 30 feet apart in the rows.

If stakes are available, set long-caned plants in hills. The year after setting the plants, drive a stake into the ground 1 foot from the plant. Tie the canes to the stakes at a point halfway between the ground and the tips of the canes, and again near the ends of the canes.

Pruning

Most varieties of red raspberries are stout-caned. They may be planted in hills and grown without training the canes to stakes. If the canes tend to bend over to the ground, they can be cut back until they are self supporting.

Black and purple raspberries need not be tied; just top them to keep them from growing too tall. Top black raspberries at a height of 18 to 24 inches. Top purple raspberries at a height of 30 to 36 inches.

This topping is done by cutting off the ends of the canes as they reach the proper height. Canes should not be topped when they are wet or when rain is forecast that day.

Toward the end of the first season, the canes send out laterals (side branches). The next season small branches grow from buds on the laterals. Fruit is borne on these small branches.

The laterals should be pruned back in the spring, before growth starts. Fruit from pruned laterals is larger and of better market quality than fruit from unpruned laterals.

Cut the laterals back so that two buds per lateral are left on slim canes, up to six buds per lateral on stout canes.

Thinning

Raspberry canes are biennial; they grow the first year, fruit the second, then die. Only the crown and the roots are perennial. Old canes should be removed as soon as their fruit is harvested.

New canes grow from buds on the base of the old canes. Two new shoots usually come up each year, often three or more shoots come up. In addition, suckers grow directly from the roots of red raspberries. The new canes and suckers should be thinned immediately after harvest. Remove weak new shoots and most of the suckers from red raspberries. Leave about seven strong canes per hill.

To thin black or purple raspberries, remove canes that are under ½ inch in diameter. Most black raspberry plants have four or five canes that are over ½ inch, but if all the canes are smaller than this, cut out all but the two largest canes.

FERTILIZING

To get maximum yields from your raspberry plantation, apply fertilizer each year in early spring just as new growth begins.

Stable manure, if available, is best for fertilizing.

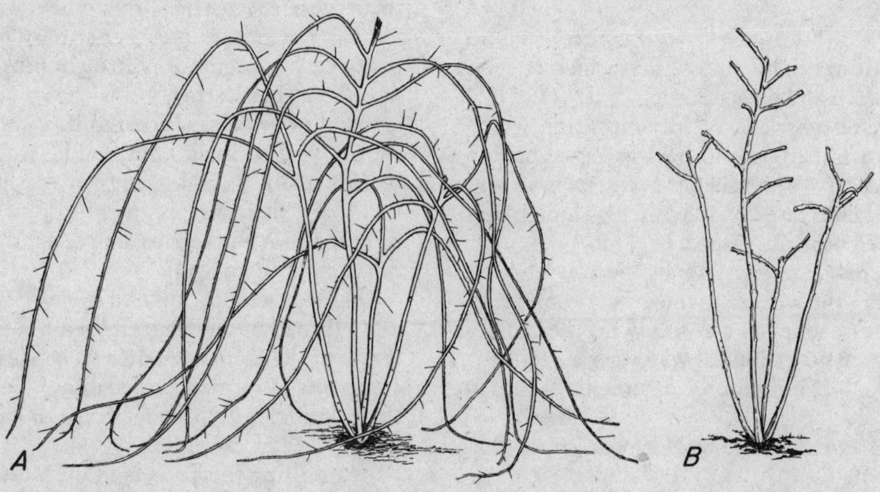

Left. *Black raspberry plant before pruning.* Right. *The same plant after pruning*

It supplies organic matter as well as nutrients. Apply 10 tons per acre. If stable manure is not available, use commercial 5–10–5 fertilizer. Apply it as a top dressing at a rate of 500 to 600 pounds per acre or spread about ½ cupful in a wide band no closer than about 6 inches from the crown around each hill.

CULTIVATING

Raspberry plantations should be cultivated thoroughly and frequently enough to prevent grass and weeds from getting started.

Begin cultivating in early spring and cultivate as often as necessary to keep weeds down. Continue cultivating until harvest time, resume cultivating after harvest, and continue it until late summer.

Do not cultivate in the fall; this tends to stimulate new growth, which is susceptible to winter injury.

To avoid harming shallow roots of the plants, cultivate only 2 or 3 inches deep near the rows. For best results and greatest safety, cultivate by shallow disking.

To reduce cost of cultivation the first year, grow other crops between the rows of raspberries. Grow crops that need cultivation in spring and early summer.

Good crops for this purpose are cabbage, cauliflower, beans, peas and summer squash. Do not grow potatoes, tomatoes or eggplant with raspberry varieties.

Do not grow grain crops; they are not cultivated and they take too much of the moisture and nutrients needed by the raspberry plants.

Do not grow intercrops after the first year; raspberry plants of bearing size need all the soil nutrients and moisture for satisfactory production.

USING HERBICIDES

Herbicides can be used as weed control aids in raspberry plantings. The use of herbicides supplements cultivation and does not replace it.

Herbicides are most useful in controlling weeds within rows or hills, where otherwise hand hoeing would be necessary. The middles between rows and hills should be cultivated regularly even though herbicides are used near the raspberry plants.

For established plantings, spray the rows with a herbicide before the weeds and new canes emerge in early spring. Use one of the following herbicides mixed with 20 to 40 gallons of water per acre:

- Dichlobenil (2,6-dichlorobenzonitrile), 2 to 4 pounds.
- Simazine [2-chloro-4,6-bis (ethylamino)-*s*-triazine], 2 to 4 pounds.

For each acre of light-textured soils, use 2 pounds or less of dichlobenil and simazine, and for heavy-textured soils, use 2 to 4 pounds per acre.

Do not apply dichlobenil at the time of shoot emergence. Dichlobenil or simazine treatments are generally effective throughout the growing season. Supplement treatments with mechanical cultivation as needed. Do not repeat use of herbicides in one season.

IRRIGATING

Raspberries need a large amount of water. Irrigation is essential in dry regions and often is profitable even in humid regions.

Irrigated plants are more vigorous and yield fruit over a longer season than unirrigated plants.

In semiarid and arid regions, begin irrigating at the same time you begin irrigating other garden crops.

Apply 1 to 2 inches of water once a week during the fruiting season and once every two or three weeks during the rest of the dry season, Light sandy soil needs more frequent irrigation than heavier soils.

In humid regions, irrigation pays if soil moisture is deficient during the time the fruit is growing and ripening. If a drought occurs from blossoming time until the end of harvest, apply 1 to 1½ inches of water once a week.

HARVESTING

Berries that are firm, ripe and sound bring the highest market price. To get maximum income from your raspberry plantation:

- Pick at least twice a week.
- Handle berries as carefully as possible.
- Discard all decaying, injured or overripe berries.

The plantation should be picked over frequently to harvest the berries when they are at their best. During hot or wet weather it may be necessary to pick every other day. Six to eight pickers per acre are needed for harvesting.

Handle the berries as carefully as possible. Use the thumb, index finger, and middle finger to pick the berries. Do not hold berries in the hand after picking. Place them gently in the cup or basket; do not drop them. After berries are placed in the basket, do not handle them again.

Discard overripe, injured or decaying berries. Separate firm fruit and very ripe fruit at time of picking. If two baskets are fitted in a waist carrier, one basket can be used for firm fruit suitable for shipping and the other for fully ripened fruit for canning or freezing.

After filling the baskets in the waist carrier, transfer them to a hand carrier, which always should be kept in the shade.

PREVENTING WINTER INJURY

In parts of Colorado and in the western North Central states, raspberry canes need protection from cold, drying winter winds. Usually the canes can be protected sufficiently by bending all of them over in the same direction and holding them close to the ground with clods of earth. The earth clods are removed in the spring.

Danger of winter injury to raspberries can be reduced by locating the plantation on an elevated site. Cold air settles to low areas. Winter temperatures are colder and spring frosts occur later in valleys and hollows than in surrounding upland areas.

PESTS AND DISEASES

Nematodes

One of the most harmful pests to raspberry plantings is the nematode. Several types of nematodes attack raspberries, and some transmit virus diseases or increase root rots.

To combat nematode infestation, treat the soil with nematicides that contain dibromochloropane (DBCP), dichloropropanes and dichloropropanes mixture (DD), sodium methyldithiocarbamate (SMDC), or a mixture of DD and methylisothiocyanate (DD–MENCS).

DD and DBCP control only nematodes, while the others listed are general soil sterilants. DD, which controls nematodes only, and SNDC and DD–MENCS, which are general soil sterilants, should be used as preplant treatments only. DBCP, which controls nematodes only, may be used as a preplant treatment, or may be used at a lower rate at the time of planting or after planting.

Rates of application of the above chemicals vary, depending on soil conditions and method of application. Therefore, follow the manufacturer's directions for specific recommendations.

Although insects sometimes are harmful to raspberry plantings, they are not as destructive as diseases. Raspberries are attacked by mosaics and other virus diseases, crown gall, wilt and anthracnose.

Disease damage can be kept to a minimum if these general suggestions are followed:

- Choose disease-resistant varieties.
- Plant only healthy stock.
- Plant black or purple varieties in fields that have not recently been used for tomatoes, potatoes or eggplant.
- Remove old canes after harvest.
- Keep the field clean of weeds and fallen leaves.
- Destroy seriously diseased plants. Use pesticides when needed.

For specific information on control of insects or diseases, consult your county agricultural agent of your state agricultural experiment station.

PROPAGATING

Raspberries are not difficult to propagate. Many growers propagate new stock for themselves and sell propagated stock to nurserymen. Often, the first harvest from a new raspberry plantation is new planting stock, rather than fruit.

Black and purple raspberries are propagated by burying the tips of the canes; they root and form new plants. Red raspberry plants are propagated from suckers and from root cuttings.

To prepare black or purple raspberry plants for propagation, pinch off the tips of the canes when they are 12 to 18 inches high. The canes branch freely and form a large number of tips for burying.

In late summer, loosen the soil around each plant and bury the tips of the canes 2 to 4 inches deep. Point the tips straight downward in the soil.

The following spring, cut the new tip plants away from the parent plants by severing the old cane. Leave 4 to 8 inches of old cane on the new plants. After the old cane is cut, the new plants are ready to be set out in the field.

The simplest way to propagate red raspberry plants is by transplanting suckers in early spring. Usually, large suckers from the previous year are transplanted, but new suckers can be transplanted also. These current-year suckers are small, but they grow rapidly after they are transplanted.

To propagate red raspberry plants from root cuttings, dig pieces of root from around established plants in early spring. Cut the roots into 2- to 3-inch lengths and scatter the cuttings on the surface of a nursery bed. Cover them with 2 inches of soil.

New plants, which come up from root cuttings during the growing season, can be set out in the field the following spring.

Instead of digging roots of red raspberries for propagation, you can remove all the old plants from a section of the field. Pieces of roots are left in the soil; new plants grow from these pieces. The new plants can be set out in the field the next spring. Usually another stand of plants will grow the second year. This system of propagation yields a large number of new plants.

IX

GROWING GRAPES AND WALNUTS

CHAPTER 34

American Bunch Grapes

THE GRAPE VARIETIES known as American bunch grapes were derived primarily from wild grape species native to North America. Most have some mixture of European varieties in their ancestry.

Although American bunch grapes make up only about 10 percent of the total United States grape crop, they are grown over a far wider area than other types of grapes—vinifera (European grapes) and muscadine grapes. Vinifera grapes are grown in California and other Southwestern states; muscadine grapes are grown in the South Atlantic and Gulf states. Varieties of American bunch grapes are available to suit most climatic conditions.

American bunch grapes are an important commercial fruit and also one of the most popular and extensively grown fruits in home plantings. They are easy to grow, bear early and regularly, and are small but long-lived plants. Insects and diseases are usually easily controlled.

The grapes are grown for fresh fruit and for wine, juice, jams, jellies and frozen products.

CLIMATE AND SOIL

Growing American bunch grapes is limited or entirely unsatisfactory only in:

- Arid sections without irrigation. Production is often limited in the West and Southwest by lack of rainfall or water for irrigation.
- Locations with very short growing seasons.
- Locations with extremely severe winter temperatures.
- Areas having high temperatures and extremely high humidity. These grapes are susceptible to several diseases which thrive under hot, humid conditions.

Grapes will grow in many different soils. The fertile, deep and well-drained loams are best, but soils that contain sand, gravel, shale, slate or clay can be used. Soils underlaid with hardpan are not well adapted, nor are those that are shallow and underlaid with gravel or sand. Avoid extremely wet or extremely dry soils. Vine growth is usually improved by organic matter in the soil.

Bunch grapes are adapted to a fairly wide range of acid to moderately alkaline soils. If the soil pH is below 5 (highly acid), liming will usually improve growth. If the soil pH is above 8 (highly alkaline), it may be necessary to use rootstocks adapted to alkaline soils.

Good drainage is essential; if the land is not well drained it is not good grape soil, regardless of other desirable soil characteristics.

The soil exerts considerable influence on the crop. Excessively rich soils and those with a high organic content produce a heavy but later-maturing crop with a low sugar content. Light soils tend to produce light yields of early-maturing fruit with a high sugar content and a comparatively weak vine growth.

Regional Adaptation

Factors to consider when choosing grape varieties for a given location include:

Minimum winter temperature: Varieties differ in their ability to survive low temperatures. This ability depends on the genetic origin of the variety and on conditions which affect the maturing of the vines in the fall.

Growing season: Varieties also differ in the number of frost-free days required for the fruit to develop and ripen. Time of ripening is a general indication of where a variety can be grown successfully.

Midseason varieties ripen about the same time as Concord and have a fairly wide area of adaptation. Concord requires at least 170 frost-free days to reach proper maturity.

The early-ripening varieties ripen 2 to 4 weeks before Concord and are grown in areas that are cooler or have a shorter growing season than the

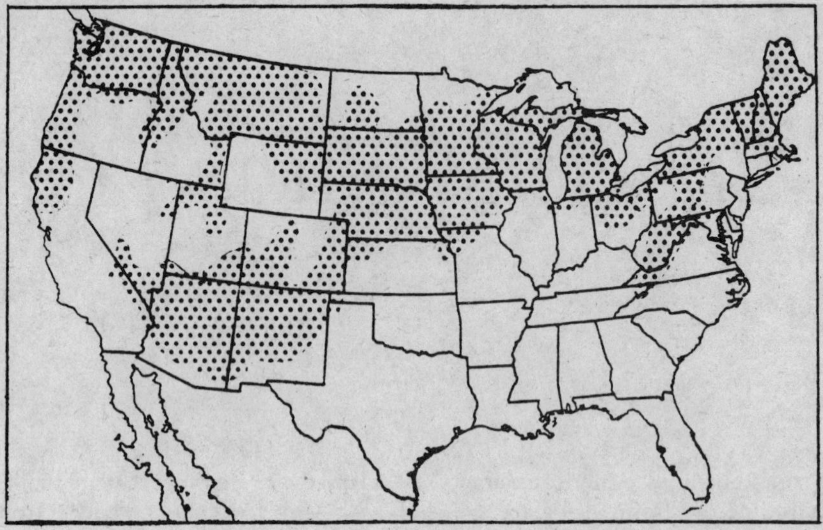

Areas where early-ripening varieties are adapted

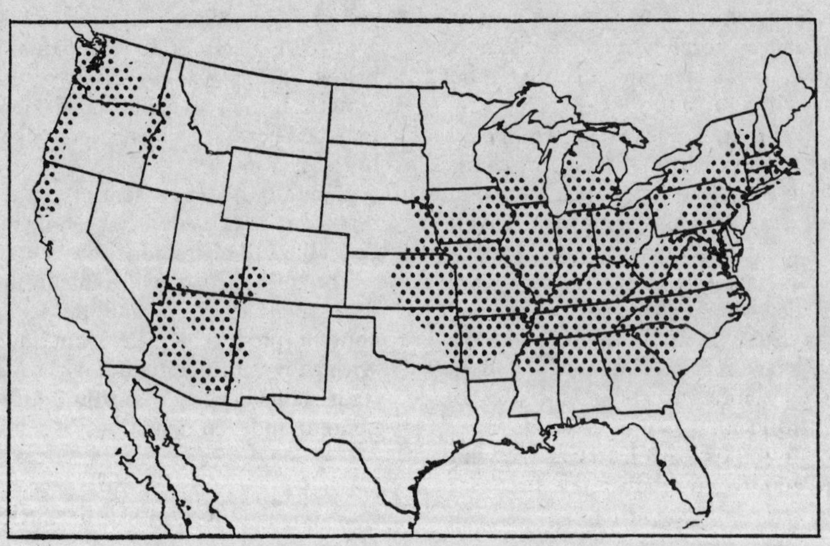

Areas where midseason varieties are adapted. These are also the areas where Concord is generally grown.

midseason area. These areas may be either farther north or at higher elevations. Early-ripening varieties grown in long-season conditions will ripen during hot weather and may have poor quality, flavor and color.

Late-season varieties are best adapted to the South, where there is a long, warm growing season. Late-ripening varieties grown in short-season conditions will not ripen in most years. In the midseason area they generally produce good-quality fruit but may not ripen sufficiently in some seasons.

Vineyard site: A favorable site often permits a variety to be grown much farther north than it could be otherwise. In a poor site, varieties which do well in the general area may fail.

Disease and insect resistance: Varieties that are susceptible to diseases or insects may not be successful in as wide an area as varieties that are resistant.

Economics: If you depend on an annual income from the grape harvest, select varieties carefully. Choose from varieties that have proved successful in the local area. Be sure there is a market for the varieties you select. If you are interested in growing a variety that has not been fully tested locally or that does not have an established market, try it out on a small scale.

If you are willing to risk an occasional crop failure, you can choose from a much larger number of varieties.

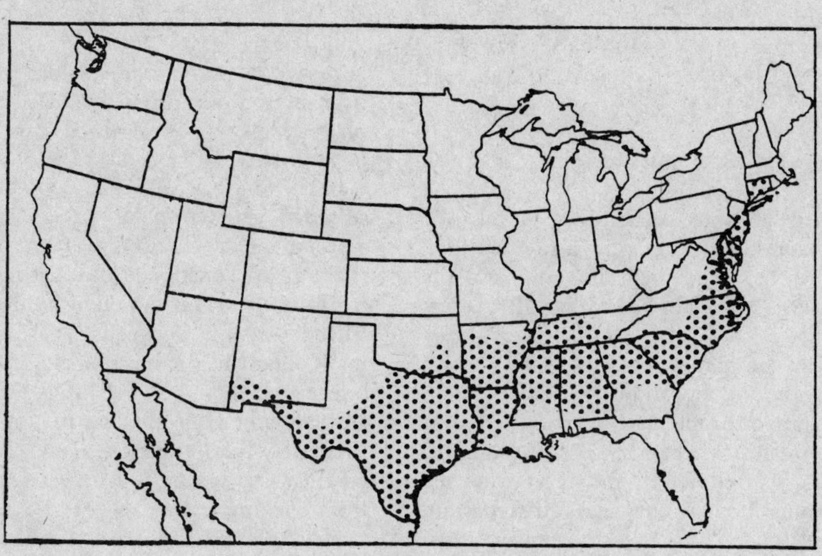

Areas of adaptation for late varieties

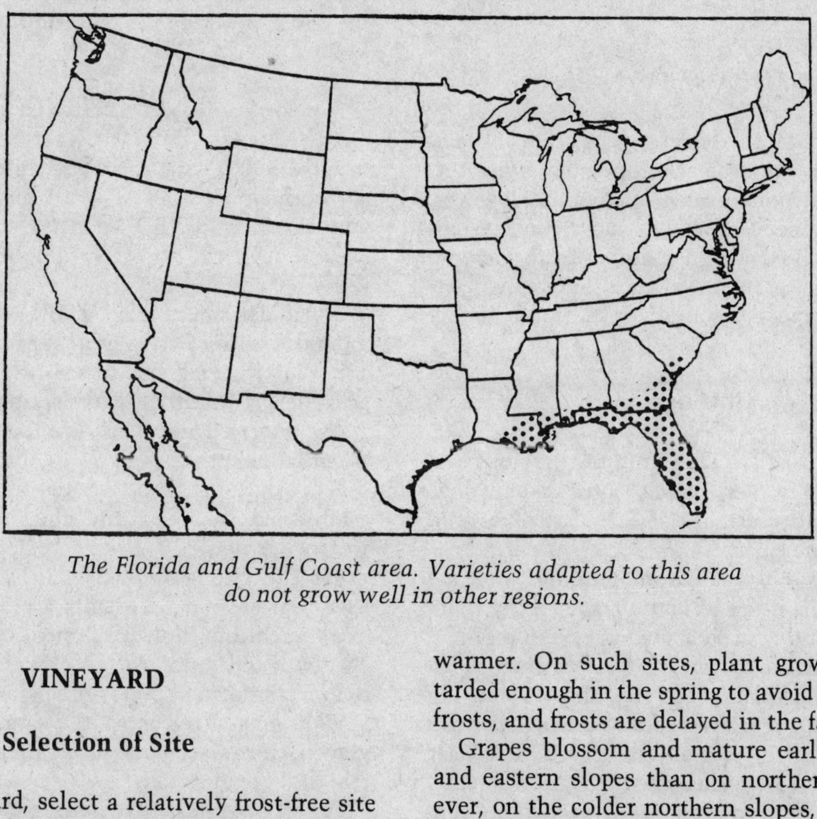

The Florida and Gulf Coast area. Varieties adapted to this area do not grow well in other regions.

VINEYARD

Selection of Site

For the vineyard, select a relatively frost-free site with well-drained soil. Level or gently sloping land that is somewhat elevated is best. Steep slopes are subject to erosion, are unsuited to mechanical harvesters and make spraying difficult during wet periods, when disease control is most important.

Sites to the south and east of large lakes are very favorable. Large bodies of water change temperature slowly and have a moderating effect on the surrounding area—summers are cooler and winters are warmer. On such sites, plant growth may be retarded enough in the spring to avoid injury from late frosts, and frosts are delayed in the fall.

Grapes blossom and mature earlier on southern and eastern slopes than on northern slopes. However, on the colder northern slopes, growth may be retarded enough in the spring to avoid injury from late frosts. Western slopes are exposed to prevailing winds, which in some areas may be strong enough to cause damage. Where the rows run east and west as on a northern or southern slope, prevailing winds from the west dry the dew and rain from the foliage quickly, which helps to prevent diseases.

Direction of the slope may be important at the northern limit of a variety's range where a few days' delay in ripening may cause a crop loss; elsewhere, it is a minor consideration.

Land Preparation

If the vineyard land has been in sod or has not been cultivated for some time, grow a row crop for at least one season before preparing the land for grapes, so that weeds will not be so difficult to control.

Before planting the grapes, plow the land deeply and disk it until the soil is well pulverized.

Straight rows are desirable, but plant on the contour to prevent erosion if necessary. Where required, contour planting is well worth the extra time required to lay it out. Your county agricultural agent or your local technician for the soil conservation district can advise on land preparation for contour planting.

PROPAGATION

Vines of American bunch grapes are usually grown on their own roots—propagated from cuttings of the previous season's growth. However, rootstocks may be used to provide a root system resistant to phylloxera or nematodes or to increase the vigor of weak-growing varieties. Scion and rootstock may be joined by grafting or by chip budding.

Cuttings

Cuttings are usually taken from the previous season's growth. However, mallet cuttings—cuttings that bear a small portion, or heel, of two-year-old wood—root more easily.

Cuttings may be taken from prunings anytime during the dormant season, but if taken early there is less chance of the wood being winter injured.

Select well-matured wood at least ⅓ inch in diameter. Make the basal cut just below a bud. For varieties of the Concord type, select canes with buds 3 to 5 inches apart, and make the cuttings at least three buds long. For weaker-growing varieties, such as Delaware, select canes with shorter joints and leave more buds per cutting. To facilitate handling and bundling, make the cuttings of a variety approximately the same length, regardless of the number of buds.

For ease in handling and planting, tie the cuttings into bundles of 25 to 100 with all buds pointing in the same direction. Bundles may be stored by tying them with wire and burying them in well-drained soil. Bundles may also be stored in a cool cellar or under refrigeration (40° to 45° F.) Put the bundles in boxes of moist sand or sawdust to prevent cuttings from drying out. Small quantities can be stored in plastic bags with moistened sawdust, peat moss or paper towels.

In the South, cuttings may be planted in the nursery any time from fall to early spring; in colder areas, plant in early spring. Plant before any root or shoot growth occurs on the cuttings.

The nursery soil should be well prepared, well fertilized and free of weeds. Set the cuttings 4 to 6 inches apart in the rows, which may be spaced 2 to 4 feet apart. Plant the cuttings with one bud above ground, and firm the earth around them. Where there may be alternate freezing and thawing, mulch cuttings set in the fall or winter to protect them from heaving.

Black plastic film can be used to control weeds in a nursery planting. Prepare the soil, then lay 3-foot-wide black plastic strips, burying the edges. Insert the cuttings through the plastic.

PLANTING

In the South, vines may be planted as soon as they are dormant in the fall. Fall planting allows the vines to start growth as soon as the weather permits, even though the soil may not be in condition to work.

In colder areas, fall-planted vines must be mounded with earth to protect against frost heaving and winter damage. Because of this extra work and possible loss of vines, early spring planting is generally preferred north of Arkansas, Tennessee and Virginia. In spring, grapevines should be planted as soon as the soil can be worked so they will be well established by the time the hot, dry summer weather arrives.

Set the strongest one-year-old plants available. Two-year-old nursery plants are seldom worth the extra premium nurseries must charge for them. Two-year-old vines will not bear fruit any sooner than well-grown one-year-old plants.

Plant grapevines about the same depth that they grew in the nursery, and prune them to a single stem two or three buds long.

For most varieties, including Concord, space the plants 8 to 10 feet apart in the row. Less vigorous varieties, such as Delaware, may be spaced 7 to 8 feet apart. Vines in single-row plantings are set the same distance apart as those in a vineyard. They may be more vigorous than those in a vineyard, because of less competition for nutrients and moisture.

Set two or three vines between wooden posts. Do not set vines against the posts because the roots may be injured when the posts are replaced, and the wood preservative in treated posts may be toxic to the plants.

Where concrete or steel posts are used, the grape hoe is easier to use if vines are set at the posts and midway between them.

Set vines directly under the trellis; vines out of line may be constantly injured during cultivation.

TRELLIS CONSTRUCTION

The trellis consists of two or more wires attached to wood, concrete or steel posts. Construction is essentially the same as for a sturdy wire fence.

Durable types of wood posts include black locust, Osage-orange, red cedar, white oak and "fat" pine. Less durable types of wood may be treated with a preservative, such as creosote or pentachlorophenol, to increase their durability.

Reinforced concrete and heavy steel posts are expensive, but are the most durable type. Steel posts must be heavy enough to resist bending in a strong wind when the vines have heavy foliage. They should be used only in soils heavy enough to hold them in line.

If the vineyard is in an exposed area, an occasional steel post among wood or concrete posts will ground the trellis and may prevent damage to the vines from lightning.

End posts should be longer and heavier than line posts and must be well braced. Failure of an end post weakens the entire trellis. Set end posts 3 feet in the ground and line posts 2 feet. In contour planting, line posts may require extra bracing.

No. 9 wire is ordinarily used for trellises, but the lower wires can be as light as No. 11. Staple the wires on the windward side of the posts. Do not drive the staples tight—allow the wires to slide under them to facilitate tightening. The wires should be tightened each spring before the vines are tied.

Vineyard rows are usually spaced 10 to 12 feet apart to allow free movement of cultural equipment without injury to the vines.

If mechanical harvesters will be used, leave at least 20 feet at the ends of the rows for turning.

PRUNING

Grapes require heavy annual pruning. Proper pruning is essential for consistent yields and good quality fruit.

Pruning prevents overproduction of fruit by limiting the number of fruit-producing buds. Underpruned vines become weak and produce small clusters. If vines are overpruned, however, they become excessively vegetative.

Grapevines should be pruned during the dormant season.

Where winters are relatively mild, prune any time during the dormant season when the temperature is above freezing. Frozen canes are brittle and easily broken.

Where winter temperatures are low enough to injure the canes, wait until late winter or early spring when you can select uninjured canes for fruiting. Pruning prior to severe freezes can increase winter injury.

Vines pruned late in the spring will "bleed" freely, but this is not injurious. Vines pruned just before growth starts, or after the buds swell, leaf out a little later than those pruned earlier. While the delay in leafing out may be sufficient to avoid injury from late frosts, it is difficult to prune and tie the vines after growth starts without destroying many of the buds.

INSECTS AND DISEASES

For quality fruit, American bunch grapes should be sprayed at least three times to control insects and diseases. Additional applications may be necessary in wet seasons or in areas where certain insects and diseases are more common or for disease-susceptible varieties.

Unsprayed vines in home gardens may occasionally produce fine clusters, but not as a rule. Spraying is easier than removing rotted and insect-infested grapes.

For information about insects and diseases consult your county agricultural agent or other plant information agency.

CHAPTER 35

Black Walnuts

THE BLACK WALNUT TREE is native to much of the United States east of the Great Plains. It is a desirable shade and ornamental tree, and will produce nut crops on a wide variety of sites and soil types within its natural range. The tree can be grown for shade or ornamental purposes a few hundred miles outside of its natural range, but may not produce nuts in those areas.

To grow black walnuts for home use:

- Plant trees of improved varieties.
- Plant trees in early spring in fertile, well-drained soil.
- Provide sufficient moisture and nutrients.
- Control diseases and insect pests.

VARIETIES

Several improved, grafted varieties of black walnut trees are available. They are far superior to native trees grown from seed.

Three of the most widely planted of the improved varieties are 'Thomas', 'Ohio', and 'Myers'. They start bearing nuts the second or third year after they are planted, while native trees do not start bearing nuts until about ten years after being planted.

At five or six years of age, 'Thomas' and 'Ohio' each produce about ¼ bushel of nuts, and 'Myers' produces about ⅛ bushel of nuts. At 15 to 20 years of age, 'Thomas' and 'Ohio' produce about 2 bushels of nuts, 'Myers' produces about 1 bushel of nuts, and native trees produce about ¼ bushel of nuts.

Nuts produced by native trees usually have thick and heavy shells. 'Thomas' and 'Ohio' nuts have thinner shells, and 'Myers' nuts have the thinnest shells of all.

Walnut anthracnose is the most serious disease of the native trees. 'Ohio' is resistant to the disease, but in years of severe infection it may be defoliated. 'Myers' usually is more resistant to anthracnose than native trees, but less so than 'Ohio'. 'Thomas' is the least resistant of the three improved varieties.

Improved varieties of black walnuts do not come from seed. They are propagated by grafting scions (twigs) from trees of the desired varieties onto the main stems of two or three-year-old native seedlings. The scions develop into tree crowns that bear nuts of their own varieties.

Little information is available to indicate the best varieties for different localities. Local nurseries usually sell varieties that are best suited to their own localities.

For the greatest possible nut production, plant trees of two or more varieties. Usually, pistillate (female) flowers produce nuts after being pollinated by staminate flowers of the same tree. In very early or very late spring, the pistillate flowers may not be ready when the pollen is shed. Different varieties have overlapping pollen-receptivity periods and can pollinate each other.

All black walnut trees tend to bear heavy nut crops every second year and light ones in between.

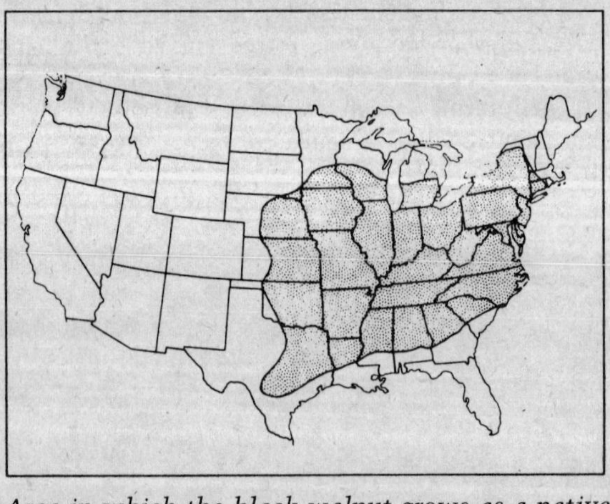

Area in which the black walnut grows as a native tree

Black walnut tree

Exact cultural practices to offset alternate-year bearing have not been developed.

PLANTING

Sites

Black walnut trees grow best in rich, loose soils of limestone origin that are at least 4 feet deep. Since the trees develop deep taproots, the subsoil should be easily penetrated by roots.

The soil must be well drained and not strongly acid. The trees will not grow well on bottomland, where the soil is often saturated with water. They will not grow well or produce large nut crops on eroded hillsides or other land that will not support good corn crops. Reliable indicators of suitable land are good stands of white oak and tulip-poplar.

Planting Times

The most favorable time to plant black walnut trees in most areas is in early spring. New roots will then be able to grow quickly to replace those lost in transplanting.

In the South, you can plant young trees in the fall or winter. Trees planted north of the Ohio and Potomac Rivers in fall and winter will not grow new roots before the ground freezes and so may die.

Flowers of black walnut: S, Staminate (male) flowers; P, pistillate (female) flowers

Spacing

Black walnut trees planted for either ornamental use or nut production should be spaced at least 60 feet apart. Branches and roots will then have enough space in which to spread out.

Setting Trees

For trees up to 7 feet tall, dig a hole 2 feet deep and 3 feet wide. Place the tree at the same depth in the hole as it stood in the nursery bed and spread the roots out well. Refill the hole with topsoil. Tamp the soil down around the roots until the ground is firm. Then form a basin around the edge of the hole with extra soil and soak the soil immediately.

FERTILIZER AND LIME REQUIREMENTS

Fertilizing

Black walnut trees need large amounts of nitrogen and potassium for best growth and nut production. They need small amounts of phosphorus.

Apply mixed fertilizers each year. Spread them evenly under the tree branches when the buds begin to swell in early spring.

Mixed fertilizers having analyses of 5–10–5 and 10–10–10 give good results. One good rule is to apply 1 pound of 5–10–5 fertilizer, or ½ pound of 10–10–10 fertilizer for each year of tree age. Do not use any during the first spring, however, because of the danger of injuring roots.

To fertilize trees in yards, apply a little more under the branches than you would normally use on your lawn.

Some trees are grown near barns or in stock or poultry yards to provide shade. They benefit from the natural addition of manures and usually flourish.

Liming

In strongly acid soils, important nutrients are often unavailable to black walnut trees. If your soil is strongly acid, apply enough lime to change the pH to 6 or 6.5. Do not overlime; overliming makes zinc in the soil unavailable to the tree.

Soils east of the Mississippi River are sometimes deficient in magnesium. Crushed dolomitic limestone, which contains magnesium oxide, will correct this and reduce the acidity of your soil.

Your county agricultural agent can test the soil for its acidity and arrange for an analysis of its nutrient needs. You may also send a soil sample to your state agricultural experiment station for analysis.

HARVESTING NUTS

Lightly colored walnut kernels have a milder flavor than dark ones. If you prefer light kernels, harvest the nuts as soon as they drop from the trees in the fall. Leaving them on the ground until the hulls partially decompose causes a discoloration of the kernels.

The hulls are thick and fleshy at maturity. They can be mashed and removed by hand, but mechanical devices make the job easier. Vegetable peelers used in restaurants and hand- and power-operated corn shellers will remove the hulls satisfactorily.

The rear wheel of an automobile can be an effective hull remover. Fit one of the rear wheels with a tire chain and jack up the rear with just enough room beneath the tire for the nuts to pass. The chain will remove the hulls as the nuts are forced through the trough formed by the turning wheel.

After the hulls are off, the nuts should be washed thoroughly and spread out away from direct sunlight to dry. Drying will take two or three weeks. The nuts can then be stored in a cool, dry place until needed.

It is difficult to extract kernels in large pieces from most varieties of black walnut because of the thick shell and convolutions of the kernel. The nuts can be tempered by soaking them in water for one or two hours, then keeping them moist overnight in a closed container. The kernels absorb enough moisture to become tough, yet remain loose in the shell.

X

GROWING VEGETABLES

CHAPTER 36

Vegetables in the Home Garden

NOTE: ANY GARDENER USING this book, which is intended for use countrywide, also needs local information, especially on the earliest and latest safe planting dates for vegetables, and any special garden practices and varieties that are best for that location.

SELECTING A SITE

A backyard or some other plot near your home in full sunlight is the most convenient spot for a home vegetable garden. However, poor drainage, shallow soil, and shade from buildings or trees may mean the garden must be located in an area farther from the house.

In planning your garden, consider what and how much you will plant. It is better to have a small, well-maintained garden than a large one that is neglected and full of weeds. Diagram the garden rows on paper and note the length you wish to assign to each vegetable. Use a scale of a selected number of feet to an inch. Then you can decide how much seed and how many plants to buy.

Consider also the possibility of working your vegetables in plots in front of your shrubbery. Many vegetables are ornamental in appearance. Some vegetables can be grown in your flower beds; others can be grown entirely in containers.

The amount of sunlight your garden gets must also be considered. Leafy vegetables, for example, can be grown in partial shade, but vegetables producing fruit must be grown in direct sunlight.

Protecting the Garden

Usually the garden should be surrounded by a fence sufficiently high and close-woven to keep out dogs, rabbits and other animals. The damage done by stray animals during a season or two can equal the cost of a fence. A fence also can serve as a trellis for beans, peas, tomatoes and other crops that need support.

In most sections of the country, rodents of various kinds damage garden crops. In the East, moles and mice cause much injury. Moles burrow under the plants, causing the soil to dry out around the roots. Mice either work independently or follow the burrows made by moles, destroying newly planted seeds and young plants. In the West, ground squirrels and prairie dogs damage vegetable gardens. Most of these pests can be partially controlled with traps.

SOIL, DRAINAGE AND SUNSHINE

Fertile, deep, friable, well-drained soil is necessary for a successful garden. The exact type of soil is not so important as that it be well drained, well supplied with organic matter, retentive of moisture and reasonably free of stones. The kind of subsoil also is vitally important. Hard shale, rock ledges, gravel beds, very deep sand or a hardpan under the surface soil is likely to make the development of high-grade garden soil extremely difficult or impossible. On the other hand, infertile soil that has good physical properties can be made productive by using organic matter, lime, commercial fertilizer and other soil-improving materials.

Good drainage is essential. Soil drainage may often be improved by installing agricultural tile, by digging ditches, and sometimes by plowing deep into the subsoil. The garden should be free of low places where water might stand after a heavy rain. Water from surrounding land should not drain into the garden, and there should be no danger of flooding by overflow from nearby streams.

Good air drainage is necessary to lessen the danger of damage by frost. A garden on a slope that has free movement of air to lower levels is most likely to escape late spring and early autumn frost damage.

A gentle slope of not more than 1½ percent facing

in a southerly direction helps early crops get started. In sections that have strong winds, a windbreak of board fence, hedge or trees on the windward side of the garden is recommended. Hedges and other living windbreaks should be far enough away from the garden to prevent shade or roots from interfering with the garden crops.

The garden should get the direct rays of the sun all day if possible. Some crops can tolerate partial shade, but no amount of fertilizer, water or care can replace needed sunshine. Even where trees do not shade garden crops, tree roots may penetrate far into the soil and rob crops of moisture and plant food.

Damage to garden crops by tree roots may be largely prevented by digging a trench 1½ to 2 feet deep between the trees and the garden, cutting all the tree roots that cross the trench. Then put a barrier of waste sheet metal or heavy roofing paper along one wall of the trench and refill it. This usually prevents root damage for several years.

Preparing the Soil

Good soil for growing vegetables must be protected by proper cultivation, use of organic matter, maintenance of soil fertility and control of plant pests. Properly prepared soil provides a desirable medium for root development, absorbs water and air rapidly, and usually does not crust excessively.

Tillage practices do not automatically create good garden soil. Tillage is needed to control weeds, to mix mulch or crop residues into the soil, and to alter soil structure. Unnecessary tillage increases crusting on the soil surface, and if the soil is wet, tillage compacts it.

Fertility requirements differ between long and short growing seasons and among soil types. In almost every state, the extension service will test soils and provide fertilizer recommendations.

Plant pests compete with garden crops and impair their growth. These pests include weeds, insects, fungi, bacteria, viruses and nematodes. They must be controlled or the garden will not succeed. However, chemical controls must be used carefully to prevent damage to neighboring crops or subsequent crops. When mechanical and chemical controls do not work, crops that are resistant to the pests should be planted in the area for a season or two.

The time and method of preparing the garden for planting depend on the type of soil and the location. Heavy clay soils in the North are frequently benefited by fall plowing and exposure to freezing and thawing during the winter, but when the garden is cover-cropped, it should not be plowed until early spring. In general, garden soils should be cover-cropped during the winter to control erosion and to add organic matter. Gardens in the dry-land areas should be plowed and left rough in the fall so that the soil will absorb and retain moisture that falls during the winter. Sandy soils, as a rule, should be cover-cropped, then spring-plowed. Whenever there is a heavy sod or growth of cover crop, the land should be plowed well in advance of planting and the soil disked several times to aid in the decay and incorporation of the material. Land that receives applications of coarse manure either before or after plowing should have the same treatment.

Soil should not be plowed or worked while wet unless the work will certainly be followed by severe freezing weather. Sandy soils and those containing high proportions of organic matter—peats and mucks for example—bear plowing and working at higher moisture content than do heavy clay soils. The usual test is to squeeze together a handful of soil. If it sticks together in a ball and does not readily crumble under slight pressure by the thumb and finger, it is too wet for plowing or working. When examining soil to determine if it is dry enough to work, samples should be taken both at the surface and a few inches below. The surface may be dry enough for working but the lower layers too wet. Soil that sticks to the plow or to other tools is usually too wet. A shiny, unbroken surface of the turned furrow is another indication of a dangerously wet soil condition.

Fall-plowed land should be left rough until spring, when it may be prepared by disking, harrowing or other methods. Spring-plowed land should be worked into a suitable seedbed immediately after plowing. Seeds germinate and plants grow more readily on a reasonably fine, well-prepared soil than on a coarse, lumpy one, and thorough preparation greatly reduces the work of planting and caring for the crops. It is possible, however, to overdo the preparation of some heavy soils. They should be brought to a somewhat granular condition rather than a powdery-fine one for planting. Spading instead of plowing is sometimes advisable in preparing small areas, such as beds for extra-early crops of lettuce, onions, beets and carrots.

Organic Matter

Organic matter improves soil as a growing medium for plants. It helps release nitrogen, minerals and other nutrients for plant use when it decays. A mulch of partially rotted straw, compost or undecomposed crop residue on the soil helps keep the soil surface from crusting, retards water loss from the soil, and keeps weeds from growing.

Practically any plant material can be composted for use in the garden. Leaves, old sod, lawn clippings, straw and plant refuse from the garden or kitchen can be used. Often, leaves can be obtained from neighbors who do not use them, or from street sweepings.

The purpose of composting plant refuse or debris is to decay it so that it can be easily worked into the soil and will not be unsightly when used in the garden. Composting material should be kept moist and supplied with commercial fertilizer, particularly nitrogen, to make it decay faster and more thoroughly.

Compost ready for use in the garden

The usual practice in building a compost pile is to accumulate the organic material in some out-of-the-way place in the garden. It can be built on open ground or in a bin made of cinder blocks, rough boards or wire fence. The sides of the bin should not be airtight or watertight. A convenient time to make a compost pile is in the fall when leaves are plentiful.

In building the compost pile, spread out a layer of plant refuse about 6 inches deep and add ½ pound, or one cupful, of 10–10–10, 10–20–10, or 10–6–4 fertilizer to each 10 square feet of surface. Then add 1 inch of soil and enough water to moisten but not to soak it. This process is repeated until the pile is 4 to 5 feet high. Make the top of the pile concave to catch rainwater.

If alkaline compost is wanted, ground limestone can be spread in the pile at the same rate as the fertilizer.

The compost pile will not decay rapidly until the weather warms up in spring and summer. In midsummer, decay can be hastened by forking over the pile so moisture can get to parts that have remained dry. The compost should be ready for use by the end of the first summer.

For a continuing supply of compost, a new pile should be built every year. Compost can be used as a mulch, or worked into flower beds and the vegetable garden.

When properly prepared and thoroughly decayed, compost is not likely to harbor diseases or insects. If the compost is used in soil where an attempt is made to control plant diseases, or if it is mixed with soil used for raising seedlings, the soil should be disinfected with chemicals recommended by your county agricultural agent or state agricultural college.

Commercial Fertilizers

Commercial fertilizers may be used to advantage in most farm gardens, the composition and rate of application depending on locality, soil and crops to be grown. On some soils with natural high fertility, only nitrogen or compost may be needed. The use of fertilizers that also contain small amounts of copper, zinc, manganese and other minor soil elements is necessary only in districts known to be deficient in those elements. State experiment station recommendations should be followed. Leafy crops, such as spinach, cabbage, kale and lettuce, which often require more nitrogen than other garden crops, may be stimulated by side dressings. As a rule, the tuber and root crops, including potatoes, sweet potatoes, beets, carrots, turnips and parsnips, need a higher percentage of potash than other vegetables.

The quantity of fertilizer to use depends on the natural fertility of the soil, the amounts of organic matter and fertilizer used in recent years, and the crops being grown. Tomatoes and beans, for example, normally require only moderate amounts of fertilizer, especially nitrogen; whereas onions, celery, lettuce, the root crops and potatoes respond profitably to relatively large applications. In some cases,

Setting the plants

300 pounds of commercial fertilizer may be sufficient on a half-acre garden; in other cases, as much as 1,000 to 1,200 pounds can be used to advantage.

As a rule, commercial fertilizers should be applied either a few days before planting or when the crops are planted. A good practice is to plow the land, spread the fertilizer from a pail or with a fertilizer distributor, then harrow the soil two or three times to get it in proper condition and at the same time mix the fertilizer with it. If the soil is left extremely rough by the plow, it should be lightly harrowed once before fertilizing. For row crops, like potatoes and sweet potatoes, the fertilizer may be scattered in the rows, taking care to mix it thoroughly with the soil before the seed is dropped or, in the case of sweet potatoes, before the ridges are thrown up.

Application of the fertilizer in furrows along each side of the row at planting time does away with the danger of injury to seeds and plants that is likely to follow direct application of the material under the row. The fertilizer should be placed so that it will lie 2 to 3 inches to one side of the seed and at about the same level as, or a little lower than, the seed.

The roots of most garden crops spread to considerable distances, reaching throughout the surface soil. Fertilizer applied to the entire area, therefore, will be reached by the plants, but not always to best advantage. Placing fertilizer too near seedlings or young plants is likely to cause burning of the roots. The fertilizer should be sown alongside the rows and cultivated into the topsoil, taking care to keep it off the leaves as far as practicable.

Heavy yields of top-quality vegetables cannot be obtained without an abundance of available plant food in the soil. However, failure to bear fruit and even injury to the plants may result from the use of too much plant nutrient, particularly chemical fertilizers, or from an unbalanced nutrient condition in the soil. Because of the small quantities of fertilizer required for short rows and small plots it is easy to apply too much fertilizer. The chemical fertilizers to be applied should always be weighed or measured. Table 3 shows how much fertilizer to apply to each 50 or 100 feet of garden row or to each 100 to 2,000 square feet of garden area.

If it is more convenient to measure the material than to weigh it, pounds of common garden fertilizer, ammonium phosphate or muriate of potash may be converted roughly to pints or cups by allowing 1 pint, or 2 kitchen measuring cups, to a pound. For example, Table 1 gives 0.25 pound for a 100-pound-per-acre application to 100 square feet. This would call for about ¼ pint, or ½ cup, of fertilizer. Ground limestone weighs about 1⅓ times as much as the same volume of water; therefore, measured quantities of this material should be about ¼ less than those calculated as equivalent to the weights in the table. For example, ¾ pint of ground limestone weighs about 1 pound. Ammonium sulfate and granular ammonium nitrate are much lighter, weighing about 7⁄10 as much as the same volumes of water; therefore, volumes of these substances calculated by the foregoing method should be increased by about ⅓.

Table 3

Approximate rates of fertilizer application per 50 or 100 feet of garden row, and per 100 to 2,000 square feet of garden area, corresponding to given rates per acre.

Measurement	Weight of fertilizer to apply when the weight to be applied per acre is—			
	100 pounds	400 pounds	800 pounds	1,200 pounds
Space between rows, and row length (feet):	*Pounds*	*Pounds*	*Pounds*	*Pounds*
2 wide, 50 long	0.25	1.0	2.0	3.0
2 wide, 100 long	.50	2.0	4.0	6.0
2½ wide, 50 long	.30	1.2	2.4	3.6
2½ wide, 100 long	.60	2.4	4.8	7.2
3 wide, 50 long	.35	1.4	2.8	4.2
3 wide, 100 long	.70	2.8	5.6	8.4
Area (square feet):				
100	.25	1.0	2.0	3.0
500	1.25	5.0	10.0	15.0
1,000	2.50	10.0	20.0	30.0
1,500	3.75	15.0	30.0	45.0
2,000	5.00	20.0	40.0	60.0

Liming

Lime, ground limestone, marl or ground oyster shells on garden soils serves a threefold purpose: (1) To supply calcium and other plant nutrients; (2) to reduce soil acidity; (3) to improve the physical character of certain heavy soils. As a rule, asparagus, celery, beets, spinach and carrots are benefited by moderate applications of lime, especially on soils that are naturally deficient in calcium. Dolomitic limestone should be used on soils deficient in magnesium. Most garden vegetables do best on soils that are slightly acid and may be injured by the application of lime in excess of their requirements. For this reason lime should be applied only when tests show it to be necessary. In no case should the material be applied in larger quantities than the test indicates. Most garden soils that are in a high state of fertility do not require the addition of lime.

With good drainage, plenty of organic matter in the soil, and the moderate use of commercial fertilizers, the growth requirements of nearly all vegetables may be fully met.

Lime, when needed, is spread after plowing and is well mixed with the topsoil by harrowing, disking or cultivating. Burned lime or hydrated lime should not be applied at the same time as commercial fertilizers or mixed with them, because loss of nitrogen is likely to result, thus destroying part of the plant-nutrient value. As a rule, lime should be applied in the spring, because some of it may be washed from the soil during winter. Any of the various forms of lime, such as hydrated and air-slaked lime, may be used, but the unburned, finely ground, dolomitic limestone is best. Fifty-six pounds of burned lime or 74 pounds of hydrated lime is equivalent to 100 pounds of ground limestone. Finely ground oyster shells and marl are frequently used as substitutes for limestone. Lime should not be used on land that is being planted to potatoes unless the soil is extremely acid, because very low soil acidity increases the development of potato scab.

CHOOSING GARDEN TOOLS

Very few tools are necessary for a small garden. It is better to buy a few simple high-grade tools that will serve well for many years than equipment that is poorly designed or made of cheap or low-grade materials that will not last. In most instances, the only tools needed are a spade or spading fork, a steel bow rake, a 7-inch common hoe, a strong cord for laying off rows, a wheelbarrow and a garden hose long enough to water all parts of the garden. A trowel can be useful in transplanting but it is not essential. If the soil is properly prepared, plants can be set more easily with the hands alone than with a trowel.

For gardens that are from 2,000 to 4,000 square feet, a wheel hoe is very useful because it can be used for most work usually done with a common hoe, and with much less effort. The single-wheel type is probably the easiest to handle and best for use as an all-purpose wheel hoe. Other styles are available and may be used if preferred.

The cultivating tools, or attachments, for the wheel hoe should include one or more of the so-called hoe blades. They are best for weeding and are used more than the cultivator teeth or small plow usually supplied with a wheel hoe.

For gardens over 4,000 square feet, a rotary garden tiller is useful in preparing the soil for planting and controlling weeds.

Many gardeners who do little or no farming have the choice of hiring equipment for garden-land preparation or buying their own. Equipment for hire too often is unavailable when needed, so that a favorable season for planting may be missed. Country gardeners, in increasing numbers, are turning to small farm and garden tractors for land preparation, cultivation, lawn mowing and hauling sprayers in gardens and orchards. Those who garden every year and who have large homesteads usually find this equipment a good investment. The size and type of equipment needed depend on the amount of work to be done, the contour of the land, and the character of the soil. For cultivating and other light work a 2- to 3-horsepower tractor is used. If plowing or other heavy work is involved, a larger tractor is desirable. Modern outfits of this size are well adapted to cultivating small areas. A medium-size tractor suitable for cultivating a large garden can also be used for plowing.

The rotary tiller, which is capable of preparing light to medium soils for planting in one operation, has been widely adopted by gardeners who have such soils. In the hands of a careful operator and on land that is not too hard and heavy and is reasonably free from stones, roots and other obstructions, this machine has many desirable features. It can be adjusted to cultivate very shallowly or to plow the soil and make it fit for planting. Tools such as sweeps may be attached, thereby adapting the machine to straddle-row cultivating.

Use of well-adapted implements in preparing garden land greatly lessens the work required in cultivating. Clean, sharp, high-grade tools greatly lessen garden labor. For larger gardens, a wheel-type hand fertilizer distributor, a sprayer or duster (preferably a wheelbarrow-type power sprayer), and a seed drill are generally profitable. Minor tools include two pointed iron stakes and weeders.

If sufficient water is available, irrigation equipment is necessary in many areas, and highly desirable in nearly all gardens. Furrow application requires careful planning and laying out of the garden area and precise handling of the soil to ensure even distribution of water. Overhead pipes with nozzles at short intervals, temporary lines of lightweight pipe with rotating sprinklers, and porous hose laid along the rows are extensively used. The most common practice is to use a length or two of garden hose, with or without sprinklers, fed by faucets on temporary or permanent lines of pipe through the garden.

In winter, when there is little heat from the sun, little water is used by plants, so irrigation is not needed in most areas. However, in summer, rainfall is usually inadequate and irrigation is essential for maximum production.

ARRANGING THE GARDEN

No one plan or arrangement for a garden can suit all conditions. Each gardener must plan to meet his own problem. Careful planning will lessen the work of gardening and increase the returns from the labor. Planting seeds and plants at random always results in waste and disappointment. Suggestions for planning a garden are here presented with the idea that they can be changed to suit the individual gardener.

The first consideration is whether the garden is to be in one unit or in two. With two plots, lettuce, radishes, beets, spinach and other vegetables requiring little space are grown in a small kitchen garden, and potatoes, sweet corn, pumpkins, melons and other vegetables requiring more room are planted in a separate patch, such as between young orchard tree rows or in other areas where conditions are especially suitable for their culture.

The cultivation methods to be employed are important in planning the garden. When the work is to be done mainly with a garden tractor, the site and the arrangement should be such as to give the longest practicable rows. On slopes of more than 1½ percent, especially on light-textured soil, the rows should extend across the slope at right angles, or on the contours where the land is uneven. The garden should be free from paths across the rows, and turning spaces of 10 to 12 feet should be provided at the ends. The rows for small-growing crops may be closer together for hand cultivation than for cultivation with power equipment.

Any great variation in the composition of the soil within the garden should be taken into consideration when deciding on where to plant various crops. If part of the land is low and moist, such crops as celery, onions and late cucumbers should be placed there. If part is high, warm and dry, that is the proper spot for early crops, especially those needing a soil that warms up quickly.

Permanent crops, such as asparagus and rhubarb, should be planted where they will not interfere with the annual plowing of the garden and the cultivation of the annual crops. If a hotbed, a coldframe or a special seedbed is provided, it should be either in one corner of, or outside, the garden.

Tall-growing crops should be planted where they will not shade or interfere with the growth of smaller crops. There seems to be little choice as to whether the rows do or do not run in a general east-and-west or in a general north-and-south direction, but they should conform to the contours of the land.

Succession of Crops

Except in dry-land areas, all garden space should be kept fully occupied throughout the growing season. In the South, this means the greater part of the year. In fact, throughout the South Atlantic and Gulf coast regions it is possible to have vegetables growing in the garden every month of the year.

In arranging the garden, all early-maturing crops may be grouped so that as soon as one crop is removed another takes its place. It is desirable, however, to follow a crop not with another of its kind, but with an unrelated crop. For example, early peas or beans can very properly be followed by late cabbage, celery, carrots or beets; early corn or potatoes can be followed by fall turnips or spinach. It is not always necessary to wait until the early crop is entirely removed; a later one may be planted between the rows of the early crop—for example, sweet corn between potato rows. Crops subject to attack by the same diseases and insects should not follow each other.

In the extreme North, where the growing season is relatively short, there is very little opportunity for succession cropping. In dry-land areas, intercropping generally is not feasible, because of limited moisture supply. Therefore, plenty of land should be provided to accommodate the desired range and volume of garden crops.

Late Summer and Fall Garden

Although gardening is commonly considered mainly as a spring and early-summer enterprise, the late-summer and fall garden deserves attention too. Second and third plantings of crops adapted to growing late in the season not only provide a supply of fresh vegetables for the latter part of the season but often give better products for canning, freezing and storing. Late-grown snap and lima beans and spinach, for example, are well adapted to freezing and canning; beets, carrots, celery and turnips, to storage. In the South, the late-autumn garden is as important as the early-autumn one.

SELECTING SEED

Except in special cases, it pays the gardener to buy seed from reputable seedsmen and not to depend on home-grown supplies. Very fine varieties that do extremely well in certain areas have been grown for long periods from locally produced seed, and such practices are to be commended, provided adequate measures are taken to keep the strains pure.

Vegetables that are entirely, or readily, cross-pollinated *among plants of their kind* include corn, cucumbers, melons, squash, pumpkins, cress, mustard, brussels sprouts, cabbage, cauliflower, collards, kale, kohlrabi, spinach, onion, radish, beet and turnip. Those less readily cross-pollinated are eggplant, pepper, tomato, carrot and celery. Beans, peas, okra and lettuce are generally self-pollinated, but occasionally cross-pollinated; lima beans sometimes rather extensively cross-pollinated. Because sweet corn will cross with field corn, it is unwise to save sweet corn seed if field corn is growing in the same neighborhood. Hybrid sweet corn should not be saved for seed. The custom of saving seed from a choice watermelon is safe, provided no citrons or other varieties of watermelons are growing nearby. Likewise, seed from a muskmelon is safe even though it may have been grown side by side with cucumbers. Beans other than lima do not readily cross, and their seed also may be saved. Cabbage, kohlrabi, kale, collards, broccoli and cauliflower all intercross freely, so each must be well isolated from the others if seed is to be saved.

Seeds should be ordered well in advance of planting time, but only after the preparation of a garden plan that shows the size of the plantings and the quantity of seed required. Table 4 shows the quantity of seed required for a given space, but allowance should be made for the possible need of replanting. Crops and varieties that are known to be adapted to the locality should be selected. The agricultural experiment station of each state, county agricultural agents and experienced gardeners are usually able to give advice about varieties of vegetables that are adapted to the area. Standard sorts of known quality and performance are usually the best choice.

Disease-resistant strains and varieties of many important vegetables are now so generally available that there is little reason for risking the loss of a crop through planting susceptible sorts. This phase of the subject is treated in detail under the individual crops.

Some seeds retain their vitality longer than others. Seeds may be divided into three groups as follows:

(1) Comparatively short-lived, usually not good after one to two years—corn, leek, onion, parsley, parsnip, rhubarb and salsify.

(2) Moderately long-lived, often good for three to five years—asparagus, beans, brussels sprouts, cabbage, carrot, cauliflower, celery, kale, lettuce, okra, peas, pepper, radish, spinach, turnip and watermelon.

(3) Long-lived, may be good for more than five years—beet, cucumber, eggplant, muskmelon and tomato.

STARTING THE PLANTS

Table 4 gives in general the proper depth of planting for seed of the various vegetables, the quantity of seed or number of plants required for 100 feet of row, and the correct spacing of rows and of plants within the row. Special planting suggestions are given in the cultural hints for the various garden crops.

Earliness, economy of garden space and lengthening of the growing season may be obtained by setting the plants of many vegetables instead of sowing the seed directly in the garden. Moreover, under average conditions, it is almost impossible with delicate plants, such as celery, to establish good stands from seed sown directly in place in the garden.

In the warmer parts of the United States, practically all vegetable plants may be started in specially prepared beds in the open with little or no covering. In the temperate and colder regions, if an early garden is desired, it is essential that certain crops, such as tomatoes, peppers, eggplant, early cabbage, cauliflower and early head lettuce, be started indoors in hotbeds or in coldframes. Occasionally onion, beet, cucumber, squash and melons are started under cover and transplanted.

Starting Plants in the House

Seeds can be germinated and seedlings started in a box, pan or flower pot of soil in a window. In addition to having at least six hours of direct sunlight each day, the room must be kept reasonably warm at all times.

Washed fine sand and shredded sphagnum moss are excellent media in which to start seeds. Place a layer of easily drained soil in the bottom of a flat and cover this soil with a layer—about ¾ inch thick—of either fine sand or sphagnum moss. Press the sand or moss to form a smooth, firm seedbed.

Then, using a jig, make furrows in the seedbed ½ inch deep. Water the sand or moss thoroughly and allow it to drain.

Sow seeds thinly in the rows and cover the seeds lightly with a second layer of sand or moss. Sprinkle the flat, preferably with a fine mist, and cover the flat with a sheet of clear plastic film. The plastic film diffuses and subdues the light and holds moisture in the soil and air surrounding the seeds. Plastic films offer advantages over glass coverings in that they are light in weight and are nonshattering.

Place the seeded and covered flat in a location that is reasonably warm at all times and has six hours of direct sunlight each day. The flat will require no further attention until after the seedlings have developed their first true leaves. They are then ready to transplant to other containers.

It is seldom possible to keep the transplanted plants in house windows without their becoming spindling and weak. For healthy growth, place them in a hotbed, coldframe or other place where they will receive an abundance of sunshine, ample ventilation and a suitable temperature.

Strong, vigorous seedlings can be started under 40-watt fluorescent tubes. These tubes should be 6 to 8 inches above the seedlings. Temperatures

Table 4

Quantity of seed and number of plants required for 100 feet of row, depths of planting, and distances apart for rows and plants

Crop	Requirement for 100 feet of row: Seed	Requirement for 100 feet of row: Plants	Depth for planting seed	Distance apart: Rows: Horse- or tractor-cultivated	Distance apart: Rows: Hand-cultivated	Distance apart: Plants in the row
			Inches	*Feet*		
Asparagus	1 ounce	75	1 -1½	4 -5	1½ to 2 feet	18 inches.
Beans:						
Lima, bush	½ pound		1 -1½	2½-3	2 feet	3 to 4 inches.
Lima, pole	½ pound		1 -1½	3 -4	3 feet	3 to 4 feet.
Snap, bush	½ pound		1 -1½	2½-3	2 feet	3 to 4 inches.
Snap, pole	4 ounces		1 -1½	3 -4	2 feet	3 feet.
Beet	2 ounces		1	2 -2½	14 to 16 inches	2 to 3 inches.
Broccoli:						
Heading	1 packet	50– 75	½	2½-3	2 to 2½ feet	14 to 24 inches.
Sprouting	1 packet	50– 75	½	2½-3	2 to 2½ feet	14 to 24 inches.
Brussels sprouts	1 packet	50– 75	½	2½-3	2 to 2½ feet	14 to 24 inches.
Cabbage	1 packet	50– 75	½	2½-3	2 to 2½ feet	14 to 24 inches.
Cabbage, Chinese	1 packet		½	2 -2½	18 to 24 inches	8 to 12 inches.
Carrot	1 packet		½	2 -2½	14 to 16 inches	2 to 3 inches.
Cauliflower	1 packet	50– 75	½	2½-3	2 to 2½ feet	14 to 24 inches.
Celeriac	1 packet	200–250	⅛	2½-3	18 to 24 inches	4 to 6 inches.
Celery	1 packet	200–250	⅛	2½-3	18 to 24 inches	4 to 6 inches.
Chard	2 ounces		1	2 -2½	18 to 24 inches	6 inches.
Chervil	1 packet		½	2 -2½	14 to 16 inches	2 to 3 inches.
Chicory, witloof	1 packet		½	2 -2½	18 to 24 inches	6 to 8 inches.
Chives	1 packet		½	2½-3	14 to 16 inches	In clusters.
Collards	1 packet		½	3 -3½	18 to 24 inches	18 to 24 inches.
Cornsalad	1 packet		½	2½-3	14 to 16 inches	1 foot.
Corn, sweet	2 ounces		2	3 -3½	2 to 3 feet	Drills, 14 to 16 inches; hills, 2½ to 3 feet.
Cress Upland	1 packet		⅛- ¼	2 -2½	14 to 16 inches	2 to 3 inches.
Cucumber	1 packet		½	6 -7	6 to 7 feet	Drills, 3 feet; hills, 6 feet.
Dasheen	5 to 6 pounds	50	2 -3	3½-4	3½ to 4 feet	2 feet.
Eggplant	1 packet	50	½	3	2 to 2½ feet	3 feet.
Endive	1 packet		½	2½-3	18 to 24 inches	12 inches.
Fennel, Florence	1 packet		½	2½-3	18 to 24 inches	4 to 6 inches.
Garlic	1 pound		1 -2	2½-3	14 to 16 inches	2 to 3 inches.
Horseradish	Cuttings	50–75	2	3 -4	2 to 2½ feet	18 to 24 inches.
Kale	1 packet		½	2½-3	18 to 24 inches	12 to 15 inches.
Kohlrabi	1 packet		½	2½-3	14 to 16 inches	5 to 6 inches.
Leek	1 packet		½-1	2½-3	14 to 16 inches	2 to 3 inches.
Lettuce, head	1 packet	100	½	2½-3	14 to 16 inches	12 to 15 inches.
Lettuce, leaf	1 packet		½	2½-3	14 to 16 inches	6 inches.
Muskmelon	1 packet		1	6 -7	6 to 7 feet	Hills, 6 feet.
Mustard	1 packet		½	2½-3	14 to 16 inches	12 inches.
Okra	2 ounces		1 -1½	3 -3½	3 to 3½ feet	2 feet.
Onion:						
Plants		400	1 -2	2 -2½	14 to 16 inches	2 to 3 inches.
Seed	1 packet		½-1	2 -2½	14 to 16 inches	2 to 3 inches.
Sets	1 pound		1 -2	2 -2½	14 to 16 inches	2 to 3 inches.
Parsley	1 packet		⅛	2 -2½	14 to 16 inches	4 to 6 inches.
Parsley, turnip-rooted	1 packet		⅛- ¼	2 -2½	14 to 16 inches	2 to 3 inches.
Parsnip	1 packet		½	2 -2½	18 to 24 inches	2 to 3 inches.
Peas	½ pound		2 -3	2 -4	1½ to 3 feet	1 inch.
Pepper	1 packet	50–70	½	3 -4	2 to 3 feet	18 to 24 inches.
Physalis	1 packet		½	2 -2½	1½ to 2 feet	12 to 18 inches.
Potato	5 to 6 pounds, tubers		4	2½-3	2 to 2½ feet	10 to 18 inches.
Pumpkin	1 ounce		1 -2	5 -8	5 to 8 feet	3 to 4 feet.
Radish	1 ounce		½	2 -2½	14 to 16 inches	1 inch.
Rhubarb		25–35		3 -4	3 to 4 feet	3 to 4 feet.
Salsify	1 ounce		½	2 -2½	18 to 26 inches	2 to 3 inches.
Shallots	1 pound (cloves)		1 -2	2 -2½	12 to 18 inches	2 to 3 inches.
Sorrel	1 packet		½	2 -2½	18 to 24 inches	5 to 8 inches.
Soybean	½ to 1 pound		1 -1½	2½-3	24 to 30 inches	3 inches.
Spinach	1 ounce		½	2 -2½	14 to 16 inches	3 to 4 inches.
Spinach, New Zealand	1 ounce		1 -1½	3 -3½	3 feet	18 inches.
Squash:						
Bush	½ ounce		1 -2	4 -5	4 to 5 feet	Drills, 15 to 18 inches; hills, 4 feet.
Vine	1 ounce		1 -2	8 -12	8 to 12 feet	Drills, 2 to 3 feet; hills, 4 feet.
Sweet potato	5 pounds, bedroots	75	2 -3	3 -3½	3 to 3½ feet	12 to 14 inches.
Tomato	1 packet	35–50	½	3 -4	2 to 3 feet	1½ to 3 feet.
Turnip greens	1 packet		¼- ½	2 -2½	14 to 16 inches	2 to 3 inches.
Turnips and rutabagas	½ ounce		¼- ½	2 -2½	14 to 16 inches	2 to 3 inches.
Watermelon	1 ounce		1 -2	8 -10	8 to 10 feet	Drills, 2 to 3 feet; hills, 8 feet.

A double layer of plastic film supported by semicircular galvanized pipe makes a highly satisfactory portable coldframe.

should be about 60° F. at night and 70° F. during the day. Best results are obtained if the fluorescent fixture is next to a window to increase the amount of light reaching the young plants.

Soil pellets are the simplest and easiest method for starting plants and are readily available from garden-supply stores and other sources. Soil pellets are a well-balanced synthetic soil mixture and are free of soilborne diseases and weeds.

Special Devices for Starting Plants

In determining the type of equipment for starting early plants, the gardener must consider the temperature and other climatic conditions in his locality, as well as the nature of the plants to be started. Hardy plants, such as cabbage, need only simple, inexpensive facilities, but such heat-loving tender seedlings as peppers and eggplant must have more elaborate facilities for successful production. In the warmer parts of the United States, and in well-protected locations elsewhere, a coldframe or a sash-covered pit on the sunny side of a building usually suffices. In colder sections, or in exposed areas elsewhere, some form of artificial heat is essential. Where only a little protection against cold damage, at infrequent intervals, is needed, a coldframe in which a temporary bank of lamps can be placed may be sufficient. The hotbed, lean-to, or sash greenhouse heated by manure, pipes, flues or electricity are all widely used, the choice depending on conditions. A comparatively small plantgrowing structure will provide enough plants for several gardens, and joint efforts by a number of gardeners will usually reduce the labor of producing plants.

The plant-growing structure should always be on well-drained land free from danger of flooding. A sunny southern exposure on a moderate slope, with trees, a hedge, a board fence, or other form of windbreak on the north and west, makes a desirable site. Plenty of sunshine is necessary.

Hotbeds and other plant-growing devices require close attention. They must be ventilated at frequent intervals, and the plants may require watering more than once daily. Convenience in handling the work is important. Sudden storms may necessitate closing the structure within a matter of minutes. Plant growing at home should not be undertaken by persons obliged to be away for extended periods, leaving the plant structure unattended.

A tight well-glazed structure is necessary where the climate is severe; less expensive facilities are satisfactory elsewhere.

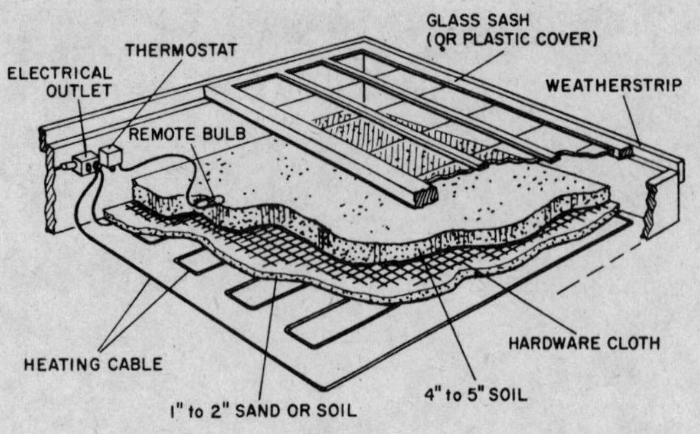

An electrically heated glass hotbed

Covers for hotbeds and coldframes may be glass sash, fiber glass, plastic film, muslin or light canvas.

In the moderate and cooler sections of the country, standard 3- by 6-foot hotbed sash is most satisfactory. Even this requires supplementary covering with canvas, blankets, mats or similar material during freezing weather. The amount of covering is determined by the degree of heat supplied the structure, the severity of the weather, and the kind of plants and their stage of development. Farther south, where less protection is necessary, a muslin cover may be all that is needed and for only a part of the time.

Many substitutes for glass as coverings for hotbeds and coldframes are on the market. The most widely used substitutes are various kinds of clear plastic film. Some of these have a lifespan of only one season, and others a lifespan of three to five years.

Clear plastic film transmits as much light as glass in the visible range, and more light than glass in the ultraviolet and infrared ranges.

The film comes as flat sheets (on rolls) and in tubular form. Flat-sheet film is used for tacking onto wooden frames; the tubular form is used for enclosing metal tubular frames with a tight double layer of film.

Large plant hoods made from semicircular aluminum or galvanized steel pipe and fitted with a sleeve of tubular plastic film make excellent coldframes or seasonal row covers. When used in this way, a double layer of plastic film provides an air space that insulates against 4° F. to 7° F. of frost temperature change.

Electrically heated plant beds are ideal for the home gardener, provided electric rates are not too high. The beds may be built any size. Because they are equipped with thermostatic control, they require a minimum of attention. It is now possible to buy frames—completely equipped with heating cables, switches and thermostats—ready to assemble and set in position. Fill the frames with soil or plant boxes and connect to a source of current. Small frames may be removed at the end of the season and stored; larger frames are usually treated as a permanent installation.

Hardening Plants

Plants should be gradually hardened, or toughened, for two weeks before planting in the open garden. This is done by slowing down their rate of growth to prepare them to withstand such conditions as chilling, drying winds, shortage of water or high temperatures. Cabbage, lettuce, onion and many other plants can be hardened to withstand frost; others, such as tomatoes and peppers, cannot. Withholding water and lowering the temperature are the best ways to harden a plant. This may be done in a glass or plastic coldframe.

About ten days before being planted in the open ground, the young plants in beds or flats are blocked out with a large knife. Blocking, or cutting the roots, causes new roots to form quickly near the plants, making recovery from transplanting in the open easier. Blocking also makes it easier to remove the plants from the bed or flat with minimum injury.

Southern-grown Plants

Vegetable plants grown outdoors in the South are shipped to all parts of the country. They are grown cheaply and usually withstand shipment and resetting very well. They may not always be as good as homegrown plants, but they save the trouble of starting them in the house or in a hotbed. Plants of beets, brussels sprouts, cabbage, cauliflower, lettuce, onions, peppers and tomatoes are extensively grown and shipped; tomato, cabbage and onion plants make up the bulk of the shipments. The plants are usually wrapped in bundles of 50 each and shipped by either mail or express. Tomato and pepper plants are packed with a little damp moss around the roots, but onion and cabbage plants are usually packed with bare roots. Shipments involving large numbers of bundles are packed in ventilated hampers or slatted crates and usually are sent by motor truck or rail express. Shipments by air mail and air express are increasing.

The disadvantages of using southern-grown plants are the occasional delays in obtaining them and the possibility of transmitting such diseases as the wilt disease of the tomato, black rot of cabbage, and disorders caused by nematodes. State-certified plants that have been carefully inspected and found as free of these troubles as can be reasonably determined are available. Southern-grown plants are now offered for sale by most northern seedsmen, by mail-order houses, and often by local hardware and supply houses.

Transplanting

The term "transplanting" means shifting of a plant from one soil or culture medium to another. It may refer to the shifting of small seedlings from the seedbed to other containers where the plants will have more space for growth, or it may mean the setting of plants in the garden row where they are to develop for the crop period. Contrary to general belief, transplanting does not in itself stimulate the plant or make it grow better; actually growth is temporarily checked, but the plant is usually given more space in which to grow. Every effort should be made during transplanting to interrupt the growth of the plant as little as possible.

Plants started in seed flats, flower pots and other containers in the house, or in the hotbed, the greenhouse or elsewhere should be shifted as soon as they can be handled to boxes, flower pots, plant bands, or other containers where they will have more room to develop. If shifted to flats or similar containers, the plants should be spaced 2 or more inches apart. This provides room for growth until the plants can be moved to their permanent place in the garden. Most gardeners prefer to place seedlings singly in flower pots, paper cups with the bottoms pierced for drainage, plant bands, berry boxes, or other containers. When the plants are set in the garden, the containers are carefully removed.

Soil for transplanting should be fertile, usually a mixture of rich topsoil and garden compost, with a very light addition of a commercial garden fertilizer.

Moistening the seedbed before removing the seedlings and care in lifting and separating the delicate plants make it possible to shift them with little damage to the root system and with only minor checks to their growth. Plants grown singly in separate containers can be moved to the garden with almost no disturbance to the root system, especially those that are hardened for a week or two before being set outdoors. Plants being hardened should be watered sparingly, but just before they are set out, they should be given a thorough soaking.

Plants grown in the hotbed or greenhouse without being shifted from the seedbed to provide more room and those shipped from the South usually have very little soil adhering to the roots when they are set in the garden. Such plants may require special care if transplanting conditions are not ideal; otherwise they will die, or at least suffer a severe shock that will greatly retard their development. The roots of these plants should be kept covered and not allowed to dry out. Dipping the roots in a mixture of clay and water helps greatly in bridging the crucial transplanting period. Planting when the soil is moist also helps. Pouring a half pint to a pint of water, or less for small plants, into the hole around the plant before it is completely filled is usually necessary. A starter solution made by mixing ½ pound of 4–12–4 or 5–10–5 commercial fertilizer in 4 gallons of water may be used instead of plain water. It is usually beneficial. Finally, the freshly set plants should be shaded for a day or two with newspapers.

Plants differ greatly in the way they recover from the loss of roots and from exposure to new conditions. Small plants of tomatoes, lettuce, beets, cabbage and related vegetables are easy to transplant. They withstand the treatment better than peppers, eggplant and the vine crops. When started indoors and moved to the field, the vine crops should be seeded directly in berry baskets or containers of the same size that can be transferred to the garden and removed without disturbing the root systems. Beans and sweet corn can be handled in the same manner, thereby often gaining a week or two in earliness.

PLANTING THE GARDEN

One of the most important elements of success in growing vegetables is planting, or transplanting, each crop at the time or times that are best for the operation in each locality. Temperatures often differ so much between localities not many miles apart that the best planting dates for a specific vegetable may differ by several days or even two weeks, depending on the immediate locality within a larger area.

The gardener naturally wants to make the first planting of each vegetable as early as he can without too much danger of its being damaged by cold. Many vegetables are so hardy to cold that they can be planted a month or more before the average date of the last freeze, or about six weeks before the frost-free date. Furthermore, most, if not all, cold-tolerant crops actually thrive better in cool weather than in hot, and should not be planted late in the spring in the southern two thirds of the country where summers are hot. Thus the gardener must time his planting not only to escape cold but also, with certain crops, to escape heat. Some vegetables that will not thrive when planted in late spring in areas having rather hot summers may be sown in late summer, however, so that they will make most of their growth in cooler weather. (See Table 5.)

Opposite each vegetable in Table 6, the first date in any column is the *earliest generally safe* date that the crop can be sown or transplanted by the gardener using that column. (No gardener needs to use more than one of the columns.) The second date is the latest date that is likely to prove satisfactory for the planting. All times in between these two dates may not, however, give equally good results. Most of the crops listed do better when planted not too far from the earlier date shown.

To determine the best time to plant any vegetable in the spring in your locality:

1. Find your location on the map on page 273, and then, the solid line on the map that is closest to this location.
2. Find the date shown on the solid line. This is the average date of the last killing frost. The first number represents the month; the second number, the day. Thus, 3–10 is March 10. Once you know the date, you are through with the map.
3. Turn again to Table 6; find the column that has your date over it; and draw a heavy line around this entire column. It is the only date column in the table that you will need.
4. Find the dates in the column that are on a line with the name of the crop you want to plant. These dates show the period during which the crop can safely be planted. The best time is on, or soon after, the first of the two dates. A time halfway between them is very good; the second date is not so good.

For areas in the Plains region that warm up quickly in the spring and are subject to dry weather, very early planting is essential to escape heat and drought. In fact, most of the cool-season crops do not thrive when spring-planted in the southern part of the Great Plains and southern Texas.

Table 7 is used with the map on page 278 in the same way to find that dates for late plantings. The recommendations for late plantings and for those in the South for overwintered crops are less exact and less dependable than those for early planting. Factors other than direct temperature effects—summer rainfall, for example, and the severity of diseases and insects—often make success difficult, especially in the Southeast, although some other areas having the same frost dates are more favorable. A date about halfway between the two shown in Table 7 will generally be best, although in most areas fair success can be expected within the entire range of dates shown.

Along the northern half of the Pacific coast, warm-weather crops should not be planted quite so late as the frost date and table would indicate. Although frost comes late, very cool weather prevails for some time before frost, retarding late growth of crops like sweet corn, lima beans and tomatoes.

Table 5

Some common vegetables grouped according to the approximate times they can be planted and their relative requirements for cool and warm weather

Cold-hardy plants for early-spring planting		Cold-tender or heat-hardy plants for later-spring or early-summer planting			Hardy plants for late-summer or fall planting except in the North (plant 6 to 8 weeks before first fall freeze)
Very hardy (plant 4 to 6 weeks before frost-free date)	Hardy (plant 2 to 4 weeks before frost-free date)	Not cold-hardy (plant on frost-free date)	Requiring hot weather (plant 1 week or more after frost-free date)	Medium heat-tolerant (good for summer planting)	
Broccoli	Beets	Beans,	Beans,	Beans, all	Beets
Cabbage	Carrot	snap	lima	Chard	Collard
Lettuce	Chard	Okra	Eggplant	Soybean	Kale
Onions	Mustard	New Zea-	Peppers	New Zea-	Lettuce
Peas	Parsnip	land	Sweet po-	land	Mustard
Potato	Radish	spinach	tato	spinach	Spinach
Spinach		Soybean	Cucum-	Squash	Turnip
Turnip		Squash	ber	Sweet	
		Sweet corn	Melons	corn	
		Tomato			

CARING FOR THE GARDEN

Watering

In most areas the garden requires a moisture supply equivalent to about 1 inch of rain a week during the growing season for best plant growth. It requires roughly that amount of watering a week to maintain good production if the moisture stored in the soil becomes depleted and no rain falls over periods of weeks. An inch of rain is equivalent to about 28,000 gallons on an acre, or 900 gallons on a 30- by 50-foot garden.

It is much better to give the garden a good soaking about once a week than to water it sparingly more often. Light sprinklings at frequent intervals do little, if any, good. The best way to apply water, when the soil and slope are suitable, is to run it the length of furrows between the rows until the soil is well soaked. If the soil is very sandy or the surface too irregular for the furrow method, sprinklers or porous irrigating hose must be used.

Controlling Weeds

Weeds rob cultivated plants of water, nutrients and light. Some weeds harbor diseases, insects and nematodes that reinfest garden crops in succeeding years.

As soon as the soil can be properly worked after each rain or irrigation, it should be thoroughly hoed or cultivated to kill weeds that have sprouted and to leave the surface in a loose, friable condition to absorb later rainfall. The primary value of hoeing or cultivating is weed control. This cultivation should be shallow so as to avoid injuring the vegetable plant

MEAN DATE OF LAST 32° (F.) TEMPERATURE IN SPRING

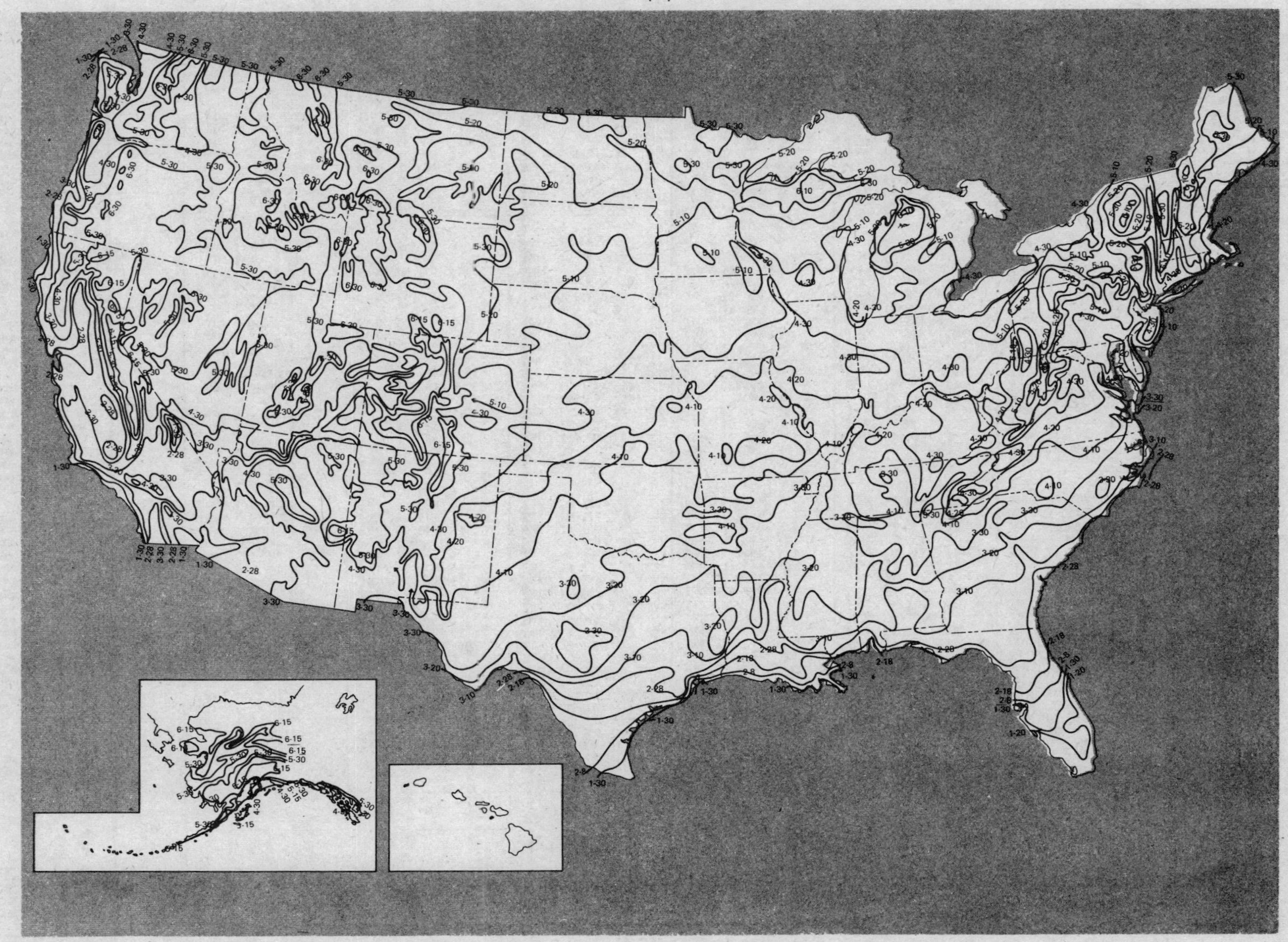

Average dates of the last killing frost in spring

Table 6

Earliest dates, and range of dates, for safe spring planting of vegetables in the open

Crop	Planting dates for localities in which average date of last freeze is—						
	Jan. 30	Feb. 8	Feb. 18	Feb. 28	Mar. 10	Mar. 20	Mar. 30
Asparagus [1]					Jan. 1–Mar. 1	Feb. 1–Mar. 10	Feb. 15–Mar. 20.
Beans, lima	Feb. 1–Apr. 15	Feb. 10–May 1	Mar. 1–May 1	Mar. 15–June 1	Mar. 20–June 1	Apr. 1–June 15	Apr. 15–June 20.
Beans, snap	Feb. 1–Apr. 1	Feb. 1–May 1	Mar. 1–May 1	Mar. 10–May 15	Mar. 15–May 15	Mar. 15–May 25	Apr. 1–June 1.
Beet	Jan. 1–Mar. 15	Jan. 10–Mar. 15	Jan. 20–Apr. 1	Feb. 1–Apr. 15	Feb. 15–June 1	Feb. 15–May 15	Mar. 1–June 1.
Broccoli, sprouting [1]	Jan. 1–30	Jan. 1–30	Jan. 15–Feb. 15	Feb. 1–Mar. 1	Feb. 15–Mar. 15	Feb. 15–Mar. 15	Mar. 1–20.
Brussels sprouts [1]	Jan. 1–30	Jan. 1–30	Jan. 15–Feb. 15	Feb. 1–Mar. 1	Feb. 15–Mar. 15	Feb. 15–Mar. 15	Mar. 1–20.
Cabbage [1]	Jan. 1–15	Jan. 1–Feb. 10	Jan. 1–Feb. 25	Jan. 15–Feb. 25	Jan. 25–Mar. 1	Feb. 1–Mar. 1	Feb. 15–Mar. 10.
Cabbage, Chinese	(2)	(2)	(2)	(2)	(2)	(2)	(2)
Carrot	Jan. 1–Mar. 1	Jan. 1–Mar. 1	Jan. 15–Mar. 1	Feb. 1–Mar. 1	Feb. 10–Mar. 15	Feb. 15–Mar. 20	Mar. 1–Apr. 10.
Cauliflower [1]	Jan. 1–Feb. 1	Jan. 1–Feb. 1	Jan. 10–Feb. 10	Jan. 20–Feb. 20	Feb. 1–Mar. 1	Feb. 10–Mar. 10	Feb. 20–Mar. 20.
Celery and celeriac	Jan. 1–Feb. 1	Jan. 10–Feb. 10	Jan. 20–Feb. 20	Feb. 1–Mar. 1	Feb. 20–Mar. 20	Mar. 1–Apr. 1	Mar. 15–Apr. 15.
Chard	Jan. 1–Apr. 1	Jan. 10–Apr. 1	Jan. 20–Apr. 15	Feb. 1–May 1	Feb. 15–May 15	Feb. 20–May 15	Mar. 1–May 25.
Chervil and chives	Jan. 1–Feb. 1	Jan. 1–Feb. 1	Jan. 1–Feb. 1	Jan. 15–Feb. 15	Feb. 1–Mar. 1	Feb. 10–Mar. 10	Feb. 15–Mar. 15.
Chicory, witloof					June 1–July 1	June 1–July 1	June 1–July 1.
Collards [1]	Jan. 1–Feb. 15	Jan. 1–Feb. 15	Jan. 1–Mar. 15	Jan. 15–Mar. 15	Feb. 1–Apr. 1	Feb. 15–May 1	Mar. 1–June 1.
Cornsalad	Jan. 1–Feb. 15	Jan. 1–Feb. 15	Jan. 1–Mar. 15	Jan. 1–Mar. 1	Jan. 1–Mar. 15	Jan. 1–Mar. 15	Jan. 15–Mar. 15.
Corn, sweet	Feb. 1–Mar. 15	Feb. 10–Apr. 1	Feb. 20–Apr. 15	Mar. 1–Apr. 15	Mar. 10–Apr. 15	Mar. 15–May 1	Mar. 25–May 15.
Cress, upland	Jan. 1–Feb. 1	Jan. 1–Feb. 15	Jan. 15–Feb. 15	Feb. 1–Mar. 1	Feb. 10–Mar. 15	Feb. 20–Mar. 15	Mar. 1–Apr. 1.
Cucumber	Feb. 15–Mar. 15	Feb. 15–Apr. 1	Feb. 15–Apr. 15	Mar. 1–Apr. 15	Mar. 15–Apr. 15	Apr. 1–May 1	Apr. 10–May 15.
Eggplant [1]	Feb. 1–Mar. 1	Feb. 10–Mar. 15	Feb. 20–Apr. 1	Mar. 10–Apr. 15	Mar. 15–Apr. 15	Apr. 1–May 1	Apr. 15–May 15.
Endive	Jan. 1–Mar. 1	Jan. 1–Mar. 1	Jan. 15–Mar. 1	Feb. 1–Mar. 1	Feb. 15–Mar. 15	Mar. 1–Apr. 1	Mar. 10–Apr. 10.
Fennel, Florence	Jan. 1–Mar. 1	Jan. 1–Mar. 1	Jan. 15–Mar. 1	Feb. 1–Mar. 1	Feb. 15–Mar. 15	Mar. 1–Apr. 1	Mar. 10–Apr. 10.
Garlic	(2)	(2)	(2)	(2)	(2)	Feb. 1–Mar. 1	Feb. 10–Mar. 10.
Horseradish [1]							Mar. 1–Apr. 1.
Kale	Jan. 1–Feb. 1	Jan. 10–Feb. 1	Jan. 20–Feb. 10	Feb. 1–20	Feb. 10–Mar. 1	Feb. 20–Mar. 10	Mar. 1–20.
Kohlrabi	Jan. 1–Feb. 1	Jan. 10–Feb. 1	Jan. 20–Feb. 10	Feb. 1–20	Feb. 10–Mar. 1	Feb. 20–Mar. 10	Mar. 1–Apr. 1.
Leek	Jan. 1–Feb. 1	Jan. 1–Feb. 1	Jan. 1–Feb. 15	Jan. 15–Feb. 15	Jan. 25–Mar. 1	Feb. 1–Mar. 1	Feb. 15–Mar. 15.
Lettuce, head [1]	Jan. 1–Feb. 1	Jan. 1–Feb. 1	Jan. 1–Feb. 1	Jan. 15–Feb. 15	Feb. 1–20	Feb. 15–Mar. 10	Mar. 1–20.
Lettuce, leaf	Jan. 1–Feb. 1	Jan. 1–Feb. 1	Jan. 1–Mar. 15	Jan. 1–Mar. 15	Jan. 15–Apr. 1	Feb. 1–Apr. 1	Feb. 15–Apr. 15.
Muskmelon	Feb. 15–Mar. 15	Feb. 15–Apr. 1	Feb. 15–Apr. 15	Mar. 1–Apr. 15	Mar. 15–Apr. 15	Apr. 1–May 1	Apr. 10–May 15.
Mustard	Jan. 1–Mar. 1	Jan. 1–Mar. 1	Feb. 15–Apr. 15	Feb. 1–Mar. 1	Feb. 10–Mar. 15	Feb. 20–Apr. 1	Mar. 1–Apr. 15.
Okra	Feb. 15–Apr. 1	Feb. 15–Apr. 15	Mar. 1–June 1	Mar. 10–June 1	Mar. 20–June 1	Apr. 1–June 15	Apr. 10–June 15.
Onion [1]	Jan. 1–15	Jan. 1–15	Jan. 1–15	Jan. 1–Feb. 1	Jan. 15–Feb. 15	Feb. 10–Mar. 10	Feb. 15–Mar. 15.
Onion, seed	Jan. 1–15	Jan. 1–15	Jan. 1–15	Jan. 1–Feb. 15	Feb. 1–Mar. 1	Feb. 10–Mar. 10	Feb. 20–Mar. 15.
Onion, sets	Jan. 1–15	Jan. 1–15	Jan. 1–15	Jan. 1–Mar. 1	Jan. 15–Mar. 10	Feb. 1–Mar. 20	Feb. 15–Mar. 20.
Parsley	Jan. 1–30	Jan. 1–30	Jan. 1–30	Jan. 15–Mar. 1	Feb. 1–Mar. 10	Feb. 15–Mar. 15	Mar. 1–Apr. 1.
Parsnip			Jan. 1–Feb. 1	Jan. 15–Feb. 15	Jan. 15–Mar. 1	Feb. 15–Mar. 15	Mar. 1–Apr. 1.
Peas, garden	Jan. 1–Feb. 15	Jan. 1–Feb. 15	Jan. 1–Mar. 1	Jan. 15–Mar. 1	Jan. 15–Mar. 15	Feb. 1–Mar. 15	Feb. 10–Mar. 20.
Peas, black-eye	Feb. 15–May 1	Feb. 15–May 15	Mar. 1–June 15	Mar. 10–June 20	Mar. 15–July 1	Apr. 1–July 1	Apr. 15–July 1.
Pepper [1]	Feb. 1–Apr. 1	Feb. 15–Apr. 15	Mar. 1–May 1	Mar. 15–May 1	Apr. 1–June 1	Apr. 10–June 1	Apr. 15–June 1.
Potato	Jan. 1–Feb. 15	Jan. 1–Feb. 15	Jan. 15–Mar. 1	Jan. 15–Mar. 1	Feb. 1–Mar. 1	Feb. 10–Mar. 15	Feb. 20–Mar. 20.
Radish	Jan. 1–Apr. 1	Jan. 1–Apr. 1	Jan. 1–Apr. 1	Jan. 1–Apr. 1	Jan. 1–Apr. 15	Jan. 20–May 1	Feb. 15–May 1.
Rhubarb [1]							
Rutabaga				Jan. 1–Feb. 1	Jan. 15–Feb. 15	Jan. 15–Mar. 1	Feb. 1–Mar. 1.
Salsify	Jan. 1–Feb. 1	Jan. 10–Feb. 10	Jan. 15–Feb. 20	Jan. 15–Mar. 1	Feb. 1–Mar. 1	Feb. 15–Mar. 1	Mar. 1–15.
Shallot	Jan. 1–Feb. 1	Jan. 1–Feb. 10	Jan. 1–Feb. 20	Jan. 1–Mar. 1	Jan. 15–Mar. 1	Feb. 1–Mar. 10	Feb. 15–Mar. 15.
Sorrel	Jan. 1–Mar. 1	Jan. 1–Mar. 1	Jan. 15–Mar. 1	Feb. 1–Mar. 10	Feb. 10–Mar. 15	Feb. 10–Mar. 20	Feb. 20–Apr. 1.
Soybean	Mar. 1–June 30	Mar. 1–June 30	Mar. 10–June 30	Mar. 20–June 30	Apr. 10–June 30	Apr. 10–June 30	Apr. 20–June 30.
Spinach	Jan. 1–Feb. 15	Jan. 1–Feb. 15	Jan. 1–Mar. 1	Jan. 1–Mar. 1	Jan. 15–Mar. 10	Jan. 15–Mar. 15	Feb. 1–Mar. 20.
Spinach, New Zealand	Feb. 1–Apr. 15	Feb. 15–Apr. 15	Mar. 1–Apr. 15	Mar. 15–May 15	Mar. 20–May 15	Apr. 1–May 15	Apr. 10–June 1.
Squash, summer	Feb. 1–Apr. 15	Feb. 15–Apr. 15	Mar. 1–Apr. 15	Mar. 15–May 15	Mar. 15–May 1	Apr. 1–May 15	Apr. 10–June 1.
Sweet potato	Feb. 15–May 15	Mar. 1–May 15	Mar. 20–June 1	Mar. 20–June 1	Apr. 1–June 1	Apr. 10–June 1	Apr. 20–June 1.
Tomato	Feb. 1–Apr. 1	Feb. 20–Apr. 10	Mar. 1–Apr. 20	Mar. 10–May 1	Mar. 20–May 10	Apr. 1–May 20	Apr. 10–June 1.
Turnip	Jan. 1–Mar. 1	Jan. 1–Mar. 1	Jan. 10–Mar. 1	Jan. 20–Mar. 1	Feb. 1–Mar. 1	Feb. 10–Mar. 10	Feb. 20–Mar. 20.
Watermelon	Feb. 15–Mar. 15	Feb. 15–Apr. 1	Feb. 15–Apr. 15	Mar. 1–Apr. 15	Mar. 15–Apr. 15	Apr. 1–May 1	Apr. 10–May 15.

[1] Plants.
[2] Generally fall-planted

Table 6

Earliest dates, and range of dates, for safe spring planting of vegetables in the open—Continued

Crop	Planting dates for localities in which average date of last freeze is—						
	Apr. 10	Apr. 20	Apr. 30	May 10	May 20	May 30	June 10
Asparagus [1]	Mar. 10–Apr. 10	Mar. 15–Apr. 15	Mar. 20–Apr. 15	Mar. 10–Apr. 30	Apr. 20–May 15	May 1–June 1	May 15–June 1.
Beans, lima	Apr. 1–June 30	May 1–June 20	May 15–June 15	May 25–June 15			
Beans, snap	Apr. 10–June 30	Apr. 25–June 30	May 10–June 30	May 10–June 30	May-15–June 30	May 25–June 15	
Beet	Mar. 10–June 1	Mar. 20–June 1	Apr. 1–June 15	Apr. 15–June 15	Apr. 25–June 15	May 1–June 15	May 15–June 15.
Broccoli, sprouting [1]	Mar. 15–Apr. 15	Mar. 25–Apr. 20	Apr. 1–May 1	Apr. 15–June 1	May 1–June 15	May 10–June 10	May 20–June 10.
Brussels sprouts [1]	Mar. 15–Apr. 15	Mar. 25–Apr. 20	Apr. 1–May 1	Apr. 15–June 1	May 1–June 15	May 10–June 10	May 20–June 10.
Cabbage [1]	Mar. 1–Apr. 1	Mar. 10–Apr. 1	Mar. 15–Apr. 10	Apr. 1–May 15	May 1–June 15	May 10–June 15	May 20–June 1.
Cabbage, Chinese	([2])	([2])	([2])	Apr. 1–May 15	May 1–June 15	May 10–June 15	May 20–June 1.
Carrot	Mar. 10–Apr. 20	Apr. 1–May 15	Apr. 10–June 1	Apr. 20–June 15	May 1–June 1	May 10–June 1	May 20–June 1.
Cauliflower [1]	Mar. 1–Mar. 20	Mar. 15–Apr. 20	Apr. 10–May 10	Apr. 15–May 15	May 10–June 15	May 20–June 1	June 1–June 15.
Celery and celeriac	Apr. 1–Apr. 20	Apr. 10–May 1	Apr. 15–May 1	Apr. 20–June 15	May 10–June 15	May 20–June 1	June 1–June 15.
Chard	Mar. 15–June 15	Apr. 1–June 15	Apr. 15–June 15	Apr. 20–June 15	May 10–June 15	May 20–June 1	June 1–June 15.
Chervil and chives	Mar. 1–Apr. 1	Mar. 10–Apr. 10	Mar. 20–Apr. 20	Apr. 1–May 1	Apr. 15–May 15	May 1–June 1	May 15–June 1.
Chicory, witloof	June 10–July 1	June 15–July 1	June 15–July 1	June 1–20	June 1–15	June 1–15	June 1–15.
Collards [1]	Mar. 1–June 1	Mar. 10–June 1	Apr. 1–June 1	Apr. 15–June 1	May 1–June 1	May 10–June 1	May 20–June 1.
Cornsalad	Feb. 1–Apr. 1	Feb. 15–Apr. 15	Mar. 1–May 1	Apr. 1–June 1	Apr. 15–June 1	May 1–June 15	May 15–June 15.
Corn, sweet	Apr. 10–June 1	Apr. 25–June 15	May 10–June 15	May 10–June 1	May 15–June 1	May 20–June 1	
Cress, upland	Mar. 10–Apr. 15	Mar. 20–May 1	Apr. 10–May 10	Apr. 20–May 20	May 1–June 1	May 15–June 1	May 15–June 15.
Cucumber	Apr. 20–June 1	May 1–June 15	May 15–June 15	May 20–June 15	June 1–15		
Eggplant [1]	May 1–June 1	May 10–June 1	May 15–June 10	May 20–June 15	June 1–15		
Endive	Mar. 15–Apr. 15	Mar. 25–Apr. 15	Apr. 1–May 1	Apr. 15–May 15	May 1–30	May 1–30	May 15–June 1.
Fennel, Florence	Mar. 15–Apr. 15	Mar. 25–Apr. 15	Apr. 1–May 1	Apr. 15–May 15	May 1–30	May 1–30	May 15–June 1.
Garlic	Feb. 20–Mar. 20	Mar. 10–Apr. 1	Mar. 15–Apr. 15	Apr. 1–May 1	Apr. 15–May 15	May 1–30	May 15–June 1.
Horseradish [1]	Mar. 10–Apr. 10	Mar. 20–Apr. 20	Apr. 1–30	Apr. 15–May 15	Apr. 20–May 20	May 1–30	May 15–June 1.
Kale	Mar. 10–Apr. 1	Mar. 20–Apr. 10	Apr. 1–20	Apr. 10–May 1	Apr. 20–May 10	May 1–30	May 15–June 1.
Kohlrabi	Mar. 10–Apr. 10	Mar. 20–May 1	Apr. 1–May 10	Apr. 10–May 15	Apr. 20–May 20	May 1–30	May 15–June 1.
Leek	Mar. 1–Apr. 1	Mar. 15–Apr. 15	Apr. 1–May 1	Apr. 15–May 15	May 1–May 20	May 1–15	May 1–15.
Lettuce, head [1]	Mar. 10–Apr. 1	Mar. 20–Apr. 15	Apr. 1–May 1	Apr. 15–May 15	May 1–June 30	May 10–June 30	May 20–June 30.
Lettuce, leaf	Mar. 15–May 15	Mar. 20–May 15	Apr. 1–June 1	Apr. 15–June 15	May 1–June 30	May 10–June 30	May 20–June 30.
Muskmelon	Apr. 20–June 1	May 1–June 15	May 15–June 15	June 1–June 15			
Mustard	Mar. 10–Apr. 20	Mar. 20–May 1	Apr. 1–May 10	Apr. 15–June 1	May 1–June 30	May 10–June 30	May 20–June 30.
Okra	Apr. 20–June 15	May 1–June 1	May 10–June 1	May 20–June 10	June 1–20		
Onion [1]	Mar. 1–Apr. 1	Mar. 15–Apr. 10	Apr. 1–May 1	Apr. 10–May 1	Apr. 20–May 15	May 1–30	May 10–June 10.
Onion, seed	Mar. 1–Apr. 1	Mar. 15–Apr. 1	Mar. 15–Apr. 15	Apr. 1–May 1	Apr. 20–May 15	May 1–30	May 10–June 10.
Onion, sets	Mar. 1–Apr. 1	Mar. 10–Apr. 1	Mar. 10–Apr. 10	Apr. 10–May 1	Apr. 20–May 15	May 1–30	May 10–June 10.
Parsley	Mar. 10–Apr. 10	Mar. 20–Apr. 20	Apr. 1–May 1	Apr. 15–May 15	May 1–20	May 10–June 1	May 20–June 10.
Parsnip	Mar. 10–Apr. 10	Mar. 20–Apr. 20	Apr. 1–May 1	Apr. 15–May 15	May 1–20	May 10–June 1	May 20–June 10.
Peas, garden	Feb. 20–Mar. 20	Mar. 10–Apr. 10	Mar. 20–May 1	Apr. 1–May 15	Apr. 15–June 1	May 1–June 15	May 10–June 15.
Peas, black-eye	May 1–July 1	May 10–June 15	May 15–June 1				
Pepper [1]	May 1–June 1	May 10–June 1	May 15–June 10	May 20–June 10	May 25–June 15	June 1–15	
Potato	Mar. 10–Apr. 1	Mar. 15–Apr. 10	Mar. 20–May 10	Apr. 1–June 1	Apr. 15–June 15	May 1–June 15	May 15–June 1.
Radish	Mar. 1–May 1	Mar. 10–May 10	Mar. 20–May 10	Apr. 1–June 1	Apr. 15–June 15	May 1–June 15	May 15–June 1.
Rhubarb [1]	Mar. 1–Apr. 1	Mar. 10–Apr. 10	Mar. 20–Apr. 15	Apr. 1–May 1	Apr. 15–May 10	May 1–20	May 15–June 1.
Rutabaga			May 1–June 1	May 1–June 1	May 1–20	May 10–20	May 20–June 1.
Salsify	Mar. 10–Apr. 15	Mar. 20–May 1	Apr. 1–May 15	Apr. 15–June 1	May 1–June 1	May 10–June 1	May 20–June 1.
Shallot	Mar. 1–Apr. 1	Mar. 15–Apr. 15	Apr. 1–May 1	Apr. 10–May 1	Apr. 20–May 10	May 1–June 1	May 10–June 1.
Sorrel	Mar. 1–Apr. 15	Mar. 15–May 1	Apr. 1–May 15	Apr. 15–June 1	May 1–June 1	May 10–June 10	May 20–June 10.
Soybean	May 1–June 30	May 10–June 20	May 15–June 15	May 25–June 10			
Spinach	Feb. 15–Apr. 1	Mar. 1–Apr. 15	Mar. 20–Apr. 20	Apr. 1–June 15	Apr. 10–June 15	Apr. 20–June 15	May 1–June 15.
Spinach, New Zealand	Apr. 20–June 1	May 1–June 15	May 1–June 15	May 10–June 15	May 20–June 15	June 1–15	
Squash, summer	Apr. 20–June 1	May 1–June 15	May 1–30	May 10–June 10	May 20–June 15	June 1–20	June 10–20.
Sweet potato	May 1–June 1	May 10–June 10	May 20–June 10				
Tomato	Apr. 20–June 1	May 5–June 10	May 10–June 15	May 15–June 10	May 25–June 15	June 5–20	June 15–30.
Turnip	Mar. 1–Apr. 1	Mar. 10–Apr. 1	Mar. 20–May 1	Apr. 1–June 1	Apr. 15–June 1	May 1–June 15	May 15–June 15.
Watermelon	Apr. 20–June 1	May 1–June 15	May 15–June 15	June 1–June 15	June 15–July 1		

[1] Plants.
[2] Generally fall-planted

Table 7

Latest dates, and range of dates, for safe fall planting of vegetables in the open

Crop	Planting dates for localities in which average dates of first freeze is—					
	Aug. 30	Sept. 10	Sept. 20	Sept. 30	Oct. 10	Oct. 20
Asparagus [1]					Oct. 20–Nov. 15	Nov. 1–Dec. 15.
Beans, lima				June 1–15	June 1–15	June 15–30.
Beans, snap		May 15–June 15	June 1–July 1	June 1–July 10	June 15–July 20	July 1–Aug. 1.
Beet	May 15–June 15	May 15–June 15	June 1–July 1	June 1–July 10	June 15–July 25	July 1–Aug. 5.
Broccoli, sprouting	May 1–June 1	May 1–June 1	May 1–June 15	June 1–30	June 15–July 15	July 1–Aug. 1.
Brussels sprouts	May 1–June 1	May 1–June 1	May 1–June 15	June 1–30	June 15–July 15	July 1–Aug. 1.
Cabbage [1]	May 1–June 1	May 1–June 1	May 1–June 15	June 1–July 10	June 1–July 15	July 1–20.
Cabbage, Chinese	May 15–June 15	May 15–June 15	June 1–July 1	June 1–July 15	June 15–Aug. 1	July 15–Aug. 15.
Carrot	May 15–June 15	May 15–June 15	June 1–July 1	June 1–July 10	June 1–July 20	June 15–Aug. 1.
Cauliflower [1]	May 1–June 1	May 1–July 1	May 1–July 1	May 10–July 15	June 1–July 25	July 1–Aug. 5.
Celery [1] and celeriac	May 1–June 1	May 15–June 15	May 15–July 1	June 1–July 5	June 1–July 15	June 1–Aug. 1.
Chard	May 15–June 15	May 15–July 1	June 1–July 1	June 1–July 5	June 1–July 20	June 1–Aug. 1.
Chervil and chives	May 10–June 10	May 1–June 15	May 15–June 15	(2)	(2)	(2)
Chicory, witloof	May 15–June 15	May 15–June 15	May 15–June 15	June 1–July 1	June 1–July 1	June 15–July 15.
Collards [1]	May 15–June 15	May 15–June 15	May 15–June 15	June 15–July 15	July 1–Aug. 1	July 15–Aug. 15.
Cornsalad	May 15–June 15	May 15–July 1	June 15–Aug. 1	July 15–Sept. 1	Aug. 15–Sept. 15	Sept. 1–Oct. 15.
Corn, sweet			June 1–July 1	June 1–July 1	June 1–July 10	June 1–July 20.
Cress, upland	May 15–June 15	May 15–July 1	June 15–Aug. 1	July 15–Sept. 1	Aug. 15–Sept. 15	Sept. 1–Oct. 15.
Cucumber			June 1–15	June 1–July 1	June 1–July 1	June 1–July 15.
Eggplant [1]				May 20–June 10	May 15–June 15	June 1–July 1.
Endive	June 1–July 1	June 1–July 1	June 15–July 15	June 15–Aug. 1	July 1–Aug. 15	July 15–Sept. 1.
Fennel, Florence	May 15–June 15	May 15–July 15	June 1–July 1	June 1–July 1	June 15–July 15	June 15–Aug. 1.
Garlic	(2)	(2)	(2)	(2)	(2)	(2)
Horseradish [1]	(2)	(2)	(2)	(2)	(2)	(2)
Kale	May 15–June 15	May 15–June 15	June 1–July 1	June 15–July 15	July 1–Aug. 1	July 15–Aug. 15.
Kohlrabi	May 15–June 15	June 1–July 1	June 1–July 15	June 15–July 15	July 1–Aug. 1	July 15–Aug. 15.
Leek	May 1–June 1	May 1–June 1	(2)	(2)	(2)	(2)
Lettuce, head [1]	May 15–July 1	May 15–July 1	June 1–July 15	June 15–Aug. 1	July 15–Aug. 15	Aug. 1–30.
Lettuce, leaf	May 15–July 15	May 15–July 15	June 1–Aug. 1	June 1–Aug. 1	July 15–Sept. 1	July 15–Sept. 1.
Muskmelon			May 1–June 15	May 15–June 1	June 1–June 15	June 15–July 20.
Mustard	May 15–July 15	May 15–July 15	June 1–Aug. 1	June 15–Aug. 1	July 15–Aug. 15	Aug. 1–Sept. 1.
Okra			June 1-20	June 1–July 1	June 1–July 15	June 1–Aug. 1.
Onion [1]	May 1–June 10	May 1–June 10	(2)	(2)	(2)	(2)
Onion, seed	May 1–June 1	May 1–June 10	(2)	(2)	(2)	(2)
Onion, sets	May 1–June 1	May 1–June 10	(2)	(2)	(2)	(2)
Parsley	May 15–June 15	May 1–June 15	June 1–July 1	June 1–July 15	June 15–Aug. 1	July 15–Aug. 15.
Parsnip	May 15–June 1	May 1–June 15	May 15–June 15	June 1–July 1	June 1–July 10	(2)
Peas, garden	May 10–June 15	May 1–July 1	June 1–July 15	June 1–Aug. 1	(2)	(2)
Peas, black-eye					June 1–July 1	June 1–July 1.
Pepper [1]			June 1–June 20	June 1–July 1	June 1–July 1	June 1–July 10.
Potato	May 15–June 1	May 1–June 15	May 1–June 15	May 1–June 15	May 15–June 15	June 15–July 15.
Radish	May 1–July 15	May 1–Aug. 1	June 1–Aug. 15	July 1–Sept. 1	July 15–Sept. 15	Aug. 1–Oct. 1.
Rhubarb [1]	Sept. 1–Oct. 1	Sept. 15–Oct. 15	Sept. 15–Nov. 1	Oct. 1–Nov. 1	Oct. 15–Nov. 15	Oct. 15–Dec. 1.
Rutabaga	May 15–June 15	May 1–June 15	June 1–July 1	June 1–July 1	June 15–July 15	July 10–20.
Salsify	May 15–June 1	May 10–June 10	May 20–June 20	June 1–20	June 1–July 1	June 1–July 1.
Shallot	(2)	(2)	(2)	(2)	(2)	(2)
Sorrel	May 15–June 15	May 1–June 15	June 1–July 1	June 1–July 15	July 1–Aug. 1	July 15–Aug. 15.
Soybean				May 25–June 10	June 1–25	June 1–July 5.
Spinach	May 15–July 1	June 1–July 15	June 1–Aug. 1	July 1–Aug. 15	Aug. 1–Sept. 1	Aug. 20–Sept. 10.
Spinach, New Zealand				May 15–July 1	June 1–July 15	June 1–Aug. 1.
Squash, summer	June 10–20	June 1–20	May 15–July 1	June 1–July 1	June 1–July 15	June 1–July 20.
Squash, winter			May 20–June 10	June 1–15	June 1–July 1	June 1–July 1.
Sweet potato					May 20–June 10	June 1–15.
Tomato	June 20–30	June 10–20	June 1–20	June 1–20	June 1–20	June 1–July 1.
Turnip	May 15–June 15	June 1–July 1	June 1–July 15	June 1–Aug. 1	July 1–Aug. 1	July 15–Aug. 15.
Watermelon			May 1–June 15	May 15–June 1	June 1–June 15	June 15–July 20.

[1] **Plants.**
[2] **Generally spring-planted.**

Table 7
Latest dates, and range of dates, for safe fall planting of vegetables in the open—
Continued

Crop	Planting dates for localities in which average date of first freeze is—					
	Oct. 30	Nov. 10	Nov. 20	Nov. 30	Dec. 10	Dec. 20
Asparagus [1]	Nov. 15–Jan. 1	Dec. 1–Jan. 1				
Beans, lima	July 1–Aug. 1	July 1–Aug. 15	July 15–Sept. 1	Aug. 1–Sept. 15	Sept. 1–30	Sept. 1–Oct. 1.
Beans, snap	July 1–Aug. 15	July 1–Sept. 1	July 1–Sept. 10	Aug. 15–Sept. 20	Sept. 1–30	Sept. 1–Nov. 1.
Beet	Aug. 1–Sept. 1	Aug. 1–Oct. 1	Sept. 1–Dec. 1	Sept. 1–Dec. 15	Sept. 1–Dec. 31	Sept. 1–Dec. 31.
Broccoli, sprouting	July 1–Aug. 15	Aug. 1–Sept. 1	Aug. 1–Sept. 15	Aug. 1–Oct. 1	Aug. 1–Nov. 1	Sept. 1–Dec. 31.
Brussels sprouts	July 1–Aug. 15	Aug. 1–Sept. 1	Aug. 1–Sept. 15	Aug. 1–Oct. 1	Aug. 1–Nov. 1	Sept. 1–Dec. 31.
Cabbage [1]	Aug. 1–Sept. 1	Sept. 1–15	Sept. 1–Dec. 1	Sept. 1–Dec. 31	Sept. 1–Dec. 31	Sept. 1–Dec. 31.
Cabbage, Chinese	Aug. 1–Sept. 15	Aug. 15–Oct. 1	Sept. 1–Oct. 15	Sept. 1–Nov. 1	Sept. 1–Nov. 15	Sept. 1–Dec. 1.
Carrot	July 1–Aug. 15	Aug. 1–Sept. 1	Sept. 1–Nov. 1	Sept. 15–Dec. 1	Sept. 15–Dec. 1	Sept. 15–Dec. 1.
Cauliflower [1]	July 15–Aug. 15	Aug. 1–Sept. 1	Aug. 1–Sept. 15	Aug. 15–Oct. 10	Sept. 1–Oct. 20	Sept. 15–Nov. 1.
Celery [1] and celeriac	June 15–Aug. 15	July 1–Aug. 15	July 15–Sept. 1	Aug. 1–Dec. 1	Sept. 1–Dec. 31	Oct. 1–Dec. 31.
Chard	June 1–Sept. 10	June 1–Sept. 15	June 1–Oct. 1	June 1–Nov. 1	June 1–Dec. 1	June 1–Dec. 31.
Chervil and chives	(2)	(2)	Nov. 1–Dec. 31	Nov. 1–Dec. 31	Nov. 1–Dec. 31	Nov. 1–Dec. 31.
Chicory, witloof	July 1–Aug. 10	July 10–Aug. 20	July 20–Sept. 1	Aug. 15–Sept. 30	Aug. 15–Oct. 15	Aug. 15–Oct. 15.
Collards [1]	Aug. 1–Sept. 15	Aug. 15–Oct. 1	Aug. 25–Nov. 1	Sept. 1–Dec. 1	Sept. 1–Dec. 31	Sept. 1–Dec. 31.
Cornsalad	Sept. 15–Nov. 1	Oct. 1–Dec. 1	Oct. 1–Dec. 1	Oct. 1–Dec. 31	Oct. 1–Dec. 31	Oct. 1–Dec. 31.
Corn, sweet	June 1–Aug. 1	June 1–Aug. 15	June 1–Sept. 1			
Cress, upland	Sept. 15–Nov. 1	Oct. 1–Dec. 1	Oct. 1–Dec. 1	Oct. 1–Dec. 31	Oct. 1–Dec. 31	Oct. 1–Dec. 31.
Cucumber	June 1–Aug. 1	June 1–Aug. 15	June 1–Aug. 15	July 15–Sept. 15	Aug. 15–Oct. 1	Aug. 15–Oct. 1.
Eggplant [1]	June 1–July 1	June 1–July 15	June 1–Aug. 1	July 1–Sept. 1	Aug. 1–Sept. 30	Aug. 1–Sept. 30.
Endive	July 15–Aug. 15	Aug. 1–Sept. 1	Sept. 1–Oct. 1	Sept. 1–Nov. 15	Sept. 1–Dec. 31	Sept. 1–Dec. 31.
Fennel, Florence	July 1–Aug. 1	July 15–Aug. 15	Aug. 15–Sept. 15	Sept. 1–Nov. 15	Sept. 1–Dec. 1	Sept. 1–Dec. 1.
Garlic	(2)	Aug. 1–Oct. 1	Aug. 15–Oct. 1	Sept. 1–Nov. 15	Sept. 15–Nov. 15	Sept. 15–Nov. 15.
Horseradish [1]	(2)	(2)	(2)	(2)	(2)	(2)
Kale	July 15–Sept. 1	Aug. 1–Sept. 15	Aug. 15–Oct. 15	Sept. 1–Dec. 1	Sept. 1–Dec. 31	Sept. 1–Dec. 31.
Kohlrabi	Aug. 1–Sept. 1	Aug. 15–Sept. 15	Sept. 1–Oct. 15	Sept. 1–Dec. 1	Sept. 15–Dec. 31	Sept. 1–Dec. 31.
Leek	(2)	(2)	Sept. 1–Nov. 1	Sept. 1–Nov. 1	Sept. 1–Nov. 1	Sept. 15–Nov. 1
Lettuce, head [1]	Aug. 1–Sept. 15	Aug. 15–Oct. 15	Sept. 1–Nov. 1	Sept. 1–Dec. 1	Sept. 15–Dec. 31	Sept. 15–Dec. 31.
Lettuce, leaf	Aug. 15–Oct. 1	Aug. 25–Oct. 1	Sept. 1–Nov. 1	Sept. 1–Dec. 1	Sept. 15–Dec. 31	Sept. 15–Dec. 31.
Muskmelon	July 1–July 15	July 15–July 30				
Mustard	Aug. 15–Oct. 15	Aug. 15–Nov. 1	Sept. 1–Dec. 1	Sept. 1–Dec. 1	Sept. 1–Dec. 1	Sept. 15–Dec. 1.
Okra	June 1–Aug. 10	June 1–Aug. 20	June 1–Sept. 10	June 1–Sept. 20	Aug. 1–Oct. 1	Aug. 1–Oct. 1.
Onion [1]		Sept. 1–Oct. 15	Oct. 1–Dec. 31	Oct. 1–Dec. 31	Oct. 1–Dec. 31	Oct. 1–Dec. 31.
Onion, seed			Sept. 1–Nov. 1	Sept. 1–Nov. 1	Sept. 1–Nov. 1	Sept. 15–Nov. 1.
Onion, sets		Oct. 1–Dec. 1	Nov. 1–Dec. 31	Nov. 1–Dec. 31	Nov. 1–Dec. 31	Nov. 1–Dec. 31.
Parsley	Aug. 1–Sept. 15	Sept. 1–Nov. 15	Sept. 1–Dec. 31	Sept. 1–Dec. 31	Sept. 1–Dec. 31	Sept. 1–Dec. 31.
Parsnip	(2)	(2)	Aug. 1–Sept. 1	Sept. 1–Nov. 15	Sept. 1–Dec. 1	Sept. 1–Dec. 1.
Peas, garden	Aug. 1–Sept. 15	Sept. 1–Nov. 1	Oct. 1–Dec. 1	Oct. 1–Dec. 31	Oct. 1–Dec. 31	Oct. 1–Dec. 31.
Peas, black-eye	June 1–Aug. 1	June 15–Aug. 15	July 1–Sept. 1	July 1–Sept. 10	July 1–Sept. 20	July 1–Sept. 20.
Pepper [1]	June 1–July 20	June 1–Aug. 1	June 1–Aug. 15	June 15–Sept. 1	Aug. 15–Oct. 1	Aug. 15–Oct. 1.
Potato	July 20–Aug. 10	July 25–Aug. 20	Aug. 10–Sept. 15	Aug. 1–Sept. 15	Aug. 1–Sept. 15	Aug. 1–Sept. 15.
Radish	Aug. 15–Oct. 15	Sept. 1–Nov. 15	Sept. 1–Dec. 1	Sept. 1–Dec. 31	Aug. 1–Sept. 15	Oct. 1–Dec. 31.
Rhubarb [1]	Nov. 1–Dec. 1					
Rutabaga	July 15–Aug. 1	July 15–Aug. 15	Aug. 1–Sept. 1	Sept. 1–Nov. 15	Oct. 1–Nov. 15	Oct. 15–Nov. 15.
Salsify	June 1–July 10	June 15–July 20	July 15–Aug. 15	Aug. 15–Sept. 30	Aug. 15–Oct. 15	Sept. 1–Oct. 31.
Shallot	(2)	Aug. 1–Oct. 1	Aug. 15–Oct. 1	Aug. 15–Oct. 15	Sept. 15–Nov. 1	Sept. 15–Nov. 1.
Sorrel	Aug. 1–Sept. 15	Aug. 15–Oct. 1	Aug. 15–Oct. 15	Sept. 1–Nov. 15	Sept. 1–Dec. 15	Sept. 1–Dec. 31.
Soybean	June 1–July 15	June 1–July 25	June 1–July 30	June 1–July 30	June 1–July 30	June 1–July 30.
Spinach	Sept. 1–Oct. 1	Sept. 15–Nov. 1	Oct. 1–Dec. 1	Oct. 1–Dec. 31	Oct. 1–Dec. 31	Oct. 1–Dec. 31.
Spinach, New Zealand	June 1–Aug. 1	June 1–Aug. 15	June 1–Aug. 15			
Squash, summer	June 1–Aug. 1	June 1–Aug. 10	June 1–Aug. 20	June 1–Sept. 1	June 1–Sept. 15	June 1–Oct. 1.
Squash, winter	June 10–July 10	June 20–July 20	July 1–Aug. 1	July 15–Aug. 15	Aug. 1–Sept. 1	Aug. 1–Sept. 1.
Sweet potato	June 1–15	June 1–July 1	June 1–July 1	June 1–July 1	June 1–July 1	June 1–July 1.
Tomato	June 1–July 1	June 1–July 15	June 1–Aug. 1	Aug. 1–Sept. 1	Aug. 15–Oct. 1	Sept. 1–Nov. 1.
Turnip	Aug. 1–Sept. 15	Sept. 1–Oct. 15	Sept. 1–Nov. 15	Sept. 1–Nov. 15	Oct. 1–Dec. 1	Oct. 1–Dec. 31.
Watermelon	July 1–July 15	July 15–July 30				

[1] Plants.
[2] Generally spring-planted.

MEAN DATE OF FIRST 32° (F.) TEMPERATURE IN AUTUMN

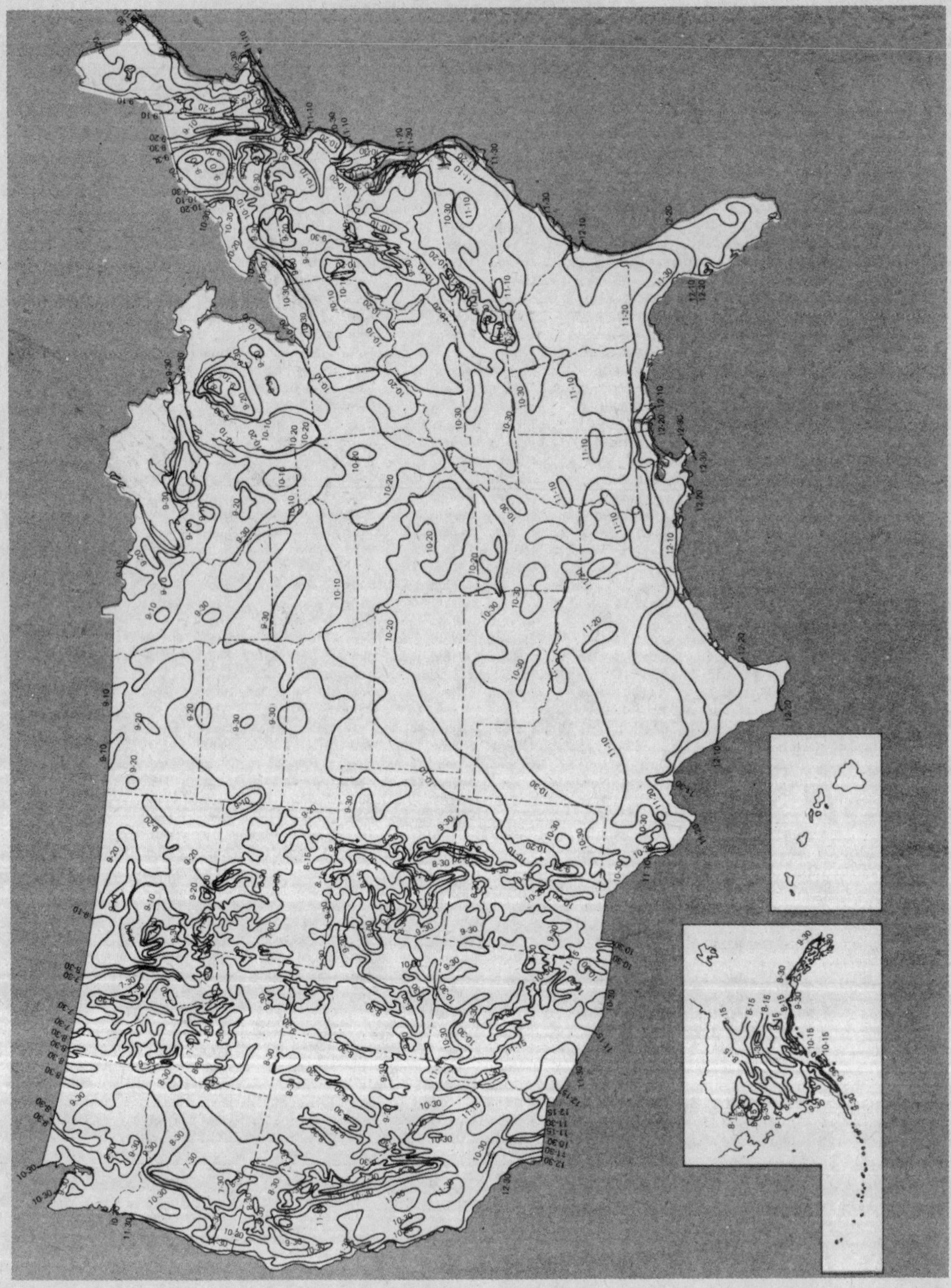

Average dates of first killing frost in autumn

Black plastic film conserves moisture, controls weeds, warms the soil, and hastens maturity of vegetable crops.

roots that lie near the surface. Although it is desirable to keep the surface soil loose, there is little to be gained by hoeing or cultivating oftener than necessary to keep weeds out of the garden.

In small gardens, weeds can be controlled with black polyethylene mulch supplemented by hand weeding such as pulling, hoeing and wheel hoeing. Mulching vegetable crops with organic material also is a common practice in small gardens.

The best organic mulches are partially decomposed hay, straw or grass clippings. The mulch should be applied 4 to 6 inches deep when the plants are about 6 inches tall. Cabbage, tomato and other transplants usually are tall enough soon after they are set in the garden. Before applying mulch, hoe out all small weeds. Not only does mulch control weeds, it also conserves moisture, keeps the soil from packing and increases the humus necessary for vigorous plant growth.

Controlling Diseases and Insects

Garden crops are subject to attack by a number of diseases and insects. Preventive measures are best, but if an attack occurs and the gardener is not familiar with the insect or disease and the proper treatment to protect his crop, he is advised to consult the county agent or write immediately to his experiment station.

Among the most important disease-control measures are the use of disease-free seeds and plants, and the use of disease-resistant varieties. Great progress has been made within recent years in the development of varieties that are resistant to certain diseases.

GROWING SPECIFIC VEGETABLES

Perennial Vegetables

The larger vegetable gardens need a number of perennials. Asparagus, horseradish and rhubarb are the most important, but chives, bottom-multiplier onions and some of the flavoring and condiment plants, chiefly sage and mint, are also desirable. Unfortunately, asparagus, horseradish and rhubarb are not adapted to conditions in the lower South.

All the perennial crops should be grouped together along one side of the garden where they will not interfere with work on the annual crops.

ASPARAGUS

Asparagus is among the earliest of spring vegetables. An area about 20 feet square, or a row 50 to 75 feet long, will supply plenty of fresh asparagus for a family of five or six persons, provided the soil is well enriched and the plants are given good attention. More must be planted if a supply is to be canned or frozen.

Asparagus does best where winters are cold enough to freeze the ground to a depth of a few inches at least. In many southern areas the plants make a weak growth, producing small shoots. Elevation has some effect, but, in general, the latitude of south-central Georgia is the southern limit of profitable culture.

The crop can be grown on almost any well-drained, fertile soil, and there is little possibility that the soil will be too rich, especially through the use of manure. Loosen the soil far down, either by subsoil plowing or by deep spading before planting. Throw the topsoil aside and spade manure, leaf mold, rotted leaves or peat into the subsoil to a depth of 14 to 16 inches; then mix from 5 to 10 pounds of a complete fertilizer into each 75-foot row or 20-foot bed.

When the soil is ready for planting, the bottom of the trench should be about 6 inches below the natural level of the soil. After the crowns are set and covered to a depth of an inch or two, gradually work the soil into the trench around the plants during the first season. When set in beds, asparagus plants should be at least 1½ feet apart each way; when set in rows, they should be about 1½ feet apart with the rows from 4 to 5 feet apart.

Asparagus plants, or crowns, are grown from seed. The use of one-year-old plants only is recommended. These should have a root spread of at least 15 inches, and larger ones are better. The home gardener will usually find it best to buy his plants from a grower who has a good strain of a recognized variety. 'Mary Washington' and 'Waltham Washington' are good varieties that have the added merit of being rust resistant. 'Waltham Washington' is an improved strain of 'Mary Washington'. It contains very little of the purple overcast predominant in the 'Mary Washington', is a high yielder and has good green color clear into the ground line. In procuring asparagus crowns, it is always well to be sure that they have not been allowed to dry out.

Clean cultivation encourages vigorous growth; it behooves the gardener to keep his asparagus clean from the start. In a large farm garden, with long rows, most of the work can be done with a horse-drawn cultivator or a garden tractor. In a small garden where the rows are short or the asparagus is planted in beds, however, hand work in necessary.

For a 75-foot row, an application of manure and 6 to 8 pounds of a high-grade complete fertilizer once each year are recommended. Manure and other fertilizer may be applied either before or after the cutting season.

Remove no shoots the year the plants are set in the permanent bed, keep the cutting period short the year after setting. Remove all shoots during the cutting season in subsequent years. Cease cutting about July 1 to 10 and let the tops grow. In the autumn, remove and burn the dead tops.

Asparagus rust and asparagus beetles are the chief enemies of the crop.

HORSERADISH

Horseradish is adapted to the north temperate regions of the United States, but not to the South, except possibly in the high altitudes.

Any good soil except possibly the lightest sands and heaviest clays, will grow horseradish, but it does best on a deep, rich, moist loam that is well supplied with organic matter. Avoid shallow soil; it produces rough, prongy roots. Mix organic matter with the soil a few months before the plants or cuttings are set. Some fertilizer may be used at the time of planting and more during the subsequent seasons. A top dressing of organic matter each spring is advisable.

Horseradish is propagated either by crowns or by root cuttings. In propagating by crowns, a portion of an old plant consisting of a piece of root and crown buds is merely lifted and planted in a new place. Root cuttings are pieces of older roots 6 to 8 inches long and of the thickness of a lead pencil. They may be saved when preparing the larger roots for grating, or they may be purchased from seedsmen. A trench 4 or 5 inches deep is opened with a hoe and the root cuttings are placed at an angle, with their tops near the surface of the ground. Plants from these cuttings usually make good roots the first year. As a rule, the plants in the home garden are allowed to grow from year to year, and portions of the roots are removed as needed. Pieces of roots and crowns remaining in the soil are usually sufficient to re-establish the plants.

There is very little choice in the matter of varieties of horseradish. Be sure, however, to obtain good healthy planting stock of a strain that is giving good results in the area where it is being grown. 'New Bohemian' is perhaps the best known sort sold by American seedsmen.

RHUBARB

Rhubarb thrives best in regions having cool, moist summers and winters cold enough to freeze the ground to a depth of several inches. It is not adapted to most parts of the South, but in certain southern areas of higher elevation it does fairly well. A few hills along the garden fence will supply all that a family can use.

Any deep, well-drained, fertile soil is suitable for rhubarb. Spade the soil or plow it to a depth of 12 to 16 inches and mix in rotted manure, leaf mold, decayed hardwood leaves, sods or other form of organic matter. The methods of soil preparation suggested for asparagus are suitable for rhubarb. As rhubarb is planted in hills 3 to 4 feet apart, however, it is usually sufficient to prepare each hill separately.

Rhubarb plants may be started from seed and transplanted, but seedlings vary from the parent plant. The usual method of starting the plants is to obtain pieces of crowns from established hills and set them in prepared hills. Top-dress the planting with a heavy application of organic matter in either early spring or late fall. Organic matter applied over the hills during early spring greatly hastens growth, or forces the plant.

A pound of complete commercial fertilizer high in nitrogen applied around each hill every year ensures an abundant supply of plant food. The plants can be mulched with green grass or weeds.

Remove seed stalks as soon as they form. No leaf stems should be harvested before the second year and but few until the third. Moreover, the harvest season must be largely confined to early spring. The hills should be divided and reset every seven or eight years. Otherwise, they become too thick and produce only slender stems.

'Crimson', 'Red Valentine', 'MacDonald', 'Canada Red', and 'Victoria' are standard varieties. Use only the leaf stalk as a food. *Rhubarb leaves contain injurious substances, including oxalic acid. Never use them for food.*

SORREL

Sorrel is a perennial that is usually started from seeds. It requires a rich, mellow, well-drained soil. Rows may be of any convenient distance apart. Thin the plants to about 8 inches apart in the rows. If the leaves alone are gathered and the plants are cultivated to prevent the growth of weeds, a planting should last three or four years. 'French Broad Leaf' is a well-known variety.

Greens

Greens are usually the leaves and leaf stems of immature plants, which in their green state are boiled for food. Young, tender branches of certain plants, New Zealand spinach, for example, are also used this way. All the plants treated here as greens, except New Zealand spinach, are hardy vegetables, most of them adapted to fall sowing and winter culture over the entire South and in the more temperate parts of the North. Their culture may be extended more widely in the North by growing them with some protection, such as mulching or frames.

CHARD

Chard, or Swiss Chard, is a type of beet that has been developed for its tops instead of its roots. Crop after crop of the outer leaves may be harvested without injuring the plant. Only one planting is necessary, and a row 30 to 40 feet long will supply a family for the entire summer. Each seed cluster contains several seeds, and fairly wide spacing of the seeds facilitates thinning. The culture of chard is practically the same as that of beets, but the plants grow larger and need to be thinned to at least 6 inches apart in the row. Chard needs a rich, mellow soil, and it is sensitive to soil acidity.

CHICORY, WITLOOF

Witloof Chicory, or French Endive, is grown for both roots and tops. It is a hardy plant, not especially sensitive to heat or cold. It does, however, need a deep, rich, loamy soil without too much organic matter. The tops are sometimes harvested while young. The roots are lifted in autumn and placed in a box or bed of moist soil in a warm cellar for forcing. They must be covered with a few inches of sand. Under this covering the leaves form in a solid head, known on the market as witloof.

The culture of chicory is simple. Sow the seeds in spring or early summer in drills about 18 inches apart. Later, thin the plants to 6 or 8 inches apart in the rows. If sown too early the plants shoot to seed and are worthless for forcing. The kind known as witloof is most generally used.

COLLARDS

Collards are grown and used somewhat like cabbage. They withstand heat better than other members of the cabbage group, and are well liked in the South for both summer and winter use. Collards do not form a true head, but a large rosette of leaves, which may be blanched by tying the leaves together.

CORNSALAD

Cornsalad is also known as Lamb's-Lettuce and Fetticus. Sow the seed in early spring in drills and cultivate the plants the same as lettuce or mustard. For an extra-early crop, plant the seed in the autumn and cover the plants lightly through the winter. In the southern states the covering is not necessary, and there the plants are ready for use in February and March. The leaves are frequently used in their natural green state, but they may be blanched by covering the rows with anything that will exclude light.

KALE

Kale, or Borecole, is hardy and lives over winter in latitudes as far north as northern Maryland and southern Pennsylvania and other areas where similar winter conditions prevail. It is also resistant to heat and may be grown in summer. Its real merit, however, is its use as cool-weather greens.

Kale is a member of the cabbage family. The best garden varieties are low-growing, spreading plants, with thick, more-or-less crinkled leaves. 'Vates Blue Curled', 'Dwarf Blue Scotch', and 'Siberian' are well-known garden varieties.

No other plant is so well adapted to fall sowing

throughout a wide area of both North and South or in areas characterized by winters of moderate severity. Kale may well follow some such early-season vegetable as green beans, potatoes or peas.

In the autumn the seed may be broadcast very thinly and then lightly raked into the soil. Except for spring sowings, made when weeds are troublesome, sow kale in rows 18 to 24 inches apart and later thin the plants to about 1 foot apart.

Kale may be harvested either by cutting the entire plant or by taking the larger leaves while young. Old kale is tough and stringy.

MUSTARD

Mustard grows well on almost any good soil. As the plants require but a short time to reach the proper stage for use, frequent sowings are recommended. Sow the seeds thickly in drills as early as possible in the spring or, for late use, in September or October. The forms of Indian mustard, the leaves of which are often curled and frilled, are generally used. 'Southern Curled' and 'Green Wave' are common sorts.

NEW ZEALAND SPINACH

New Zealand Spinach is not related to common spinach. It is a large plant, with thick, succulent leaves and stems, and grows with a branching, spreading habit to a height of 2 or more feet. It thrives in hot weather and is grown as a spinach substitute in seasons when ordinary spinach cannot withstand the heat. New Zealand spinach thrives on soils suitable for common spinach. Because of their larger size, these plants must have more room. The rows should be at least 3 feet apart, with the plants about 1½ feet apart in the rows. As prompt germination may be difficult, the seeds should be soaked for one or two hours in water at 120° F. before being planted. They may be sown, 1 to 1½ inches deep, as soon as danger of frost is past. Successive harvests of the tips may be made from a single planting, as new leaves and branches are readily produced. Care must be taken not to remove too large a portion of the plant at one time.

SPINACH

Spinach is a hardy cool-weather plant that withstands winter conditions in the South. In most of the North, spinach is primarily an early-spring and late-fall crop, but in some areas, where summer temperatures are mild, it may be grown continuously from early spring until late fall. It should be emphasized that summer and winter culture of spinach is possible only where moderate temperatures prevail.

Spinach will grow on almost any well-drained, fertile soil where sufficient moisture is available. It is very sensitive to acid soil. If a soil test shows the need for less acidity, apply lime to the part of the garden used for spinach, regardless of the treatment given the rest of the area.

The application of 100 pounds of rotted manure and 3 to 4 pounds of commercial fertilizer to each 100 square feet of land is suitable for spinach in the home garden. Broadcast both manure and fertilizer and work them in before sowing the seed.

'Long Standing Bloomsdale' is perhaps the most popular variety seeded in spring. It is attractive, grows quickly, is very productive, and will stand for a moderate length of time before going to seed. 'Virginia Savoy' and Hybrid No. 7 are valuable varieties for fall planting, as they are resistant to yellows, or blight. Hybrid No. 7 is also resistant to downy mildew (blue mold). These two varieties are very cold-hardy but are not suitable for the spring crop, as they produce seed stalks too early. For horse or tractor cultivation, the rows of the garden should be not less than 24 inches apart; when land is plentiful they may be 30 inches apart. For wheel hoe or hand work, the rows should be 14 to 16 inches apart. Spinach may be drilled by hand in furrows about 1 inch deep and covered with fine earth not more than ½ inch deep, or it may be drilled with a seed drill, which distributes the seed more evenly than is ordinarily possible by hand. Thin the plants to 3 or 4 inches apart before they crowd in the row.

TURNIP GREENS

Varieties of Turnips usually grown for the roots are also planted for the greens. 'Shogrin' is a favorable variety for greens. It is resistant to aphid damage and produces fine-quality white roots if allowed to grow. 'Seven Top' is a leafy sort that produces no edible root. As a rule, sow turnips to be used for greens thickly and then thin them, leaving all but the greens to develop as a root crop. Turnip greens are especially adapted to winter and early-spring culture in the South. The cultural methods employed are the same as those for turnip and rutabaga roots (see page 287).

Salad Vegetables

The group known as salad crops includes vegetables that are usually eaten raw with salt, pepper, vinegar, and salad oil, or with mayonnaise or other dressings. This classification is entirely one of convenience; some vegetables not included in this group are used in the same way. Some members of this class may be cooked and used as greens.

CELERY

Celery can be grown in home gardens in most parts of the country at some time during the year. It is a cool-weather crop and adapted to winter culture in the lower South. In the upper South and in the North it may be grown either as an early-spring or as a late-fall crop. Farther north in certain favored locations it can be grown throughout the summer.

Rich, moist but well-drained, deeply prepared, mellow soil is essential for celery. As long as these requirements are met, soil varying from sand to clay loam and to peat may be used. Unless the ground is very fertile, plenty of organic material supplemented by liberal applications of commercial fertilizer is necessary. For a 100-foot row of celery, 5 pounds of a high-grade complete fertilizer thoroughly mixed with the soil are none too much. Prepare the celery row a week or two before setting the plants.

The most common mistake with celery is failure to allow enough time for growing the plants. About ten weeks are needed to grow good celery plants. Celery seed is small and germinates slowly. A good method is to place the seeds in a muslin bag and soak them overnight, then mix them with dry sand, distribute them in shallow trenches in the seed flats or seedbed, and cover them with leaf mold or similar material to a depth of not more than ½ inch. Keep the bed covered with moist burlap sacks. Celery plants are very delicate and must be kept free from weeds. They are made more stocky by being transplanted once before they are set in the garden, but this practice retards their growth. When they are to be transplanted before being set in the ground, the rows in the seed box or seedbed may be only a few inches apart. When they are to remain in the box until transplanted to the garden, however, the plants should be about 2 inches apart each way. In beds, the rows should be 10 to 12 inches apart, with seedlings 1 to 1½ inches apart in the row.

For hand culture, celery plants are set in rows 18 to 24 inches apart; for tractor cultivation, 30 to 36 inches apart. The plants are spaced about 6 inches in the row. Double rows are about 1 foot apart. Set celery on a cool or cloudy day, if possible; and if the soil is at all dry, water the plants thoroughly. If the plants are large, it is best to pinch off the outer leaves 3 or 4 inches from the base before setting. In bright weather it is well also to shade the plants for a day or two after they are set. Small branches bearing green leaves, stuck in the ground, protect the plants from intense sun without excluding air. As soon as the plants attain some size, gradually work the soil around them to keep them upright. Be careful to get no soil into the hearts of the plants. Early celery is blanched by excluding the light with boards, paper, drain tiles or other devices. Late celery may be blanched also by banking with earth or by storing in the dark. But banking celery with soil in warm weather causes it to decay.

Late celery may be kept for early-winter use by banking with earth and covering the tops with leaves or straw to keep them from freezing, or it may be dug and stored in a cellar or a coldframe, with the roots well embedded in moist soil. While in storage it must be kept as cool as possible without freezing.

For the home garden 'Golden Detroit', 'Summer Pascal' ('Waltham Improved'), and 'Golden Plume' are adapted for the early crop to be used during late summer, fall, and early winter. For storage and for use after the holiday season, it is desirable to plant some such variety as 'Green Light' or 'Utah 52–70'.

ENDIVE

Endive closely resembles lettuce in its requirements, except that it is less sensitive to heat. It may be substituted for lettuce when the culture of lettuce is impracticable. In the South, it is mainly a winter crop. In the North, it is grown in spring, summer and autumn and is also forced in winter. 'Full Heart Batavian' and 'Salad King' are good varieties. Broadleaved endive is known on the markets as escarole.

Cultural details are the same as those for head lettuce. When the plants are large and well formed, draw the leaves together and tie them so that the heart will blanch. For winter use, lift the plants with a ball of earth, place them in a cellar or coldframe where they will not freeze, and tie and blanch them as needed.

LETTUCE

Lettuce can be grown in any home garden. It is a cool-weather crop, being as sensitive to heat as any vegetable grown. In the South, lettuce culture is confined to late fall, winter and spring. In colder parts of the South, lettuce may not live through the winter. In the North, lettuce culture is limited for practical purposes to spring and autumn. In some favored locations, such as areas of high altitude or in far-northern latitudes, lettuce grows to perfection in summer. Planting at the wrong season is responsible for most of the failures with this crop.

Any rich soil is adapted to lettuce, although the plant is sensitive to acid soil. A commercial fertilizer with a heavy proportion of phosphorus is recommended.

Start spring lettuce indoors or in a hotbed and transplant it to the garden when the plants have four or five leaves. Gardeners need not wait for the end of light frosts, as lettuce is not usually harmed by a temperature as low as 28° F., if the plants have been properly hardened. Allow about six weeks for growing the plants. For the fall crop the seed may be sown directly in the row and thinned; there is no gain in transplanting.

For tractor cultivation, set lettuce plants 12 to 15 inches apart in rows 30 to 36 inches apart; for hand culture, about 14 to 16 inches apart each way. Where gardeners grow leaf lettuce, or desire merely the leaves and not well-developed heads, the spacing in the rows may be much closer. In any case it is usually best to cut the entire plant instead of removing the leaves.

There are many excellent varieties of lettuce, all of which do well in the garden when conditions are right. Of the loose-leaf kinds, 'Black-Seeded Simpson', 'Grand Rapids', 'Slobolt' and 'Saladbowl' are among the best. 'Saladbowl' and 'Slobolt' are heat resistant and very desirable for warm-weather culture. Of the heading sorts, 'Buttercrunch', 'White Boston', 'Fulton', and 'Great Lakes' are among the best. The 'White Boston' requires less time than the three others. Where warm weather comes early, it is seldom worth while to sow head-lettuce seed in the open ground in the spring with the expectation of obtaining firm heads.

PARSLEY

Parsley is hardy to cold but sensitive to heat. It thrives under much the same temperature conditions as kale, lettuce and spinach. If given a little protection it may be carried over winter through most of the North.

Parsley thrives on any good soil. As the plant is delicate during its early stages of growth, however, the land should be mellow.

Parsley seeds are small and germinate slowly. Soaking in water overnight hastens the germination. In the North, it is a good plan to sow the seeds indoors and transplant the plants to the garden, thereby getting a crop before hot weather. In the South, it is usually possible to sow the seed directly in drills. For the fall crop in the North, row seeding is also practiced. After seeding, it is well to lay a board over the row for a few days until the first seedlings appear. After its removal, day-to-day watering will ensure germination of as many seeds as possible. Parsley rows should be 14 to 16 inches apart, with the plants 4 to 6 inches apart in the rows. A few feet will supply the family, and a few plants transplanted to the coldframe in the autumn will give a supply during early spring.

UPLAND CRESS

Upland Cress, sometimes erroneously called peppergrass, is a hardy plant. It may be sown in all the milder parts of the country in autumn. In the colder sections it is sown in early spring as soon as the ground can be worked. The seeds are small and must not be covered deeply. After the plants are well established, thin them to 4 to 6 inches apart in the rows. This is a short-season crop that should be planted in quick succession to ensure a steady supply.

Root Vegetables

Potatoes in the North and sweet potatoes in the South are grown in almost every garden. Beets, carrots and turnips are also widely grown in gardens. The vegetables in this group may be used throughout the growing season and also be kept for winter.

BEETS

The Beet is well adapted to all parts of the country. It is fairly tolerant of heat; it is also resistant to cold. However, it will not withstand severe freezing. In the northern states, where winters are too severe, the beet is grown in spring, summer and autumn.

Beets are sensitive to strongly acid soils, and it is wise to apply lime if a test shows the need for it. Good beet quality depends on quick growth; for this the land must be fertile, well drained and in good physical condition.

Midsummer heat and drought may interfere with seed germination. By covering the seeds with sandy soil, leaf mold or other material that will not bake, and by keeping the soil damp until the plants are up, much of this trouble can be avoided. Make successive sowings at intervals of about three weeks in order to have a continuous supply of young, tender beets throughout the season.

Where cultivating is by hand, the rows may be about 16 inches apart; where it is by tractor, they must be wider. Beet seed as purchased consists of small balls, each containing several seeds. On most soils the seed should be covered to a depth of about 1 inch. After the plants are well established, thin them to stand 2 to 3 inches apart in the rows.

'Early Wonder', 'Crosby Egyptian' and 'Detroit Dark Red' are standard varieties suitable for early home-garden planting, while 'Long Season' remains tender and edible over a long season.

CARROTS

Carrots are usually grown in the fall, winter and spring in the South, providing an almost continuous supply. In the North, carrots can be grown and used through the summer and the surplus stored for winter. Carrots will grow on almost any type of soil as long as it is moist, fertile, loose and free from clods and stones, but sandy loams and peats are best. Use commercial fertilizer.

Because of their hardiness, carrots may be seeded as early in the spring as the ground can be worked. Succession plantings at intervals of three weeks will ensure a continuous supply of tender carrots. Cover carrot seed about ½ inch on most soils; less, usually about ¼ inch, on heavy soils. With care in seeding, little thinning is necessary; carrots can stand some crowding, especially on loose soils. However, they should be no thicker than ten to 15 plants per foot of row.

'Chantenay', 'Nantes' and 'Imperator' are standard varieties. Carrots should be stored before hard frosts occur; otherwise the roots may be injured by cold.

CELERIAC

Celeriac, or Turnip-rooted Celery, has been developed for the root instead of the top. Its culture is the same as that of celery, and the enlarged roots can be used at any time after they are big enough. The late-summer crop of celeriac may be stored for winter use. In areas having mild winters the roots may be left in the ground and covered with a mulch of several inches of straw or leaves, or they may be lifted, packed in moist sand and stored in a cool cellar.

CHERVIL

Chervil comes in two distinct types, Salad Chervil and Turnip-rooted Chervil. Salad chervil is grown somewhat like parsley. The seeds must be bedded in damp sand for a few weeks before being sown; otherwise, their germination is very slow.

Turnip-rooted chervil thrives in practically all parts of the country where the soil is fertile and the moisture sufficient. In the South, the seeds are usually sown in the fall, but they may not germinate until spring. In the North, the seeds may be sown in the autumn to germinate in the spring; or the plants may be started indoors in later winter and transplanted to open ground later on. The spacing and culture of chervil are about the same as for beets and carrots.

DASHEEN

The Dasheen, a large-growing plant, is related to the ordinary elephant's-ear and looks like it. It is a long-season crop, adapted for culture only in the South, where there is normally a very warm frostless season of at least seven months. It needs a rich loamy soil, an abundance of moisture with good drainage, and a fairly moist atmosphere. Small tubers—from 2 to 5 ounces in weight—are used for planting in much the same way as potatoes. Planting may be done two or three weeks before frosts are over, and the season may be lengthened by starting the plants indoors and setting them out after frost is past. Set the plants in 3½- to 4-foot rows, about 2 feet apart in the rows. Dasheen tubers may be dug and dried on the ground in much the same way as sweet potatoes, and stored at 50° F. with ventilation.

PARSNIPS

The Parsnip is adapted to culture over a wide portion of the United States. It must have warm soil and weather at planting time, but does not thrive in midsummer in the South.

In many parts of the South, parsnips are grown and used during early summer. They should not reach maturity during midsummer, however. Furthermore, it is difficult to obtain good germination in the summer, which limits their culture during the autumn.

Any deep, fertile soil will grow parsnips, but light, friable soil, with no tendency to bake, is best. Stony or lumpy soils are objectionable; they may cause rough, prongy roots.

Parsnip seed must be fresh—not more than a year old—and it is well to sow rather thickly and thin to about 3 inches apart. Parsnips germinate slowly, but it is possible to hasten germination by covering the seed with leaf mold, sand, a mixture of sifted coal ashes and soil, peat or some similar material that will not bake. Rolling a light soil over the row or trampling it firmly after seeding usually hastens and improves germination. 'Hollow Crown' and 'All American' are suitable varieties.

Parsnips may be dug and stored in a cellar or pit or left in the ground until used. Roots placed in cold storage gain in quality faster than those left in the ground, and freezing in the ground in winter improves the quality.

There is no basis for the belief that parsnips that remain in the ground over winter and start growth in the spring are poisonous. All reported cases of poisoning from eating so-called wild parsnips have been traced to water hemlock (*Cicuta*), which belongs to the same family and resembles the parsnip somewhat. *Be very careful to identify wild plants that look like the parsnip before using them.*

POTATOES

Potatoes, when grown under favorable conditions, are one of the most productive of all vegetables in terms of food per unit area of land.

Potatoes are a cool-season crop; they do not thrive in midsummer in the southern half of the country. Any mellow, fertile, well-drained soil is suitable for potato production. Stiff, heavy clay soils often produce misshapen tubers. Potatoes respond to a generous use of commercial fertilizer, but if the soil is too heavily limed the tubers may be scabby.

Commercial 5–8–5 or 5–8–7 mixtures applied at 1,000 to 2,000 pounds to the acre (approximately 7½ to 15 pounds to each 100-foot row) usually provide enough plant food for a heavy crop. The lower rate of application is sufficient for very fertile soils; the higher rate for less fertile ones. Commercial fertilizer can be applied at the time of planting, but it should be mixed with the soil in such a way that the seed pieces will not come in direct contact with it.

In the North, plant two types of potatoes—one to provide early potatoes for summer use, the other for storage and winter use. Early varieties include 'Irish Cobbler', 'Early Gem', 'Norland', 'Norgold Russet' and 'Superior'. Best late varieties are 'Katahdin', 'Kennebec', 'Chippewa', 'Russet Burbank', 'Sebago' and the golden nematode-resistant 'Wanseon'. 'Irish Cobbler' is the most widely adapted of the early varieties, and 'Katahdin' of the late. In the Great Plains states, 'Pontiac' and 'Red La Soda' are preferred for summer use; the 'Katahdin' and 'Russet Burbank' for winter. In the Pacific Northwest, the 'Russet Burbank', 'White Rose', 'Kennebec' and 'Early Gem' are used. In the southern states, 'Irish Cobbler', 'Red La Soda', 'Red Pontiac' and 'Pungo' are widely grown. The use of certified seed is always advisable.

In preparing seed potatoes for planting, cut them into blocky rather than wedge-shaped pieces. Each piece should be about 1½ ounces in weight and have at least one eye. Medium-sized tubers weighing 5 to 7 ounces are cut to best advantage.

Plant early potatoes as soon as weather and soil conditions permit. Fall preparation of the soil often makes it possible to plant the early crop without delay in late winter or early spring. Potatoes require two to three weeks to come up, depending on depth of planting and the temperature of the soil. In some sections the ground may freeze slightly, but this is seldom harmful unless the sprouts have emerged. Prolonged cold and wet weather after planting is likely to cause the seed pieces to rot. Hence, avoid too early planting. Young potato plants are often damaged by frost, but they usually renew their growth quickly from uninjured portions of the stems.

Do not dig potatoes intended for storage until the tops are mature. Careful handling to avoid skinning is desirable, and protection from long exposure to light is necessary to prevent their becoming green and unfit for table use. Store in a well-ventilated place where the temperature is low, 45° F. to 50° F. if possible, but where there is no danger of freezing.

RADISHES

Radishes are hardy to cold, but they cannot withstand heat. In the South they do well in autumn, winter and spring. In the North they may be grown in spring and autumn, and in sections having mild winters they may be grown in coldframes in winter. In high altitudes and in northern locations with cool summers, radishes thrive from early spring to late autumn.

Radishes are not sensitive to the type of soil so long as it is rich, moist and friable. Apply additional fertilizer when the seeds are sown; conditions must be favorable for quick growth. Radishes that grow slowly have a too-pungent flavor and are undesirable.

Radishes mature the quickest of our garden crops. They remain in prime condition only a few days, which makes small plantings at weekly or ten-day intervals advisable. A few yards of row will supply all the radishes a family will consume during the time the radishes are at their best.

There are two types of radishes—the mild, small, quick-maturing sorts such as 'Scarlet Globe', 'French Breakfast' and 'Cherry Belle', all of which reach edible size in from 20 to 40 days; and the more pungent, large winter radishes such as 'Long Black Spanish' and 'China Rose', which require 75 days or more for growth. Plant winter radishes so they will reach a desirable size in the autumn. Gather and store them like other root crops.

SALSIFY

Salsify, or Vegetable Oyster, may be grown in practically all parts of the country. It is similar to parsnips in its requirements but needs a slightly longer growing season. For this reason it cannot be grown as far north as parsnips. Salsify, however, is somewhat more hardy and can be sown earlier in the spring.

Thoroughly prepare soil for salsify to a depth of at least 1 foot. Lighten heavy garden soil by adding sand or comparable material. Salsify must have plenty of plant food.

'Sandwich Island' is the best-known variety. A half-ounce of seed will sow a 50-foot row, enough for most families. Always use fresh seed; salsify seed retains its vitality only one year.

Salsify may be left in the ground over winter or lifted and stored like parsnips or other root crops.

SWEET POTATOES

Sweet Potatoes succeed best in the South, but they are grown in home gardens as far north as southern New York and southern Michigan. They can be grown even farther north in sections having especially mild climates, such as the Pacific Northwest. In general, sweet potatoes may be grown wherever there is a frost-free period of about 150 days with relatively high temperature. 'Jersey Orange', 'Nuget' and 'Nemagold' are the commonest, dry-fleshed varieties; 'Centennial', 'Porto Rico' and 'Goldrush' are three of the best of the moist type.

A well-drained, moderately deep sandy loam of medium fertility is best for sweet potatoes. Heavy clays and very deep, loose-textured soils encourage the formation of long stringy roots. For best results the soil should be moderately fertilized throughout. If applied under the rows, the fertilizer should be well mixed with the soil.

In most of the area over which sweet potatoes are grown, it is necessary to start the plants in a hotbed because the season is too short to produce a good crop after the weather warms enough to start plants outdoors. Bed roots used for seed close together in a hotbed and cover them with about 2 inches of sand or fine soil, such as leaf mold. It is not safe to set the plants in the open ground until the soil is warm and the weather settled. Before setting the plants in the ground, ventilate the hotbed freely to harden them.

The plants are usually set on top of ridges, 3½ to 4 feet apart, with the plants about 12 inches apart in the row. When the vines have covered the ground, no further cultivation is necessary, but some additional hand weeding may be required.

Dig sweet potatoes a short time before frost, on a bright, drying day when the soil is not too wet to work easily. On a small scale they may be dug with a spading fork, great care being taken not to bruise or injure the roots. Let the roots lie exposed for two or three hours to dry thoroughly; then put them in containers and place them in a warm room to cure. The proper curing temperature is 85° F. Curing for about ten days is followed by storage at 50° to 55° F.

TURNIPS AND RUTABAGAS

Turnips and Rutabagas, similar cool-season vegetables, are among the most commonly grown and widely adapted root crops in the United States. They are grown in the South chiefly in the fall, winter and spring; in the North, largely in the spring and autumn. Rutabagas do best in the more northerly areas; turnips are better for gardens south of the latitude of Indianapolis, Indiana, or northern Virginia.

Turnips reach a good size in from 60 to 80 days, but rutabagas need about a month longer. Because they are susceptible to heat and hardy to cold, these crops should be planted as late as possible for fall use, allowing time for maturity before hard frost. In the South, turnips are very popular in the winter and spring. In the North, however, July to August seeding, following early potatoes, peas or spinach, is the common practice.

Land that has been in a heavily fertilized crop, such as early potatoes, usually gives a good crop without additional fertilizing. The soil need not be prepared deeply, but the surface should be fine and smooth. For spring culture, row planting similar to that described for beets is the best practice. The importance of planting turnips as early as possible for the spring crop is emphasized. When seeding in rows, cover the seeds lightly; when broadcasting, rake the seeds in lightly with a garden rake. A half-ounce of seed will sow a 300-foot row or broadcast 300 square feet. Turnips may be thinned as they grow, and the tops used for greens.

Although there are both white-fleshed and yellow-fleshed varieties of turnips and rutabagas, most turnips are white-fleshed and most rutabagas are yellow-fleshed. 'Purple Top White Globe' and 'Just Right' are the most popular white-fleshed varieties of turnip; 'Golden Ball' ('Orange Jelly') is the most popular yellow-fleshed variety. 'American Purple Top' is the commonly grown yellow-fleshed rutabaga; 'Sweet German' ('White Swede', 'Sweet Russian') is the most widely used white-fleshed variety. For turnip greens, the 'Seven Top' variety is most suitable. This winter-hardy variety overwinters in a majority of locations in the United States.

TURNIP-ROOTED PARSLEY

The root is the edible portion of Turnip-rooted Parsley. The flesh is whitish and dry, with much the same flavor as celeriac.

Turnip-rooted parsley requires the same climate, soil and culture as parsley. It can withstand much cold, but is difficult to start in dry, hot weather. This vegetable may remain in the ground until after hard frosts. It may be lifted and stored like other root crops.

Vine Vegetables

The vine crops, including cucumbers, muskmelons, pumpkins, squashes, watermelons and citrons, are similar in their cultural requirements. In their importance to the home gardener, they do not compare with some other groups, especially the root crops and the greens, but there is a place in most gardens for at least bush squashes and a few hills of cucumbers. They all make rank growth and require much space. In large gardens, muskmelons and watermelons are often desirable.

CUCUMBERS

Cucumbers are a warm-weather crop. They may be grown during the warmer months over a wide portion of the country but are not adapted to winter growing in any but a few of the most southerly locations. Moreover, the extreme heat of midsummer in some locations is too severe, and so cucumber culture must be limited there to spring and autumn.

The cucumber demands an exceedingly fertile,

mellow soil high in decomposed organic matter from the compost pile. Also, an additional application of organic matter and commercial fertilizer is advisable under the rows or hills. Be sure the organic matter contains no remains of any vine crops; they might carry injurious diseases. Three or four wheelbarrow loads of well-rotted organic matter and 5 pounds of commercial fertilizer to a 50-foot drill or each ten hills are enough. Mix the organic matter and fertilizer well with the top 8 to 10 inches of soil.

For an early crop, the seed may be started in berry boxes or pots, or on sods in a hotbed, and moved to the garden after danger of late frost is past. During the early growth and in cool periods, cucumbers may be covered with plant protectors made of panes of glass with a top of cheesecloth, parchment paper or muslin. A few hills will supply the needs of a family.

When the seed is planted in drills, the rows should be 6 or 7 feet apart, with the plants thinned to 2 to 3 feet apart in the rows. In the hill method of planting, the hills should be at least 6 feet apart each way, with the plants thinned to 2 in each hill. It is always wise to plant 8 or 10 seeds in each hill, thinned to the desired stand. Cover the seeds to a depth of about ½ inch. If the soil is inclined to bake, cover seeds with loose earth, such as a mixture of soil and coarse sand, or other material that will not harden and keep the plants from coming through.

When cucumbers are grown primarily for pickling, plant one of the special small-size pickling varieties, such as 'Chicago Pickling' or 'National Pickling'; if they are grown for slicing, plant such varieties as 'White Spine' or 'Straight Eight'. It is usually desirable to plant a few hills of each type; both types can be used for either purpose.

Cucumbers require almost constant vigilance to prevent destructive attacks by cucumber beetles. These insects not only eat the foliage but also spread cucumber wilt and other serious diseases.

Success in growing cucumbers depends largely on the control of diseases and insect pests that attack the crop.

Removal of the fruits before any hard seeds form materially lengthens the life of the plants and increases the size of the crop.

GOURDS

Gourds have the same general habit of growth as pumpkins and squashes and should have the same general cultural treatment, except that most species require some form of support or trellis to climb upon.

Gourds are used in making dippers, spoons, ladles, salt and sugar containers and many other kinds of household utensils. They are also used for birdhouses and the manufacture of calabash pipes. But they are of interest chiefly because of their ornamental and decorative possibilities. The thin-shelled, or hard-drying, gourds are the most durable and are the ones that most commonly serve as decorations. The thick-fleshed gourds are more in the nature of pumpkins and squashes and are almost as perishable.

A variety of gourds

The thin-shelled gourds of the *Lagenaria* group are gathered and cured at the time the shells begin to harden, the fruits become lighter in weight, and the tendrils on the vines near the gourds begin to shrivel and dry. For best results, give the gourds plenty of time to cure. Some kinds require six months or a year to cure.

The thick-shelled gourds of the *Cucurbita* group are more difficult to cure than the thin-shelled ones. Their beauty is of short duration; they usually begin to fade after three or four months.

All types of gourds should be handled carefully. Bruises discolor them and cause them to soften and decay.

MUSKMELON

The climatic, soil and cultural requirements of Muskmelons are about the same as for cucumbers, except that they are less tolerant of high humidity and rainy weather. They develop most perfectly on light-textured soils. The plants are vigorous growers and need a somewhat wider spacing than cucumbers.

'Hearts of Gold', 'Hale's Best' and Rocky Ford (the last-named a type, not a variety) are usually grown in the home garden. Where powdery mildew is prevalent, resistant varieties such as 'Gulf Stream', 'Dulce', and 'Perlita' are better adapted. 'Osage' and 'Pride of Wisconsin' (Queen of Colorado) are desirable home-garden sorts, particularly in the northern states. 'Sweet Air' (Knight) is a popular sort in the Maryland-Virginia area.

The Casaba and Honey Dew are well adapted only to the West, where they are grown under irrigation.

PUMPKIN

Pumpkins are sensitive to both cold and heat. In the North they cannot be planted until settled weather; in the South they do not thrive during midsummer.

The gardener is seldom justified in devoting any part of a limited garden area to pumpkins, because many other vegetables give greater returns from the same space. However, in gardens where there is plenty of room and where they can follow an early crop like potatoes, pumpkins can often be grown to advantage.

The pumpkin is one of the few vegetables that thrives under partial shade. Therefore it may be grown among sweet corn or other tall plants. 'Small Sugar' and 'Connecticut Field' are well-known orange-yellow-skinned varieties. 'Kentucky Field' has a grayish-orange rind with salmon flesh. All are good-quality, productive varieties.

Hills of pumpkins, containing one to two plants, should be at least 10 feet apart each way. Pumpkin plants among corn, potato or other plants usually should be spaced 8 to 10 feet apart in every third or fourth row.

Gather and store pumpkins before they are injured by hard frosts. They keep best in a well-ventilated place where the temperature is a little above 50° F.

SQUASH

Squashes are among the most commonly grown garden plants. They do well in practically all parts of the United States where the soil is fertile and moisture sufficient. Although sensitive to frost, squashes are more hardy than melons and cucumbers. In the warmest parts of the South they may be grown in winter. The use of well-rotted composted material thoroughly mixed with the soil is recommended.

There are two classes of squash varieties: summer and winter. The summer class includes the Bush Scallop, known in some places as the Cymling, the Summer Crookneck, Straightneck, and Zucchini. It also includes the vegetable marrows, of which the best known is Italian Vegetable Marrow (Cocozelle). All the summer squashes and the marrows must be used while young and tender, when the rind can be easily penetrated by the thumbnail. The winter squashes include varieties such as Hubbard, Delicious, Table Queen (Acorn), and Boston Marrow. They have hard rinds and are well adapted for storage.

Summer varieties, like yellow straightneck, should be gathered before the seeds ripen or the rinds harden, but the winter sorts will not keep unless well-matured. They should be taken in before hard frosts and stored in a dry, moderately warm place, such as on shelves in a basement with a furnace. Under favorable conditions such varieties as hubbard may be kept until midwinter.

WATERMELON

Only gardeners with a great deal of space can afford to grow Watermelons. Moreover, they are rather particular in their soil requirements, a sand or sandy loam being best. Watermelon hills should be at least 8 feet apart. The plan of mixing a half-wheelbarrow load of composted material with the soil in each hill is good, provided the compost is free from the remains of cucurbit plants that might carry diseases. A half-pound of commercial fertilizer also should be thoroughly mixed with the soil in the hill. It is a good plan to place several seeds in a ring about 1 foot in diameter in each hill. Later the plants should be thinned to two to each hill.

'New Hampshire Midget', 'Rhode Island Red', and 'Charleston Gray' are suitable varieties for the home garden. 'New Hampshire Midget' and 'Sugar Baby' are small, extra-early, widely grown, very productive varieties. The oval fruits are about 5 inches in diameter; they have crisp, red flesh and dark seeds. 'Rhode Island Red' is an early variety. The fruits are medium in size, striped and oval; they have a firm rind and bright pink-red flesh of choice quality. 'Charleston Gray' is a large, long, high-quality, gray-green watermelon with excellent keeping and shipping qualities. It is resistant to anthracnose and fusarium wilt and requires a long growing season.

The preserving type of watermelon—Citron—is not edible when raw. Its culture is the same as that for watermelon.

Legumes

Beans and peas are among our oldest and most important garden plants. The popularity of both is enhanced by their wide climatic and soil adaptation.

BEANS

Green Beans, both snap and lima, are more important than dry beans to the home gardener. Snap beans cannot be planted until the ground is thoroughly warm, but succession plantings may be made very two weeks from that time until seven or eight weeks before frost. In the lower South and Southwest, green beans may be grown during the fall, winter and spring, but they are not well adapted to midsummer. In the extreme South, beans are grown throughout the winter.

Green beans are adapted to a wide range of soils as long as the soils are well drained, resonably fertile and of such physical nature that they do not interfere with germination and emergence of the plants. Soil that has received a general application of manure and fertilizer should need no additional fertilization. When beans follow early crops that have been fertilized, the residue of this fertilizer is often sufficient for the beans.

On very heavy soils it is well to cover the planted row with sand, a mixture of sifted coal ashes and sand, peat, leaf mold or other material that will not bake. Bean seed should be covered not more than 1 inch in heavy soils and not more than 1½ inches in sandy soils. When beans are planted in hills, they may be covered with plant protectors. These covers make it possible to plant somewhat earlier.

'Tendercrop', 'Topcrop', 'Tenderette', 'Contender', 'Harvester', and 'Kinghorn Wax' are good bush varieties of snap beans. 'Dwarf Horticultural' is an outstanding green-shell bean. Brown-seeded or white-seeded 'Kentucky Wonder' are the best pole varieties for snap pods. White navy, or pea beans, white or red kidney, and the horticultural types are excellent for dry-shell purposes.

Two types of lima beans, called butter beans in the South, are grown in home gardens. Most of the more northerly parts of the United States, including the northern New England states and the northern parts of other states along the Canadian border, are not adapted to the culture of lima beans. Lima beans need a growing season of about four months with relatively high temperature; they cannot be planted safely until somewhat later than snap beans. The small butter beans mature in a shorter period than the large-seeded lima beans. The use of plant protectors over the seeds is an aid in obtaining earliness.

Fordhook 242 bush lima beans are vigorous, productive, and heat-resistant.

Lima beans may be grown on almost any fertile, well-drained, mellow soil, but it is especially desirable that the soil be light-textured and not subject to baking, as the seedlings cannot force their way through a hard crust. Covering with some material that will not bake, as suggested for other beans, is a wise precaution when soils are heavy. Lima beans need a soil somewhat richer than is necessary for kidney beans, but the excessive use of fertilizer containing a high percentage of nitrogen should be avoided.

Both the small- and large-seeded lima beans are available in pole and bush varieties. In the South, the most commonly grown lima bean varieties are 'Jackson Wonder', 'Nemagreen', 'Henderson Bush', and 'Sieva Pole'; in the North, 'Thorogreen', 'Dixie Butterpea', and 'Thaxter' are popular small-seeded bush varieties. 'Fordhook 242' is the most popular midseason large, thick-seeded bush lima bean. 'King of the Garden' and 'Challenger' are the most popular large-seeded pole lima bean varieties.

Pole beans of the kidney and lima types require some form of support, as they normally make vines several feet long. A 5-foot fence makes the best support for pole beans. A more complicated support can be prepared from 8-foot metal fence posts spaced about 4 feet apart and connected horizontally and diagonally with coarse stout twine to make a trellis. Bean plants usually require some assistance to get started on these supports. Never cultivate or handle bean plants when they are wet; to do so is likely to spread disease.

ENGLISH PEAS

English Peas are a cool-weather crop and should be planted early. In the lower South, they are grown at all seasons except summer; farther north, in spring and autumn. In the northern states and at high altitudes, they may be grown from spring until autumn, although in many places summer heat is too severe and the season is practically limited to spring. A few succession plantings may be made at ten-day intervals. The later plantings rarely yield as well as the earlier ones. Planting may be resumed as the cool weather of autumn approaches, but the yield is seldom as satisfactory as that from the spring planting.

'Alaska' and other smooth-seeded varieties are frequently used for planting in the early spring because of the supposition that they can germinate well in cold, wet soil. 'Thomas Laxton', 'Greater Progress', 'Little Marvel', 'Freezonia' and 'Giant Stride' are recommended as suitable early varieties with wrinkled seeds. 'Wanda' has considerable heat resistance. 'Alderman' and 'Lincoln' are approximately two weeks later than 'Greater Progress', but under favorable conditions yield heavily. 'Alderman' is a desirable variety for growing on brush or a trellis. Peas grown on supports are less liable to destruction by birds.

SUGAR PEAS

Sugar Peas (edible podded peas) possess the tenderness and fleshy podded qualities of snap beans and the flavor and sweetness of fresh English peas. When young, the pods are cooked like snap beans; the peas are not shelled. At this stage, pods are stringless, brittle, succulent and free of fiber or parchment. However, if the pods develop too fast, and are not good to use like snap beans, the seeds may be eaten as shelled peas, and are of the best flavor before they have reached full size. 'Dwarf Gray Sugar' is the earliest and dwarfest sugar pea. It is ideal for home gardens, especially where space is limited and seasons are short. A larger and later variety, 'Mammoth Melting Sugar', is resistant to fusarium wilt and requires support to climb upon.

BLACKEYE PEAS

Blackeye Peas, also known as Cowpeas or Southern Table Peas, are highly nutritious, tasty and easily grown. Do not plant until danger of frost has passed because they are very susceptible to cold. Leading varieties are 'Dixilee', 'Brown Crowder', 'Lady', 'Conch', 'White Acre', 'Louisiana Purchase', 'Texas Purple Hull 49', 'Knuckle Purple Hull', and 'Monarch Blackeye'. 'Dixilee' is a later variety of southern pea. Quality is excellent and it yields considerably more than the old standbys. It is also quite resistant, or at least tolerant, to nematodes. This fact alone makes it a desirable variety wherever this pest is present. 'Monarch Blackeye' is a fairly new variety of blackeye and much better adapted to southern conditions.

Heavy applications of nitrogen fertilizer should not be used for Southern table peas. Fertilize moderately with a low-nitrogen analysis such as 4–12–12.

For the effort necessary to grow them, few if any other vegetables will pay higher dividends than Southern table peas.

SOYBEANS

The soil and cultural requirements and methods of growing Soybeans are essentially the same as for bush forms of common beans. Soybeans, however, are slower growing than most garden beans, requiring three to five months for maturity, and warmer weather. They also grow taller, the larger, later varieties requiring a greater distance between rows than dwarf snap beans. Small, early varieties may be planted in rows as close as 2 feet, but the larger, later ones require 3 feet between rows. The planting dates given in Table 4 are for midseason varieties (about 120 days), neither the earliest nor the latest kinds. Differences in time of development among varieties are so great that the gardener must choose the proper variety and know its time of maturity in making plans for planting in any particular locality. 'Kanrich' and 'Giant Green' are the most widely grown varieties.

In cooler sections the rate of development will be slower. Only the early varieties should be grown in the more northerly states, and the medium or late varieties in the South. Plantings should be made principally when tomatoes and other long-season, warm-weather crops are put in the garden.

For use as a green vegetable, soybean pods should be harvested when the seeds are fully grown but before the pods turn yellow. Most varieties produce beans in usable condition over a period of a week to ten days. The green beans are difficult to remove from the pods unless the pods are boiled or steamed four to five minutes, after which they are easily shelled.

The yields per unit area of land are about the same as are usually obtained with peas, and are thus less than can be obtained with many other vegetables. On this account, they appear of major interest only to gardeners having medium-to-large gardens.

Cabbage Group

The cabbage, or cole, group of vegetables is noteworthy because of its adaptation to culture in most parts of the country having fertile soil and sufficient moisture, and because of its hardiness to cold.

BROCCOLI

Heading Broccoli is difficult to grow—therefore, only sprouting broccoli is discussed here. Sprouting broccoli forms a loose flower head (on a tall, green, fleshy, branching stalk) instead of a compact head or curd found on cauliflower or heading broccoli. It is one of the newer vegetables in American gardens, but has been grown by Europeans for hundreds of years.

Sprouting broccoli is adapted to winter culture in areas suitable for winter cabbage. It is also tolerant of heat. Spring-set plants in the latitude of Washington, D.C., have yielded good crops of sprouts until midsummer and later under conditions that caused cauliflower to fail. In the latitude of Norfolk, Virginia, the plant has yielded good crops of sprouts from December until spring.

Sprouting broccoli is grown in the same way as cabbage. Plants grown indoors in the early spring and set in the open about April 1 begin to yield sprouts about ten weeks later. The fall crop may be handled in the same way as late cabbage, except that the seed is sown later. The sprouts carrying flower buds are cut about 6 inches long, and other sprouts arise in the axils of the leaves, so that a continuous harvest may be obtained. 'Green Comet', 'Calabrese' and 'Waltham 29' are among the best-known varieties.

Sprouting broccoli with center head and side shoots

BRUSSELS SPROUTS

Brussels Sprouts are somewhat more hardy than cabbage and will live outdoors over winter in all the milder sections of the country. They may be grown as a winter crop in the South and as early and late as cabbage in the North. The sprouts, or small heads, are formed in the axils (the angle between the leaf stem and the main stalk) of the leaves. As the heads begin to crowd, break the lower leaves from the stem of the plant to give them more room. Always leave the top leaves; the plant needs them to supply nourishment. For winter use in cold areas, take up the plants that are well laden with heads and set them close together in a pit, a coldframe or a cellar, with some soil tamped around the roots. Keep the stored plants as cool as possible without freezing. 'Jade Cross', a true F_1 hybrid, has a wide range of adaptability.

CABBAGE

Cabbage ranks as one of the most important home-garden crops. In the lower South, it can be grown in all seasons except summer, and in latitudes as far north as Washington, D.C., it is frequently set in the autumn, as its extreme hardiness enables it to live over winter at relatively low temperatures and thus become one of the first spring garden crops. Farther north it can be grown as an early summer crop and as a late fall crop for storage. Cabbage can be grown throughout practically the entire United States.

Cabbage is adapted to widely different soils as long as they are fertile, of good texture and moist. It is a heavy feeder; no vegetable responds better to favorable growing conditions. Quality in cabbage is closely associated with quick growth. Both compost and commercial fertilizer should be liberally used. In addition to the applications made at planting time, a side dressing or two of nitrate of soda, sulfate of ammonia or other quickly available nitrogenous fertilizer is advisable. These may be applied sparingly to the soil around the plants at intervals of three weeks, not more than 1 pound being used to each 200 square feet of space, or, in terms of single plants, ⅓ ounce to each plant. For late cabbage the supplemental feeding with nitrates may be omitted. Good seed is especially important. Only a few seeds are needed for starting enough plants for the home garden, as two or three dozen heads of early cabbage are as many as the average family can use. Early 'Jersey Wakefield' and 'Golden Acre' are standard early sorts. 'Copenhagen Market' and 'Globe' are excellent midseason kinds. Flat Dutch and Danish Ballhead are largely used for late planting.

Where cabbage yellows is a serious disease, resistant varieties should be used. The following are a few of the wilt-resistant varieties adapted to different seasons: 'Wisconsin Hollander', for late storage; 'Wisconsin All Seasons', a kraut cabbage, somewhat earlier; 'Marion Market' and 'Globe', round-head cabbages, for midseason; and 'Stonehead' for an early, small, round-head variety.

Cabbage plants for spring setting in the North may be grown in hotbeds or greenhouses from seeding made a month to six weeks before planting time, or may be purchased from southern growers who produce them outdoors in winter. The winter-grown, hardened plants, sometimes referred to as frostproof, are hardier than hotbed plants and may be set outdoors in most parts of the North as soon as the ground can be worked in the spring. Northern gardeners can have cabbage from their gardens much earlier by using healthy southern-grown plants or well-hardened, well-grown hotbed or greenhouse plants. Late cabbage, prized by northern gardeners for fall use and for storage, is grown from plants produced in open seedbeds from sowings made about a month ahead of planting. Late cabbage may well follow early potatoes, peas, beets, spinach or other early crop. Many gardeners set cabbage plants between potato rows before the potatoes are ready to dig, thereby gaining time. In protected places, or when plant protectors are used, it is possible always to advance dates somewhat, especially if the plants are well hardened.

CHINESE CABBAGE

Chinese Cabbage is more closely related to mustard than to cabbage. It is variously called Crispy Choy, Chihili, Michili, and Wong Bok. Also, it is popularly known as Celery Cabbage, although it is unrelated to celery. The nonheading types deserve greater attention.

Chinese cabbage seems to do best as an autumn crop in the northern tier of states. When fullgrown, it is an attractive vegetable. It is not especially successful as a spring crop, and gardeners are advised not to try to grow it at any season other than fall in the North or in winter in the South.

Chinese cabbage is a desirable autumn crop in the northern states.

The plant demands a very rich, well-drained but moist soil. The seeds may be sown and the plants transplanted to the garden, or the seed may be drilled in the garden rows and the plants thinned to the desired stand.

CAULIFLOWER

Cauliflower is a hardy vegetable, but it will not withstand as much frost as cabbage. Too much warm weather keeps cauliflower from heading. In the South, its culture is limited to fall, winter and spring; in the North, to spring and fall. However, in some areas of high altitude, and when conditions are otherwise favorable, cauliflower culture is continuous throughout the summer.

A good head of cauliflower on a plant mulched with hay

Cauliflower is grown on all types of land from sands to clay and peats. Although the physical character is unimportant, the land must be fertile and well drained. Manure and commercial fertilizer are essential.

The time required for growing cauliflower plants is the same as for cabbage. In the North, the main cause of failure with cauliflower in the spring is delay in sowing the seed and setting the plants. The fall crop must be planted at such a time that it will come to the heading stage in cool weather. Snowball and Purple Head are standard varieties of cauliflower. Snow King is an extremely early variety with fair sized, compact heads of good quality; it has very short stems. Always take care to obtain a good strain of seed; poor cauliflower seed is most objectionable. The Purple Head variety, well adapted for the home garden, turns green when cooked.

A necessary precaution in cauliflower culture with all varieties except Purple Head is to tie the leaves together when the heads, or buttons, begin to form. This keeps the heads white. Cauliflower does not keep long after the heads form; one or two dozen heads are enough for the average garden in one season.

KOHLRABI

Kohlrabi is grown for its swollen stem. In the North, the early crop may be started like cabbage and transplanted to the garden, but usually it is sown in place. In the South, kohlrabi may be grown almost any time except midsummer. The seeds may be started indoors and the plants transplanted in the garden; or the seeds may be drilled in the garden rows and the plants thinned to the desired stand. Kohlrabi has about the same soil and cultural requirements as cabbage, principally a fertile soil and enough moisture. It should be harvested while young and tender. Standard varieties are 'Purple Vienna' and 'White Vienna'.

Onion Group

Practically all members of the onion group are adapted to a wide variety of soils. Some of them can be grown at one time of the year or another in any part of the country that has fertile soil and ample moisture. They require but little garden space to produce enough for a family's needs.

A pot of chives grown in a kitchen window

CHIVES

Chives are small onionlike plants that will grow in any place where onions do well. They are frequently planted as a border, but are equally well adapted to culture in rows. Being a perennial, chives should be planted where they can be left for more than one season.

Chives may be started from either seed or clumps of bulbs. Once established, some of the bulbs can be lifted and moved to a new spot. When left in the same place for several years the plants become too thick; occasionally dividing and resetting are desirable.

GARLIC

Garlic is more exacting in its cultural requirements than are onions, but it may be grown with a fair degree of success in almost any home garden where good results are obtained with onions.

Garlic is propagated by planting the small cloves, or bulbs, which make up the large bulbs. Each large bulb contains about ten small ones. Carefully separate the small bulbs and plant them singly.

The culture of garlic is practically the same as that of onions. When mature, the bulbs are pulled, dried and braided into strings or tied in bunches, which are hung in a cool, well-ventilated place.

In the South, where the crop matures early, care must be taken to keep the garlic in a cool, dry place; otherwise it spoils. In the North, where the crop matures later in the season, storage is not so difficult, but care must be taken to prevent freezing.

LEEKS

The Leek resembles the onion in its adaptability and cultural requirements. Instead of forming a bulb, it produces a thick, fleshy cylinder like a large green onion. Leeks are started from seeds, like onions. Usually the seeds are sown in a shallow trench, so that the plants can be more easily hilled up as growth proceeds. Leeks are ready for use any time after they reach the right size. Under favorable conditions they grow to 1½ inches or more in diameter, with white parts 6 to 8 inches long. They may be lifted in the autumn and stored like celery in a coldframe or a cellar.

Leeks are used for almost any purpose that onions are used for.

ONIONS

Onions thrive under a wide variety of climatic and soil conditions, but do best with an abundance of moisture and a temperate climate without extremes of heat or cold through the growing season. In the

South, the onion thrives in the fall, winter and spring. Farther north, winter temperatures may be too severe for certain types. In the North, onions are primarily a spring, summer and fall crop.

Any type of soil will grow onions, but it must be fertile, moist and in the highest state of tilth. Both compost and commercial fertilizer, especially one high in phosphorus and potash, should be applied to the onion plot. A pound of compost to each square foot of ground and 4 or 5 pounds of fertilizer to each 100 square feet are about right. The soil should be very fine and free from clods and foreign matter.

Onions may be started in the home garden by the use of sets, seedlings or seed. Sets, or small dry onions grown the previous year—preferably not more than ¾ inch in diameter—are usually employed by home gardeners. Small green plants grown in an outdoor seedbed in the South, or in a hotbed or a greenhouse, are also in general use. The home-garden culture of onions from seed is satisfactory in the North where the summers are comparatively cool.

Sets and seedlings cost about the same; seeds cost much less. In certainty of results the seedlings are best; practically none form seed stalks. Seed-sown onions are uncertain unless conditions are extremely favorable.

Several distinct types of onions may be grown. The Potato (Multiplier) and Top (Tree) onions are planted in the fall or early spring for use while green. 'Yellow Bermuda', 'Granex', and 'White Granex' are large, very mild, flat onions for spring harvest in the South; they have a short storage life. 'Sweet Spanish' and the hybrids 'Golden Beauty', 'Fiesta', 'Bronze', 'Perfection', 'El Capitan' are large, mild, globular onions suited for growing in the middle latitudes of the country; they store moderately well. 'Southport White Globe', 'Southport Yellow Globe', 'Ebenezer, Early Yellow Globe', 'Yellow Globe Danvers' and the hybrid 'Abundance' are all firm-fleshed, long-storage onions for growing as a main crop in the Northeast and Midwest. 'Early Harvest' is an early F_1 hybrid adapted to all northern regions of the United States. Varieties that produce bulbs may also be used green.

SHALLOT

The shallot is a small onion of the Multiplier type. Its bulbs have a more delicate flavor than most onions. Its growth requirements are about the same as those of most other onions. Shallots seldom form seed and are propagated by means of the small cloves or divisions, into which the plant splits during growth. The plant is hardy and may be left in the ground from year to year, but best results are had by lifting the clusters of bulbs at the end of the growing season and replanting the smaller ones at the desired time.

Fleshy-fruited Vegetables

The fleshy-fruited, warm-season vegetables, of which the tomato is the most important, are closely related and have about the same cultural requirements. All must have warm weather and fertile, well-drained soil for good results.

EGGPLANT

Eggplant is extremely sensitive to the conditions under which it is grown. A warm-weather plant, it demands a growing season of from 100 to 140 days with high average day and night temperatures. Also, the soil must be well warmed up before eggplant can safely be set outdoors.

In the South, eggplants are grown in spring and autumn; in the North, only in summer. The more northerly areas, where a short growing season and low summer temperatures prevail, are generally unsuitable for eggplants. In very fertile garden soil, which is best for eggplant, a few plants will yield a large number of fruits.

Sow eggplant seeds in a hotbed or greenhouse, or, in warm areas, outdoors about eight weeks before the plants are to be transplanted. It is important that the plants be kept growing without check from low or drying temperatures or other causes. They may be transplanted like tomatoes. Good plants have stems that are not hard or woody; one with a woody stem rarely develops satisfactorily. 'Black Beauty', 'Early Beauty Hybrid', and 'Jersey King Hybrid' are good varieties.

PEPPERS

Peppers are more exacting than tomatoes in their requirements, but may be grown over a wide range in the United States. Being hot weather plants, peppers cannot be planted in the North until the soil has warmed up and all danger of frost is over. In the South, planting dates vary with the location, fall planting being practiced in some locations. Start pepper plants six to eight weeks before needed. The seeds and plants require a somewhat higher temperature than those of the tomato. Otherwise they are handled in exactly the same way.

Hot peppers are represented by such varieties as 'Red Chili' and 'Long Red Cayenne'; the mild-flavored by 'Penn Wonder', 'Ruby King', 'Worldbeater', 'California Wonder', and 'Yale Wonder', which mature in the order given.

TOMATOES

Tomates grow under a wide variety of conditions and require only a relatively small space for a large production. Of tropical American origin, the tomato does not thrive in very cool weather. It will, however, grow in winter in home gardens in the extreme South. Over most of the upper South and the North it is suited to spring,summer and autumn culture. In the more northern areas, the growing season is likely to be too short for heavy yields, and it is often desirable to increase earliness and the length of the growing season by starting the plants indoors. By adopting a few precautions, the home gardener can grow tomatoes practically everywhere, given fertile soil with sufficient moisture.

A liberal application of compost and commercial fertilizer in preparing the soil should be sufficient for tomatoes under most conditions. Heavy applications of fertilizer should be broadcast, not applied in the row; but small quantities may be mixed with the soil in the row in preparing for planting.

Start early tomato plants from five to seven weeks before they are to be transplanted to the garden. Enough plants for the home garden may be started in a window box and transplanted to small pots, paper drinking cups with the bottoms removed, plant bands (round or square), or other soil containers. In boxes, the seedlings are spaced 2 to 3 inches apart. Tomato seeds germinate best at about 70° F., or ordinary house temperature. Growing tomato seedlings, after the first transplanting, at moderate temperatures, with plenty of ventilation, as in a coldframe, gives stocky, hardy growth. If desired, the plants may be transplanted again to larger containers, such as 4-inch clay pots or quart cans with holes in the bottom.

Tomato plants for all but the early spring crop are usually grown in outdoor seedbeds. Thin seeding and careful weed control will give strong, stocky plants for transplanting. A list of tomato varieties for home garden use in areas other than the Southwest is given in Table 8.

Table 8
Tomato Varieties for Areas Other Than the Southwest

VARIETY	AREA
Ace	West
Atkinson	South
C17	East, Midwest
Fireball VF	East, North
Floradel	South
R1350	East, Midwest
Homestead-24	South
Manalucie	South
Marion	South
Morton Hybrid	North, East
Moscow VR	West
Small Fry	All areas
Spring Giant	East, Midwest
Supermarket	South
Supersonic	East, Midwest
Tropi-Gro	South
VFW-8	West

In the Southwest, 'Pearson', 'Early Pack No. 7', 'VF 36', 'California 145', 'VF 13L', and 'Ace' are grown.

Tomatoes are sensitive to cold. Never plant them until danger of frost is past. By using plant protectors during cool periods the home gardener can set tomato plants somewhat earlier than would otherwise be possible. Hot, dry weather, like midsummer weather in the South, is also unfavorable for planting tomatoes. Planting distances depend on the variety and on whether the plants are to be pruned and staked or not. If pruned to one stem, trained and tied to stakes or a trellis, they may be set 18 inches apart in 3-foot rows; if not, they may be planted 3 feet apart in rows 4 to 5 feet apart. Pruning and staking have many advantages for the home gardener. Cultivation is easier, and the fruits are always clean and easy to find. Staked and pruned tomatoes are, however, more subject to losses from blossom-end rot than those allowed to grow naturally.

Miscellaneous Vegetables

FLORENCE FENNEL

Florence Fennel is related to celery and celeriac. Its enlarged, flattened leafstalk is the portion used. For a summer crop, sow the seeds in the rows in spring; for an autumn and winter crop in the South, sow them toward the end of the summer. Thin the plants to stand about 6 inches apart. When the leafstalks have grown to about 2 inches in diameter the plants may be slightly mounded up and partially blanched. They should be harvested and used before they become tough and stringy.

OKRA

Okra, or Gumbo, has about the same degree of hardiness as cucumbers and tomatoes and may be grown under the same conditions. It thrives on any fertile, well-drained soil. An abundance of quickly available plant food will stimulate growth and ensure a good yield of tender, high-quality pods.

As okra is a warm-weather vegetable, the seeds should not be sown until the soil is warm. The rows should be from 3 to 3½ feet apart, depending on whether the variety is dwarf or large-growing. Sow the seeds every few inches and thin the plants to stand 18 inches to 2 feet apart in the rows. 'Clemson Spineless', 'Emerald', and 'Dwarf Green' are good varieties. The pods should be picked young and tender, and none allowed to ripen. Old pods are unfit for use and soon exhaust the plant.

PHYSALIS

Physalis, known also as Groundcherry and Husk Tomato, is closely related to the tomato and can be grown wherever tomatoes do well. The kind ordinarily grown in gardens produces a yellow fruit about the size of a cherry. The seeds may be started indoors or sown in rows in the garden.

SWEET CORN

Sweet Corn requires plenty of space and is adapted only to the larger gardens. Although a warm-weather plant, it may be grown in practically all parts of the United States. It needs a fertile, well-drained, moist soil. With these requirements met, the type of the soil does not seem to be especially important, but a clay loam is almost ideal for sweet corn.

In the South, sweet corn is planted from early spring until autumn, but the corn earworm, drought and heat make it difficult to obtain worthwhile results in midsummer. The ears pass the edible stage very quickly, and succession plantings are necessary to ensure a constant supply. In the North, sweet corn cannot be safely planted until the ground has thoroughly warmed up. Here, too, succession plantings need to be made to ensure a steady supply. Sweet corn is frequently planted to good advantage after early potatoes, peas, beets, lettuce or other early, short-season crops. Sometimes, to gain time, later corn may be planted before the early crop is removed.

Sweet corn may be grown in either hills or drills, in rows at least 3 feet apart. It is well to plant the seed rather thickly, and thin to single stalks 14 to 16 inches apart or three plants to each 3-foot hill. Experiments have shown that in the eastern part of the country there is no advantage in removing suckers from sweet corn. Cultivation sufficient to control weeds is all that is needed.

Hybrid sweet corn varieties, both white and yellow, are usually more productive than the open-pollinated sorts. As a rule, they need a more fertile soil and heavier feeding. They should be fertilized with 5–10–5 fertilizer about every three weeks until they start to silk. Many are resistant to disease, particularly bacterial wilt. Never save seed from a hybrid crop for planting. Such seed does not come true to the form of the plants from which it was harvested.

Good yellow-grained hybrids, in the order of the time required to reach edible maturity, are 'Spancross', 'Marcross', 'Golden Beauty', 'Golden Cross Bantam', and 'Ioana'. White-grained hybrids are 'Evergreen' and 'Country Gentleman'.

Well-known open-pollinated yellow sorts are 'Golden Bantam' and 'Golden Midget'. Open-pollinated white sorts, in the order of maturity, are 'Early Evergreen', 'Country Gentleman' and 'Stowell Evergreen'.

CHAPTER 37

Minigardens for Vegetables

YOU'D LIKE TO BE A GARDENER, but you live in a room, an apartment or a townhouse—and you think you have no place for a garden. But if you have a windowsill, a balcony or a doorstep you have enough space for a minigarden.

Growing vegetables in a minigarden can be fun for youngsters as well as for the not so young. You don't need to be familiar with growing plants if you have the patience to follow a few instructions.

The basic materials you will need for minigardening are some containers, some synthetic soil and some seeds.

CONTAINERS

To start a minigarden of vegetables, you will need a container large enough to hold the plant when it's fully grown. You can use plastic or clay pots, an old pail, a plastic bucket, a bushel basket, a wire basket or a wooden box. Most any container is satisfactory—from tiny pots for your kitchen windowsill to large wooden boxes for your patio.

The size and number of the containers can very with the space you have and the number of plants you want to grow. Six-inch pots are satisfactory for chives. Radishes, onions and a variety of miniature tomato ('Tiny Tim') will do well in 10-inch pots. For the average patio, 5-gallon plastic trash cans are suitable. They are easy to handle and provide enough space for the larger vegetable plants. Half-bushel or bushel baskets also work well if you have room for them.

Readymade containers of plastic, metal and wood are so widely available that it is not necessary to build your own containers. Many are designed especially for growing plants. Others can easily be modified for growing plants, particularly pails, tubs, baskets and trash containers. Plastic laundry baskets, for example, are attractive and can be modified by lining them with plastic sheeting.

If you use solid plastic containers, allow for drainage. Drill four or more ¼-inch holes, spaced evenly along the sides, near the bottom. Don't drill the holes in the bottom itself. Then, to further help drainage, put about ½ inch of coarse gravel in the bottom of each container.

Wood containers, such as a bushel basket, will last three to five years if painted both inside and outside with a safe wood preservative.

SYNTHETIC SOIL

You can buy a soil substitute, or synthetic soil, prepared from a mixture of horticultural vermiculite, peat moss and fertilizer. This mixture, sold by seed dealers and garden-supply centers, comes ready to use. For minigardening it has several advantages over soil. It is free of plant-disease organisms and weed seeds, it holds moisture and plant nutrients well, and it is very lightweight and portable.

Lettuce is a good minigarden crop. It is a fast-growing, cool-weather crop and can be grown in a small container without much sunlight.

You can prepare your own soil substitute from horticultural grade vermiculite, peat moss, limestone, superphosphate and 5–10–5 fertilizer. To 1 bushel each of vermiculite and shredded peat moss, add 1¼ cups of ground limestone (preferably dolomitic), ½ cup of 20-percent superphosphate and 1 cup of 5–10–5 fertilizer. This material should be mixed thoroughly. If the material is very dry, add a little water to it to reduce the dust during mixing.

SEEDS

Your success in minigardening will depend partly on the quality of seed you plant. Vegetable-seed envelopes are stamped with the year in which they should be planted; check the date to see that seed is not old. Old seed often germinates poorly and does not grow vigorously. Don't use last year's seed.

Seeds of many varieties of each plant are available. Miniature vegetable varieties are best for minigardens. When possible, select disease- and insect-resistant varieties.

LIGHT

Vegetable plants grow better in full sunlight than in the shade. Some vegetables need more sun than others. Leafy vegetables (lettuce, cabbage, mustard greens) can stand more shade than root vegetables (beets, radishes, turnips). Root vegetables can stand more shade than vegetable fruit plants (cucumbers, peppers, tomatoes), which do very poorly in the shade. Plant your vegetable fruit plants where they will get the most sun, and your leafy vegetables and root vegetables in the shadier areas.

PLANTING DATES

Planting or transplanting vegetables at the proper time helps ensure success. The best planting date in one area may be days or weeks from the best date in another. This is because temperatures can differ greatly from one place to another—even a few miles apart. City temperatures, for example, are usually 5 to 10 degrees higher than those in the suburbs.

(The frost-free date in spring usually is two to three weeks later than the average date of the last freeze—about the date that oak leaves become full grown. See also Guide beginning on page 300.) Your local cooperative extension service agent can tell you the average frost-free dates in spring and fall for your locality.

STARTING PLANTS INDOORS

You can give some plants a jump on the growing season by starting them indoors on windowsills that have plenty of sunlight. Then, after the weather gets warmer, you can transplant them into larger containers and move them outdoors.

Start your plants in small aluminum baking pans, plastic trays, pots or cardboard milk cartons.

Use readymade peat pellets or peat pots; both are available from garden-supply centers. Peat pellets

Guide to Cultural Requirements of Vegetables

Plant	Light	When to plant	Days from seed to harvest	Space between plants (inches)	Planting depth (inches)	When to harvest
BEETS	Tolerate partial shade.	2 to 4 weeks before frost-free date.	50 to 60	2 to 3	½	When 1 to 2 inches in diameter.
Comment: *Thin plants when 6 to 8 inches high; use thinnings for greens.*						
CABBAGE	Tolerates partial shade.	Set out plants 4 to 6 weeks before frost-free date.	65 to 120, depending on variety.	12 to 18	½ (for seed); bury roots of plants.	When head is hard and rounded.
Comment: *Can also be set out for a fall crop.*						
CARROTS	Tolerate partial shade.	2 to 4 weeks before frost-free date.	65 to 80	2 to 3	½	For small carrots, when ½ to 1 inch in diameter.
Comment: *To get several harvests, make plantings at 3-week intervals until 3 months before fall freezing date.*						
CHIVES	Grow in partial shade, as in kitchen window.	Set out plants 4 to 6 weeks before frost-free date (can also be started from seed).	60 to 70	2 to 3 (in clusters).	½	Clip as needed for salads, toppings.
Comment: *Bulbs should be divided occasionally, so that they do not get too thick.*						
CUCUMBERS	Require full sunlight.	Set out plants 1 week after frost-free date.	70 to 80	18	½ (for seed); bury roots of plants.	For best yield, pick before hard seeds form.
Comment: *Need hot weather. Use container of at least 5-gallon size. Start seeds in pots or berry boxes about 3 weeks before time to set out. During early growth, cover with a paper or plastic tent during cool nights.*						
EGGPLANT	Needs full sunlight.	Set out plants on frost-free date; they require warm soil.	100 to 140	One plant to a 3-gallon container.	½ (for seed); bury roots of plants.	When fruits are mature.
Comment: *Hard to grow in northern part of U.S. because of high heat requirement and long growing season. Cover the plants during cool periods. You might want to try the new dwarf varieties. Start seeds indoors 8 to 9 weeks before transplanting time.*						
KALE	Tolerates partial shade.	6 to 8 weeks before first fall freeze.	55 to 70	6	½	When tall enough for greens; cut whole plants or take larger leaves.
Comment: *Very winter hardy. Plant also in early fall for winter crops.*						
LEEK	Tolerates partial shade.	4 to 6 weeks before frost-free date.	130	2 to 3	½	When 1 inch in diameter and white part is 5 to 6 inches long.
Comment: *Leek is a decorative and winter-hardy plant.*						
LEAF LETTUCE	Tolerates partial shade.	4 to 6 weeks before frost-free date and 6 to 8 weeks before first fall freeze.	30 to 35	4 to 6	¼	Cut leaves when large enough to use.
Comment: *Lettuce is a cool-weather crop. It can be started inside early and set out even before frosts end. Plants will tolerate temperatures as low as 28° F. You can make several later plantings for summer lettuce unless hot weather hinders growth.*						

Plant	Light	When to plant	Days from seed to harvest	Space between plants (inches)	Planting depth (inches)	When to harvest
MUSTARD GREENS	Tolerate partial shade.	2 to 4 weeks before frost-free date until 6 to 8 weeks before first fall freeze.	35 to 40	4 to 5	¼	When large enough to make greens.
Comment: Can be grown throughout the summer. You can make plantings at 10-day intervals for successive crops.						
ONIONS	Green onions grow in partial shade; mature bulbs need full sun.	Plant bulb sets 4 to 6 weeks before frost-free date.	100 to 120 (less time for green onions).	2 to 3	1 to 1½	When large enough for green onions (8 to 10 inches tall); after they dry out they are usable as cooking onions.
Comment: Onions like lots of moisture.						
PARSLEY	Does well in partial shade; will grow on kitchen windowsills.	Set out plants 4 to 6 weeks before frost-free date.	85	6 to 8	¼	Clip for garnish.
Comment: Sensitive to heat. Parsley seeds germinate slowly; soak them in water overnight before planting. Cover container for a few days after planting to keep soil moist. Start indoors if possible.						
PEPPERS	Require full sunlight.	Set out plants 1 week after frost-free date.	110 to 120	14 to 18	½ (for seed); bury roots of plants.	When peppers are 2 to 3 inches in diameter (depends on variety).
Comment: Require hot weather. If you start your own seeds indoors, plant 5 or 6 weeks before transplanting time. Allow one plant per 1-gallon container.						
RADISHES (mild)	Do well in partial shade.	2 to 4 weeks before frost-free date.	25 to 35	1	½	When ½ to 1 inch in diameter.
Comment: Cannot withstand heat. The faster they grow, the better the quality. Be sure they get fertilizer at seeding time. Radishes are at their best for only a few days, so you may wish to make several plantings at 1-week intervals. You may also want to try the hotter, large, winter radishes, which need 75 days or more growing time and are planted to mature just before fall frost.						
SUMMER SQUASH	Does best in full sunlight.	On frost-free date.	50 to 60	One plant per 5-gallon container.	1 to 2	Depends on variety; see your seed package.
Comment: Plant the bush types of this vegetable.						
SWISS CHARD	Tolerates partial shade.	2 to 4 weeks before frost-free date.	30 to 40	4 to 5	½	When leaves are 3 inches or more in length.
Comment: Only one planting is necessary; new leaves replace the harvested leaves. Outer leaves may be harvested without injuring the plant. Each seed cluster contains several seeds.						
TOMATOES	Require full sunlight.	Transplant on frost-free date (start seeds 5 to 7 weeks before transplanting).	55 to 100	One plant per 1- to 3-gallon container.	½ (for seed); bury roots of plants.	When tomatoes turn pink or almost red.
Comment: Dwarf tomatoes offer a large return for a small space. They need warm weather. The Tiny Tim and other dwarf varieties do well in containers.						
TURNIPS	Tolerate partial shade.	4 to 6 weeks before frost-free date and 6 to 8 weeks before first fall freeze.	30 to 80 (30 days for greens).	3 to 4, when harvesting for greens.	½	Thin when large enough to make greens; leave others to mature (2 inches or more in diameter).
Comment: Turnips are a cool-season vegetable.						

contain synthetic soil that swells up several times its original size when water is added.

Clean your containers with hot soapy water, rinse them well, and fill them with the peat pots or the peat pellets. If you use the pellets, add water and wait until they expand.

Then make a planting hole with your finger or some tool to the correct depth for the kind of seed you are planting. Put in two or three seeds. Cover the seeds with peat moss and moisten with water. Then enclose the container in a plastic bag until the seedlings emerge. If more than one seedling comes up, pull out the less vigorous ones.

Transplant seedlings to larger containers when the first two leaves are fully developed. Water them thoroughly before transplanting. Be careful not to disturb the roots.

HARDENING

Plants should be gradually "hardened," or toughened, for two weeks before being moved outdoors. This is done by withholding water and lowering the temperature. Hardening slows down the plants' rate of growth to prepare them to withstand such conditions as chilling, drying winds or high temperatures.

Lettuce, cabbage and many other plants can be toughened to withstand frost; others, such as tomatoes and peppers, cannot be hardened.

FERTILIZER

Apply 1 level teaspoon of 5–10–5 fertilizer per square foot of soil about three weeks after the plants have reached the two-leaf stage and again every three weeks. Mix the fertilizer into the top ½ inch of soil and water thoroughly. This will keep your plants growing rapidly and producing well.

WATERING

Vegetables need a water supply equal to about 1 inch of rain every week during the growing season. Since you are gardening in containers instead of a garden plot, you can control moisture easily. Water each time the soil becomes dry down to a depth of ⅛ inch. Overwatering will slowly kill your plants. During hot, dry weather you may need to water three times a week.

If you use a sprinkler can, do not water so late in the evening that the leaves of plants stay wet at night. Wet leaves encourage plant diseases. It is important for you to fill the bottom of your plant containers with gravel or similar material. This allows for good drainage. If your soil becomes waterlogged, the plants will die from lack of oxygen.

CULTIVATING

Weeds rob plants of water, nutrients, space and light. If weeds come up in your minigarden, pull them by hand or use a small hand weeder to loosen the soil and remove the weeds while they are still small. Be careful not to injure the roots.

ORNAMENTAL VEGETABLES

If you want to grow ornamental vegetables, there are several attractive varieties that are pretty as well as tasty. Here are a few suggestions.

Salad Bowl lettuce produces many curled, wavy, bright-green leaves. If you want color in your lettuce, grow the Ruby variety. This is a beautiful, nonheading salad lettuce with fancy, frilled leaves that are bright red.

Another bright-red vegetable is a swiss chard variety called Rhubarb. It looks like rhubarb and is easy to grow.

A kale variety called Flowering Kale from the Orient has bright red-and-green leaves.

All tomato varieties are decorative. 'Tiny Tim,' a miniature tomato, is an especially colorful plant that adds color and taste to any salad.

DISEASES AND INSECTS

Vegetables grown in minigardens are as susceptible to attack by diseases and insects as those grown in a garden plot. This is especially true if they are grown near other plants. If attack occurs, consult your cooperative extension service agent or other state and county agricultural service.

CHAPTER 38

Cauliflower and Broccoli

CAULIFLOWER AND BROCCOLI are popular members of the cabbage family.

There are two types of broccoli—heading and sprouting. The curd (head) of heading broccoli is white and compact, like cauliflower. Heading broccoli takes longer to mature than cauliflower, however. Sprouting broccoli has green heads that are branched, rather than compact.

In this chapter "cauliflower" refers to both cauliflower and heading broccoli; "broccoli" refers only to sprouting broccoli.

GENERAL NEEDS AND ADAPTATION

Cauliflower is difficult to grow. It needs:

- Fertile, moist soil, rich in organic matter and nitrogen
- Good drainage
- A cool, humid climate
- A frost-free growing season.

Cauliflower grown on light soil must be kept well watered.

Because its needs are so precise, cauliflower is grown in only a few areas, chiefly on Long Island and in western New York, in Texas, in the Colorado mountains and on the Washington and California coasts. Small amounts are grown elsewhere.

Broccoli's requirements are similar to those of cauliflower, but it is not as exacting and thus can be grown in a much wider area. Much of the broccoli grown in the southern and South Atlantic States is shipped to northern markets, fresh or frozen.

Because frozen broccoli keeps well in storage, it can be shipped long distances. This has opened up new markets.

VARIETIES

Cauliflower

Cauliflower varieties are not well defined. Strains within a variety differ in plant size, in foliage and in how the inner leaves protect the developing curd from discoloration by sunlight. Poor strains are apt to develop small leaves that extend through the curd, lowering market value.

To make sure you get a good strain, buy high-grade seed from a reputable dealer. Good yields more than make up for the extra expense of good seed.

Here are descriptions of some typically good varieties, from earliest to latest:

Early Snowball does well in areas with a short growing season. It matures in 50 to 60 days after transplanting and is the most important short-season variety. Plants are dwarf, compact and fast growing. The leaves are medium green and grow upright, turning outward at the tips. The curd is uniform, solid and ivory white. It has excellent flavor and quality.

Super Snowball is good for canning or freezing. It matures in 55 to 60 days. The plants are dwarf and the leaves are blue-green, long and spreading. The curd is solid and white.

Snowdrift is large and vigorous. The curd is large, free of leaflets, and well protected by the inner leaves during its early development. It matures in 60 to 65 days.

Danish Giant, also called *Dry Weather*, grows well in drier climates. It is grown mainly in the Midwestern states. The curd is white and large, averaging about 7 inches across. It matures in 70 to 80 days.

Winter cauliflowers take up to 150 days to mature. They are grown mainly on the California coast, where the growing season is very long. Varieties are available for planting on definite dates from June to November for harvest from November to May. Some of the best, from the earliest to the latest, are: *Early Pearl, Christmas, February, March, St. Valentine* and *Late Pearl.* Names of the varieties reflect the harvest dates.

Broccoli

Most American-grown broccoli is of the Italian green type called 'Calabrese'.

New varieties are being developed to meet increasing demands. Some are especially adapted to specific areas. Others are suited for freezing.

Here are some of the popular varieties:

Atlantic can be planted densely for a high per-acre yield. Plants are dwarf and compact, with fast-developing heads that are medium to large, round and compact. It is a distinctive short-season type suited for a fall harvest in the Northeastern Alantic Coast states.

Coastal is an early variety grown in the Far West. Plants are very short and compact. There is little division among clusters in the head. The buds are small, with a good, lasting color. Since the heads are rather uniform, they can be harvested in only three or four cuttings.

DeCicco is a popular early Calabrese variety. It is very productive, with many side shoots that are good for freezing. Plants are light green and medium tall. It will grow in spring, summer and fall.

Green Sprouting Medium is an important shipping and freezing variety. It is a mid-season Calabrese, grown mainly on the Pacific coast and in the Southwest. It is too late for the northern and eastern States. Plants are large and vigorous, with large, compact central heads and a heavy yield of side heads after central heads are harvested.

Green Sprouting Late, a long-season Calabrese, is grown mainly in California for early spring harvest. It would probably grow well in the South Atlantic states, too, but it is not grown there at present.

Waltham 29 can be grown in many regions, but is particularly suited for the Northeastern and Atlantic Coast states for fall harvesting.

It produces over a moderately long season and is generally blue-green and fairly uniform. Plants are stocky, with large, broad central heads. They develop many side heads that are good for freezing. Hybrid broccoli is now being developed and is gaining in importance where commercial operations require once-over mechanical harvesting.

FERTILIZING

Cauliflower and broccoli need fertile soil for good yields. Poor soil can be enriched by using fertilizer.

Before applying fertilizer and lime, have your soil tested for phosphorus, potassium, acidity and soil type. Soil tests for fertilizer recommendations are made by state rather than federal agencies in all states except California and Illinois. In these two states, as well as in the others, commercial laboratories provide this service. Most states charge for testing soils. Consult your county agricultural agent or the soil specialist at your state agricultural college for soil tests.

Without a soil test, here is an example of what one acre of loamy soil might require:

- 1,000 pounds of a 10–10–10 fetilizer plowed down with the stubble.
- 50 pounds of ammonium nitrate or 100 pounds of nitrate of soda as a side-dressing about two weeks after plants have recovered from transplanting shock.

A second side-dressing about two weeks before the head is harvested.

For maximum cauliflower and broccoli growth:

- Grow a well-fertilized green-manure crop. About 30 percent of the nitrogen used on the green-manure crop will be recovered by the succeeding cauliflower and broccoli crop.
- When using fertilizer high in phosphorous, place it in bands near the seed to decrease phosphorous fixation by the soil. Plow down the nitrogen and potassium fertilizer to speed the decomposition of plant residues.
- Use about 1 pint of starter solution of 5 pounds of 5–20–10 fertilizer per 100 gallons of water on each transplant, or use commercial fertilizer starter solution according to manufacturer's instructions.

Nitrogen deficiency can cause "buttons"—small, premature heads—particularly in cauliflower. Lack of water or poor drainage can also cause buttons. In addition, yellowing leaves indicate deficiency of nitrogen and a need to side-dress with nitrogen.

Discolored, pithy cores are a sign of boron deficiency. Discolored, deformed curds appear in cauliflower; in broccoli, an early symptom is browning of the florets.

In both manganese and magnesium deficiencies, the older leaves lose their green color, except for the veins.

If these symptoms appear, consult your county agricultural agent or the soil specialist at your state agricultural college.

CONTROLLING WEEDS

Effective weed control is necessary to produce good-quality cauliflower and broccoli. Herbicides are useful where mechanical cultivation supplemented by hand weeding is ineffective or impractical.

The same herbicides at the same rates may be used on cauliflower and broccoli. The following is a choice of herbicides for use on:

Seeded plants: Trifluralin (*a,a,a,*-trifluoro-2, 6-dinitro-*N*, *N*-dipropyl-*p*-to-luidine) at a rate of ¾ pound active ingredient per acre, before seeding.

DCPA (dimethyl tetrachlorotere-phthalate) at a rate of 10 pounds active ingredient per acre, before emergence of seedlings.

Nitrofen (2,4-dichlorophenyl *p*-nitrophenyl ether) at a rate of 4 to 6 pounds active ingredient per acre, before or after emergence of seedlings.

Transplanted plants: Trifluralin at a rate of ¾ pound active ingredient per acre, before planting. Nitralin (4-(methylsulfonyl)-2, 6-dinitro-N,*N*-dipropylaniline) at a rate of ¾ to 1½ pounds active ingredient per acre before or after planting.

DCPA at a rate of 10 pounds active ingredient per acre, after planting.

Nitrofen at a rate of 4 to 6 pounds active ingredient per acre, after planting.

Using a rototiller or a disk, incorporate trifluralin and nitralin into the soil to a depth of 2 to 3 inches.

DCPA needs moisture for best results. If it does not rain within a week after application, irrigate the soil with ½ to ¾ inches of water.

Wait two weeks after plants are set or after seedlings appear before applying nitrofen. Nitrofen is not effective unless weeds are small.

Use lower rates of application on sandy soils.

STARTING THE PLANTS

When the plant cauliflower and broccoli depends on the area, how long the variety takes to mature, and when you plan to harvest.

Cauliflower and broccoli can be planted from mid-April to late fall in California for a long harvest, but in the eastern states they must be planted in time for a summer or fall harvest.

In most of California, mild climate permits growing all seedlings in open beds for transplanting to the field. Elsewhere, this is done for summer and fall crops only, and plants for spring harvest must be started in hotbeds or greenhouses. Seedlings need a loose, easily pulverized loam that is not too fertile. Avoid soil that tends to crust on top.

If plants are started in open beds, plant the seed thinly in rows 12 to 14 inches apart. It is best to use a seeder. If the seed is broadcast, weed control is difficult. Cover lightly with ¼ to ½ inch of soil.

If you start plants under glass, you may sow the seed in rows or broadcast. Sow thinly so seedlings have room to develop. Thin when they reach the four-leaf stage; allow 2 inches between plants. Leave them to grow until field conditions permit transplanting.

With proper handling, 3 to 4 ounces of seed will produce enough seedlings to plant 1 acre; 1 ounce of seed will produce about 3,000 plants.

If beds or flats have been used for other plants in the cabbage family, be sure they are free of clubroot, blackleg, black rot, ring spot, and damping-off. These diseases can remain in the soil.

If weather permits, either cauliflower or broccoli may be started in the field. Set the seeder to drop three or four seeds in one place. Be sure to thin early to avoid overcrowding.

TRANSPLANTING TO THE FIELD

Plants are usually transplanted by hand for small plantings, and by plant-setting equipment for large plantings.

Set plants in rows 2½ to 3 feet apart. Distances between plants in rows vary from 15 to 36 inches, depending on the variety and strain. In the West, plants are usually spaced rather widely.

Do not set plants until danger of frost is past. In cauliflower, cold causes stunting and premature heading. Broccoli is less sensitive than cauliflower, but it can be damaged by frost.

Avoid planting cauliflower or broccoli in fields planted in cabbage, turnips, kale or similar crops during the previous four to five years. All are susceptible to damage by the same diseases and insects.

As the plants grow, cultivate shallowly for weed control or for mulching. Deep cultivation causes root injury, especially late in the season.

Cauliflower needs a lot of moisture for a good yield. Most western growers irrigate. Some eastern growers rely on rainfall, and their crops are often injured by drought.

Broccoli will grow well under drier conditions than cauliflower.

BLANCHING CAULIFLOWER

Exposure to sunlight discolors the cauliflower curd and can produce off-flavors. While curds are still small, the inner leaves protect them from sunlight. But, in most varieties, as the curds grow they force the inner leaves apart.

Some large, late varieties have very long, upright leaves which protect the curd until it is ready for harvest. Other varieties, like the Snowball types, must be blanched—that is, tied for protection.

To blanch, gather the longest leaves together over the curd and tie them with soft twine, raffia or tape. Since the plants grow and the curds develop at different rates, you must go through the field every two or three days to tie each plant when the curd begins to show through the small central leaves.

You may want to use twine of a different color each day. In this way, you can tell that heads tied with a certain color will be ready for harvest on approximately the same date.

Broccoli does not need to be blanched.

CHAPTER 39

Table Beets

TABLE, OR GARDEN, BEETS are grown in a wide range of soils and climates. Since beets produce their best color and quality in a cool climate, they are grown in the southern third of the United States as fall, winter and spring crops; in the middle third as early summer or late fall crops; and in the northern third as summer and early fall crops.

SOILS

Table beets are grown in a variety of soils such as mucks, sands, sandy loams and silt loams. It is generally difficult to get good stands on soils that have high clay content or those that pack or crust after a sprinkling or a rain. Early crops require sandy loam soils that warm up quickly in the spring. Heavier and more compact soils, as clay loams, are satisfactory for late spring or fall crops.

For best results the soil should be deep, well-drained, friable and adequately supplied with organic matter. Green-manure crops, crop residues, animal manures or composts—whichever is most practical—should be used to maintain soil fertility.

Beet

FERTILIZERS AND LIME

The land and amount of commercial fertilizer needed will depend on the soil type, natural fertility and the amount of fertilizer applied to previous crops.

In general, truck gardens require up to 2,000 pounds per acre and home gardens require up to 4½ pounds per 100 square feet. The mixture of fertilizer normally recommended is 10–10–10. On soils low in potash, 8–16–16 or 5–10–30 may be used.

In large-scale plantings, broadcast muriate of potash (0–0–60) to correct potash deficiencies. On muck soils, use a high-potash, low-nitrogen fertilizer.

When a truck garden is about half grown, a top-dressing of up to 150 pounds per acre of ammonium nitrate (or equivalent) may be used. For home gardens, use from ½ to 1 pound for each 100 feet of row. Internal blackspot of beets can be controlled by application of boron to the soil.

Beets grow best at a soil acidity from pH 6.0 to 6.8 but will tolerate neutral soils, and, in some districts, alkaline soils.

Soil acidity should be determined by an accurate soil test. If necessary, use ground limestone to lower the acidity (raise pH value). Many states maintain soil-testing services. Check with your county agricultural agent for instructions on how to take soil samples and where to send them for testing.

VARIETIES

Beets are classified according to the shape of the root and the time of maturing. For example, 'Crosby Egyptian', 'Green Top Bunching', 'Ruby Queen', and 'Early Wonder' are flat or globular early-maturing varieties. 'Detroit Dark Red' and 'Perfected Detroit' are globular and medium early-maturing varieties. 'Long Dark Blood', or 'Long Smooth Blood' are late-maturing varieties.

The roots of most beets are dark red or purplish. However, when beets are grown in hot weather, the roots may develop light-colored zones. In cool weather these zones are less conspicuous. The light-colored zones tend to disappear when the beets are cooked. Sugar content in the root is highest when beets are grown in cool temperatures and good sunlight.

'Crosby Egyptian' and 'Early Wonder' varieties are generally recommended when rapid growth to market-size is desired.

Both are slightly flattened and have alternate zones of purplish flesh in warm weather. Plantings that reach harvest stage in cool weather have darker flesh and less prominent differences in color zones.

For processing and where quick maturity is not important, 'Detroit Dark Red', 'Perfected Detroit', 'Ruby Queen' and 'Red Pak' are most commonly grown. Certain varieties, such as 'Crosby Green Top', are grown for beet greens, but other varieties can be used if harvested at the proper time.

Monogerm varieties with superior quality and uniformity have recently been developed. Examples of monogerm varieties are 'Pacemaker', 'Mono-King', 'Explorer' and 'Monogerm'.

PLANTING AND CULTURE

Young beet seedlings are tender. To help them become established, work the soil into a friable condition free of trash, clods and surface irregularities before planting.

Cover the seed 1 inch in sandy soils, about ¾ inch in sandy loams, and not deeper than ½ inch in finer-textured soils. It is important that the cover depth is both uniform and correct to assure even germination.

For home gardens worked by hand, rows may be as close as 12 inches; for commercial plantings, they are normally 18 to 24 inches apart.

For drainage or irrigation purposes, plant beets on formed beds in paired rows that are 40 inches apart from center. Sow seeds at the rate of 5 to 6 per foot of row, 10 to 12 pounds per acre, or 1 ounce for 100 feet of row. If beets are grown for processing, increase seedling rate to 14 to 16 pounds of seed per acre.

When multigerm seed is used, remove excess plants to avoid crowding. Thin the seedlings when they are large enough to be handled but before they greatly exceed 2 inches in height. Later thinning may cause damage. Three to four plants per foot of row should be left upon final thinning.

To achieve uniform stands and an earlier crop, home gardeners should sow 4 or 5 seeds per inch in

Thin beets so they are spaced 3 inches apart in the row.

rows 3 inches apart. Transplant the seedlings 3 inches apart in the row when they are 2 to 3 inches high.

Beets may be planted from three to four weeks before the average date of the last killing spring frost to six weeks before the average date of the first autumn frost except during very hot weather.

Beet seeds will germinate at soil temperatures from 40° to 85° F., with the optimum being 65° to 75° F.

An example of poor-quality beets

WEEDS

Mechanical cultivation can control weeds between the beet rows, but herbicides are needed to control weeds in the rows.

Herbicides registered for use in planting table beets include cycloate and pyrazon. Cycloate is effective against annual grasses and should be applied before the beets and weeds emerge. Pyrazon will control many broadleaf weeds when used before emergence of beets and weeds.

State experiment station weed specialists can provide specific information on the herbicides to be used in their areas. Be sure to read and follow the label carefully.

Herbicides are not generally recommended for use in home gardens because of the difficulty in correctly treating small areas. Hand weeding and hoeing are usually adequate in small garden areas.

PEST CONTROL

The nature and severity of pests of table beets varies with growing areas. For this reason, only general suggestions for pest control are made. Consult your county agricultural agent for more specific information. Read and follow the directions for use and the precautions indicated on the label of the pesticide to be used.

Leaf miners and aphids are the most common insect pests of beets; but webworms, flea beetles and others may cause extensive damage to the crop.

Check frequently for insects and start control measures before damage occurs.

Aphids and leaf miners may be controlled with diazinon; flea beetles with carbaryl; and webworms with pyrethrins.

Cercospora leaf spot, the most common disease of beets, is identified by circular spots with reddish brown or purplish margins. The infected area later turns gray and drops out, giving the leaf a spothole appearance. Crop rotation, sanitation and the use of fungicides, such as captan, control this disease.

Damping-off and seed rot can be reduced by seed treatment with captan or thiram.

HARVESTING AND HANDLING

Beets are usually harvested when 1¾ to 2 inches in diameter.

If you wish to bunch beets, do this immediately after they are pulled from the soil. Put together beets of similar size and appearance. Remove dead or damaged leaves.

STORAGE

Beets maturing in the late fall can be stored in cold, moist root cellars as long as three to five months. The plants will stand frost and mild freezing, but they must be removed from the field before hard freezing occurs.

For long storage, clip the tops close to the roots and sort out all diseased or decaying matter. Slatted crates or baskets are good containers; large bins are not.

The storage space should have a relative humidity of 95 to 98 percent to prevent excessive shrinkage. Keep the temperature as near to 32° F. as possible; take care not to freeze the roots. Under these conditions, bunched beets with tops may be stored for ten to 15 days. Higher temperatures shorten storage life and reduce quality.

Commercial storage at 32° F. with a humidity of 95 percent is satisfactory.

CHAPTER 40

Tomatoes in the Home Garden

TOMATOES ARE ONE of the most popular vegetables grown in home gardens. They grow under a wide variety of conditions with a minimum of effort, and they require relatively little space for a large production.

Of tropical American origin, tomatoes do not thrive in very cool weather. They are suited to spring, summer, and autumn culture over most of the North and upper South, and they will grow in winter in the extreme South.

Each tomato plant may be expected to yield 8 to 10 pounds of fruit. The number of plants needed will depend on the size of your family. To spread the tomato harvest over the growing season, stagger planting dates at two- to three-week intervals.

VARIETIES

Some tomato varieties are adapted to only certain areas of the country; others are more widely adapted. Choose a variety that is suitable to your

Tomato Varieties for the Home Garden

Variety	Climatic Adaptation	Disease [1] Resistance
Ace VF	Semiarid	V,F
Beefmaster	Humid	V,F,N
Better Boy	General	V,F,N
Burpee VF	Humid	V,F
C1327	Humid	V,F
Fireball VF	Humid	V,F
H1350	Humid	V,F
Homestead 24	Humid	F
Jet Star	Humid	V,F
Manalucie	Humid	F,S,C
Moscow VR	Semiarid	V
Ramapo	Humid	V,F
Small Fry	General	V,F
Supermarket	Humid	F,S
Supersonic	Humid	V,F
Tropic	Humid	V,F,S
VFN-8	Semiarid	V,F,N
Walter	Humid	F1&2,S
Wonder Boy	Humid	V,F,N

[1] V—Verticillium Wilt
F—Fusarium Wilt (1 and 2 indicates resistance to the common race and the recently discovered second race)
N—Root Knot Nematodes
S—Stemphylium (gray leaf spot)
C—Cladosporium (leaf mold)

part of the country and is resistant to fusarium and verticillium wilts. These diseases are likely to be a problem, and the only practical method of control is to grow resistant varieties.

A list of tomato varieties for home gardens is given on page 309.

PLANTING

Tomatoes grow best in fertile, well-drained soil, but they will grow in almost any kind of soil. Choose a site that receives direct sunrays all day.

SOIL PREPARATION

The time and method of preparing the soil for planting depend on the type of soil and the location of your garden.

In general, a cover crop should be grown in the garden during the winter to add organic matter to the soil. This is especially important with sandy soils that contain little organic matter.

Spade the cover crop into the soil in early spring well in advance of planting.

Heavy clay soils in northern areas benefit from fall tilling and exposure to freezing and thawing during the winter. Also, gardens in dry areas should be tilled in the fall and left rough so that the soil will absorb and retain moisture that falls during the winter.

Do not spade or work soil while it is wet unless the work will be followed by severe freezing weather. To test for moisture, squeeze a handful of soil. If it sticks together in a ball and does not readily crumble under slight pressure, it is too wet for working. Take the soil samples at both the surface and a few inches below. Sometimes, although the surface may be dry enough, the lower layers are too wet for working.

Moisture may also be tested by inserting a shovel into the soil. If soil sticks to the shovel, it is usually too wet to work.

Fertilizing During Soil Preparation

Fertilizers applied during soil preparation will help tomato plants grow rapidly and produce well. The kind and amount of fertilizer you need depend on your locality and the natural fertility of your soil.

Generally, a 5–10–5 fertilizer (5 percent nitrogen, 10 percent phosphoric acid, and 5 percent potash) gives good results. Sometimes just manure or a nitrogen fertilizer is needed. Fertilizers that contain small amounts of iron, zinc, manganese and other minor soil elements are necessary only if your soil is deficient in these elements.

Soil composition is best determined by a soil test. Contact your county agricultural agent or state experiment station for information on soil tests.

Fertilizer should be applied either a few days before planting or when the tomatoes are planted. A good practice is to spade the garden plot, spread the fertilizer by hand or with a fertilizer distributor, then go over the soil two or three times with a rake to get it in granular condition and to mix in the fertilizer. If the soil is left extremely rough, cultivate it once lightly before fertilizing.

Because of the small quantities of fertilizer required for some garden plots, it is easy to apply too much. Chemical fertilizers should be weighed before application.

The Table below shows how much fertilizer to use for each 100 to 2,000 square feet of garden area. For example, if your garden measures 500 square feet and a soil test indicates that 400 pounds of a 5–10–5 fertilizer is needed for 1 acre, you find in the Table that you should use 5 pounds.

Liming

Use lime only when a soil test shows it is needed. Do not apply lime in larger quantities than the test indicates. Most garden soils that are in a high state of fertility do not require additional lime.

Rates of Chemical Fertilizer to Apply per 100 to 2,000 Square Feet of Garden Area

GARDEN AREA	Weight of fertilizer to apply when the soil test report suggests the application of a mixed fertilizer (e.g. 5–10–5, 10–6–4) in the following amounts (pounds per acre)			
	100	400	800	1,200
SQUARE FEET	POUNDS	POUNDS	POUNDS	POUNDS
100	.25	1.0	2.0	3.0
500	1.25	5.0	10.0	15.0
1,000	2.50	10.0	20.0	30.0
1,500	3.75	15.0	30.0	45.0
2,000	5.00	20.0	40.0	60.0

If needed, however, any of the various forms of lime, such as hydrated and air-slaked lime, may be used; but the unburned, finely ground dolomitic limestone is best. Fifty-six pounds of burned lime or 74 pounds of hydrated lime is equivalent to 100 pounds of ground limestone. Finely ground oyster shells and marl may be used as substitutes for limestone.

Sometimes tomato plants need the calcium provided by lime to help prevent blossom-end rot.

When using lime, spread it after plowing and mix it thoroughly into the topsoil. Although it can be applied in the fall or winter, it is best to apply lime in the spring because some of it may be washed from the soil during winter.

SEEDING OUTDOORS

In areas with a long growing season, tomatoes may be seeded directly into the garden.

Work the soil into a somewhat granular condition. Sow the seeds in rows 4 to 5 feet apart. Keep the soil moist until the seeds germinate.

When the seedlings have three leaves, thin them out so they are spaced about one every 1½ to 3 feet.

SEEDING INDOORS

In the more northern areas, the growing season is likely to be too short for heavy tomato yields; therefore it is desirable to increase the length of the growing season by starting tomato plants indoors.

Sow the tomato seeds five to seven weeks before the plants are to be transplanted into the garden. The seeds may be planted directly into small pots and growing containers, or you may sow them in flats and later transplant them individually into growing containers.

The first method involves less handling of the small plants, and there is less chance for the spread of tobacco mosaic virus. Also, with this method seedlings develop more rapidly because the roots are not disturbed by transplanting.

However, seeding into flats and transplanting into pots is preferred by some gardeners because less space is required initially and weak seedlings can be discarded, leaving only the best plants for transplanting.

Loam or sandy soil, sand, shredded sphagnum peat moss, vermiculite and perlite may be used in various combinations to start seedlings.

Some of these combinations are:

1 part compost, 1 part sand, 2 parts topsoil
1 part peat moss, 1 part vermiculite
1 part peat moss, 2 parts sand

Growing tomatoes in the home garden

1 part peat moss, 1 part perlite or sand, 1 part soil
1 part compost, 1 part vermiculite
1 part peat moss, 1 part vermiculite, 1 part perlite

Various prepared mixtures for starting seeds are available commercially.

To ensure good germination of tomato seed, the soil must be kept moist. Temperatures of 70° to 80° F. are best during the germination period.

To help maintain proper temperature and moisture for germinating seeds, cover the flats or pots with panes of glass or sheets of plastic until the seedlings break through the soil surface. After germination, remove the cover and water the soil—but only as often as necessary to keep it moist to the touch.

Seeding into Flats

When seeding into flats, place seven to eight seeds per inch in rows and cover the seeds with ½ inch of starting mixture.

Transplant young seedlings into growing containers as soon as the stems have straightened and the leaves have opened—which is usually ten to 14 days after sowing the seed. The earlier the seedlings are transplanted, the quicker they recover from the shock of being uprooted. Use 3- or 4-inch clay or peat pots or paper drinking cups with a hole punched in the bottom.

When transplanting young tomato seedlings, hold the plant by one of the leaves; even slight pressure on the stems can cause permanent injury. A rich topsoil with a very light addition of commercial garden fertilizer or one of the artificial soil preparations may be used to grow the transplants.

The best temperatures for growing transplants are from 65° to 75° F. during the day and 60° to 65° at night. The young plants should be exposed to as much sunlight as possible. For best results, keep the plants in a hotbed or coldframe. If neither is available, keep them in front of a window with a western or southern exposure.

Seeding into Containers

When seeding in pots or some of the new plant-growing containers, fill the pots with starting mixture to within about ½ inch from the top of the pot. Plant one to three seeds ⅓ to ½ inch deep in the center of each pot. After germination, pots with more than one seedling should be thinned to a single plant.

Transplanting to Garden

Plant tomato seedlings outside when the soil has warmed and there is little threat of frost. If there is danger of frost after the plants are put outside, protect them with paper or plastic coverings, newspapers or boxes. Remove the covers during the day.

Set tomato plants into the garden at about the same depth as they were growing indoors. It is not necessary to remove the containers if they are made of peat or paper. However, if clay containers were used, knock the plants out of the pots before transplanting.

After replanting, press the soil firmly around the plant so that a slight depression is formed to hold water. Then pour approximately 1 pint water (to which fertilizer has been added) around each plant to wash the soil down around the roots. Use 2 tablespoons of granular 5–10–5 fertilizer per gallon of water.

Distances between plants depend on the variety used and on whether the tomato plants are to be pruned and staked. If plants will be staked, plant them 18 inches apart in rows 3 feet apart. If plants will grow unstaked, plant them 3 feet apart in rows 4 to 5 feet apart.

CARE

Watering

Tomatoes need about 1 inch of water per week. If rainfall is deficient, water plants thoroughly once a week.

Heavy soakings at weekly intervals are better than many light sprinklings. Do not wet the foliage any more than is necessary while watering.

More frequent watering may be needed if the soil is sandy.

Fertilizing

Tomato plants benefit from fertilization while growing. When the first fruit is about the size of a half-dollar, scatter uniformly around the plant a heaping teaspoon of 5–10–5 fertilizer 8 to 10 inches from the stem. Mix the fertilizer into the top ½ inch of soil and water thoroughly. Repeat once or twice a month.

If the soil is very low in fertility, more frequent fertilization may be necessary. Poor foliage color and stunted growth indicate a need for additional fertilizer.

Staking

Staking makes it easier to cultivate and harvest tomatoes and helps prevent fruit rots. However, staked plants are more subject to losses from blossom-end rot than plants allowed to grow naturally.

If you plan to stake your tomatoes, insert the stakes soon after transplanting to prevent root damage.

Use wood stakes that are about 8 feet long and 1½ inches wide. Push the stakes into the soil about 2 feet. Tie soft twine or strips of rag tightly around the stake 2 to 3 inches above a leaf stem, then loop the twine loosely around the main stem not far below the base of the leaf stem and tie with a square knot. Or use plant ties made of tape reinforced with wire to fasten plants to stakes.

Wire fencing about 6 feet high may also be used to support a tomato plant. Form a circle around the plant with the fence.

Pruning

Prune tomatoes once a week. Remove the small shoots that appear at the point where the leaf stem joins the main stem. Do not disturb the fruit buds, which appear just above or below the points where the leaves are attached to the leaf stem.

It is best to prune by hand. Grasp the shoot with your thumb and forefinger. Bend the shoot sharply to one side until it snaps; then pull it off in the opposite direction. Reversing the direction is necessary to prevent injury to the leaf axil or the main stem.

Controlling Weeds

Weeds compete with tomato plants for water, nutrients, and sunlight. Weeds also harbor insects and diseases and may be hosts for nematodes.

Cultivating: The area around tomatoes should be kept free of weeds. Weeds can be removed by hand or with a hoe or cultivator. Loosen the soil with a hoe or cultivator so water can soak into the soil around the plant and reach the roots.

Soil fumigation: Fumigating the soil with methyl bromide before planting is an excellent way to control practically all weeds and nematodes and many diseases in the tomato garden.

Plow or spade up the soil, then work it over with a harrow or rake. Place a plastic sheet over the area to be treated. Cover the edges of the sheet with soil to keep the methyl bromide from escaping; release the gas (in the quantity recommended by the manufacturer) under the plastic sheet. Keep cover in place 48 hours, then remove it. Cultivate the soil for aeration.

Tomatoes may be planted 72 hours after aeration. Precautions for the use of methyl bromide are given on the manufacturer's label and should be carefully followed.

Mulching: Mulches help keep weeds down. They also reduce water loss from the soil and stabilize soil temperature.

Rolls of black polyethylene, paper, and aluminum mulch are available in most garden stores. Straw or leaves may also be used as mulch.

When using plastic, paper or aluminum mulch, treat the soil with a broadcast application of fertilizer before applying the mulch. If you use organic mulch, it should be at least 2 inches deep on the soil to provide insulation, to hold water, and to control weeds.

Herbicides: Many home gardeners have found herbicides a convenient and efficient means for controlling weeds in tomato plantings. Amiben or DCPA, applied to the soil immediately after transplanting, effectively controls weeds without injuring the plants. Follow directions on the manufacturer's label for use of these herbicides.

Carefully directed sprays of full-strength Stoddard solvent cleaning fluid will kill established weeds between mulched rows without damage to the tomato plants. Use this spray when there is no wind. Apply a low pressure that gives a coarse spray. Thoroughly wet the weeds.

BLOSSOM DROP

Home gardeners often find that blossoms drop off prematurely and the fruit fails to develop. Blossom drop is caused by (1) cold temperatures; (2) hot temperatures; or (3) excessive nitrogen fertilization. Nothing can be done to remedy the situation, and you can only wait for later flowers to produce fruit. Rarely does a plant continue to drop its flowers.

HARVEST

To get the best flavor and color, harvest tomatoes after they are fully ripe. If tomatoes are picked green, they can be ripened at temperatures between 55 and 72° F.

Light will increase the color of tomatoes somewhat, but light is not essential to ripening. When tomatoes are placed in direct sunlight, the added heat often deteriorates their quality.

INSECT CONTROL

Several insect species damage tomatoes. Flea beetles, tomato fruitworms and hornworms may be controlled with carbaryl; aphids and leaf miners with diazinon; and spider mites with dicofol. The insecticides can be obtained at a garden-supply store. Follow the directions and heed all precautions on the label. For further information, see Chapter 41.

CHAPTER 41

Insects and Diseases of Vegetables

INSECTICIDES AND FUNGICIDES

Insecticide Dusts and Sprays

You can use an insecticide as a dust or a spray. Dusts come ready to use; they require no mixing. They can be applied with less expensive equipment than that needed for sprays. Most sprays must be mixed by the home gardener. They are easier to control than dusts during application.

Follow safety precautions (page 318) when working with pesticides.

Do not apply an insecticide unless it is necessary to prevent damage to your vegetables. Very few of the insect pests in your garden will cause appreciable damage if you protect their predators and parasites by avoiding unnecessary applications of insecticides. (See "Beneficial Insects," page 340.) However, if you do have a pest that usually causes serious damage unless an insecticide is used, apply the insecticide when the infestation first appears.

Watch for spider mites, cabbage caterpillars, the Colorado potato beetle and the Mexican bean beetle; these are some of the insects likely to need prompt treatment with insecticides. Repeat the treatment in a week or ten days if infestation continues. Do not treat for soil insects, such as cutworms, wireworms and white grubs, unless they have caused damage or unless you find them when preparing the soil.

Dusts recommended here are available from pesticide dealers or garden-supply stores. You may find it desirable to buy a dust containing a fungicide (to kill disease organisms) and one or more insecticides (to kill insects). Such a preparation is very practical for garden use; it controls a larger variety of pests than a dust containing only one fungicide or insecticide. You may wish to obtain two or more dusters and fill each with a dust suited for a particular purpose.

Unless otherwise specified, purchase dusts that contain the following percentages of active ingredient:

	Percent
Carbaryl	4
Dicofol	2
Endosulfan	3
Malathion	4
Methoxychlor	5
Naled	4
Rotenone	¾
Toxaphene	10

Apply an even, light coating of dust at the rate of 1 ounce per 50 feet of row or 125 square feet. Force it through the foliage so it reaches both sides of the leaves. Apply dust when the air is still.

Few sprays come ready to use in the home vegetable garden. It is usually necessary to prepare sprays by mixing wettable powders or emuslifiable concentrates with water. These materials contain different percentages of active ingredient (different strengths).

The Table opposite shows how to mix sprays in strengths recommended in this chapter. References to sprays are under "What to do" headings in the "Insects and Diseases" list beginning on page 319.

The Table gives proportions for mixing a small quantity of spray. If you require a large quantity, use proportionately more of each ingredient in the mixture. If you use a material in which the *percentage of active ingredient* (strength) differs from that mentioned in the table, mix proportionately more or less of it with the water.

If you use a wettable powder, stir it vigorously in a small amount of water to make a smooth paste, or slurry. Add this to the full amount of water, and stir until completely mixed. When applying wettable-powder sprays, shake the applicator frequently to keep the powder from settling to the bottom of the spray chamber.

If you use an emulsifiable concentrate, shake the container thoroughly before measuring out the amount needed for the spray mixture. Apply 1 quart of spray per 50 feet of row, or 125 square feet.

Fungicide Dusts and Sprays

You can use a fungicide as a dust or a spray. Sprays are usually preferable for prevention of plant diseases in the home garden; they stick to the plant surfaces better than dusts. They are most effective if applied with a compressed-air sprayer.

Fungicide dusts are effective if used properly. For best results, apply a fungicide before there is evidence of plant damage. Repeat the treatment every week or ten days. More frequent applications may be necessary during moist weather, when plant diseases tend to be most severe.

Whether you use a dust or a spray, only those parts of the plant that are actually coated with the fungicide are protected.

Following is a discussion of the fungicides recommended in this chapter, and a guide to the kinds of dusts and sprays to use. References to them are made under "What to do" headings in the "Insects and Diseases" list beginning on page 319.

Copper Fungicides

The fixed copper compounds such as basic copper sulfate, copper oxychloride and cuprous oxide are effective in preventing such plant diseases as late blight of potatoes and tomatoes, leaf blight of celery, and downy mildew of cucumbers and melons. These compounds are sold under various trade names; they should be used as directed on the container labels.

If you prefer a dust to a spray, use a fixed copper dust containing 5 to 7 percent of actual copper.

Insecticide Spray Formulations and Mixing Proportions

INSECTICIDE	FORMULATION[1]	AMOUNT OF FORMULATION TO MIX WITH 1 GALLON OF WATER
Carbaryl	50 percent WP	2 level tablespoons.
Chlordane	40 percent WP	1½ level tablespoons.
	or	
	45 percent EC	2 teaspoons.
Diazinon	25 percent EC	2 teaspoons.
Dicofol	18.5 percent WP	1 level tablespoon.
	or	
	18.5 percent EC	1 teaspoon.
Dimethoate	23.4 percent EC	1 teaspoon.
Endosulfan	50 percent WP	1 level tablespoon.
	or	
	2 pounds per gallon EC	2 teaspoons.
Malathion	57 percent EC	2 teaspoons.
Methoxychlor	50 percent WP	2 level tablespoons.
Naled	8 pounds per gallon EC	1 teaspoon.
Pyrethrum	Ready-prepared spray	([2]).
Rotenone	Derris or cube root powder (5 percent rotenone content).	4 level tablespoons.[3]
Sulfur	Wettable sulfur	3 level tablespoons.
Toxaphene	40 percent WP	3 level tablespoons.

[1] WP = wettable powder; EC = emulsifiable concentrate. If the available formulation contains more or less of the indicated active ingredient, mix proportionately more or less of the material with 1 gallon of water.

[2] Mix with water as directed on the container label.

[3] First, mix the powder with a small quantity of water; then add remaining water.

Organic Fungicides

Organic fungicides such as captan, ferbam, maneb, nabam, zineb and ziram are frequently used instead of copper fungicides. They are sold under various trade names, some of which are listed below:

Common Name	*Trade name*
Captan	Captan 50—W, Orthocide 50
Ferbam	Fermate, Karbam Black, Ferradow, Ferberk
Maneb	Manzate, Dithane M–22
Zineb	Dithane Z–78, Parzate Zineb Fungicide, Ortho Zineb 65 (Wettable)
Ziram	Zerlate, Zirberk, Karbam White, Corozate

Ferban is not used as extensively for vegetable-disease control as the other organic fungicides listed above. It is effective for control of certain blackberry and raspberry diseases.

To prepare a spray, mix one of the purchased products with water according to directions on the package.

Use a dust containing 5 to 10 percent of the fungicide.

Note: Mention of a proprietary product in this book is not a guarantee or warranty of the product. Such mention does not imply its approval to the exclusion of other products that may also be suitable.

Seed-treatment Chemicals

Certain chemicals, dusted on the seed of some crops, act as protective fungicides to reduce injury caused by seed decay and damping-off. They are sold under various trade names, some of which are listed below:

Common Name	*Trade Name*
Thiram	Arasan 75, Thiram–50
Chloranil	Spergon
Dichlone	Phygon Seed Protectant
Captan	Orthocide–75 Seed Protectant Captan 50–W

Follow these directions for treating a small quantity of seed:

1. Tear off the corner of the seed packet.
2. Dip the small blade of a penknife into the dust.
3. Lift out as much dust as will go on the tip of the blade.
4. Insert dust through the hole in the packet.
5. Fold down corner of packet.
6. Shake the seed thoroughly.

The directions on the fungicide package will tell you how much dust to use for treating a large quantity of seed. Place the dust and seed in a closed container. Shake the container one to two minutes.

Do not eat treated seed or feed it to livestock.

Compatibility of Pesticides

The following pesticides—insecticides and fungicides—are compatible with one another and may be

Table of Measures

The following tables of measures are useful in preparing small quantities of insecticide for garden application.

Liquid measures:

3 teaspoons = 1 tablespoon	2 cups = 1 pint
2 tablespoons = 1 fluid ounce	2 pints = 1 quart
8 fluid ounces = 1 cup	4 quarts = 1 gallon

Approximate quantities of powder required to weigh 1 ounce:

Carbaryl wettable powder	6 level tablespoons
Chlordane wettable powder	5 level tablespoons
Dicofol wettable powder	5 level tablespoons
Malathion wettable powder	4 level tablespoons
Methoxychlor wettable powder	4 level tablespoons
Sulfur wettable powder	3 level tablespoons
Toxaphene wettable powder	3 level tablespoons

used together in spray mixtures. Any pesticide in the list can be used with any one or several of the others.

Chlordane	Maneb
Diazinon	Naled
Dicofol	Pyrethrum
Dimethoate	Rotenone
Endosulfan	Thiram
Ferbam	Toxaphene
Malathion	Zineb

The other pesticides recommended in this chapter for use on the green foliage of plants are also compatible except as follows:

Emulsifiable concentrate of methoxychlor may cause injury to foliage if mixed with sulfur, ferbam, maneb, thiram, zineb or ziram. Methoxychlor wettable powder is compatible with these fungicides.

Mixtures of the fixed coppers with diazinon, ferbam, ziram, maneb, thiram or zineb may decompose upon standing.

Mixtures of captan with emulsifiable concentrates of methoxychlor, chlordane, dicofol, endosulfan or malathion may cause injury to the foliage. Captan is compatible with wettable powders of these insecticides.

SPRAYING AND DUSTING EQUIPMENT

There are many kinds of sprayers and dusters available under different trade names. You can apply insecticides and fungicides easily and efficiently if you use good equipment manufactured expressly for the purpose. Below are some points to consider in selecting sprayers and dusters.

Sprayers

Hand atomizers: Hand atomizers vary in capacity from ½ pint to 3 quarts. They are very useful for applying all-liquid pesticides to small plantings. Wettable powders tend to clog the nozzles.

Choose an atomizer with an adjustable nozzle that can be turned upward or downward and that will deliver a continuous spray. The nozzle and spray chamber should be made of a noncorrosive material and should be so constructed that they can be easily cleaned.

Compressed-air sprayers: Compressed-air sprayers, which are usually made of galvanized steel, range in capacity from 1 to 5 gallons. They are the most satisfactory sprayers to use in the garden. Some types are not equipped with an agitator and must be shaken frequently during spraying.

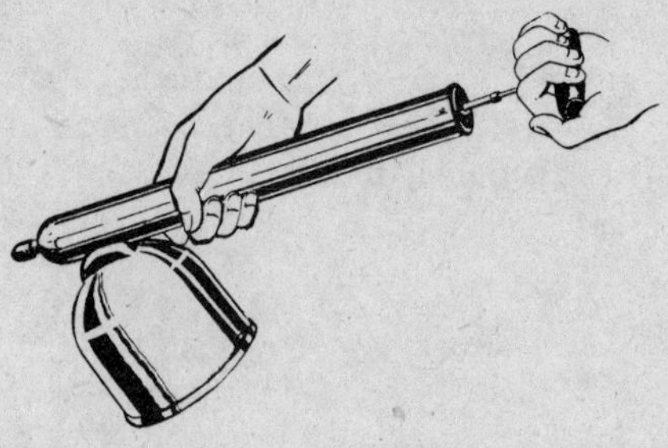

This hand atomizer has a copper spray chamber. Some hand atomizers come with removable glass chambers that resemble fruit jars.

This compressed-air sprayer holds 2 gallons of spray, and it operates at about 50 pounds of pressure, which is obtained by a plunger-type hand pump. The handle of the pump also serves as the handle of the sprayer.

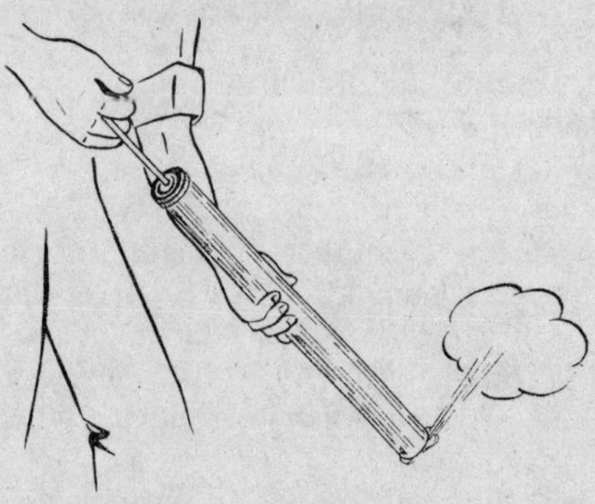

This plunger-type duster is ideal for treating individual plants and small areas.

Dusters

Plunger: Plunger-type dusters range in capacity from 1 to 3 pounds. They are the most practicable applicators for the small garden. They are usually equipped with tube and nozzle attachments, which permit the dust to be directed to the underside of leaves.

Fan or crank: Fan- or crank-type dusters have capacities up to 15 pounds and can be used satisfactorily in small and large areas. These dusters are more efficient and durable than other types of hand dusters.

PRECAUTIONS

Pesticides used improperly can be injurious to man, animals and plants. Follow the directions and heed all precautions on the labels.

Store pesticides in original containers—out of reach of children and pets—and away from foodstuff.

Apply pesticides selectively and carefully. Do not apply a pesticide when there is danger of drift to other areas. Avoid prolonged inhalation of a pesticide spray or dust. When applying a pesticide it is advisable that you be fully clothed.

After handling a pesticide, do not eat, drink or smoke until you have washed. In case a pesticide is swallowed or gets in the eyes, follow the first aid treatment given on the label and get prompt medical attention. If a pesticide is spilled on your skin or clothing, remove clothing immediately and wash skin thoroughly. Launder clothing before wearing.

Chlordane, diazinon, dimethoate, naled and toxaphene can be absorbed directly through the skin in harmful quantities. When working with these pesticides in any form, take extra care not to let them come in contact with the skin.

Apply a pesticide only to those crops on which it is recommended. Do not apply more than is recommended. Allow a sufficient waiting period—at least one day before a harvest, or longer if the label specifies. Wash all treated vegetables before eating.

Carbaryl: Do not apply carbaryl to asparagus, beans, carrot, cucumber, eggplant, melons, okra, peas, peppers, pumpkin, squash, sweet corn or tomato within one day before a harvest; or to broccoli, brussels sprouts, cabbage, cauliflower, head lettuce, kohlrabi, parsnip, radish or rutabaga within three days before a harvest. Do not apply carbaryl to blackberry or raspberry within seven days; or chard, Chinese cabbage, collards, kale, leaf lettuce, mustard or spinach within 14 days. Do not apply carbaryl to table beet or turnip within 14 days before a harvest (three days if tops won't be used for food or feed). Do not apply carbaryl to onion or potato.

Chlordane: Do not apply chlordane to any plant after the appearance of foliage or fruit that is to be eaten or fed to livestock. Do not repeat soil application of chlordane for at least three years. Do not apply chlordane to soil within two years before planting asparagus, carrot, parsnip or radish.

Diazinon: Do not apply diazinon to peas or tomato within one day before a harvest; or to melons or winter squash within three days; or to broccoli, cauliflower or peppers within five days; or to beans, blackberry, brussels sprouts, cabbage, cucumber, raspberry, or summer squash within seven days; or to carrot, celery, collard, kale, lettuce, onion, parsnip, radish, spinach, or turnip within ten days; to table beet within 14 days; or to potato within 35 days before a harvest. Do not apply diazinon to foliage of asparagus, eggplant, kohlrabi, okra, pumpkin, mustard or rutabaga.

Dicofol: Do not apply dicofol to blackberry, cucumber, melons, peppers, squash, raspberry or tomato within two days, or to beans within seven days before a harvest. Do not use dicofol on beans or potatoes.

Dimethoate: Do not apply dimethoate to peppers within one day before a harvest, to tomato within seven days, or to spinach within 14 days.

Endosulfan: Do not apply endosulfan to cucumber, eggplant, pepper, potato, pumpkin, squash or tomato within one day before a harvest; or to broccoli or cabbage within seven days; or to brussels sprouts or cauliflower within 14 days; or to collards, kale, mustard, spinach or turnip within 21 days before a harvest. Do not apply more than once to kale, mustard, spinach or turnip. Do not feed treated plants to livestock. Do not apply to beets, beans, kohlrabi or chard. Apply only to plants for which it is recommended on the label.

Fungicides: Do not apply zineb to beet or carrot within seven days before a harvest if the tops are to be used as food. Do not apply ferbam or ziram to carrot within seven days before a harvest if the tops are to be used as food. Do not apply zineb to chard or spinach within seven days before a harvest. Do not apply ferbam to blackberry or raspberry within 40 days. Do not apply ziram to potato. Do not apply ferbam to potato or sweet potato. Fungicides may be used up to one day before a harvest on other crops for which they are recommended.

Malathion: Do not apply malathion to asparagus, beans, blackberry, cucumber, melons, okra, squash, tomato or raspberry within one day before a harvest; or to broccoli, eggplant, onion, peas, peppers, pumpkin, rutabaga or turnip (including tops) within three days; or to sweet corn within five days; or to beet tops, brussels sprouts, cabbage, carrot, cauliflower, celery, collard, kale, kohlrabi, head lettuce, mustard, radish or spinach within seven days; or leaf lettuce within 14 days before a harvest.

Methoxychlor: Do not apply methoxychlor to cantaloupe, cucumber, eggplant, kohlrabi, peppers, pumpkin, squash, tomato or turnip (if tops are not to be used) within one day before a harvest; or to asparagus, beans, blackberry, blackeye pea, cabbage or raspberry, within three days; or to beet or carrot (if tops are not to be used), cauliflower, pea, radish, rutabaga or sweet corn within seven days; or to beet tops, broccoli, brussels sprouts, carrot tops, collard, kale, lettuce, spinach, or turnip tops within 14 days before a harvest. Do not apply methoxychlor to onions or okra.

Naled: Do not apply naled to broccoli, brussels sprouts, cabbage, cauliflower, chard, cucumber, eggplant, lettuce, melons, peppers, pumpkin, spinach, squash, tomato or turnip within one day before a harvest. Do not apply naled to beans, table beet, blackberry, celery, collards, kale, kohlrabi, mustard, okra, onion, peas, potato, raspberry or sweet corn.

Toxaphene: Do not apply toxaphene to tomato within three days or to eggplant or peppers within five days before a harvest. Do not apply to celery after bunch begins to form or stalk is half grown. Do not apply to other crops after appearance of parts to be eaten or fed to livestock. Do not apply toxaphene to asparagus, beets, chard, endive, melons, mustard, potato, squash, sweet potato or turnip.

Dispose of empty pesticide containers by wrapping them in several layers of newspaper and placing them in your trash can.

It is difficult to remove all traces of a herbicide (weed killer) from equipment. Therefore, to prevent injury to desirable plants, do not use the same equipment for insecticides and fungicides that you use for a herbicide.

OTHER CONTROL MEASURES

Insecticides and fungicides, although effective in controlling a large number of garden pets, will not eradicate all insects or cure all diseases. Plant diseases can rarely be cured, but must be controlled by prevention.

The following measures will help prevent losses caused by insects and diseases:

1. Use fertile, well-drained soil and a good grade of fertilizer.
2. Plant crops that are suited to the soil and climate.
3. Keep down weeds and grass.
4. Purchase disease-free seed. Buy certified seed where possible.
5. Treat seed with chemicals to protect against decay and damping-off.
6. Purchase disease-free plants; make sure they do not have swellings on the roots, cankers on the stems or spots on the leaves.
7. Grow disease-resistant varieties if available. Resistant varieties are available for only a few diseases of certain crops. Some of these varieties are highly resistant; others give partial protection.
8. Destroy plants of each annual crop as soon as harvest is completed.
9. Avoid unnecessary use of insecticides that may kill friendly insects. See "Beneficial Insects," page 340.

INSECTS AND DISEASES

Asparagus

ASPARAGUS BEETLE

Description: Adult: Metallic blue to black; orange to yellow markings; ¼ inch long. Larva: Olive green to dark gray; ⅓ inch long. Eggs, which are laid on spears of female beetles, look like shiny black specks.

Damage: Adults and larvae eat foliage; shoots are disfigured.

Distribution: Throughout United States.

What to do: Apply a dust or spray containing carbaryl, malathion or rotenone. *Caution:* Do not apply carbaryl, malathion or rotenone within one day before a harvest. Do not repeat applications of carbaryl within three days.

RUST (FUNGUS)

Symptoms and damage: Elongated, orange-red, powdery pustules (blisters) on stems and foliage; early death of plant tops; reduction in following year's crop. Disease is worst during moist seasons. Fungus lives on remains of diseased tops of previous year.

Distribution: Throughout United States.

What to do: Grow rust-resistant varieties such as 'Mary Washington' and 'Waltham Washington'; use a dependable strain of seed. Cut diseased tops close to the ground and burn them in the fall.

Beans

BEAN APHID (PLANT LOUSE)

Description: Adult and young: Tiny black insect; looks like cabbage aphid. Bean aphids cluster on stems and under leaves.

Damage: Leaves curl and thicken; plants become yellow and unthrifty. Aphids spread virus of common bean mosaic.

Distribution: Throughout United States; infestations localized.

What to do: Apply a dust or spray containing diazinon, malathion or naled.

BEAN LEAF BEETLE

Description: Reddish to yellowish; black spots on back; up to ¼ inch long.

Damage: Eats regular-shaped holes in leaves.

Distribution: In all eastern states; damage usually restricted to small areas.

What to do: Apply a dust or spray containing carbaryl or rotenone to underside of leaves.

CORN EARWORM

Description: Green, brown or pink; light stripes along sides and on back; up to 1¾ inches long. When insect occurs on tomatoes, it is called tomato fruitworm.

Damage: Eats holes in pods; attacks beans in the fall. Damage is worst in warm coastal areas.

Distribution: Throughout United States.

What to do: Apply carbaryl or methoxychlor as for leafhoppers, below.

LEAFHOPPERS

Description: Several species. Adults: Green; wedge-shaped; up to ⅛ inch long; they fly quickly when disturbed. Nymphs resemble adults but are smaller; they crawl sidewise like crabs.

Damage: Adults and nymphs attack beans. Leaves of beans curl or roll downward, crinkle and tend to become yellow or bronze. Some plants are dwarfed and may die.

Distribution: Throughout United States.

What to do: Apply a dust or spray containing carbaryl, malathion or methoxychlor.

Caution: Do not apply methoxychlor within three days before harvesting or carbaryl or malathion within one day before a harvest.

LIMA-BEAN POD BORER

Description: Pink with pale-yellow head; up to ⅝ inch long; wriggles violently when disturbed.

Damage: Bores through lima bean pods and eats seed. Seldom a pest of snap beans.

Distribution: Southern part of United States; most damaging in California.

What to do: Apply carbaryl as for leafhoppers.

Lima-bean pod borer

LYGUS BUGS

Description: Several related species including tarnished plant bug. Flat, oval; mottled with white, yellow and black splotches that give it a tarnished appearance; ¼ inch long. When disturbed these active insects fly or move to opposite side of stems; are seldom seen.

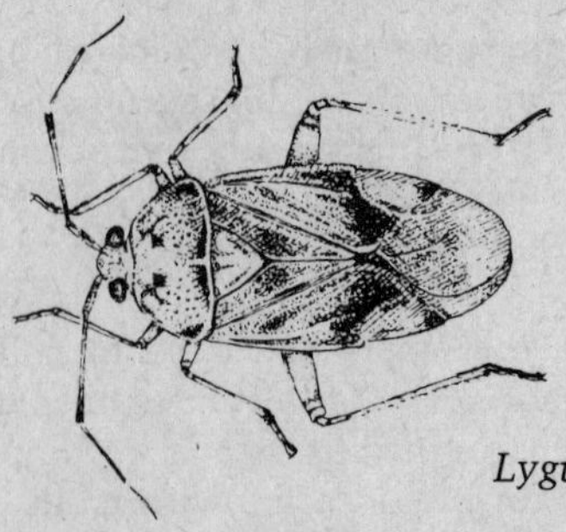

Lygus bug

Damage: Adults and nymphs pierce and suck juices from the pods, stems and blossoms. This feeding causes blossoms and young pods to drop from the plants. Feeding on the older pods causes the pods and seed to be pitted and undesirable for food. The pods may also be deformed.

Distribution: Throughout United States.

What to do: Dust or spray with carbaryl as for leafhoppers. Clean up and destroy weeds and trash in the fall to prevent overwintering.

MEXICAN BEAN BEETLE

Description: Adults: Copper-colored; oval; ¼ inch long; 16 black spots on its back. Larva: Orange to yellow; fuzzy or spiny; up to ⅓ inch long.

Damage: Adults and larvae feed on pods and on underside of leaves; pods and leaves are skeletonized.

Distribution: In most states east of Rocky Mountains.

What to do: Apply a dust or spray containing carbaryl, malathion, methoxychlor or rotenone to underside of leaves.

SEED-CORN MAGGOT

Description: Yellowish white; legless; ¼ to ⅓ inch long.

Damage: Bores into sprouting seed and prevents development of plants; particularly destructive to early planted seed.

Distribution: Throughout United States.

What to do: Purchase insecticide-treated seed and plant in warm weather; cool, wet periods retard germination and make seed more susceptible to maggot injury. Replant immediately if maggot damage is heavy.

SPOTTED CUCUMBER BEETLE

Description: Yellowish green; 12 black spots on back; ¼ inch long.

Damage: Eats holes in leaves; chews on pods.

Distribution: East of Rocky Mountains. (Closely related species are found throughout United States.)

What to do: Apply carbaryl, methoxychlor or malathion as for leafhoppers.

ANTHRACNOSE (FUNGUS)

Symptoms and damage: Brown sunken spots, which have pink centers, on pods; elongated dark-red cankers on stems and leaf veins; rusty-brown spots on ripe seeds. Disease is most common during cool, moist summers. Fungus is carried on seeds and lives in soil on remains of diseased plants.

Distribution: Central, northeastern and southeastern states.

What to do: Rotate crops. Follow recommendations for bacterial blights, below.

BACTERIAL BLIGHTS

Symptoms and damage: Large, dry, brown spots on leaves, often surrounded by yellow borders; water-soaked spots with reddish margins on pods; reddish cankers on stems. Plants may be girdled. Bacteria are carried on seed.

Distribution: Throughout United States, but seldom found west of the Rocky Mountains.

What to do: Plant western-grown seed. Do not plant discolored seeds or those that come from spotted pods. Avoid working in the garden when plants are wet; disease spreads more rapidly on wet foliage.

COMMON BEAN MOSAIC (VIRUS)

Symptoms and damage: Mottled (light and dark green) and curled leaves; stunted plants; reduced yields. Virus is carried in seed and spread by aphids (plant lice).

Distribution: Throughout United States.

What to do: Grow common mosaic-resistant varieties such as 'Topcrop', 'Tendercrop', 'Contender', 'Wade', 'Puregold Wax', 'Kentucky Wonder' (pole), and 'Blue Lake' (pole).

RUST (FUNGUS)

Symptoms and damage: Red to black pustules (blisters) on leaves. Leaves turn yellow and drop. Fungus lives through winter on remains of diseased plants.

Distribution: Throughout United States, except in some semiarid regions.

What to do: Apply sulfur spray or undiluted sulfur dust. Grow varieties such as 'Harvester', 'Tenderwhite', 'Tendergreen', 'Kingham', 'Cherokee Wax', and 'Rust Resistant Kentucky Wonder' (pole), which have some resistance to rust.

SEED DECAY (FUNGI)

Symptoms and damage: Seed rot in soil. Disease is most common during cool, moist weather. Fungi live in soil.

Distribution: Throughout United States.

What to do: Purchase treated seed.

Beets and Chard

BEET WEBWORM

Description: Yellow to green; a black stripe and numerous black spots on back; up to 1¼ inches long.

Damage: Eats leaves and buds of young plants. Rolls and folds leaves; ties them together with webs.

Distribution: Throughout United States; especially troublesome in western states.

What to do: Apply a pyrethrum dust containing 0.2 percent pyrethrins (active ingredients) or apply a pyrethrum spray.

Beet webworm

BLISTER BEETLES

Description: Many species. Gray, black or striped; slender; ½ to ¾ inch long.

Damage: The beetles eat leaves.

Distribution: Throughout United States; infestations localized; usually occur late in season.

What to do: Apply a dust or spray containing carbaryl or methoxychlor. Handpick beetles; wear gloves while picking as the beetles discharge a caustic fluid that may blister the skin.

Blister beetle

DAMPING-OFF (FUNGI)

Symptoms and damage: Seed decay in soil; young plants collapse and die. Fungi live in soil.

Distribution: Throughout United States.

What to do: Treat seeds with a protective fungicide.

LEAF SPOT (FUNGUS)

Symptoms and damage: Numerous small, round spots with light-tan centers and dark-brown borders on leaves. Fungus is carried on seed and lives in soil or on remains of diseased plants.

Distribution: East of Rocky Mountains.

What to do: Apply a dust or spray containing a fixed copper fungicide or apply zineb. Disease usually is not severe enough to require regular treatments.

Blackberries, Dewberries, Raspberries

ORANGE TORTRIX

Description: Yellow to green larva; light-brown head; up to ½ inch long.

Damage: Feeds in berries or within a web on leaves.

Distribution: Destructive to bramble berries in California, Oregon and Washington.

What to do: Apply a dust or spray containing carbaryl in spring when the plants begin to grow. Repeat treatments at ten-day intervals until the plants begin to bloom. *Caution:* Do not apply carbaryl within seven days before a harvest.

RASPBERRY CROWN BORER

Description: Larva: White, grublike, ¼ to 1¼ inches long. Egg: Oval, deep reddish brown, about 1/16 inch long, laid under surface of leaf. Adult: Clear-winged moth that resembles a common wasp; black body crossed by yellow bands.

Damage: In fall the young larvae burrow into the bark of plants, near the soil. Older larvae hollow out crowns of plants.

Distribution: Northern part of United States.

What to do: Drench the crowns and lower canes of the plants with diazinon spray when the eggs hatch in early September or October. Repeat the treatment in about two weeks. *Caution:* Do not apply diazinon while fruit is present.

RASPBERRY FRUITWORMS

Description: Several species. Adults: Yellow to brown beetles; ¼ inch long. Larvae: Brown and white; up to ⅛ inch long.

Damage: Adults make long, narrow slits in blossom buds and newly formed leaves; larvae feed in berries.

Distribution: In northern states.

What to do: Apply a dust or spray containing rotenone to foliage seven days after the first blossoms appear. Repeat three times at ten-day intervals.

Raspberry Fruitworm

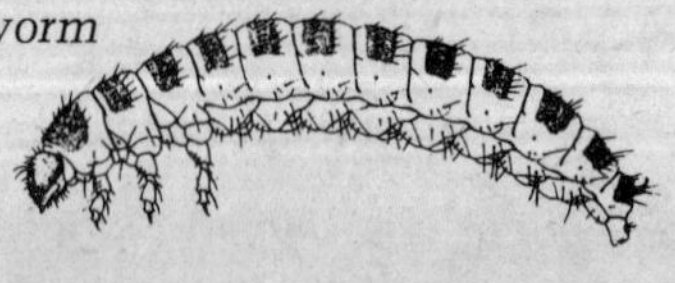

RED-NECKED CANE BORER

Description: Adults: Dark-bronze or black beetle; shiny, copper-red neck; slender; about ¼ inch long. Larvae: White; flat head; slender; up to ¾ inch long.

Damage: Adults eat margins of leaves; larvae tunnel canes, causing spindle-shaped swellings on surfaces.

Distribution: Eastern half of United States.

What to do: Apply a dust or spray containing rotenone immediately before plants bloom; repeat in two weeks. Cut off infested canes well below the points of injury and destroy them.

ROSE CHAFER

Description: Gray or fawn-colored beetle; reddish-brown head: long-legged and slender, ½ inch long.

Damage: Feeds on foliage, buds, flowers and fruits of blackberry, raspberry, cabbage, beans, beets and pepper.

Distribution: Eastern United States.

What to do: Apply a dust or spray containing methoxychlor.

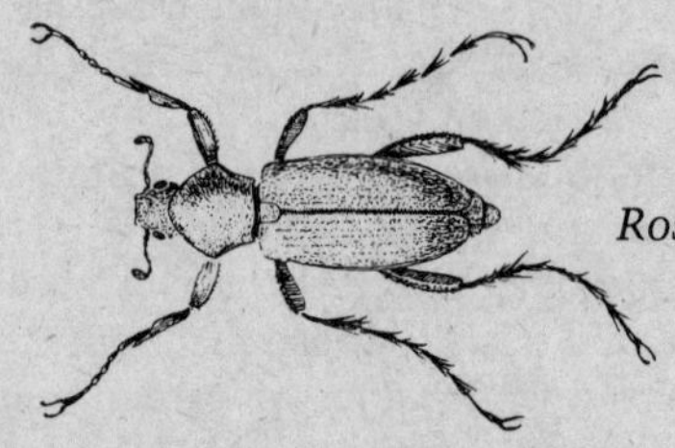

Rose chafer

ROSE SCALE

Description: White, circular and scaly; ⅛ inch in diameter.

Damage: Incrusts bark at base of canes; weakens or kills canes by feeding on sap.

Distribution: Throughout United States.

What to do: Keep down weeds in the planting. Remove and destroy infested canes. Apply a dust or spray containing malathion. If the scales persist until the dormant season, apply a spray containing ½ cup of a summer oil emulsifiable concentrate in 1 gallon of water; do not mix this spray with other pesticides, and do not apply it to plants that have green foliage.

ANTHRACNOSE (FUNGUS)

Symptoms and damage: Small gray spots with dark margins on leaves; purplish spots (about 1 inch in diameter) with ash-gray centers and raised, purplish margins on canes. Spotted canes may crack lengthwise. Fruits of many varieties of blackberries are not badly damaged; but those of 'Lawton' are particularly susceptible. Disease also attacks raspberries. Fungus lives on remains of diseased canes of previous year.

Distribution: Throughout United States.

What to do: Make three applications of ferbam. Make first application when leaves are exposed ½ to ¾ inch; second, just before blossoms open; third, after blossoming. In North Carolina and regions southward, cut all canes close to the ground and destroy them after harvest. In the North, prune away only the fruiting canes.

DOUBLE BLOSSOM (FUNGUS)

Symptoms and damage: Twisted and wrinkled petals; abnormally large flower buds. Short, broom-like growths emerge from infected buds; no berries grow at these points. Diseased canes produce poor fruits. New canes infected in early summer show no outer symptoms until following spring. Fungus lives in infected blossoms and canes.

Distribution: Chiefly in southeastern states.

What to do: Remove and destroy infected blossoms. In North Carolina and regions southward, cut all canes close to ground after harvest and destroy them.

Cabbage and Related Plants

CABBAGE APHID (PLANT LOUSE)

Description: Adults and young: Tiny green to powdery blue; soft-bodied; covered with a fine whitish wax. Aphids cluster on leaves.

Damage: Curled and distorted leaves; stunted plants. Aphids may severely damage cabbage, collards, brussels sprouts, broccoli and kale.

Distribution: Throughout United States; particularly troublesome in the South.

What to do: Remove and destroy heavily damaged plants early in season. Cut off and destroy old leaves from infested collard, broccoli, cauliflower and kale plants. Apply a dust or spray containing diazinon, malathion, or naled.

CABBAGE LOOPER

Description: Pale-green measuring worm; light stripes down back; up to 1½ inches long; doubles up, or loops, when it crawls.

Damage: Feeds on underside of leaves, producing ragged holes; large loopers burrow into heads.

Distribution: Throughout United States.

What to do: Apply a spray or dust containing endosulfan, malathion or naled. Direct the insecticide to the underside of the leaves. Repeat treatment once a week as long as needed.

CABBAGE WEBWORM

Description: Dull grayish-yellow; fat; 5 brownish-purple stripes down back; up to ½ inch long.

Damage: Bores into buds and stems, killing young plants. Feeds under a protective web that it produces. Does little or no damage to spring crop.

Distribution: Southern United States.

What to do: Apply a dust or spray containing endosulfan, malathion, or naled. In the South, where the insect causes heavy damage to young plants in late summer and early fall, apply the insecticide as soon as the plants appear.

DIAMONDBACK MOTH CATERPILLAR

Description: Larvae: Light green; slender; up to ⅓ inch long. Larva wriggles rapidly when disturbed, and often drops from the plant and hangs by a silken thread, which it produces.

Damage: Larva eats small holes in leaves and buds; adult (diamondback moth) does no damage.

Distribution: Throughout United States.

What to do: Apply the treatment for cabbage looper.

IMPORTED CABBAGEWORM

Description: Velvety green; up to 1¼ inches long.

Damage: Feeds on underside of leaves, producing ragged holes; bores into heads.

Distribution: Throughout United States.

What to do: Same as for the cabbage looper.

HARLEQUIN BUG

Description: Adults and young: Black; brilliantly colored with red or yellow; shield-shaped; up to ⅜ inch long.

Damage: Plants wilt; leaves turn brown as if scalded.

Distribution: In southern part of United States, from California to Virginia; infestations localized.

What to do: Apply a dust or spray containing endosulfan or naled. Handpick bugs and crush egg masses (effective if done often).

Harlequin bug

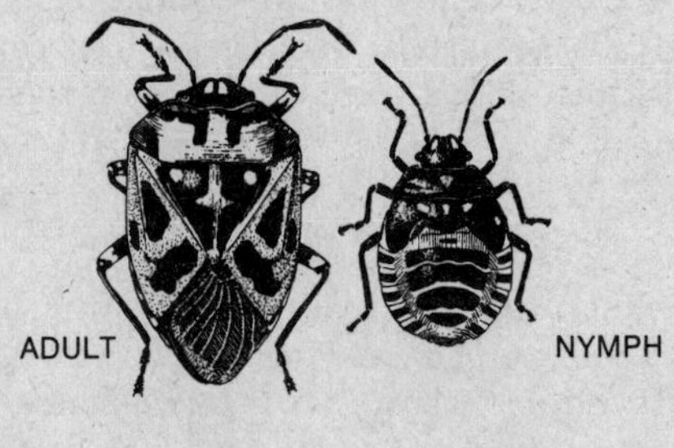

ROOT MAGGOTS

Description: Several species (include seed-corn and cabbage maggots). Yellowish white; legless, ¼ to ⅓ inch long.

Damage: Destructive in seedbeds and on young transplants. Maggots tunnel roots and stems, causing rot; plants wilt and die.

Distribution: Seed-corn maggot, throughout

United States; cabbage maggot, in northern part of country.

What to do: Before planting seed apply 6 ounces of 2 percent diazinon granules to each 100 square feet of soil surface. Mix thoroughly with the upper 4 inches of soil. If transplants are used, water each with 1 cup of diazinon spray.

BLACKLEG (FUNGUS)

Symptoms and damage: Ashen-gray spots speckled with tiny black dots on leaves and stems; stems girdled; plants wilt and die. Most common on cauliflower, broccoli and brussels sprouts. Fungus is carried on seed and lives on crop refuse in soil.

Distribution: In Central, southern, and eastern states.

What to do: Use Pacific Coast seed free from blackleg fungus. Do not plant in soil that has grown cabbage.

BLACK ROT (BACTERIAL)

Symptoms and damage: Blackened veins; stems show a blackened ring when cut across. Leaves turn yellow and drop. Plants may die. Bacteria are carried on seed and live in soil.

Distribution: In Central, southern, and eastern states.

What to do: See Blackleg, above.

CLUBROOT (SLIME MOLD)

Symptoms and damage: Large, irregular swellings, or "clubs," on roots; unthrifty and stunted plants. Disease attacks plants in seedbeds and in field. May severely damage cabbage, cauliflower, broccoli, brussels sprouts and kohlrabi. Slime mold lives in soil and enters roots.

Distribution: Throughout United States.

What to do: Grow seedlings in clean soil. Do not grow cabbage in soil where disease has occurred. Do not set plants that have swellings on roots. Rotate crops.

DAMPING-OFF (FUNGI)

Symptoms and damage: Seed decay in soil; young plants collapse and die. Fungi live in soil.

Distribution: Throughout United States.

What to do: Treat seeds with a protective fungicide.

RHIZOCTONIA DISEASE (FUNGUS)

Symptoms and damage: Seedling stems dark and shrunken just above soil (injury called "wire stem"); lower leaves of older plants droop, decay and turn dark, but do not drop. In cabbage, base of head may rot. Fungus lives in soil.

What to do: Do not set plants that have wire stem. Rotate crops if possible.

YELLOWS OR WILT (FUNGUS)

Symptoms and damage: Yellowish-green leaves; stunted plants; lower leaves drop. Disease first attacks one side of plant. May severely damage cabbage, kohlrabi and kale. Cauliflower, broccoli, and brussels sprouts are resistant. Fungus lives in soil and enters roots.

Distribution: Throughout United States.

What to do: Plant seed in clean soil. Grow yellows-resistant varieties such as 'Jersey Queen', 'Resistant Detroit', 'Marion Market', 'Badger Market', 'Globe', 'Wisconsin Ballhead' and 'Wisconsin All-Season'. Spraying is of no value.

Carrots

CARROT CATERPILLAR

Description: Green; banded with black and yellow markings; up to 2 inches long.

Damage: Eats leaves; destroys tops. Seldom numerous enough to reduce yield.

Distribution: Throughout United States.

What to do: Handpick caterpillars.

Carrot caterpillar

Carrot rust fly

CARROT RUST FLY

Description: Larvae: Yellowish white; legless; up to ⅓ inch long.

Damage: Larva tunnels into fleshy roots; destroys fibrous roots.

Distribution: In Northeast; also in coastal Washington and Oregon.

What to do: Before planting apply 6 ounces of 2 percent diazinon granules to each 100 square feet of soil surface. Mix thoroughly with the upper 4 inches of soil; wait 1 week before planting.

LEAF BLIGHT (FUNGUS)

Symptoms and damage: Black or brown spots appear on leaves and leaf stalks; older leaves dry and die. Fungus is carried on seed and lives in remains of infected plants in the soil.

Distribution: Throughout United States.
What to do: Rotate crops. If plants show damage, apply a spray containing a fixed copper or organic fungicide; or use copper or organic fungicide dust.

YELLOWS (VIRUS)

Symptoms and damage: Yellowed young leaves (at center of crown) followed by appearance of a large number of yellowed shoots; reddened and twisted old leaves. Roots are small and of poor quality. Virus, which causes aster yellows, attacks other cultivated and wild plants; it is spread by leafhoppers and lives through winter in perennial plants.
Distribution: Throughout United States.
What to do: Same as for six-spotted leafhopper on lettuce.

Celery

CELERY LEAF TIER

Description: Greenish: up to ¾ inch long.
Damage: Eats holes in leaves and stalks. Rolls and folds leaves; ties them together with webs.
Distribution: Throughout United States.
What to do: Make two applications of a pyrethrum dust containing 0.2 percent of pyrethrins (active ingredient) ½ hour apart. First application should drive tiers from webs and second should kill them.

Celery leaf tier

DAMPING-OFF (FUNGI)

Symptoms and damage: Seed decay in soil; young plants collapse and die. Fungi live in soil.
Distribution: Throughout United States.
What to do: Treat seed with a protective fungicide.

EARLY BLIGHT (FUNGUS)

Symptoms and damage: Small, circular, yellowish-brown spots on old leaves. Spots enlarge and later are ashen gray. Disease affects stalks. Fungus is spread by rain and lives in soil.
Distribution: Throughout United States.
What to do: Apply a spray containing a fixed copper fungicide, zineb or ziram, or a dust containing copper, zineb or ziram. Remove and destroy plant debris in the fall. Rotate crops. If blight damage is heavy, grow 'Emerson Pascal', a blight-resistant variety. *Caution:* Remove residues of zineb and ziram by stripping, trimming and washing.

LATE BLIGHT (FUNGUS)

Symptoms and damage: Small yellow spots on old leaves and stalks. Spots turn dark gray and are speckled with tiny black dots. Fungus is carried on seed and lives in the soil.
Distribution: Throughout United States.
What to do: Same as for early blight, above. If disease is common, spraying or dusting should begin in the seedbed; as advised above, grow 'Emerson Pascal', a blight-resistant variety.

PINK ROT (FUNGUS)

Symptoms and damage: Water-soaked spots and white-to-pink cottony growth at base of stalks. Stalks rot and turn bitter. Fungus, which also attacks cabbage and lettuce, lives in soil for several years.
Distribution: In northeastern, North Central and southern states.
What to do: Rotate crops, if possible. Avoid successive planting of celery, lettuce or cabbage in same soil. Remove and destroy diseased plants.

YELLOWS (FUNGUS)

Symptoms and damage: Yellowed leaves; stunted plants. Some plants may die. Fungus lives in soil and enters roots.
Distribution: In Central and eastern states.
What to do: Plant seed in clean soil. Do not set diseased plants. If self-blanching varieties are wanted, grow yellows-resistant varieties such as 'Michigan Golden', 'Florida Golden' and 'Forbes Golden Plume'. Green celeries are generally resistant.

Cucumbers

PICKLEWORM

Description: Yellowish white; brownish head; up to ¾ inch long. Numerous dark spots on young worm.
Damage: Feeds on flowers and leaf buds; tunnels flowers, terminal buds, vines and fruits.
Distribution: Southeastern part of U.S. as far north as Connecticut, Illinois, Iowa and Kansas. Winters in southern Florida and Texas; spreads northward late in season.
What to do: Very early spring plantings are seldom damaged. Apply a dust or spray containing carbaryl. Begin treating plants at first sign of worms in blossoms and buds; worms must be killed before they enter the fruits. Repeat treatment once a week. *Caution:* Do not apply insecticides within one day before a harvest.

STRIPED CUCUMBER BEETLE

Description: Adults: Yellow to black; 3 black stripes down back, ⅕ inch long. Larvae: White; slender; brownish at the ends; up to ⅓ inch long.

Damage: Adults feed on leaves, stems and fruit, and spread bacterial wilt. Larvae bore into roots and stems below soil line. Insects usually attack young plants. Damaged plants wilt and sometimes die.

Distribution: East of Rocky Mountains; related species are found in some western states.

What to do: Apply a dust or spray containing carbaryl, malathion or methoxychlor as soon as plants appear. Repeat treatment once or twice a week. *Caution:* Do not apply insecticides within one day before a harvest.

ANTHRACNOSE (FUNGUS)

Symptoms and damage: Reddish-brown circular spots on leaves; elongated tan cankers on stems; round, sunken spots with pinkish-tan centers (later turning dark) on fruits. Also attacks muskmelons and watermelons. Damage worst in warm, moist weather. Fungus is carried on seeds and lives in soil.

Distribution: Central, eastern and southern states.

What to do: Do not grow cucumbers or melons in same soil oftener than once in three years. Spray or dust the plants with captan or ziram. If mildew is present, apply a spray containing a fixed copper fungicide or an organic fungicide, but do not apply ferbam.

BACTERIAL WILT

Symptoms and damage: Large vines gradually wilt and die (no yellowing of leaves); young plants die rapidly. Old plants may first have only one shoot affected. Bacteria, spread by cucumber beetles, enter and plug water vessels of stems, leaves.

Distribution: North, Central and northeastern states.

What to do: Remove and destroy wilted plants found early in season. Follow same recommendations as for striped cucumber beetle, above.

DAMPING-OFF (FUNGI)

Symptoms and damage: Seeds decay in soil; young plants collapse and die. Fungi live in soil.

Distribution: Throughout United States.

What to do: Treat seed with a protective fungicide.

DOWNY MILDEW (FUNGUS)

Symptoms and damage: Yellowish, angular spots on older leaves, fruits not affected. Leaves dry, curl, and die. Also attacks muskmelons and watermelons. Fungus is not carried on seeds and does not overwinter in soil.

Distribution: Atlantic Coast and Gulf States.

What to do: Apply a dust or spray containing a fixed copper fungicide or an organic fungicide, but do not apply ferbam. Grow mildew-resistant varieties such as 'Palmetto', 'Santee', 'Ashley', 'Stono', 'Smoothie', 'Fletcher' and 'Palomar'.

MOSAIC (VIRUS)

Symptoms and damage: Mottled (green and yellow) and curled leaves; warty, misshapen and spotted fruits; stunted plants; reduced yields. Also attacks muskmelon, squash, pepper, celery, and tomatoes. Virus lives in perennial weeds—milkweed, ground cherry, catnip—and is spread by aphids (plant lice).

Distribution: Throughout United States.

What to do: Remove and destroy perennial weeds. Grow mosaic-resistant cucumber varieties such as 'Niagara', 'Ohio MR 200', 'Sensation Hybrid', 'Burpee Hybrid', 'Surecrop Hybrid' and 'Table Queen'—slicing varieties; and 'Ohio MR 17', 'Ohio MR 25', 'Yorkstate Pickling', 'Wisconsin SMR 18' and 'Spartan Dawn F. Hybrid'—pickling varieties.

ROOT KNOT (NEMATODE)

Symptoms and damage: Galls, or swellings, on roots; stunted plants. Galls on small roots are tiny; compound galls on large roots are up to an inch in diameter. Pearly-white specks inside galls are egg masses of root-knot nematode, which lives in soil. Damages many kinds of plants.

Distribution: In southern areas; most common south of 40° latitude.

What to do: If the soil is heavily infested, the best thing to do is to move garden to another location, if possible. For some crops and in some locations, the treatment of the soil with nematocides is practicable.

SCAB (FUNGUS)

Symptoms and damage: Sunken dark-brown spots on fruits. Gummy substance oozes from fruits. In moist weather, spots are covered by grayish-olive fungus growth. Some small brown spots on leaves and stems. Fungus also attacks summer squash, particularly crookneck and yellow straightneck. Damage worse in cool, moist weather. Fungus lives in soil.

Distribution: North Central and northeastern states.

What to do: Do not grow cucumbers or squash in

same soil oftener than once in three years. Grow scab-resistant varieties such as 'Highmoor', 'Ashe' and 'Fletcher'—slicing varieties; and 'Wisconsin SR 6' and 'Wisconsin SMR 12'—pickling varieties. Spraying or dusting is not vary effective against scab.

Eggplant

EGGPLANT LACEBUG

Description: Adults: Grayish to light brown; flat; lacelike wings; ⅙ inch long. Nymphs: Yellowish; louselike; spiny; up to ⅒ inch long.

Damage: Adults and nymphs feed in groups on undersides of leaves. Leaves turn yellow and brown; plants usually die.

Distribution: The South.

What to do: Apply a dust or spray containing malathion. *Caution:* Do not apply malathion to eggplant within three days before a harvest.

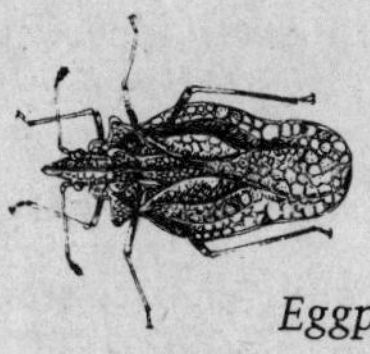

Eggplant lacebug

DAMPING-OFF (FUNGI)

Symptoms and damage: Seed decay in soil; young plants collapse and die. Fungi live in soil.

Distribution: Throughout United States.

What to do: Treat seeds with a protective fungicide.

FRUIT ROT (FUNGUS)

Symptoms and damage: Brown and shrunken stems at soil line; brown or gray spots on leaves; large, ringed, circular tan or brown spots covered with small pustules (blisters) on fruits. Fungus is carried on seed and lives in soil.

Distribution: Throughout United States.

What to do: Grow rot-resistant varieties such as 'Florida Beauty' and 'Florida Market'.

WILT (FUNGI)

Symptoms and damage: Slow wilting and stunting of plants. Plants sometimes die. Fungi live in soil.

Distribution: Throughout United States.

What to do: Do not plant eggplant in soil that has recently grown tomatoes or potatoes. Rotate crops.

Lettuce

CABBAGE LOOPER

Description: Pale-green measuring worm; light stripes down back; up to 1½ inches long; doubles up, or loops, when it crawls.

Damage: Feeds on undersides of leaves, producing ragged holes.

Distribution: Throughout United States.

What to do: Apply a dust or spray containing malathion or naled.

SIX-SPOTTED LEAFHOPPER

Description: Adults and young: Light greenish yellow; slender; wedge-shaped; very active; several pairs of tiny black dots on face; up to ⅛ inch long. Looks like the potato leafhopper, but is broader. Prefers open areas.

Damage: Spreads the virus of aster yellows to lettuce, carrots and asters.

Distribution: Throughout United States.

What to do: Plant lettuce in sheltered areas—near hedges, buildings, etc. Apply a dust or spray containing carbaryl, malathion or methoxychlor when plants are ½ inch high, repeat treatment once a week. Leafhoppers must be controlled on all host plants or they will continue to spread disease to lettuce.

DROP (FUNGUS)

Symptoms and damage: Wilting of outer leaves; watery soft rot on stems and old leaves; wilted and decayed plants. Disease worst in moist weather.

Distribution: Central, eastern, and southern states.

What to do: Avoid close planting and poorly drained soil. Ridge soil slightly about plants to prevent water from accumulating.

TIPBURN (PHYSIOLOGIC)

Symptoms and damage: Margins of the tender leaves turn brown and dry. Most severe damage on head lettuce.

Distribution: Throughout United States.

What to do: Grow tipburn-resistant varieties such as 'Great Lakes', 'Cornell 456' and 'Pennlake'.

YELLOWS (VIRUS)

Symptoms and damage: Yellowing, blanching, curling and twisting of inner leaves. Virus, which causes aster yellows, attacks other cultivated and wild plants. Virus lives in perennial plants and is spread by leafhoppers.

Distribution: Throughout United States.
What to do: Same as for six-spotted leafhopper.

Muskmelon and Cantaloupe

APHIDS (PLANT LICE)

Description: Many species. Adults and young are tiny, green to black, and soft-bodied; they cluster on undersides of leaves or on stems or roots.
Damage: Curled and distorted leaves; stunted plants. Severely damage turnip, melons, cucumber, peas, beans, tomato, potato, celery, pepper, spinach and cabbage. Aphids transmit certain virus diseases of vegetables.
Distribution: Throughout United States.
What to do: Apply a dust or spray containing diazinon, malathion or naled. Repeat treatments weekly as needed. Apply malathion to cucumber, squash and cantaloupe only when the plants are dry. Do not apply to crops not specified on container label.

PICKLEWORM

Description: Yellowish white; brownish head; up to ¾ inch long. Numerous dark spots on young worm.
Damage: Feeds on flowers and leaf buds; tunnels flowers, terminal buds, vines and fruits.
Distribution: Southeastern part of United States, as far north as Connecticut, Illinois, Iowa and Kansas. Winters in southern Florida and Texas, spreads northward late in season.
What to do: Very early spring plantings are seldom damaged. Apply a dust or spray containing carbaryl. Begin treating plants at first sign of worms in blossoms or buds; worms must be killed before they enter fruits. Repeat treatment once a week. Do not treat within one day before a harvest.

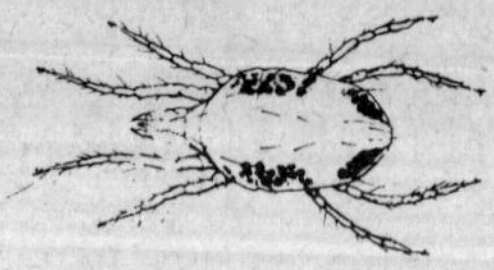

Spider mite

SPIDER MITES

Description: Several species. Adults and young: Tiny (barely visible to naked eye); red or greenish red. Found on undersides of leaves. Not classified as insects.
Damage: Yellow specks and fine webs on leaves, plants and fruits are stunted. Attack beans, blackberry, cucumber, melons and tomato.
Distribution: Throughout United States.
What to do: Apply a dust or spray containing dicofol. Partial control may be obtained by applying a dust containing 25 to 30 percent of sulfur or by applying a spray containing sulfur. *Caution:* Sulfur may cause injury to cucumber and melons.

STRIPED CUCUMBER BEETLE

Description: Adults: Yellow to black; 3 black stripes down back; ⅕ inch long. Larvae: White; slender; brownish at the ends; up to ⅓ inch long.
Damage: Adults feed on leaves, stems and fruit, and spread bacterial wilt of cantaloupe and cucumber. Larvae bore into roots and also feed on stems at or below soil line. Insects usually attack young plants. Damaged plants wilt and sometimes die.
Distribution: East of Rocky Mountains; related species are found throughout United States.
What to do: Apply a dust or spray containing malathion or methoxychlor as soon as plants appear. Repeat treatment once or twice a week as needed. Do not apply these insecticides within one day before a harvest.

DOWNY MILDEW (FUNGUS)

Symptoms and damage: Irregular brownish spots on older leaves; fruits not affected. Leaves dry, curl and die. Also attacks cucumbers and watermelons. Fungus is not carried on seed, does not overwinter in soil.
Distribution: Atlantic Coast and Gulf States.
What to do: Apply a dust or spray containing a fixed copper or organic fungicide, but do not use ferbam. Grow mildew-resistant varieties such as 'Delta Gold', 'Georgia 47', 'Edisto 47', 'Perlita', 'Home Garden' and 'Gulfstream'.

LEAF SPOT (FUNGUS)

Symptoms and damage: Numerous small round brown spots on leaves; no spotting of fruits. Many leaves may be killed. Fungus lives on remains of diseased vines in soil.
Distribution: Central, southern and Atlantic States.
What to do: Do not grow melons or cucumbers in same soil oftener than once in three years. Apply a dust or spray containing a fixed copper or organic fungicide, but do not use ferbam.

MOSAIC (VIRUSES)

Symptoms and damage: Mottled green-and-yellow, curled leaves; stunted plants; reduced yields. Mosaic diseases are caused by watermelon mosaic viruses 1 and 2 in the South and West, by tobacco ringspot virus in the Central United States east of the Rocky Mountains, and by cucumber mosaic and squash mosaic viruses nationally. Viruses live in perennial weeds, in soil, or in seed. Squash mosaic viruses are carried in squash and muskmelon seed; tobacco ringspot virus is soil-born; watermelon mosaic viruses and cucumber mosaic viruses are spread by aphids; and squash mosaic virus is spread by cucumber beetles.

Distribution: Throughout United States.

What to do: Remove and destroy perennial weeds and diseased plants. Do not plant seed from infected plants. Follow recommendations for aphids and striped cucumber beetle.

Mustard

See under "Turnips and Mustard," page 340.

Okra

CORN EARWORM

Description: Green, brown or pink; up to 1¾ inches long.

Damage: Eats holes in pods.

Distribution: Where okra is grown.

What to do: Handpick and destroy worms and damaged pods. Apply a dust or spray containing carbaryl.

ROOT KNOT (NEMATODE)

Symptoms and damage: Galls, or swellings, on roots; stunted plants. Galls on small roots are tiny; compound galls on large roots are up to an inch in diameter. Pearly-white specks inside galls are egg masses of root-knot nematode, which lives in soil. Damages many kinds of plants.

Distribution: In southern areas; most common south of 40° latitude.

What to do: See "Root Knot" under "Cucumbers," page 325.

WILT (FUNGI)

Symptoms and damage: Yellow and wilted leaves; stunted plants. Occasionally does serious damage.

Distribution: In the South.

What to do: Do not grow okra in soil where wilt has occurred, or in any soil oftener than once in three years.

Onion

ONION MAGGOT

Description: White root maggot; legless; up to ⅓ inch long.

Damage: Burrows into bulbs.

Distribution: Northern United States.

What to do: Apply a dust or spray containing malathion. Do not apply malathion within three days before a harvest.

ONION THRIPS

Description: Adults: Yellow or brownish; winged; active; about 1/25 inch long. Larvae: White; wingless; look like adults but are smaller.

Damage: Adults and larvae suck out juices from plants. White blotches appear on leaves; tips of leaves wither and turn brown.

Distribution: Throughout United States.

What to do: Apply a dust or spray containing diazinon or malathion. *Caution:* Do not apply diazinon within ten days or malathion within three days before a harvest.

Onion thrip

SMUT (FUNGUS)

Symptoms and damage: Black pustules (blisters) filled with masses of fungus on leaves. Disease often kills young plants. Fungus overwinters in soil.

Distribution: Northern states.

What to do: Avoid planting in soil where disease has occurred, if possible. Or sprinkle a formaldehyde solution (1 teaspoon to 1 quart of water) over seeds before covering row with soil.

Peas (Black-eye)

COWPEA CURCULIO

Description: Adults: Black; humpbacked; snout beetle; ¼ inch long. Larvae: Whitish; legless; yellowish head; up to ⅓ inch long.

Damage: Adults eat small holes in pods and peas. Larvae feed within the green seed.

Distribution: South Atlantic and Gulf States.

What to do: Apply a dust or spray containing carbaryl. Treat plants when blossoms are open. Repeat treatment in three and six days. *Caution:* Do not apply carbaryl within one day before a harvest.

Cowpea curculio

Peas (Garden)

PEA WEEVIL

Description: Adults: Brownish; white, black and grayish markings; ⅕ inch long. Larvae: White; small brown head and mouth; up to ⅓ inch long.

Damage: Adults feed in blossoms and lay eggs on young pods. Larvae burrow into green seed.

Distribution: Throughout United States; most troublesome in Utah, Idaho, Washington, Oregon, California, New York.

What to do: Apply a dust or spray containing malathion or methoxychlor. Treat plants while in blossom and before first pods form.

ROOT MAGGOTS

Description: Several species (includes seed-corn and cabbage maggots. Yellowish white; legless; ¼ to ⅓ inch long when full grown.

Damage: Bore into sprouting seeds and prevent development of plants. Destructive in seedbeds and on young transplants. Tunnel roots and stems; plants wilt and die. Attack beans, peas, carrot, melons, spinach, cabbage, turnip, onion and radish. Particularly destructive to early-season plantings.

Distribution: Throughout United States.

What to do: Consult your state agricultural experiment station or county agent for information on seed treatments for root-maggot control in your area. Also see recommendations for controlling the seed-corn maggot on beans, the onion maggot, and root maggots on cabbage and radish.

ASCOCHYTA POD SPOT (FUNGUS)

Symptoms and damage: Irregular light-colored spots with dark margins on pods; concentric circular spots with tiny dark dots on leaves; spots on stems near soil. Fungus is carried on seed and lives on remains of old infected vines.

Distribution: Central, southern and northeastern states.

What to do: Remove and burn diseased vines after crop is picked. Plant western-grown seed.

BACTERIAL BLIGHT

Symptoms and damage: Large water-soaked spots on pods; irregular dark spots on leaves; cream-colored shining ooze in centers of spots. Bacteria are carried on seed and live in remains of vines.

Distribution: Throughout United States, except in semiarid regions of the West.

What to do: Plant western-grown seed (infection less likely than in seed grown east of Rocky Mountains).

FUSARIUM WILT (FUNGUS)

Symptoms and damage: Yellowed leaves; wilted plants. Interiors of stems are lemon yellow. Disease sometimes kills plants. Fungus lives in soil and enters through roots.

Distribution: Throughout United States.

What to do: Grow wilt-resistant varieties such as 'Alaska', 'Alderman', 'Progress No. 9', 'World Record' and 'Giant Stride'.

ROOT ROTS (FUNGUS)

Symptoms and damage: Yellowish, unthrifty plants; rotted and yellowish-brown, red or black stems (below ground) and roots. Disease often kills plants at flowering time. Fungus lives in soil.

Distribution: Throughout United States.

What to do: Avoid growing peas continually in same soil. Make sure soil is well-drained; excessive moisture favors disease.

SEED DECAY (FUNGI)

Symptoms and damage: Seeds rot in soil. Disease is most common during cool, moist weather. Fungi live in soil.

Distribution: Throughout United States.

What to do: Treat seed with a protective fungicide.

Peppers

PEPPER WEEVIL

Description: Adults: Black snout beetle; gray or yellow markings; ⅛ inch long. The snout is about half the length of the body. Larvae: Grayish-white; pale-brown head; legless; up to ¼ inch long.

Damage: Adults feed on foliage, blossom buds and tender pods; larvae feed within buds and pods. Large pods are misshapen and discolored; buds and pods may drop off plants.

Distribution: From Florida and southern Georgia to southern California.

What to do: Apply a dust or spray containing toxaphene every week or 10 days. *Caution:* Do not apply this insecticide within five days before harvest.

Pepper weevil

ANTHRACNOSE (FUNGUS)

Symptoms and damage: Large dark-brown or black spots (whose centers have black specks) on fruits. Sun-scalded fruits often attacked by another fungus that causes spotting similar to anthracnose. Fungus is carried on seed and lives in soil.

Distribution: Central, southern and Atlantic Coast states.

What to do: Plant clean seed. Treat plants with a dust or spray containing zineb.

BACTERIAL SPOT

Symptoms and damage: Small yellowish-green spots on young leaves; spots (1/8 to 1/4 inch in diameter) with dead, straw-colored centers and dark margins on old leaves; small, rough, corky-looking spots on fruits. Old leaves turn yellow and drop. Bacteria are carried on seed and live in soil.

Distribution: In all but semiarid regions.

What to do: Plant seed in new seedbed soil. If plants show damage, apply a dust or spray containing a fixed copper fungicide.

BLOSSOM-END ROT (PHYSIOLOGIC)

Symptoms and damage: Light-colored, sunken, water-soaked spots near blossom end of fruits. Spots enlarge; 1/3 of fruit may become dark and shriveled. Fungi may grow over spots.

Distribution: Throughout United States.

What to do: Avoid excessive use of nitrogenous fertilizer and use ample amounts of superphosphate and lime. Maintain even soil moisture at all times.

CERCOSPORA LEAF SPOT (FUNGUS)

Symptoms and damage: Circular, water-soaked spots on leaves and stems. Spots enlarge 1/4 to 1/2 inch in diameter, turn white in centers, and have dark margins. Infected leaves often drop. Occasionally does serious damage. Fungus is carried on seed.

Distribution: Most common in southeastern and Gulf states.

What to do: Same as for bacterial spot.

DAMPING-OFF (FUNGI)

Symptoms and damage: Seed decay in soil; young plants collapse and die. Fungi live in soil.

Distribution: Throughout United States.

What to do: Treat seeds with a protective fungicide.

MOSAIC (VIRUSES)

Symptoms and damage: Mottled green-and-yellow, curled leaves; fruits sometimes are yellowed or show green ring spots; stunted plants; reduced yields. Disease is caused by tomato- or cucumber-mosaic viruses.

Distribution: Throughout United States.

What to do: Follow recommendations for cucumber mosaic and tomato mosaic. Grow varieties such as 'Keystone Resistant Giant', 'Liberty Bell', 'Yolo Wonder' and 'Rutgers World Beater No. 13'; these are resistant to tomato mosaic but not to cucumber mosaic.

Potatoes

BLISTER BEETLE

Description: Many species. Gray, black, or striped; slender; 1/2 to 3/4 inches long.

Damage: Beetles eat leaves.

Distribution: Throughout United States; usually occur late in season. Infestations localized.

What to do: Apply a dust or spray containing methoxychlor. Hand-pick beetles. Wear gloves while picking; the beetles discharge a caustic fluid that may blister the skin.

Blister beetle

COLORADO POTATO BEETLE

Description: Adults: Yellow; black-striped; 3/8 inch long. Larvae: Brick-red; humpback; up to 3/5 inch long.

Damage: Adults and larvae defoliate eggplant, potato and tomato; they are especially destructive to small plantings.

Distribution: In all states except California and Nevada; principal damage in eastern states.

What to do: Apply a dust or spray containing carbaryl. See "Precautions," page 318. Hand-pick beetles and crush egg masses (effective if done often).

GARDEN SYMPHYLAN

Description: White; fragile; 12 pairs of legs on adult (fewer legs on young); up to 3/8 inch long. Not classified as insect. Found in moist soils that contain decayed plant material, particularly near greenhouses.

Damage: Eats numerous tiny holes, or pits, into underground portions of plants; eats off tiny roots and root hairs. Roots of injured plants have blunted appearance. Damages beans, potato, beet, carrot, celery and spinach.

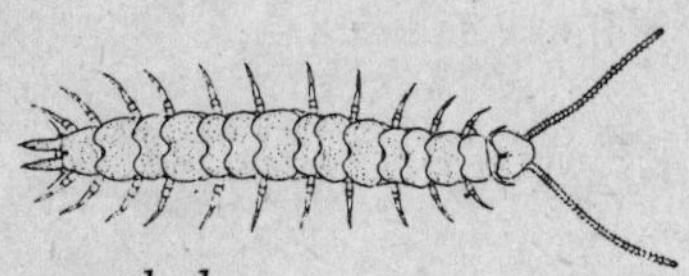

Garden symphylan

Distribution: Throughout humid areas of United States.

What to do: Difficult to control. Have your soil fumigated by your local pest-control operator.

GRASSHOPPERS

Description: Many species. Adults and nymphs: Brown, gray, black or yellow; strong hind legs; up to 2 inches long. Most grasshoppers are strong flyers.

Damage: Feed on any available vegetation; when abundant, they may destroy complete plantings of such crops as lettuce and potato.

Distribution: Throughout United States; they are especially troublesome in Central and northwestern states.

Grasshopper

What to do: Apply a dust or spray containing malathion.

LEAFHOPPERS

Description: Several species. Adults: Green; wedge-shaped; up to ⅛ inch long; they fly quickly when disturbed. Nymphs resemble adults but are smaller; they crawl sidewise like crabs.

Damage: Adults and nymphs attack potatoes and cause hopperburn. Tips and sides of potato leaves curl upward, turn yellow to brown, and become brittle. Potato and western potato leafhoppers are most destructive.

Distribution: Potato leafhopper: eastern United States; Western potato leafhoppers: parts of Southwest.

What to do: Apply a dust or spray containing malathion or methoxychlor.

POTATO TUBERWORM

Description: Pinkish white; brown head; up to ½ inch long.

Damage: Tunnels in stems, leaves and tubers; shoots wilt and die.

Distribution: Some southern states and California; infestations localized.

What to do: Keep garden free of weeds and keep potato plants deeply hilled with soil. Apply a dust or spray containing endosulfan.

Potato tuberworm

WHITE-FRINGED BEETLES

Description: Several species. Adults: Dark-gray snout beetles; light band along the side of the body; ½ inch long. Larvae: Yellowish white; curved; legless; fleshy; up to ½ inch long.

Damage: Larvae feed on roots and tubers of potato and turnip.

Distribution: Southeastern United States, infestation localized.

What to do: Treat infested soil with chlordane as for white grubs, below.

White-fringed beetle

ADULT

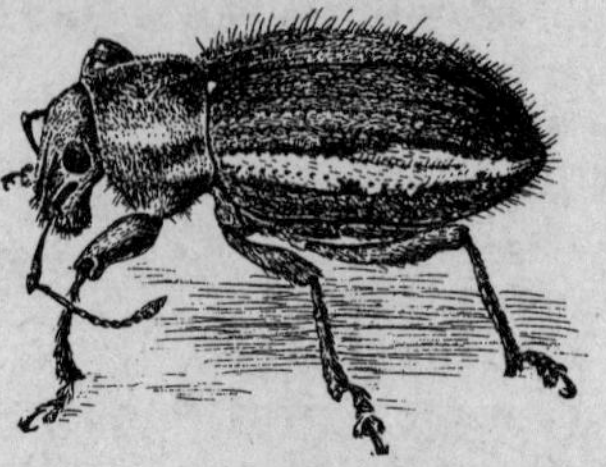

Adult

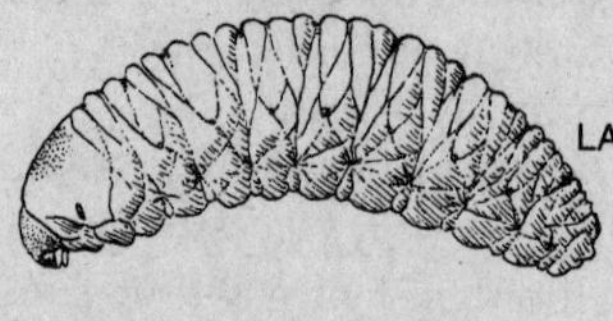

LARVA

WHITE GRUBS

Description: Several species. White or light yellow; hard brown heads; curved; ½ inch to 1½ inches long when full-grown. White grubs live in soil and are larvae of May beetles. They require three years to mature.

Damage: Larvae feed on roots and underground parts of potato and many other plants. Adults feed on tree foliage.

Distribution: Throughout United States.

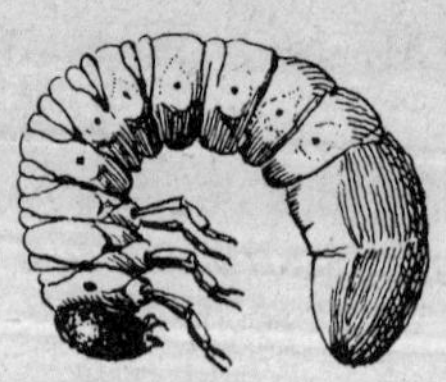

White grub

What to do: Grasslands are likely to be infested with white grubs; avoid planting vegetables in newly plowed grasslands. Treat infested soil with chlordane. Apply 5 ounces (1⅓ cups) of 40 percent chlordane wettable powder or 45 percent chlordane emulsifiable concentrate in 2½ gallons of water per 1,000 square feet of soil surface. Work the spray into the top 3 inches of soil. *Caution:* Do not apply chlordane within two years before planting asparagus, carrot, radish or parsnip. Do not repeat soil applications of chlordane within three years.

WIREWORMS

Description: Many species. Yellow to white; dark head and tails; slender; ½ to 1½ inches long when full-grown. Resemble a jointed wire.

Damage: Puncture and tunnel stems, roots and tubers. Severely damage beans, carrot, beet, celery, lettuce, onion, potato, sweet potato and turnip.

Distribution: Throughout United States, particularly in irrigated lands of western states.

What to do: Avoid planting vegetables in infested soil.

Treat infested soil with diazinon at least one week before planting. Use 6 ounces of 2 percent diazinon granules on each 100 square feet of soil surface. Thoroughly work into top 6 inches of soil immediately after application. If granules are not available, use 4 fluid ounces of 25 percent diazinon emulsifiable concentrate in 2½ gallons of water.

In the North Central and northeastern states chlordane is effective. Apply 5 ounces (1⅓ cups) of 40 percent chlordane wettable powder or 45 percent chlordane emulsifiable concentrate in 2½ gallons of water per 1,000 square feet of soil surface. Work the spray into the top 6 to 8 inches of soil. *Caution:* Do not apply chlordane within two years before planting asparagus, carrot, radish or parsnip. Do not repeat soil applications of chlordane within three years.

COMMON SCAB (FUNGUS)

Symptoms and damage: Rough scabby, raised or pitted spots on tubers. Fungus is carried on tubers and lives in soil.

Distribution: Throughout United States.

What to do: Plant clean tubers. Do not grow potatoes in soil where disease has occurred. Do not use lime, wood ashes or fresh stable manure on infested soil. Grow scab-resistant varieties, such as 'Cayuga', 'Cherokee', 'Early Gem', 'Menominee', 'Ontario', and 'Seneca'.

EARLY BLIGHT (FUNGUS)

Symptoms and damage: Leaves show small, irregular, dark-brown spots, which often enlarge and have targetlike markings. Disease injures foliage, reduces yields. Fungus is carried in soil, may be present in tubers.

Distribution: Central, southern, and eastern states, and parts of the West and Northwest that have overhead irrigation.

What to do: Plant clean tubers. Apply a dust or spray containing a fixed copper or organic fungicide. Rake and burn plant debris. Do not apply ferbam or ziram.

LATE BLIGHT (FUNGUS)

Symptoms and damage: Dark, irregular dead areas on leaves and stems. Infected tubers may rot in storage. Disease may kill plants early in season; it is worse in cool, moist weather. Fungus is carried in tubers.

Distribution: Most common in North Central, northeastern and Atlantic states.

What to do: Plant clean tubers. Apply a dust or spray containing a fixed copper or organic fungicide every seven to ten days, but do not use ferbam or ziram. Grow blight-resistant varieties such as 'Sebago', 'Kennebec', 'Saco', 'Pungo', 'Cherokee' and 'Plymouth'. Do not dig up tubers from diseased plants until tops are dead and dry.

LEAF ROLL (VIRUS)

Symptoms and damage: Upward rolling of lower leaves; yellow and stunted plants; brown specks in tubers. Virus is carried in tubers and spread by aphids.

Distribution: Throughout United States.

What to do: Plant clean tubers; use certified seed potatoes. Grow disease-resistant varieties. 'Katahdin' and 'Saco' are resistant to tuber discoloration and have some resistance to leaf rolling. 'Kennebec', 'Sebago' and 'Chippewa' are also resistant to tuber discoloration but leaves may roll. Destroy infected plants as soon as leaf roll is detected; control the aphids.

MOSAIC (VIRUSES)

Symptoms and damage: Mottled light- and dark-green, curled leaves; stunted plants; reduced yields. Caused by several viruses that are carried in tubers and spread by aphids.

Distribution: Throughout United States.

What to do: Plant clean tubers; use certified seed potatoes. Grow following varieties (resistant to some forms of mosaic): 'Cherokee', 'Chippewa', 'Katahdin', 'Kennebec', 'Pungo', 'Saco', and 'Sebago'. Destroy infected plants as soon as mosaic is detected; control the aphids.

WILT AND DRY ROT (FUNGI)

Symptoms and damage: Yellow leaves; drooping plants; brown rings inside stems and tubers. Infected tubers rot in storage. Fungi are carried in tubers and live in soil.

Distribution: Throughout United States.

What to do: Do not plant internally discolored tubers; plant certified seed potatoes. Do not grow potatoes in soil where disease has occurred. Plant resistant varieties—'Menominee' and 'Ona' are two.

Radishes

ROOT MAGGOTS

Description: Several species (including seed-corn and cabbage maggots). Yellowish white; legless; ¼ to ⅓ inch long.

Damage: Maggots tunnel edible roots.

Distribution: Throughout United States.

What to do: Before planting apply 6 ounces of 2 percent diazinon granules to each 100 square feet of soil surface. Mix thoroughly with the upper 4 inches of soil; wait one week before planting.

Raspberries

ANTHRACNOSE (FUNGUS)

Symptoms and damage: Small gray spots that have dark margins on leaves; purplish spots (about 1 inch in diameter) that have ash-gray centers and raised purplish margins or canes. Badly infected canes are girdled; canes crack lengthwise. Fruits often fail to ripen normally, or they wither on canes. Black-raspberry canes are more susceptible than those of red varieties. Fungus lives on diseased canes.

Distribution: Throughout United States.

What to do: Plant clean nursery stock. Make three applications of ferbam. Make first application when leaves are exposed ½ to ¾ inch, second just before blossoms open; third after blossoming. Cut and burn fruiting canes after harvest. Remove and destroy new canes that become badly infected.

LEAF CURL (VIRUS)

Symptoms and damage: Leaves are curled and rounded; tissue between veins is arched upward; fruits ripen prematurely and are not edible. Symptoms first appear at tip of a single cane; following season all canes affected; in a few years shoots may be only a few inches high. Virus attacks both red and black varieties; it is spread by aphids.

Distribution: From Ohio westward.

What to do: Same as for mosaic, next column.

LEAF SPOT (FUNGUS)

Symptoms and damage: Circular or irregular gray spots, about ⅛ inch in diameter, on leaves; stunted canes; reduced yields. Severely spotted leaves drop; canes may be nearly bare in fall. Disease worse in hot weather. Fungus lives in diseased leaves on ground.

Distribution: Eastern United States, particularly in the South.

What to do: Apply ferbam three times at intervals of three or four weeks. Make first application after harvest, when old canes have been removed.

MOSAIC (VIRUS)

Symptoms and damage: Red raspberries: Raised dark-green spots surrounded by yellow-green tissue on leaves; stunted plants; reduced yields. Leaves that develop in hot weather show only faint symptoms. *Black raspberries:* Dwarfed and mottled leaves; stunted plants. Virus may kill tips of shoots; severely stunted plants die. Other viruses cause leaves to become flecked with yellow and green, dwarfed, yellowed, and to curl upward at edges. Mosaic viruses are spread by aphids.

Distribution: Throughout United States.

What to do: Plant virus-free stocks. Do not plant healthy plants near diseased ones. Remove and destroy diseased plants; dig up roots to prevent new shoots from appearing.

ORANGE RUST (FUNGUS)

Symptoms and damage: Spindly shoots; small, pale-green leaves; blisterlike pustules on undersides of leaves. Pustules burst, releasing reddish-orange fungus spores. When disease occurs in old hills, only a few canes rust the next spring; in new plantings, infected canes do not blossom, and plants are rusted as long as they live. Attacks black raspberries; rarely affects red varieties. Fungus lives in diseased canes.

Distribution: Throughout United States.

What to do: Plant only rust-free stock. If young plants show rust, dig and burn them. If plants in old hills are infected, cut and burn parts of crowns that are injured; remainder of plant may be saved.

Rhubarb

RHUBARB CURCULIO

Description: Yellow-dusted snout beetle ½ to ¾ inch long.

Damage: Punctures stems.

Distribution: New England to Idaho, south to Florida and Louisiana.

What to do: Hand-pick. Remove and destroy dock plants growing near garden; beetle breeds in dock plants.

Rhubarb curculio

ROOT ROT OR CROWN ROT (FUNGUS)

Symptoms and damage: Brown sunken spots at base of leaf stalks; decayed stalks; wilted leaves. Disease spreads rapidly in row. Fungus is carried on roots and lives in soil.

Distribution: Central and eastern states.

What to do: Remove and destroy diseased plants. Do not use roots from beds where disease has occurred. Apply a fixed copper spray deep into crowns of plants.

Spinach

BLIGHT OR YELLOWS (VIRUS)

Symptoms and damage: Yellowed and curled leaves; stunted plants; reduced yields. Disease caused by cucumber-mosaic virus, spread by aphids.

Distribution: Throughout United States.

What to do: Grow blight-resistant varieties—'Virginia Savoy' and 'Old Dominion'—and resistant hybrids—56 and 612. Remove and destroy perennial weeds. Follow recommendations for control of aphids on page 328, under "Muskmelon and Cantaloupe."

BLUE MOLD (FUNGUS)

Symptoms and damage: Yellow spots on upper surfaces of leaves; downy purple or blue-colored mold on underside of leaves. Disease is worse during cool, humid weather.

Distribution: Southeastern and Central states.

What to do: Grow resistant varieties—'Dixie Market' and 'Dixie Savoy' (savoy), and resistant hybrids—7 (semisavoy), and 424 and 425 (smooth leaf). Spray susceptible plants with zineb.

SEED DECAY (FUNGI)

Symptoms and damage: Seed rot in soil. Disease most common in cool, moist weather. Fungi live in soil.

Distribution: Throughout United States.

What to do: Treat seed with a protective fungicide.

Squash and Pumpkin

PICKLEWORM

Description: Yellowish white; brownish head; up to ¾ inch long. Numerous dark spots on young worm.

Damage: Feeds on flowers and leaf buds; tunnels flowers, terminal buds, vines and fruits.

Distribution: Winters in Florida and Texas; may spread as far north as Connecticut, Illinois, Iowa and Kansas late in season.

What to do: Very early spring plantings are seldom damaged. Apply dust or spray containing carbaryl. Begin treatments at first sign of worms in blossoms and buds; worms must be killed before they enter fruits. Repeat treatment once a week.

SQUASH BUG

Description: Adults: Brownish, flat back stink bug, ⅝ inch long. Nymphs: Vary from bright green with red head and legs to dark greenish-gray with black head and legs; up to ⅜ inch long. Egg clusters are shiny brick-red; are found leaves.

Damage: Adults and nymphs feed in colonies; they suck sap from leaves and stems. Plants wilt and die.

Distribution: Throughout United States.

What to do: Hand-pick adults and eggs. Trap bugs under boards placed on soil around plants; collect and destroy bugs every morning. Treat plants with a dust or spray containing carbaryl.

Squash bug

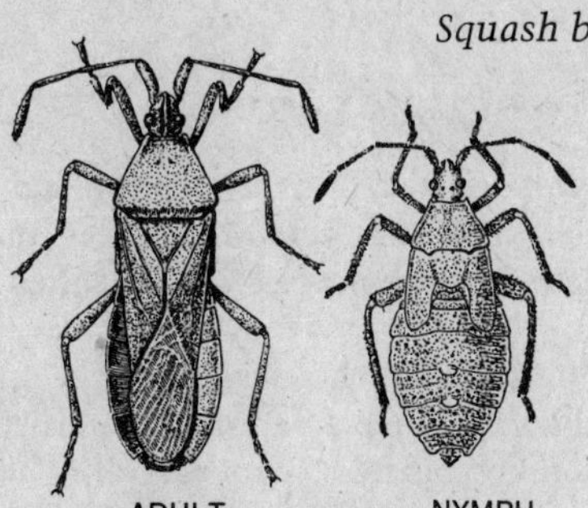

SQUASH VINE BORER

Description: Larvae: White; up to 1 inch long.

Damage: Bores in vines; eats holes in stem near base of runner. Runner wilts.

Distribution: East of Rocky Mountains.

What to do: Locate points of injury. Split one side of stem with razor blade or sharp knife and puncture worm. Put a mound of moist dirt around each cut stem to prevent drying and to induce root growth beyond point of injury. Partial control may be obtained by applying a dust or spray containing carbaryl or endosulfan. Begin applications when runners develop; repeat treatment once a week.

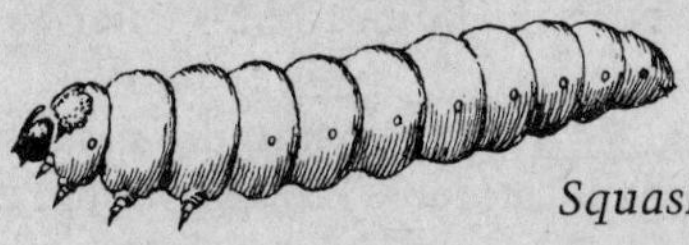

Squash vine borer

STRIPED CUCUMBER BEETLE

Description: Adults: Yellow to black; 3 black stripes down back; ⅕ inch long. Larvae: White; slender; brownish at the ends; up to ⅓ inch long.

Damage: Adults feed on leaves, stems and fruit; they spread bacterial wilt and squash mosaic. Larvae bore into roots and also feed on stems at or below soil line. Damaged plants wilt and sometimes die.

Distribution: East of Rocky Mountains; related species found in West.

What to do: Apply a dust or spray containing carbaryl, malathion or methoxychlor.

MOSAIC (VIRUSES)

Symptoms and damage: Yellow spots on leaves and occasionally on fruits; stunted plants; reduced yields. Most common on straightneck and crookneck summer squash. Disease causal agents are same as for muskmelon mosaic viruses.

Distribution: Throughout United States.

What to do: Remove and destroy diseased plants and perennial weeds. Follow recommendations for control of striped cucumber beetle and aphids.

Sweet Corn

CORN EARWORM

Description: Green, brown or pink; light stripes along sides and on back; up to 1¾ inches long. When insect occurs on tomatoes, it is called tomato fruitworm.

Damage: Early in the season feeds on central shoot (budworm damage); later burrows through silk and feeds on kernels near tip of ear.

Distribution: Throughout United States.

What to do: To prevent budworm damage, spray entire plant. To prevent damage to ear, spray silks until they are wet. Use 3 level tablespoons of 50 percent carbaryl wettable powder per gallon of water. Apply the day after silks appear. Repeat four times, at two-day intervals.

CORN SAP BEETLES

Description: Several species. Adults: Usually black; 3/16 inch long. Larvae: White to cream-colored; maggotlike; active; up to ¼ inch long; they scatter over ear when exposed to light.

Damage: Adults seldom do damage. Larvae eat into kernels of roasting ears.

Distribution: Eastern United States, and as far west as Colorado.

What to do: Apply a spray containing malathion six days after silks appear; repeat treatment ten days later.

EUROPEAN CORN BORER

Description: Pale pink or brown; dark-brown head; up to 1 inch long.

Damage: Feeds in stalks and ears; may enter ear at base, side or tip. Also feeds on foliage and pods of pepper.

Distribution: From Georgia to Maine and westward to Montana, Colorado and Oklahoma.

European corn borer

What to do: Apply a carbaryl or diazinon spray to ear shoots and centers of leaf whorls at first sign of borers. Repeat treatment at least three times at five-day intervals. Use about 1½ gallons of spray per 100 stalks; apply it until runoff occurs at the base of the plants.

JAPANESE BEETLE

Description: Adults: Shiny metallic green; oval; coppery-brown outer wings; about ½ inch long and ¼ inch wide. Larvae: White body; brown head; up to 1 inch long when full grown.

Damage: Adults may attack foliage of raspberry, blackberry, beans and okra, and silk and foliage of sweet corn. Larvae feed on roots of grasses and other plants.

Distribution: From southern Maine southward into Georgia and westward to the Mississippi River and Iowa.

What to do: For control of adults, apply a dust or spray containing carbaryl or malathion to infested foliage. Treat lawns and turf areas with milky disease spores to kill larvae in soil.

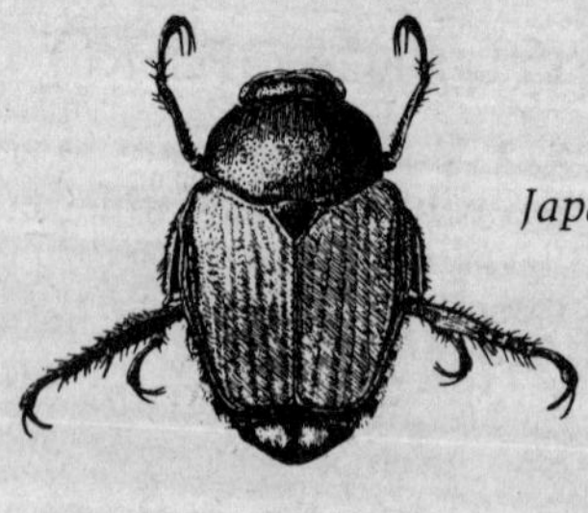

Japanese beetle

BACTERIAL WILT

Symptoms and damage: Wilted and dwarfed plants; tassels whiten early. Yellow bacterial slime oozes from cut stalks. The bacteria are carried on seed; also carried by insects that spread them in the field.

Distribution: Central, southern, and eastern states.

What to do: Grow wilt-resistant varieties such as 'Stowell's Evergreen', 'Golden Cross Bantam', 'Marcross', 'Spancross', or 'Whipcross'. Most white late varieties are somewhat resistant; other resistant varieties are listed by seedsmen.

SEED DECAY AND SEEDLING BLIGHT (FUNGI)

Symptoms and damage: Seed decay in soil; young plants die. Fungi are carried in seed and live in the soil.

Distribution: Throughout United States.

What to do: Treat seed with a protective fungicide.

SMUT (FUNGUS)

Symptoms and damage: Large, irregularly shaped white galls, or outgrowths, form on stalks, ears and tassels. Galls burst, releasing masses of black fungus spores. Fungus lives in soil.

Distribution: Throughout United States.

What to do: Remove and destroy galls. Do not use diseased plants in making compost.

Sweet Potato

SWEET POTATO WEEVIL

Description: Adults: Reddish snout beetle; shiny; antlike; slender-bodied; bluish-black head; ¼ inch long. Larvae: White; legless; pale-brown head; up to ⅜ inch long.

Damage: Adults seldom cause damage. Larvae tunnel through sweet potatoes and vines.

Distribution: Parts of Texas, Louisiana, Mississippi, Alabama, Florida, Georgia, South Carolina.

What to do: The weevil does not hibernate, so there must be food available for it to survive the winter. To prevent the weevil's survival, destroy volunteer plants in the field. Destroy all infested sweet potatoes in storage. Well before spring, clean out storage places and destroy all plant material. Plant weevil-free seed stock or plants.

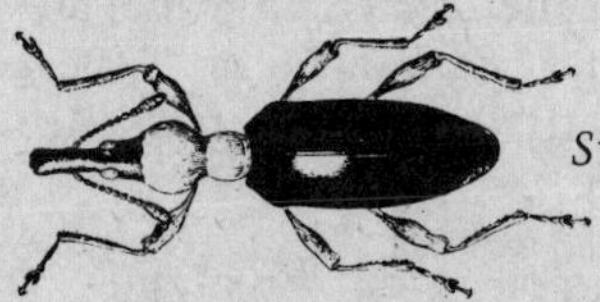

Sweetpotato weevil

BLACK ROT (FUNGUS)

Symptoms and damage: Black, sunken, roundish spots on sweet potatoes; black cankers on underground parts of stems. Fungus overwinters in diseased roots and in the soil, and attacks slips in plant bed. Disease is spread in storage.

Distribution: Throughout United States.

What to do: Use plants that have clean, white roots. Remove and destroy diseased plants. Do not plant sweet potatoes in the same soil every year.

STEM ROT OR WILT (FUNGUS)

Symptoms and damage: Yellowed and wilted plants. When cut across, stems have a black discoloration; roots, a black ring. Fungus overwinters in fleshy roots and in the soil and infects roots and stems of young plants.

Distribution: Throughout United States.

What to do: Same as for black rot.

Tomatoes

CUTWORMS

Description: Many species. Cutworms are dull gray, brown or black, and may be striped or spotted. They are stout, soft-bodied and smooth, and up to 1¼ inches long; they curl up tightly when disturbed.

Damage: Cut off plants above, at, or below soil surface. Some cutworms feed on leaves, buds or fruits; others feed on the underground portions of plants. Particularly destructive to early-season plants of pepper, tomato, cabbage and related crops, peas and beans.

Distribution: Throughout United States.

What to do: Apply a 10 percent toxaphene dust, or spray with toxaphene. Apply the insecticide to the soil surface when the garden is being prepared for planting. Ready-mixed poison baits containing 3 percent of toxaphene are effective against species that feed above the soil surface. If you use bait, spread it in the late afternoon at the rate of 1 pound per 1,000 square feet. Do not apply toxaphene to foliage of cucumbers or melons; it may injure the plants. See "Precautions," page 318. *Note:* You can prevent cutworm injury to transplants without using an insecticide. Place a stiff 3-inch cardboard collar around the stems; allow it to extend about 1 inch into the soil and to protrude 2 inches above the soil; clear the stem by about ½ inch.

FLEA BEETLES

Description: Many species. Black, brown or striped; jumping beetles; about 1⁄16 inch long.

Damage: Attacks potato, tomato, eggplant, pepper, beet, spinach, turnip, radish and cabbage and related crops. Young plants, especially transplants, are severely damaged; leaves look as if they had been shot full of holes.

Distribution: Throughout United States.

What to do: Apply a dust or spray containing carbaryl or endosulfan.

HORNWORMS

Description: Two species. Green; diagonal lines on sides; prominent horn on rear end; up to 4 inches long.

Damage: Eat foliage and fruit of eggplant, pepper and tomato.

Distribution: Throughout United States; infestations localized.

What to do: Handpick worms. If damage is heavy, apply a dust or spray containing carbaryl or endosulfan.

Hornworm

LEAF MINERS

Description: Larvae: Yellow, ⅛ inch long, live in leaves. Adult fly: Tiny; black and yellow. Several generations of this insect develop in a summer.

Damage: Larvae make long, slender, winding white tunnels in the leaves of tomato, pepper and spinach.

Distribution: Throughout United States. Damage usually is not appreciable in northern states.

What to do: Apply a spray containing diazinon or dimethoate.

MOLE CRICKETS

Description: Several species. Adults and nymphs: Light brown; large, beady eyes; short, stout front legs with shovel-like feet; up to 1½ inches long.

Damage: Make burrows in soil; uproot young plants in seed beds.

Distribution: In Florida and in coastal areas of North Carolina, South Carolina, Georgia, Alabama and Mississippi.

What to do: Apply diazinon before planting, as for wireworms. If mole crickets are damaging established plants, apply a ready-mixed 3 percent chlordane bait. If you use bait, apply it to the soil surface in the late afternoon following rain or watering. Use about 1 pound of bait per 1,000 square feet of soil surface.

Mole crickets

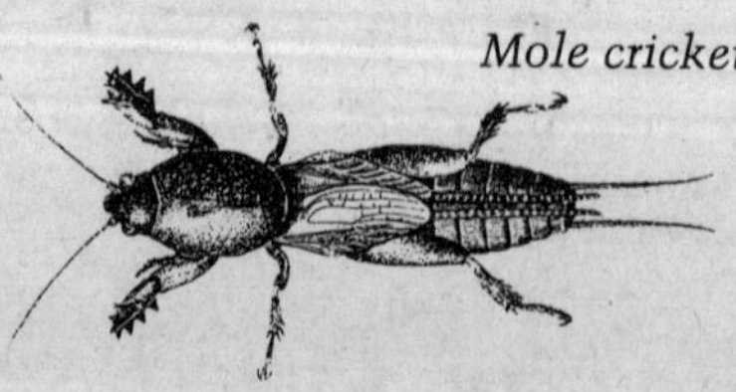

STALK BORER

Description: Slender, up to 1¼ inches long. *Young borer:* Creamy white; dark purple bank around the body; several brown or purple stripes running lengthwise down the body. *Full-grown borer:* Creamy white to light purple, without band and stripes.

Damage: Eats tunnel in stem, causing plant to wither and die. Tunnel usually has opening up to ¼ inch in diameter at its lower end.

Stalk borer

Distribution: Eastern part of United States.

What to do: Remove and destroy weeds; the insect breeds in weeds. Plant may be saved by puncturing the insect. To locate the borer, split the stems lengthwise above opening to tunnel. Bind split stem and keep plant watered.

STINK BUGS

Description: Several species. Adults: Brown, green or black, with or without markings; shield-shaped; up to ⅝ inch long and ⅓ inch wide. Nymphs: Resemble adults but are smaller. Stink bugs discharge a foul odor.

Damage: Adults and nymphs suck sap from tomato, bean and okra. Plants are weakened; buds and young fruits are malformed. Pimples or wartlike growths appear on okra and bean pods.

Distribution: Throughout United States, particularly in the South.

What to do: Do not allow weeds to grow in or around garden. Apply a dust or spray containing carbaryl, endosulfan, or naled. See "Precautions," page 318.

TOMATO FRUITWORM

Description: Green, brown or pink; light stripes along sides and on back; up to 1¾ inches long. When insect occurs on corn, it is called corn earworm.

Damage: Eats holes in fruits and buds.

Distribution: Throughout United States, particularly in South and California.

What to do: Apply a dust or spray containing carbaryl. Make first application when plants are 1 or 2 feet across or when fruit begins to set. Repeat treatment three times at two-week intervals. See "Precautions," page 318.

TOMATO RUSSET MITE

Description: Not visible to naked eye; mite can be seen with a 20-power hand lens. It is white and pear-shaped. Not classified as insect.

Damage: Lower stems become bronze or russet; damage spreads up the plant and to underside of leaves; fruit may become bronzed. Plants have smoked appearance.

Distribution: Mite is most common in California, but localized infestations have been scattered over the United States.

What to do: Apply a dust containing 25 to 50 percent of dusting sulfur when fruit begins to set, or use a spray containing sulfur. Repeat treatment every two weeks. *Caution:* Higher dosages of sulfur dust may injure plants.

BLOSSOM-END ROT (PHYSIOLOGIC)

Symptoms and damage: Large, dark, sunken, leathery spots at the blossom end of fruits, caused by a deficiency of calcium. Most common during droughts when soil dries rapidly while plants are making a vigorous growth.

Distribution: Throughout United States.

What to do: Use ample amounts of lime and superphosphate. Avoid excessive use of nitrogenous fertilizers. When watering garden, maintain even moisture in soil.

DAMPING-OFF (FUNGI)

Symptoms and damage: Seed decay in soil; young plants collapse and die. Fungi live in soil.

Distribution: Throughout United States.

What to do: Treat seed with a protective fungicide.

EARLY BLIGHT (FUNGUS)

Symptoms and damage: Leaves show small irregular dark-brown spots that often enlarge into circular spots with targetlike markings. Brown cankers on stems that may girdle plants at ground line. Dark, leathery, decayed spots at stem end of fruits. Disease is worse in warm, moist weather. Fungus may be carried on seeds; lives in soil.

Distribution: Throughout United States, except semiarid regions.

What to do: Use clean plants. Apply a dust or spray containing a fixed copper or organic fungicide to plants every seven to ten days.

FUSARIUM WILT (FUNGUS)

Symptoms and damage: Gradual yellowing and wilting of foliage, beginning with lower leaves; browning of woody tissue under the outer green portion of the stem. Plants may die. Fungus lives in soil and enters through roots.

Distribution: Throughout United States, particularly in southern states.

What to do: Grow wilt-resistant varieties such as 'Homestead', 'Manapal', 'Floradel', 'Manalucie', 'KC 146', 'Marion', 'Kokomo', 'Enterpriser', 'Porte', 'H 1350', 'Campbell's 17', 'Pinkshipper'; (pink), and 'Sunray' (yellow).

LATE BLIGHT (FUNGUS)

Symptoms and damage: Dark water-soaked spots on leaves; large water-soaked spots on fruits; white fungus growths on undersides of leaves and occasionally on fruits during moist weather. Spots on leaves enlarge and turn brown; leaves wither. Spots on fruits turn brown and remain firm. Disease is worse in cool, moist weather. Fungus also causes late blight of potatoes.

Distribution: In humid areas, particularly east of the Mississippi River.

What to do: Apply a dust or spray containing a fixed copper or organic fungicide, but do not apply ferbam or ziram. Repeat treatment every seven to ten days.

LEAF SPOT (FUNGUS)

Symptoms and damage: Small spots that have light centers and dark margins on leaves; dark specks in centers of spots. Many leaves may be killed, and crop reduced. Disease worse in warm, moist weather. Fungus lives in soil and on perennial weeds.

Distribution: North Central, northeastern and southeastern states.

What to do: Remove vines or turn under in the fall. Destroy perennial weeds. Rotate crops. Apply a dust or spray containing a fixed copper or organic fungicide.

MOSAIC (VIRUS)

Symptoms and damage: Mottled green-and-yellow, curled foliage; stunted plants (if attacked early in season); reduced yields. Caused by tobacco-mosaic virus, which is often present in manufactured tobacco; smokers may carry it on their hands and transmit it to tomato plants. The disease is spread by persons who handle plants, and also by aphids. Virus is not carried in seed and does not live long in soil.

Distribution: Throughout United States.

What to do: Avoid handling young plants. If you smoke, wash hands with soap and water before working in the garden; do not smoke while working with tomato plants.

ROOT KNOT (NEMATODE)

Symptoms and damage: Galls, or swellings, on roots; stunted plants. Galls on small roots are tiny; compound galls on large roots may be an inch in diameter. Pearly-white specks inside galls are egg masses of root-knot nematode, which lives in soil. Damages many kinds of plants.

Distribution: In southern areas; most common south of 40° latitude.

What to do: See "Root Knot" under "Cucumbers," page 325.

VERTICILLIUM WILT (FUNGUS)

Symptoms and damage: Symptoms of verticillium wilt are easily mistaken for those of fusarium wilt; both diseases cause branches to wilt and die. However, the symptoms of verticillium wilt usually appear at the same time on all branches of a plant, whereas those of fusarium wilt may appear on a single shoot that will wilt and die before the rest of the plant is affected. The fungus that causes verticillium wilt lives in the soil. Fruit of plants it attacks may sunburn when exposed to the sun, and the plants also may die.

Distribution: California, Utah, Washington, Colorado, North Central and northeastern states and southern Florida.

What to do: Grow resistant varieties such as 'H 1350', 'Porte', 'Enterpriser', 'Pearson' types VF6 and VF36, and 'Campbell's 17'. These varieties are also resistant to fusarium wilt. 'VR Moscow' and 'Loran Blood' are resistant to verticillium wilt only. Sprays and dusts are not effective against verticillium wilt.

Turnips and Mustard

HARLEQUIN BUG

Description: Adults and nymphs: Black and brilliantly colored with red or yellow; shield-shaped; up to ⅜ inch long.

Damage: Plants wilt; leaves turn brown as if scalded.

Distribution: In southern part of United States from California to Virginia. Infestations localized.

What to do: Apply a dust or spray containing endosulfan. See "Precautions," page 318.

TURNIP APHID (PLANT LOUSE)

Description: Tiny; greenish; looks like cabbage aphid but is not covered with whitish wax. Feeds in colonies on undersides of leaves.

Damage: Curled leaves and yellowed plants.

Distribution: Throughout United States, except in the northwestern states.

What to do: Apply a dust or spray containing malathion every seven to ten days, beginning as soon as true leaves form. See "Precautions," page 318.

VEGETABLE WEEVIL

Description: Adults: Dull grayish brown; 2 oval pale-gray marks on back; ⅜ inch long. Larvae: Light-green body and light-yellow to brown head; ⅝ inch long when full-grown.

Damage: Adults and larvae feed on leaves and roots of turnip, cabbage and related plants.

Distribution: Southern United States.

What to do: Apply a dust or spray containing rotenone.

Watermelon

ANTHRACNOSE (FUNGUS)

Symptoms and damage: Round, water-soaked spots on fruits; dark spots on leaves, which may give vines a scorched appearance. At first, spots on fruits are small and raised; later they enlarge and become sunken; they have dark centers, which may show a pinkish fungus growth in moist weather. Fungus also affects cucumber and muskmelon; it is carried on seed and lives in soil on remains of diseased plants.

Distribution: Throughout United States.

What to do: 'Congo', 'Fairfax', 'Charleston Gray' and 'Blackstone' are resistant varieties. Follow seed treatment, spraying and dusting recommendations for anthracnose on cucumbers.

WILT (FUNGUS)

Symptoms and damage: Stunted seedlings; wilted vines; reduced yields. Plants eventually die. Wilting starts at tips of runners and slowly spreads to entire vine. Fungus is carried on seed, lives indefinitely in soil and enters through roots. (Not identical with bacterial wilt of cucumber and muskmelon.)

Distribution: In the South and in California; in some Central states.

What to do: Grow wilt-resistant varieties such as 'Kleckley No. 6', 'Improved Stone Mountain No 5', 'Fairfax', 'Charleston Gray', 'Hawkesbury', 'Missouri Queen', 'Miles', 'Leesburg', 'Klondike R–7', and 'Baby Klondike'.

BENEFICIAL INSECTS

Certain insects cause no damage and are beneficial to man. They destroy other insects that are injurious to vegetables, and thus are friends of the gardener. Learn to recognize beneficial insects, and avoid destroying them. Following are descriptions of a few of the important beneficial insects.

ANT LION (DOODLEBUG)

Description: Rough; sickle-shaped jaws; brown, up to ½ inch long. Lives at bottom of conical pits in sand.

Benefit: Feeds on ants and other insects. Does not damage plants.

Distribution: Many parts of United States; most abundant in South.

APHID LION

Description: Adults: Fragile; hairlike antennae; golden eyes; gauzy, green wings. Places eggs singly on stalk. Larvae: Elongate body, tapering at both ends; large, sickle-shaped jaws; prominent, projecting hairs; yellowish or mottled with red or brown; about ⅓ inch long.

Benefit: Larvae feed on aphids, mealybugs, scales, thrips and mites.

Distribution: Throughout United States.

ASSASSIN BUGS

Description: Several species. Long legs; light brown, ½ to ¾ inch long. These insects walk over plants in a slow, clumsy manner. Their forelegs are usually in a prayerful position and are used to capture and hold other insects.

Benefit: Assassin bugs feed on the immature forms of insects.

Distribution: Throughout United States.

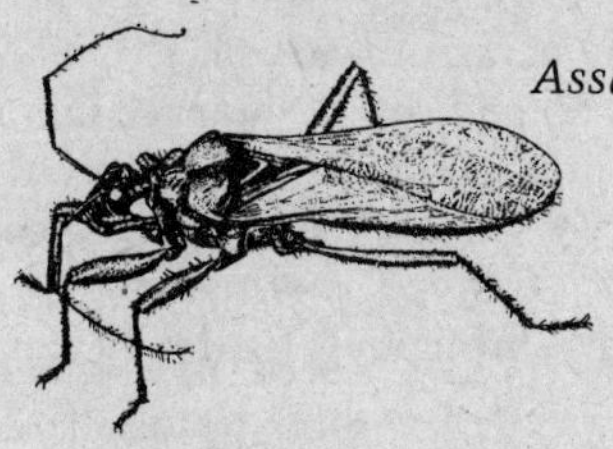

Assassin bug

DAMSEL BUGS

Description: Several species. Resemble assassin bugs; pale gray; about ⅜ inch long; forelegs used for capturing prey.

Benefit: Damsel bugs feed on aphids, fleahoppers and small larvae of insects.

GROUND BEETLES

Description: Many species. Adults: Broadly oval, elongate bodies; narrow heads; color usually dull black or brown. Commonly occur on ground surface under stones or loose trash. They hide by day, are active at night, and run rapidly when disturbed. Larvae: Bodies are slender, flattened and slightly tapering to the tail, which terminates in two spines or bristlelike processes.

Benefit: Adults and larvae feed on caterpillars and other insects.

Distribution: Throughout United States.

LADY BEETLES

Description: Many species. Adults: Oval; shiny; red or tan, with or without black spots; about ⅕ inch long. Larvae: Carrot-shaped; warty; blue, orange or gray; 1⁄16 to ¼ inch long.

Benefit: Feed on aphids, spider mites, scales and mealybugs. Do not damage plants.

Distribution: Throughout United States.

Lady beetle

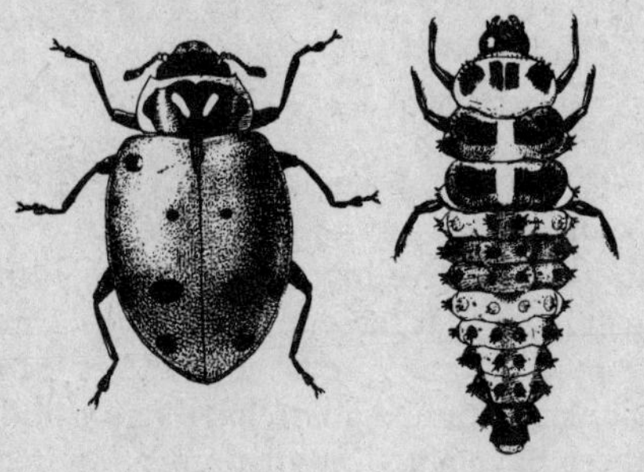

MINUTE PIRATE BUGS

Description: Several species. Adults: Oval, flat; about 1⁄16 inch long. Most species are black, marked with white spots or streaks. Nymphs: Similar to adults; amber. Found on flowers and under loose bark.

Benefit: Adults and larvae feed on small insects such as mites; they also feed on eggs and larvae of many destructive insects.

Distribution: Throughout United States.

Minute pirate bug

PRAYING MANTISES

Description: About 20 species. Bodies of most species are green; wings are green with brown front margins. Large abdomens, slender thoraxes, wedge-shaped, movable heads. Front legs are large and have spines for grasping prey. Sizes range from 2½ to 5 inches in length.

In fall, females lay eggs in masses on shrubs or tall

Praying mantis

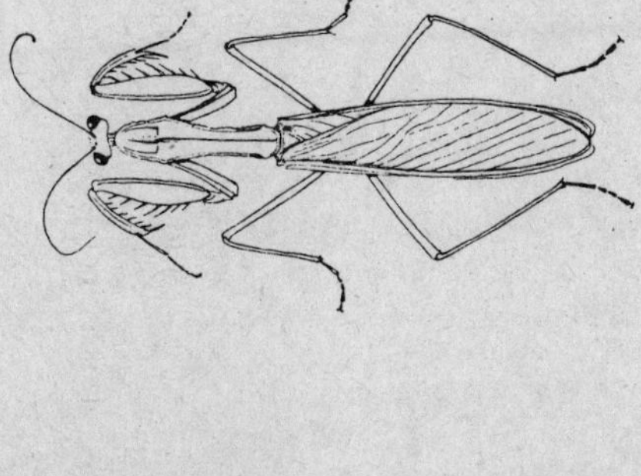

grasses and cover them with a frothy fluid that hardens. Young mantises hatch in spring; they resemble adults, but lack wings.

Benefit: Young mantises feed on aphids and other small insects. Older mantises devour many kinds of larger insects that they capture in the garden.

Distribution: Throughout United States; prevalent in northeastern parts.

SPIDERS AND MITES

Description: Eight-legged; not classified as insects. Many species. Range in size from the orb-weaving black-and-yellow garden spiders and large hunting spiders that have leg spreads of 2 inches or more to microscopic, predaceous mites 1/50 inch or less in length. Some spiders have hairy bodies and legs; others have smooth, glistening surfaces; color may be black, brown, yellow, black or gray. Color of predaceous mites may be gray or pinkish gray. Some spiders construct webs for snarling their prey; others run or jump to capture their prey.

Benefit: All spiders and predaceous mites feed by sucking out the body juices of other insects. Large, web-forming spiders attack large flying and crawling insects; small, hunting and jumping spiders attack small insects such as flies, beetles, caterpillars, aphids and leafhoppers. Predaceous mites are important in the natural destruction of many plant-feeding pests including spider mites, cyclamen mites, aphids, thrips, larvae and the eggs of many insects.

Distribution: Many species of spiders and mites occur throughout the United States.

SYRPHID FLIES

Description: Many species. Adults: Bright yellow and black; 1/4 to 1/3 inch long; hover above flowers and plants. Larvae: Sluglike; brown, gray or mottled.

Benefit: Larvae eat insects. Single larva eats aphids at rate of one per minute. Harmless to plants.

Distribution: Throughout United States.

WASPS

Description: Many species of parasitic and predaceous wasps, varying widely in size, color and general body structure.

Wasps

Benefit: Tiny parasitic wasps lay their eggs in the bodies of insects, and the developing larvae kill the pests. Large predaceous wasps, which are well known to every gardener, feed on young caterpillars, which they first paralyze by stinging.

Distribution: Throughout United States.

Index

Aarons-beard, 120
Abelia, glossy, 105, 117
Acacia, 109, 142
Achillea, 54
Achimenes, 85
Aconite, winter, 78
Activated charcoal, 25
African violets, 27
Ageratum, 40, 42
Air pollution, 108–109
Alabama fothergilla, 111–112
Aldenham crabapple, 150
Alder tree, 109
Algerian ivy, 105
Alkanet, 55
Allium, 77, 85
Allspice, Carolina, 105, 109, 116
Alyssum, 54–55
Amaryllis, 77, 85–86
American beech tree, 142
American birch tree, 136
American bunch grapes, *see* Grapes
American holly, 142, 214
American linden tree, 136
Anchusa, 55
Andromeda, 105
  Japanese, 110–111
Anemone, 55, 77–78
Anemone-flowered clematis, 122
Annuals, flowering, 39–50
  cultivating, 45
  cutting, 47
  drying flowers, 47
  insects, 46–47
  mulches, 45
  old flowers, removing, 46
  planting times, 44
  seedlings, raising, 50
  seeds, buying, 39–40
  selection of, 39
  soil preparation, 40–44
  started plants, 44–45
  starting plants indoors, 47–50
  sowing seed outdoors, 45
  thinning, 45
  transplanting, 50
  watering, 45
Ant lions, 340–341
Anthemis, 55
Anthracnose, 225, 321–323, 326, 330–331, 334, 340
Aphid lions, 341
Aphids, 96, 153, 168, 202, 206, 225, 308, 313, 328
Apple scab, 153
Apple trees, 146
Apricot trees, 164–168
  cultivating, 167
  diseases, 167
  fertilizers, 166–167
  harvesting, 167
  insects, 167–168
  planting, 165
  pruning, 165–166
  thinning the fruit, 166
  varieties, 164
Arabis, 55
Aralia, 109, 111
  false, 27–28
Arborvitae, 142
Arbutus, 109
Armeria, 55
Arnold crabapple, 151
Arrowwood, 111
Artemisia, 55–56
Artificial lighting, 106
Ascochyta pod spot, 330
Ash, 109
Asian magnolias, 160–161
Asparagus, 279–280
  diseases, 319
  insects, 319
Asparagus beetle, 319
Asparagus fern, 28
Assassin bugs, 341
Asters, 56
  Stokes', 63
Astilbe, 56
Aubrieta, 56
Aucuba, 111
Automatic watering system, 103
Autumn crocus, 105
Avocado, 28, 109
Azalea lacebugs, 173
Azaleas, 171–174
  buying, 171
  diseases, 174
  fertilizers, 173
  flame, 111
  insects, 173–174
  mulches, 173
  planting, 171–172
  pruning, 173
  swamp, 121
  watering, 173
  weeding, 173

Babysbreath, 40, 42, 59
Bacterial blights, 321, 330
Bacterial canker, 167
Bacterial soft rot, 95
Bacterial spot, 331
Balloonflower, 62
Balsam, 40, 42
Barberry, 105
  warty, 111
Barren wort, 207
Bean aphid, 319
Bean leaf beetle, 319–320
Beans, 289–290
  diseases, 319–321
  insects, 319–321
Bearberry, 207

Bearded iris, 92, 93
Beardless iris, 92, 93
Beardlip, 61–62
Beautyberry, 115
Bechtel crabapple, 151
Bee-balm, 61
Beet curlytop disease, 225
Beet webworm, 321
Beetles
  asparagus, 319
  bean leaf, 319–320
  blister, 206, 321, 331
  Colorado potato, 331
  corn sap, 336
  flea, 308, 313, 337–338
  fuller rose, 198
  ground, 341
  Japanese, 163, 168, 336
  lady, 341
  leaf-feeding, 198
  Mexican bean, 320
  spotted cucumber, 320
  striped cucumber, 326, 328, 335–336
  white-fringed, 332
Beets, table, 284, 300, 306–308
  culture, 307–308
  diseases, 321
  fertilizers, 306
  harvesting, 308
  insects, 308, 321
  liming, 306
  planting, 307–308
  soil, 306
  storage, 308
  varieties, 307
  weeds, 308
Begonias, 56, 86, 105
  wax, 105
Bellflower, 105
Beneficial insects, 340–342
Bittersweet, 121
Black larch tree, 136
Black oak tree, 136
Black raspberries, 243
Black rot, 324, 337
Black walnut tree, *see* Walnut tree, black
Blackberries, 235–238
  diseases, 322–323
  fertilizers, 236
  insects, 322–323
  intercropping, 236
  planting, 235–236
  pruning, 238
  thinning, 238
  thornless, 239–242
    cultivation, 240–241
    diseases, 241
    fertilizers, 240
    harvesting, 241
    insects, 241
    intercropping, 239
    planting, 239
    pruning, 240
    training, 240
    trellis construction, 239–240
    varieties, 239, 241–242
    watering, 240
    winter protection, 241
  training, 236–238
  types of, 235
Blackeye peas, 291
  insects, 329
Blackleg, 324
Bleeding heart, 58, 105
Blister beetles, 206, 321, 331
Blossom-end rot, 331, 339
Blue mold, 335
Blue spruce tree, 142
Bluebeard, 115
Bluebells, 80
  Spanish, 105
  Virginia, 105
Bone meal, 25
Bonsai, 175–187
  choosing a style, 176–179
  containers for, 183–184
  displaying, 187
  fertilizers, 185
  growth media, 185
  as house plants, 180–181
  obtaining plants, 181–182
  potting, 184–185
  principles of, 175–176
  propagating, 186–187
  seasonal care, 185–186
  shaping and pruning, 182–183
  trees and shrubs, 179–180
  watering, 186
  wiring, 183
Borers, 168
Boston fern, 28–29
  Boston ivy, 105
Bottlebrush buckeye, 115
Botrytis, 197, 230
Boxwood leaf miner, 191
Boxwood mites, 191–192
Boxwood psyllid, 191
Boxwoods, 105, 109, 188–192
  care of, 188–191
  common, 188
  diseases, 191
  English, 188
  fertilizers, 188–189
  hardiness, 188
  insects, 191–192
  pesticides for, 192
  pruning, 189–190
  sites and soil, 188
  species and varieties, 188
  transplanting, 190
  treating infected plant, 192
Brazilian pepper tree, 142
Breeder tulips, 80
Broad-leaved evergreens, pruning, 130
Broccoli, 291–292, 303–305
  fertilizers, 304
  general needs, 303
  starting plants, 305
  transplanting, 305
  varieties, 303–304
  weed control, 304–305
Brown rot, 167
Brussels sprouts, 292
Buckeye, bottlebrush, 115
Bugleweed, 105, 207
Bulbs
  spring-flowering, 77–84
    care of, 82–83
    forcing, 83–84
    planting, 82
    planting indoors, 84
    selection of, 81
  summer-flowering, 85–91
    care of, 90–91
    planting, 89–90
    selection of, 89
Bush cinquefoil, 119
Bushclover, shrubby, 119–120
Butterflybush, 116
  orange-eye, 116
Buttonbush, 116

Cabbage, 292–293, 300
  celery, 293
  Chinese, 293
  diseases, 323–324
  insects, 323–324
Cabbage aphid, 323
Cabbage loopers, 323, 327
Cabbage webworm, 323
Cabbageworm, imported, 323
Caladium, 86, 105
Calendula, 40, 42
Calla, 86
Calliopsis, 40, 42, 50
Camellias, 105, 109, 193–195
  buying, 193

care of, 194–196
common, 111
diseases, 196–197
fertilizers, 195
insects, 197–198
mountain, 120
mulches, 194
planting, 193–194
potted plants, 196
pruning, 195
sasanqua, 111
silky, 120
species of, 193
transplanting, 195
watering, 194–195
weeding, 195
Candytuft, 40, 42, 50
Canker, 196
Canna, 86–87
Cantaloupe
diseases, 328–329
insects, 328–329
Canterbury bells, 56
Capeweed, 207–208
Carmine crabapple, 151
Carnation, 57
Carolina allspice, 105, 109, 116
Carolina yellow jessamine, 105
Carrot caterpillars, 324
Carrot rust flies, 324
Carrots, 284–285, 300
diseases, 324–325
insects, 324–325
Catalpa, 136
Caterpillars, 154
carrot, 324
diamondback moth, 323
Cauliflower, 293, 303–305
blanching, 305
fertilizers, 304
general needs, 303
starting plant, 305
transplanting, 305
varieties, 303–304
weed control, 304–305
Cedar apple rust, 153
Celeriac, 285
Celery, 283
diseases, 325
insects, 324
turnip-rooted, 285
Celery cabbage, 293
Celery leaf tier, 325
Centaurea, 57
Cerastium, 57
Cercospora leaf spot, 331
Charcoal, activated, 25
Chard, 281
diseases, 321
insects, 321
Swiss, 281, 301
Chaste-tree, 116
Chemicals, seed-treatment, 316
Cherry laurel tree, 142
Cherry tree, ornamental, 109
Chervil, 285
Chestnut oak tree, 136
Chicory, witloof, 281
China-aster, 40, 42, 50
Chinaberry tree, 142
Chinese cabbage, 293
Chinese evergreen, 29
Chinese holly, 214
Chinese lantern, 57
Chinese lilac, 218
Chionodoxa, 78
Chives, 294, 300
Chlorosis, 174, 197
Christmas rose, 59, 105
Chrysanthemums, 63, 199–202
diseases, 202
fertilizers, 201
growing, 201–202
hardiness, 199
insects, 202
plant selection, 199
planting, 200–201
propagating, 201
types of, 199–200
Clematis, 121–122
anemone-flowered, 122
Jackman, 122
scarlet, 122
sweet autumn, 122
Clove pink, 57
Clubroot, 324
Cockscomb, 40, 42, 50
Coleus, 40, 42, 105
Collards, 281
Colorado potato beetles, 331
Columbine, 57, 105
Common bean mosaic, 321
Common boxwood, 188
Common camellia, 111
Common lilac, 218
Common scab, 333
Coneflower, 63
Coniferous evergreens, pruning, 130–131
Conifers, shaping, 131
Copper fungicides, 315
Coral bells, 61, 105
Coralberry, 208
Coreopsis, 57
Corn, sweet, 297
diseases, 336–337
insects, 336–337
Corn earworm, 206, 320, 329, 336
Corn sap beetles, 336
Cornflower, 40, 42, 50
Cornsalad, 281
Cosmos, 40, 42, 50
Cotoneaster, 109, 208
Cottage tulips, 80
Cowberry, 208
Cowpea curculio, 329
Crabapples, flowering, 150–154
diseases, 153
fertilizers, 152–153
insects, 153–154
mulches, 152
planting, 152
pruning, 153
varieties of, 150–152
watering, 152
weeding, 152
Crape myrtle, 116
Creeping lilyturf, 208
Creeping thyme, 208
Cress, upland, 284
Crested iris, 92, 93
Crocus, 78
autumn, 105
Crown gall bacteria, 167
Crown elongation, 231
Crown rot, 335
Crownvetch, 208
Cucumber beetles, 206
Cucumbers, 287–288, 300
diseases, 325–327
insects, 325–327
Cutworms, 337
Cypress, 109
Cytosporina, 167

Daffodils, 80
Peruvian, 87–88
Dahlia mosaic, 206
Dahlias, 40, 42, 50, 87, 203–206
care of, 205
classes of, 203–204
diseases, 206
fertilizers, 205
insects, 206
planting, 204–205
propagating, 205–206
watering, 205
Daisies
English, 58
painted, 63

Daisies (*Cont.*)
- Shasta, 58
- South African, 209

Damping-off, 47–48, 72, 321, 324–327, 331, 339
Damsel bugs, 341
Darwin tulips, 80
Dasheen, 285
Daylily, 61, 87, 208
Deciduous holly, 215
Deciduous shrubs, pruning, 125–129
Deciduous trees, planting seasons, 137
Delphinium, 58
Desert willow, 142
Devils-walkingstick, 117
Dewberries, 235
- diseases, 322–323
- insects, 322–323

Diamondback moth caterpillar, 323
Dianthus, 58
Dicentra, 58
Dichondra, 208
Dieback, 196
Dieffenbachia, 30–31, 109
Dogwood, flowering, 105, 155–159
- cultivated varieties, 155
- diseases, 157–158
- fertilizers, 156
- gray, 111
- heat and drought injury, 158
- herbicide damage, 158
- insects, 158–159
- mulches, 156
- planting, 155–156
- pruning, 157
- transplanting, 157
- watering, 156
- weeding, 156

Dogwood borer, 158
Dogwood club-gall midges, 159
Dogwood twig borer, 159
Dolgo crabapple, 151
Doodlebugs, 340–341
Dorothea crabapple, 151
Double blossom, 323
Double tulips, 80
Downy mildew, 326, 328
Dracaenas, 29–30, 109
Drooping leucothoë, 112
Drop fungus, 327
Dry rot, 333–334
Dumb cane, 30–31
Dusting equipment, 317–318
Dusty miller, 55–56
Dutchman's breeches, 58
Dutchman's pipe, 105
Dwarf bamboo, 208
Dwarf fruit trees, *see* Fruit trees, dwarf
Dwarf hollygrape, 208
Dwarf iris, 79
Dwarf Korean lilac, 218
Dwarf lilyturf, 208
Dwarf polygonum, 208

Early blight, 325, 333, 339
Eggplant, 295, 300
- diseases, 327
- insects, 327

Eggplant lacebug, 327
Elephant's ear, 105
Eleyi crabapple, 151
Elm tree, 109
Emerald feather, 28
Endive, 281, 283
English boxwood, 188
English daisy, 58
English holly, 214
English ivy, 105, 112, 208
English peas, 290–291
Environment, controlling, 106–107
Eranthis, 78
Erect blackberries, 235
European corn borers, 206, 336
Evergreen holly, 214
Evergreen shrubs, pruning, 129–131
Evergreen trees, planting seasons, 137
Everlasting sweetpeas, 63–64

False aralia, 27–28
False spirea, 118
Fatsia, 109
Fennel, Florence, 296
Fern
- asparagus, 28
- Boston, 28–29

Fig tree, 109
Fire blight, 153
Flame azalea, 111
Flathead borers, 158–159
Flatheel apple tree borers, 154
Flax, 61
Flea beetles, 308, 313, 337–338
Florence fennel, 296
Flower thrips, 231
Flowering annuals, *see* Annuals, flowering
Flowering crabapples, *see* Crabapples, flowering
Flowering dogwood, *see* Dogwood, flowering
Flowering onion, 77, 85
Flowering perennials, *see* Perennials, flowering
Flowering raspberry, 117
Flowering tobacco, 105
Forget-me-nots, 40, 42, 105
Formal pruning, 126
Fothergilla, Alabama, 111–112
Four-o'clocks, 40, 42
Fox grape, 105
Foxglove, 58–59, 105
Fragrant sarcococca, 113
Franklin tree, 123
French endive, 281
Fringewood, 112
Fritillaria, 78
Froebel spirea, 120
Fruit rot, 327
Fruit trees, dwarf, 146–149
- apple, 146–147
- early fruit production, 147
- fertilizers, 149
- mulches, 149
- pear, 147
- planting and training, 148–149
- pruning, 147–148
- size of, 147
- soil, 147

Fruitworms, tomato, 313, 338
Fuller rose beetles, 198
Fungicides
- compatibility of, 316–317
- control measures, 319
- copper, 315
- dusts and sprays, 315
- organic, 316
- precautions, 318–319
- for vegetables, 314–319

Fungus rots, 95
Fusarium wilt, 330, 339

Gaillardia, 40, 42, 50, 59
Galanthus, 78–79
Garden beets, *see* Beets, table
Garden loam, 25, 100
Garden mulches, 21–22
Garden peas
- diseases, 330
- insects, 330

Garden peonies, 226
Garden symphylan, 331–332
Garden tools, 265

Gardenias, 31
Garlic, 294
Gayfeather, 61
Geraniums, strawberry, 210
Germander, 117, 208
Geum, 59
Ginkgo tree, 109, 136
Gladiolus, 87
Globe flower, 64, 105
Globe-amaranth, 40, 42
Glory bower, 117
Glory-of-the-snow, 78, 105
Glossy abelia, 105, 117
Glossy privet, 112
Glove amaranth, 50
Gloxinia, 87
Gold dust tree, 105
Golddrop, 119
Golddust, 54–55
Golden daisy, 55
Golden rain tree, 123, 142
Golden St. Johns-wort, 120
Goldflower St. Johns-wort, 120
Goldmoss stonecrop, 208–209
Gourds, 288
Grape hyacinth, 79–80, 105
Grape ivy, 31
Grapes, 251–255
  climate, 251–252
  diseases, 255
  fox, 105
  insects, 255
  planting, 254–255
  propagation, 254
  pruning, 255
  soil, 251–252
  trellis construction, 255
  vineyard site, selection of, 253–254
Grasshoppers, 332
Gray dogwood, 111
Gray mold, 225
Green ash tree, 142
Ground beetles, 341
Ground blackberries, 235
Ground cover, 207–213
  care of, 212
  planting, 210–212
  propagating, 212–213
  types of, 207–210
Ground-ivy, 209
Gumbo, 296
Gypsophila, 59

Hackberry, 136, 142
Halls honeysuckle, 122
Hardy asters, 56
Hardy begonias, 56
Hardy garden carnations, 57
Hardy plants, transplanting, 13
Harlequin bug, 323, 340
Heading broccoli, 303
Heartleaf bergenia, 209
Heath, 117
Heather, 117
Hedge pruning, 127
Helianthemum, 59
Helleborus, 59
Hemerocallis, 61, 87
Hemlock, 142
Herbicides, 246
Hercules-club, 117
Heuchera, 61
Hibiscus, 61, 109
High-pressure sodium lamps, 106
Himalayan lilac, 218
Hippeastrum, 85–86
Hollies, 105, 214–217
  care of, 215–216
  Chinese, 214
  diseases, 216–217
  English, 214
  failure to fruit, 216
  fertilizers, 216
  insects, 216, 217
  Japanese, 112, 209, 214
  kinds of, 214–215
  mulches, 215
  planting, 215
  pruning, 216
  selecting, 215
  watering, 216
  weeding, 216
Holly bud moths, 217
Holly leaf miners, 217
Holly mahonia, 105
Hollygrape, Oregon, 112
Hollyhock, 61
Honesty, 105
Honeylocust tree, 142
Honeysuckle, 105, 122, 209
  Halls, 122
  swamp, 121
  sweet, 122
Hornworms, 313, 338
Horsechestnut tree, 136
Horseradish, 280
House hydrangea, 117–118
House plants, 23–36
  buying, 23
  fertilizers, 26
  grooming, 24
  humidity, 26
  location for, 23–24
  plant selection, 27–36
  pots, saucers and trays, 24–25
  potting, 24
  soils, 25
  tools, 24
  watering, 25
  See also names of house plants
Hungarian lilac, 218
Hyacinth, 79
  grape, 79–80, 105
Hydrangea, 117–118
  oakleaf, 105

Iceland poppy, 62
Iceplant, 209
Impatiens, 40, 42, 105
Imported cabbageworm, 323
Incandescent lamps, 106
Informal pruning, 126
Insecticides
  compatibility of, 316–317
  control measures, 319
  dusts and sprays 314–315
  precautions, 318–319
  for vegetables, 314–319
Insects, beneficial, 340–342
Iris, 61, 79, 87, 92–96
  care of, 94
  description of, 92–93
  diseases, 95
  insects, 96
  planting, 93–94
  propagating, 94
Iris borer, 96
Iris leaf spot, 95
Iris mosaic, 95
Iris thrips, 96
Ismene, 87–88
Ivy
  Algerian, 105
  Boston, 105
  English, 105, 112, 208
  grape, 31
  ground-, 209

Jacaranda tree, 142
Jackman clematis, 122
Jade plant, 31–32
Japanese andromeda, 110–111
Japanese barberry, 105
Japanese beetles, 163, 168, 336
Japanese crabapples, 151
Japanese holly, 112, 209, 214
Japanese iris, 92, 93

Japanese pagoda tree, 123
Japanese pittosporum, 109, 112
Japanese skimmia, 113
Japanese spurge, 209
Japanese stewartia, 120
Japanese tree lilac, 218
Japanese white spirea, 120
Japonica, 105
Jetbead, 112
Juneberry, 105
Juniper, 209

Kale, 281, 300
Kalm St. Johns-wort, 120–121
Kashmir false-spirea, 118
Katherine crabapple, 151
Kohlrabi, 293–294

Lace bugs, 202
Lady beetles, 341
Lamb's lettuce, 281
Lamps, 106
Largeleaf lilac, 218
Larkspur, 40, 42
Late blight, 325, 333, 339
Laurel, mountain, 105, 112
Leaf blight, 324–325
Leaf curl, 231, 334
Leaf lettuce, 300
Leaf miners, 202, 308, 313, 338
Leaf spot, 95, 321, 328, 333, 334, 339
Leaf-feeding beetles, 198
Leafhoppers, 225, 320, 332
Leatherwood, 118
Lebanon squill, 80
Leeks, 294, 300
Lemoinei crabapple, 151
Lettuce, 283–284
  diseases, 327–328
  insects, 327–328
  lamb's, 281
  leaf, 300
Leucojum, 79
Leucothoë, 105, 112
Liatris, 61
Lighting, artificial, 106
Lilac borers, 221
Lilacs, 109, 218–221
  care of, 219
  diseases, 221
  insects, 221
  planting, 219
  propagating, 219–221
  summer, 116
  types of, 218–219
Lilium hybrids, 88
Lily, 105
  spider, 88
Lily-flowered tulips, 80
Lily-of-the-valley, 79, 105
Lima-bean pod borers, 320
Linum, 61
Littleleaf lilac, 218
Live oak tree, 142
Loam, garden, 25, 100
Locust tree, 109
Lopping shears, 132
Lunaria, 61
Lupine, 40, 42, 61
Lycoris, 88
Lygus bugs, 320
Lythrum, 61

Maackia, 124
Madagascar periwinkle, 105
Maggots, onion, 329
Magnolia scales, 163
Magnolias, 160–163
  Asian, 160–161
  buying, 161
  diseases, 162–163
  fertilizers, 162
  insects, 162–163
  mulches, 162
  native, 160
  planting, 161–162
  pruning, 162
  southern, 142
  watering, 162
Maidenhair tree, 109
Maple tree, 109
Mapleleaf viburnum, 113
Marigolds, 40, 42, 50
Mallow, 61
Meal, bone, 25
Mealybugs, 198
Memorial rose, 209
Mercury lamps, 106
Mexican bean beetles, 320
Mexican shell flower, 89
Midget crabapple, 151
Mimosa, 124
Minigardens for vegetables, *see* Vegetable gardens, minigardens
Mint, 109, 136, 142
Minute pirate bugs, 341
Mites, 168, 198, 342
Mole crickets, 338
Monarda, 61
Money plant, 61
Montbretia, 88–89
Morning-glory, 40, 42, 50
Mosaic, 231, 326, 328–329, 331, 333, 334, 336, 339
Moss, peat, 25, 100
Moss phlox, 62
Moss sandwort, 209
Mother-in-law plant, 30–31
Mountain camellia, 120
Mountain laurel, 105, 112
Muscari, 79–80
Muskmelons, 288–289
  diseases, 328–329
  insects, 328–329
Mustard greens, 282, 301
  diseases, 340
  insects, 340
Myrtle, 112

Nandina, 112, 118
Narcissus, 80, 105
Nasturtium, 40, 42
Native magnolias, 160
Nematodes (root knot), 95, 192, 202, 247, 326, 329, 339–340
New Jersey-tea, 118–119
New Zealand spinach, 282
Norfolk Island pine, 32
Norway maple, 142
Nut orchid, 85

Oak tree, 109, 136
Oakleaf hydrangea, 105, 117–118
Ocean-spray, 119
Okra, 296
  diseases, 329
  insects, 329
Onion maggots, 329
Onion thrips, 329
Onions, 294–295, 301
  diseases, 329
  flowering, 77, 85
  insects, 329
Orange rust, 334
Orange tortrix, 322
Orange-eye butterflybush, 116
Orchid, nut, 85
Oregon hollygrape, 112
Organic fungicides, 316
Oriental fruit moth, 168
Oriental poppy, 62
Ornamental cherry tree, 109
Ornamental vegetables, 302
Ornamentals, 99–109
  air pollution problems, 108–109

controlling environment, 106–107
fertilizers, 103
growing area, 99–100
growing media, preparation of, 100–101
lighting, 104–106
mulches, 104
plant damage, 108
planting, 101–103
trees and shrubs, transplanting, 13–20
digging up, 16
fertilizers, 19
hardy plants, 13
heeling-in, 15
mulches, 19
planting, 17–18
protecting from sun and wind damage, 19–20
pruning, 18
soil preparation, 15
watering, 18–19
wild plants, 14
watering, 103
winter care, 107–108
Ornithogalum, 80
Overgrown plants, pruning, 126
Oxalis, 80
Oyster, vegetable, 286
Oyster-shell scale, 192, 221
Ozone, 109

Pachysandra, 209
Pagoda flower, 61–62
Pagoda tree, Japanese, 123
Painted daisy, 63
Palm, parlor, 32–33
Pansies, 41, 43, 222–225
care, 224–225
cultivating, 225
diseases, 225
fertilizers, 224–225
insects, 225
kinds of, 222
pesticide precautions, 225
planting, 222–223
propagating, 224
tufted, 64
watering, 224
Paper birch tree, 136
Parkman crabapple, 151
Parlor palm, 32–33
Parrot tulips, 80
Parsley, 284, 301
turnip-rooted, 287
Parsnips, 285
Pea weevils, 330
Peach trees, 109
Pear trees, 147
Peas
blackeye, 291
insects, 329
English, 290–291
garden
diseases, 330
insects, 330
sugar, 291
Peat moss, 25, 100
Pecan tree, 142
Peegee hydrangea, 117–118
Penstemon, 61–62
Peonies, 62, 89, 226–231
buying, 227
care, 228–229
diseases, 230–231
dividing, 230
failure to bloom, 230
fertilizers, 229
flowers, 229–230
insects, 230–231
kinds of, 226, 227
method of growing, 226–227
mulches, 228
planting, 227–228
watering, 229
Pepper weevils, 330
Pepperbush, 121
sweet, 113
Peppers, 295, 301
diseases, 330–331
insects, 330–331
Perennials
cultivating, 68
flowering, 53–73
buying plants or seeds, 64–65
dividing, 69–72
fertilizers, 67–68
mulches, 67
old flowers, removing, 72
planting the garden, 65–72
seedlings, raising, 73
selection of, 54–64
soil preparation, 53–54
staking, 68–69
starting plants indoors, 72
transplanting, 73
watering, 67
Periwinkle, 209, 212
Madagascar, 105
Perlite, 25
Persian lilac, 218
Peruvian daffodil, 87–88
Pesticides
compatibility of, 316–317
control measures, 319
precautions, 318–319
Petunias, 41, 43, 50, 109
Philodendron, 33, 109
windowleaf, 33–34
Phlox, 41, 43, 50, 62
Photochemical smog
plants resistant to, 109
plants sensitive to, 109
Physalis, 297
Phytophthora blight, 216–217, 230
Pickleworm, 325, 328, 335
Pine tree, 109
Norfolk Island, 32
Scotch, 142
Pink rot, 325
Pinks, 41, 43, 58
Pinkweeper crabapple, 151
Pittosporum, 109, 112
Plant bugs, 202, 206
Plantain lily, 105
Platycodon, 62
Plum curculio, 168
Plum tree, 109
Polianthes, 89
Poppy, 41, 43, 50, 62
Portulaca, 41, 43, 50
Potato tuberworms, 332
Potatoes, 285–286
diseases, 331–334
insects, 331–334
sweet, 286–287
diseases, 337
insects, 337
Potentilla, 119
Potting soil, 25
Powdery mildew, 153, 221
Praying mantids, 341–342
Primrose, 62
Prince Georges crabapple, 151
Privet, 105
glossy, 112
Pruning, 125–132
controlling shape, 127
deciduous shrubs, 125–129
spring-flowering, 126–128
summer-flowering, 128–129
equipment for, 132
evergreen shrubs, 129–131
broad-leaved, 130
coniferous, 130–131
formal, 126
hedge pruning, 127
informal, 126
overgrown plants, 126

Pruning (*Cont.*)
  treating wounds, 132
  vines, 131–132
Pruning saw, 132
Pruning shears, 132
Pumpkins, 289
  insects, 335–336
Purple passion plant, 34
Purple raspberries, 243
Puschkinia, 80
Pyracantha firethorn, 109
Pyrethrum, 63

Radishes, 286, 301
  insects, 334
Rainbow rockcress, 56
Ranunculus, 80
Raspberries, 243–247
  cultivating, 246
  diseases, 247, 322–323, 334
  fertilizers, 245–246
  flowering, 117
  harvesting, 246–247
  herbicides for, 246
  insects, 247, 322–323, 334
  irrigation for, 246
  planting, 243–244
  propagating, 247
  soil preparation, 243–244
  training, 244–245
  types of, 243
  winter protection, 247
Raspberry crown borer, 322
Raspberry fruitworms, 322
Red cedar tree, 136
Red hot poker, 64
Red maple tree, 136, 142
Red mulberry tree, 136
Red raspberries, 243
Redbud, 105, 142
Redbud crabapple, 151–152
Red-necked cane borers, 322
Redwood tree, 136
Rhizoctonia disease, 324
Rhododendrons, 109, 171–174
  buying, 171
  diseases, 174
  fertilizers, 173
  insects, 173–174
  mulches, 173
  planting, 171–172
  pruning, 173
  rosebay, 112
  watering, 173
  weeding, 173
Rhubarb, 280–281
  diseases, 334–335
  insects, 334–335
Rhubarb curculio, 334
Ring pox, 167
Ring spot, 167, 206
Rockcress, 55, 56
Root maggots, 323–324, 330, 334
Root rots, 330, 335
Rose chafers, 231, 322
Rose scale, 322
Rose-acacia, 109
Rosebay rhododendron, 112
Roses, 119
  Christmas, 59, 105
  memorial, 209
  sun, 59
Rose-of-Sharon, 119
Rouen lilac, 218
Rubber tree plant, 34–35
Rudbeckia, 41, 43, 50, 63
Running blackberries, 235
Rust, 95, 225, 319, 321
Rutabagas, 287

Sage, 109
St. Johns-wort, 105, 120–121, 209
  golden, 120
  goldflower, 120
  Kalm, 120–121
  shrubby, 121
Salal, 113
Salpiglossis, 41, 43, 50
Salsify, 286
Salvia, 63, 109
San Jose scale, 221
Sand, 25, 100
Sand strawberry, 209
Sarcococca, 209
  fragrant, 113
Sargent crabapple, 152
Sasanqua camellia, 111
Saw, pruning, 132
Scab, 153, 326–327
Scabiosa, 41, 43, 50
Scale insects, 231
Scales, 159, 168, 197–198
Scarlet clematis, 122
Scarlet oak tree, 136
Scarlet sage, 41, 43, 50
Schefflera, 35
Scheidecker crabapple, 152
Scilla, 80
Sclerotinia, 197
Scotch pine, 142
Sea pink, 55
Sea-lavender, 63
Seed decay, 321, 330, 335, 337
Seed-corn maggots, 320
Seedling blight, 337
Seed-treatment chemicals, 316
Sequoia tree, 136
Shade trees
  buying and planting, 136–139
    deciduous, 137
    evergreen, 137
    planting seasons, 137
    preparing the planting hole, 138
    setting the tree, 138–139
    spacing, 137
    steps in planting, 139
    temporary storage, 137
  care after planting, 139–140
Shallots, 295
Shasta daisy, 58
Shears
  lopping, 132
  pruning, 132
Shellback hickory tree, 136
Shot-hole fungus, 167
Showy stewartia, 120
Shrubby bushclover, 119–120
Shrubby St. Johns-wort, 121
Shrubs
  for shady areas, 110–114
    kinds of shade, 110
    planting and care, 113–114
    selection of, 110–113
    soil preparation, 113
  for summer color, 115–121
Siberian iris, 92, 93
Siberian wallflower, 63
Silk tree, 124
Silky camellia, 120
Silver fleece vine, 122
Six-spotted leafhopper, 327
Skimmia, Japanese, 113
Smog, photochemical
  plants resistant to, 109
  plants sensitive to, 109
Smut, 329, 337
Snake plant, 35–36
Snapdragon, 41, 43, 50
Snowberry, 105
Snowdrop, 78–79, 105
Snowflake, 79
  summer, 105
Snowhill hydrangea, 117–118
Snow-in-summer, 57
Sodium lamps, high-pressure, 106
Soft scale, 217
Sorrel, 281
Sorrel tree, 124

Sourwood tree, 124
South African daisy, 209
Southern magnolia, 142
Southern red mite, 217
Soybeans, 291
Spanish bluebell, 105
Speedwell, 64
Spider lily, 88
Spider mites, 153, 173–174, 206, 225, 313, 328
Spider plant, 36, 41, 43
Spiders, 342
Spinach, 282
  diseases, 335
  New Zealand, 282
Spirea, 105, 109, 120
  false, 118
  Froebel, 120
  Japanese white, 120
Spittle bugs, 202
Spotted cucumber beetles, 320
Spraying equipment, 317
Spring-flowering bulbs, *see* Bulbs, spring-flowering
Sprouting broccoli, 303
Spurge, Japanese, 209
Squash bug, 335
Squash vine borers, 335
Squashes, 289
  insects, 335–336
  summer, 301
Squill, 80
Stalk borers, 338
Star of Bethlehem, 80, 105
Stem rot, 337
Stewartia, 120
Stink bugs, 338
Stock, 41, 43
Stokes' aster, 63
Stokesia, 63
Strawberry, sand, 209
Strawberry geranium, 210
Strawflower, 41, 43
Striped cucumber beetles, 326, 328, 335–336
Sugar maple tree, 136, 142
Sugar peas, 291
Summer lilac, 116
Summer phlox, 62
Summer snowflake, 105
Summer squash, 301
Summer-cypress, 41, 43
Summer-flowering bulbs, *see* Bulbs, summer-flowering
Summersweet, 113, 121
Sun rose, 59
Sunflower, 41, 43, 50
Swamp azalea, 121
Swamp honeysuckle, 121
Sweet alyssum, 41, 43
Sweet autumn clematis, 122
Sweet corn, *see* Corn, sweet
Sweet honeysuckle, 122
Sweet pepperbush, 113
Sweet potato weevil, 337
Sweet potatoes, 286–287
  diseases, 337
  insects, 337
Sweetbay, 113
Sweetgum, 136
Sweetpeas, 41, 43, 63–64
Sweetwilliam, 64
Swiss chard, 281, 301
Sycamore tree, 109
Sydney wattle tree, 142
Syrphid flies, 342

Table beets, *see* Beets, table
Tall iris, 79
Tamarix, 121
Tar spot, 216
Tea crabapple, 152
Thornless blackberries, *see* Blackberries, thornless
Thrips, 202, 206
Tigridia, 89
Tipburn, 327
Tomato fruitworms, 313, 338
Tomato russet mites, 338–339
Tomatoes, 295–296, 301, 309–313
  blossom drop, 313
  care, 312–313
  diseases, 337–340
  fertilizers, 312
  harvest, 313
  insects, 313, 337–340
  liming, 310–311
  planting, 310–311
  pruning, 312
  seeding, 311–312
  soil preparation, 310
  staking, 312
  transplanting, 312
  varieties, 309–310
  watering, 312
  weed control, 312–313
Tools, garden, 265
Trailing blackberries, 235
Tree lilacs, 218
Tree peonies, 226
Trees
  for summer color, 123–124
  for use and beauty, 141–145
    availability, 143
    caring for trees in the city, 143–145
    fertilizers, 144–145
    form, 142
    hardiness, 141
    planting, 143–144
    protecting from insects, diseases and mechanical injury, 145
    pruning, 145
    selection of, 141–143
    size, 142
    undesirable characteristics, 142
    watering, 145
  See also names and types of trees
Tritoma, 64
Trollius, 64
Trumpet vine, 122–123
Tuberose, 89
Tufted pansy, 64
Tulip tree, 136, 142
Tulip tree scales, 163
Tulips, 80–81
Turnip aphids, 340
Turnip greens, 282
Turnip-rooted celery, 285
Turnip-rooted parsley, 287
Turnips, 287, 301
  diseases, 340
  insects, 340
Twig blight, 216–217

Umbrella tree, 35
Upland cress, 284

Valley oak tree, 142
Van Eseltine crabapple, 152
Vegetable gardens, 261–297
  arrangement of, 265–266
  cabbage group, 291–294
  care, 272–279
  diseases, 279
  drainage, 261–265
  fertilizers, 263–264
  fleshy-fruited vegetables, 295–296
  garden tools, choosing, 265
  greens, 281–282
  hardening plants, 270
  insects, 279
  legumes, 289–291

Vegetable gardens (*Cont.*)
  liming, 264–265
  minigardens, 298–302
    containers, 298
    cultivating, 302
    diseases, 302
    fertilizers, 302
    hardening plants, 302
    harvesting dates, 300–301
    insects, 302
    light, 299
    ornamental vegetables, 302
    planting dates, 299–301
    seeds, 299
    starting plants indoors, 299–302
    synthetic soil, 298–299
    watering, 302
  onion group, 294–295
  organic matter, 262–263
  perennial vegetables, 279–281
  planting, 271–272
  planting dates for vegetables, 274–277
  root vegetables, 284–287
  salad vegetables, 282–284
  seed selection, 266–267
  site selection, 261
  soil, 261–265
  southern-grown plants, 270–271
  starting plants, 267–271
    in the house, 267–269
    special devices for, 269–270
  sunshine, 261–265
  transplanting, 271
  vine vegetables, 287–289
  watering, 272
  weed control, 272–279
Vegetable oyster, 286
Vegetable weevils, 340
Vegetables
  diseases, 314–342
  fungicides for, 314–319
  insecticides for, 314–319
  insects, 314–342
  ornamental, 302
  See also names of vegetables
Velvet plant, 34
Verbena, 41, 43, 50
Verbena bud moth, 96
Vermiculite, 25
Veronica, 64
Verticillium wilt, 340
Viburnum, 105, 109
  mapleleaf, 113
Vinca, 41, 43
Vines
  pruning, 131–132
  for summer color, 121–123
  See also names of vines
Violets, 105
  African, 27
Virginia bluebell, 105

Walnut anthracnose, 256
Walnut trees, 109
  black, 256–258
    fertilizers, 258
    harvesting, 258
    liming, 258
    planting, 257–258
    varieties, 256–257
Wandering Jew, 36, 210
Warty barberry, 111
Wasps, 342
Watering system, automatic, 103
Watermelons, 289
  diseases, 340
Wax begonia, 105
Wax myrtle, 142
Wax scales, 163
Webworms, 308, 323
Weeping lantana, 210
White ash tree, 142
White fringe, 112
White grubs, 332–333
White oak tree, 136, 142
White spruce tree, 136
Whiteflies, 198
White-fringed beetles, 332
Wild bergamot, 61
Wild plants, transplanting, 14–15
Willow tree, 109, 142
Willow oak tree, 136, 142
Wilt, 230, 326, 327, 329, 330, 333–340
Windflower, 55, 77–78
Windowleaf philodendron, 33–34
Winter aconite, 78
Winterberry, 105
Wintercreeper, 113, 210
Wintergreen, 210
Wireworms, 333
Wishbone flower, 105
Witloof chicory, 281
Wormwood, 55–56

Yarrow, 54
Yellowroot, 113
Yellows, 225, 324, 325, 327–328, 335
Yellowwood tree, 136
Yew, 105
Yucca, 109

Zinnia, 41, 43, 50